Successful
College
Writing

Successful College Writing

Third Edition

SKILLS • STRATEGIES • LEARNING STYLES

Kathleen T. McWhorter

NIAGARA COUNTY COMMUNITY COLLEGE

Bedford / St. Martin's

Boston ◆ New York

For Bedford/St. Martin's

Developmental Editor: Beth Ammerman
Senior Production Editor: Michael Weber
Senior Production Supervisor: Nancy Myers
Art Director: Lucy Krikorian
Text Design and Cover Design: Anna Palchik
Copy Editor: Rosemary Winfield
Indexer: Kirsten Kite
Photo Research: Martha Friedman
Cover Art: Wolf Kahn, *Dark Pines,* 2000. Oil on canvas, 22 × 34 inches. Art © Wolf Kahn/Licenced by VAGA, New York, NY.
Composition: Monotype, LLC
Printing and Binding: R.R. Donnelley & Sons Company

President: Joan E. Feinberg
Editorial Director: Denise B. Wydra
Editor in Chief: Nancy Perry
Director of Marketing: Karen Melton Soeltz
Director of Editing, Design, and Production: Marcia Cohen
Managing Editor: Erica T. Appel

Library of Congress Control Number: 2005928581 (with Handbook)
2005928582 (without Handbook)

Manufactured in the United States of America.

1   0   9   8   7
f   e   d

For information, write: Bedford/St. Martin's, 75 Arlington Street, Boston, MA 02116 (617-399-4000)

ISBN-10: 0–312–43232–1 (Student Edition with Handbook)
0–312–44131–2 (Student Edition without Handbook)
0–312–44132–0 (Instructor's Annotated Edition)
ISBN-13: 978–0–312–43232–4 (Student Edition with Handbook)
978–0–312–44131–9 (Student Edition without Handbook)
978–0–312–44132–6 (Instructor's Annotated Edition)

Acknowledgments

Acknowledgments and copyrights are continued at the back of the book on pages 969–971, which constitute an extension of the copyright page.

My goal in writing *Successful College Writing* was to create a first-year composition text that covers the skills other college-level texts assume students already possess. The overwhelmingly positive response from instructors who have used the first and second editions confirms my own experience: Many students today need a review of basic writing conventions before they can be equipped with college-level skills in writing, reading, or critical thinking. *Successful College Writing* in its third edition continues to address this reality.

Through its unique, highly visual, student-centered approach, *Successful College Writing* teaches students essential skills while guiding them through the writing strategies and activities that form the core of composition instruction. With this revision, I sought to provide more guidance for students to think critically about and evaluate their own work, to add coverage of topics that are integral to students' success in college, and to strengthen the proven features of *Successful College Writing*.

PROVEN FEATURES OF *SUCCESSFUL COLLEGE WRITING*

True to its goal of offering more coverage of essential skills, *Successful College Writing* provides abundant guidance and support for inexperienced writers along with thorough help with reading and study skills.

Extensive Support for Inexperienced College Writers Throughout

Every chapter of *Successful College Writing* provides practical, student-oriented instruction, along with extra help for those students who need it.

Detailed coverage of each stage of the writing process. Part Two of the text, "Strategies for Writing Essays," consists of five chapters that cover each stage of the writing process in detail, with plenty of skill-building exercises, many of them collaborative; a running student example; and Essay in Progress activities that lead students through each step in writing an essay.

Appealing, helpful visuals.   Because inexperienced writers often are more comfortable with images than with text, *Successful College Writing* employs a visual approach to writing instruction. The Quick Start at the beginning of each chapter provides an engaging image for students to respond to. In addition, Graphic Organizers—maps that display relationships among ideas—present students with an alternative to traditional outlines. Students are encouraged to use the Graphic Organizers as tools both for analyzing readings and for planning and revising their own essays. Finally, Revision Flowcharts help students read their own essays as well as those of their peers with a critical eye, and other figures and boxes reinforce points made in the text and summarize information for students.

Practical, step-by-step writing assignments.   Each chapter in Part Three covers one of the patterns of development that students will frequently encounter in college and on the job. The chapters in Part Three, as well as the chapter on writing arguments in Part Four and on writing a literary analysis in Part Six, include Guided Writing Assignments that lead students step by step through the process of writing an essay. These guided assignments give student writers the support they need, whether they are working in class or on their own. The assignments will also appeal to faculty members who often have limited time to become familiar with a complex textbook.

Comprehensive coverage of research and documentation.   Because many students are called upon to work with sources early in their college careers and because technological advancements and the Internet have made such source-based writing increasingly difficult, *Successful College Writing* provides three full chapters on writing with sources, covering both electronic and print sources. Students learn to locate sources and take effective notes, evaluate a source's relevancy and reliability, synthesize and integrate sources, avoid plagiarism, and properly use MLA and APA documentation formats.

Unique emphasis on learning styles.   Because students learn in different ways, they learn to write in different ways as well, yet most writing texts do not take these differences into account. *Successful College Writing* encourages students to explore alternative writing strategies and provides the tools to approach writing as a flexible, multifaceted process, alleviating some of the frustration students often feel.

In this text, I focus on four learning styles that are relevant for writing: verbal versus spatial learning, creative versus pragmatic learning, concrete versus abstract learning, and social versus independent learning. A brief questionnaire in Chapter 1 enables students to assess their learning styles. Recognizing that no one strategy works for every student, the text includes a variety of strategies for generating ideas

Learning Style Options   and revising an essay. Alternative strategies are identified by the "Learning Style Options" icon throughout the text.

Thorough reference handbook.   The handbook in Part Seven covers basic grammar, sentence problems, punctuation, mechanics, spelling, and ESL troublespots. It also reinforces students' learning with plenty of opportunities for practice. The handbook includes hand-corrected examples, key grammatical terms defined in the margin, helpful charts and boxes, and sentence and paragraph exercises. Cross-references direct students to additional grammar exercises online at Exercise Central.

Emphasis on Reading and Study Skills

Over the years, my work with students has convinced me that skills taught in isolation are seldom learned well or applied. Because reading and study skills are essential to successful writing, instruction in these skills is integrated throughout *Successful College Writing*. By becoming proficient, enthusiastic readers, students learn to be better writers and improve their chances for success not only in the writing classroom but also in their other courses as well.

Complete chapter on active, critical reading.   To provide students with solid, proven strategies for working with text, the Guide for Active Reading in Chapter 2 helps students improve their comprehension and build skills that they can apply to the readings within this text as well as to those that they encounter in their other college classes.

Thorough coverage of reading skills throughout.   The reading skills that are taught in Chapter 2 are reinforced in each of the chapters on the patterns of development. As students develop their writing skills by writing a particular type of essay, they simultaneously learn practical strategies for reading that type of essay. In addition, Chapter 16, "Reading Arguments," gives students guidelines for analyzing and evaluating arguments.

High-interest readings.   Students who enjoy what they are reading become more proficient readers. Therefore, the professional and student readings in this text were carefully chosen to interest students as well as to function as strong rhetorical models. The professional readings come from a wide range of sources, including newspapers, popular magazines, special-interest magazines, textbooks, and scholarly journals, representing the diverse texts students encounter in both their personal and academic lives.

Attention to study skills.   *Successful College Writing* gives students practical survival strategies that they can use not only in their writing course but in all their college courses. In addition to guidelines for reading different types of texts, *Successful College Writing* includes excerpts from college textbooks in marketing, biology, and communication; practical advice on study strategies in Chapter 22 on essay examinations; and useful advice on college life and study skills in the updated Keys to Academic Success section.

NEW TO THE THIRD EDITION

My goals for the revision of *Successful College Writing*—based on feedback from instructors and students who used the text—were to strengthen the proven features that help students write clearly, read carefully, and think critically and to add features that reflect recent changes in the field of composition.

Greater Emphasis on Assessment and Self-Evaluation

Learning to assess their own work and monitor their progress is one of the most difficult challenges students face. To help them develop these metacognitive skills, I've added several new features to the Third Edition.

New Evaluating Your Progress boxes.   Appearing at the end of Chapters 8–15 and 17, Evaluating Your Progress boxes guide students in assessing their learning and seeking additional help when needed. For each method of development, students are asked to evaluate their success in using the method, analyze what they learned from the professional readings they were assigned, and identify errors in proofreading and editing on graded papers.

Enhanced Keys to Academic Success.   The Keys to Academic Success section in the front of the book has been revised to be more interactive and to focus on self-assessment and evaluation. Students are asked to list goals, evaluate a course syllabus, complete an academic image self-evaluation checklist, identify opportunities to communicate with their instructors, adapt note-taking strategies to specific courses, identify useful online reference sources, list effective study and review strategies, and complete a stress mini-quiz.

New section on compiling portfolios.   A new section in Chapter 22 discusses how to prepare writing portfolios and use them to track progress. A model reflective letter gives students an example of how compiling a portfolio can assist them in reviewing and evaluating the development of their writing through the semester.

New reading quizzes.   Available on the book's Web site are short-answer quizzes that can be used either by students individually or by instructors in class to evaluate reading comprehension.

New Sections and Ancillaries Provide More Help for Important Skills

New chapter on classroom communication skills.   Chapter 23 offers advice that will help students function effectively in the college classroom. Topics include developing critical listening skills, asking and answering questions, working on collaborative projects, and giving oral presentations. Giving an oral presentation is presented as analogous to writing an essay: Students learn to overcome apprehension; plan, organize, and draft a presentation; and rehearse and deliver the presentation. A useful table addresses students' most common concerns and problems.

New material on learning from student writing.   Many writing textbooks contain student writing samples, but few tell students how to learn from studying the writing of others. A new section in Chapter 2 shows students how to approach student writing samples and how to use them to improve their own writing.

New material on learning from instructor comments.   Instructors spend a great deal of time grading and commenting on student papers, yet many students only note the grade they receive and do not benefit from the comments. A new section in Chapter 6 discusses how to benefit from instructor comments and includes a sample paper with instructor comments.

Expanded print workbook.   The print workbook, *Additional Exercises,* now provides coverage of more topics, giving students extra practice for the most common writing problems. In addition to the wealth of grammar exercises, the workbook contains a grammar diagnostic test, more ESL exercises, paragraph development and outlining exercises, and research and documentation tutorials.

Revision of the Research and Documentation Section

Updated, reorganized working with sources chapters.   Part Five of the book has been revised to help students easily find and understand the information they need. Chapter 18 gives advice on planning a paper and evaluating sources, Chapter 19 provides detailed information on doing research and taking notes, and Chapter 20 features a step-by-step guide to writing a research paper and documenting sources properly.

More visual aids throughout Part Five.   New graphics and boxed elements help students grasp important topics such as avoiding plagiarism and using proper documentation.

Thirteen New Professional Readings

The new readings provide strong models and spark ideas for student writing. These brief, accessible readings focus on subjects that are relevant and interesting to students, such as athletes' unsportsmanlike behavior, SUVs, low-paying jobs, racial discrimination in the workplace, monster truck rallies, cell phones, and the death penalty. Well-known writers such as Amy Tan, William Safire, and Barbara Ehrenreich are represented.

USEFUL ANCILLARIES FOR INSTRUCTORS AND STUDENTS

The print and electronic ancillaries that accompany *Successful College Writing* offer plenty of support for both students and instructors. The exercise book is numbered to correspond with the handbook available in the full version of the text. The Instructor's Annotated Edition and the Instructor's Resource Manual are valuable resources for all instructors but are especially helpful for adjunct instructors, who often don't receive their teaching assignments until the last minute.

Print Ancillaries

- **Instructor's Annotated Edition**, with annotations prepared by Kathleen McCoy with Lale Davidson, Adirondack Community College. This useful volume provides abundant teaching tips, including suggestions for collaborative activities and applying learning styles to the writing classroom; computer hints; notes on additional resources; and answers to exercises and questions following readings.

- **Instructor's Resource Manual**, by Kathleen T. McWhorter; Michael Hricik, Westmoreland County Community College; Mary Applegate, D'Youville College; and Rebecca J. Fraser, Nassau Community College. This extensive collection of materials provides extra support for adjuncts and new instructors. It includes sample syllabi along with chapters on teaching with *Successful College Writing*, helping underprepared students in the first-year writing classroom, evaluating student writing, and using the writing center. It also provides a bibliography of books and articles in rhetoric and composition.

- **Transparency Masters.** These reproducible masters include Graphic Organizers, Revision Flowcharts, and other helpful charts and images from the text; all images are also available in PDF format on the book's Web site.

- **Additional Exercises for** *Successful College Writing*, by Carolyn Lengel and Jess Carroll. Available free with the text, these additional exercises are keyed specifically to the handbook.

- **The Bedford/St. Martin's ESL Workbook.** This comprehensive exercise workbook covers grammar issues for multilingual students with varying English-language skills and cultural backgrounds. To reinforce each lesson, instructional introductions are followed by illustrative examples and exercises. Answers are provided at the back.

Electronic Ancillaries

- **Exercise Central.** This extensive collection of interactive online grammar exercises is easy to use and convenient for students and instructors alike. Multiple exercise sets on every grammar topic ensure that students get as much practice as they need. Customized feedback turns skills practice into a learning experience, and the reporting feature allows both students and instructors to monitor and assess the students' progress. Exercise Central can be accessed through the Book Companion Site for *Successful College Writing*.

- **Book Companion Site**. bedfordstmartins.com/successfulwriting. The Web site provides interactive versions of the Graphic Organizers, reading comprehension quizzes, and downloadable versions of the print ancillaries. The site also provides access to **Re:Writing**, an online collection of free, open, and easy-to-access resources for the writing class. Here you'll find plagiarism tutorials, model documents, style and grammar exercises, visual analysis activities, research guides, bibliography tools, and much more.

- **Exercise Central to Go: Writing and Grammar Practices for Basic Writers**. This CD-ROM for basic writers has hundreds of practice items for writing and editing skills. Drawn from the popular Exercise Central Web site, the exercises provide instant feedback and have been extensively class-tested. No Internet connection is necessary.

- **Testing Tool Kit: A Writing and Grammar Test Bank CD-ROM**. This bank of nearly 2,000 test items (covering writing, grammar, and more) allows instructors to create secure, customized tests and quizzes to assess students' writing and grammar competency and gauge their progress.

- **Comment**. This easy-to-use peer review and instructor response Web site enables students to share their work and receive feedback from their instructor and other students.

- **iX**. Available free with *Successful College Writing*, this CD-ROM allows students to analyze and manipulate the elements of visuals, giving students a more thorough understanding of how visual rhetoric works.

- **iClaim**. This innovative CD-ROM features six tutorials on fundamental qualities good arguments share. An illustrated glossary defines fifty key terms from argument theory and classical rhetoric, and a visual index provides direct access to more than seventy multimedia arguments on the CD-ROM. Available free with *Successful College Writing*.

- **iCite**. This new research and documentation CD-ROM brings research to life with animation and four interactive tutorials that explore fundamental concepts about working with sources. A gallery of sources provides concrete practice recognizing, evaluating, incorporating, and citing a wide range of real-life sources from across the disciplines. Available free with *Successful College Writing*.

ACKNOWLEDGMENTS

A number of instructors and students from across the country have helped me to develop and revise *Successful College Writing*. I would like to express my gratitude to the following instructors, who served as members of the advisory board for the first edition. They provided detailed, valuable comments and suggestions about the manuscript as well as student essays and additional help and advice during its development: Marvin Austin, Columbia State Community College; Sarah H. Harrison, Tyler Junior College; Dan Holt, Lansing Community College; Michael Mackey, Community College of Denver; Lucille M. Schultz, University of Cincinnati; Sue Serrano, Sierra College; Linda R. Spain, Linn-Benton Community College; and Jacqueline Zimmerman, Lewis and Clark Community College.

I would also like to thank the following instructors and their students, who class tested chapters from *Successful College Writing* and provided valuable feedback about how its features and organization worked in the classroom: Mary Applegate, D'Youville College; Michael Hricik, Westmoreland County Community College; Lee Brewer Jones, DeKalb College; Edwina Jordan, Illinois Central College; Susan H. Lassiter, Mississippi College; Mildred C. Melendez, Sinclair Community College; Steve Rayshich, Westmoreland County Community College; Barbara J. Robedeau, San Antonio College; and Deanna White, University of Texas at San Antonio.

The following instructors have given me the benefit of their experience and expertise by reviewing early drafts of *Successful College Writing*; I am very grateful to them for all of their comments and advice: Andrea Berta, University of Texas at El Paso; Larry T. Blades, Highline Community College; Laurie Warshal Cohen, Seattle Central Community College; Mark Coley, Tarrant County College; Patricia Delamer, University of Dayton; Marla Dinchak, Glendale Community College; Elizabeth Griffey, Florida Community College at Jacksonville; Avon Bisson Hadoulis, Long Island University, C. W. Post Campus; Michael Hricik, Westmoreland County Community College; Becky Johnen, West Virginia Northern Community College; Lee Brewer Jones, DeKalb College; Edwina Jordan, Illinois Central College; Peter Jordan, Tennessee State University; Earnest Lee, Carson-Newman College; Jane Maher, Nassau Community College; Mildred C. Melendez, Sinclair Community College; Dianne S. Metzar, Broome Community College; Gunhild T. Miller, Rockland Community College (SUNY); Patrice A. Quarg, Community College of Baltimore County — Catonsville Campus; Barbara J. Robedeau, San Antonio College; Eileen B. Seifert, DePaul University; Lauren Sewell, University of Tennessee at Chattanooga; Bill M. Stiffler, Harford Community College; William Tucker, Eastern Michigan University; Susan A. VanSchuyver, Oklahoma City Community College; Deanna M. White, University of Texas at San Antonio; and Ruth Windhover, Highline Community College.

In addition, I benefited from the experience of those instructors who reviewed the second edition, and I am grateful for their wonderful suggestions and helpful advice: Gwen S. Argersinger, Mesa Community College — Red Mountain; Rita Quillen, Mountain Empire Community College; Gary L. Buxton, Black River Technical College; Kathleen Chrismon, Northeastern Oklahoma A&M College; Adelle Mery, University of Texas — Pan American; James A. Anderson, Johnson & Wales University — Florida Campus; Tracy Brunner, Broward Community College — South Campus; Belton Hammond, Brevard College; Donna Revtai, Broward Community College — Central Campus; Mark Underwood, Southwest Texas Junior

College; Laura Hamilton, Rogue Community College; Corla Dawson, Missouri Western State College; Brenda Stevens Fick, Community College of Baltimore County—Dundalk; Ana B. Hernandez, Miami Dade College—Wolfson Campus; Connie Humphreys, Northeastern Junior College; Robin Newcomer, Olympic College; Linda E. Smith, Fort Hays State University; Jacqueline Bradley, Southern Methodist University; Lourdes Rodriguez-Florido, Broward Community College; Shirley Roberts, Brookhaven College; Susan Bamberg, Shelton State Community College; Wynora Freeman, Shelton State Community College; Patricia Hanahoe-Dosch, Passaic County Community College; Amy McCauley, Ivy Tech State College, Region 5; and Keri Turner, Nicholls State University.

For useful comments on the chapters on argument, I would like to thank Heather Graves, DePaul University, and Gary Mitchner, Sinclair Community College. For their advice on the research coverage, I am grateful to Barbara Fister; Valerie Balkun, Johnson and Wales University; Carmella Braniger, Oklahoma State University; Carol Callahan, Southern State Community College; Deborah Carmichael, Oklahoma State University; Susan M. Doody, Durham Technical Community College; Robert Headley, Southern State Community College; Bernard LaChance, Cerro Coso Community College; Jacquelyn Leonardi, Oklahoma State University; Catherine Palmer, University of California, Irvine; and Bret L. Scaliter, Crafton Hills Community College. For useful comments on the ESL chapters in the handbook, I would like to thank Craig Kleinman, City College of San Francisco, and Bob Hemmer.

I am indebted to the valuable research conducted by George Jensen, John DiTiberio, and Robert Sternberg on learning-style theory that informs the pedagogy of this book. For their comments on the coverage of learning styles in this text, I would like to thank John K. DiTiberio, Saint Louis University; Ronald A. Sudol, Oakland University; and Thomas C. Thompson, The Citadel. My thanks go to Mary Jane Feldman, Niagara County Community College, for designing the field test of the Learning Styles Inventory and conducting the statistical analysis of the results. I would also like to thank the instructors and students who participated in a field test of the Learning Styles Inventory: Laurie Warshal Cohen, Seattle Central Community College; Lee Brewer Jones, DeKalb College; Edwina Jordan, Illinois Central College; Jennifer Manning, John Jay College; Mildred Melendez, Sinclair Community College; Paul Resnick, Illinois Central College; and Deanna M. White, University of Texas at San Antonio.

I am grateful to the following students whose essays appear in this text: Tracey Aquino, Andrew Decker, Nicholas Destino, Stanford DeWinter, Robin Ferguson, Heather Gianakos, David Harris, Michael Jacobsohn, Christine Lee, Kyle Mares, Ryan Porter, Maria Rodriguez, Harley Tong, and Aphonetip Vasavong.

Judy Voss deserves much credit and recognition for her thoughtful editing of the research and documentation chapters, as does Rosemary Winfield for her careful and judicious copyediting of my final draft. I also want to thank Susan Alexander for her clerical work in preparing the manuscript and Elizabeth Gruchala-Gilbert for her research assistance.

Many people at Bedford/St. Martin's have contributed to the creation and development of *Successful College Writing*. Each person with whom I have worked is a true professional; each demonstrates high standards and expertise; each is committed to producing a book focused on student needs. First of all, I would like to thank Carla Samodulski and Kristin Bowen for their many contributions to the development of the first edition.

To Chuck Christensen, former president of Bedford/St. Martin's, I attribute much of my success in writing college textbooks. Twenty-four years ago, I signed a contract for my first textbook with Chuck. Under his guidance, it became a bestseller. From Chuck I learned how to translate what I teach to the printed page. Joan Feinberg, current president, has become another trusted adviser. I value her editorial experience and appreciate the creative energy she brings to each issue and to each conversation. I also must thank Nancy Perry, editor in chief, for her forthright advice and for valuable assistance in making some of the more difficult decisions about the book.

I also appreciate the advice and guidance that Karen Melton Soeltz, marketing director, and her colleagues have provided at various junctures in the writing of this text. To Michael Weber, senior project editor, I extend my thanks for conscientiously and carefully guiding the book through production. Laura King, editorial assistant, has helped prepare the manuscript in innumerable ways, and Nathan Odell, associate editor, expertly oversaw the revision of the ancillary materials. I thank them both.

I owe the largest debt of gratitude to Beth Ammerman, editor, for her valuable guidance and assistance in preparing this revision. Her awareness of the book's audience, her creative revision suggestions, her help in identifying appropriate professional readings, her careful editing, and her attention to detail have strengthened the third edition significantly. She helped me to reinforce the book's strengths and to retain its focus on providing extra help to the student. I particularly value her knowledge of the freshman composition field and appreciate her analytical and organizational skills. She is an editor from whom I have learned a great deal and with whom I am pleased and fortunate to have worked.

Finally, I must thank the many students who inspired me to write this book. From them I have learned how to teach, and they have shown me how they think and learn. My students, then, have made the largest contribution to this book, for without them I would have little to say and no reason to write.

Kathleen T. McWhorter

Contents

6   REVISING CONTENT AND ORGANIZATION   147

7 EDITING SENTENCES AND WORDS   *173*

PART THREE   PATTERNS OF DEVELOPMENT   *197*

8 NARRATION: RECOUNTING EVENTS   *199*

12 COMPARISON AND CONTRAST: SHOWING SIMILARITIES AND DIFFERENCES *371*

13 CLASSIFICATION AND DIVISION: EXPLAINING CATEGORIES AND PARTS   *417*

PART FIVE   WRITING WITH SOURCES   *637*

18 PLANNING A PAPER WITH SOURCES   *639*

19 FINDING SOURCES AND TAKING NOTES *663*

20 WRITING A PAPER USING SOURCES *695*

PART SIX   ACADEMIC APPLICATIONS   *757*

21 READING AND WRITING ABOUT LITERATURE   *759*

PART SEVEN   HANDBOOK
Writing Problems and How to Correct Them   *833*

Thematic Contents

LANGUAGE AND LITERATURE

POPULAR CULTURE

SPORTS AND HOBBIES

To the Student

As a college student, you probably have many responsibilities. You may need to balance the demands of college with the needs of your family and the requirements of your job. In addition, you are probably attending college to make a change in your life — to better your prospects. You may not have chosen a specific career path yet, but you eventually want a rewarding, secure future. Consequently, you are ready to pursue a course of study that will lead you there.

I have been teaching students like you for over thirty years in numerous colleges. I have written this book to help you achieve your goals by becoming a successful college writer. In writing the book, I have taken into account your busy lifestyle and made this book practical and easy to read. As simply and directly as possible, the text explains what you need to know to sharpen your writing skills. You will also find it easy to locate the information you need within the text. You can use the brief contents on the inside front cover, the detailed contents, or the comprehensive index to locate information. In addition, numerous flowcharts, boxes, and other visual aids appear throughout to help you quickly find the information or writing assistance you need. (You will find a list of helpful flowcharts, figures, and boxes near the back of the text.) I also show how the writing strategies you are learning apply to other college courses and to the workplace. Throughout the book you will find tips for completing reading and writing assignments in your other college courses, and the Keys to Academic Success section contains useful study-skills advice, as well.

How This Book Can Help You Succeed

There are no secrets to success in writing — no tricks or miracle shortcuts. Rather, becoming a successful student writer requires hard work, guidance and feedback, and skills and strategies. You must provide the hard work; your instructor and classmates will provide you with the guidance and feedback. This book introduces you to the skills and strategies that successful writers need to know. Specifically, this book will help you succeed in your writing course in the following ways.

- **By emphasizing the connection between reading and writing.** You have been reading nearly your entire life. You could probably read sentences and paragraphs before you could write them. This book shows you how reading and writing are connected and how to use your reading skills to improve your writing.

- **By helping you become and stay involved with the course by including readings on topics and issues of interest and concern to college students.** The readings in this book have been selected from a wide range of sources—including newspapers, popular magazines, special-interest magazines, textbooks, and scholarly journals—that represent the diverse texts you will encounter in both your personal life and your academic life.

- **By offering you both professional and student models of good writing.** As you work with the essays in this book, you will discover that both professional writers and student writers follow the same principles in organizing and presenting their ideas. You will also have opportunities to examine, react to, and discuss the ideas presented in these essays and to relate those ideas to your own life.

- **By helping you discover the writing strategies that work best for you.** You may have noticed that you don't learn in the same way as your best friend or the person who sits next to you in class. For example, some students learn better by listening, while others learn better by reading. Because not all students learn in the same way, Chapter 1 includes a Learning Style Inventory that will help you discover how you learn. As you work through the writing assignments throughout the book, you will find lists of Learning Style Options that suggest different ways that you can approach a given writing task. Feel free to experiment with these options; try one and then another. You will probably discover some techniques that work better or take less time than those you are currently using.

- **By helping you identify and eliminate frequently occurring problems with sentence structure, grammar, punctuation, and mechanics.** Sections in Chapter 5, "Drafting an Essay," and in Chapter 7, "Editing Sentences and Words," provide strategies for fixing errors that students commonly make. In addition, Chapters 8–15 and 17 all provide editing and proofreading tips particular to the type of essays you will be writing in each chapter. Part 7, "Handbook: Writing Problems and How to Correct Them," covers important grammar rules and provides exercises that allow you to practice applying those rules. For more help, a student workbook, *Additional Exercises for Successful College Writing*, is available, and *Exercise Central*, available on the companion Web site, offers online grammar practice.

How to Use This Book

In writing this book, I have included many features that I use when I am actually teaching a class. Each is described below along with suggestions for how the feature can help you become a skilled, successful writer.

A Guide to Active Reading

Chapter 2, "Reading and Writing about Text," includes specific, practical strategies that will help you get the most out of the selections in this book as well as the reading assignments in your other courses. The Guide to Active Reading on page 23 explains, step by step, how to improve your comprehension and build your critical reading skills.

Detailed Coverage of Each Stage of the Writing Process

Part 2 of the text, "Strategies for Writing Essays," includes five chapters (Chapters 3–7) that cover each stage of the writing process in detail. Each step in the process is illustrated by the example of a student, Christine Lee, as she generates ideas for, drafts, and revises an essay. Chapter 6, "Revising Content and Organization," includes an important section on working with classmates to revise an essay (p. 155), with plenty of practical suggestions for you to use both as a writer seeking advice and as a peer reviewer.

Student Essays

Throughout the text, student essays illustrate different types of writing or different writing strategies. These student examples are usually found in sections titled "Students Write." A section in Chapter 2, "How to Approach Student Writing," explains how to read and examine student essays and apply what you learn to improve your writing. In addition, use the questions following these student essays to help you discover how other students apply the techniques you are learning in their writing.

Computer Tips

Today more than ever before, computers affect every aspect of the writing process. Using a computer at home or at a computer lab on campus can help you to write and revise your papers more efficiently, and using the Internet for research opens up an almost unlimited number of sources for you to consider. Throughout the text, I suggest particular ways that computers, and specifically word processing programs, can be especially helpful as you write and revise an essay. This advice is designated by the icon ▨ .

Graphic Organizers

Throughout the text you will find Graphic Organizers — diagrams that offer a visual approach to organizing and revising essays. These organizers present a picture or map of an essay. A sample Graphic Organizer appears on page xl. As you draft and revise, you can refer frequently to the graphic organizer for the

GRAPHIC ORGANIZER

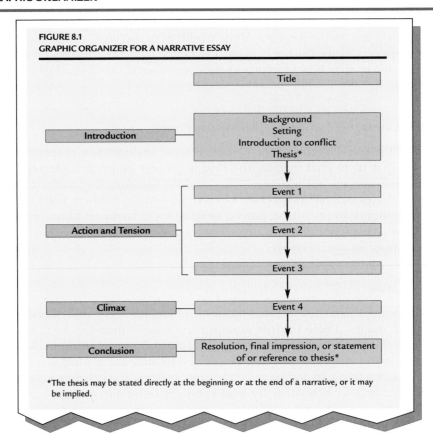

FIGURE 8.1
GRAPHIC ORGANIZER FOR A NARRATIVE ESSAY

particular type of essay you are writing. The text also demonstrates how to draw your own organizers to help you analyze a reading, structure your ideas, and write and revise drafts.

Guided Writing Assignments

Chapters 8–15, 17, and 21 contain writing guides that "walk you through" a writing assignment step by step. The Guided Writing Assignments are shaded, as in the sample on page xli. You can refer to this guide as often as you need to while you complete the assignment in the chapter or other similar assignments. Think of it as a tutorial to which you can always turn for tips, examples, and advice.

Revision Flowcharts

Many chapters include flowcharts that will help you identify what you need to revise in a first draft. Each flowchart lists key questions to ask about a draft and

PART OF A GUIDED WRITING ASSIGNMENT

A GUIDED WRITING ASSIGNMENT

The following guide will help you write a process analysis essay. It may be a how-to or a how-it-works essay. Although you will focus on process analysis, you may need to integrate one or more other patterns of development in your essay.

The Assignment

Write a process analysis essay on one of the following topics or one that you choose on your own. Be sure the process you choose is one that you know enough about to explain to others or can learn about through observation or research. Your audience consists of readers who are unfamiliar with the process, including your classmates.

How-to Essay Topics

1. How to improve _____ (your study habits, your wardrobe, your batting average)

A PORTION OF A REVISION FLOWCHART

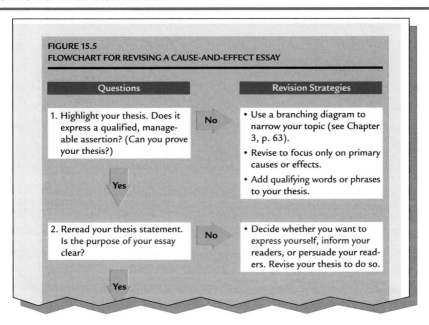

FIGURE 15.5
FLOWCHART FOR REVISING A CAUSE-AND-EFFECT ESSAY

Questions	Revision Strategies
1. Highlight your thesis. Does it express a qualified, manageable assertion? (Can you prove your thesis?) — **No**	• Use a branching diagram to narrow your topic (see Chapter 3, p. 63). • Revise to focus only on primary causes or effects. • Add qualifying words or phrases to your thesis.
Yes ↓	
2. Reread your thesis statement. Is the purpose of your essay clear? — **No**	• Decide whether you want to express yourself, inform your readers, or persuade your readers. Revise your thesis to do so.
Yes ↓	

offers suggestions for how to revise to correct any weaknesses you uncover. (See the sample on page xli.) You can also use the questions in the appropriate revision flowchart to guide classmates who are reviewing your essay.

Evaluating Your Progress Boxes

At the end of Chapters 8–15 and 17, you will find boxes titled "Evaluating Your Progress," which provide an opportunity for you to review and reflect on your mastery of chapter content. Specifically, each box asks you to consider what you have learned in the chapter, evaluate how successfully you were able to apply your learning to your writing, and identify areas in which you need further practice. Reviewing your progress in this way not only helps you identify and focus on the skills you need to work harder on but also reinforces what you have learned and shows you how your writing is developing over the course of the semester.

EVALUATING YOUR PROGRESS BOX

EVALUATING YOUR PROGRESS
Part A: Using Comparison and Contrast

Write a paragraph that evaluates your use of comparison and contrast. Be sure to

- Identify one everyday, one academic, and one workplace situation in which comparison and contrast would be a useful method for organizing information.
- What method of organization did you use in your comparison and contrast essay(s)? Did you discover any disadvantages or limitations of the method? How would your essay(s) have changed if you had used a different method of organization?
- Identify any problems or trouble spots you experienced in using comparison and contrast, and explain how you dealt with them.

Part B: Analyzing Comparison and Contrast Readings

The readings in this chapter are models of essays using comparison and contrast. Some use a subject-by-subject organization; others use a point-by-point organization. What do you perceive to be the strengths of each method?

Part C: Proofreading and Editing

List the errors your instructor identified in your comparison and contrast essay(s). For more help with these problems, refer to Exercise Central (www.bedfordstmartins.com/successfulwriting).

Writing Using Sources

Often, as you write and revise an essay you will find that you need facts, statistics, or the viewpoint of an expert to strengthen your own ideas. Chapter 18, "Planning a Paper with Sources," shows you where to start and gives helpful advice for evaluating different types of sources. Chapter 19, "Finding Sources and Taking Notes" explains how to locate sources in the library and on the Internet and how to extract the information you need. Chapter 20, "Writing a Paper Using Sources," demonstrates how to use, integrate, and document information from sources within an essay. For your convenience, this book includes guidelines for using two widely recommended styles for documenting sources: MLA (green-shaded pages) and APA (brown-shaded pages). In addition, color-coded visuals provide clear models for documenting books, articles, and Web sites.

Handbook

Part 7, "Handbook: Writing Problems and How to Correct Them," is a user-friendly reference that you can consult to review problem areas or to check rules about grammar, punctuation, or mechanics. Refer to this section often to help make your papers error free. Your instructor may also refer you to this part of the book by writing either revision symbols (such as *cs* for "comma splice") or the numbers and letters of specific sections (such as *7a* for a pronoun reference problem) on your papers. You can refer to the list of revision symbols included at the

DOCUMENTATION DIAGRAM

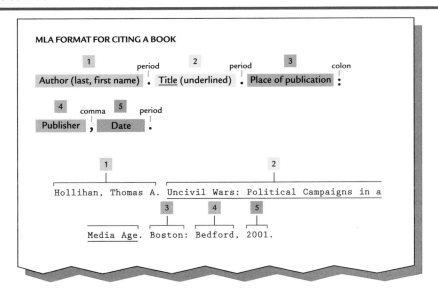

back of the book or to the complete contents for the handbook included on the last page of the text and on the inside back cover to find the information you need. You can also look up grammar concepts, punctuation marks, or problem areas in the index.

A Final Word

In my high school and early college years, I was an OK writer but never a skilled writer. I certainly never imagined myself writing a textbook, and yet *Successful College Writing* is my tenth college textbook. How did I learn to write well? I learned from my college writing courses and from my instructors, both in English classes and in other disciplines as well. I learned from my husband, who used to read and comment on my papers while we were in college. I learned from friends and classmates; I continue to learn from colleagues, editors, and most important from my own students, who deserve clear and concise expression. Never stop learning: I know I will not. I wish you success.

Kathleen T. McWhorter

Keys to Academic Success

Focus, skill, and organization: these are the essential ingredients for academic success. Success begins when you view yourself as a successful student, plan your time, use your course syllabus, and take advantage of the facilities and services available on your campus. Success also demands new skills. You must project a positive academic image, communicate with your instructors, take effective notes, and use those notes to study. Finally, college success requires organizing and managing your life. This involves organizing your study area, locating and using the right learning tools, staying focused while writing and studying, and managing stress.

This brief set of keys can help you unlock your potential as a student, but there are no shortcuts to academic success. Education is a process, not a product. It requires the courage to challenge your old ideas about literature, writing, politics, science, and many other subjects. It also requires a willingness to take risks and to change how you think, how you study, and how you write.

FOCUSING ON ACADEMIC SUCCESS

You can start preparing for college success even before you enter the classroom. To begin make sure you

- see yourself as a successful student,
- plan your valuable time,
- use your course syllabus, and
- discover college services.

See Yourself as a Successful Student

The students in the photograph on page xlvi have achieved an important goal in their lives—college graduation. They are successful students, exuberant about having reached their goal. Do you consider yourself a successful student? No

doubt you are enthusiastic about jumping into your college studies, but you may be concerned about how you will juggle a job, your family life, and school. You also may be wondering whether you have the skills and abilities necessary to get the grades you want. Having doubts and concerns is normal, but it is important to think positively and to focus on success. Here are a few success strategies.

- **Define success.** *Success* means different things to different people, and you need to decide what success means to you. Is a rewarding career your highest priority? Are relationships with family and friends important? What about helping others? Define what *success* means to you, and decide how college fits into your definition of success.

- **Develop long-term goals that will lead to success.** Once you have defined *success,* you need to determine the long-term goals that will get you there. What do you intend to accomplish this term? This year? In the next four years? Complete the planner on the next page to help you define your goals. List where you would like to be and what you would like to be doing at each of the times listed. You may have multiple goals, so list as many as apply.

- **Take responsibility for achieving those goals.** Only you are in charge of your own learning and reaching your goals. You can do as little or as much as you want to achieve your goals, but you take the responsibility either way.

- **Visualize success.** To keep your goals in mind, close your eyes and imagine yourself achieving your goals. For example, picture yourself finishing your first year of college with high marks or walking across the stage at graduation. Never visualize failure.

SUCCESS ACTIVITY 1: GOALS TABLE

List what you expect to accomplish in the next two weeks.	1. 2.
List what you expect to have accomplished by the end of this semester.	1. 2. 3.
List what you will accomplish within the next year.	1. 2. 3.
List what you will have accomplished upon graduation.	1. 2. 3.
Where do you see yourself five years after you graduate?	1. 2. 3.

- **Develop essential skills that will help you achieve success.** Success is not a matter of luck; it is a matter of specific skills, such as communicating effectively and visualizing success, that will help you achieve success. Think of your writing class as a place to develop these skills.

SUCCESS ACTIVITY 2: SETTING GOALS

Write a paragraph describing your academic and professional goals. Include the specific steps you need to take to achieve those goals.

Plan Your Valuable Time

Examine the two student schedules shown in Figures 1 and 2 on the next page. Which student is more likely to meet his or her deadlines? Why?

FIGURE 1: PLANNER WITH DUE DATES

November	November
10 Monday	Thursday 13 *10 am Essay 3 due*
11 Tuesday *3 pm History exam*	Friday 14 *1 pm Anthro quiz*
12 Wednesday	Saturday 15
	Sunday 16

FIGURE 2: PLANNER WITH DETAILED SCHEDULE

November	November
10 Monday *am—outline English Essay 3* *6 pm History study group*	Thursday 13 *10 am Essay 3 due* *5–8 pm Work* *9–10 pm Study Anthro chapters*
11 Tuesday *am—Draft Essay 3* *3 pm History exam* *6–8 pm Work* *Read Anthro Ch. 21*	Friday 14 *am—Review Anthro notes and chapter highlighting* *1 pm Anthro quiz*
12 Wednesday *10 am Writing Center—review Essay 3* *Read Anthro Chs. 21–22*	Saturday 15 *9–4 Work*
	Sunday 16 *Read Bio Ch. 17* *Review Bio lab* *Read History Ch. 15*

The student planner in Figure 1 shows only test dates and assignment deadlines. Figure 2 shows a planner that details how and when the student will meet those deadlines. The student who uses the planner in Figure 2 is likely to complete his or her work with less stress and worry.

The biggest challenge for most first-year college students is managing time. The most successful students spend two hours outside of the classroom for every hour spent in the classroom (more for reading- or writing-intensive courses). College students are required to spend only twelve to eighteen hours per week in class or lab. The remainder of the time is unstructured, and as a result, many students never seem to get organized. Others are overwhelmed by the workload and the challenge of integrating college study into already busy lives. Still others tend to study non-stop: by never finding free time for relaxation, they set themselves up for burnout.

To avoid these traps and manage your time effectively, you need to establish goals and plan your activities.

Establish Positive, Realistic, Short-Term Goals

The first step in managing your time is establishing goals that are positive and realistic. Keep in mind a broad, long-term goal, like earning a bachelor's degree in elementary education in four years, before setting short-term goals that you can achieve more quickly. A short-term goal could be finishing an assigned paper by next Friday. Setting a time frame is a critical step toward accomplishing each of your goals.

Plan Your Activities

If you let days "just happen," you're not likely to accomplish much. You need to plan your activities. You may prefer a tightly structured or loosely structured plan — or something in between. Consider the following three types of plans — term, weekly, and daily — and choose the one that works best for you. If you are not sure, experiment by trying out all three.

The term plan.   Once you have a sense of the work that you will need to complete for each of your courses, block out four to six hours per week for each course. Remember, the rule of thumb is that for every hour spent in class you should plan to work two hours outside of class. Study for each course during the same time period each week. For instance, you might reserve Monday, Wednesday, and Thursday evenings between 8:00 and 10:00 P.M. for your writing course. This plan establishes a routine for study. The tasks you work on each week will vary, but you will always be certain you have enough time to get everything done. If you have trouble starting on assignments, this plan may be the best one for you.

The weekly plan.   Take ten minutes at the beginning of each week to specify when you'll work on each course, taking into account upcoming assignments. Figure 2 is a good example of how to organize a weekly plan.

Regardless of which plan you choose, you need to purchase a student planner or pocket calendar for recording assignments, due dates for papers, and upcoming exams. You'll also want to schedule time to work on your coursework, whether you schedule this time daily, weekly, or across the term. Keep this planner or calendar with you at all times and check it daily. It will help you get and stay organized.

Each evening before you begin studying, assess what needs to be done and determine the order in which you will do these tasks. Although you may be tempted to tackle short or easy tasks first, it is usually best to work on the most challenging assignments first, when your concentration is at its peak.

Use Your Course Syllabus

The **syllabus** is the most important document you will receive in your first week of class. Some instructors place the syllabus on the course's Web site as well. A syllabus usually describes how the course operates. It includes information on the required texts, attendance policy, grading system, course objectives, weekly assignments or readings, due dates of papers, and dates of exams. Think of a syllabus as a course guide or course planner that directs you through your writing class. Examine the following excerpt from a sample syllabus illustrating how an instructor might organize a writing course.

FIGURE 3: EXCERPTED SAMPLE SYLLABUS FOR A COLLEGE WRITING COURSE

I. General Information

Course Title:	English Composition I	*Course Number:*	ENG 161
Prerequisite:	English 070 or placement test	*Semester:*	Fall
Instructor:	John Gillam	*Phone:*	(724) 555-7890
Email:	gillam@indiana.edu	*Office Hours*	
		& Location:	MWF 3–5
		English Department offices in Ryan Hall	

A good way to contact your instructor. *(margin note, points to Email)*

Important — be sure to use them. *(margin note, points to Office Hours & Location)*

II. Text
McWhorter, Kathleen T. *Successful College Writing*, 2nd Edition: New York: Bedford, 2003.

III. General Course Objectives
1. The student will learn to organize his or her thoughts into a meaningful written work.
2. The student will easily recognize grammar mistakes.
3. The student will be familiar with different types of writing.
4. The student will be able to use several different writing styles.

Planning and organizing is expected. *(margin note, points to objective 1)*

Grammar is important. *(margin note, points to objective 2)*

IV. Specific Course Objectives
1. The student will write papers using the following strategies: description, illustration, process analysis, comparison and contrast, classification and division, and cause and effect.

What you will be graded on. *(margin note, points to IV. Specific Course Objectives)*

Learn these strategies. *(margin note, points to objective 1)*

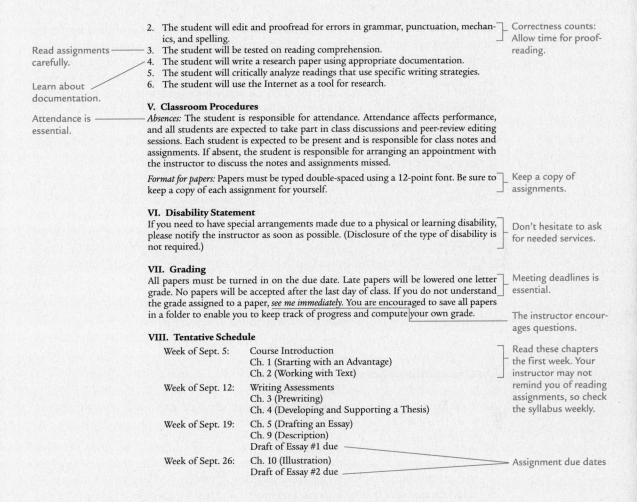

Read assignments carefully.

Learn about documentation.

Attendance is essential.

2. The student will edit and proofread for errors in grammar, punctuation, mechanics, and spelling.
3. The student will be tested on reading comprehension.
4. The student will write a research paper using appropriate documentation.
5. The student will critically analyze readings that use specific writing strategies.
6. The student will use the Internet as a tool for research.

Correctness counts: Allow time for proofreading.

V. Classroom Procedures

Absences: The student is responsible for attendance. Attendance affects performance, and all students are expected to take part in class discussions and peer-review editing sessions. Each student is expected to be present and is responsible for class notes and assignments. If absent, the student is responsible for arranging an appointment with the instructor to discuss the notes and assignments missed.

Format for papers: Papers must be typed double-spaced using a 12-point font. Be sure to keep a copy of each assignment for yourself.

Keep a copy of assignments.

VI. Disability Statement

If you need to have special arrangements made due to a physical or learning disability, please notify the instructor as soon as possible. (Disclosure of the type of disability is not required.)

Don't hesitate to ask for needed services.

VII. Grading

All papers must be turned in on the due date. Late papers will be lowered one letter grade. No papers will be accepted after the last day of class. If you do not understand the grade assigned to a paper, *see me immediately.* You are encouraged to save all papers in a folder to enable you to keep track of progress and compute your own grade.

Meeting deadlines is essential.

The instructor encourages questions.

VIII. Tentative Schedule

Week of Sept. 5:	Course Introduction
	Ch. 1 (Starting with an Advantage)
	Ch. 2 (Working with Text)
Week of Sept. 12:	Writing Assessments
	Ch. 3 (Prewriting)
	Ch. 4 (Developing and Supporting a Thesis)
Week of Sept. 19:	Ch. 5 (Drafting an Essay)
	Ch. 9 (Description)
	Draft of Essay #1 due
Week of Sept. 26:	Ch. 10 (Illustration)
	Draft of Essay #2 due

Read these chapters the first week. Your instructor may not remind you of reading assignments, so check the syllabus weekly.

Assignment due dates

A course syllabus can be prepared in various styles. Some instructors prefer to use a weekly format for a syllabus and then give specific assignments in class. The sample syllabus in Figure 3 is formatted this way. Some instructors avoid dates by using a general outline of assignments and requirements and then craft the assignment schedule as the class masters each topic. Still other instructors prefer a highly structured syllabus that lists daily assignments as well as required readings, long-term writing assignments, and group work. Whatever format the syllabus takes, be sure to read it carefully at the beginning of the course and to check it regularly so that you are prepared for class. Mark all deadlines on your calendar. Ask your instructor any questions you may have about the syllabus, course structure, deadlines, and his or her expectations about course objectives. Note his or her answers on your syllabus or in your course notebook.

Pay particular attention to the course objectives section of the syllabus, where your instructor states what he or she expects you to learn in the course. Objectives also provide clues about what the instructor feels is important and how he or she views the subject matter. Since the course objectives state what you are expected to learn, papers and exams will measure how well you have met these objectives.

Make a copy of each course syllabus. Keep one syllabus in the front of your notebook for easy reference during class or while you are studying. Keep another syllabus in a file folder at home in case you lose your notebook on campus.

SUCCESS ACTIVITY 3: GETTING THE MOST FROM YOUR SYLLABUS

Review the syllabus that your writing class instructor distributed. Write a paragraph describing your expectations and concerns about your writing course based on the syllabus. Be sure to include information on the questions listed below. If the syllabus does not contain the information, consult your college catalog for general policies and your instructor for specific questions.

1. What are you expected to learn in the course?
2. What kind of essays will you write?
3. What are the grading and attendance policies?
4. Is class participation expected and required? Is it part of your grade?
5. Is research required? Is Internet usage required or expected?

Discover College Services

Identifying and using your college's support services can make the difference between frustration and success. Here's how to increase your success by using college support services.

- **Find out what is available.** Academic services include writing centers, computer labs, math labs, library tours, free workshops, academic skills centers, learning specialists, counseling services, and peer tutoring in specific courses. You can find out when and where these services are offered and how to use them by checking the campus bulletin boards, newspaper, or Web site. These valuable services can give you an important academic advantage: Don't hesitate to use them. Many or all of these services are free; all you need to do is request them.

- **Visit your college's writing center and learn what services it offers.** Writing centers offer individualized help with planning, organizing, drafting, and revising papers, usually for any college course, not just your writing class. Computers are often available for your use at either the writing center or the computer lab. The staff or tutors can help you learn how to use them.

SUCCESS ACTIVITY 4: USING COLLEGE SERVICES

For each college service listed below, visit it or research the services it offers. Record the information in the space provided. Then choose two or three of these services and write a paragraph in which you evaluate the usefulness of each service to you.

College Service	Services Offered
Writing center	
Learning lab or academic support center	
Computer lab	
Library	
Counseling and testing center	
Placement office	

DEVELOPING SKILLS FOR SUCCESS

College success requires more than just doing the assigned work. It is learning how to

- project a positive academic image,
- communicate with instructors, and
- take effective notes.

Present Yourself as a Successful Student

How you act and respond in classes determine what you get out of them.

Do

Make thoughtful contributions to class discussions
Maintain eye contact with instructor
Ask questions if information is unclear to you
Refer to assigned readings in class
Be courteous to classmates when you speak

Don't

Work on homework during class
Sleep or daydream in class
Remain silent during class discussion
Interrupt others or criticize their contributions

Once you see yourself as a serious student, you are ready to project that positive academic image to your instructors and classmates. Don't underestimate the value of communicating daily — through your words and actions — that you are a hard-working student who takes your college experience seriously. A student who takes his or her studies seriously is more likely to be taken seriously and to find the assistance he or she needs.

SUCCESS ACTIVITY 5: ACADEMIC IMAGE QUIZ

Rate your academic image by checking "Always," "Sometimes," or "Never" for each of the following statements.

	Always	Sometimes	Never
I arrive at classes promptly.	❑	❑	❑
I sit near the front of the room.	❑	❑	❑
I look and act alert and interested in the class.	❑	❑	❑
I make eye contact with instructors.	❑	❑	❑
I complete reading assignments before class.	❑	❑	❑
I ask thoughtful questions.	❑	❑	❑
I participate in class discussions.	❑	❑	❑
I complete all assignments on time.	❑	❑	❑
I turn in neat, complete, well-organized papers.	❑	❑	❑
I refrain from carrying on conversations with other students while the instructor is addressing the class.	❑	❑	❑
I say "hello" when I meet instructors on campus.	❑	❑	❑

To be successful, it is not enough to change your image; you must also actively participate in class at every opportunity. Keep in mind the following suggestions.

- **Prepare to participate.** As you read an assignment, make notes and jot down questions to use as a starting point for class participation.

- **Organize your remarks.** Plan in advance what you will say or ask in class. Work on stating your ideas clearly.

- **Say something early in a discussion.** The longer you wait, the more difficult it will be to say something that has not already been said.

- **Keep your comments brief.** You will lose your classmates' attention if you ramble. Your instructor may ask you to explain your ideas further.

- **Be sensitive to the feelings of others.** Make sure that what you say does not offend or embarrass other class members.

Participation in class involves more than just speaking out. It also involves making a serious effort to focus on the discussion and to record important ideas that others may have. Be sure to take notes on class discussions, record whatever the instructor writes on the chalkboard, keep handouts from PowerPoint presentations, and jot down ideas for future writing assignments.

SUCCESS ACTIVITY 6: ACADEMIC IMAGE

Write a brief statement about how you think others perceive you as a student. Refer to the above list of tips about building a positive academic image. What tips do you normally follow? Which do you most need to work on?

Communicate with Your Instructors

Why is this student likely to get a good grade in her writing class?

Meeting regularly with your instructor will help you understand and meet the course objectives. Take advantage of your instructor's office hours, or speak to him or her after class. Use the following tips to communicate with your instructors.

- **Don't be afraid to approach your instructors.** At first, some of your instructors may seem distant or unapproachable. In fact, they enjoy teaching and working with students. Don't be afraid to talk to your instructors, but don't expect them to become your best friends. Instead, your instructors will answer questions you have about a reading, help you with problems you may experience with an assignment, and suggest directions to take with a topic for a paper or research project.

- **Learn your instructors' office hours.** Most instructors keep office hours—times during which they are available and ready to talk with you and answer your questions. Some instructors give out their email addresses so you can communicate with them by computer. You have to take the initiative to contact them.

- **Prepare for meetings with your instructor.** Write out specific questions in advance. If you need help with a paper, be sure you bring along all the work (drafts, outlines, research sources) you have done so far.

- **Stay in touch with your instructor.** If you absolutely cannot attend class for a particular reason, be sure to notify your instructor and explain. Unexcused absences generally lower your grade and suggest that you are not taking your studies seriously. In addition, if personal problems interfere with your schoolwork, let your instructors know. They can refer you to the counseling services on campus and may grant you an extension for work missed for an unavoidable family or other emergency.

You will find that your instructors are happy to help you and are willing to serve as valuable sources of information on research, academic decisions, and careers in their respective fields.

SUCCESS ACTIVITY 7: COMMUNICATING WITH INSTRUCTORS

Using the chart on the next page, list the name of each of your instructors; also include the course he or she teaches. Considering factors such as class size and organization, subject matter, assignments, tests and exams, and so forth, identify at least one opportunity to communicate with each of your instructors.

Instructor and Course	Opportunities to Communicate
1.	
2.	
3.	
4.	
5.	

Take Effective Class Notes and Use Them Well

To become a successful student, you also need to take careful notes on your classes and review those notes. Plan on reviewing notes at least once each week. Researchers have shown that most people retain far more information when they interact with it using more than one sense. For instance, if a student only listens to a lecture or discussion, he or she probably will forget most of it within a couple of weeks, well before the next exam. However, if a student takes accurate notes and reviews them regularly, then he or she is likely to retain the main points and supporting details needed to understand the concepts discussed in the class. Following are two of the most popular and efficient methods of taking notes on class lectures, discussions, and readings.

Two-Column Method

This note-taking method is valuable for all learners. Draw a vertical line from the top of a piece of paper to the bottom. The left-hand column should be about half as wide as the right-hand column.

In the wider, right-hand column, record ideas and facts as they are presented in a lecture or a discussion. In the narrower, left-hand column, note your own questions as they arise during the class. When you go home and review your notes, add summaries of major concepts and sections to the left-hand margin. This method allows you to quickly review an outline or overview of a lecture by reading the left-hand column and to study specific information and examples in the right-hand column. See the figure on the next page.

Modified Outline Method

The modified branch or outline method uses bullets for main ideas and dashes for detailed information within a section. The more detailed the information gets, the farther to the right you indent your outline entries.

COLUMNAR NOTE-TAKING

Writing as Process	*Prewriting — taking notes, writing ideas, drawing a cluster diagram, researching, writing questions, noting what you already know, outlining, etc.*
	Writing — drafting
(How many drafts does the average writer complete?)	*Rewriting — revision = "to see again"*
	2 types: global = major rehaul (reconsidering, reorganizing)
	local = rewording, correcting grammar (editing for correctness & style)
NOT linear	*Writing is not a linear process. May go back to prewriting after writing, etc.*

THE MODIFIED OUTLINE METHOD OF NOTE-TAKING

Writing is a process.
- *Prewriting*
  - *Taking notes*
  - *Writing ideas*
  - *Drawing a cluster diagram*
  - *Researching*
  - *Writing questions*
  - *Noting what you already know*
  - *Outlining*
- *Writing*
  - *First drafts*
    - *On paper*
    - *On cards*
    - *On computer*
  - *Later drafts*
- *Rewriting, or revision (means "to see again")*
  - *Global*
    - *Major revision*
    - *Reconsidering ideas*
    - *Reorganizing*
  - *Local*
    - *Rewording for style*
    - *Rewriting for correct grammar, spelling, punctuation*

Good note-taking is a hallmark of a successful student. It gets easier with practice, and developing your own symbols over time will help make note-taking quicker and more consistent for you. Borrow notes from a good student when you cannot be in class. When you take good notes and review them regularly, you are replacing the inefficient and exhausting strategy of cramming for exams — a strategy that loads information into your memory only temporarily — with a system of learning that allows deeper, longer-term retention of information.

ORGANIZING AND MANAGING YOUR LIFE

The final key to academic success is managing your tasks at home. You will need to

- organize a writing and study area,
- locate the right learning tools,
- stay focused, and
- manage stress.

Organize a Writing and Study Area

Which student has created a workable area for reading, writing, and studying?

The student in the disorganized space is not working efficiently and probably is not getting as much accomplished as she had hoped. The other student is studying efficiently in an uncluttered work space, free from distraction. You don't need

a lot of room to create an appropriate space for studying and writing. Use the following suggestions to organize an efficient work area.

- **Work in the same location daily.** As you become accustomed to working in the same spot each day, you will form a psychological association between the place and the reading and writing tasks that you are accomplishing there. Eventually, your mind will focus on academic tasks as soon as you enter this area.

- **Choose a setting that is conducive to writing and studying.** Your work area should be relatively free of distractions, well lit, comfortable, and equipped with all the tools you need — pens, pencils, paper, a clock, a computer, a calculator, a pencil sharpener. Be sure to keep a dictionary and a thesaurus nearby as well.

- **Find a quiet area.**
  - If you live on campus, your dormitory room probably includes a desk or work area. If your dorm is noisy, consider studying in the library or another quiet place. Libraries offer free carrel space where you can work without distractions. Many also offer study rooms for group work or secluded areas with upholstered chairs if you do not need a desk.
  - If you live off campus, find a place where you won't be disturbed by family or roommates. Your work area need not be a separate room, but it should be a place where you can spread out your materials and find them undisturbed when you return. Otherwise, you may waste a great deal of time setting up your work, figuring out where you left off, and getting started again. In addition, you should find a quiet place on campus where you can study between classes.

SUCCESS ACTIVITY 8: ORGANIZING YOUR WORK SPACE

Using the suggestions listed above and those you learned through discussion with your classmates, write a paragraph describing what you can do to organize an area that is conducive to study and writing.

Locate the Right Learning Tools

How often do you need to look up a word in a dictionary? Have you ever used an online dictionary? (If not, visit www.m-w.com.) Do you prefer using a hard-bound or online dictionary? Each has its advantages, and which dictionary you use depends on your purpose and your personal preferences.

To be successful in college, you will need the right learning tools. Your textbooks are essential, but you also will need quick access to other sources of information. Be sure you have each of the following handy in your writing and study area.

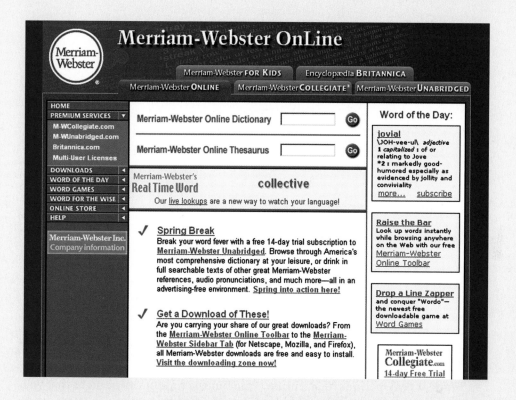

- The URL of an online dictionary (such as www.m-w.com)
- A reliable hard-bound collegiate dictionary, such as *Merriam-Webster's Collegiate Dictionary, The Oxford Dictionary of American English,* or *The American Heritage Dictionary*
- A paper-bound pocket dictionary to carry to class or to the library
- A thesaurus (dictionary of synonyms), such as *Roget's Thesaurus.* You may have a thesaurus as part of your word processing program.
- The URLs of Internet search engines. See Chapter 19, page 675, for suggestions.
- The URL of an online reference desk, such as www.refdesk.com, for factual information
- CDs for saving and transporting your work
- Classmates' and instructors' email addresses
- Specialized accessories your classes may require, such as a graphing calculator or a foreign language dictionary

SUCCESS ACTIVITY 9: USING ONLINE REFERENCES

Record below the online reference sources that you have found useful or helpful. Compare your list with those of other students and add any sources to your list that seem useful.

Online Reference Sources

1.

2.

3.

4.

Stay Focused and "Study Smarter"

Does either of these situations sound familiar?

"I just read a whole page, and I can't remember anything I read!"
"Every time I start working on this assignment, my mind wanders."

If so, you may need to improve your concentration. No matter how intelligent you are or what skills or talents you possess, if you cannot keep your mind on your work, your classes, including your writing class, will be unnecessarily difficult. Try the following concentration skills to help you "study smarter," not harder.

- **Work at peak periods of attention.** Find out the time of day or night that you are most efficient and least likely to lose concentration. Do not try to work when you are tired, hungry, or distracted by others.

- **Work on difficult assignments first.** Your mind is freshest as you begin to work. Putting off difficult tasks until last may be tempting, but you need your fullest concentration when you begin challenging assigments.

- **Vary your activities.** Do not complete three reading assignments consecutively. Instead, alternate assignments: for example, read, then write, then work on math problems, then read another assignment, and so on.

- **Use writing to keep you mentally and physically active.** Highlight and annotate as you read. These processes will keep you mentally alert.

- **Approach assignments critically.** Ask questions as you read. Make connections with what you have already learned and with what you already know about the subject.

- **Challenge yourself with deadlines.** Before beginning an assignment, estimate how long it should take and work toward completing the task within that time limit.

- **Keep a list of distractions.** When working on an assignment, stray thoughts about other pressing things are bound to zip through your mind. You might remember that your car has to be inspected tomorrow or that you have to buy your mother's birthday present next week. When these thoughts occur to you, jot them down so that you can unclutter your mind and focus on your work.

- **Reward yourself.** Use fun activities, such as emailing a friend or getting a snack, as a reward when you have completed an assignment.

SUCCESS ACTIVITY 10

Not all students study the same way, and most students study differently for different courses. List below the courses you are taking this semester. For each, identify a study strategy that works for that course. Compare your list with those of other students and add useful techniques you have discovered.

Course	Study Strategies to Try
1.	
2.	
3.	
4.	
5.	

Manage Stress

The pressures and obligations of school lead many students to feel overwhelmed and overstressed. As a successful student, you need to monitor your stress. Take the following quiz to assess your stress level.

If you answered yes more than once or twice, you may be feeling overwhelmed by stress. Stress is a natural reaction to the challenges of daily living, but if you are expected to accomplish more or perform better than you think you can, stress can become overwhelming. You can respond to stress either positively or negatively. For example, you can use stress to motivate yourself and start a project or assignment, or you can let it interfere with your ability to function mentally and physically. Here are some effective ways to change your thinking and habits and reduce stress.

- **Establish your priorities.** Decide what is more and less important in your life. Let's say you decide college is more important than your part-time job, for example. Once you have decided this, you won't worry about requesting a work schedule to accommodate your study schedule because studying is your priority.

SUCCESS ACTIVITY 11: STRESS MINI QUIZ

	Always	Sometimes	Never
1. I worry that I do not have enough time to get everything done.	❑	❑	❑
2. I regret that I have no time to do fun things each week.	❑	❑	❑
3. I find myself losing track of details and forgetting due dates, promises, and appointments.	❑	❑	❑
4. I worry about what I am doing.	❑	❑	❑
5. I have conflicts or disagreements with friends or family.	❑	❑	❑
6. I lose patience with small annoyances.	❑	❑	❑
7. I seem to be late, no matter how hard I try to arrive on time.	❑	❑	❑
8. I have difficulty sleeping.	❑	❑	❑
9. My eating habits have changed.	❑	❑	❑
10. I find myself needing a cigarette, drink, or prescription drug.	❑	❑	❑

- **Be selfish and learn to say no.** Many people feel stress because they are trying to do too many things for too many people—family, friends, classmates, and coworkers. Allow your priorities to guide you in accepting new responsibilities.

- **Simplify your life by making fewer choices.** Avoid simple daily decisions that needlessly consume time and energy. For example, instead of having to decide what time to set your alarm clock each morning, get up at the same time each weekday morning. Set out your clothes before you go to bed. Choose fixed study times and adhere to them without fail.

- **Focus on the positive.** Do not say, "I'll never be able to finish this assignment on time." Instead ask yourself, "What do I have to do to finish this assignment on time?"

- **Separate work, school, and social problems.** Create mental compartments for your worries. Don't spend time in class thinking about a problem at work. Leave work problems at work. Don't think about a conflict with a friend while attempting to write a paper. Deal with problems at the appropriate time.

- **Keep a personal journal.** Writing is not just for school. Taking a few minutes to write down details about your worries and your emotions can go a long way toward relieving stress. Be sure to include your goals and how you plan to achieve them.

SUCCESS ACTIVITY 12: MANAGING STRESS

Using the guidelines above, write a brief paragraph listing ways you successfully manage stress or ways you could improve how you manage stress.

PART 1

Academic Quick Start

Starting with an Advantage

The three photographs on the opposite page illustrate three important parts of most students' lives—classes, jobs, and friends and family.

Writing Quick Start

Open a new computer file, or take out a blank sheet of paper and write at the top, "I am a (an) _____." Under this statement, write a vertical list of the numbers 1 through 10. Working rapidly, complete the statement by writing down next to the numbers whatever words or phrases come to mind that describe you. Try to be as honest as possible. Remember, there are no right or wrong answers. Responses such as "great math student," "procrastinator," "good outfielder," or "slow reader" are all acceptable. Once your list is complete, take a few minutes to reread it. Then renumber the items in order of importance.

What did your list tell you about yourself? Did this exercise help you see what is important in your life? Many kinds of writing help you explore and learn about yourself and your values, especially journal writing and personal essays. You will learn more about these and other kinds of writing throughout college.

College is a challenging, often competitive environment. Hard work and a strong commitment to learning are essential to success: You must be willing to devote time and effort to reading, writing, and learning. If you are like most students, however, you have other commitments—to a job or a family or perhaps to both. The main purpose of this book is to help you succeed in your writing course, but you'll find that many of the suggestions offered here will help you with your other courses as well.

One key to academic success is to give yourself a competitive edge that will help you learn efficiently and get the most out of the time you spend studying and writing. Analyzing your learning style, discussed later in this chapter, will help you gain such an advantage. You will not only discover how you learn but also discover effective approaches to improve your learning and writing. First, let's consider why writing skills are so important and look at some general writing strategies.

WHY STRIVE TO IMPROVE YOUR WRITING SKILLS?

Most college students ask themselves the following two questions:

- How can I improve my grades?
- How can I improve my chances of getting a good job?

The answer to both questions is the same: Improve your writing, reading, and thinking skills. The following sections explain how these skills, especially writing, are essential to your success in college and on the job.

Writing Skills Help You Succeed in College and in Your Career

College courses such as psychology, biology, and political science demand that you read articles, essays, reports, and textbooks and then react to and write about what you have read. In many courses, you demonstrate what you have learned by writing exams, reports, and papers.

Writing is important on the job, as well. In most jobs, workers need to communicate effectively with supervisors, coworkers, patients, clients, and customers. You can expect to write plenty of letters, email messages, memos, and reports. The 2000-2001 study performed by the Collegiate Employment Research Institute found that employers consistently want the "total package" in recent college graduates. Employers want job candidates who have not only the technical knowledge to work but also strong oral and written communication skills.*

Because your writing course offers both immediate and long-range benefits, it is one of the most important college courses you will ever take. You will learn how to express your ideas clearly, structure convincing arguments, prepare research papers, and write essay exams. Your writing course will also help you improve your reading and thinking skills. As you read, respond to, and write about the readings, you will learn how to analyze, synthesize, and evaluate ideas.

Writing Facilitates Learning and Recall

You can often remember something more easily if you write it down. Taking notes, outlining, summarizing, or annotating focuses your attention on and gets you thinking about the course material. In addition, writing facilitates learning by engaging two senses at once. Whereas you take in information visually by reading or aurally by listening, writing engages your sense of touch as you put your pen to paper or your fingers on a keyboard. In general, the more senses you use in a learning task, the more easily learning occurs and the more you remember about the task later on. Writing also forces you to think about the subject matter at hand as you sort, connect, and define ideas.

Writing Clarifies Thinking

Writing forces you to think through a task. Getting your ideas down on paper or on a computer screen helps you evaluate them. Writing, then, is a means of sorting ideas, exploring relationships, weighing alternatives, and clarifying values.

Writing Helps You Solve Problems

When you solve problems, you identify possible actions that may change undesirable situations (your car won't start) to desirable ones (your car starts). Writing makes problem solving easier by helping you define the problem. That is, by describing the problem in writing, you can often see new aspects of it.

One student, for example, had a father-in-law who seemed hostile and uncooperative. The student described her problem in a letter to a friend: "He looks at me as if I'm going to take his son to the end of the earth and never bring him

---

*Philip D. Gardner, *Recruiting Trends, 2001–2002* (East Lansing, MI: Collegiate Employment Research Institute, Michigan State University, 2002).

back." When she reread this statement, the student realized that her father-in-law may have resented her because he was afraid of losing contact with his son and began to think of ways to reassure her father-in-law and strengthen their relationship. Writing about the problem helped the student define it and discover ways to solve it. Similarly, writing can help you think through confusing situations, make difficult decisions, and clarify your position on important issues.

DEVELOPING STRATEGIES FOR WRITING

For more help with study strategies, time management, and other academic strategies, see Keys to Academic Success, p. xlv.

Establishing a study area, planning your time, and using academic services such as the writing center are all strategies that will help you succeed in your courses. Other strategies will also make a big difference in your writing: Starting with a positive attitude, keeping a journal, and planning to get the most out of conferences with your writing instructor.

Start with a Positive Attitude

You have the potential and ability to be a successful writer. To approach your writing course positively and to get the most out of it, use the following suggestions.

1. **Think of writing as a process.** Writing is not a single act of getting words down on paper. Instead, it is a series of steps — planning, organizing, drafting, revising, and editing and proofreading. In addition, most writers go back and forth among these steps. Chapters 3 to 7 cover these steps of the writing process.

2. **Be patient.** Writing is a skill that improves gradually. Don't expect to see dramatic differences in your writing immediately. As you draft and revise your essays, your writing will improve in small ways that build on one another.

3. **Expect writing to take time, often more time than you planned.** Realize, too, that on some days writing will be easier than on other days.

4. **Focus on learning.** When you are given a writing assignment, ask, "What can I learn from this?" As you learn more about your own writing process, write down your observations (see the section on journal writing below).

5. **Use the support and guidance available to you.** Your instructor, your classmates, and this book can all help you become a better writer. In Parts 3 and 4 of the text, Guided Writing Assignments will lead you, step-by-step, through each chapter assignment. You will find tips, advice, and alternative ways of approaching the assignment.

6. **Look for ideas in the readings.** The essays in this book have been chosen to spark your interest and to touch on current issues. Think of every assigned reading as an opportunity to learn about a topic that you might not otherwise have the time to read or think about. Chapter 2 provides a Guide to Active Reading and a Guide to Responding to Text that offer helpful strategies for getting the most out of the reading assignments in this book and responding to what you have read.

7. **Attend all classes.** Writing is a skill, not a set of facts you can read about in a book; it is best learned through interactions with your instructor and classmates.

Keep a Writing Journal

Use a **writing journal** to record daily impressions, reflect on events or on reading assignments, comment on experiences and observations, explore relationships among people or ideas, ask questions, and test ideas. You should write in your journal frequently; write every day, if possible. You can keep your writing journal in a notebook or a computer file and use it to record your ideas.

Benefits of Journal Writing

- **A journal is a place to practice writing.** Writing can best be improved through practice. Record conversations, summarize or react to meaningful experiences, or release pent-up frustrations. Remember, regardless of what you write about, you are writing and thereby improving your skills.

- **A journal is a place to experiment.** Try out new ideas, and express things that you are learning about yourself—your beliefs and values. Experiment with different voices, different topics, and different approaches to a topic.

- **A journal is a place to warm up.** Like an athlete, a writer benefits from warming up. Use a journal to activate your thought processes, loosen up, and stretch your mind before you tackle your writing assignments.

- **A journal is a place to reflect on your writing.** Record problems, strategies you have learned, and ways to start assignments. You might also find it helpful to keep an error log and a misspelled word log.

- **A journal is a source of ideas for papers.** If you are asked to choose your own topic for an essay, leaf through your journal. You'll find plenty of possibilities.

- **A journal is a place to respond to readings.** Use it to collect your thoughts about and respond to a reading before writing an assigned essay. (You will learn more about response journals in Chapter 2.)

How to Get Started

Your first journal entry is often the most difficult one to write. Once you've written a few entries, you'll begin to feel more comfortable. Here's how to get started.

1. Write in a spiral-bound notebook, or type your entries on a computer, print them out, and compile them in a notebook. Be sure to date each entry.

2. Set aside five to ten minutes each day for journal writing. "Waiting times" at the bus stop, at the laundromat, or in long lines provide opportunities for journal writing, as do "down times," such as the ten minutes before a class begins or the few minutes between finishing dinner and studying.

3. Concentrate on capturing your ideas—not on being grammatically correct. Try to write correct sentences, but do not focus on grammar and punctuation.

4. If you are not sure what to write about, consult Figure 1.1. Coding your entries as shown in the figure will make you more aware of your thought processes and help you to distinguish different types of entries.

5. Reread your journal entries on a regular basis. By doing so, you will discover that rereading entries is similar to looking at old photographs: They will bring back vivid snippets of the past for reflection and appreciation.

WRITING ACTIVITY 1

Write a journal entry describing your reaction to one or more of your classes this semester. For example, you might write about which classes you expect to be most or least difficult, most or least enjoyable, and most or least time consuming.

Get the Most out of Writing Conferences

Many writing instructors schedule periodic writing conferences with individual students. These conferences are designed to give you and your instructor an opportunity to discuss your work and your progress in the course. Such conferences are opportunities for you to get help with your writing skills. If the conferences are optional, be sure to schedule one.

The following tips will help you get the most out of a writing conference.

1. Arrive on time or a few minutes early.

2. Bring copies of the draft essay you are currently working on as well as previously returned papers. Have them in hand, not buried in your book bag, when your conference begins, since you may want to refer to them.

3. Reread recently returned papers ahead of time, so that your instructor's comments are fresh in your mind. Also review your notes from any previous conferences.

4. Allow your instructor to set the agenda, but come prepared with a list of questions you need answered.

FIGURE 1.1
STARTING POINTS FOR JOURNAL WRITING

Codes for Your Journal Entries	Type of Writing	Ideas for Subjects
< >	Describing	a daily event a sporting event an object a cartoon or photograph an overheard conversation
!!	Reacting to	a person a world, national, local, or campus event a passage from a book a magazine or newspaper article a film, song, or concert a television program a radio personality a fashion or fad
←	Recollecting	an important event a childhood experience an impression or dream a favorite relative or friend
?	Questioning	a policy a trend a position on an issue
↔	Comparing or contrasting	two people two events or actions two issues
ex	Thinking of examples of	a personality type a type of teacher, supervisor, or doctor
+ −	Judging (evaluating)	a rule or law a decision a musician or other performer an assignment a radio or television personality a political candidate

5. Take notes, either during or immediately after the conference. Include the comments and suggestions offered by your instructor. You might also consider writing a journal entry that summarizes the conference.

6. Revise the draft essay you and your instructor discussed as soon as possible, while the suggestions for revision you received are still fresh in your mind.

ASSESSING YOUR LEARNING STYLE

Depending in part on a person's past experiences, personality, and prior learning, each person learns and writes in a unique way. Discovering your learning style will give you an important advantage in your writing course and in your other courses. In this section and the following one, you will assess how you learn by using a Learning Style Inventory. You will learn specific strategies to learn more effectively, capitalizing on your strengths and overcoming your weaknesses.

What Is Your Learning Style?

Have you noticed that you do better with some types of academic assignments than with others? Hands-on assignments may be easier than conducting research, for example. Have you discovered that it is easier to learn from some instructors than from others? You may prefer instructors who give plenty of real-life examples or those who show relationships by drawing diagrams. Have you noticed differences in how you and your friends study, solve problems, and approach assignments? You may be methodical and analytical, whereas a friend may get flashes of insight. You may be able to read printed information and recall it easily, but a friend may find it easier to learn from class lectures or a videotape. Have you noticed that some students prefer to work alone on a project, while others enjoy working as part of a group?

These differences can be explained by what is known as **learning style,** or the set of preferences that describes how you learn. The following Learning Style Inventory is intended to help you assess your learning style. After you have completed the Learning Style Inventory, you'll find directions for scoring on page 14.

LEARNING STYLE INVENTORY

Directions: Each numbered item presents two choices. Select the one alternative that best describes you. There are no right or wrong answers. In cases in which neither choice suits you, select the one that is closer to your preference. Check the letter of your choice next to the question number on the answer sheet on page 14.

1. In a class, I usually
   a. make friends with just a few students.
   b. get to know many of my classmates.

2. If I were required to act in a play, I would prefer to
   a. have the director tell me how to say my lines.
   b. read my lines the way I think they should be read.

3. Which would I find more helpful in studying the processes by which the U.S. Constitution can be amended?
   a. a one-paragraph summary
   b. a diagram

4. In making decisions, I am more concerned with
   a. whether I have all the available facts.
   b. how my decision will affect others.

5. When I have a difficult time understanding how something works, it helps most if I can
   a. see how it works several times.
   b. take time to think the process through and analyze it.

6. At a social event, I usually
   a. wait for people to speak to me.
   b. initiate conversation with others.

7. I prefer courses that have
   a. a traditional structure (lectures, assigned readings, periodic exams, and assignments with deadlines).
   b. an informal structure (class discussions, flexible assignments, and student-selected projects).

8. If I were studying one of the laws of motion in a physics course, I would prefer to have my instructor begin the class by
   a. stating the law and discussing examples.
   b. giving a demonstration of how the law works.

9. Which set of terms best describes me?
   a. fair and objective
   b. sympathetic and understanding

10. When I learn something new, I am more interested in
    a. the facts about it.
    b. the principles behind it.

11. As a volunteer for a community organization that is raising funds for a hospice, I prefer the following tasks.
    a. stuffing envelopes for a mail campaign
    b. making phone calls asking for contributions

12. I would begin an ideal day by

    a. planning what I want to do during each hour of the day.
    b. doing whatever comes to mind.

13. If I wanted to learn the proper way to prune a rosebush, I would prefer to

    a. have someone explain it to me.
    b. watch someone do it.

14. It is more important for me to be

    a. consistent in thought and action.
    b. responsive to the feelings of others.

15. If I kept a journal or diary, it would most likely contain entries about

    a. what happens to me each day.
    b. the insights and ideas that occur to me each day.

16. If I decided to learn a musical instrument, I would prefer to take

    a. one-on-one lessons.
    b. group lessons.

17. If I worked in a factory, I would prefer to be a

    a. machine operator.
    b. troubleshooter.

18. I learn best when I

    a. write down the information.
    b. form a mental picture of the information.

19. If I gave a wrong answer in class, my main concern would be

    a. finding out the correct answer.
    b. what others in class thought of me.

20. I prefer television news programs that

    a. summarize events through film footage and factual description.
    b. deal with the issues behind the events.

21. Whenever possible, I choose to

    a. study alone.
    b. study with a study group.

22. In selecting a topic for a research paper, my more important concern is

    a. choosing a topic for which there is adequate information.
    b. choosing a topic I find interesting.

23. If I took apart a complicated toy or machine to repair it, to help me reassemble it I would

    a. write a list of the steps I followed when taking it apart.
    b. draw a diagram of the toy or machine.

24. As a member of a jury for a criminal trial, I would be primarily concerned with
    a. determining how witness testimony fits with the other evidence.
    b. judging the believability of witnesses.
25. If I were an author, I would most likely write
    a. biographies or how-to books.
    b. novels or poetry.
26. A career in which my work depends on that of others is
    a. less appealing than working alone.
    b. more appealing than working alone.
27. When I am able to solve a problem, it is usually because I
    a. worked through the solution step by step.
    b. brainstormed until I arrived at a solution.
28. I prefer to keep up with the news by
    a. reading a newspaper.
    b. watching television news programs.
29. If I came upon a serious auto accident, my first impulse would be to
    a. assess the situation.
    b. comfort any injured people.
30. I pride myself on my ability to
    a. remember numbers and facts.
    b. see how ideas are related.
31. To solve a personal problem, I prefer to
    a. think about it myself.
    b. talk it through with friends.
32. If I had one last elective course to take before graduation, I would choose one that presents
    a. practical information that I can use immediately.
    b. ideas that make me think and stimulate my imagination.
33. For recreation, I would rather do a
    a. crossword puzzle.
    b. jig-saw puzzle.
34. I can best be described as
    a. reasonable and levelheaded.
    b. sensitive and caring.
35. When I read a story or watch a film, I prefer one with a plot that is
    a. clear and direct.
    b. intricate and complex.

Answer Sheet

Directions: Check either *a* or *b* in the boxes next to each question number.

	Column One			Column Two			Column Three			Column Four			Column Five	
	a	*b*		*a*	*b*		*a*	*b*		*a*	*b*		*a*	*b*
1			2			3			4			5		
6			7			8			9			10		
11			12			13			14			15		
16			17			18			19			20		
21			22			23			24			25		
26			27			28			29			30		
31			32			33			34			35		
Total														

Directions for Scoring

1. On your answer sheet, add the checkmarks in each *a* and *b* column, counting first the number of *a*s checked and then the number of *b*s.

2. Enter the number of *a*s and *b*s you checked in the boxes at the bottom of each column.

3. Transfer these numbers to the Scoring Grid on page 15. Enter the number of *a* choices in column one in the blank labeled "Independent," the number of *b* choices in column one in the blank labeled "Social," and so on.

4. Circle your higher score in each row. For example, if you scored 2 for Independent and 5 for Social, circle "5" and "Social."

5. Your higher score in each row indicates a characteristic of your learning style. If the scores in a particular row are close to one another, such as 3 and 4, this suggests that you do not have a strong preference for either approach to learning. Scores that are far apart, such as 1 and 6, suggest that you favor one way of learning over the other.

Interpreting Your Scores

The Learning Style Inventory is divided into five parts; each question in the inventory assesses one of five aspects of your learning style. Here is how to interpret the five aspects of your learning style.

SCORING GRID

COLUMN	NUMBER OF CHECKMARKS	
	Choice a	*Choice b*
One		
	Independent	Social
Two		
	Pragmatic	Creative
Three		
	Verbal	Spatial
Four		
	Rational	Emotional
Five		
	Concrete	Abstract

1. *Independent or Social*

These scores indicate the level of interaction with others that you prefer. *Independent* learners prefer to work and study alone. They focus on the task at hand rather than on the people around them and are often goal-oriented and self-motivated. *Social* learners are more people-oriented and prefer to learn and study with classmates. They often focus their attention on those around them and see a task as an opportunity for social interaction.

2. *Pragmatic or Creative*

These scores suggest how you prefer to approach learning tasks. *Pragmatic* learners are practical and systematic. They approach tasks in an orderly, sequential manner. They like rules and learn step by step. *Creative* learners, in contrast, approach tasks imaginatively. They prefer to learn through discovery or experiment. They enjoy flexible, open-ended tasks and tend to dislike following rules.

3. *Verbal or Spatial*

These scores indicate the way you prefer to take in and process information. *Verbal* learners rely on language, usually written text, to acquire information. They are skilled in the use of language and can work with other symbol systems as well. *Spatial* learners prefer to take in information by studying graphics such as drawings, diagrams, films, or videos. They can visualize in their minds how things work or how things are positioned in space.

4. Rational or Emotional

These scores suggest your preferred approach to decision making and problem solving. *Rational* learners are objective and impersonal; they rely on facts and information when making decisions or solving problems. Rational learners are logical, often challenging or questioning a task. They enjoy prioritizing, analyzing, and arguing. In contrast, *emotional* learners are subjective; they focus on feelings and values. Emotional decision makers are socially conscious and often concerned with what others think. In making a decision, they seek harmony and may base a decision in part on the effect it may have on others. Emotional decision makers are often skilled at persuasion.

5. Concrete or Abstract

These scores indicate how you prefer to perceive information. *Concrete* learners pay attention to what is concrete and observable. They focus on details and tend to perceive tasks in parts or steps. Concrete learners prefer actual, tangible tasks and usually take a no-nonsense approach to learning. *Abstract* learners look at a task from a broader perspective. They tend to focus on the "big picture" or an overview of a task. Abstract learners focus on large ideas, meanings, and relationships.

A Word about Your Findings

The results of the Learning Style Inventory probably confirmed some things you already knew about yourself as a learner and provided you with some new insights as well. Keep in mind, though, that there are other ways to measure learning style.

- The inventory you completed is an informal measure of your learning style. Other, more formal measures — including Kolb's *Learning Style Inventory,* the *Canfield Instructional Styles Inventory,* and the *Myers-Briggs Type Indicator* — may be available at your college's counseling or academic skills center.

- The inventory you completed measures the five aspects of learning style that are most relevant to the writing process. However, many other aspects of learning style exist.

- You are the best judge of the accuracy of the results of this inventory and how they apply to you. If you think that one or more of the aspects of your learning style indicated by the inventory do not describe you, trust your instincts.

How to Use Your Findings

Now that you have identified important characteristics of your learning style, you are ready to use the findings to your advantage — to make learning easier and improve your writing skills. As you do so, keep the following suggestions in mind.

1. **If you have a strength in one area, you can still act in the opposite way.** For example, if you scored highly on the pragmatic scale, you are still capable of creative thinking as well.

2. **Learning style tendencies are not fixed, unchangeable characteristics.** Although you may have a higher score on the independent scale, for example, you can learn to function effectively in groups.

3. **Experiment with approaches that are not necessarily suited to your learning style.** Some students find that when they try a new approach, it works better than they expected. A verbal learner, for example, may discover that drawing a diagram of how a process works is an effective learning strategy.

4. **Learning style is not an excuse to avoid learning.** Don't make the mistake of saying, "I can't write poetry because I'm not a creative learner." Instead, use what you know about your learning style to guide your approach to each task. If you are a pragmatic learner, try writing a poem about a tangible object or place or a real event.

APPLYING YOUR LEARNING STYLE TO YOUR WRITING

Writing is a process that involves planning, organizing, drafting, revising, and editing and proofreading. You'll learn more about each of these steps in Chapters 3 to 7. It is important to realize that you can approach each step in the writing process in more than one way. For example, one of the first steps in that process is to select a topic to write about. There are a number of ways to go about this task. A social learner may prefer to brainstorm about possible topics with a friend. A verbal learner may find that flipping through a newsmagazine brings topics to mind. A spatial learner may see a photograph that generates ideas for topics. Someone who is a social as well as a spatial learner may prefer to select a topic by discussing photographs with a classmate.

Let's consider an example involving two hypothetical students. Yolanda and Andrea, classmates in a first-year writing course, are assigned to write an essay describing an event that has influenced their lives. Yolanda writes a list of possible events and arranges them in order of importance in her life. After selecting one of these events, she draws a diagram showing the circumstances that led up to the event and the effects that the event had on her. Before she begins writing, Yolanda decides on the best way to organize her ideas and creates an outline.

Andrea lets her mind roam freely over various events in her life while she is out jogging. All of a sudden an idea comes to mind, and she knows what she wants to write about. She jots down everything she can recall about the event, in the haphazard order that each remembered detail comes to her. From these notes, she selects ideas and writes her first draft. Andrea writes numerous drafts, experimenting with different organizations. Finally, she produces an essay with which she is satisfied.

Although Yolanda and Andrea approach the same assignment in different ways, they both write effective essays. Yolanda prefers a deliberate and systematic approach because she is a pragmatic learner. Andrea, a creative learner, prefers a less structured approach, one that allows ideas to come to her in any form. Yolanda spends a great deal of time planning before writing, while Andrea prefers to experiment with various versions of her paper.

Because students' learning styles differ, this book presents alternative strategies for generating ideas and for revising your writing. These choices are indicated by the marginal note "Learning Style Options" (see p. 50 for an example). The following advice will help you take advantage of these learning style alternatives.

1. **Select an alternative that fits with how you learn.** If you are writing an essay on insurance fraud and are given the choice of interviewing an expert on insurance fraud or finding several articles in the library on the topic, choose the option that best suits the way you prefer to acquire information.

2. **Experiment with options.** To sustain your interest and broaden your skills, you should sometimes choose an option that does not match your preferred learning style. For example, if you are an independent learner, conducting an interview with the insurance fraud expert may help you strengthen your interpersonal skills.

3. **Don't expect the option that is consistent with your learning style to require less attention or effort.** Even if you are a social learner, an interview must still be carefully planned and well executed.

4. **Keep logs of the skills and approaches that work for you and the ones you need to work on.** The logs may be part of your writing journal (see p. 7). Be specific: Record the assignment, the topic you chose, and the skills you applied. Analyze your log, looking for patterns. Over time, you will discover more about the writing strategies and approaches that work best for you.

Your learning style profile also indicates your strengths as a writer. As with any skill, you should try to build on your strengths, using them as a foundation. Work with Figure 1.2 to identify your strengths. First, circle or highlight the characteristics that you scored higher on in the five areas of learning style. Then refer to the right-hand column to see your strengths as a writer in each area.

WRITING ACTIVITY 2

Write a two-page essay describing your reactions to the results of the Learning Style Inventory. Explain how you expect to use the results in your writing course or other courses.

WRITING ACTIVITY 3

Using your responses to the Writing Quick Start on page 3 and the results of the Learning Style Inventory, write a two-page profile of yourself as a student or as a writer.

FIGURE 1.2
YOUR STRENGTHS AS A WRITER

Learning Style Characteristic	Strengths as a Writer
Independent	You are willing to spend time thinking about a topic and are able to pull ideas together easily.
Social	You usually find it easy to write from experience. Writing realistic dialogue may be one of your strengths. You tend to have a good sense of who you are writing for (your audience) and what you hope to accomplish (your purpose).
Pragmatic	You can meet deadlines easily. You recognize the need for organization in an essay. You tend to approach writing systematically and work through the steps in the writing process.
Creative	You tend to enjoy exploring a topic and often do so thoroughly and completely. Your writing is not usually hindered or restricted by rules or requirements.
Verbal	You may have a talent for generating ideas to write about and expressing them clearly.
Spatial	You can visualize or draw a map of the organization of your paper. Descriptions of physical objects, places, and people come easily.
Rational	You tend to write logically developed, well-organized essays. You usually analyze ideas objectively.
Emotional	Expressive and descriptive writing usually go well for you. You have a strong awareness of your audience.
Concrete	You find it easy to supply details to support an idea. You are able to write accurate, detailed descriptions and observations. You can organize facts effectively and present them clearly.
Abstract	You can develop unique approaches to a topic; you can grasp the point to which supporting ideas lead.

Reading and Writing about Text

The photograph on the opposite page is taken from a mass communication textbook. Your mass communication instructor has asked your class to study the photograph and discuss its significance.

Writing Quick Start

Write a paragraph explaining what you think the photograph means and why it might have been included in the communication textbook.

To explain the meaning of the photograph, you had to think beyond the obvious action it portrays. You had to interpret and evaluate the photograph to arrive at its possible meaning. To complete this evaluation, you did two things. First, you grasped what the photograph showed; then you analyzed what it meant.

Reading involves a similar process of comprehension and evaluation. First, you must know what the author *says;* then you must interpret and respond to what the author *means.* Both parts of the process are essential. This chapter will help you succeed with both parts of the reading process.

In this chapter, you will learn to be a more active reader, a reader who becomes engaged and involved with a reading assignment by analyzing, challenging, and evaluating ideas. The chapter contains a Guide to Active Reading (p. 23) in which you will learn what to do before, during, and after reading to strengthen your comprehension and increase your recall. You will also learn how to approach difficult assignments and how to draw a diagram, called a *graphic organizer,* that will help you grasp both the content and organization of an assignment. The chapter also includes a Guide to Responding to Text (p. 41) that offers several useful strategies for responding to text. These include summarizing, linking the reading to your own experiences, analyzing the reading by asking critical questions, using annotation, keeping a response journal, and using a response worksheet.

As you improve your ability to read and respond thoroughly and carefully, you'll learn more about what you read. You'll also do better on exams and quizzes that ask you to apply, connect, and evaluate ideas.

The examples in the accompanying box demonstrate why active, critical reading and active response are essential to your success in college and on the job.

SCENES FROM COLLEGE AND THE WORKPLACE

- In an *art history* class, your instructor assigns a critical review of a museum exhibit that your class recently visited. She asks you to read the review and write an essay agreeing or disagreeing with the critic's viewpoint and expressing your own views.

- For a *zoology* course, your instructor distributes an excerpt from the book *When Elephants Weep: The Emotional Lives of Animals* and asks you to write a paper summarizing and analyzing the author's position.

- You are working as an *inspector* for the Occupational Safety and Health Administration (OSHA). Part of your job is to read, interpret, and evaluate corporate plans to comply with OSHA safety standards.

CHANGING SOME MISCONCEPTIONS ABOUT READING

Much misinformation exists about how to read effectively and efficiently. This section dispels some popular misconceptions about reading.

- **Not everything on a page is equally important.** Whether you are reading an article in a sports magazine, a biography of a president, or an essay in this book, each text contains a mixture of important and not-so-important ideas and information. Your task as a reader is to sort through the material and evaluate what you need to know.

- **You should not read everything the same way.** What you read, how rapidly and how carefully you read, what you pay attention to, and what, if anything, you skip are all affected by your intent. For instance, if your psychology instructor assigns an article from *Psychology Today* as a basis for class discussion, you would read it differently than if you were preparing for a quiz based on the article. Your familiarity with a topic also affects how you read. Effective readers vary their reading techniques to suit what they are reading and why they are reading it.

  For more on how to read selectively by scanning and skimming, see Working with Text: Reading Sources in Chapter 18 (p. 658).

- **Reading material once is often not sufficient.** In many academic situations, you will need to read chapters, articles, or essays more than once to discover the author's position, summarize the author's key ideas, and analyze the reliability and sufficiency of the supporting evidence that he or she provides.

- **Not everything in print is true.** Just as you don't believe everything you hear, neither should you believe everything you read. Be sure to read with a critical, questioning eye and, at times, with a raised eyebrow. To evaluate a text, consider the authority of the author and the author's purpose for writing. As you read, try to distinguish facts from opinions, value judgments, and generalizations. If you were to read an article titled "Woman Loses 30 Pounds in One Week," for example, your critical, questioning eye would probably be wide open. Be sure to keep that eye open when you read scholarly essays as well.

A GUIDE TO ACTIVE READING

When you attend a ball game or watch a soap opera, do you get actively involved? If you are a baseball fan, at ball games you cheer some players and criticize others, evaluate plays and calls, offer advice, and so forth. Similarly, if you are a soap-opera fan, you get actively involved in your favorite program. You react to sudden turns of events, sympathize with some characters, and despise others. By contrast, if you are not a fan of a baseball team or soap opera, you might watch the game or show passively, letting it take its course with little or no personal involvement or reaction. Like fans of a sports team or soap opera, active readers get involved with the material they read. They question, think about, and react to ideas using the process outlined in Figure 2.1.

The accompanying chart (see p. 25) shows how active and passive readers approach a reading assignment in different ways. As you can see, active readers get involved by using a step-by-step approach. The sections that follow explain each of these active reading steps in more detail.

Preview before Reading

You probably wouldn't pay to see a movie unless you knew something about it. Similarly, you should not start reading an essay without checking its content to get a sense of what it is about. **Previewing** is a quick way to familiarize yourself with an essay's content and organization. Previewing also enables you to decide what you need to know from the material. Previewing has a number of other benefits as well.

- It helps you get interested in the material.
- It provides you with a mental outline of the material before you read it.

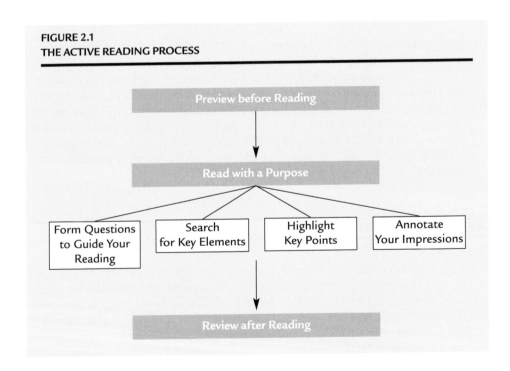

FIGURE 2.1
THE ACTIVE READING PROCESS

APPROACHES TO READING: ACTIVE VERSUS PASSIVE

Passive Reading	*Active Reading*
Passive readers begin reading.	Active readers begin by reading the title, evaluating the author, and thinking about what they already know about the subject. Then they decide what they need to know before they begin reading.
Passive readers read the essay only because it is assigned.	Active readers read the essay while looking for answers to questions and key elements.
Passive readers read but do not write.	Active readers read with a pen in hand. They highlight or underline, annotate, and write notes as they read.
Passive readers close the book when finished.	Active readers review, analyze, and evaluate the essay.

- It enables you to concentrate more easily on the material because you know what to expect.
- It helps you remember more of what you read.

To preview a reading assignment, use the guidelines in the following list. Remember to read *only* the parts of an essay that are listed.

1. **Read the title, subtitle, and author.** The title and subtitle may tell you what the reading is about. Check the author's name to see if it is one you recognize.
2. **Read the introduction and the first paragraph.** These sections often provide an overview of the essay.
3. **Read any headings and the first sentence following each one.** Headings, taken together, often form a mini-outline of the essay. The first sentence following a heading often explains the heading further.
4. **For an essay without headings, read the first sentence in a few of the paragraphs on each page.**
5. **Look at any photographs, tables, charts, and drawings.**
6. **Read the conclusion or summary.** A conclusion will draw the reading to a close. If the reading concludes with a summary, it will give you a condensed view of the reading.

7. **Read any end-of-assignment questions.** These questions will help focus your attention on what is important in the reading and on what you might be expected to know after you have read it.

The following essay, "Purse Snatching," has been highlighted to illustrate the parts you should read while previewing. Preview it now.

Purse Snatching

The issue not yet confronted is the barrier to being treated equally when it comes to money.

Donna Lopiano

1   It appears that we are at a crossroads in women's sports. As Jesse Jackson said of the civil rights movement, "We have moved from the battlefield of access to opportunity to the battlefield of access to capital." Through government legislation like Title IX and the pressure of societal sanction and criticism, we have removed the participation barriers that once confronted women in the world of sport, especially sport at government-supported educational institutions. The right to play has been established. However, the issue that has not yet been confronted is the barrier to being treated equally when it comes to money.

2   Few see the fairness, for example, in our 1999 U.S.A. Women's World Cup soccer champions being promised $12,500 if they won compared to the approximately $300,000 received by male World Cup champs. Now the U.S. women will receive almost $50,000 as a result of the public outcry over how the event's huge profits (estimates hover at $2 to $5 million) would be spent. And few would argue against the position that the women's pro tennis tour is more appealing and interesting to the public than the men's tour and should command equal if not higher salaries for its players. Yet women's professional tennis purses are 25 percent smaller than those of men.

3   The Women's National Basketball Association (WNBA) players had trouble negotiating minimum salary guarantees of $20,000 to $30,000 a year — a tiny fraction of what most NBA players make. Meanwhile, it took almost 30 years for the NBA to average 10,000 spectators a game and only two years for the WNBA to reach that mark.

4   Where are the women in auto racing at Indy, NASCAR, or CART events — truly the most lucrative of all professional sports — when it comes to endorsements, winnings, and the profits of team ownership? The answer is nowhere, since virtually no women regularly participate in auto racing. With regard to salaries, profit sharing, or

access to significant dollars to begin professional leagues or gain entry into high-stakes sports competition, women are still behind the eight ball.

Instead of paying women athletes what they're worth, there seems to be a concerted effort to sexualize them. By commenting on the looks of the U.S. women's soccer team, the media blatantly suggest that these athletes' physical appearance is more important and of greater interest than their athletic achievements. When Brandi Chastain took her shirt off following the winning goal, displaying considerable muscle as well as a sports bra that more than covered the territory, the media acted like they were looking at a Victoria's Secret catalog as opposed to a world championship soccer match. How many women jog on city streets and work out in health clubs every day wearing less?

The media and the medical establishment, despite evidence to the contrary, are quick to posit that the reason for a spate of anterior cruciate knee injuries in women is because women are physically inferior to men (our knees are ill-constructed and our hormones wreak havoc on our bodies). Are these predominantly male professionals maybe too eager to reinforce the strength and dominance of males and dismiss women in sport?

I travel all over the country as a public speaker. I love talking to high school boys because they reflect the male view before the veil of political correctness disguises their true feelings. Young boys believe that it's terribly important for me to acknowledge that males are better athletes than females. Males jump higher, throw farther, run faster, dunk basketballs better, and are more interesting to watch than female athletes. They listen intently as I ask, "Who is the better athlete, Mike Tyson or Sugar Ray Leonard?" Initially struck silent by the question, they then respond with considerable chagrin, "That's not a fair question! Those are boxers in different weight classes. They don't compete against each other. They are both great boxers." To which I quietly respond, "Exactly." Why the need to affirm male dominance? Why the need to hog the marbles?

Women's sport has proved it has a market. What the marketplace needs is people who are willing to risk and share capital to exploit that market. One would think that sex discrimination would take a backseat to making money and good business decisions. How many more wildly successful events need to occur before people talk positively about an investment in the women's sports market and act to take advantage of this opportunity? When will questioning the physical ability of female athletes go away? When will efforts to undermine the women's sports industry cease? Ultimately, it comes down to a matter of will and being gender blind when exploiting business opportunities. We're not there yet. ∎

EXERCISE 2.1

Based only on your preview of the essay "Purse Snatching," answer the following questions as either true or false to determine whether you have gained a sense of the essay's content and organization. If most of your answers are correct, you will know that previewing worked. (For the answers to this exercise, see p. 56.)

_____ 1. The reading is primarily about the financial inequity between men's and women's sports.

_____ 2. Auto racing is not a lucrative sport.

_____ 3. The author suggests that women's sports have proven to be sound business opportunities.

_____ 4. In basketball, there is a large discrepancy between men's and women's salaries.

_____ 5. World Cup soccer championships pay men and women equally.

Read with a Purpose

If you tried to draw the face side of a one-dollar bill from memory, you would probably remember little about its appearance. In much the same way, if you read an essay thinking, "Well, it was assigned, so I had better read it," you probably won't remember much of what you read. Why does this happen? According to a psychological principle known as *intent to remember*, you remember what you decide to remember. So if you begin reading an essay without first deciding what you need to know and remember, you won't be able to recall any more about the essay than you could about the dollar bill.

Form Questions to Guide Your Reading

Before you begin reading, you will want to improve your intent to remember. Look again at the guidelines for previewing on page 24. You can use these parts of an essay to form questions. Then, as you read, you can answer those questions and thereby strengthen your comprehension and memory of the material. The following suggestions will help you start devising your questions.

- **Use the title of an essay to devise questions.** Then read to find the answers. Here are a few examples of titles and relevant questions.

Essay Title	**Question**
"Part-time Employment Undermines Students' Commitment to School"	Why does part-time employment undermine commitment to school?
"Human Cloning: Don't Just Say 'No'"	What are good reasons to clone humans?

- **Use headings to devise questions that will guide your reading.** For example, in an essay titled "Territoriality," Joseph DeVito explains the concept of territoriality. His headings include "Types of Territoriality" and "Territorial

Encroachment." Each of these headings can easily be turned into a question that becomes a guide as you read: What are the types of territoriality? and What is territorial encroachment and how does it occur?

Not all essays lend themselves to these particular techniques. For some essays, you may need to dig deeper into the introductory and final paragraphs to form questions. Or you may discover that the subtitle is more useful than the title. Look again at your preview of "Purse Snatching." Using the subtitle and the introductory paragraph of that essay, you might decide to look for answers to this question: Why does financial inequity exist between men's and women's sports?

Search for Key Elements

When you know what to look for as you read, you will read more easily, read faster, and do less rereading. When you read assigned articles, essays, or chapters, search for the following key elements.

1. **The meaning of the title and subtitle** In some essays, the title announces the topic and reveals the author's point of view. In others, the meaning or the significance of the title becomes clear only after you have read the entire essay.

2. **The introduction** The opening paragraph should provide background information, announce the subject of the essay, and get the reader's attention.

3. **The author's main point** The author's main point is often stated directly in the **thesis statement.** The thesis states the one big idea that the piece of writing explains, explores, or supports. For example, in an essay about who should receive organ transplants, the thesis might state the writer's position on the issue: "Whether a person smokes or drinks alcohol should be a factor in determining whether he or she is eligible for an organ transplant." The thesis is often placed in the first or second paragraph of an essay to let the reader know what lies ahead. But it may at times appear at the end of an essay instead. Occasionally, an essay's thesis will be implied or suggested rather than stated directly.

    For more about thesis statements, see Chapter 4, p. 92.

4. **The support and explanation** The body of the piece of writing should support or give reasons for the author's main point. For example, if an essay's thesis is that gay marriages should be legalized, then the body of the essay should offer reasons to support that position. Each paragraph in the body has a topic sentence, which states what the paragraph is about. Each topic sentence should in some way explain or support the essay's thesis statement.

5. **The conclusion** The concluding paragraph or paragraphs of an essay may restate the author's main point, offer ideas for further thought, or suggest new directions.

You'll learn much more about each part of an essay in Chapters 3 to 7.

Now read the entire essay "Purse Snatching" with a purpose — to know and to remember the material. Remember to look for key elements as you read.

Purse Snatching

The issue not yet confronted is the barrier to being treated equally when it comes to money.

Donna Lopiano

Donna Lopiano is the execcutive director of the Women's Sports Foundation. This essay was first published in Ms. *magazine in 1999. As you read, pay attention to the marginal notes that identify and explain various parts of the essay.*

1   It appears that we are at a crossroads in women's sports. As Jesse Jackson said of the civil rights movement, "We have moved from the battlefield of access to opportunity to the battlefield of access to capital." Through government legislation like Title IX and the pressure of societal sanction and criticism, we have removed the participation barriers that once confronted women in the world of sport, especially sport at government-supported educational institutions. The right to play has been established. However, the issue that has not yet been confronted is the barrier to being treated equally when it comes to money.

2   Few see the fairness, for example, in our 1999 U.S.A. Women's World Cup soccer champions being promised $12,500 if they won compared to the approximately $300,000 received by male World Cup champs. Now the U.S. women will receive almost $50,000 as a result of the public outcry over how the event's huge profits (estimates hover at $2 to $5 million) would be spent. And few would argue against the position that the women's pro tennis tour is more appealing and interesting to the public than the men's tour and should command equal if not higher salaries for its players. Yet women's professional tennis purses are 25 percent smaller than those of men.

3   The Women's National Basketball Association (WNBA) players had trouble negotiating minimum salary guarantees of $20,000 to $30,000 a year—a tiny fraction of what most NBA players make. Meanwhile, it took almost 30 years for the NBA to average 10,000 spectators a game and only two years for the WNBA to reach that mark.

4   Where are the women in auto racing at Indy, NASCAR, or CART events—truly the most lucrative of all professional sports—when it comes to endorsements, winnings, and the profits of team ownership? The answer is nowhere, since virtually no women regularly participate in auto racing. With regard to salaries, profit sharing, or access to significant dollars to begin professional leagues or gain

entry into high-stakes sports competition, women are still behind the eight ball.

Instead of paying women athletes what they're worth, there seems to be a concerted effort to sexualize them. By commenting on the looks of the U.S. women's soccer team, the media blatantly suggest that these athletes' physical appearance is more important and of greater interest than their athletic achievements. When Brandi Chastain took her shirt off following the winning goal, displaying considerable muscle as well as a sports bra that more than covered the territory, the media acted like they were looking at a Victoria's Secret catalog as opposed to a world championship soccer match. How many women jog on city streets and work out in health clubs every day wearing less?

5 Support: gives reasons for salary inequity

The media and the medical establishment, despite evidence to the contrary, are quick to posit that the reason for a spate of anterior cruciate knee injuries in women is because women are physically inferior to men (our knees are ill-constructed and our hormones wreak havoc on our bodies). Are these predominantly male professionals maybe too eager to reinforce the strength and dominance of males and dismiss women in sport?

6 Support: explains media and medical bias

I travel all over the country as a public speaker. I love talking to high school boys because they reflect the male view before the veil of political correctness disguises their true feelings. Young boys believe that it's terribly important for me to acknowledge that males are better athletes than females. Males jump higher, throw farther, run faster, dunk basketballs better, and are more interesting to watch than female athletes. They listen intently as I ask, "Who is the better athlete, Mike Tyson or Sugar Ray Leonard?" Initially struck silent by the question, they then respond with considerable chagrin, "That's not a fair question! Those are boxers in different weight classes. They don't compete against each other. They are both great boxers." To which I quietly respond, "Exactly." Why the need to affirm male dominance? Why the need to hog the marbles?

7 Support: Men's and women's sports are distinct and should not be compared.

Women's sport has proved it has a market. What the marketplace needs is people who are willing to risk and share capital to exploit that market. One would think that sex discrimination would take a backseat to making money and good business decisions. How many more wildly successful events need to occur before people talk positively about an investment in the women's sports market and act to take advantage of this opportunity? When will questioning the physical ability of female athletes go away? When will efforts to undermine the women's sports industry cease? Ultimately, it comes down to a matter of will and being gender blind when exploiting business opportunities. We're not there yet. ■

8 Conclusion: affirms thesis statement

Questions that suggest reasons why change is justifiable

Final word on current status

Highlight Key Points

As you read, you will encounter many new ideas. You will find some ideas more important than others. You will agree with some and disagree with others. Later, as you write about what you have read, you will want to return to the main points to refresh your memory. To locate and remember these points easily, it is a good idea to read with a highlighter or pen in hand. Highlighting is an active reading strategy because it forces you to sort and sift important from less important ideas.

Develop a system of highlighting that you can use as you read to identify ideas you plan to reread or review later on. Use the following guidelines to make your highlighting as useful as possible.

1. **Decide what kinds of information to highlight before you begin.** What types of tasks will you be doing as a result of your reading? Will you write a paper, participate in a class discussion, or take an exam? Think about what you need to know, and tailor your highlighting to the particular needs of the task.
2. **Read first; then highlight.** First read a paragraph or section; then go back and mark what is important within it. This approach will help you control the tendency to highlight too much.
3. **Be selective.** If you highlight every idea, none will stand out.
4. **Highlight key elements, words, and phrases.** Mark the thesis statement, the topic sentence in each paragraph, important terms and definitions, and key words and phrases that relate to the thesis.

Annotate Your Impressions

Annotating is a way to keep track of your impressions, reactions, and questions as you read. When you annotate, you jot down your ideas about what you are reading in the margins of the essay. Think of your annotations as a personal response to the author's ideas: You might question, agree with, or express surprise at those ideas. Your annotations can take several forms, including questions that come to mind, personal reactions (such as disagreement or anger), or brief phrases that summarize important points. Later on, when you are ready to write about or discuss the reading, your annotations will help you focus on major issues and questions. Following is a partial list of what you might annotate.

- Important points (such as the thesis) that initiate personal responses
- Sections about which you need further information
- Sections in which the author reveals his or her reasons for writing
- Ideas you disagree or agree with
- Inconsistencies

Sample annotations for a portion of "Purse Snatching" are shown in Figure 2.2 below.

EXERCISE 2.2

Reread "Purse Snatching" on page 30. Highlight and annotate the essay as you read.

FIGURE 2.2
SAMPLE ANNOTATIONS

Where are the women in auto racing at Indy, NASCAR, or CART events — truly the most lucrative of all professional sports — when it comes to endorsements, winnings, and the profits of team ownership? The answer is nowhere, since virtually <u>no women regularly participate in auto racing</u>. With regard to salaries, profit sharing, or access to significant dollars to begin professional leagues or gain entry into high-stakes sports competition, women are still behind the eight ball.

> *Why?*

Instead of paying women athletes what they're worth, there seems to be a concerted effort to sexualize them. By commenting on the looks of the U.S. women's soccer team, the media blatantly suggest that these athletes' physical appearance is more important and of greater interest than their athletic achievements. When Brandi Chastain took her shirt off following the winning goal, displaying considerable muscle as well as a sports bra that more than covered the territory, the media acted like they were looking at a <u>Victoria's Secret catalog</u> as opposed to a world championship soccer match. How many women jog on city streets and work out in health clubs every day wearing less?

> *This is one example; are there others?*

> *interesting comparison*

The media and the medical establishment, <u>despite evidence to the contrary</u>, are quick to posit that the reason for a spate of anterior cruciate knee injuries in women is because women are physically inferior to men (our knees are ill-constructed and our hormones wreak havoc on our bodies). Are these predominantly male professionals maybe too eager to reinforce the strength and dominance of males and dismiss women in sport?

> *Why doesn't the author include this evidence?*

> *Is medicine still predominantly male?*

Review after Reading

Do you simply close a book or put away an article after you have read it? If so, you are missing an opportunity to reinforce your learning. If you are willing to spend a few minutes reviewing and evaluating what you read, you can increase dramatically the amount of information you remember.

To review material after reading, you use the same steps used to preview a reading (see p. 24). You should do your review immediately after you have finished reading. Reviewing does not take much time. Your goal is to touch on each main point one more time, not to embark on a long and thorough study. Pay particular attention to the following elements.

- The headings
- Your highlighting
- Your annotations
- The conclusion

As you already know, active reading involves much more than moving your eyes across lines of print. It is a process of actively searching for ideas and sorting important ideas from less important ones. You may need to read an essay more than once. Comprehension is often gradual. On the first reading, you may grasp some ideas but not others. On the second reading, other ideas may become clear. Do not hesitate to reread.

As part of your review, it is also helpful to write a brief summary of the essay. See the section on summarizing later in this chapter for detailed suggestions on how to write a summary (p. 42).

UNDERSTANDING DIFFICULT TEXT AND VISUALS

All students experience difficulty with a reading assignment at one time or another. Perhaps this will happen because you just can't "connect" with the author or because you find the topic uninteresting or the writing style confusing. Regardless of the problem, however, you know you must complete the assignment. Table 2.1 lists some typical problems that students experience with difficult reading material and identifies strategies for solving them.

Draw a Graphic Organizer

If you are having difficulty following a long or complicated essay, try drawing a graphic organizer—a diagram of the structure of an essay's main points. Even if you are not a spatial learner, you will probably find a graphic organizer helpful.

TABLE 2.1
DIFFICULT READINGS: SPECIFIC PROBLEMS AND STRATEGIES FOR SOLVING THEM

Problems	Strategies
You cannot concentrate.	1. Take limited breaks. 2. Tackle the assignment at peak periods of attention. 3. Divide the material into sections. Make it your goal to complete one section at a time. 4. Give yourself a reasonable deadline for completing the assignment.
The sentences are long and confusing.	1. Read aloud. 2. Divide each sentence into parts, and analyze the function of each part. 3. Express each sentence in your own words.
The ideas are complicated and hard to understand.	1. Reread the material several times. 2. Rephrase or explain each idea in your own words. 3. Make outline notes. 4. Study with a classmate; discuss difficult ideas. 5. Look up the meanings of unfamiliar words in a dictionary.
The material seems disorganized or poorly organized.	1. Study the introduction for clues to organization. 2. Pay more attention to headings. 3. Read the summary or conclusion. 4. Try to discover the organization by writing an outline or drawing a graphic organizer (see pp. 37 and 38).
You cannot get interested in the material.	1. Think about something you've experienced that is related to the topic. 2. Work with a classmate, discussing each section as you go.
You cannot relate to the writer's ideas or experiences.	1. Find out some background information about the author. 2. Put yourself in the writer's position. How would you react?
The subject is unfamiliar; you lack background information on the subject.	1. Obtain a more basic text or other source that moves slower, offers more explanation, and reviews fundamental principles and concepts. 2. For unfamiliar terminology, consult a specialized dictionary within the field of study. 3. Ask your instructor to recommend useful references.

Just as a map shows the relationship of streets and highways to one another, a graphic organizer shows you how an essay's main points are related. Think of a graphic organizer as a means of tracking the author's flow of ideas.

To draw detailed graphic organizers using a computer, visit www .bedfordstmartins.com /successfulwriting.

Drawing a graphic organizer is an active way to review and connect major ideas. The graphic organizer format is shown in Figure 2.3. When you draw a graphic organizer, be sure it includes all the key elements of an essay listed on page 29. An example of a graphic organizer for "Purse Snatching" appears in Figure 2.4. Work through the organizer and reread the essay (pp. 30–31), paragraph by paragraph, at the same time.

Read Visuals

Much of what you read is accompanied by visuals — drawings, photographs, diagrams, graphs, charts, and so forth. A writer may use a visual to clarify an idea, reveal trends, condense information, emphasize a particular idea, or illustrate a particular point of view. For example, an article espousing the value of a college education may contain a graph comparing lifetime average salaries of college graduates with high school graduates to emphasize the dramatic differences in income and to demonstrate the value of higher education. An argument for increased U.S. aid to developing countries may use a photograph of a sickly, emaciated child to emphasize poignantly the effects of a recent famine while drawing out feelings of shock or pity to make the reader sympathetic.

Writers may also use visuals to help readers visualize a place or setting, understand a complicated process, or remember important information. Visuals are a powerful means of communication, and writers use them deliberately and creatively to shape the message they are sending to the reader. Visuals make a reader more receptive to a printed page by creating interest, offering easy access to information, or emphasizing important concepts.

It is worthwhile to spend time studying and analyzing visuals that accompany text. Because they supplement or enhance the meaning of the text, they give you a more complete understanding of the text. To analyze a visual, ask yourself the following questions.

- **What is the background of the visual?** Where is it from? How does it connect the article or essay? Why was it included?
- **What does the visual show?** Who or what is in the image? What action is occurring or has occurred? What information is presented?
- **What does the visual mean?** What is important? What is the intended message?
- **What does the visual suggest?** How does it make you feel? What should you remember? What questions or issues does it raise?

FIGURE 2.3
GRAPHIC ORGANIZER: KEY ELEMENTS TO INCLUDE

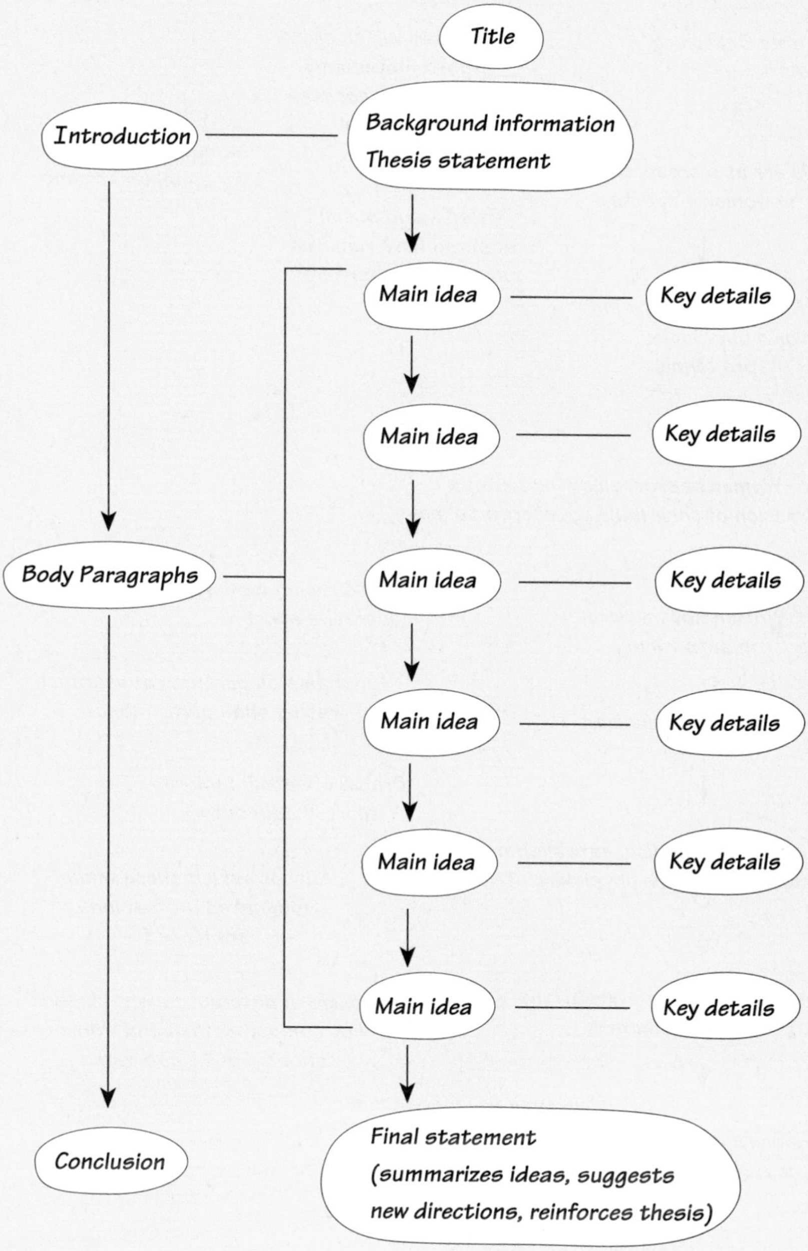

```
                                    ( Title )

  ( Introduction )—————( Background information
                          Thesis statement )
                                    |
                                    v
                              ( Main idea )————( Key details )
                                    |
                                    v
                              ( Main idea )————( Key details )
                                    |
                                    v
  ( Body Paragraphs )————       ( Main idea )————( Key details )
                                    |
                                    v
                              ( Main idea )————( Key details )
                                    |
                                    v
                              ( Main idea )————( Key details )
                                    |
                                    v
                              ( Main idea )————( Key details )
                                    |
                                    v
  ( Conclusion )              ( Final statement
                               (summarizes ideas, suggests
                               new directions, reinforces thesis) )
```

FIGURE 2.4
GRAPHIC ORGANIZER FOR "PURSE SNATCHING"

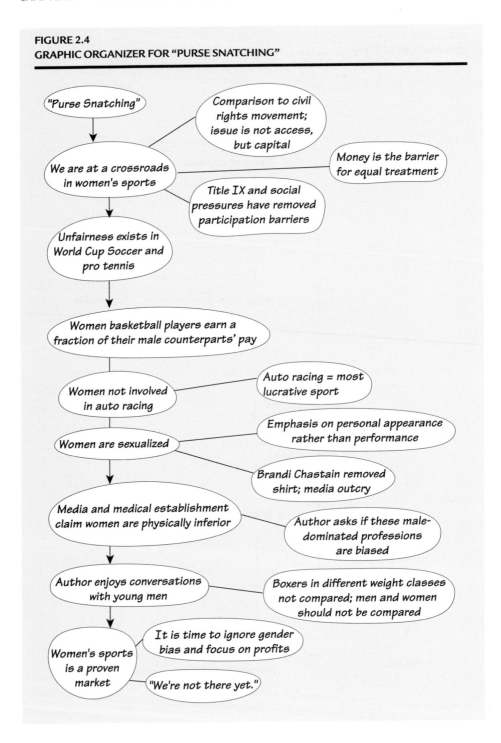

In "Purse Snatching," Lopiano refers to the various media interpretations of Brandi Chastain's removal of her shirt in a victory pose. The photograph of Chastain (below) demonstrates Lopiano's point: The media focuses on sexual issues rather than the skills and competitive nature of female athletes.

EXERCISE 2.3
1. Answer the questions listed on page 36 to analyze the photo of Brandi Chastain.
2. Use the questions listed on page 36 to analyze the photo at the beginning of this chapter on page 20.

Brandi Chastain of the U.S. women's soccer team removes her shirt in triumph after kicking in the final goal, winning the World Cup. This photo is mentioned in the essay "Purse Snatching."

RESPONDING TO TEXT

Active reading is one step in understanding a text, but equally important is responding to a text or an essay. Once you respond to material, you understand it better.

There are a number of different ways you can respond to something you have read. In your everyday life, you might read an advertisement for a digital camera and respond by taking action—purchasing it. If you read a review of a movie that sounds interesting, you might respond by emailing a friend and suggesting a time to see it. In your college career, you may read a key chapter of your psychology textbook and respond by writing an outline because the material is likely to be on your next exam. Response, then, can take a variety of forms.

When an instructor assigns a reading, some form of response is always expected. You might be expected to participate in a class discussion, summarize the information as part of an essay exam, or research the topic further and report your findings. One of the most common types of response that instructors assign is called a *response paper*. A **response paper** requires you to read an essay, analyze it, and write about some aspect of it. In some assignments, your instructor may suggest a particular direction for the paper. At other times, your instructor may not suggest where to start; it will be up to you to decide how you are going to respond to what you have read.

In a response paper, your instructor does not want you simply to summarize an essay, although that summarizing may be a useful way to begin planning a response (see the next section). You may include a brief summary as part of your introduction, but you should concentrate on analyzing the essay. Focus on interpreting and evaluating what you have read. Keep in mind, however, that you should not attempt to discuss all of your reactions. Instead, choose one key idea, one question the essay raises, or one issue it explores.

Before beginning any response paper, make sure you understand the assignment. If you are uncertain of what your instructor expects, be sure to ask. You may also want to check with other students to find out how they are approaching the assignment. If your instructor does not mention length requirements, be sure to ask how long the paper should be.

For example, suppose your instructor asks you to read an article titled "Advertising: A Form of Institutional Lying" that tries to show that advertisements deceive consumers by presenting half-truths, distortions, and misinformation. Your instructor asks you to write a two-page paper about the essay but gives you no other directions. In writing this response paper, you might take one of the following approaches.

- Discuss how you were once deceived by an advertisement, as a means of confirming the author's main points.

- Evaluate the evidence and examples the author provides to support his claim; determine whether the evidence is relevant and sufficient.

- Discuss the causes or effects of deception in advertising that the author overlooks (you might need to consult other sources to take this approach).

- Evaluate the assumptions the author makes about advertising or about consumers.

For an assignment like this one, or for any response paper, how do you decide on an issue to write about? How do you come up with ideas about a reading? The following guide will help you.

A GUIDE TO RESPONDING TO TEXT

This guide presents a step-by-step process to discover ideas for response papers, as shown in Figure 2.5. Notice that the Guide begins with summary writing to check and clarify your understanding, moves to connecting the ideas to your own experiences, and then offers numerous strategies for analyzing the reading. Each of these steps is discussed below within the context of a reading assignment.

FIGURE 2.5
ACTIVE RESPONSE TO A READING

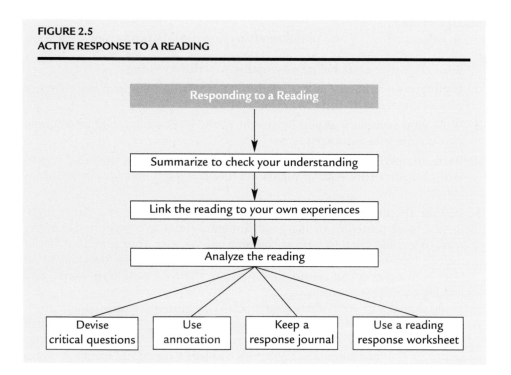

Summarize to Check Your Understanding

A **summary** is a brief statement of major points, and whether or not we recognize it, we all practice summarizing every day. When a friend asks, "What was the movie about?" we reply with a summary of the plot. A summary presents only the main ideas, not details. Your summary of a movie would not include specific scenes or dialogue, for example. When summarizing print text, a summary is about one-fifth of the original, or less, depending on the amount of detail needed. Summarizing is an excellent way to check whether you have understood what you have read. There is no sense in trying to respond and write about something you do not understand clearly. If you have difficulty writing a summary, this is a sign that you do not fully know what is important in the reading. Reread the essay; try a different approach than you used on earlier readings. For example, try working through the reading with a classmate or writing an outline of difficult sections of the reading.

Summaries make it easier for you to keep track of a writer's important ideas and can be reviewed easily and quickly in preparation for a class discussion or exam. Summarizing is also an excellent way to clarify ideas and improve your retention of the material.

For more on journal writing, see Chapter 1, p. 7.

Many students keep a journal in which they write summaries of essays as well as other responses to what they read. Journal writing is a good way to generate and record ideas about an essay, and your journal entries can serve as useful sources of ideas for writing papers.

To write an effective and useful summary, use the following seven guidelines.

1. **Read the entire essay before attempting to write anything.**

2. **Highlight or annotate as you read.** These markings will help you pick out what is important to include in your summary.

3. **Write your summary as you reread the essay.** Work paragraph by paragraph as you write your summary.

4. **Write an opening sentence that states the author's thesis, the most important idea the entire essay explains.** Be sure to express this idea in your own words.

5. **Include the author's most important supporting ideas.** Use either highlighted topic sentences or marginal summary notes as a guide for knowing what to include. Each paragraph contains one key idea. Your summary should include each of these key ideas. If you have highlighted key ideas during or after reading, you can reread them, restate them in your own words, and include them in your summary.

   Marginal summary notes briefly state the content of each paragraph. If you write marginal summary notes similar to those on pages 30–31, these will be helpful when you write a summary. You can easily convert these notes into sentences for your summary. Figure 2.6 displays a list of the summary notes written for "Purse Snatching" along with sentences that have been generated

FIGURE 2.6
CONVERTING MARGINAL SUMMARY NOTES TO SUMMARY SENTENCES

MARGINAL NOTE	SUMMARY SENTENCE
(para. 2) unfairness in soccer and tennis	In both World Cup soccer and pro tennis, there are vast differences between men's and women's salaries.
(para. 3) compares salaries in men's and women's basketball	Women basketball players (WNBA) earn only a fraction of what men players (NBA) earn.
(para. 4) women do not participate in high-paying auto racing	Auto racing is the most lucrative sport but has no women participants.
(para. 6) gives reasons for salary inequity	Women are treated as sexual objects, as shown by the coverage of Brandi Chastain removing her shirt.

from the marginal notes, which then become part of the summary that follows.

6. **Present the ideas in the order in which they appear in the original source.** Be sure to use transitions (connecting words) as you move from one supporting idea to another.

7. **Reread your summary to determine if it contains sufficient information.** Ask yourself this question: Would your summary be understandable and meaningful to someone who has not read the essay? If it would not, revise your summary to include additional information.

Here is a sample summary for the essay "Purse Snatching" that a student wrote using the preceding seven steps.

    Although the right to participate in women's professional
sports is now well established, financial equality with men
participants does not exist. In both World Cup soccer and pro
tennis, there are vast differences between men's and women's
salaries. In professional basketball, women players earn a fraction of what men players are paid. Auto racing, the most lucrative of all sports, has few, if any, women participants. Women
are at a financial disadvantage not only in salary but also for
endorsements, winnings, and profit sharing. Financial inequity may
exist because women are treated as sexual objects, as shown by
the recent media coverage of Brandi Chastain removing her shirt.

The media and the medical profession suggest that women are
physically inferior to men. The author contends that boxers in
different weight categories are not compared and, likewise, that
men and women participating in the same sport should not be compared. Sex discrimination should be less important than financial
considerations, but financial inequity still exists.

Notice that the summary covers the main point of each of the paragraphs in the
essay. Notice, too, that the summary is written in the student writer's own words
and that the phrases were not copied from the essay. Finally, notice that the order
of ideas in the summary parallels the order of ideas presented in the reading.

EXERCISE 2.4

Write a summary of the section of this chapter titled Changing Some Misconceptions
about Reading, p. 23.

Link the Reading to Your Own Experiences

One way to get ideas flowing for a response paper is to think about how the reading relates to your own experiences. It is a way of building a bridge between you
and the author, between your ideas and those expressed by the author.

- **Begin by looking for useful information in the essay and considering how
  you could apply or relate that information to other real-life situations.**
  Think of familiar situations or examples that illustrate the subject. Your reading
  of "Purse Snatching," for example, might lead you to think of other situations
  in which sports inequity exists. While the article considers inequity in professional sports, you might write a journal entry about inequities that exist among
  Little League teams or among women in high school or collegiate athletics.

- **Try to think beyond the reading itself.** Recall other material you have read and
  events you have experienced that are related to the reading. In thinking about
  "Purse Snatching," for example, you might recall an article about the WNBA or
  a men's or women's tennis match on television. The following paragraph shows
  how one student connected "Purse Snatching" to his own experiences.

I watch a lot of tennis because I used to play tennis in
high school. For the Wimbledon tournament in London, I remember
the commentators talked about the strict dress codes. For example, all the players have to wear white. Women also have to
wear tennis skirts and cannot wear shorts. In other sports like
golf, basketball, and soccer, the women's uniforms look like
the men's uniforms. Then they would cut to commercials featur-

ing Anna Kournikova and Venus Williams. In her commercial, Kournikova, who was really not highly ranked in the sport, is featured for her beauty. In her commercial, Williams, who eventually won the tournament, was featured for her drive and competitive nature. It is likely that not only is there a double standard for men and women tennis players, but there is a double standard for women athletes as well.

This writer discovered two possible topics to write about — the double standard in professional organizations and the differences between how male and female athletes are viewed.

- **Let your mind jump from idea to idea.** While writing in your journal or working with a classmate, jot down facts about, questions about, and examples of the subject. If you work quickly and write whatever comes to mind, this process will create a flow of thoughts and ideas related to the subject.

For more on the flow of thought, see Brainstorming in Chapter 3, p. 73.

- **Use the key-word response method for generating ideas.** Choose one or more key words that describe your initial response, such as *angered, amused, surprised, confused, annoyed, curious,* or *shocked.* For example, fill in the following blank with key words describing your response to "Purse Snatching."

"After reading the essay, I felt _____."

The key-word response you just wrote will serve as a point of departure for further thinking. Start by explaining your response; then write down ideas as they come to you, trying to approach the reading from many different perspectives. Here is the result of one student's key-word response to "Purse Snatching."

After reading "Purse Snatching," I <u>felt depressed and at the same time somewhat relieved.</u> I had no idea of the extent to which such discrimination existed in professional sports. It is depressing that after all of the reforms and advances required by Title IX, the problem still exists. In a way, though, it was gratifying to know that professional sports are not exempt from sexual discrimination. Everything is always magnified and blown out of proportion in professional sports. Sports have become an unreal fantasy where superathletes perform extraordinary feats, becoming superheroes. The problem of sexual discrimination makes professional sports seem almost human instead of superhuman.

For more on freewriting, see Chapter 3, p. 69.

This key-word response led the student to two possible topics — athletes as superheroes and professional sports as a fantasy experience.

EXERCISE 2.5

Review the four preceding techniques for connecting the subject of an essay to your own experiences. Choose one of those techniques, and try it out on the topic of inequity in women's sports.

Analyze the Reading

Analyzing, like summarizing, is a skill we use every day. After you see a movie, you ask a friend, "So, what did you think of it?" You are asking your friend to evaluate the film—to look at its parts and its overall effect. In response, your friend may analyze the plot, criticize the photography, or comment on the credibility of the characters, for example. Analysis of text, then, is a broad opportunity to comment on any aspect of the essay. You might, for example, discuss one of the author's ideas, his or her fairness or accuracy, his or her method of presentation, the adequacy of the supporting evidence provided, the intended audience, or the author's purpose. There are a variety of methods to use to discover ideas for analysis. These include devising critical questions, using annotation, keeping a response journal, and using a response worksheet.

Devise Critical Questions

Asking critical questions is a useful method for analysis and for discovering ideas for a response paper. Ask why things are the way they are, how they happened, and what makes them work—that is, look at causes, effects, and consequences. Ask questions and then answer them. Suppose you are assigned to read an essay about mercy killing. You might ask yourself, "Under what circumstances is it done? Who is involved? Who should make the decision?" In answering these questions, you'll probably recall having read or heard about cases of medically assisted suicide or about legislation governing it. Such questions and answers can also be entered in your journal. Here are some critical questions you might ask about "Purse Snatching."

- Why is discrimination stronger in sports than elsewhere, such as in the workplace?
- Do some men resent women breaking into what was once a male domain?
- Why are there almost no women involved in auto racing? What restrictions, if any, limit their participation? What other sports have few or no women participants?
- How has the women's sports industry been undermined, and who is responsible?

The answers to any of the preceding questions might serve as the basis for a paper responding to "Purse Snatching." Here are three sample questions and the answers that one student wrote in response to them after reading the essay.

Will female athletes ever become as popular as their male counterparts when it comes to team sports?

I think patience is the key here. The degree of popularity, respect, and salaries desired by female team sports athletes won't occur overnight. The all-male major leagues have been around for over a century. Also, we have to remember how African American sports figures had to struggle to fit in and prove themselves worthy of their game.

Why did Brandi Chastain remove her shirt?

Perhaps she did so in the exuberance of the moment, but why choose an action with a sexual connotation? Chastain played into the hands of the media by giving them a controversial behavior to report. She could have thrown her shoes, tossed a soccer ball, or just shouted exuberantly.

Why did the media give so much coverage to Chastain's removal of her shirt?

Perhaps her action was a media ploy to draw media attention to the sporting event. Perhaps the media reports what people want to hear and see. Is the public more interested in women as women or as athletes?

Her questions and answers enabled this student to discover several more possible writing topics — behavior of women athletes, media coverage of women athletes, and the general popularity of women's athletics.

ESSAY IN PROGRESS 1

Write a list of critical questions about the reading "Purse Snatching" on page 30 or another essay assigned by your instructor. Use *why, how,* and *what* questions to generate ideas about inequity in women's sports.

Use Annotation

In the Guide to Active Reading, you learned to annotate as you read. Annotation can also be used to analyze and respond to a reading after you have read it the first time and while you are preparing to write about it. As you read an essay for the second time, record additional reactions that occur to you. Some students prefer to use a different color of ink to record their second set of annotations. Refer to the sample student annotation shown in Figure 2.2 (p. 33).

ESSAY IN PROGRESS 2

Reread "Purse Snatching" or the other assigned essay, this time adding annotations that record your reactions to and questions about the essay as you read.

Keep a Response Journal

A response journal is a section of your writing journal (see Chapter 1, p. 7) in which you record your reactions, questions, and comments about readings. There are two ways you can organize a response journal; experiment with each format until you discover the one that works best for you.

The open-page format.   On a blank page, write, outline, draw, or create a diagram to express your reactions to an essay. Because the open-page format encourages you to let your ideas flow freely, it may work particularly well for creative and spatial learners. Figure 2.7 shows one student's open-page response journal entry for "Purse Snatching." This entry suggests several possible topics to write about—how women athletes dress, how endorsements affect images of women athletes, and how commercials create negative images of women athletes.

The two-column format.   Divide several pages of your journal into two vertical columns. If you journal on a computer, you can insert a table with two columns. Label the left side "Quotations" and the right side "Responses." Under "Quotations," jot down five to ten quotations from the text. Choose remarks that seem important—that state an opinion, summarize a viewpoint, and so forth. In the right column, directly opposite each quotation, write your response to the quotation. You might explain it, disagree with or question it, relate it to other information in the reading or in another reading, or tie it to your own experiences. The two-column for-

FIGURE 2.7
SAMPLE OPEN-PAGE JOURNAL FORMAT

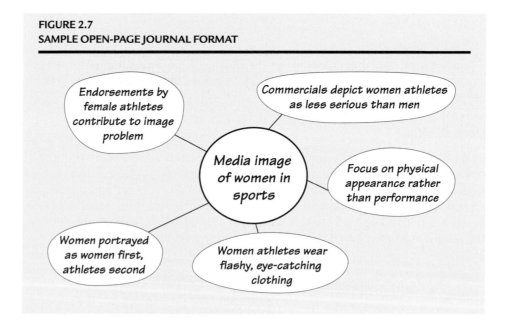

mat forces you to think actively about an essay while you question what you have read and draw connections. Figure 2.8 follows the two-column format.

In this entry, the writer has uncovered several possible topics—the dispersion of available funds for sporting events, the attire and behavior of female athletes, and male viewpoints and political correctness. Because the two-column format provides more structure, students who tend to be pragmatic or concrete learners may find it effective.

You may find it useful to paraphrase the quotation before writing your response. Paraphrasing forces you to think about the meaning of the quotation,

For more on paraphrasing, see Chapter 19, p. 684.

FIGURE 2.8
SAMPLE TWO-COLUMN JOURNAL FORMAT

Quotations	Responses
"Why the need to hog the marbles?"	This statement implies that there are only so many marbles. If there is limited money, then the question becomes how it should be divided between men and women. It would seem that the most money should go to the sporting events that are most profitable.
"How many women jog on city streets and work out in health clubs every day wearing less?"	The fact that some women do wear body-revealing sports clothing does not justify an athlete removing clothing during a public sporting event.
"I love talking to high school boys because they reflect the male view before the veil of political correctness disguises their true feelings."	Do men feel the need to veil their feelings? It could be possible that their attitudes have changed instead of being disguised. Are most men concerned with political correctness in expressing their attitudes about sports?

and ideas for writing may come to mind as a result. To use paraphrasing, add a "Paraphrase" column to your journal between the "Quotation" column and the "Response" column.

ESSAY IN PROGRESS 3

For "Purse Snatching" or another essay, write a response in your journal using the open-page format or the two-column format.

Use a Reading Response Worksheet

An easy way to record all of your ideas about a reading all in one place is to use a reading response worksheet. The worksheet guides your response while directing your thinking. A blank response sheet is shown in Figure 2.9 on p. 51. Notice that it includes space for recording your first impressions, a summary, connections to your own experiences, ideas for analysis, and additional sources.

USING YOUR LEARNING STYLE

If you are a *verbal* learner, a *social* learner, or both, you probably find reading a comfortable and convenient way to obtain information. If you are a *spatial* learner, though, you may prefer the graphic images of video and film to those of printed material. Regardless of your learning style, most of your assignments will be in print form for the foreseeable future. Therefore, it is up to you to use your learning style in a way that enhances your reading and writing. The following guidelines for active reading and response are tailored to the various learning styles.

Learning Style Options

- If you are a *spatial* learner, create mental pictures of people and places. For example, while reading the essay "Purse Snatching," you might create a mental image of a female athlete in a sports competition. In addition, use graphic organizers and diagrams to organize the ideas in an essay. As you annotate, use symbols to connect the ideas within and between paragraphs (for example, see the symbols listed for the reading response journal on p. 9).

- If you are a *social* learner, discuss a reading assignment with a classmate both before and after reading. Preview the essay together, sharing ideas about the topic. After reading the essay, discuss your reactions to it. In both instances, use the Guide to Active Reading in this chapter (p. 23) and the Guide to Responding to Text (p. 41) to get started.

- If you are an *abstract* learner, a *creative* learner, or both, you may tend to overlook details while focusing instead on the "big ideas" and overall message of a reading. Be sure to highlight important points and to concentrate on facts and supporting details.

FIGURE 2.9
SAMPLE READING RESPONSE WORKSHEET

READING RESPONSE WORKSHEET

TITLE: _____

AUTHOR: _____

FIRST IMPRESSIONS: _____
_____
_____

SUMMARY: _____
_____
_____
_____
_____

CONNECTIONS TO YOUR OWN EXPERIENCES: _____
_____
_____
_____

ANALYSIS (issue, aspect, feature, problem)

1. _____
_____
_____

2. _____
_____
_____
_____

ADDITIONAL SOURCES OR VISUALS (if needed)

1. _____
_____

2. _____
_____

3. _____
_____

- If you are a *concrete* learner, a *pragmatic* learner, or both, you may like to focus on details instead of seeing how ideas fit together and contribute to an author's overall message. Use graphic organizers to help you create a larger picture. Try to make the essay as "real" as possible; visualize events occurring or the author writing. You might visualize yourself interviewing the author, alone or with a panel of classmates.

- If you are an *emotional* learner, you may generally focus on people or events and overlook the way an author uses them to convey an overall message. Keep this question in mind: How does the author use these people or events to get his or her message across?

- If you are a *rational* learner, you may zero in on a logical presentation of ideas and overlook more subtle shades of meaning. Be sure to annotate in order to draw out your personal reactions to a piece of writing.

ESSAY IN PROGRESS 4

Discuss "Purse Snatching" with a classmate. Make notes as you discuss. If you chose another essay, pair up with a classmate who also chose that essay, or ask your classmate to read the essay you have chosen.

ESSAY IN PROGRESS 5

Write a two- to four-page paper in response to "Purse Snatching" or the essay you have chosen. Use the following steps to shape the ideas you generated in Essays in Progress 1 to 4.

1. **Reread the writing you did in response to the reading.** Look for ideas, comments, statements, or annotations that seem worthwhile and that are important enough to become the basis of your essay.
2. **Look for related ideas.** Try to find ideas that fit together to produce a viewpoint or position toward the reading.
3. **Do not attempt to cover all your ideas.** Your essay should not analyze every aspect of the essay. Instead, you should choose some feature or aspect on which to focus.
4. **Write a sentence that states your central point.** This sentence will become your thesis statement. It should state what your essay will assert or explain.
5. **Collect ideas and evidence from the reading to support your ideas.** Your ideas should be backed up by specifics in the reading.
6. **Organize your ideas into essay form.** Your paper should have a title, introduction, body, and conclusion.
7. **Revise your essay.** Evaluate and revise your essay to be sure that you have explained your ideas fully and that you have provided clear support for each of your ideas by referring to the reading.
8. **Proofread for accuracy and correctness.** Use the Suggestions for Proofreading in Chapter 7 (p. 191).

For more on thesis statements, see Chapter 4. For more on organizing your ideas, see Chapter 5. To help you revise your essay, see Chapter 6. For more on editing and proofreading, see Chapter 7.

HOW TO APPROACH THE STUDENT ESSAYS IN THIS BOOK

Use the following suggestions when reading student essays.

- **Never get discouraged when reading a student essay.** Each writer has a unique style and unique ideas. Try to use some of the techniques that the writer uses. For example, if a writer begins his or her essay with a striking statistic, consider whether you could use a striking statistic to begin your essay.

- **Read an essay several times.** During your first reading, concentrate on the writer's message. Then read the essay again as many times as necessary to analyze its writing features. For example, first notice how the writer supported the thesis statement, and then look at the language used to create a particular impression.

- **Think of student essays as trial balloons.** You will see some techniques that you may want to try and some things that you are fairly sure would not work for you. For example, one writer may use transitions to make ideas easier to follow, but another writer may use an organization that you would find difficult to apply to your topic.

How to Focus on Writing Features

Use the following suggestions to help you get the most from student essays.

- **Read with a pen or marker in hand.** As you discover writing techniques that are emphasized in the chapter, mark or annotate them.

- **Focus on characteristics.** Each chapter in Part 3 presents the characteristics of a particular method of organization. Consider how the student essay demonstrates some or all of that method's characteristics.

- **Focus on techniques.** Each chapter in Part 3 offers specific techniques and suggestions for writing a particular type of essay. Review these techniques and observe how the writer applied them.

- **Focus on what is new and different.** Ask yourself the following questions as you read: What is the writer doing that you haven't seen before? What is unique and nontraditional? What catches your attention? What works particularly well? What techniques might be fun to try? What techniques would be challenging to try?

- **Use student essays to train your critical eye.** Although student essays are reasonably good models, they are not perfect. Look for ways the essays can be improved. Once you can see ways to improve someone else's essay, you will be better equipped to analyze and improve your own writing.

• Use graphic organizers to grasp the essay's structure. In Part 3, a graphic organizer is presented for each method of organization. Compare the essay to the graphic organizer, noticing how the essay contains each element.

STUDENTS WRITE

Tracey Aquino was a student at Johnson & Wales University when she wrote the following essay. Her essay, written in response to "Purse Snatching," was assigned by her writing instructor. As you read, notice how Aquino analyzes Lopiano's points about female athletics.

The Games We Play: Inequality in the Pro-Sports Workplace
Tracey Aquino

1   Donna Lopiano in her article "Purse Snatching" states that professional female athletes are not getting their fair share of salary and respect compared to professional male athletes. Feminists may cheer upon hearing Lopiano's point of view, and some sports fans may grumble about it. "Purse Snatching" may justify feminist ways of thinking, but Lopiano's argument does not account for the necessary time it will take for the exposure and investment in female team athletics to grow.

2   Perhaps the question we should ask is *why* this is such a big problem, especially for team sports. Lopiano never asks, Why aren't female team players getting as much pay and respect as their male counterparts? The answer could be only a matter of time. Professional female leagues have only gained media exposure in the past decade, whereas all-male professional leagues have been well known since the late 1800s. After over a century of building a strong relationship with spectators and host cities, male professional team sports have become a prominent part of American culture. Professional female leaguers will have to wait a little longer before they see the money and adoration they want.

3   Lopiano states that the Women's National Basketball Association averages 10,000 spectators a game--a feat reached in only two years as opposed to the 30 years it

took the NBA. After stating this statistic, Lopiano declares that the $30,000-per-year salary of a WNBA player is only a small percentage of what most NBA players make. What she fails to recognize is that not only does attendance matter but that television exposure has a direct effect on investment and salaries. With additional television exposure the WNBA can expect to generate interest and popularity, and with increased popularity will come successful investors willing to field six- or seven-figure salaries for the players.

WNBA games suffer from being aired primarily on the Lifetime television network, a specialty cable channel aimed at women. When a WNBA game is aired only on Lifetime, the WNBA is neglecting male viewers who do not watch cable channels marketed toward women. Compare this audience to the one who watches a sports channel or a major national network. If popularity is the door to a six- or seven-figure salary, exposure via a gender-specific cable channel is not the key. The WNBA and similar female team sporting leagues need to grow their audience to grow their revenue.

4

Lopiano implies that this problem is based on investment. If new interest can be found from better exposure, however, new investors will be attracted and richly compensated. Women's soccer and basketball players have proven over time to be worthy of their fans, of which they have many. With a comparison to boxing, Lopiano disproves the argument that women are physically inferior to men and therefore men's team sports are better. When women play against women, there is no inferiority because everyone is on equal ground. On the court or on the field, professional female athletes show true stamina and spirit. With the proper media outlets, more fans and investors will be attracted to female team sports. But this will take time.

5

If Lopiano wants positive action taken for women's rights in sports, she must first realize that fame and fortune happen not overnight but over time. Sexism will always be a factor in the workplace, even if that work-

6

```
place is a basketball court, a tennis court, or a soccer
field. Female athletes have a long road to pave ahead of
them in the fight for fairness, but in time, exposure,
audiences, investment, and salaries will grow.
```

Analyzing the Reading

1. What is Aquino's thesis (central point)?
2. What kind of information does Aquino include to support her thesis?
3. What additional information, if any, would you recommend that Aquino include in her essay?

Reacting to the Reading: Discussion and Journal Writing

1. Is television and advertising exposure a result of popularity, or does it build and increase popularity? Explain your answer.
2. Do you agree with Aquino that it may be only a matter of time before the inequity in men's and women's sports is resolved? Explain your answer.
3. Write a journal entry describing a situation in which you observed or experienced women being treated differently than men.
4. What steps not mentioned by Aquino or Lopiano might be effective in increasing equity between men's and women's sports?

Applying Your Skills: Writing about the Reading

Use your highlighting, annotating, and graphic organizers as sources of ideas for the following writing assignments based on "Purse Snatching."

1. Write an essay describing a female athlete that you know personally or that you watch on professional sports. Describe the traits that make this person a good athlete.
2. Discuss whether it is fair to compare men's and women's performance in other areas such as education or in the workplace, given that men and women seem to approach tasks differently and may have different priorities.
3. Discuss whether spending more money on women's sports will make them more popular.

ANSWERS TO EXERCISE 2.1

1. True   2. False   3. True   4. True   5. False

PART 2

Strategies for
Writing Essays

Prewriting: How to Find and Focus Ideas

Study the photo on the opposite page. What is happening in the photo? What do you think the man could be reacting to?

Writing Quick Start

Take out a sheet of paper or open a new computer file, and write whatever comes to mind about the photo and what you think might be happening in it. You might write about times when you've felt the same emotions you think the man is expressing, or you might write about times when you've seen people express strong emotions in a public place. Try to write nonstop for at least five minutes, jotting down or typing whatever ideas cross your mind. Don't stop to evaluate your writing or to phrase your ideas in complete sentences or correct grammatical form. Don't worry about correctness; just record your thinking.

You have just used *freewriting*, a method of discovering ideas about a topic. Read over what you wrote. Suppose you were asked to write an essay about joy or exuberance. Do you see some starting points and usable ideas in your freewriting? In this chapter, you will learn more about freewriting as well as a number of other methods, in addition to those described in Chapter 2, that will help you find ideas to write about. You will also learn how to focus an essay by considering why you are writing (your purpose), who you are writing for (your audience), and what perspective you are using to approach your topic (point of view). These steps are all part of the beginning of the process of writing an essay, as illustrated in Figure 3.1.

CHOOSING AND NARROWING A TOPIC

When you begin an essay assignment, it's a good idea to take time to choose a broad topic and then to narrow it to be manageable within the assigned length of your paper. Skipping this step is one of the biggest mistakes you can make in beginning a writing assignment. You can waste a great deal of time working on an essay only to discover that the topic is too large or that you don't have enough to say about it.

Choosing a Topic

In some writing situations, your instructor will assign the topic. In others, your instructor will allow you to write on a topic of your choice. Or you may be given a number of possible topics to choose from, as in the Guided Writing Assignments in Chapters 8 to 15, 17, and 21 of this text. In the latter cases, use the following guidelines to choose a successful topic.

1. **Invest time in making your choice.** It may be tempting to grab the first topic that comes to mind, but you will produce a better essay if you work with a topic that interests you and that you know something about.

2. **Choose a topic that is substantive, meaningful, and worthwhile.** Even if you start with a mundane subject, you can take it in surprising directions. If you are interested in soap operas, for example, you might write about why people watch them or do some research to discover who writes them or how they are made.

3. **Focus on questions and ideas rather than topics.** You may find it easier to think of questions or ideas rather than topics. For example, the question "Do television commercials really sell products?" may come to mind more easily than the broad topic of advertising or television commercials.

FIGURE 3.1
AN OVERVIEW OF THE WRITING PROCESS

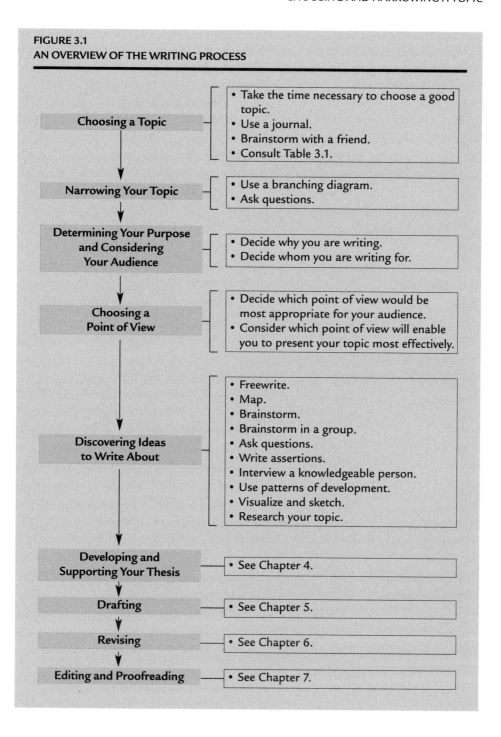

Choosing a Topic
- Take the time necessary to choose a good topic.
- Use a journal.
- Brainstorm with a friend.
- Consult Table 3.1.

Narrowing Your Topic
- Use a branching diagram.
- Ask questions.

Determining Your Purpose and Considering Your Audience
- Decide why you are writing.
- Decide whom you are writing for.

Choosing a Point of View
- Decide which point of view would be most appropriate for your audience.
- Consider which point of view will enable you to present your topic most effectively.

Discovering Ideas to Write About
- Freewrite.
- Map.
- Brainstorm.
- Brainstorm in a group.
- Ask questions.
- Write assertions.
- Interview a knowledgeable person.
- Use patterns of development.
- Visualize and sketch.
- Research your topic.

Developing and Supporting Your Thesis
- See Chapter 4.

Drafting
- See Chapter 5.

Revising
- See Chapter 6.

Editing and Proofreading
- See Chapter 7.

4. **Use your journal as a source of ideas.** Chapter 1 describes how to keep a writing journal, and Chapter 2 explains how to use a response journal. If you have not begun keeping a journal, start one now; try writing in it for a few weeks to see if it is helpful.

5. **Discuss possible topics with a friend.** Conversations with friends may help you discover worthwhile topics and give you feedback on topics you have already thought of.

6. **Use freewriting or another prewriting technique.** The prewriting techniques described in this chapter can help you discover an interesting topic and decide whether you have enough to say about it (see pp. 69–83).

7. **Consult Table 3.1 or Table 3.3 (p. 82).** A number of specific sources of ideas for essay topics are listed in Table 3.1. Table 3.3 groups Chapter 3 topics into broad categories.

TABLE 3.1
SOURCES OF IDEAS FOR ESSAY TOPICS

Source	What to Look For	Example
Your classes	Listen for issues, controversies, and new ideas that might be worth exploring.	A discussion in your education class on education reform leads you to the topic of standardized testing.
Daily activities	Take note of memorable or meaningful incidents at work and at sporting or social events.	A health inspector's visit at work suggests an essay on restaurant food safety.
Newspapers and magazines	Flip through recent issues; look for articles that might lead to promising topics.	You find an interesting article on a hip-hop musician and decide to write about her career.
Radio and television	Listen to your favorite radio station for a thought-provoking song, or look for ideas in television programs and commercials.	Commercials for diet soda suggest an essay on the diet food industry.
The world around you	Look within your household or outside of it. Notice people, objects, interactions.	You notice family members reading books or newspapers and decide to write about the value of leisure time.

▎ ESSAY IN PROGRESS 1
▎ Using the suggestions on pages 60 and 62 and in Table 3.1 to stimulate your thinking, list
▎ at least three broad topics.

Narrowing a Topic

Once you have chosen a topic, the next step is to narrow it so that it is manageable within the length of the essay your instructor has assigned. If you are assigned to write a two- to four-page essay, for example, a broad topic such as divorce is too large. However, you might write about one specific cause of divorce or its effects on children.

To narrow a topic, limit it to a specific part or aspect. The following techniques—branching and questioning—will help you do so. Later in the chapter, you will learn other techniques for narrowing a broad topic (see pp. 69–83).

Using a Branching Diagram

Start by writing your broad topic at the far left side of your paper or computer screen. Then subdivide the topic into three or more subcategories or aspects. Here is an example for the broad topic of wild game hunting.

Then choose one subcategory and subdivide it further, as shown here.

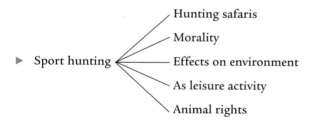

Continue narrowing the topic in this way until you feel you have found one that is both interesting and manageable.

Keep in mind that once you begin planning, researching, and drafting the essay, you may need to narrow your topic even further. The following example shows additional narrowing of the topic of effects on environment.

▶ Effects on environment — Prized species may become endangered.
— Hunters may spoil pristine wilderness areas.
— Regulated hunting helps control animal populations.

Any one of these narrowed topics would be workable for a two- to four-page essay. Did you notice that as the narrowing progressed, the topics changed from words and phrases to statements of ideas?

EXERCISE 3.1

Use branching diagrams to narrow three of the following broad topics to more manageable topics for a two- to four-page essay.

1. Divorce
2. Safe transportation
3. Population explosion
4. Military spending
5. Birth control
6. Early childhood education

ESSAY IN PROGRESS 2

Narrow one of the broad topics you chose in Essay in Progress 1 to a topic manageable for a two- to four-page essay.

Asking Questions to Narrow a Broad Topic

Use questions that begin with *who, what, where, when, why,* and *how* to narrow your topic. Questioning will lead you to consider and focus your attention on specific aspects of the topic. Here is an example of questioning for the broad topic of divorce.

Questions	*Narrowed Topics*
Why does divorce occur?	• Lifestyle differences as a cause of divorce • Infidelity as a cause of divorce
How do couples divide their property?	• Division of assets during a divorce
Who can help couples work through a divorce?	• Role of divorce mediators • Marital counselor's or attorney's role in divorce
What are the effects of divorce on children?	• Emotional effects of divorce on children • Financial effects of divorce on children
When might it be advisable for a couple considering divorce to remain married?	• Couples who stay together for the sake of their children • Financial benefit of remaining married

As you can see, the questions about divorce produced several workable topics. At times, however, you may need to ask additional questions to get to a topic that is sufficiently limited. The topic "emotional effects of divorce on children," for example, is still too broad for an essay. Asking questions such as "What are the most typical emotional effects?" and "How do divorcing parents prevent emotional problems?" would lead to more specific topics.

EXERCISE 3.2

Use questioning to narrow three of the following subjects to topics that would be manageable within a two- to four-page essay.

1. Senior citizens
2. Mental illness
3. Environmental protection
4. Affirmative action
5. Television programming

THINKING ABOUT YOUR PURPOSE, AUDIENCE, AND POINT OF VIEW

Once you have decided on a manageable topic, you are ready to determine your purpose and consider your audience.

Determining Your Purpose

A well-written essay should have a specific **purpose** or goal. There are three main purposes for writing—to *express* yourself, to *inform* your reader, and to *persuade* your reader. For example, an essay might express the writer's feelings about an incident of road rage that he or she observed. Another essay may inform readers about the primary causes of road rage. Still another essay might attempt to persuade readers to vote for funding to investigate the problem of road rage in the local community.

As you plan your draft essay, ask yourself two critical questions.

- Why am I writing this essay?
- What do I want this essay to accomplish?

Some essays can have more than one purpose. An essay on snowboarding, for example, could be both informative and persuasive: It could explain the benefits of snowboarding and then urge readers to take up the sport because it is good aerobic exercise.

Considering Your Audience

If you were getting ready to go to a rock concert, you probably would not choose the same outfit you would wear to a job interview. You would select clothing to suit the event and situation. Likewise, if you were describing a student orientation session to a friend, you would use a different tone and select different details than you would if you were describing the orientation in an article for the student newspaper. Consider the following examples.

TELLING A FRIEND

Remember I told you how nervous I am about attending college in the fall? Well, guess what? I went to my student orientation over the weekend, and it was much better than I had expected! I even met one of my psych teachers — they call them "instructors" here — and he was so nice and down-to-earth that now I'm starting to get excited about going to college. Some of the welcoming speeches were really boring, but after that things got better. All the students were so friendly that before long I was talking to them as if we had known each other for a long time. I'm really glad I got to go. Now I'm sure I made the right decision about college.

WRITING FOR THE STUDENT NEWSPAPER

College student orientations are often thought to be stuffy affairs where prospective students attempt to mix with aloof professors. For this reason, I am pleased to report that the college orientation held on campus last weekend was a major success and not a pointless endeavor after all. Along with my fellow incoming first-year students, I was impressed with the friendliness of instructors and the camaraderie that developed between students and faculty. I would have preferred fewer "welcome-to-the-college" speeches, but once they were over, practical information on registration, grading policies, and college services followed. The college arranged for us to meet our advisers — not to chart our academic futures but to lay the groundwork for a solid working relationship. With most self-doubt erased, I can begin my college career with newly found confidence.

Notice how the two examples differ in terms of word choice, sentence structure, and type of information that is provided. The tone varies as well: The paragraph spoken to a friend has a casual tone, whereas the article written for the student newspaper is more formal.

Considering your **audience** — the people who read your essay — is an important part of the writing process. Many aspects of your writing — how you express yourself (the type of sentence structure you use, for example), which words you choose, what details and examples you include, and what attitude you take toward your topic — all depend on the audience. Your **tone** — how you sound to your audience — is especially important. If you want your audience to feel comfortable with your writing, be sure to write in a manner that appeals to them.

How to Consider Your Audience

As you consider your audience, keep the following points in mind.

- **Your readers are not present and cannot observe or participate in what you are writing about.** If you are writing about your apartment, for example, they cannot visualize it unless you describe it in detail.

- **Your readers do not know everything you do.** They may not have the same knowledge about and experience with the topic that you do, and they may not know what specialized terms mean.

- **Your readers may not necessarily share your opinions and values.** If you are writing about raising children and assume that strict discipline and authoritative parenting are undesirable, for example, some readers may not agree with you.

- **Your readers may not respond in the same way you do to situations or issues.** Some readers may not see any humor in a situation that you find funny. An issue that you consider only mildly disturbing may make some readers angry.

The following box lists questions you can ask to analyze your audience.

- **What does your audience know or not know about your topic?** If you are proposing a community garden project to an audience of city residents who know little about gardening, you would need to describe the pleasures and benefits of gardening to capture their interest.

- **What is the education, background, and experience of your audience?** If you are writing your garden-project proposal for an audience of low-income residents, you might emphasize how much money they could save by growing vegetables, but if you are proposing the project to middle-income residents, you might stress instead how relaxing gardening can be and how a garden can beautify a neighborhood.

- **What attitudes, beliefs, opinions, or biases is your audience likely to hold?** If, for example, your audience believes that most development is harmful to the environment, and you are writing an essay urging your audience to agree to a new community garden, consider emphasizing how the garden will benefit the environment and decrease development.

- **What tone do your readers expect you to take?** Suppose you are writing to your local city council urging council members to sanction the community garden. Although the council has been stalling on the issue and is environmentally insensitive, your tone should be serious, respectful, and nonaccusatory. As respected community leaders, the council members expect to be treated with deference.

When Your Audience Is Your Instructor

Instructors occasionally direct students to write for a particular audience, such as readers of a certain magazine or newspaper, but usually you can assume that your audience is your instructor. You should not, however, automatically assume that he or she is an expert on your topic. In most cases, it is best to write as if your instructor were unfamiliar with your topic. He or she wants to see if you understand the topic and can write and think clearly about it. For academic papers, then, you should provide enough information to demonstrate your knowledge of the subject. Include background information, definitions of technical terms, and relevant details to make your essay clear and understandable.

EXERCISE 3.3

1. Write a one-paragraph description of a current television commercial for a particular product. Your audience is another college student.
2. Write a description of the same commercial for one of the following writing situations.
   a. An assignment in a business marketing class: Analyze the factors that make the advertisement interesting and appealing. Your audience is a marketing instructor.
   b. A letter to the company that produces the product: Describe your response to the advertisement. Your audience is the consumer relations director of the company.
   c. A letter to your local television station: Comment favorably on or complain about the advertisement. Your audience is the station director.

Choosing a Point of View

Point of view is the perspective from which you write an essay. There are three types—*first, second,* and *third person.* In choosing a point of view, consider your topic, your purpose, and your audience.

Think of point of view as the "person" you become as you write. For some essays, you may find first-person pronouns (*I, me, mine, we, ours*) effective and appropriate, such as in an essay narrating an event in which you participated. For other types of essays, second-person pronouns (*you, your, yours*) are appropriate, as in an essay explaining how to build a fence: "First, *you* should measure. . . ." At times, the word *you* may be understood but not directly stated, as in "First, measure. . . ." Many textbooks, including this one, use the second person to address student readers.

In academic writing, the third-person point of view is prevalent. The third-person point of view is less personal and more formal than both the first person and the second person. The writer uses people's names and third-person pronouns (*he, she, they*). Think of the third person as public rather than private or personal. The writer reports what he or she sees.

| EXERCISE 3.4

Working with a classmate, discuss which point of view (first, second, or third person) would be most appropriate in each of the following writing situations.

1. An essay urging students on your campus to participate in a march against hunger to support a local food drive
2. A description of a car accident on a form that your insurance company requires you to submit in order to collect benefits
3. A paper for an ecology course on the effects of air pollution caused by a local industry

DISCOVERING IDEAS TO WRITE ABOUT

Many students report that one of the most difficult parts of writing an essay is finding enough to say about a narrowed topic. For many students, writing is easier when they make the effort to do some thinking and planning first. You wouldn't leave for a vacation without choosing a route and a destination beforehand. Similarly, you should not start writing a paper until you have a route and destination for it in mind. Before writing actual sentences and paragraphs, you should have some sense of your purpose and how you will accomplish it and organize your ideas. In the following sections, you will learn a number of useful strategies for discovering ideas to write about. Experiment with each before deciding which will work for you. Depending on your learning style, you will probably discover that some strategies work better than others. You may also find that the technique you choose for a given essay may depend in part on your topic.

Chapters 4 and 5 will show you how to focus your ideas and organize them into an effective essay. In addition, in the Guided Writing Assignments in Chapters 8 to 15 and 17, you will use various strategies for choosing and narrowing a topic and generating ideas about it.

Freewriting

When you use **freewriting**, you write nonstop for a specific period of time, usually five to ten minutes. As you learned in the activity that opens this chapter, freewriting involves writing whatever comes to mind, regardless of its relevance to your topic. If nothing comes to mind, just write the topic, your name, or "I can't think of anything to write." Then let your mind run free: Explore ideas, make associations, jump from one idea to another. The following tips will help you.

- Be sure to write nonstop. Writing often forces thought.
- Don't be concerned with grammar, punctuation, or spelling.
- Write fast! Try to keep up with your thinking. (Most people can think faster than they can write.)

- Record ideas as they come to you and in whatever form they appear—words, phrases, questions, or sentences.
- If you are freewriting on a computer, darken the screen so you are not distracted by errors, formatting issues, and the words you have already written.

Next, reread your freewriting, and highlight or underline ideas that seem useful. Look for patterns and connections. Do several ideas together make a point, reflect a sequence, or suggest a larger, unifying idea? Here is an annotated excerpt from one student's freewriting on the broad topic of violence in the media.

Portrayal of violence

Negative impact on viewers

Portrayal of minority and ethnic groups

There seems to be a lot of <u>violence</u> in the media these days, particularly on TV. For example, last night when I watched the news, the camera man showed people <u>getting shot in the street.</u> What kind of people watch this stuff? I'd rather watch a movie. It really bothered me because people get so turned off by such an ugly, <u>gruesome scene</u> that they won't want to watch the news anymore. Then we'll have a lot of <u>uninformed citizens.</u> There are too many already. Some people do not even know who the vice president of the U.S. is. A negative thing-- that is the media <u>has a negative impact</u> on anyone or group who want to do something about violence in the inner city. And they create <u>negative impressions of minority and ethnic groups</u>, too. If the media shows one Latino man committing a crime, viewers falsely assume <u>all Latinos</u> are criminals. It's difficult to think of something positive that can be done when you're surrounded by so much violence. It's all so overwhelming. What we need in the inner city is not more coverage of violence but viable solutions to the violence we have. The media coverage of violent acts only serves to make people think that this violence is a normal state of affairs and nothing can be done about it.

A number of different subtopics surfaced from this student's freewriting:

The media's graphic portrayal of violence
The media's negative impact on viewers
The media's portrayal of minority and ethnic groups

Any one of these could be narrowed into a manageable topic for an essay.

If you are a creative learner or feel restricted by organization and structure, *Learning Style Options* freewriting may appeal to you because it allows you to give your imagination free rein.

EXERCISE 3.5

Set a clock or timer for five minutes and freewrite on one of the following broad topics. Then review and highlight your freewriting, identifying usable ideas with a common theme that might serve as a topic for an essay. Starting with this potential topic, freewrite for another five minutes to narrow your topic further and develop your ideas.

1. Rock 'n' roll
2. Web sites
3. How to be self-sufficient
4. Urban problems
5. Job interviews

Mapping

Mapping, or **clustering**, is a visual way to discover ideas and relationships. It is also a powerful tool for some writers. Here is how it works.

1. Write your topic in the middle of a blank sheet of paper, and draw a box or circle around it.

2. Think of ideas that are related to or suggested by your topic. As you think of them, write them down in clusters around the topic, connecting them to the topic with lines (see Figure 3.2). Think of your topic as a tree trunk and the related ideas as branches.

3. Draw arrows and lines or use highlighting to show relationships and connect groups of related ideas.

4. Think of still more ideas, clustering them around the ideas already on your map.

 5. If possible, experiment with mapping on a computer, using a graphics program such as the draw function available in Microsoft Word. You can then cut and paste items from your map into an outline or draft of your essay.

The sample map in Figure 3.2 was done by a student working on the topic of the costs of higher education. In this map, the student compared attending a local community college and attending an out-of-town four-year college. A number of different subtopics evolved, including the following.

- Transportation costs
- Social life
- Availability of degree programs
- Room and board costs

FIGURE 3.2
SAMPLE MAP

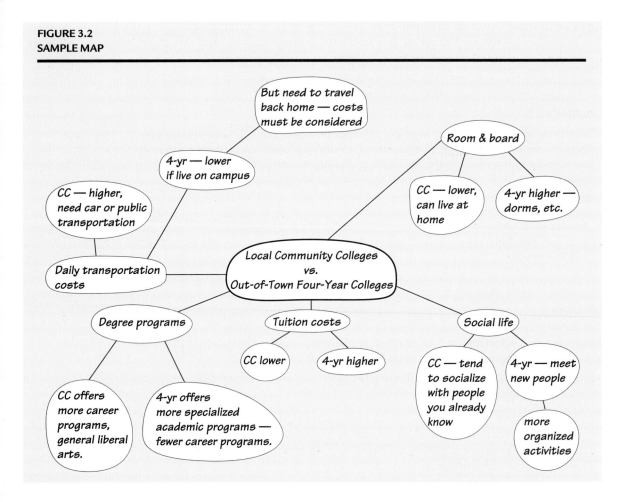

Learning Style Options

Mapping may appeal to you if you prefer a spatial method of dealing with information and ideas. It also appeals to creative learners who like to devise their own structure or framework within which to work.

EXERCISE 3.6

Narrow one of the following topics. Then select one of your narrowed topics, and draw a map of related ideas as they come to mind.

1. Presidential politics
2. Daydreaming
3. The function of jewelry
4. Radio stations
5. Year-round schooling

Brainstorming

When you do **brainstorming**, you list everything you can think of about your topic. Record impressions, emotions, and reactions as well as facts. List them as you think of them, recording brief words or phrases rather than complete sentences. Give yourself a time limit; it will force ideas to come faster. If you use a computer, you might use bullets or the indent function to brainstorm.

The following example shows a student's brainstorming on the narrowed topic of the disadvantages of home schooling. Home schooling is a form of education in which children do not attend school and are taught at home by parents.

TOPIC: DISADVANTAGES OF HOME SCHOOLING

```
- Child not exposed to other children
- Parent may not be an expert in each subject
- Libraries not easily accessible
- Wide range of equipment, resources not available
- Child may be confused by parent playing the role of
    teacher
- Child does not learn to interact with other children
- Child does not learn to compete against others
- Parents may not enforce standards
- Parents may be unable to be objective about child's
    strengths and weaknesses
- Child may learn only parent's viewpoint--not exposed to
    wide range of opinions
- Special programs (art, music) may be omitted
- Child may feel strong pressure to achieve
- Services of school nurse, counselors, reading special-
    ists not available
```

Two clusters of topics are evident — unavailable services and resources and problems of social development. In the sample, ideas that belong in the first cluster are highlighted in yellow; ideas that belong in the second cluster are highlighted in gray. Once the student selected a cluster of topics, he did further brainstorming to generate ideas about his narrowed topic.

Brainstorming is somewhat more structured than freewriting because the writer focuses only on the topic at hand instead of writing whatever comes to mind. If you are a pragmatic learner, brainstorming may help you release your creative potential.

Learning Style Options

Group Brainstorming

Brainstorming can also work well when it is done in groups of two or three classmates. Use a chalkboard in an empty classroom, share a large sheet of paper, sit together in front of a computer screen, or use networked computers. Say your ideas aloud as you write. You'll find that your classmates' ideas will trigger more of your own. **Group brainstorming** often appeals to students who are social learners and who find it stimulating and enjoyable to exchange ideas with other students.

EXERCISE 3.7

Choose one of the following subjects and narrow it to a manageable topic for a two- to four-page paper. Then brainstorm, either alone or with one or two classmates, to generate ideas to write about.

1. Value of music
2. National parks
3. Misuse of credit cards
4. Teenage fashions
5. Telemarketing

Questioning

Questioning is another way to discover ideas about a narrowed topic. Working either alone or with a classmate, write down every question you can think of about your topic. As with other prewriting strategies, focus on ideas, not correctness. Don't judge or evaluate ideas as you write. It may help to imagine that you are asking an expert on your topic anything that comes to mind.

Here is a partial list of questions one student generated on the narrow topic of the financial problems faced by single parents.

```
Why do many female single parents earn less than male single
   parents?
How can single parents afford to pay for day care?
Is there a support group for single parents that offers financial
   advice and planning?
How do single parents find time to attend college to improve
   their employability?
How can women force their former husbands to keep up with child
   support payments?
How can single female parents who don't work outside the home
   still establish credit?
```

```
Are employers reluctant to hire women who are single parents?
Is it more difficult for a working single parent to get a
   mortgage than for a couple in which only one spouse works?
```

These questions yielded several possible ideas for further development—income disparity, financial planning, establishment of credit, and child support.

Beginning a question with "What if . . ." is a particularly good way to extend your thinking and look at a topic from a fresh perspective. Here are a few challenging "What if . . ." questions about the financial situation of single parents:

```
What if the government provided national day care or paid for day
   care?
What if single parents were not allowed to deduct more than one
   child on their income tax?
What if there were financial support groups for single parents?
```

You may find questioning effective if you are an analytical, inquisitive person, and social learners will enjoy using this technique with classmates. Since questions often tend to focus on specifics and details, questioning is also an appealing strategy for concrete learners.

Learning Style Options

EXERCISE 3.8

Working either alone or with a classmate, choose one of the following topics, narrow it, and write a series of questions to discover ideas about it.

1. The campus newspaper
2. Learning a foreign language
3. Financial aid regulations
4. Late-night talk radio shows
5. Government aid to developing countries

Writing Assertions

The technique of **writing assertions** forces you to look at your topic from a number of different perspectives. Begin by writing five to ten statements that take a position on or make an assertion about your topic. Here are a few possible assertions for the topic of the growing popularity of health food.

```
Supermarkets have increased their marketing of health foods.
Health food is popular because buying it makes people think they
   are hip and current.
```

```
Health food is popular because it is chemical-free.
Health food tricks people into thinking they have a healthy
   lifestyle.
```

Review your list of assertions, choose one statement, and try brainstorming, freewriting, or mapping to generate more ideas about it.

Learning Style Options Abstract learners who prefer to deal with wholes rather than parts or who tend to focus on larger ideas rather than details often find this technique appealing.

EXERCISE 3.9

Working either alone or with one or two classmates, write assertions about one of the following topics.

1. Advertising directed toward children
2. Buying a used car from a private individual
3. Needed improvements in public education
4. Characteristics of a good teacher
5. Attempts to regulate speech on campus

Interviewing

Interview a classmate about your topic; then ask your classmate to interview you about your topic. As you ask each other questions, make notes on interesting issues and subtopics that arise. Use questions that begin with *who, what, when, where, why,* and *how* to get your interview started.

Here is a transcription of a conversation between two students on the topic of how holidays are celebrated.

MARY:	How did you celebrate holidays at your house when you were a child? Let's start by talking about a particularly memorable holiday.
CHRISTINA:	Well, on Christmas Eve — coming from a traditional Italian American family — my mother always prepared a meatless dinner.
MARY:	Such as?
CHRISTINA:	Eel and codfish. We also had squid and pasta with a fish sauce.
MARY:	Was it good? Did you eat it?
CHRISTINA:	No, it was like doing penance. We tried. But mostly we waited for the dessert — which was Italian cookies like cuccidati and ciccalane. But as we got older, we appreciated the tradition more and ate the fish — but no fish sauce.
MARY:	What other traditions did you have?
CHRISTINA:	For one, we sang Christmas songs. That is, everyone but my mother. She whistled. My father's favorite song was "O Holy Night," and sometimes he held our dog, Mickey, on his arm while he sang, and Mickey's eyes got big and his ears perked up — like he was enjoying it, too.

MARY: What else did you do on Christmas Eve?

CHRISTINA: We went to midnight mass. We always walked to church as a family. It took about an hour.

From this interview, narrowed topics emerged—special holiday foods and the importance of family and tradition. In addition, Christina recalled a number of details about Christmas Eve celebrations that she might use in an essay.

Interviewing provides both social interaction and an opportunity to focus on details and specifics. Also, since it involves questioning, interviewing appeals to students who enjoy analyzing ideas and issues.

Learning Style Options

EXERCISE 3.10

Interview a classmate on one of the following topics.

1. Nicknames, uses and abuses
2. A favorite sports team
3. A part-time job as a learning experience
4. Long-term goals after college
5. The effects of peer pressure

Using the Patterns of Development

In Parts 3 and 4 of this book, you will learn nine ways to develop an essay—narration, description, illustration, process, comparison and contrast, classification and division, definition, cause and effect, and argument. These methods are often called *patterns of development.* In addition to providing ways to develop an essay, the patterns of development may be used to generate ideas about a topic. Think of the patterns as doors through which you can gain access to your topic. Just as a building or room looks different depending on which door you enter, so you will see your topic in various ways by approaching it through different patterns of development.

Once you work through the chapters in Parts 3 and 4, you will become more familiar with the patterns of development; for now, the list of questions in Table 3.2 will help you approach your topic through these different "doors." For any given topic, some questions will work better than others. If your topic is voter registration, for example, the questions listed for definition and process would be more helpful than those listed for description.

As you write your answers to the questions, also record any related ideas that come to mind. If you are working on a computer, create a table listing the patterns in one column and your questions in another. This way, you can brainstorm ideas about various rhetorical approaches. Pragmatic and creative learners will find this technique helpful.

Here are the answers that one student wrote in response to questions rel*e* to the topic of extrasensory perception (ESP).

TABLE 3.2
USING THE PATTERNS OF DEVELOPMENT TO EXPLORE A TOPIC

Pattern of Development	Questions to Ask
Narration (Chapter 8)	What stories or events does this topic remind you of?
Description (Chapter 9)	What does the topic look, smell, taste, feel, or sound like?
Illustration (Chapter 10)	What examples of this topic are particularly helpful in explaining it?
Process (Chapter 11)	How does this topic work? How do you do this topic?
Comparison and Contrast (Chapter 12)	To what is the topic similar? In what ways? Is the topic more or less desirable than those things to which it is similar?
Classification and Division (Chapter 13)	Of what larger group of things is this topic a member? What are its parts? How can the topic be subdivided? Are there certain types or kinds of the topic?
Definition (Chapter 14)	How do you define the topic? How does the dictionary define it? What is the history of the term? Does everyone agree on its definition? Why or why not? If not, what points are in dispute?
Cause and Effect (Chapter 15)	What causes the topic? How often does it happen? What might prevent it from happening? What are its effects? What may happen because of it in the short term? What may happen as a result of it over time?
Argument (Chapters 16 and 17)	What issues surround this topic?

```
Narration (What stories does my topic remind me of?)
• Stories about ghosts, haunted houses--particularly the famous
  one in Amityville on Long Island
• Stories of cats with ESP--they find their way to the new house
  when their owners move away and leave them behind (sometimes
  traveling across states).

Description (What does my topic look, feel, smell, taste, or
sound like?)
```

- Some people report experiencing dizziness, eerie feelings, foggy vision, unnatural sounds, cold winds.

Illustration (What examples of my topic come to mind?)
- Feelings of déjà vu--that you have experienced something before
- When a husband and wife or two friends have the same thought simultaneously

Process (How does my topic work?)
- The theory is that ESP works by way of one person transmitting a thought telepathically (not through the usual senses) to another person. This is said to happen particularly in times of distress (for example, a wife "has a feeling" that her husband's plane will crash and sends a telepathic message to him not to board the plane).

Comparison and Contrast (What is similar to my topic?)
- Some people might say ESP is similar to guessing.
- Strange coincidences--two movies with similar plots released at the same time

Classification and Division (How can my topic be classified or divided?)
- ESP may be subdivided by time--those who experience events in advance, those who experience events as they are happening, and those who experience events after they have happened.

Definition (How can my topic be defined?)
- ESP, or extrasensory perception, is the ability to perceive information not through the ordinary senses but as a result of a "sixth sense" (as yet undeveloped in most people).
- Scientists disagree on whether ESP exists and how it should be tested.

Cause and Effect (Why does my topic happen? What are its effects?)
- Scientists do not know the cause of ESP and have not confirmed its existence, just the possibility of its existence.
- The effects of ESP are that some people know information that they would (seemingly) have no other way of knowing.
- Some people with ESP claim to have avoided disasters such as airplane crashes.

<u>Argument (What issues surround my topic?)</u>

• Is ESP always a desirable trait?
• Can ESP be learned or developed?

A number of interesting topics and ideas emerged from this student's answers, including types of ESP, ESP research, precognition, and mental telepathy.

Learning Style Options   Using the patterns of development helps to direct or focus your mind on specific issues related to a topic. The strategy may appeal to you if you are a pragmatic learner who enjoys structured tasks or a creative learner who likes to analyze ideas from different viewpoints.

EXERCISE 3.11

Use the patterns of development to generate ideas on one of the following topics. Refer to Table 3.2 (p. 78) to form questions based on the patterns.

1. Buying only American-made products
2. The increase in incidents of carjacking
3. Community policing in urban areas
4. Effects of labor union strikes on workers
5. Internet chat sessions

Visualizing or Sketching

Especially if you enjoy working with graphics, **visualizing** or actually **sketching** your topic may be an effective way to discover ideas. If you are writing a description of a person, for example, close your eyes, and visualize that person in your mind. Imagine what he or she is wearing; study facial expressions and gestures.

Here is what one student "saw" when visualizing a shopping mall.

As I walked through the local mall, I crossed the walkway to get to Sears and noticed a large group of excited women all dressed in jogging suits; they were part of a shopping tour, I think. I saw a tour bus parked outside. Across the walkway was a bunch of teenagers, shouting and laughing and commenting on each other's hairstyles. They all wore T-shirts and jeans; some had body adornments--pierced noses and lips. They seemed to have no interest in shopping. Their focus was on one another. Along the walkway came an obvious mother-daughter pair. They seemed to be on an outing, escaping from their day-to-day routine for some shopping, joking, and laughing. Then I noticed a tired-looking elderly couple sitting on one of the benches. They seemed to enjoy just sitting there and watching the people walk by, every now and then commenting on the fashions they observed people wearing.

After visualizing the mall, this student came up with several possible topics related to malls as social gathering places as well as a number of subtopics — body piercing, tour-group shopping, and teenage behavior. Visualization is a technique particularly well suited to spatial and creative learners.

Learning Style Options

EXERCISE 3.12

Visualize one of the following situations. Make notes on or sketch what you "see." Include as many details as possible.

1. A traffic jam
2. A couple obviously "in love"
3. A class you recently attended
4. The campus snack bar
5. A sporting event

Researching Your Topic

Do some preliminary research on your topic in the library or on the Internet. Find three or four related books or articles in the library or online sources of information. Reading what others have written about your topic may suggest new approaches, reveal issues or controversies, and help you determine what you do and do not already know about the topic. This method is especially useful when you are working on an assigned essay with an unfamiliar topic or when you have chosen a topic you want to learn more about.

For more information on locating, using, and crediting sources, refer to Chapters 18 and 20.

Take notes while reading sources. In addition, be sure to record the publication data you will need to cite each source (author, title, publisher, page numbers, and so on). If you use ideas or information from sources in your essay, you must give credit to the sources of the borrowed material. While research may be particularly appealing to concrete or rational learners, all students may need to use it at one time or another depending on their topic.

EXERCISE 3.13

Do library or Internet research to generate ideas on one of the narrowed topics listed here.

1. A recent local disaster (hurricane, flood)
2. Shopping for clothes on the Internet or on television
3. Preventing terrorism in public buildings
4. Controlling children's access to television programs
5. Advantages or disadvantages of belonging to a health maintenance organization (HMO)

EXERCISE 3.14

Choose two prewriting techniques discussed in this chapter that appeal to you. Experiment with each method by generating ideas about one of the topics in the following list or any of the topics from the previous exercises in the chapter. These topics are listed in Table 3.3. Use a different topic for each prewriting technique you choose.

1. Nuisance phone calls
2. Budgeting money
3. Dorm life
4. Pop music icons
5. Couch potatoes

ESSAY IN PROGRESS 3

Keeping your audience and purpose in mind, use one of the prewriting strategies discussed in this chapter to generate details about the topic you narrowed in Essay in Progress 2.

TABLE 3.3
BROAD TOPICS FROM CHAPTER 3 EXERCISES

Family Matters	Divorce
	Early childhood education
	Senior citizens
	Year-round schooling
	Teenage fashions
	Controlling children's access to television programs
College Life	The campus newspaper
	Learning a foreign language
	Financial aid regulations
	Characteristics of a good teacher
	Attempts to regulate speech on campus
	A part-time job as a learning experience
	Long-term goals after college
	A class you recently attended
	The campus snack bar
	Dorm life
Community Concerns	Safe transportation
	The increase in incidents of carjacking
	Community policing in urban areas
	A traffic jam
	A recent local disaster (hurricane, flood)
	Needed improvements in public education

(Continued on next page)

TABLE 3.3 *(Continued)*

National Government	Military spending
	Environmental protection
	Affirmative action
	Urban problems
	Presidential politics
	National parks
	Government aid to developing countries
	Effects of labor union strikes on workers
	Preventing terrorism in public buildings
World Issues	Population explosion
	AIDS
	Terrorism
Consumer Culture	Misuse of credit cards
	Telemarketing
	Advertising directed toward children
	Buying a used car from a private individual
	Buying only American-made products
	Shopping for clothes on the Internet or on television
	Nuisance phone calls
	Budgeting money
Entertainment Culture	Television programming
	Rock 'n' roll
	Radio stations
	Value of music
	Late-night talk radio shows
	A favorite sports team
	A sporting event
	Pop music icons
	Couch potatoes
Technology Issues	World Wide Web sites
	Internet chat sessions
Everyday Life	How to be self-sufficient
	Job interviews
	Daydreaming
	The function of jewelry
	Nicknames, uses and abuses
	The effects of peer pressure
	A couple obviously "in love"
	Advantages or disadvantages of belonging to a health maintenance organization (HMO)

STUDENTS WRITE

In this and the remaining four chapters of Part 2, we will follow the work of Christine Lee, a student in a first-year writing course who was assigned to write about a recent trend or fad in popular culture.

Lee decided to use questioning to narrow her topic and freewriting to generate ideas about the topic. Here is an example of her questioning.

SAMPLE QUESTIONING

What are some recent fads or trends?

        Trivia shows

        Yoga

        Extreme sports

        Alternative parties in politics

        Cell phones

        Reality TV

Lee decided to explore two of these experiences further: alternative parties in politics and reality TV. She did so by asking another question.

Why are these trends popular?

1. Alternative parties in politics
        They give voters more choice.
        They often appeal to minorities, special-interest groups, and
           young voters.
        They support radical platforms like legalizing drugs and
           abolishing the IRS.
        People find little difference between the two major parties
           these days.

2. Reality TV
        People are more likely to identify with real people, not
           actors.
        The shows are usually contests, which keep viewers watching
           until the last episode.
        They are unscripted and often unpredictable.
        Survivor was popular because money was involved.

After looking over the answers to her questions, Lee chose reality TV as her topic, and she decided to focus on its evolution and popularity. The following excerpt from her freewriting shows how she started to develop her topic.

SAMPLE FREEWRITING

When Survivor was first on TV everyone was watching and talking about it at school and work. It was new and different, and it was interesting to watch how people started to act when a million dollars was at stake. Everybody had a favorite and someone else they loved to hate. After that season it seemed like every network had two or three reality shows they were trying out. They get more and more ridiculous and less tasteful with every new show. Now I'm getting tired of all these "real" people as they defend their pettiness by saying "It's just a game." In the end I'll go back to watching Friends because it's funny (which Big Brother never is), and ER because they talk about serious issues that real people deal with. Maybe we'd all like to think that we wouldn't be as petty and mean as all of these contestants, but with all of these "real" people on TV these days, I can't relate to a single one of them.

As you work through the remaining chapters of Part 2, you will see how Lee develops her tentative thesis statement in Chapter 4, her first draft in Chapter 5, and her final draft in Chapter 6. In addition, in Chapter 7, you will also see a portion of her final draft, edited and proofread to correct sentence-level errors.

Developing and Supporting a Thesis

Study the cartoon on the opposite page; it humorously depicts a serious situation.

Writing Quick Start

Working alone or with one or two class-mates, write a statement that expresses the main point of the cartoon. Your state-ment should not just describe what is hap-pening in the cartoon. It should also state the idea that the cartoonist is trying to communicate to his audience.

The statement you have just written is an assertion around which you could build an essay. Such an assertion is called a *thesis statement*. In this chapter, you will learn how to write effective thesis statements and how to support them with evidence. Developing a thesis is an important part of the writing process shown in Figure 4.1, which lists the skills presented in this chapter while placing them within the context of the writing process.

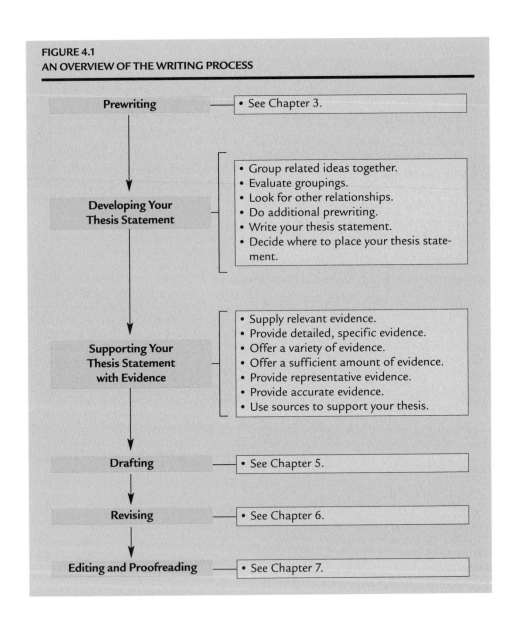

FIGURE 4.1
AN OVERVIEW OF THE WRITING PROCESS

Prewriting —— • See Chapter 3.

Developing Your Thesis Statement
- Group related ideas together.
- Evaluate groupings.
- Look for other relationships.
- Do additional prewriting.
- Write your thesis statement.
- Decide where to place your thesis statement.

Supporting Your Thesis Statement with Evidence
- Supply relevant evidence.
- Provide detailed, specific evidence.
- Offer a variety of evidence.
- Offer a sufficient amount of evidence.
- Provide representative evidence.
- Provide accurate evidence.
- Use sources to support your thesis.

Drafting —— • See Chapter 5.

Revising —— • See Chapter 6.

Editing and Proofreading —— • See Chapter 7.

WHAT IS A THESIS STATEMENT?

A **thesis statement** is the main point of an essay. It explains what the essay will be about and expresses the writer's position on the subject. It may also give clues about how the essay will develop or how it will be organized. Usually a thesis statement is expressed in a single sentence. When you write, think of a thesis statement as a promise to your reader. The rest of your essay delivers on your promise.

Here is a sample thesis statement.

> Playing team sports, especially football and baseball, develops skills and qualities that can make you successful in life because these sports demand communication, teamwork, and responsibility.

In this thesis, the writer identifies the topic—team sports—and states the position that team sports, especially football and baseball, equip players with important skills and qualities. After reaching the end of this statement, the reader expects to discover what skills and qualities football and baseball players learn and how these contribute to success in life.

DEVELOPING YOUR THESIS STATEMENT

A thesis statement usually evolves or develops as you explore your topic during prewriting: Do not expect to be able to sit down and simply write one. As you prewrite, you may discover a new focus or a more interesting way to approach your topic. Expect to write several versions of a thesis statement before you find one that works. For some topics, you may need to do some reading or research to get more information about your topic or tentative thesis. Your thesis may change, too, as you write your paper. As you organize supporting evidence, draft, and revise, you may again make changes in the focus or direction of your essay.

For more on prewriting, see Chapter 3.

For more on library and Internet research, see Chapter 19.

Your learning style can influence how you develop a thesis statement. Some students find it helpful to generate facts and details about a narrow topic and then write a thesis statement that reveals a large idea that is demonstrated by the details (pragmatic and concrete learners). Other students find it easier to begin with a broad idea, focus it in a thesis statement, and then generate details to support the thesis (creative and abstract learners).

Learning Style Options

Coming Up with a Working Thesis Statement

To come up with a preliminary or working thesis for your paper, use the following suggestions.

Highlight Details That Seem to Fit Together

As you reread your prewriting, look for and highlight the details that seem to fit together or that all have to do with the same subtopic. Some students recopy their highlighted details on a separate sheet of paper or index cards or cut and paste them in a separate computer file to make it easier to rearrange the details into meaningful groups.

Here is the brainstorming that one student did on the broad topic of *animal intelligence*. As she reread her brainstorming, she noticed that most of her details dealt with the intelligence of dogs, so she highlighted those details as well as others she thought might help her come up with a working thesis.

SAMPLE BRAINSTORMING

Topic: Animal Intelligence

dogs seem smarter than cats

hard to know about wild animals

female dogs instinctively know how to deliver and care for their
   puppies

how to separate intelligence from instinct?

how can we measure intelligence?

there are different types

understanding commands is intelligence

choosing the best food source is intelligence

some dogs smarter than others

may vary by canine breed

dolphins have click-whistle communication system

dogs avoid danger

dogs may have learned some behaviors from ancestry as wolves

finding shelter

avoiding predators--is this instinct?

how dogs avoid predators may require intelligence

dogs can learn new behaviors--tricks

elephants recognize family members

cats know how to mark their scent on humans

my dog knows when I'm angry or depressed

ex-neighbor's dog used to pick up and bring empty water dish to her

retrievers can solve problems

most dogs adapt to new situations, new owners

not sure if dogs respond more to human language or nonverbal
   messages

```
birds can learn to imitate human speech
dogs learn to become housebroken
cats know to use litter boxes
retrievers have memory--remember where a decoy dropped
rescue dogs solve problems--missing persons
retriever rolls up clothing in order to carry it more easily
```

Look for Groups of Related Details

Look at the details you have highlighted, and try to find groups or sets of details that all have to do with the same subtopic. Group these similar details together, and write a word or phrase that describes each group of related ideas.

For example, the student working on animal intelligence noticed in her brainstormed list that the details she highlighted could be grouped into three general categories—details about learning, details about problem solving, and details about instinct. Here is how the student rearranged her list of ideas into these three categories, rephrasing some items and adding new details as she worked.

```
Learning

learn to take commands
learn new tricks
learn to read master's emotions
learn to adapt to new owners
learn housebreaking
retrievers have memory--decoy; serve as guide dogs for blind
  people


Problem Solving

roll up clothing to carry it more easily
rescue dogs find victims
can warn owners about upcoming epileptic seizures
can carry empty water dish to owner


Instinct

females deliver and care for puppies
avoid danger
avoid predators
seek shelter
automatically raise hair on back in response to aggression
```

Evaluate Your Groupings

Once you've grouped similar details together, the next step is to decide which group or groups of ideas best represent the focus your paper should take. In some instances, one group of details will be enough to develop a working thesis for your paper. At other times, you need to use the details in two or three groups. From your clusters or groupings of details, you may be able to identify topics of paragraphs to include in your essay.

The student working on a thesis for the topic of animal intelligence evaluated her three groups of details and decided that instinct was unrelated to her topic. Consequently, she decided to write about learning and problem solving.

Do Additional Prewriting

For more on prewriting, see Chapter 3.

If you are not satisfied with how you have grouped or arranged your details, you probably don't have enough details to come up with a good working thesis. If you need more details, use prewriting to generate more ideas. Be sure to try a different prewriting strategy than the one you used previously. A new strategy may help you see your narrowed topic from a different perspective. If your second prewriting does not produce better results, consider refocusing or changing your topic. If a narrowed topic is not workable, it is better to revise it now rather than after you have spent time and effort drafting your essay.

> **ESSAY IN PROGRESS 1**
>
> If you used a prewriting strategy to generate details about your topic in response to Essay in Progress 3 in Chapter 3 (p. 82), review your prewriting, highlight useful ideas, and identify several sets of related details among those you have highlighted.

Writing an Effective Thesis Statement

A thesis statement should introduce your narrowed topic, revealing what your essay is about, and state the point you will make about that topic. Your thesis statement, or a sentence following it, may also preview the organization of your essay. Use the following guidelines to write an effective thesis statement or to evaluate and revise your working thesis.

1. **Make an assertion.** An **assertion,** unlike a fact, takes a position, expresses a viewpoint, or suggests your approach toward the topic.

LACKS AN ASSERTION	Hollywood movies, like *Pearl Harbor* and *A Beautiful Mind,* are frequently based on true stories.
REVISED	Hollywood movies, like *Pearl Harbor* and *A Beautiful Mind,* manipulate true stories to cater to the tastes of the audience.

   The first thesis states a fact; the revised thesis develops an idea about the fact.

2. **Be specific and provide enough detail.** Try to provide as much information as possible about your main point.

TOO GENERAL	I learned a great deal from my experiences as a teenage parent.
REVISED	From my experiences as a teenage parent, I learned to accept responsibility for my own life and for that of my son.

The first thesis is too general because it does not suggest what the student learned.

3. **Focus on one central point.** Limit your essay to one major idea.

FOCUSES ON SEVERAL POINTS	This college should improve its tutoring services, sponsor more activities of interest to Latino students, and speed up the registration process for students.
REVISED	To better represent the student population it serves, this college should sponsor more activities of interest to Latino students.

The first thesis makes three separate points, each of which could become the main point of an essay. The revised thesis makes one specific point.

4. **Offer an original perspective on your narrowed topic.** If your thesis seems dull or ordinary, it probably needs more work. Search your prewriting for an interesting angle on your narrowed topic.

TOO ORDINARY	Many traffic accidents are a result of carelessness.
REVISED	When a driver has an accident, it can change his or her entire approach to driving.

The first thesis makes an assertion that few would dispute.

5. **Avoid making an announcement.** Don't use phrases such as "This essay will discuss" or "The subject of my paper is." Instead, state your main point directly.

MAKES AN ANNOUNCEMENT	The point I am trying to make is that people should not be allowed to smoke on campus.
REVISED	The college should prohibit smoking on campus.

6. **Do not hesitate to revise or change your thesis.** As you work on your essay, you may realize that your thesis is still too broad, or you may discover a more interesting approach to your narrowed topic.

7. **Use your thesis to preview the organization of the essay.** Consider using your thesis to mention the two or three key concepts on which your essay will focus, in the order in which you will discuss them.

EXERCISE 4.1

Working in a group of two or three students, discuss what is wrong with each of the following thesis statements. Then revise each thesis to make it more effective.

1. In this paper, I will discuss the causes of asthma, which include exposure to smoke, chemicals, and allergic reactions.
2. Jogging is an enjoyable aerobic sport.
3. The crime rate is decreasing in American cities.
4. Living in an apartment has many advantages.
5. Children's toys can be dangerous, instructional, or creative.

If you find it difficult to come up with a working thesis statement, one or more of the following strategies may help you.

- Arrange your details chronologically, according to their occurrence in time. You may discover a trend or sequence.

  WORKING THESIS   A speaker can use numerous strategies to prepare for a speech, including planning, researching, rehearsing, and thinking positively.

- Divide your details into similarities and differences.

  WORKING THESIS   The famous Kentucky Derby is similar to most other horse races, and yet the consequences of winning are more far-reaching than those of any other race.

- Divide your details into causes and effects.

  WORKING THESIS   Because the justices who sit on the U.S. Supreme Court are appointed by the president, their attitudes and viewpoints always become a political issue during confirmation hearings.

- Divide your details into advantages and disadvantages.

  WORKING THESIS   A divorce may provide immediate benefits but also cause unexpected long-range problems for both the couple and their children.

ESSAY IN PROGRESS 2

Keeping your audience in mind, select one or more of the groups of ideas you identified in Essay in Progress 1, and write a working thesis statement based on these ideas.

Placing the Thesis Statement

Your thesis statement can appear anywhere in your essay, but it is usually best to place it in the first paragraph as part of your introduction. When your thesis appears at the beginning of the essay, your readers will know what to pay attention to and what to expect in the rest of the essay. When your thesis is placed later in the essay, you can build up to the thesis gradually in order to prepare readers for it.

Using an Implied Thesis

In some professional writing, especially in narrative or descriptive essays, the writer may not state the thesis directly. Instead, the thesis may be strongly implied by the details the writer chooses and the way those details are organized. Although professional writers may use an implied thesis, academic writers, including professors and students, generally state their thesis. You should always include a clear statement of your thesis for your college papers.

SUPPORTING YOUR THESIS STATEMENT WITH EVIDENCE

Once you have written a working thesis statement, the next step is to develop evidence that supports your thesis. **Evidence** is any type of information, such as examples, statistics, or expert opinion, that clarifies, explains, or justifies your thesis and will convince your reader that your thesis is reasonable or correct. This evidence, organized into well-developed paragraphs, makes up the body of your essay. To visualize the basic structure of an essay, look ahead to Figure 5.2 (p. 109).

Choosing Types of Evidence

Although there are many types of evidence, it is usually best not to use them all. Analyze your purpose, audience, and thesis to determine which types of evidence will be most effective. If your audience is unfamiliar with your topic, help them become more familiar with it by providing definitions, historical background, an explanation of process, and factual and descriptive details. If your purpose is to persuade, use comparison and contrast, advantages and disadvantages, examples, problems, quotations, and statistics to make your argument. Table 4.1 lists various types of evidence and gives examples of how each type could be used to support a working thesis on acupuncture. Note that many of the types of evidence correspond to the patterns of development discussed in Parts 3 and 4 of this text.

EXERCISE 4.2

1. Working in a group of two to three students, discuss and list the types of evidence that could be used to support the following thesis statement for an informative essay.

   > The pressure to become financially independent is a challenge for many young adults and often causes them to develop social and emotional problems.

2. For each audience listed here, discuss and record the types of evidence that would offer the best support for the preceding thesis.
   a. Young adults
   b. Parents of young adults
   c. Counselors of young adults

TABLE 4.1
TYPES OF EVIDENCE USED TO SUPPORT A THESIS

WORKING THESIS	Acupuncture, a form of alternative medicine, is becoming more widely accepted in the United States.
Types of Evidence	*Example*
Definition	Explain that in acupuncture, needles are inserted into specific points of the body to control pain or relieve symptoms.
Historical background	Explain that acupuncture is a medical treatment that originated in ancient China.
Explanation of a process	Explain the principles on which acupuncture is based and how scientists think it works.
Factual details	Explain who uses acupuncture, on what parts of the body it is used, and under what circumstances it is applied.
Descriptive details	Explain what acupuncture needles look and feel like.
Narrative story	Relate a personal experience that illustrates the use of acupuncture.
Causes or effects	Discuss one or two theories that explain why acupuncture works. Offer reasons for its increasing popularity.
Classification	Explain types of acupuncture treatments.
Comparison and contrast	Compare acupuncture to other forms of alternative medicine, such as massage and herbal medicines. Explain how acupuncture differs from these other treatments.
Advantages and disadvantages	Describe the pros (nonsurgical, relatively painless) and cons (fear of needles) of acupuncture.
Examples	Describe situations in which acupuncture has been used successfully: by dentists, in treating alcoholism, for pain control.
Problems	Explain that acupuncture is not always practiced by medical doctors; licensing and oversight of acupuncturists may thus be lax.
Statistics	Indicate how many acupuncturists practice in the United States.
Quotations	Quote medical experts who attest to the effectiveness of acupuncture as well as those who question its value.

Collecting Evidence to Support Your Thesis

Prewriting may help you collect evidence for your thesis. Try a different prewriting strategy than the one you used previously to arrive at a working thesis statement. Depending on your learning style, select one or more of the following suggestions to generate evidence that supports your thesis.

Learning Style Options

1. Complete the worksheet shown in Figure 4.2 on pages 98–99. For one or more types of evidence listed in the left column of the worksheet, give examples that support your thesis in the right column. Collect evidence only for those types that are appropriate for your thesis.

2. Visualize yourself speaking to your audience. What would you say to convince your audience of your thesis? Jot down ideas as they come to you.

3. On a sheet of paper or in a computer file, develop a skeletal outline of major headings. Leave plenty of blank space under each heading. Fill in ideas about each heading as they come to you.

For more on outlining, see Chapter 5, p. 114.

4. Draw a graphic organizer of your essay, filling in supporting evidence as you think of it.

5. Discuss your thesis statement with a classmate; try to explain why he or she should accept your thesis as valid.

See p. 34 in Chapter 2 for instructions on drawing a graphic organizer. For samples of graphic organizers for each pattern of development, see Parts 3 and 4. To draw detailed graphic organizers using a computer, visit www .bedfordstmartins.com /successfulwriting.

ESSAY IN PROGRESS 3

Using the preceding list of suggestions for collecting evidence to support a thesis, generate at least three different types of evidence to support the working thesis statement you wrote in Essay in Progress 2.

Choosing the Best Evidence

In collecting evidence in support of a thesis, you will probably generate more than you need. Consequently, you will need to identify the evidence that best supports your thesis and that suits your purpose and audience. Your learning style can also influence the way you select evidence and the kinds of evidence you favor. If you are a creative or an abstract learner, for example, you may tend to focus on large ideas and overlook the need for supporting detail. However, if you are a pragmatic or concrete learner, you may tend to generate too many facts and details, in which case you would need to select the most essential information and then concentrate on organizing your evidence logically.

Learning Style Options

The following guidelines will help you select the types of evidence that will best support your thesis.

1. **Make sure the evidence is relevant.** All of your evidence must clearly and directly support your thesis. Irrelevant evidence will distract your readers and

**FIGURE 4.2
A WORKSHEET FOR COLLECTING EVIDENCE**

Purpose: _____

Audience: _____

Point of View: _____

Thesis Statement: _____

_____

Type of Evidence	Actual Evidence
Definition	
Historical background	
Explanation of a process	
Factual details	
Descriptive details	
Narrative story	
Causes or effects	
Classification	
Comparison and contrast	
Advantages and disadvantages	
Examples	

(Continued on next page)

FIGURE 4.2 *(Continued)*

Type of Evidence	Actual Evidence
Problems	
Statistics	
Quotations	

cause them to question the validity of your thesis. If your thesis is that acupuncture is useful for controlling pain, you would not need to describe other, less popular alternative therapies.

2. **Provide specific evidence.** Avoid general statements that will neither engage your readers nor help you make a convincing case for your thesis. For instance, to support the thesis that acupuncture is becoming more widely accepted by patients in the United States, it would be most convincing to cite statistics that demonstrate an increase in the number of practicing acupuncturists in the United States over the past five years.

   To locate detailed, specific evidence, return to your prewriting or use a different prewriting strategy to generate concrete evidence. You may also need to conduct research to find evidence for your thesis.

For more on conducting research, see Chapters 18–20.

3. **Offer a variety of evidence.** Using diverse kinds of evidence increases the likelihood that your evidence will convince your readers. If you provide only four examples of people who have found acupuncture helpful, for example, many of your readers may conclude that these few isolated examples are not convincing. If you provide statistics and quotations from experts along with an example or two, however, more readers are likely to accept your thesis. Using different types of evidence also shows readers that you are knowledgeable and informed about your topic, thus enhancing your own credibility.

4. **Provide a sufficient amount of evidence.** The amount of evidence you need will vary according to your audience and your topic. To discover whether you have provided enough evidence, ask a classmate to read your essay and tell you whether he or she is convinced. If your reader is not convinced, ask him or her what additional evidence is needed.

5. **Provide representative evidence.** Be sure the evidence you supply is typical and usual. Do not choose unusual, rare, or exceptional situations as evidence.

Suppose your thesis is that acupuncture is widely used for various types of surgery. An example of one person who underwent painless heart surgery using only acupuncture without anesthesia will not support your thesis unless the use of acupuncture in heart surgery is routine. Including such an example would mislead your reader and could bring your credibility into question.

For more on choosing reliable sources, see Chapter 18, p. 649.

6. **Provide accurate evidence.** Gather your information from reliable sources. Do not guess at statistics or make estimates. If you are not certain of the accuracy of a fact or statistic, verify it through research. For example, do not estimate the number of medical doctors who are licensed to practice acupuncture in the United States. Instead, find out exactly how many U.S. physicians are licensed to practice.

ESSAY IN PROGRESS 4

Evaluate the evidence you generated in Essay in Progress 3. Select from it the evidence that you could use to support your thesis in a two- to four-page essay.

Using Sources to Support Your Thesis

For many topics, you will need to research library or Internet sources or interview an expert on your topic to collect enough supporting evidence for your thesis. Chapter 19 provides a thorough guide to locating sources in the library and on the Internet, and it also includes tips for conducting interviews (p. 689). Chapter 20 provides guidelines for integrating and documenting sources. Also see "Using Sources to Add Details to an Essay" on page 641 of Chapter 18.

ESSAY IN PROGRESS 5

For the thesis statement you wrote in Essay in Progress 2, locate and consult at least two sources to find evidence that supports your thesis.

STUDENTS WRITE

In the Students Write section of Chapter 3, you saw how student writer Christine Lee narrowed her topic and generated ideas for her essay on a contemporary fad. You also saw how she decided to focus on reality TV.

    After reviewing her responses to questions about her topic and her freewriting, Lee decided that reality TV had become less tasteful and less interesting. She then wrote the following working thesis statement.

```
As the trend in reality TV wears on, shows are becoming both less
interesting and less tasteful.
```

To generate more details that would support her thesis, Lee did more freewriting and brainstorming to help her recall details from the shows. Here's an excerpt from what she wrote:

```
--Early shows: Cops and Candid Camera
--MTV's Real World was first recent reality show to become popular.
--Original Survivor was smart and interesting.
--Big Brother just locked people up together and forced us to
  watch them bicker.
--The Survivor series continues to be popular, while copy-cats
  like Murder in Small Town X and Fear Factor get more graphic
  and unwatchable.
--People will tire of Fear Factor quickly because there is no
  plot to follow from one episode to the next and watching people
  eat worms and hold their breaths underwater gets boring.
--Reality TV was popular because it was something different, but
  now there are dozens of these shows each season and few worth
  watching.
--Murder in Small Town X opens with a reenactment from the
  murderer's point of view and ends with the audience watching
  one of two players getting "attacked" and "killed."
```

WORKING WITH TEXT

Pet Therapy for Heart and Soul
Kerry Pechter

The following essay by Kerry Pechter was first published in 1985 in Prevention *magazine, a periodical that focuses on promoting a healthy lifestyle. Later the article appeared in a collection of essays,* Your Emotional Health and Well-Being *(1989). Pechter supports the essay's thesis with a variety of evidence. As you read, underline the thesis statement, and highlight the types of evidence that are offered to support it.*

    It's exercise hour at the Tacoma Lutheran Home in the state of   1
Washington, and P.T., an exotic yellow-crested bird called a cockatiel, is having the time of his life. He's sitting on the foot of 81-year-old

Ben Ereth, riding in circles while Ben pedals vigorously on an exercise bicycle. The bird likes it so much that if Mr. Ereth stops too soon, he'll squawk at him.

2   A bizarre sort of activity to find in a nursing home? Not at Tacoma Lutheran. Three years ago, the nursing home adopted an angora rabbit. Then a puppy. Then tropical birds. The home's elderly residents have taken to these animals with a passion. And, says Virginia Davis, director of resident services, the animals have breathed enthusiasm into what otherwise might have been a listless nursing home atmosphere.

3   "The animals help in several ways," says Davis. "One of the cockatiels gives a wolf whistle whenever anyone passes its cage. That gives them an unexpected boost in morale. And the birds seem to alleviate the tension associated with exercise. They make exercise more acceptable and relaxing."

4   What's happening at Tacoma Lutheran is just one example of an increasingly popular phenomenon called pet therapy. Although humans have adopted pets for thousands of years, only recently have social scientists taken a close look at the nature of the relationship that people form with dogs, cats, and other "companion animals."

5   At places like the Center for the Interaction of Animals and Society in Philadelphia and the Center for the Study of Human Animal Relationships and Environments (CENSHARE) in Minneapolis, they've discovered that there is something mutually therapeutic about these relationships. They say that pets relax us, help us communicate with each other, build our self-esteem, and comfort us when we're feeling down.

6   In fact, many now believe that pets play a small but very significant role in determining how well, for example, a heart attack survivor recuperates, how a family handles domestic strife, whether a disturbed teenager grows up straight, or even whether a nursing home resident like Mr. Ereth enjoys and sticks to his daily exercycle program.

7   Pet animals, in short, may affect our health.

ANIMAL MAGNETISM AT WORK

8   Pet therapists have put these capacities to work in a variety of ways. Pet therapy is very often used, for example, to combat the isolation and loneliness so common in nursing homes. At the Tacoma Lutheran Home, Davis has found that the pets help many residents break their customary silence.

9   "Animals are a catalyst for conversation," she says. "Most people can remember a story from their past about a pet animal. And people

are more comfortable talking to animals than they are to people. Sometimes a person who hasn't spoken for a long time, or one who has had a stroke and doesn't talk, will talk to an animal."

Animals also seem to draw everyone into the conversation. "Even in a nursing home, there are some people who are more attractive or responsive than others," says Phil Arkow, of the Humane Society of the Pike's Peak Region in Colorado, who drives a "Petmobile" to local nursing homes. "Human visitors try not to do it, but they inevitably focus on those who are most attractive. But animals don't make those distinctions. They focus on everyone equally." 10

A person doesn't have to live in a nursing home, however, in order to reap the benefits of a pet. Pets typically influence the communication that goes on between family members in a normal household. During a research project a few years ago, University of Maryland professor Ann Cain, Ph.D., discovered that pets help spouses and siblings express highly charged feelings. 11

"When family members want to say something to each other that they can't say directly," Dr. Cain says, "they might say it to the pet and let the other person overhear it. That also lets the listener off the hook, because he doesn't have to respond directly." 12

Though it's still in the experimental stage, researchers are discovering that watching or petting friendly animals—not only dogs and cats but almost any pet—can produce the kind of deep relaxation usually associated with meditation, biofeedback, and hypnosis. This kind of relaxing effect is so good that it can actually lower blood pressure. 13

At the University of Pennsylvania's Center for the Interaction of Animals and Society, for instance, Dr. Katcher and Dr. Friedmann monitored the blood pressure of healthy children while the children were sitting quietly or reading aloud, either with or without a dog in the room. Their blood pressure was always lower when the dog was in the room. 14

The researchers went on to discover, remarkably, that looking at fish could temporarily reduce the blood pressure of patients with hypertension. In one widely reported study, they found that the systolic and diastolic pressure of people with high blood pressure dipped into the normal range when they gazed at an aquarium full of colorful tropical fish, green plants, and rocks for 20 minutes. 15

This calming power of pets has found at least a few noteworthy applications. In Chicago, one volunteer from the Anti-Cruelty Society took an animal to a hospital and arranged for a surgical patient to be greeted by it when he awoke from anesthesia. "It's a comforting way to come back to reality," says one volunteer. "For children, pets can make a hospital seem safer. It's a reminder of home." 16

17   Animals may also have the power to soften the aggressive tendencies of disturbed adolescents. At Winslow Therapeutic Riding Unlimited, Inc., in Warwick, New York, where horseback riding is used to help handicapped children of all kinds, problem teenagers seem to behave differently when they're put on a horse.

18   "These are kids who fight in school. Some of their fathers are alcoholics," says Mickey Pulis of the nonprofit facility. "But when they come here, they're different. When they groom and tack the horses, they learn about the gentle and caring side of life.

19   "The horse seems to act like an equalizer," she says. "It doesn't care what reading levels these kids are at. It accepts them as they are."

20   Ultimately, researchers like Dr. Friedmann believe that the companionship of pets can reduce a person's risk of dying from stress-related illnesses, such as heart disease.

21   "The leading causes of mortality and morbidity in the United States are stress-related or life-style related," she says. "Pets, by decreasing the level of arousal and moderating the stress response, can help slow the progression of those diseases or even prevent them."

PETS ARE COMFORTING

22   But what is it about pets that make them capable of all this? And why do millions of people go to the trouble and expense of keeping them? Pet therapists offer several answers.

23   For one thing, animals don't talk back to us. Researchers have discovered that a person's blood pressure goes up whenever he talks to another person. But we talk to animals in a different way, often touching them at the same time, which minimizes stress.

24   Another theory holds that pets remind us of our ancestral link with other animals. "By domesticating an animal, man demonstrates his kinship to nature," Dr. Levinson once wrote. "A human being has to remain in contact with all of nature throughout his lifetime if he is to maintain good mental health."

25   Dr. Corson, on the other hand, says that we love pets because they are perpetual infants. Human infants charm us, but they eventually grow up. Pets never do. They never stop being cuddly and dependent. Likewise, pets are faithful. "Pets can offer a relationship that is more constant than relationships with people," says Dr. Cain. "You can count on them."

26   Some argue that the most important ingredient in our relationships with animals is that we can touch them whenever we want to. "Having access to affectionate touch that is not related to sex is important," says Dr. Katcher. "If you want to touch another person, you can't always do it immediately. But with pets you can." ■

Examining the Reading

1. Describe the effects of placing animals in nursing homes.
2. In what situations, other than nursing homes, are pets beneficial?
3. What reasons does Pechter offer to explain the positive effects of pets on humans?
4. Define each of the following words as it is used in the essay: *bizarre* (paragraph 2), *alleviate* (paragraph 3), *therapeutic* (paragraph 5), *catalyst* (paragraph 9), and *morbidity* (paragraph 21).

Analyzing the Reading

1. State the author's thesis in your own words. Then, using the guidelines on pages 92–93, evaluate the effectiveness of the thesis.
2. To what audience does Pechter address this essay? What purpose does the essay fulfill? How do you think the audience and purpose affect the author's choice of evidence?
3. What types of evidence does the author use to support the thesis? Which type does the author rely on most? What other types of evidence could the author have used? (Refer to Table 4.1, p. 96, for a summary of the various types of evidence.)
4. Do you think the author provides sufficient evidence for you to accept the thesis? Why or why not?
5. Cite one paragraph from the essay in which you think the author provides detailed, specific information. Explain why you chose it.

Reacting to the Reading: Discussion and Journal Writing

1. How do you think this essay would change if the writer wrote it for readers of *Dog Fancy,* a magazine for dog owners?
2. Most pet owners talk to their pets even though the pets probably do not understand most of what is said. In what sense is this "talk" therapeutic?
3. In your journal, write about other activities or types of recreation that you find relaxing or comforting because they remind you of your kinship to nature.

Drafting an Essay

The photographs on the opposite page show a few of the technologies that have reshaped the way we experience the world and interact with others. Study these photographs, and think of other recent technological innovations.

Writing Quick Start

Working alone or with two or three classmates, write a sentence that states your opinion of how electronic media have affected society. Then support this opinion with a list of details (evidence) from the three photographs and from your own knowledge of new technologies. Number your best evidence 1, your second-best evidence 2, and so on. Cross out any details that do not support your opinion, or adjust the sentence if the evidence you gathered disagrees with it. Finally, write a paragraph that begins with the sentence you wrote and includes your evidence in order of importance.

The paragraph you have just written could be part of an essay on the topic of how access to electronic media varies in developed and developing countries. To write an essay you would need to do additional prewriting and research to learn more about this topic. Then you would write a thesis statement, develop supporting paragraphs, write an effective introduction and conclusion, and choose a good title. This chapter will guide you through the process of developing an essay in support of a thesis statement, as part of the writing process shown in Figure 5.1.

THE STRUCTURE OF AN ESSAY

Think of an essay as a complete piece of writing, much as a textbook chapter is. For example, a textbook chapter might have the title "Human Rights in Developing Countries," which gives you a clear idea of the chapter's subject. The first few paragraphs of the chapter would probably introduce and define the concept of human

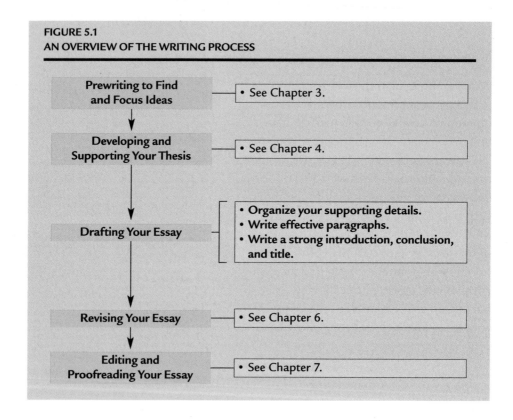

FIGURE 5.1
AN OVERVIEW OF THE WRITING PROCESS

Prewriting to Find and Focus Ideas
- See Chapter 3.

Developing and Supporting Your Thesis
- See Chapter 4.

Drafting Your Essay
- Organize your supporting details.
- Write effective paragraphs.
- Write a strong introduction, conclusion, and title.

Revising Your Essay
- See Chapter 6.

Editing and Proofreading Your Essay
- See Chapter 7.

rights. The chapter might then assert that human rights is a controversial global issue of growing importance. The rest of the chapter might explain the issue by tracing its history, examining why it is a world issue, and discussing its current status. The chapter would conclude with a summary.

FIGURE 5.2
THE STRUCTURE OF AN ESSAY: PARTS AND FUNCTIONS

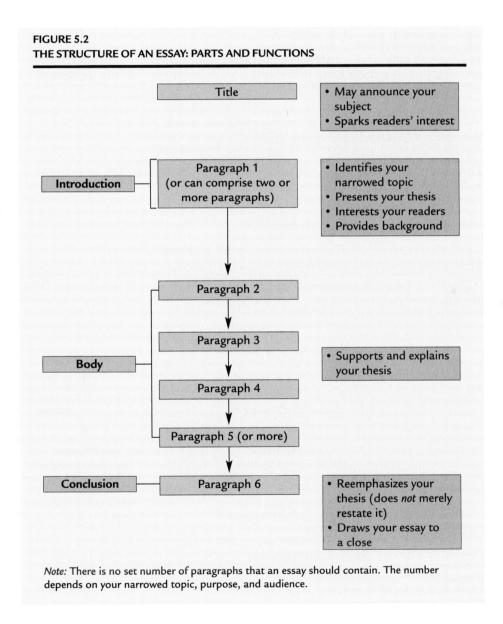

Title
- May announce your subject
- Sparks readers' interest

Introduction

Paragraph 1 (or can comprise two or more paragraphs)
- Identifies your narrowed topic
- Presents your thesis
- Interests your readers
- Provides background

Body

Paragraph 2

Paragraph 3

Paragraph 4
- Supports and explains your thesis

Paragraph 5 (or more)

Conclusion

Paragraph 6
- Reemphasizes your thesis (does *not* merely restate it)
- Draws your essay to a close

Note: There is no set number of paragraphs that an essay should contain. The number depends on your narrowed topic, purpose, and audience.

Similarly, as you can see in Figure 5.2 on page 109, an essay has a title and an introduction. It also makes an assertion (the thesis statement) that is explained and supported throughout the body of the essay. The essay ends with a final statement, its conclusion.

ORGANIZING YOUR SUPPORTING DETAILS

For more on developing a thesis and selecting evidence to support it, see Chapter 4.

The body of your essay contains the paragraphs that support your thesis. Before you begin writing these body paragraphs, decide on the supporting evidence you will use and the order in which you will present your evidence.

Selecting a Method of Organization

The three common ways to organize ideas are most-to-least (or least-to-most) order, chronological order, and spatial order.

Most-to-Least (or Least-to-Most) Order

If you choose this method of organizing an essay, arrange your supporting details from most to least (or least to most) important, familiar, or interesting. You might begin with your most convincing evidence or save your most compelling evidence for last, building gradually to your strongest point. You can visualize these two options as shown here.

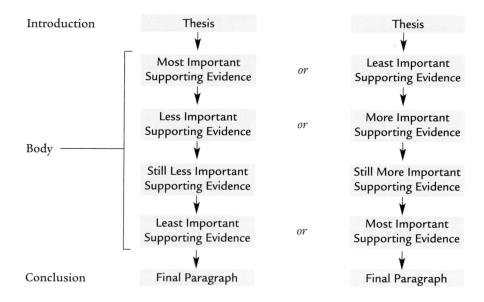

A student, Robin Ferguson, was working on the thesis statement "Working as a literacy volunteer taught me more about learning and friendship than I ever expected" and identified four primary benefits related to her thesis.

BENEFITS

- I learned about the learning process.

- I developed a permanent friendship with my student, Marie.

- Marie built self-confidence.

- I discovered the importance of reading.

Ferguson then chose to arrange these benefits from least to most important and decided that the friendship was the most important benefit. Here is how she organized her supporting evidence.

WORKING THESIS

Working as a literacy volunteer taught me more about
learning and friendship than I ever expected.

LEAST	Supporting paragraph 1:	Learned about the learning process
TO	Supporting paragraph 2:	Discovered the importance of reading for Marie
MOST	Supporting paragraph 3:	Marie increased her self-confidence
IMPORTANT	Supporting paragraph 4:	Developed a permanent friendship

EXERCISE 5.1

For each of the following narrowed topics, identify several qualities or characteristics that you could use to organize details in most-to-least or least-to-most order.

1. Three stores in which you shop
2. Three friends
3. Three members of a sports team
4. Three fast-food restaurants
5. Three television shows you watched this week

Chronological Order

When you arrange your supporting details in **chronological order,** you put them in the order in which they happened. When using this method of organization, begin the body of your essay with the first example or event, and progress through the others as they occurred. Depending on the subject of your essay, the events could be minutes, days, or years apart. Chronological order is commonly used in narrative essays and process analyses. You can visualize this order as follows.

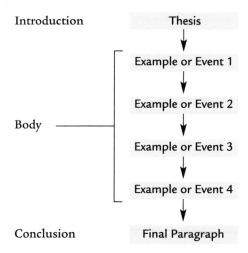

As an example, let's suppose that Robin Ferguson, writing about her experiences as a literacy volunteer, decides to demonstrate her thesis by relating the events of a typical tutoring session. In this case, she might organize her essay by narrating the events in the order in which they usually occur, using each detail about the session to demonstrate what tutoring taught her about learning and friendship.

EXERCISE 5.2

Working alone or with a classmate, identify at least one thesis statement from those listed below that could be supported by chronological paragraphs. Write a few sentences explaining how you would use chronological order to support this thesis.

1. European mealtimes differ from those of many American visitors, much to the visitors' surprise and discomfort.
2. Despite the many pitfalls that await those who shop at auctions, people can find bargains if they prepare in advance.
3. My first day of kindergarten was the most traumatic experience of my childhood, one that permanently shaped my view of education.
4. Learning how to drive a car increases a teenager's freedom and responsibility.

Spatial Order

When you use **spatial order,** you organize details about your subject according to their location or position in space. Consider, for example, how you might use spatial order to support the thesis that modern movie theaters are designed to shut out the outside world and create a separate reality within. You could begin by describing the ticket booth, then the lobby, and finally the individual theaters. Similarly, you might describe a basketball court from right to left or a person from head to toe. Robin Ferguson, writing about her experiences as a literacy volunteer, could describe her classroom or meeting area from front to back or left to right. Spatial organization is commonly used in descriptive essays as well as in classification and division essays.

You can best visualize spatial organization by picturing your subject in your mind or by sketching it on paper. "Look" at your subject systematically — from top to bottom, inside to outside, front to back. Cut it into imaginary sections or pieces and describe each piece.

You can visualize an essay that uses spatial order as follows.

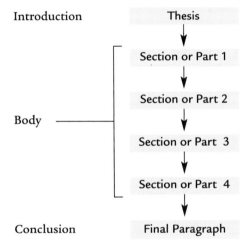

EXERCISE 5.3

Working alone or with a classmate, identify one thesis statement listed below that could be supported by means of spatial organization. Write a few sentences explaining how you would use spatial order to support this thesis.

1. Our family's yearly vacation at a cabin in Maine provides us with a much needed opportunity to renew family ties.
2. The Civic Theatre of Allentown's set for Tennessee Williams's play *A Streetcar Named Desire* was simple, yet striking and effective.
3. Although a pond in winter may seem frozen and lifeless, this appearance is deceptive.
4. A clear study space can cut down on time-wasting distractions.

ESSAY IN PROGRESS 1

Choose one of the following activities.

1. Using the thesis statement and evidence you gathered for the Essay in Progress activities in Chapter 4, choose a method for organizing your essay. Then explain briefly how you will use that method of organization.

2. Choose one of the following narrowed topics. Then, using the steps in Figure 5.1, An Overview of the Writing Process (p. 108), prewrite to produce ideas, develop a thesis, and generate evidence to support the thesis. Next, choose a method for organizing your essay. Explain briefly how you will use that method of organization.

   a. Positive or negative experiences with computers
   b. Stricter (or more lenient) regulations for teenage drivers
   c. Factors that account for the popularity of action films
   d. Discipline in public elementary schools
   e. Advantages or disadvantages of instant messaging

Preparing an Outline or Graphic Organizer

Once you have written a thesis statement and chosen a method of organization for your essay, take a few minutes to write an outline or draw a graphic organizer of the essay's main points in the order you plan to discuss them. Making an organizational plan is an especially important step when your essay is long or deals with a complex topic.

Outlining or drawing a graphic organizer can help you plan your essay as well as discover new ideas to include. Either method will help you see how ideas fit together and may reveal places where you need to add supporting information.

There are two types of outlines—informal and formal. An **informal outline,** also called a *scratch outline,* uses keys words and phrases to list main points and subpoints. An informal outline does not necessarily follow the standard outline format of numbered and lettered headings. The outline of Robin Ferguson's essay below is an example of an informal outline. Recall that she chose to use a least-to-most important method of organization.

SAMPLE INFORMAL OUTLINE

Thesis: Working as a literacy volunteer taught me more about learning and friendship than I ever expected.

Paragraph 1: Learned about the learning process
• Went through staff training program
• Learned about words "in context"

Paragraph 2: Discovered the importance of reading for Marie
• Couldn't take bus, walked to grocery store
• Couldn't buy certain products
• Couldn't write out grocery list

Paragraph 3: Marie increased her self-confidence

- Made rapid progress
- Began taking bus
- Helped son with reading

Paragraph 4: Developed a permanent friendship
- Saw each other often
- Both single parents
- Helped each other baby-sit

Conclusion: I benefited more than Marie did.

Formal outlines use Roman numerals (I, II), capital letters (A, B), arabic numbers (1, 2), and lowercase letters (a, b) to designate levels of importance. Formal outlines fall into two categories: *Sentence outlines* use complete sentences, and *topic outlines* use only key words and phrases. In a topic or sentence outline, less important entries are indented, as in the sample formal outline below. Each topic or sentence begins with a capital letter.

FORMAT FOR A FORMAL OUTLINE

I. First main topic
    A. First subtopic of I
    B. Second subtopic of I
        1. First detail about I.B
        2. Second detail about I.B
    C. Third subtopic of I
        1. First detail about I.C
            a. First detail or example about I.C.1
            b. Second detail or example about I.C.1
        2. Second detail about I.C
II. Second main topic

Here is a sample outline that a student wrote for an essay for her interpersonal communication class:

SAMPLE FORMAL OUTLINE

I. Types of listening
    A. Participatory
        1. Involves the listener responding to the speaker
        2. Has expressive quality
            a. Maintain eye contact
            b. Express feelings using facial expressions

```
     B.  Nonparticipatory
         1.  Involves listener listening without talking or
             responding
         2.  Allows speaker to develop his or her thoughts with-
             out interruption
     C.  Critical listening
         1.  Involves listener analyzing and evaluating the
             message
         2.  Is especially important in college classes
             a.  Listen for instructors' biases
             b.  Evaluate evidence in support of opinions
                 expressed
```

For more on parallel structure, see Chapter 7, p. 184.

Remember that all items labeled with the same designation (capital letters, for example) should be of parallel importance, and each must explain or support the topic or subtopic under which it is placed. Also, all items at the same level should be grammatically parallel.

NOT PARALLEL	I. Dietary Problems
	   A. Consuming too much fat
	   B. High refined-sugar consumption

PARALLEL	I. Dietary Problems
	   A. Consuming too much fat
	   B. Consuming too much refined sugar

If your instructor allows, you can use both phrases and sentences within an outline, as long as you do so consistently. You might write all subtopics (designated by capital letters A, B, and so on) as sentences and all supporting details (designated by 1, 2, and so on) as phrases, for instance.

Learning Style Options

For more about graphic organizers, see Chapter 2, p. 34.

If you have a pragmatic learning style or a verbal learning style or use both styles, preparing an outline will probably appeal to you. If you are a creative or spatial learner, however, you may prefer to draw a graphic organizer. Whichever method you find most appealing, begin by putting your working thesis statement at the top of a piece of paper or word-processing document. Then list your main points below your thesis. Be sure to leave plenty of space between main points. While you are filling in the details that support one main point, you will often think of details or examples to use in support of a different main point. As these details or examples occur to you, jot them down under or next to the appropriate main point of your outline or graphic organizer.

The graphic organizer shown in Figure 5.3 was done for Ferguson's essay. As you examine her graphic organizer, notice that it follows the least-to-most important method of organization, as did her informal outline on page 114.

FIGURE 5.3
SAMPLE GRAPHIC ORGANIZER

ESSAY IN PROGRESS 2
For the topic you chose in Essay in Progress 1, write a brief outline or draw a graphic organizer to show the organizational plan of your essay.

WRITING EFFECTIVE PARAGRAPHS

Your essay can be only as good as its supporting paragraphs. Therefore, each supporting paragraph in the body of your essay must be well developed. A well-developed paragraph supports your thesis, contributes to the overall effectiveness of your essay, and contains three parts:

- A well-focused topic sentence,
- Unified, specific supporting details (definitions, examples, explanations, or other evidence), and
- Transitions and repetition to show how the ideas are related.

To visualize the structure of a well-developed paragraph, see Figure 5.4.

Writing Well-Focused Topic Sentences

A **topic sentence** is to a paragraph what a thesis statement is to an essay. Just as a thesis announces the main point of an essay, a topic sentence states the main point

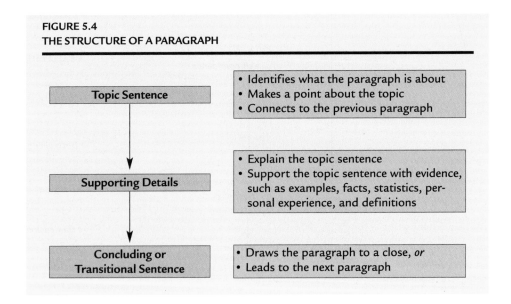

FIGURE 5.4
THE STRUCTURE OF A PARAGRAPH

Topic Sentence
- Identifies what the paragraph is about
- Makes a point about the topic
- Connects to the previous paragraph

Supporting Details
- Explain the topic sentence
- Support the topic sentence with evidence, such as examples, facts, statistics, personal experience, and definitions

Concluding or Transitional Sentence
- Draws the paragraph to a close, *or*
- Leads to the next paragraph

of a paragraph. In addition, each paragraph's topic sentence must support the thesis of the essay. The topic sentence can appear at any position in the paragraph. In the following student essay by Robin Ferguson on volunteering in a literacy program, which you have been learning about in earlier sections of this chapter, the thesis statement and topic sentences are underlined.

Robin Ferguson was a first-year college student studying to become a physical therapy assistant when she wrote this essay. She wrote it in response to an assignment in a community studies course. As you read the essay and the annotations, note how each topic sentence states the main point of the paragraph and supports the essay's thesis.

The Value of Volunteering

Robin Ferguson

	I began working as a literacy volunteer as part of a community service course I was taking last semester. The course required a community service project, and I chose literacy volunteers simply as a means of fulfilling a course requirement.	1 Background
Thesis statement	<u>Now I realize that working as a literacy volunteer taught me more about learning and friendship than I ever expected.</u>	
Topic sentence	<u>When I first went through the training program to become a literacy volunteer, I learned about the process of learning--that is, the way in which people learn new words most effectively.</u> To illustrate this concept, the person who trained me wrote a brief list of simple words on the left side of a chalkboard and wrote phrases using the same words on the right side of the chalkboard. She instructed us to read the words and then asked which words we would be most likely to remember. We all said the words on the right because they made more sense. In other words, we could remember the words in the phrases more easily because they made more sense in context. The trainer showed us several more examples of words in context so we could get a grasp of how people learn new information by connecting it to what they already know.	2 Benefit 1: learned about learning process Example

Topic sentence

3   The training I received, though excellent, was no substitute for working with a real student, however. When I began to discover what other people's lives are like because they cannot read, I realized the true importance of reading. For example, when I had my first tutoring session with my client, Marie, a forty-four-year-old single mother of three, I found out she walked two miles to the nearest grocery store twice a week because she didn't know which bus to take. When I told her I would get her a bus schedule, she confided to me that it would not help because she could not read it and therefore wouldn't know which bus to take. She also said she had difficulty once she got to the grocery store because she couldn't always remember what she needed. Since she did not know words, she could not write out a grocery list. Also, she identified items by sight, so if the manufacturer changed a label, she could not recognize it as the product she wanted.

Benefit 2: importance of reading

— Example

Topic sentence

4   As we worked together, learning how to read built Marie's self-confidence, which gave her an incentive to continue in her studies. She began to make rapid progress and was even able to take the bus to the grocery store. After this successful trip, she reported how self-assured she felt. Eventually, she began helping her youngest son, Mark, a shy first grader, with his reading. She sat with him before he went to sleep, and together they would read bedtime stories. When his eyes became wide with excitement as she read, her pride swelled, and she began to see how her own hard work in learning to read paid off. As she described this experience, I swelled with pride as well. I found that helping Marie to build her self-confidence was more rewarding than anything I had ever done before.

Benefit 3: self-confidence

— Example

Topic sentence   <u>As time went by, Marie and I developed a</u>   5   Benefit 4: friendship
<u>friendship that became permanent.</u> Because we saw
each other several times a week, we spent a lot of
time getting to know each other, and we discovered
we had certain things in common. For instance, I'm
also a single parent. So we began to share our
similar experiences with each other. In fact, we   Example
have even baby-sat for each other's children. I
would drop my children off at her house while
I taught an evening adult class, and in return, I
watched her children while she worked on Saturday
mornings.

Conclusion   As a literacy volunteer, I learned a great   6
deal about learning, teaching, and helping others.
I also established what I hope will be a lifelong
friendship. In fact, I may have benefited more
from the experience than Marie did.

A Topic Sentence Supports Your Thesis

Each topic sentence must in some way explain the thesis or show why the thesis is believable or correct. This sample thesis, for example, could be supported by the topic sentences that follow it.

> **THESIS**   Adoption files should not be made available to adult children seeking their biological parents.

TOPIC SENTENCES

- Research has shown that not all biological parents want to meet with the sons or daughters they gave up many years before.
- If a woman gives up a child for adoption, it is probable that she does not ever intend to have a relationship with that child.
- Adult children who try to contact their biological parents often meet resistance and even hostility, which can cause them to feel hurt and rejected.
- A woman who gave up her biological child because she became pregnant as a result of rape or incest should not have to live in fear that her child will one day confront her.

All of these topic sentences support the thesis because they offer valid reasons for keeping adoption files closed.

EXERCISE 5.4

For each of the following thesis statements, identify the one topic sentence in the list that does *not* support the thesis.

1. To make a marriage work, a couple must build trust, communication, and understanding.
   a. Knowing why a spouse behaves as he or she does can improve a relationship.
   b. People get married for reasons other than love.
   c. The ability to talk about feelings, problems, likes, and dislikes should grow as a marriage develops.
   d. Marital partners must rely on each other to make sensible decisions that benefit both of them.
2. For numerous products, mail-order sales are capturing a larger market share.
   a. Mail-order firms that target a specific audience tend to be most successful.
   b. The increasing number of women in the workforce accounts, in part, for increased mail-order sales.
   c. Mail-order customers may order merchandise in a variety of ways—by phone, fax, mail, or computer.
   d. Products most commonly purchased through mail order are clothing and home furnishings.

A Topic Sentence States What the Paragraph Is About

A topic sentence should be focused and state exactly what the paragraph explains. Avoid vague or general statements. Often, a topic sentence also previews the organization of the paragraph. Compare these examples of unfocused and focused topic sentences.

UNFOCUSED	Some members of minority groups do not approve of affirmative action.
FOCUSED	Some members of minority groups disapprove of affirmative action because it implies that they are not capable of obtaining employment based on their own accomplishments.
UNFOCUSED	Many students believe that hate groups shouldn't be allowed on campus.
FOCUSED	The Neo-Nazis, a group that promotes hate crimes, should not be permitted to speak in our local community college because most students find its members' views objectionable.

If you have trouble focusing your topic sentences, review the guidelines for writing an effective thesis statement in Chapter 4 (pp. 92–94), many of which also apply to writing effective topic sentences.

EXERCISE 5.5

Revise each topic sentence to make it focused and specific. At least two of your revised topic sentences should also preview the organization of the paragraph.

1. In society today, there is always a new fad or fashion in clothing.
2. People watch television talk shows because they find them irresistible.
3. Body piercing is a popular trend.
4. Procrastinating can have a negative effect on your success in college.
5. In our state, the lottery is a big issue.

A Topic Sentence Can Appear in Any Position within a Paragraph

Where you place the topic sentence will determine the order and structure of the rest of the paragraph.

Topic sentence first.   The most common and often the best position for a topic sentence is at the beginning of the paragraph. A paragraph that opens with the topic sentence should follow a logical sequence: You state your main point, and then you explain it. The topic sentence tells readers what to expect in the rest of the paragraph, making it clear and easy for them to follow. This paragraph begins by telling readers that it is about the principle of visibility in advertising.

> Advertising is first and foremost based on the principle of visibility — the customer must notice the product. Manufacturers often package products in glitzy, even garish, containers to grab the consumer's attention. For example, one candy company always packages its candy in reflective wrappers. When the hurried and hungry consumer glances at the candy counter, the reflective wrappers are easy to spot. It is only natural for the impatient customer to grab the candy and go.

Topic sentence early in the paragraph.   When one or two sentences at the beginning of a paragraph are needed to smooth the transition from one paragraph to the next, the topic sentence may follow these transitional sentences. In the following example, the topic sentence comes after two transitional sentences. Note also that the paragraph explains the main point stated in the topic sentence.

> However, visibility is not the only principle in advertising; it is simply the first. A second and perhaps more subtle principle is identity. The manufacturer attempts to lure the consumer into buying a product by linking it to a concept with which the consumer can identify. For instance, Boundaries perfume is advertised on television as the choice of "independent" women. Since independent women are admired in our culture, women identify with the concept and therefore are attracted to the perfume. Once the consumer identifies with the product, a sale is more likely to occur.

Topic sentence last.   The topic sentence can also appear last in a paragraph. You first present the supporting details and then end the paragraph with the topic sentence, which usually states the conclusion that can be drawn from the details. Common in argumentative writing, this arrangement allows you to present convincing evidence before stating your point about the issue, as the following paragraph from a student essay on gun control shows.

The saying "Guns don't kill people; people kill people" always makes me even more certain of my own position on gun control. That statement is deceptive in the same way that the statement "Heroin doesn't kill people; people kill themselves" is deceptive. Naturally, people need to pull the trigger of a gun in order to make the gun kill other people, just as it is necessary for a person to ingest heroin in order for it to kill him or her. However, these facts do not excuse us from the responsibility of keeping guns (or heroin) out of people's hands as much as possible. People cannot shoot people unless they have a gun. <u>This fact alone should persuade the government to institute stiff gun control laws.</u>

Including Unified, Specific Supporting Details

In addition to including well-focused topic sentences, effective paragraphs are unified and well developed and provide concrete details that work together to support the main point.

Effective Paragraphs Have Unity

In a unified paragraph, all of the sentences in the paragraph directly support the topic sentence. The following sample paragraph lacks unity. As you read it, try to pick out the sentences that do not support the topic sentence.

PARAGRAPH LACKING UNITY

(1) <u>Much of the violence we see in the world today may be caused by the emphasis on violence in the media.</u> (2) More often than not, the front page of the local newspaper contains stories involving violence. (3) In fact, one recent issue of my local newspaper contained seven references to violent acts. (4) There is also violence in public school systems. (5) Television reporters frequently hasten to crime and accident scenes and film every grim, violent detail. (6) The other day, there was a drive-by shooting downtown. (7) If the media were a little more careful about the ways in which they glamorize violence, there might be less violence in the world today and children would be less influenced by it.

Although sentences 4 and 6 deal with the broad topic of violence, neither is directly related to the main point about the media promoting violence that is stated in the topic sentence. Both should be deleted.

EXERCISE 5.6

Working alone or in a group of two or three students, read each paragraph, and identify the sentences that do not support the topic sentence. In each paragraph, the topic sentence is underlined.

1. (a) <u>Today many options and services for the elderly are available that did not exist years ago.</u> (b) My grandmother is eighty-five years old now. (c) Adult care for the

elderly is now provided in many parts of the country. (d) Similar to day care, adult care provides places where the elderly can go for meals and social activities. (e) Retirement homes for the elderly, where they can live fairly independently with minimal supervision, are another option. (f) My grandfather is also among the elderly at eighty-two. (g) Even many nursing homes have changed so that residents are afforded some level of privacy and independence while their needs are being met.

2. (a) <u>Just as history repeats itself, fashions have a tendency to do the same.</u> (b) In the late 1960s, for example, women wore long peasant dresses with beads; some thirty years later, the fashion magazines are featuring this same type of dress. (c) This peasant style has always seemed feminine and flattering. (d) I wonder if the fashion industry deliberately recycles fashions. (e) Men wore their hair long in the 1960s. (f) Today, some men are again letting their hair grow. (g) Goatees, considered "in" during the beatnik period of the 1950s, have once again made an appearance in the 1990s.

Effective Paragraphs Are Well Developed

A unified paragraph provides adequate and convincing evidence that supports the topic sentence. Evidence can include explanations, examples, or other kinds of information that help the reader understand and believe the assertion in the topic sentence. The following example shows an underdeveloped paragraph that is revised into a well-developed paragraph.

UNDERDEVELOPED PARAGRAPH

Email and instant messaging are important technological advances, but they have hidden limitations, even dangers. It is too easy to avoid talking to people face to face. Using email can be addictive, too. Plus, they encourage ordinary people to ignore others while typing on a keyboard.

DEVELOPED PARAGRAPH

Email and instant messaging are important technological advances, but they have hidden limitations, even dangers. While email and instant messaging allow fast and efficient communication and exchange of information, they provide a different quality of human interaction. It is too easy to avoid talking to people. It is easier to click on one's "Buddy List" and check to see if she wants to meet for dinner than it would be to look up her number and actually talk to her. Online you can post a "be right back" message, avoiding an intrusion into your life. In fact, using these services can become addictive. For example, some students on campus are obsessed with checking their email several times throughout the day. They spend their free time talking to email acquaintances across the country, while ignoring interesting people right in the same room. Because computer interaction is not face to face, email and instant messenger addicts are shortchanging themselves of real human contact. There is something to be said for responding not only to a person's words, but to their expressions, gestures, and tone of voice.

These two versions of the paragraph differ in the degree to which the ideas are developed. The first paragraph has skeletal ideas that support the topic sentence, but those ideas are not explained. For example, the first paragraph does not explain why email and instant messaging are important or provide any evidence of how or why email can be addictive. Notice that the second paragraph explains how email and instant messaging allow for fast and efficient communication and gives further information about the addictive qualities of email. The second paragraph also explains the qualities of face-to-face interaction that are absent from online communication.

To discover if your paragraphs are well developed, begin by considering your audience. Have you given them enough information to make your ideas understandable and believable? Try reading your essay aloud, or ask a friend to do so. Listen for places where you jump quickly from one idea to another without explaining the first. To find supporting evidence for a topic sentence, use a prewriting strategy from Chapter 3. Also, the same types of evidence that are shown in Table 4.1 (p. 96) to support a thesis can be used to develop a paragraph. You may need to do some research to find this evidence.

EXERCISE 5.7

Use Table 4.1 (p. 96) to suggest the type or types of evidence that might be used to develop a paragraph based on each of the following topic sentences.

1. Many people have fallen prey to fad diets, risking their health and jeopardizing their mental well-being.
2. One can distinguish experienced soccer players from rookies by obvious signs.
3. To begin a jogging routine, take a relaxed but deliberate approach.
4. The interlibrary loan system is a fast and convenient method for obtaining print materials from libraries affiliated with the campus library.
5. Southwest Florida's rapid population growth poses a serious threat to its freshwater supply.

EXERCISE 5.8

Revise the following paragraph by adding details to create a well-developed paragraph.

> Although it is convenient, online shopping is a different experience than shopping in an actual store. You don't get the same opportunity to see and feel objects. Also, you can miss out on other important information. There is much that you miss. If you enjoy shopping, turn off your computer and support your local merchants.

Effective Paragraphs Provide Specific Supporting Details

The evidence you provide to support your topic sentences should be *concrete* and *specific*. Specific details interest your readers and make your meaning clear and forceful. Look at the following two examples. The first paragraph contains vague, general statements, while the revised paragraph provides concrete details that make the distinction between psychologists and psychiatrists clear.

VAGUE

Many people are confused about the difference between a psychologist and a psychiatrist. Both have a license, but a psychiatrist has more education than a psychologist. Also, a psychiatrist can prescribe medication.

CONCRETE AND SPECIFIC

Many people are confused about the difference between psychiatrists and psychologists. Both are licensed by the state to practice psychotherapy. However, a psychiatrist has earned a degree from medical school and can also practice medicine. Additionally, a psychiatrist can prescribe psychotropic medications. A psychologist, on the other hand, usually has earned a Ph.D. but has not attended medical school and therefore cannot prescribe medication of any type.

To make your paragraphs concrete and specific, use the following guidelines.

1. **Focus on** *who, what, when, where, how,* **and** *why* **questions.** Ask yourself these questions about your supporting details, and use the answers to expand and revise your paragraph.

VAGUE	Some animals hibernate for part of the year. (*What* animals? *When* do they hibernate?)
SPECIFIC	Some bears hibernate for three to four months each winter.

2. **Name names.** Include the names of people, places, brands, and objects.

VAGUE	When my sixty-three-year-old aunt was refused a job, she became an angry victim of age discrimination.
SPECIFIC	When my sixty-three-year-old Aunt Angela was refused a job at Vicki's Nail Salon, she became an angry victim of age discrimination.

3. **Use action verbs.** Select strong verbs that will help your readers visualize the action.

VAGUE	When Silina came on stage, the audience became excited.
SPECIFIC	When Silina burst onto the stage, the audience screamed, cheered, and chanted "Silina, Silina!"

4. **Use descriptive language that appeals to the senses (smell, touch, taste, sound, sight).** Words that appeal to the senses enable your readers to feel as if they are observing or participating in the experience you are describing.

   For more about descriptive language, see Chapter 9, p. 242.

VAGUE	It's relaxing to walk on the beach.
SPECIFIC	I walked in the sand next to the ocean, breathing in the smell of the salt water and listening to the rhythmic sound of the waves.

5. **Use adjectives and adverbs.** Including carefully chosen adjectives and adverbs in your description of a person, a place, or an experience can make your writing more concrete.

VAGUE   Working in the garden can be enjoyable.

SPECIFIC   As I slowly weeded my perennial garden, I let my eyes wander over the pink meadow sweets and blue hydrangeas, all the while listening to the chirping of a bright red cardinal.

EXERCISE 5.9

Working alone or in a group of two or three students, revise and expand each sentence in the following paragraph to make it specific and concrete. Feel free to add new information and new sentences.

> I saw a great concert the other night in Dallas. Two groups were performing. The music was great, and there was a large crowd. In fact, the crowd was so enthusiastic that the second group performed one hour longer than scheduled.

Connecting Your Supporting Details with Transitions and Repetition

All of the details in a paragraph must fit together and function as a connected unit of information. When a paragraph has **coherence**, its ideas flow smoothly, allowing readers to follow their progression with ease. Using one of the methods of organization discussed earlier in this chapter can help you show the connections among details and ideas. Transitions, used both within and between paragraphs, and repeated words are also useful devices for linking details. Look back at the student essay, "The Value of Volunteering," you read earlier (see p. 119). Notice that each paragraph is organized chronologically and that transitions such as *after, eventually,* and *for example* are used to link ideas.

Coherent Paragraphs Include Transitional Words and Phrases

Transitions are words or phrases that lead your reader from one idea to another. Think of transitional expressions as guideposts or signals of what is coming next in a paragraph. Some commonly used transitions are shown in the box on page 129, grouped according to the type of connections they show.

In the two examples that follow, notice that the first paragraph is disjointed and choppy because it lacks transitions, whereas the revised version with transitions is easier to follow.

WITHOUT TRANSITIONS

Most films are structured much like a short story. The film begins with an opening scene that captures the audience's attention. The writers build up tension, preparing for the climax of the story. They complicate the situation by revealing other elements of the plot, perhaps by introducing a surprise or additional characters. They introduce a problem. It will be solved either for the betterment or to the detriment of the characters and the situation. A resolution brings the film to a close.

COMMONLY USED TRANSITIONAL EXPRESSIONS

Type of Connection	*Transitions*
Logical Connections	
Items in a series	then, first, second, next, another, furthermore, finally, as well as
Illustration	for instance, for example, namely, that is
Result or cause	consequently, therefore, so, hence, thus, because, then, as a result
Restatement	in other words, that is, in simpler terms
Summary or conclusion	finally, in conclusion, to sum up, all in all, evidently, actually
Opposing viewpoint	but, however, on the contrary, nevertheless, neither, nor, on the one/other hand, still, yet
Spatial Connections	
Direction	inside/outside, along, above/below, up/down, across, to the right/left, in front of/behind
Nearness	next to, near, nearby, facing, adjacent to
Distance	beyond, in the distance, away, over there
Time Connections	
Frequency	often, frequently, now and then, gradually, week by week, occasionally, daily, rarely
Duration	during, briefly, hour by hour
Reference to a particular time	at two o'clock, on April 27, in 2000, last Thanksgiving, three days ago
Beginning	before then, at the beginning, at first
Middle	meanwhile, simultaneously, next, then, at that time
End	finally, at last, eventually, later, at the end, subsequently, afterward

WITH TRANSITIONS

Most films are structured much like a short story. The film begins with an opening scene that captures the audience's attention. <u>Gradually</u>, the writers build up tension, preparing for the climax of the story. <u>Soon after the first scene</u>, they complicate the situation by revealing other elements of the plot, perhaps by introducing a surprise or additional characters. <u>Next</u>, they introduce a problem. <u>Eventually</u>, the problem will be solved either for the betterment or to the detriment of the characters and the situation. <u>Finally</u>, a resolution brings the film to a close.

Coherent Essays Include Transitional Clauses and Sentences

Transitional clauses and sentences show connections between sentences and paragraphs. A transitional clause or sentence signals the reader about what is to follow or shows the reader how a new sentence or paragraph is connected to the one that precedes it. It may also remind the reader of an idea discussed earlier in the essay.

In the example that follows, the underlined transitional clause connects the two paragraphs by reminding the reader of the main point of the first.

> A compliment is a brief and pleasant way of opening lines of communication and demonstrating goodwill. _____
> _____ [remainder of paragraph] _____ .
>
> <u>Although compliments do demonstrate goodwill</u>, they should be used sparingly; otherwise they may seem contrived. _____
> _____ .

Especially in lengthy essays (five pages or longer), you may find it helpful to include one or more transitional clauses or sentences that recap what you have said so far and suggest the direction of the essay from that point forward. The following example is from a student's essay on the invasion of privacy.

> Thus, the invasion of privacy is not limited to financial and consumer information; invasion of medical and workplace privacy is increasingly common. What can individuals do to protect their privacy in each of these areas?

The first sentence summarizes the four types of invasion of privacy already discussed in the essay. The second sentence signals that the discussion will shift to the preventive measures that individuals can take.

Coherent Essays Use Repeated Words to Connect Ideas

Repeating key words or their **synonyms** (words that have similar meanings) or using pronouns that refer to key words in the essay also helps readers follow your ideas. Such repetition can reinforce a main point in your essay. In the following paragraph, notice how the underlined words help to keep the reader's attention on the issue — the legal drinking age.

> Many years ago the <u>drinking age</u> in New York State was eighteen; now <u>it</u> is twenty-one. Some young adults continue to argue that <u>it</u> should be eighteen again. Whether a

young adult is twenty or twenty-one does not make a big difference when he or she is consuming alcoholic beverages, young people say. However, statistics indicate that twenty-year-olds who drink alcohol are at a greater risk for having an automobile accident than twenty-one-year-olds. That difference is the reason the drinking age was changed.

WRITING YOUR INTRODUCTION, CONCLUSION, AND TITLE

It is not necessary to start writing an essay at the beginning and write straight through to the end. In fact, some students prefer to write the body of the essay first and then the introduction and conclusion. Others prefer to write a tentative introduction as a way of getting started. Some students think of a title before they start writing; others find it easier to add a title when the essay is nearly finished. Regardless of when you write them, the introduction, conclusion, and title are important components of a well-written essay.

Writing a Strong Introduction

Your introduction creates a first, and often lasting, impression. It focuses your readers on your narrowed topic and establishes the tone of your essay — how you "sound" about your topic and what attitude you take toward your readers. Based on your introduction, your readers will form an expectation of what the essay will be about and the approach it will take. Because the introduction is crucial, take the time to get it right.

For more on tone, see Chapter 7, p. 187.

Two sample introductions to student essays follow. Although they are written on the same topic, notice how each creates an entirely different impression and set of expectations.

INTRODUCTION 1

The issue of sexual harassment has received a great deal of attention in recent years. From the highest offices of government to factories in small towns, sexual harassment cases have been tried in court and publicized on national television for all Americans to witness. This focus on sexual harassment has been, in and of itself, a good and necessary thing. However, when a little boy in first grade makes national headlines for having kissed a little girl of the same age, and the incident is labeled "sexual harassment," the American public needs to take a serious look at the definition of sexual harassment.

INTRODUCTION 2

Sexual harassment in the workplace seems to be happening with alarming frequency. As a woman who works part time in a male-dominated office, I have witnessed at least six incidents of sexual harassment aimed at me and my female colleagues on various occasions during the past three months alone. For example, in one incident, a male co-worker repeatedly made kissing sounds whenever I passed his desk, even after I explained that his actions made me uncomfortable. A female co-worker was invited to dinner several times by her male supervisor; each time she refused. The last time she refused, he made a veiled threat, "You obviously aren't happy working with me. Perhaps a transfer is in order." These incidents were not isolated, did not happen to only one woman, and were initiated by more than one man. My colleagues and I are not the only victims. Sexual harassment is on the rise and will continue to increase unless women speak out against it loudly and to a receptive audience.

In introduction 1, the writer focuses on the definition of sexual harassment. Introduction 2 has an entirely different emphasis — the frequency of incidents of sexual harassment. Each introductory paragraph reveals a different tone as well. Introduction 1 suggests a sense of mild disbelief, whereas introduction 2 suggests anger and outrage. From introduction 1, you expect the writer to examine definitions of sexual harassment and, perhaps, suggest his or her own definition. From introduction 2, you expect the writer to present additional cases of sexual harassment and suggest ways women can speak out against it.

In addition to establishing a focus and tone, your introduction should accomplish three other objectives:

- Present your thesis statement,
- Interest your reader, and
- Provide any background information your reader may need.

Introductions are often difficult to write. If you have trouble, write a tentative introductory paragraph and return to it later. Once you have written the body of your essay, you may find it easier to complete the introduction. In fact, as you work out your ideas in the body of the essay, you may think of a better way to introduce them in the opening.

Tips for Writing a Strong Introduction

The following suggestions for writing a strong introduction will help you capture your readers' interest.

1. **Ask a provocative or disturbing question.** Pose a question that will interest or intrigue your readers. Or consider posing a series of short, related questions that will direct your readers' attention to the key points in your essay.

   Should health insurance companies pay for more than one stay in a drug rehabilitation center? Should health insurance companies continue to pay for rehab services when patients consciously and consistently put themselves back into danger by using drugs again?

2. **Begin with a story or anecdote.** Choose a story or anecdote that will appeal to your audience and is relevant to or illustrates your thesis.

> I used to believe that it was possible to stop smoking by simply quitting cold turkey. When I tried this approach, I soon realized that quitting was not so simple. When I did not smoke for even a short period of time, I became so uncomfortable that I started again just to alleviate the discomfort. I realized then that in order to quit smoking, I would need a practical solution that would overcome my cravings.

3. **Offer a quotation.** The quotation should illustrate or emphasize your thesis. Consult *Bartlett's Familiar Quotations* or locate it online.

> As Indira Gandhi once said, "You cannot shake hands with a clenched fist." This truism is important to remember whenever people communicate with one another but particularly when they are attempting to resolve a conflict. Both parties need to agree that there is a problem and then agree to listen to each other with an open mind. Shaking hands is a productive way to begin working toward a resolution.

4. **Cite a little-known or shocking fact or statistic.** An unfamiliar or unusual fact or statistic can interest your readers and focus their attention on the topic of your essay.

> Between 1963 and 1993, there was a 26 percent increase in the number of college students who admitted copying academic work from another student. This increase suggests that students' attitude toward cheating changed dramatically during that thirty-year period.

5. **Move from general to specific.** Begin with the category or general subject area to which your topic belongs and narrow it to arrive at your thesis.

> The First Amendment is the basis for several cherished rights in the United States, and free speech is among them. Therefore, it would seem unlawful—even anti-American—for a disc jockey to be fired for expressing his or her views on the radio, regardless of whether those views are unpopular or offensive.

6. **State a commonly held misconception or a position that you oppose.** Your thesis would then correct the misconception or state your position on the issue.

> Many people have the mistaken notion that only homosexuals and drug users are in danger of contracting AIDS. In fact, many heterosexuals also suffer from this debilitating disease. Furthermore, the number of heterosexuals who test HIV-positive has increased substantially over the past decade. It is time the American public became better informed about the prevention and treatment of AIDS.

7. **Describe a hypothetical situation.** A situation that illustrates your thesis provides a realistic opening to your essay.

Suppose you were in a serious car accident and became unconscious. Suppose further that you slipped into a coma, with little hope for recovery. Unless you had a prewritten health-care proxy that designated someone familiar with your wishes to act on your behalf, your fate would be left in the hands of medical doctors who knew nothing about you or your preferences for treatment.

8. **Begin with an intriguing statement.** A provocative statement may encourage your readers to continue reading.

   Recent research has shown that the color pink has a calming effect on people. In fact, a prison detention center in western New York was recently painted pink to make prisoners more controllable in the days following their arrest.

9. **Begin with a striking example.** A compelling example makes your topic immediate and relevant to your readers.

   The penal system is sometimes too concerned with protecting the rights of the criminal instead of the victim. For example, during a rape trial, the victim is often questioned about his or her sexual history by the defense attorney. However, the prosecuting attorney is forbidden by law to raise the question of whether the defendant has been charged with rape in a previous trial. In fact, if the prosecution even hints at the defendant's sexual history, the defense can request a mistrial.

10. **Make a comparison.** Compare your topic to one that is familiar or of special interest to your readers.

    The process a researcher uses to locate a specific piece of information in the library is similar to the process an investigator follows in tracking a criminal; both use a series of questions and follow clues to accomplish their task.

Mistakes to Avoid

The following advice will help you avoid the most common mistakes students make in writing introductions.

1. **Do not make an announcement.** Avoid opening comments such as "I am writing to explain . . ." or "This essay will discuss. . . ."
2. **Keep your introduction short.** Often one or two paragraphs is sufficient. In some cases, more than two paragraphs may be appropriate, but an introduction that goes beyond two paragraphs will probably sound long-winded and make your readers impatient.
3. **Avoid statements that may create negative attitudes.** Statements such as "This process may seem complicated, but . . ." may make your readers apprehensive.

4. **Avoid a casual, overly familiar, or chatty tone.** Opening comments such as "Man, did it surprise me when . . ." or "You'll never in a million years believe what happened . . ." are not appropriate.

5. **Be sure your topic is clear or explained adequately for your readers.** Do not begin an essay by stating, for example, "I oppose Proposition 413 and urge you to vote against it." Before stating your position on your topic, you need to explain to readers what that legislation is and what it proposes.

Writing an Effective Conclusion

Your essay should not end abruptly with your last supporting paragraph. Instead, it should end with a conclusion—a separate paragraph that reiterates (without directly restating) the importance of your thesis and that brings your essay to a satisfying close.

Tips for Writing a Solid Conclusion

For most essays, your conclusion should summarize your main points and reaffirm your thesis. For many essays, however, you might supplement this information and make your conclusion more memorable and forceful by using one of the following suggestions.

1. **Look ahead.** Take your readers beyond the scope and time frame of your essay.

   For now, then, the present system for policing the Internet appears to be working. In the future, though, it may be necessary to put a more formal, structured procedure in place.

2. **Remind readers of the relevance of the issue.** Suggest why your thesis is important.

   As stated earlier, research has shown that implementing the seat-belt law has saved thousands of lives. These lives would almost certainly have been lost had this law not been enacted.

3. **Offer a recommendation or make a call to action.** Urge your readers to take specific steps that follow logically from your thesis.

   To convince the local cable company to eliminate pornographic material, concerned citizens should organize, contact their local cable station, and threaten to cancel their subscriptions.

4. **Discuss broader implications.** Point to larger issues not fully addressed in the essay, but do not introduce a completely new issue.

When fair-minded people consider whether the FBI should be allowed to tap private phone lines, the issue inevitably leads them to the larger issue of First Amendment rights.

5. **Conclude with a fact, a quotation, an anecdote, or an example that emphasizes your thesis.** These endings will bring a sense of closure and realism to your essay.

The next time you are tempted to send a strongly worded message over email, consider this fact: Your friends and your enemies can forward those messages, with unforeseen consequences.

Mistakes to Avoid

The following advice will help you avoid common mistakes writers make in their conclusions.

1. **Avoid a direct restatement of your thesis.** An exact repetition of your thesis will make your essay seem dull and mechanical.

2. **Avoid standard phrases.** Don't use phrases such as "To sum up," "In conclusion," or "It can be seen, then." They are routine and tiresome.

3. **Avoid introducing new points in your conclusion.** Major points belong in the body of your essay.

4. **Avoid apologizing for yourself, your work, or your ideas.** Do not say, for example, "Although I am only twenty-one, it seems to me. . . ."

5. **Avoid softening or reversing your stance in the conclusion.** If, for instance, your essay criticizes someone's behavior, do not back down by saying "After all, she's only human. . . ." This will weaken the impact of your thesis or argument.

Writing a Good Title

The title of your essay should suggest your topic and spark your readers' interest. Depending on the purpose, intended audience, and tone of your essay, your title may be direct and informative, witty, or intriguing. The following suggestions will help you write effective titles.

1. **Write straightforward, descriptive titles for most academic essays.**

   Lotteries: A Game Players Can Little Afford

2. **Ask a question that your essay answers.**

   Who Plays the Lottery?

3. **Use alliteration.** Repeating initial sounds (called **alliteration**) often produces a catchy title.

   Lotteries: Dreaming about Dollars

4. **Consider using a play on words or a catchy or humorous expression.** This technique may work well for less formal essays.

   If You Win, You Lose

5. **Avoid broad, vague titles that sound like labels.** Titles such as "Baseball Fans" or "Gun Control" provide your reader with too little information.

EXERCISE 5.10

For each of the following essays, suggest a title. Try to use each of the above suggestions at least once.

1. An essay explaining the legal rights of tenants
2. An essay opposing human cloning
3. An essay on causes and effects of road rage
4. An essay comparing fitness routines
5. An essay explaining how to choose a primary care physician

ESSAY IN PROGRESS 3

Using the outline or graphic organizer you created in Essay in Progress 2, write a first draft of your essay. Be sure to write clear and effective topic sentences that support your thesis and unified paragraphs that support each topic sentence.

DRAFTING WITH A COMPUTER

The word-processing programs that are available on most computers are ideally suited to drafting essays. First of all, because a word processor takes care of many of the mechanics of drafting (setting margins, for example), you are free to concentrate on the most important part of drafting—developing and expressing your ideas clearly. Second, when you are drafting a paragraph within your essay, you often will think of ideas for a previous or later paragraph. On a computer, you can move back and forth within your draft, cutting and pasting these ideas in the appropriate places whenever they occur to you.

When drafting an essay on computer, use its flexibility to your advantage. Experiment with different ways to express an idea, different ways to organize the essay, different positions for a topic sentence, or different word choices. For example, on a computer you can rewrite a paragraph that you are uncertain about in two or three different ways by copying it and making changes in each copy. You can then make comparisons. When comparing several drafts, you may find it helpful to print each draft so that you can place them side by side and study each.

Be sure to save your work frequently as you draft, make back-up copies for security, and note file names so that you can find your essay again easily. When you work with multiple drafts, be sure to save each draft as a different file. This way, you can keep a record of your ideas.

STUDENTS WRITE

In her first draft the writer concentrated on expressing her ideas. Consequently, it contains errors that she later corrects. See Chapter 6, pp. 168–71, and Chapter 7, pp. 194–96, for later versions of this essay.

The first draft of a narrative essay by Christine Lee follows. Lee used her freewriting (see Chapter 3) and her working thesis (see Chapter 4) as the basis for her draft, adding details that she came up with by doing additional brainstorming (see Chapter 4). Because she was writing a first draft, Lee did not worry about correcting the errors in grammar, punctuation, and mechanics you will notice. (You will see her revised draft in Chapter 6 and an excerpt that shows Lee's final editing and proofreading in Chapter 7.)

FIRST DRAFT

The Reality of Real TV

1   Do you remember life before the reality TV craze? One look at a <u>TV Guide</u> today shows an overload of reality-based programming, even with the guaranteed failure of most of these shows. Before reality TV there was mostly situational comedies and serial dramas. When <u>Survivor</u> caught every viewer's attention, every network in American believed they must also become "real" to keep up its ratings. Shows that followed it were less interesting and less tasteful in the hopes of finding a show as original, inventive, and engaging as the first <u>Survivor</u>.

2   When <u>Survivor</u> began in the summer of 2000, there was nothing else like it on TV. <u>Survivor</u> had real people in a contest in an exotic location. It had different

kinds of players. There was a certain fascination in watching these players struggle week after week for food and shelter but the million dollar prize kept viewers tuning in week after week. Viewers wanted to find out who was going to win and who was getting "voted off the island." The last contestant on the island wins. Players developed a sense of teamwork and camaraderie, as they schemed and plotted. And we as an audience were allowed to watch every minute of it.

Big Brother started as the first of the reality TV   3
spinoffs but audiences didn't have the same things to respond to. It has never been a success because they took the basic concept of Survivor and added nothing new or interesting to it. Big Brother locked a bunch of people up together in a house and forced the audience to watch them bicker over nothing. Viewers were forced to watch bored contestants bicker and fight, locked up in a house with nothing else to do. It didn't seem the kind of competition that Survivor was, even though there was a cash prize on the line. We didn't choose favorites because the players weren't up against anything, except fighting off weeks of boredom. Big Brother introduced audience participation with the television audience voting off members, which actually only gave the house members less to do and less motive to scheme and plot their allegiances like the castaways on Survivor. But Big Brother had the prize component, and it took away the housemates' access to the outside world.

Although nothing seems to capture ratings like   4
the original Survivor, networks have continued to use sensational gimmicks to appeal to the audience's basic instincts. Nothing good was carried over from Survivor, and the new shows just had extreme situations. There were shows that revolved around flirtation and sex. In shows like Chains of Love, Temptation Island, and Love Cruise, audiences watched as contestants backstabbed, cheated, lied, and connived in the name of

"love." Audiences watched because of sexual intrigue, but these sexually charged shows pushed the limits of taste.

5   Another type of reality show like Fear Factor and Murder in Small Town X gets more graphic and unwatchable, trying to push the limit of reality TV to the edge. Like watching a car wreck, viewers hold some interest in watching how far other people will go, but most were repulsed. Most people don't watch Fear Factor because watching people eat worms or getting immersed in rats is boring. Murder in Small Town X combined a murder mystery with a group of "detective" strangers living together in a small town, it forced contestants to work together in the beginning. Just as survival on a Pacific Island in itself was a new and interesting concept to viewers, the mystery aspect of Murder in Small Town X was supposed to hold viewers' attention. The controversy of the show was that it opens with a reenactment from the murderer's point of view and ends with the audience watching one of two players getting "attacked" and "killed." Viewers turned off in disgust.

6   The biggest problem with the shows that followed Survivor is that viewers are so overloaded with reality TV now that it has become as mainstream as sitcoms and dramas were but not as interesting. Survivor was popular because it was something different, but now there are dozens of these shows each season and few worth watching. They are less interesting and less tasteful, and people have stopped watching.

Analyzing the First Draft

1. Evaluate Lee's title and introduction.
2. Evaluate Lee's thesis statement.
3. Does Lee provide adequate details for her essay? If not, what additional information might she include?

4. How does Lee organize her ideas?

5. Evaluate her supporting paragraphs. Which paragraphs need more detail?

6. Evaluate the conclusion.

WORKING WITH TEXT

Black Men and Public Space
Brent Staples

Brent Staples is a journalist who has written numerous articles and editorials as well as a memoir, Parallel Time: Growing Up in Black and White *(1994). Staples holds a Ph.D. in psychology and is currently an editor at the* New York Times. *This essay, first published in* Harper's *magazine in 1986, is a good model of a well-structured essay. As you read the selection, highlight or underline the author's thesis and topic sentences.*

My first victim was a woman—white, well dressed, probably in her early twenties. I came upon her late one evening on a deserted street in Hyde Park, a relatively affluent neighborhood in an otherwise mean, impoverished section of Chicago. As I swung onto the avenue behind her, there seemed to be a discreet, uninflammatory distance between us. Not so. She cast back a worried glance. To her, the youngish black man—a broad six feet two inches with a beard and billowing hair, both hands shoved into the pockets of a bulky military jacket—seemed menacingly close. After a few more quick glimpses, she picked up her pace and was soon running in earnest. Within seconds she disappeared into a cross street. 1

That was more than a decade ago. I was twenty-two years old, a graduate student newly arrived at the University of Chicago. It was in the echo of that terrified woman's footfalls that I first began to know the unwieldy inheritance I'd come into—the ability to alter public space in ugly ways. It was clear that she thought herself the quarry of a mugger, a rapist, or worse. Suffering a bout of insomnia, however, I was stalking sleep, not defenseless wayfarers. As a softy who is scarcely able to take a knife to a raw chicken—let alone hold one to a person's throat—I was surprised, embarrassed, and dismayed all at once. Her flight made me feel like an accomplice in tyranny. It also made it clear that I was indistinguishable from the muggers who 2 occasionally seeped into the area from the surrounding ghetto. That first encounter, and those that followed, signified that a vast, unnerving gulf lay between nighttime pedestrians—particularly women—and me. And I soon gathered that being perceived as dangerous is a hazard in itself. I only needed to turn a corner into a dicey situation, or crowd some frightened, armed person in a foyer somewhere, or make an errant move after being pulled over by a policeman. Where fear and weapons meet—and they often do in urban America—there is always the possibility of death.

3   In that first year, my first away from my hometown, I was to become thoroughly familiar with the language of fear. At dark, shadowy intersections, I could cross in front of a car stopped at a traffic light and elicit the *thunk, thunk, thunk, thunk* of the driver—black, white, male, or female—hammering down the door locks. On less traveled streets after dark, I grew accustomed to but never comfortable with people crossing to the other side of the street rather than pass me. Then there were the standard unpleasantries with policemen, doormen, bouncers, cabdrivers, and others whose business it is to screen out troublesome individuals *before* there is any nastiness.

4   I moved to New York nearly two years ago and I have remained an avid night walker. In central Manhattan, the near-constant crowd cover minimizes tense one-on-one street encounters. Elsewhere—in SoHo, for example, where sidewalks are narrow and tightly spaced buildings shut out the sky—things can get very taut indeed.

5   After dark, on the warrenlike streets of Brooklyn where I live, I often see women who fear the worst from me. They seem to have set their faces on neutral, and with their purse straps strung across their chests bandolier-style, they forge ahead as though bracing themselves against being tackled. I understand, of course, that the danger they perceive is not a hallucination. Women are particularly vulnerable to street violence, and young black males are drastically overrepresented among the perpetrators of that violence. Yet these truths are no solace against the kind of alienation that comes of being ever the suspect, a fearsome entity with whom pedestrians avoid making eye contact.

6   It is not altogether clear to me how I reached the ripe old age of twenty-two without being conscious of the lethality nighttime pedestrians attributed to me. Perhaps it was because in Chester, Pennsylvania, the small, angry industrial town where I came of age in the 1960s, I was scarcely noticeable against a backdrop of gang warfare, street knifings, and murders. I grew up one of the good boys, had

perhaps a half-dozen fistfights. In retrospect, my shyness of combat has clear sources.

As a boy, I saw countless tough guys locked away; I have since buried several, too. They were babies, really — a teenage cousin, a brother of twenty-two, a childhood friend in his mid-twenties — all gone down in episodes of bravado played out in the streets. I came to doubt the virtues of intimidation early on. I chose, perhaps unconsciously, to remain a shadow — timid, but a survivor.   7

The fearsomeness mistakenly attributed to me in public places often has a perilous flavor. The most frightening of these confusions occurred in the late 1970s and early 1980s, when I worked as a journalist in Chicago. One day, rushing into the office of a magazine I was writing for with a deadline story in hand, I was mistaken for a burglar. The office manager called security and, with an ad hoc posse, pursued me through the labyrinthine halls, nearly to my editor's door. I had no way of proving who I was. I could only move briskly toward the company of someone who knew me.   8

Another time I was on assignment for a local paper and killing time before an interview. I entered a jewelry store on the city's affluent Near North Side. The proprietor excused herself and returned with an enormous red Doberman pinscher straining at the end of a leash. She stood, the dog extended toward me, silent to my questions, her eyes bulging nearly out of her head. I took a cursory look around, nodded, and bade her good night.   9

Relatively speaking, however, I never fared as badly as another black male journalist. He went to nearby Waukegan, Illinois, a couple of summers ago to work on a story about a murderer who was born there. Mistaking the reporter for the killer, police officers hauled him from his car at gunpoint and but for his press credentials would probably have tried to book him. Such episodes are not uncommon. Black men trade tales like this all the time.   10

Over the years, I learned to smother the rage I felt at so often being taken for a criminal. Not to do so would surely have led to madness. I now take precautions to make myself less threatening. I move about with care, particularly late in the evening. I give a wide berth to nervous people on subway platforms during the wee hours, particularly when I have exchanged business clothes for jeans. If I happen to be entering a building behind some people who appear skittish, I may walk by, letting them clear the lobby before I return, so as not to seem to be following them. I have been calm and extremely congenial on those rare occasions when I've been pulled over by the police.   11

12   And on late-evening constitutionals I employ what has proved to be an excellent tension-reducing measure: I whistle melodies from Beethoven and Vivaldi and the more popular classical composers. Even steely New Yorkers hunching toward nighttime destinations seem to relax, and occasionally they even join in the tune. Virtually everybody seems to sense that a mugger wouldn't be warbling bright sunny selections from Vivaldi's *Four Seasons*. It is my equivalent of the cowbell that hikers wear when they know they are in bear country.   ■

Examining the Reading

1. Explain what Staples means by "the ability to alter public space" (para. 2).
2. Staples considers himself a "survivor" (para. 7). To what does he attribute his survival?
3. What does Staples do to make himself seem less threatening to others?
4. Explain the meaning of each of the following words as it is used in the reading: *uninflammatory* (para. 1), *unwieldy* (2), *vulnerable* (5), *retrospect* (6), and *constitutionals* (12).

Analyzing the Reading

1. Evaluate Staples's opening paragraph. Does it spark your interest? Why or why not?
2. Identify Staples's thesis statement. How does the author support his thesis? What types of information does he include?
3. Cite several examples of places in the essay where Staples uses specific supporting details and transitions effectively. Explain your choices.
4. Evaluate Staples's conclusion. Does it leave you satisfied? Why or why not?
5. What is Staples's method of organization in this essay? What other method of organization could he have used?
6. Many of the paragraphs in this essay begin with clearly stated topic sentences. Identify at least one topic sentence. What kind of support does Staples offer for this topic sentence?

Reacting to the Reading: Discussion and Journal Writing

1. Why is Staples's whistling of classical music similar to hikers wearing cowbells in bear country?

2. In what other ways can an individual "alter public space"?

3. Do you think Staples should alter his behavior in public to accommodate the reactions of others? Write a journal entry explaining whether you agree or disagree with Staples's actions.

Revising Content and Organization

Looking at the photo from left to right, list everything that is going on in the picture.

Examine your list, looking for ways to make it more understandable to someone who has not seen the photo. Write a few sentences summarizing what you think is going on in the photo, and then add details to your original list to describe the photo more fully. After you make these changes, will it be easier for a reader who has not seen the photo to understand what is happening in it? Exchange papers with a classmate, examining how your classmate organized ideas. Look for parts that you find confusing and that need more detail. Write down your comments for your classmate. Finally, using your own comments and those of your classmate, make changes to improve your own description.

When you changed your list, did you include more details from the photo while leaving unimportant details out? The changes you made improved the content of your writing. In other words, you have *revised* the description of the photo.

Revising an essay works in much the same way. **Revision** is a process of making changes to improve both what your essay says and how it is said. This chapter offers several approaches to revising an essay. It lists some general suggestions, describes how to use a graphic organizer for revision, offers specific questions to guide your revision, and discusses the implications of learning style for the revision process. You will notice in Figure 6.1 that revision is an essential part of the writing process.

WHY REVISE?

A thorough, thoughtful revision can change a C paper to an A paper! Revising can make a significant difference in how well your paper achieves your purpose and how effectively it expresses your ideas to your intended audience. Although revision takes time and hard work, it pays off and produces results.

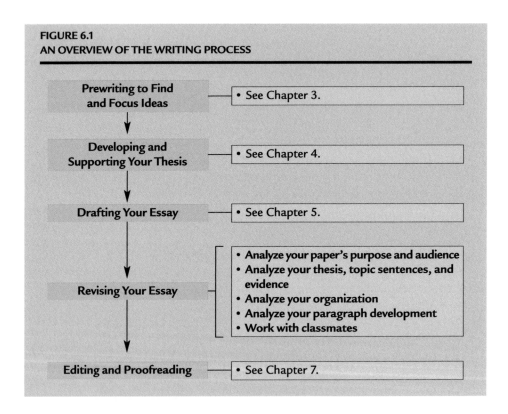

FIGURE 6.1
AN OVERVIEW OF THE WRITING PROCESS

- **Prewriting to Find and Focus Ideas** — • See Chapter 3.
- **Developing and Supporting Your Thesis** — • See Chapter 4.
- **Drafting Your Essay** — • See Chapter 5.
- **Revising Your Essay** —
  - • Analyze your paper's purpose and audience
  - • Analyze your thesis, topic sentences, and evidence
  - • Analyze your organization
  - • Analyze your paragraph development
  - • Work with classmates
- **Editing and Proofreading** — • See Chapter 7.

Most professional writers revise frequently and thoroughly, as do successful student writers. Revision is a process of looking again at your *ideas* to make them clearer and easier to understand. It is not merely a process of correcting surface errors. It may mean adding, eliminating, or reorganizing key elements within the essay. It may even mean revising your thesis statement and refocusing the entire essay.

The amount of revision you will need to do will depend, in part, on how you approach the task of writing. Some writers spend more time planning; others spend more time in revision. For example, students who tend to be pragmatic learners take a highly structured approach to writing. They plan in detail what they will say before they draft. More creative learners, however, may dash off a draft as ideas come to mind. A well-planned draft usually requires less revision than one that was spontaneously written. However, regardless of how carefully planned an essay may be, any first draft will require at least some revision.

Learning Style Options

USEFUL TECHNIQUES FOR REVISION

The following techniques will help you to get the most benefit from the time you spend revising your essays.

- **Allow time between drafting and revision.** Once you have finished writing, set your draft aside for a while, overnight if possible. When you return to your draft, you will be able to approach it from a fresh perspective.

- **Read your draft aloud.** Hearing what you have written will help you discover main points that are unclear or that lack adequate support. You will notice paragraphs that sound confusing, awkward wording, and vague or overused expressions.

- **Ask a friend to read your draft aloud to you.** When your reader hesitates, slows down, misreads, or sounds confused, it could be a signal that your message is not as clear as it should be. Keep a copy of your draft in front of you as you listen, and mark places where your reader falters or seems baffled.

- **Seek the opinions of classmates.** Ask a classmate to read and comment on your paper. This process, called **peer review**, is discussed in more detail later in this chapter (see p. 155).

- **Look for consistent problem areas.** Over the course of writing and revising several essays, many students discover consistent problem areas, such as organization or a lack of concrete details to support main points.

- **Mark your typed or printed copy.** Even if you prefer to handwrite your draft, be sure to type and print it before you revise. Because computer-generated, typed copy will seem less personal, you will be able to analyze and evaluate it more impartially. You will also be able to see a full page at a time on a printed copy, instead of only a paragraph at a time on a computer screen. Finally, on a printed copy you can write marginal annotations, circle troublesome words or sentences, and draw arrows to connect details.

- **Prepare readable copy.** If you cannot type or keyboard your paper, write on one side of the page in case you want to cut your paper into pieces and rearrange them. Leave wide margins so you have plenty of room to jot down new points or supporting details as they occur to you.

Using a Graphic Organizer for Revision

One of the best ways to reexamine your essay is to draw a graphic organizer—a visual display of your thesis statement and supporting paragraphs. A graphic organizer allows you to see how your thesis and topic sentences relate and connect to one another. It will also help you evaluate both the content and organization of your essay.

For instructions on creating a graphic organizer, see Chapter 2, page 34. If you are working on an assignment in Chapters 8 to 15 or Chapter 17, each of those chapters includes a model graphic organizer for the type of writing covered in the chapter. As you are drawing your graphic organizer, if you spot a detail or an example that does not support a topic sentence, as well as any other problems, write notes to the right of your organizer, as shown in Figure 6.2.

Another option, instead of drawing a graphic organizer, is to write an outline of your draft. For more information on outlining, see Chapter 5, page 114.

ESSAY IN PROGRESS 1

Make a graphic organizer or an outline for the draft essay you wrote in Essay in Progress 3 in Chapter 5 (p. 137) if you have not already done so, or for any essay that you are working on.

KEY QUESTIONS FOR REVISION

The five key questions listed below will help you know what to look for when you revise. Use the questions to identify broad areas of weakness in your essay.

- Does your essay clearly convey a purpose, address an appropriate audience, and state a thesis?
- Do you have enough reasons and evidence to support your thesis?
- Do the ideas in your essay fit together?
- Is each paragraph well developed?
- Does it have a strong introduction and conclusion?

FIGURE 6.2
SAMPLE GRAPHIC ORGANIZER FOR REVISION

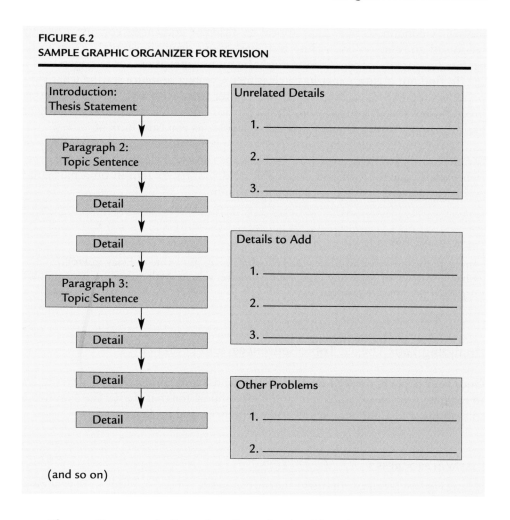

(and so on)

After reading your draft or after discussing it with a classmate, try to pinpoint areas that need improvement by answering each of these five questions. Then refer to the self-help flowcharts in the following sections. In addition to the revision suggestions and flowcharts in this chapter, the chapters in Part 3, Chapter 17 in Part 4, and Chapters 19 and 20 in Part 5 provide revision flowcharts that are tailored to the specific assignments in those chapters.

Analyzing Your Purpose and Audience

First drafts are often unfocused and may go off in several directions rather than have a clear purpose. For instance, one section of an essay on divorce may inform readers of its causes, and another section may argue that it harms children. A first

For more information about purpose and audience, see Chapter 3, pp. 65–69. For more on developing a thesis, see Chapter 4, p. 89.

draft may contain sections that appeal to different audiences. For instance, one section of an essay on counseling teenagers about drug abuse might seem to be written for parents; other sections might be more appropriate for teenagers.

To find out if your paper has a clear focus, write a sentence stating what your paper is supposed to accomplish. If you cannot write such a sentence, your essay probably lacks a clear purpose. To find a purpose, do some additional thinking or brainstorming, listing as many possible purposes as you can think of.

To find out if your essay is directed to a specific audience, write a sentence or two describing your intended readers. Describe their knowledge, beliefs, and experience with your topic. If you are unable to do so, try to zero in on a particular audience and revise your essay with them in mind.

ESSAY IN PROGRESS 2

Evaluate the purpose and audience of the draft essay you wrote in Essay in Progress 3 in Chapter 5 (p. 137) or of any essay that you have written. Make notes on your graphic organizer or annotate your outline.

Analyzing Your Thesis, Topic Sentences, and Evidence

Once your paper is focused on a specific purpose and audience, your next step is to evaluate your thesis statement and your support for that thesis. Use Figure 6.3 to examine your thesis statement, topic sentences, and evidence.

ESSAY IN PROGRESS 3

Using Figure 6.3, evaluate the thesis statement, topic sentences, and evidence of your essay in progress. Make notes on your graphic organizer or annotate your outline.

Analyzing Your Organization

Your readers will not be able to follow your ideas if your essay does not hold together as a unified piece of writing. To be sure that it does, examine your essay's organization. The graphic organizer or outline of your draft (see p. 150) that you completed will help you analyze the draft's organization and discover any flaws.

To determine if the organization of your draft is clear and effective, you can also ask a classmate to read your draft and explain to you how your essay is organized. If your classmate cannot describe its organization, it probably needs further work. Use one of the methods in Chapter 5 (pp. 110–13) or one of the patterns of development described in Parts 3 and 4 to reorganize your ideas.

FIGURE 6.3
FLOWCHART FOR EVALUATING YOUR THESIS STATEMENT, TOPIC SENTENCES, AND EVIDENCE

Questions	Revision Strategies

1. Does your essay have a thesis statement that identifies your topic and states your position or suggests your slant on the topic? (To find out, state your thesis aloud without looking at your essay; then highlight the sentence in your draft essay that matches or is close to what you have just said. If you cannot find such a sentence, you have probably not written a well-focused thesis statement.)

No →

- Reread your essay and answer this question: What one main point is most of this essay concerned with?
- Write a thesis statement that expresses that main point.
- Revise your paper to focus on that main point.
- Delete parts of the essay that do not support your thesis statement.

Yes

2. Have you given your readers all the background information they need to understand your thesis? (To find out, ask someone unfamiliar with your topic to read your essay, asking questions as he or she reads.)

No →

- Answer *who, what, when, where, why,* and *how* questions to discover more background information.

Yes

3. Have you presented enough convincing evidence to support your thesis? (To find out, place checkmarks ✔ beside the evidence in your essay, and compare the evidence against the thesis. Ask yourself this question: Would I accept the thesis, or does it need more evidence to be convincing?)

No →

- Use prewriting strategies or do additional research to discover more supporting evidence.
- Evaluate this new evidence and add the most convincing evidence to your essay.

Yes

(Continued on next page)

FIGURE 6.3 *(Continued)*

Questions	Revision Strategies
4. Does each topic sentence logically connect to and support the thesis? (To find out, underline each topic sentence. Read the thesis, and then read each topic sentence. When the connection between them is not obvious, revision is needed.)	• Rewrite the topic sentence so that it clearly supports the thesis. • If necessary, broaden your thesis so that it encompasses all your supporting points.

No

Yes

Questions	Revision Strategies
5. Is your evidence specific and detailed? (To find out, go through your draft, and reread where you placed checkmarks ✓. Does each checkmarked item answer one of these questions: *Who? What? When? Where? Why? How?* If you have not placed a checkmark in a particular paragraph or have placed a checkmark by only one sentence or part of a sentence, you need to add more detailed evidence to that paragraph.)	• Name names, give dates, specify places. • Use action verbs and descriptive language, including carefully chosen adjectives and adverbs. • Answer *who, what, when, where, why,* and *how* questions to discover more detailed evidence.

No

Yes

Analyzing Your Introduction, Conclusion, and Title

Once you are satisfied with the draft's organization, evaluate your introduction, conclusion, and title. Use the following questions as guidelines.

1. **Does your introduction interest your reader and provide needed background information?** If your essay jumps into the topic without preparing readers for it, your introduction needs to be revised. Use the suggestions on pages 132 to 135 to create interest. Ask the *W* questions—*who, what, when,*

where, why, and *how*—to determine the background information that you need.

2. **Does your conclusion draw your essay to a satisfactory close and reinforce your thesis statement?** Does the conclusion follow logically from the introduction? If not, use the suggestions for writing conclusions in Chapter 5 (pp. 135–36). Also try imagining yourself explaining the significance or importance of your essay to a friend. Use this explanation to rewrite your conclusion.

3. **Does your title accurately reflect the content of your essay?** To improve your title, write a few words that "label" your essay. Also, reread your thesis statement, looking for a few key words that can serve as part of your title. Finally, use the suggestions in Chapter 5 (pp. 136–37) to help you choose a title.

ESSAY IN PROGRESS 4

Evaluate the organization of your essay in progress. Make notes on your draft copy.

Analyzing Your Paragraph Development

Each paragraph in your essay must fully develop a single idea that supports your thesis. (Narrative essays are an exception to this rule. As you will see in Chapter 8, in a narrative essay, each paragraph focuses on a separate part of the action.)

See Chapter 5 for more on paragraph development.

In a typical first draft, paragraphs are often weak or loosely structured. They may contain irrelevant information or lack a clearly focused topic sentence. To evaluate your paragraph development, study each paragraph separately in conjunction with your thesis statement. You may need to delete some paragraphs, rework or reorganize other paragraphs, or move selected paragraphs to a more appropriate part of the essay. If you need to supply additional information to support your thesis, you may need to add paragraphs to the draft. Use Figure 6.4 to help you analyze and revise your paragraphs.

ESSAY IN PROGRESS 5

Using Figure 6.4, examine each paragraph of your essay in progress. Make notes on the draft copy of your essay.

WORKING WITH CLASSMATES TO REVISE YOUR ESSAY

Increasingly, instructors in writing and other academic disciplines use **peer review,** a process in which two or more students read and comment on each other's papers. Students might work together in class or outside of class or

FIGURE 6.4
FLOWCHART FOR EVALUATING YOUR PARAGRAPHS

Questions	Revision Strategies
1. Does each paragraph have a clearly focused topic sentence that expresses the main point of the paragraph? (To find out, underline the topic sentence in each paragraph of your draft. Then evaluate whether the topic sentence makes a statement that the rest of the paragraph supports.) **No →**	• Revise a sentence that is currently within the paragraph so that it clearly states the main point. • Write a new sentence that states the one main point of the paragraph.

Yes ↓

2. Do all sentences in each paragraph support the topic sentence? (To find out, read the topic sentence, and then read each supporting sentence in turn. The topic sentence and each supporting sentence should fit together.) **No →**	• Revise supporting sentences to make their connection to the topic sentence clear. • Delete any sentences that do not support the topic sentence.

Yes ↓

3. Does the paragraph offer adequate explanation and supporting details? (To find out, place checkmarks ✔ beside supporting details. Ask yourself this question: Is there other information readers will want or need to know?) **No →**	• Add more details if your paragraph seems skimpy. • Use the *who, what, when, where, why,* and *how* questions to generate the details you need. • Use the prewriting strategies in Chapter 3 to generate additional details.

Yes ↓

(Continued on next page)

FIGURE 6.4 *(Continued)*

Questions	Revision Strategies

4. Have you used transitional words and phrases to connect your sentences? (To find out, place brackets [ ] around transitional words and phrases. Be sure they separate main ideas. Read your paper aloud to see if it flows smoothly or sounds choppy.)

No

- Add transitional words and phrases where they are needed.
- Refer to the list of common transitions on page 129.

Yes

5. Will it be clear to your reader how each paragraph connects to those that precede and follow it? (To find out, draw brackets [ ] around transitional sentences.)

No

- Add transitional sentences where they are needed.

Yes

communicate via email or a classroom computer network. Working with classmates is an excellent way to get ideas for improving your essays. You'll also have the opportunity to discover how other students view and approach the writing process. The following suggestions will help both the writer and the reviewer get the most out of peer review.

How to Find a Good Reviewer

Selecting a good reviewer is key to getting good suggestions for revision. Your instructor may pair you with another class member or let you find your own reviewer, either a classmate or someone outside of class. Class members make good reviewers since they are familiar with the assignment and with what you have learned so far in the course. If you need to find someone outside your class, try to choose a person who has already taken the writing course you are taking, preferably someone who has done well. Best friends are not necessarily the best reviewers; they may be reluctant to offer criticism, or they may be too critical. Instead, choose someone who is serious, skillful, and willing to spend the time needed to provide useful comments. If your college has a writing center, you might ask a tutor in the center to read and comment on your draft. Consider using more than one reviewer so you can get several perspectives.

Suggestions for the Writer

To get the greatest benefit from having another student review your paper, use the following suggestions.

1. Be sure to provide readable copy; a typed, double-spaced draft is preferred.
2. If your essay is not very far along, think it through a little more, and make additions and revisions. The more developed your draft is, the more helpful the reviewer's comments will be.
3. Offer specific questions or guidelines so that the reviewer will know what to do. A sample set of Questions for Reviewers is provided below. Give your reviewer a copy of these questions, adding others that you need answered. You

---

QUESTIONS FOR REVIEWERS

1. What is the purpose of the paper?
2. Who is the intended audience?
3. Is the introduction fully developed?
4. What is the main point or thesis? Is it easy to identify?
5. Does the essay offer evidence to support each important point? Where is more evidence needed (indicate specific paragraphs)?
6. Is each paragraph clear and well organized?
7. Are transitions used to connect ideas within and between paragraphs?
8. Is the organization easy to follow? Where might it be improved, and how?
9. Does the conclusion draw the essay to a satisfying close?
10. What do you like about the draft?
11. What are its weaknesses and how could they be eliminated? Underline or highlight sentences that are unclear or confusing.

might also give your reviewer questions from one of the revision flowcharts in this chapter. If you have written an essay in response to an assignment in a later chapter, consider giving your reviewer the revision flowchart for that assignment.

4. Be open to criticism and new ideas. As much as possible, try not to be defensive; instead, look at your essay objectively, seeing it as your reviewer sees it.

5. Don't feel obligated to accept all of the advice you are given. A reviewer might suggest a change that will not work well in your paper or wrongly identify an error. If you are uncertain about a suggestion, discuss it with your instructor.

Suggestions for the Reviewer

Be honest but tactful. Criticism is never easy to accept, so keep your reader's feelings in mind. The following tips will help you provide useful comments.

1. Read the draft through completely before making any judgments or comments. You will need to read it at least twice to evaluate it.

2. Concentrate on content; pay attention to what the paper says. Evaluate the writer's train of thought; focus on the main points and how clearly they are expressed. If you notice a misspelling or a grammatical error, you can circle it, but correcting errors is not your primary task.

3. Offer some positive comments. It will help the writer to know what is good as well as what needs improvement.

4. Be specific. For instance, instead of saying that more examples are needed, tell the writer which ideas in which paragraphs are unclear without examples.

5. Use the Questions for Reviewers on page 158 to guide your review as well as any additional questions that the writer provides. If the essay was written in response to an assignment in one of the chapters in Parts 3, 4, or 5, you might use the revision flowchart in that chapter. Keep these questions in mind as you read, and try to answer each one in your response. You might make a copy of the questions and jot your responses next to each question.

6. Write notes and comments directly on the draft. Then, at the end, write a final note summarizing your overall reaction, pointing out both strengths and weaknesses. Here is a sample final note written by a reviewer.

Overall, I think your paper has great ideas, and I found that it held my interest. The example about the judge did prove your point. I think you should organize it better. The last three paragraphs do not seem connected to the rest of the essay. Maybe better transitions would help, too. Also work on the conclusion. It just says the same thing as your thesis statement.

7. If you are reviewing a draft on a computer, type your comments in brackets following the appropriate passage, or highlight them in some other way. The writer can easily delete your comments after reading them. Some word-processing programs have features for adding comments.

8. Do not rewrite paragraphs or sections of the paper. Instead, suggest how the writer might revise them.

ESSAY IN PROGRESS 6

Give your essay in progress to a classmate to read and review. Ask your reviewer to respond to the Questions for Reviewers. Revise your essay using your revision outline, your responses to Figures 6.3 and 6.4, and your reviewer's suggestions.

USING YOUR INSTRUCTOR'S COMMENTS

Another resource to use in revising your essays is the commentary your instructor provides. These comments can be used to submit a revised version of a particular essay or to improve your writing throughout the course.

Revising an Essay Using Your Instructor's Comments

Your instructor may want to review a draft of your essay and suggest revisions you can make for the final version. Some instructors allow students to revise and resubmit a paper and then give the students an average of the two grades. Either way, your instructor's comments can provide a roadmap for you to begin your revision. Review the comments on your essays carefully, looking for problems that recur, so that you can focus on these elements in your future writing.

Different instructors may use different terminology when they mark up writing assignments, but most like to point out several common problems. The marks on your essay will often address spelling and grammar errors, organization problems, and problems with the clarity or development of ideas.

Figure 6.5 shows a first draft of an essay by a student, David Harris, that has been read and marked by his instructor. The assignment was to write an essay defining a specialized term, and the student chose the salary cap in professional football as his subject. Note that the instructor has commented on a range of elements in the essay, including grammar, structure and organization, effectiveness of the introduction, paragraph unity and development, and transitions. Some spelling and punctuation errors have not been marked. Harris read the comments carefully and used them to revise his essay. His final draft appears in Chapter 14 (pp. 488–92).

FIGURE 6.5
USING YOUR INSTRUCTOR'S COMMENTS TO REVISE YOUR ESSAY

NFL Salary Cap

In the 1990s sports salaries increased at   1
record-breaking rates. The onset of free agency
caused owners to search for ways to limit the
ballooning salaries. [In previous years players   *Run-on*
were owned by a team, when a players' contract
ran out, the players needed permission to negotiate with other teams.] Beginning in the 70's   *Run-on*
and 80's, after a contract expired players were
free to negotiate with any team, this freedom
caused bidding wars that eventually raised
salaries dramatically.] A salary cap in sports
is a limit on the amount of money a team can   *Central definition is*
spend on player salaries, either as a per-player   *buried here*
limit or a total limit for the team's roster.
(http://www.wordiq.com/definition/Salary_cap)
The NFL (National Football League) instituted a
salary cap in 1994. Since that time no team has
won more than two super bowls and only the 1998   *Too specific for intro*
and 1999 broncos won consecutive Super Bowls;
the most appearances by one team is three
(http://www.superbowl.com/history/recaps). Baseball however, a sport without a salary cap, the
New York Yankees have won 4 times and made 6
total appearances (http://www.mlb.com). The
salary cap has given every team regardless of   *Nice, strong thesis!*
revenue a chance to compete for the championship
of their respective sport.   *Need more info at*
                                                       beginning on how caps
The NFL salary cap is a total team limit   2 *were started*
salary cap; in 2004 the NFL salary cap was $80.6
million (http://sports.espn.go.com/nfl/columns
/story?columnist=pasquarelli_len&id=1738866). All
NFL teams must bring their total salaries paid
down to this $80.6 million mark. A player's   *Subject-pronoun*
salary is not always the same as their value   *agreement*

List events in order

*Why baseball? Title
says "NFL . . ."*

*Intro lacks focus and
unity. What is your
main point?*

*Subject-pronoun
agreement*

Connection is unclear

according to the salary cap. Signing bonuses are distributed over the length of the contract unevenly, if the teams choose to do so. Many teams run into huge salary cap problems because of back-loaded contracts. A Super Bowl team one year could have to cut many of its star players to remain under the salary cap. In 2003 the Tampa Bay Buccaneers won the Super Bowl, but failed to make the playoffs the following year. Continued success in the NFL is a product of good management and good scouting. A rookie contract, typically, is much smaller than that of a proven player. Replacing high-priced veterans with low-cost rookies is an excellent way to manage a cap, and translates into more money for other positions.

A team in the Bowl? Or the winner?

Tie this fact in specifically, or omit it

Clarify connection for reader

Clarify connection for reader

3   The NFL salary cap is absolute, but it does change from year to year. In 2003 the NFL salary cap was $75 million, it increased by 6.6% to $80.6 million dollars in 2004 (http://sports.espn.go.com). The salary cap is not randomly set. It is a calculation of a percentage of combined revenue of each team divided by the 32 teams in the NFL. This salary cap is in effect for the whole season. If a team exceeds the salary cap at any point in the season the NFL has the right to cut any player starting from the lowest salary until the team is below the set cap. Cutting a player from a team eliminates him from team's payroll and any team can acquire him at his current contracted rate. This is the fate of many players as they reach the twilight years of their careers.

Run-on

Commas

Examples?

How is this related to subject of paragraph?

4   Sports without salary caps have had trouble keeping the level of competition equal. In Major League baseball the largest markets dominate and teams in smaller cities can not compete. The New York Yankees' salary has been the highest in the

Need transition

league since 1996, and since then they have won 4 World Series and finished first in their division every year. There is no team even close to this kind of dominance in the NFL. The salary cap keeps smaller city teams, with less revenue like The Buffalo Bills in contention.

Rest of paragraph doesn't follow from first sentence

[There are many reasons that not all sports have salary caps.] The NFL salary cap was first negotiated by the players' union and the owners union in 1994. In the same year baseball owners tried to impose a salary cap. The players' union strongly opposed this action; the union went on strike, canceling the entire postseason for the first time since World War II. It is still a highly contested topic in baseball. The NFL has benefited greatly from its addition of the salary cap. They have created their own network, The NFL Network, and fan interest is at record levels.

5

This info would be helpful at beginning

The salary cap has had a tremendous impact on the game of football, the fans of football and the owners of football teams. The limit on players' salaries keeps all teams in contention, and for that, the fans are grateful.

6

Need stronger, more developed conclusion

EXERCISE 6.1

Working either alone or in small groups, compare the first draft of David Harris's essay in Figure 6.5 with the final version on pages 488–92. Make a list of the changes Harris made to his essay in response to his instructor's comments. Also, put a checkmark next to any problems that recur throughout the first draft of the essay.

EXERCISE 6.2

If your instructor has returned a marked-up first draft to you, read the comments carefully. Then draw a line down the middle of a blank piece of paper. On the left, write the instructor's comments; on the right, jot down ways you might revise the essay in response to each. Put a checkmark next to any problems that recur throughout your essay; these are areas you will want to pay particular attention to in your future writing.

Using Your Instructor's Comments to Improve Future Essays

When you receive a graded essay back from an instructor, it is tempting to note the grade and then file away the essay. To improve your writing, however, take time to study each comment. Use the following suggestions.

- **Reread your essay more than once.** Read it once to note grammatical corrections, and then read it again to study comments about organization or content. Processing numerous comments on a wide range of topics takes more than one reading.

- **For grammar errors, make sure you understand the error.** Check a grammar handbook or ask a classmate; if the error is still unclear, check with your instructor.

- **Record grammar errors in your error log (see Chapter 7, p. 193).** When you proofread your next essay, be sure to look carefully for each of these errors.

- **If you did not get a high grade, try to determine why.** Was the essay weak in content, organization, or development?

- **Using Figures 6.3 and 6.4, highlight or mark weaknesses that your instructor identified.** When writing your next essay, refer back to these flowcharts. Pay special attention to these areas as you evaluate your next paper.

- **If any of your instructor's comments are unclear, first ask a classmate if he or she understands them.** If not, then ask your instructor, who will be pleased that you are taking time to study the comments.

CONSIDERING YOUR LEARNING STYLE

Learning Style Options

Depending on your learning style, you may tend to focus on some elements of an essay and overlook others. For example, a pragmatic learner tends to write tightly organized drafts, but the draft may lack interest, originality, or sufficient content. A creative learner may write drafts that lack organization. Writers with different learning styles may need to address different kinds of problems as they revise their drafts.

Following are some revision tips for other aspects of your learning style.

- *Independent* learners, who often need extra time for reflection, should be sure to allow sufficient time between drafting and revising. *Social* learners often find discussing revision plans with classmates particularly helpful.

- *Verbal* learners may prefer to use outlining to check the organization of their drafts, while *spatial* learners may find it more helpful to draw a graphic organizer.

- *Rational* learners should be sure their drafts do not seem dull or impersonal, adding personal examples and vivid descriptions where appropriate. *Emotional* learners, whose writing may tend to be overly personal, should state their ideas directly without hedging or showing undue concern for those who may disagree.

- *Concrete* learners, who tend to focus on specifics, should check that their thesis and topic sentences are clearly stated. *Abstract* learners, who tend to focus on general ideas, should be sure they have enough supporting details.

STUDENTS WRITE

After writing her first draft, which appears in Chapter 5 (pp. 138–40), Christine Lee used the guidelines and revision flowcharts in this chapter to help her decide what to revise. For example, she decided that she needed to add more details about what happened on the TV show *Survivor*. She also decided that she should emphasize the uninteresting details of the examples of some other reality TV shows.

Lee asked a classmate named Sam to review her essay. A portion of Sam's comments is shown below.

REVIEWER'S COMMENTS

The trend that you have chosen to write about is well-known and interesting. Beginning your introduction with a question piques the reader's interest, and your thesis is clear: Reality TV shows are becoming less interesting and tasteful. You mention why people enjoyed Survivor and why they didn't enjoy the other shows. You should also emphasize why television viewers watched Survivor. Once that point is clear, many of your ideas might fit better.

I think some specific details about the example reality TV shows you mention would help readers who are not familiar with the shows. It would also help prove your point: These shows are getting worse.

The title and conclusion could better help make this point too. The title doesn't indicate what the reality of reality TV is, and the conclusion could look ahead to what you think the fate of reality TV will be.

Using her own analysis and her classmate's suggestions, Lee created a graphic organizer to help her decide how to revise her draft, using the format for an illustration essay provided in Chapter 10 (p. 291). Lee's graphic organizer, which includes her notes for revision, is shown in Figure 6.6.

FIGURE 6.6
GRAPHIC ORGANIZER FOR CHRISTINE LEE'S FIRST DRAFT

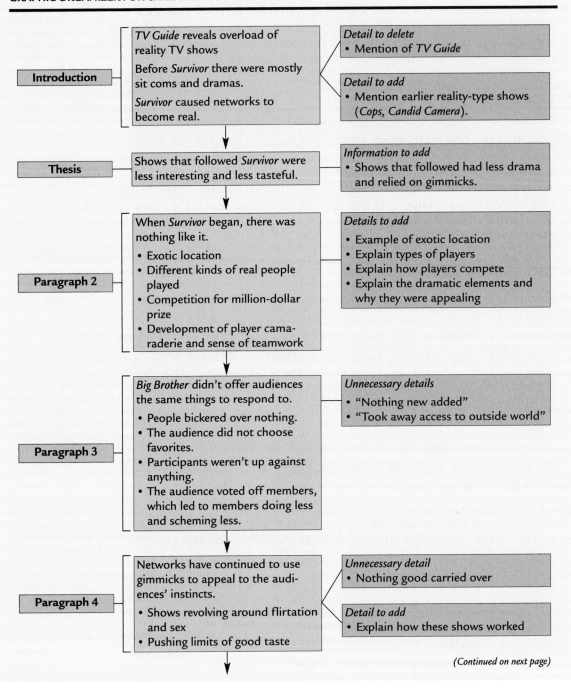

(Continued on next page)

FIGURE 6.6 (*Continued*)

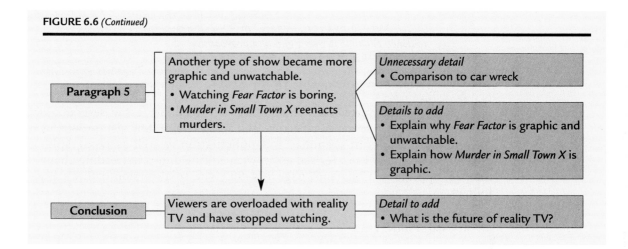

After creating the graphic organizer, Lee revised her first draft. A portion of her revised draft, with her revisions marked, follows.

REVISED DRAFT

A Trend Taken too Far:
The Reality of Real TV

Do you remember life before the reality TV craze?

~~One look at a TV Guide today shows an overload of~~

~~reality-based programming, even with the guaranteed~~

Before reality TV television viewers
~~failure of most of these shows. Before Survivor there~~
seemed mostly interested in the fictional lives of characters in
~~was only~~ situational comedies and serial dramas. Survivor
the attention of even more viewers and dominated television ratings. Television
caught every ~~viewers' attention. Every network in Ameri-~~

~~can believed they must also become "real" to keep up its~~

Survivor was engaging and dramatic, but the shows
~~ratings. Shows~~ that followed it were less interesting and
, lacking drama and relying on gimmicks.
less tasteful ~~in the hopes of finding a show as origi-~~

~~nal, inventive and engaging as the first Survivor.~~

Characters were played by professional actors and the shows were written by professional writers. Except for a few early reality-type shows such as "Cops" and "Candid Camera," this simple formula was what network television offered. Then came MTV's "The Real World" in 1992. The high ratings that this cable show garnered made network executives take notice of the genre. Eventually "Survivor" debuted in the summer of 2000.

networks changed their programming. It seemed that every network acted as though it had to become "real" to compete with *Survivor* and maintain viewer interest. The problem with networks trying to copy *Survivor* is that the original *Survivor* offered more interesting elements to its audience than any reality TV show modeled after it.

> *Survivor captured the interest of a wide viewing*
> ~~When~~ ~~Survivor began in the summer of 2000, there~~
> *audience because it was fresh and provocative.*
> ~~was nothing else like it on TV.~~ Survivor had real
> *participants. There was   where contestants competed against each other*
> ~~people in~~ a contest in an exotic location.

Before Lee submitted her final draft, she read her essay several more times, editing it for sentence structure and word choice. She also proofread it once to catch errors in grammar and punctuation as well as typographical errors. (A portion of Lee's revised essay, with editing and proofreading changes marked, appears in Chapter 7, page 194–96.) The final version of Lee's essay follows.

REVISED STUDENT ESSAY

A Trend Taken Too Far: The Reality of Real TV
Christine Lee

1   Do you remember life before the reality TV craze? Before reality TV, television viewers seemed interested only in the fictional lives of characters in situational comedies and serial dramas. Characters were played by professional actors, and the shows were written by professional writers. Except for a few early reality type shows such as Cops and Candid Camera, this simple formula was what network television offered. Then came MTV's The Real World in 1992. The high ratings that this cable show garnered made network executives take notice of the genre. Eventually Survivor debuted in the summer of 2000. When Survivor caught the attention of even more viewers and dominated television ratings, television networks changed their programming. It seemed that every network acted as though it had to become "real" to compete with Survivor and maintain viewer interest. The problem with networks trying to copy Survivor is that the original Survivor offered more interesting elements to its audience than any reality TV show modeled after it. Survivor was engaging and dramatic, but the shows that followed it were less interesting and less tasteful, lacking drama and relying on gimmicks.

<u>Survivor</u> captured the interest of a wide viewing   2
audience because it was fresh and entertaining. <u>Survivor</u>
introduced real participants in a contest where they
competed against each other in an exotic location. The
participants on <u>Survivor</u> were ethnically and socially
diverse and represented a variety of ages including
younger, middle aged, and older adults. The location for
<u>Survivor</u> was fascinating; a South Pacific island was more
interesting than any house full of people on a sitcom.
However, the most unique feature of <u>Survivor</u> was to make
the participants compete for a million-dollar prize. Contestants were divided into two camps that had to compete
to win everyday supplies, like food and shelter. At the
end of each episode, players voted, and one of them was
kicked off the show and lost his or her chance for the
million dollars. The last contestant on the island wins.
To win the game, contestants created alliances and manipulated other contestants. All of these unique elements
drew television viewers back each week.

The television audience responded favorably to the   3
dramatic elements of <u>Survivor</u>. The competition gave viewers something to speculate about as the show progressed.
Viewers' allegiance to one team over another or one
player over another developed from episode to episode.
Viewers were fascinated watching these players struggle
in primitive situations, compete in tasks of strength and
skill, and decide on how to cast their votes. The phrase
"getting voted off the island" became a recognizable saying across America. While players displayed positive
human traits like teamwork, compassion, and camaraderie,
they also schemed and plotted to win the allegiance of
their fellow players. This situation made <u>Survivor</u> dramatic, and the viewers were attracted to the drama.
Reality TV shows that followed <u>Survivor</u> had none of the
interesting elements that it had.

<u>Big Brother</u> was the first spin-off reality TV show   4
to try and repeat the success of <u>Survivor</u>, but it did
not offer the drama that <u>Survivor</u> did. In <u>Big Brother</u>,

contestants were locked in a house without any outside contact for weeks. Like Survivor, there was a cash prize on the line, but in Big Brother there were not any competitions or struggles. Contestants were expelled by a viewer phone poll, but the viewer phone poll gave the house members no motive to scheme and plot allegiances like Survivor. In fact, the contestants had little to do, and viewers were forced to watch bored contestants bicker and fight. Viewers were not interested in the players who were not up against anything except fighting off weeks of boredom. In the end, Big Brother was simply not interesting.

5   Attempts to make reality TV more interesting failed because they relied on sensational gimmicks; the first of these gimmicks was sex. Shows like Chains of Love, Temptation Island, and Love Cruise revolved around flirtation and sex where contestants competed for prizes by flirting with members of the opposite sex. In every one of these shows, members of the opposite sex were organized in a way to make them grow jealous. For example, Temptation Island featured engaged couples living in separate camps, surrounded by attractive members of the opposite sex. The premise of the show was to see if engaged couples could resist temptation and remain engaged. Viewers might have responded to the sexual intrigue, but these sexually charged situations turned viewers away pushing the limits of taste.

6   After using sex to try and interest viewers, the next wave of reality TV shows tried another gimmick--the use of graphic displays of terror and violence. Examples of this type of reality show include Murder in Small Town X and Fear Factor. Both feature graphic scenes that repulsed viewers. Murder in Small Town X featured a murder mystery where contestants worked together to solve a made-up crime. Just as survival on a Pacific Island interested viewers, the mystery plot in Murder in Small Town X was supposed to interest viewers, but the show went too far in its tasteless depiction of violence. The

show opens with a reenactment from the murderer's point of view and ends with the viewers watching one of two chosen players getting fictitiously attacked and killed. The randomness of who got killed and the graphic way it was presented turned viewers away. Similarly, <u>Fear Factor</u> has its contestants commit all manner of gross and terrifying acts, like eating worms or being immersed in live rats. Some viewers may hold some interest in watching how far the contestants will go, but the majority of viewers regard these acts with disgust. Viewers might tune in once or twice but, disgusted, will not be interested in the long run.

Viewers understandably were not interested in the tasteless and uninteresting gimmicks that were featured in the reality TV shows that followed <u>Survivor</u>. In the end, it is the viewers that determine what gets shown on television. As reality TV becomes less interesting and less tasteful, ratings will drop and there will be less reality TV, and viewers will likely return to their familiar situational comedies and serial dramas, or perhaps to another form of engaging program that may evolve.

7

Analyzing the Revision

1. Identify the major revisions that Lee made from the earlier draft in Chapter 5 (pp. 138–40). How did she carry out the plan indicated in her graphic organizer?

2. Choose one major revision that Lee made and explain why you think it improved her essay.

3. Evaluate Lee's introduction and conclusion. In what ways are they more effective than the introduction and conclusion in her first draft? What additional improvements could she make?

4. Choose one paragraph and compare the details provided in it with those in the corresponding paragraph of the first draft. Which added details are particularly effective, and why?

Editing Sentences and Words

CHAPTER QUICK START

The cartoons on the facing page take a humorous view of language; however, each makes a point about writing as well.

Writing Quick Start

Write a few sentences describing what you think the cartoons suggest about writing and about the focus of this chapter—editing sentences and words.

Once you have revised an essay for content and organization, as discussed in Chapter 6, you are ready to edit and proofread the essay. Your task is to examine individual sentences and words with care, to be sure that each conveys your meaning accurately, concisely, and in an interesting way. Even an essay with good ideas will be ineffective if its sentences are vague and imprecise or if its words convey an inappropriate tone and level of diction. Therefore, your goal at this point is to improve your revised draft through the use of clear, correct sentences and effective word choice. This chapter will help you sharpen your sentences and refine your word choice.

As shown in Figure 7.1, editing and proofreading are the final steps in the writing process. Because you are almost finished with your assignment, you may be tempted to hurry through these steps or to skip them altogether. Careful editing and proofreading will always pay off in the end, however, because an error-free essay makes a good impression on the reader.

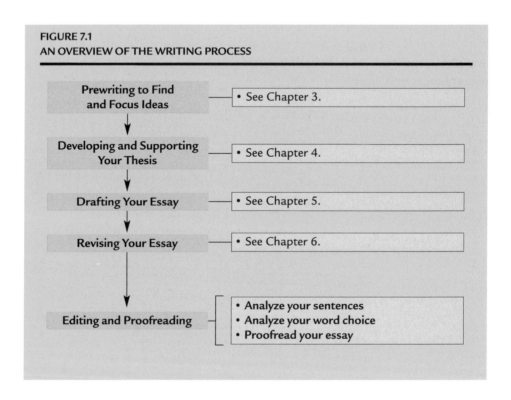

FIGURE 7.1
AN OVERVIEW OF THE WRITING PROCESS

Prewriting to Find and Focus Ideas —— • See Chapter 3.

Developing and Supporting Your Thesis —— • See Chapter 4.

Drafting Your Essay —— • See Chapter 5.

Revising Your Essay —— • See Chapter 6.

Editing and Proofreading ——
- Analyze your sentences
- Analyze your word choice
- Proofread your essay

ANALYZING YOUR SENTENCES

Effective sentences have four important characteristics: They should be clear and concise; they should be varied and should not all follow the same order; they should contain elements and parts that are parallel; and they should contain strong, active verbs. Use the questions listed in the next four headings to analyze your sentences, and use the suggestions in each section to create more effective sentences.

Are Your Sentences Concise?

Sentences that are concise convey their meaning in as few words as possible. Use the following suggestions to make your sentences concise.

1. Avoid wordy expressions. Search your essay for sentences with empty phrases that contribute little or no meaning to the sentence. Use this rule: If the sentence is clear without a particular phrase or if the phrase can be replaced by a more direct word or phrase, take it out or replace it. Here are a few examples.

▶ ~~In the near future,~~ *A* another revolution in computer technology is bound to occur. *soon.*

▶ *Since* ~~In light of the fact that~~ computer technology changes ~~every month or so~~ *monthly*, software upgrades are ~~what everybody has to do~~ *necessary*.

2. Eliminate redundancy. A common problem, **redundancy** is the unnecessary repetition of ideas using the same words or different words that have the same meaning. Here are some examples.

▶ ~~My decision to choose~~ *Choosing* accounting as my major will lead to steady, rewarding employment.

▶ ~~The type of slang I notice~~ teenagers *T* ~~using is part of the way they~~ *use slang to* establish ~~who they are and what~~ their identity ~~is~~.

3. Eliminate unnecessary sentence openings. When you first write down an idea, you may express it indirectly or awkwardly. As you revise, look for and edit sentence openings that sound indirect or tentative. Consider these examples.

▶ ~~It is my opinion that~~ **F**ast-food restaurants should post nutritional information for each menu item.

▶ ~~Many people would agree that~~ *Selecting* nutritious food and snacks ~~are~~ *is* a priority for ~~health~~ *many* conscious people.

4. Eliminate unnecessary adverbs. Using too many **adverbs** can weaken your writing. Adverbs such as *extremely*, *really*, and *very*, known as intensifiers, add nothing and can actually weaken the word they modify. Notice that the following sentence is stronger without the adverb.

*An **adverb** modifies a verb, an adjective, or another adverb.*

▶ The journalist was ~~very~~ elated when he learned that he had won a Pulitzer Prize.

Other adverbs, such as *somewhat*, *rather*, and *quite*, also add little or no meaning and are often unnecessary.

▶ The college president was ~~quite~~ disturbed by the findings of the Presidential Panel on Sex Equity.

5. Eliminate unnecessary phrases and clauses. Wordy phrases and clauses can make it difficult for readers to find and understand the main point of your sentence. This problem often occurs when you use too many **prepositional phrases** and clauses that begin with *who*, *which*, or *that*.

*A **prepositional phrase** is a group of words that begins with a preposition and includes the object or objects of the preposition and all their modifiers: above the low wooden table.*

▶ The complaints ~~of students in the college~~ *students'* encouraged the dean to create additional parking spaces ~~for cars~~ *areas*.

▶ The ~~teenagers who were~~ *teenage* mall walkers disagreed with the editorial ~~in the newspaper~~ *newspaper* ~~that supported~~ *supporting* the shopping mall regulations.

6. Avoid weak verb-noun combinations. Weak verb-noun combinations such as *wrote a draft* instead of *drafted* or *made a change* instead of *changed* tend to make sentences wordy.

▶ The attorney ~~made an assessment of~~ *assessed* the company's liability in the accident.

▶ The professor ~~gave a lecture~~ *lectured* on Asian American relations in the 1990s.

EXERCISE 7.1

Edit the following sentences to make them concise.

1. Due to the fact that Professor Wu assigned twenty-five math problems for tomorrow, I am forced to make the decision to miss this evening's lecture to be given by the vice president of the United States.
2. In many cases, workers are forced to use old equipment that needs replacing despite the fact that equipment malfunctions cost the company more than the price of new machines.
3. Bill Cosby is one of the best examples of an entertainment celebrity being given too much publicity.
4. The president of Warehouse Industries has the ability and power to decide who should and who should not be hired and who should and who should not be fired.
5. The soccer league's sponsor, as a matter of fact, purchased league jerseys for the purpose of advertisement and publicity.

Are Your Sentences Varied?

Sentences that are varied will help to hold your reader's interest and make your writing flow more smoothly. Vary the type, length, and pattern of your sentences.

How to Vary Sentence Type

There are four basic types of sentences—*simple, compound, complex,* and *compound-complex.* Each type consists of one or more clauses. A **clause** is a group of words with both a subject and a verb. There are two types of clauses. An **independent clause** can stand alone as a complete sentence. A **dependent clause** cannot stand alone as a complete sentence. It begins with a subordinating conjunction (for example, *because* or *although*) or a relative pronoun (for example, *when, which,* or *that*).

Here is a brief summary of each sentence type and its clauses.

Sentence Type	*Clauses That Comprise It*	*Example*
Simple	One independent clause	Credit card fraud is increasing in the United States.
Compound	Two or more independent clauses	Credit card fraud is increasing in the United States; it is a violation of financial privacy.
Complex	One or more dependent clauses joined to one independent clause	Because credit card fraud is increasing in America, consumers must become more cautious.

Sentence Type	Clauses That Comprise It	Example
Compound-complex	One or more dependent clauses and two or more independent clauses	Because credit card fraud is increasing in America, consumers must be cautious, and retailers must take steps to protect consumers.

Use the following suggestions to vary your sentence types.

1. **Use simple sentences for emphasis and clarity.** A **simple sentence** contains only one independent clause, but it is not necessarily short. It can have more than one subject, more than one verb, and several modifiers.

>   subject   subject   verb   verb   modifier
> ▶ Both retailers and consumers have and must exercise the responsibility to curtail
>   modifier
> fraud by reporting suspicious use of credit cards.

A short, simple sentence can be used to emphasize an important point or to make a dramatic statement.

> ▶ Credit card fraud is rampant.

If you use too many simple sentences, however, your writing will sound choppy and disjointed.

> ▶ It was a cold, drizzly spring morning. I was driving to school. A teenage hitchhiker stood alongside the road. He seemed distraught.

2. **Use compound sentences to clarify relationships.** A **compound sentence** consists of two or more independent clauses joined in one of the following ways.

- With a comma and **coordinating conjunction** (*and, but, or, nor, so, for, yet*):

  > ▶ Leon asked a question, *and* the whole class was surprised.

- With a semicolon:

  > ▶ Graffiti had been scrawled on the subway walls; passersby ignored it.

- With a semicolon and a **conjunctive adverb**:

  > ▶ Each year thousands of children are adopted; *consequently,* adoption service agencies have increased in number.

- With a **correlative conjunction**:

  > ▶ *Either* the jury will reach a verdict tonight, *or* it will recess until Monday morning.

Coordinating conjunctions (*and, but, or, nor, for, so, yet*) connect sentence elements that are of equal importance.

A **conjunctive adverb** is a word (such as *also, however,* or *still*) that links two independent clauses.

A **correlative conjunction** is a word pair (such as *not only . . . but also*) that works together to join elements within a sentence.

Use compound sentences to join ideas of equal importance. For instance, in the following sentence, both ideas are equally important and receive equal emphasis.

▶ Several researchers have proved that garlic is good for the heart; consequently, many people with heart disease use garlic in their meals.

You can also use compound sentences to explain *how* ideas are related. You can, for example, suggest each of the following relationships, depending on the coordinating conjunction you choose.

Coordinating Conjunction	Relationship	Example
and	Additional information	The three teenage vandals were apprehended, *and* their parents were required to pay damages.
but, yet	Contrast or opposites	No one wants to pay more taxes, *yet* taxes are necessary to support vital public services.
for, so	Causes or effects	Telephone calls can interrupt a busy worker constantly, *so* answering machines are a necessity.
or, nor	Choices or options	Quebec may become a separate country, *or* it may settle its differences with the Canadian government.

3. Use complex sentences to show subordinate relationships. A **complex sentence** consists of one independent clause and at least one dependent clause; either type of clause may come first. When the dependent clause appears first, it is followed by a comma. When the independent clause comes first, a comma is not used.

▶ Because the dam broke, the village flooded.
▶ The village flooded because the dam broke.

Use complex sentences to show that one or more ideas are less important than (or subordinate to) another idea. In the preceding sentence, the main point is that the village flooded. The dependent clause explains *why* the flood happened. A dependent clause often begins with a *subordinating conjunction* that indicates how the less important (dependent) idea is related to the more important (independent) idea.

Here is a list of some subordinating conjunctions and the relationships they suggest.

Subordinating Conjunction	*Relationship*	*Example*
as, as far as, as soon as, as if, as though, although, even though, even if, in order to	Circumstance	*Even though* cable television has expanded, it is still unavailable in some rural areas.
because, since, so that	Causes or effects	*Because* the movie industry has changed, the way theaters are built has changed.
before, after, while, until, when	Time	*When* prices rise, demand falls.
whether, if, unless, even if	Condition	More people will purchase satellite dishes *if* they become less expensive.

Dependent clauses can also begin with a relative pronoun (*that, who, which*).

▶ Many medical doctors *who are affiliated with a teaching hospital* use interns in their practices.

To see how complex sentences can improve your writing, study the following two paragraphs. The first paragraph consists primarily of simple and compound sentences. The revised paragraph uses complex sentences that show relationships.

ORIGINAL

Are you one of the many people who has tried to quit smoking? Well, don't give up trying. Help is here in the form of a nonprescription drug. A new nicotine patch has been developed. This patch will help you quit gradually. That way, you will experience less severe withdrawal symptoms. Quitting will be easier than ever before. You need to be psychologically ready to quit smoking. Otherwise, you may not be successful.

REVISED

If you are one of the many people who has tried to quit smoking, don't give up trying. Help is now here in the form of a nonprescription nicotine patch, which has been developed to help you quit gradually. Because you experience less severe withdrawal symptoms, quitting is easier than ever before. However, for this patch to be successful, you need to be psychologically ready to quit.

4. Use compound-complex sentences occasionally to express complicated relationships. A **compound-complex sentence** contains one or more dependent clauses and two or more independent clauses.

▶ If you expect to study medicine, you must take courses in biology and chemistry, and you must prepare for four more years of study after college.

Use compound-complex sentences sparingly; when overused, they tend to make your writing sound wordy and labored.

1. A day-care center may look respectable.
   Parents assume a day-care center is safe and run well.
2. In some states, the training required to become a day-care worker is minimal.
   On-the-job supervision and evaluation of day-care workers are infrequent.
3. Restaurants are often fined or shut down for minor hygiene violations.
   Day-care centers are rarely fined or closed down for hygiene violations.
4. More and more mothers have entered the workforce.
   The need for quality day care has increased dramatically.
5. Naturally, day-care workers provide emotional support for children.
   Few day-care workers are trained to provide intellectual stimulation.

How to Vary Sentence Length

Usually, if you vary sentence type, you will automatically vary sentence length as well. Simple sentences tend to be short, whereas compound and complex sentences tend to be longer. Compound-complex sentences tend to be the longest. You can, however, use sentence length for specific effects. Short sentences tend to be sharp and emphatic; they move ideas forward quickly, creating a fast-paced essay. In the following example, a series of short sentences creates a dramatic pace.

> ▶ The jury had little to debate. The incriminating evidence was clear and incontrovertible. The jury announced its verdict with astonishing speed.

Longer sentences, in contrast, move the reader more slowly through the essay. Notice that the lengthy sentence in this example suggests a leisurely, unhurried pace.

> ▶ While standing in line, impatient to ride the antique steam-powered train, a child begins to imagine how the train will crawl deliberately, endlessly along the tracks, slowly gathering speed as it spews grayish steam and emits hissing noises.

How to Vary Sentence Patterns

A sentence is usually made up of subject(s), verb(s), and modifiers. **Modifiers** are words (adjectives or adverbs), phrases, or clauses that describe, qualify, or limit another part of the sentence (a noun, pronoun, verb, phrase, or clause). Think of a modifier as a word or group of words that provides additional information about a part of the sentence. Here are some examples of modifiers in sentences.

WORDS AS   The *empty* classroom was unlocked. [adjective]
MODIFIERS   The office runs *smoothly*. [adverb]

PHRASES AS   The student *in the back* raised his hand.
MODIFIERS   Schools should not have the right *to mandate community service*.

CLAUSES AS   The baseball *that flew into the stands* was caught by a fan.
MODIFIERS   *When the exam was over,* I knew I had earned an A.

As you can see, the placement of modifiers may vary, depending on the pattern of the sentence. The most common sentence patterns (or sentence structures) are described here.

1. Modifier last: subject-verb-modifier. In this sentence pattern, the main message (expressed in the subject and verb) comes first, followed by information that clarifies or explains the message.

>   subject   verb   modifier
> ▶ The instructor announced that class was canceled. [clause as modifier]

In some cases, a string of modifiers follows the subject and verb.

>   subject   verb   modifiers
> ▶ The salesperson demonstrated the word-processing software, creating and deleting
>
> files, moving text, creating directories, and formatting tables.

2. Modifier first: modifier-subject-verb. Sentences that follow this pattern are called **periodic sentences.** Notice that information in the modifier precedes the main message, elaborating the main message but slowing the overall pace. The emphasis is on the main message at the end of the sentence.

>   modifier   subject verb
> ▶ Tired and depressed from hours of work, divers left the scene of the accident.

Use this sentence pattern sparingly. Too many periodic sentences will make your writing sound stiff and unnatural.

3. Modifier in the middle: subject-modifier-verb. In sentences that follow this pattern, the modifier or modifiers appear between the subject and the verb. The modifier thus interrupts the main message and tends to slow the pace of the sentence. The emphasis is on the subject because it comes first in the sentence.

>   subject   modifier   verb
> ▶ The paramedic, trained and experienced in water rescue, was first on the scene of
>
> the boating accident.

Avoid placing too many modifiers between the subject and verb in a sentence. Doing so may cause your reader to miss the sentence's key idea.

4. Modifiers used throughout. In this pattern, modifiers are used throughout a sentence.

► modifier   subject

Because human organs are in short supply, awarding an organ transplant, especially

modifier   *verb*   *modifier*

hearts and kidneys, to patients has become a controversial issue, requiring difficult

medical and ethical decisions.

By varying the order of subjects, verbs, and modifiers, you can give emphasis where it is needed as well as vary sentence patterns. In the first paragraph that follows, notice the monotonous effect of using the same subject-verb-modifier pattern in all of the sentences. In the revised paragraph, the ideas are better developed, and the main point comes alive as a result of the varied sentence patterns.

ORIGINAL

Theme parks are growing in number and popularity. Theme parks have a single purpose—to provide family entertainment centered around high-action activities. The most famous theme parks are Disney World and Disneyland. They serve as models for other, smaller parks. Theme parks always have amusement rides. Theme parks can offer other activities such as swimming. Theme parks will probably continue to be popular.

REVISED

Theme parks are growing in number and popularity. Offering high-action activities, theme parks fulfill a single purpose—to provide family entertainment. The most famous parks, Disney World and Disneyland, serve as models for other, smaller parks. Parks always offer amusement rides, which appeal to both children and adults. Added attractions such as swimming, water slides, and boat rides provide thrills and recreation. Because of their family focus, theme parks are likely to grow in popularity.

EXERCISE 7.3

Add modifiers to the following sentences to create varied sentence patterns.

1. The divers jumped into the chilly waters.
2. The beach was closed because of pollution.
3. Coffee-flavored drinks are becoming popular.
4. The dorm was crowded and noisy.
5. The exam was more challenging than we expected.

Are Your Sentences Parallel in Structure?

Parallelism means that similar ideas in a sentence are expressed in similar grammatical form. It means balancing words with words, phrases with phrases, and clauses with clauses. Use parallelism to make your sentences flow smoothly and your thoughts easy to follow. Study the following pairs of sentences. Which sentence in each pair is easier to read?

▶ The horse was large, had a bony frame, and it was friendly.

▶ The horse was large, bony, and friendly.

▶ Maria enjoys swimming and sailboats.

▶ Maria enjoys swimming and sailing.

In each pair, the second sentence sounds better because it is balanced grammatically. *Large, bony,* and *friendly* are all adjectives. *Swimming* and *sailing* are nouns ending in *-ing.*

The following sentence elements should be parallel in structure.

1. **Nouns in a series should be parallel.**

   ▶ A thesis statement, ~~that is clear,~~ *clear* strong supporting paragraphs, and ~~a~~ conclusion *an interesting* ~~that should be interesting~~ are all elements of a well-written essay.

2. **Adjectives in a series should be parallel.**

   ▶ The concertgoers were rowdy and ~~making a great deal of noise.~~ *noisy.*

3. **Verbs in a series should be parallel.**

   ▶ The sports fans jumped and ~~were applauding~~ *applauded*.

4. **Phrases and clauses within a sentence should be parallel.**

   ▶ The parents who supervised the new playground were pleased ~~about~~ *that* the preschoolers ~~playing~~ *played* congenially and that everyone enjoyed the sandbox.

5. **Items being compared should be parallel.** When items within a sentence are compared or contrasted, use the same grammatical form for each item.

   ▶ It is usually better to study for an exam over a period of time than ~~cramming~~ *to cram* the night before.

EXERCISE 7.4

Edit the following sentences to eliminate problems with parallelism.

1. The biology student spent Saturday morning reviewing his weekly textbook assignments, writing a research report, and with lab reports.
2. The career counselor advised Althea to take several math courses and that she should also register for at least one computer course.
3. Three reasons for the popularity of fast-food restaurants are that they are efficient, offer reasonable prices, and most people like the food they serve.
4. Driving to Boston is as expensive as it is to take the train.
5. While at a stop sign, it is important first to look both ways and then proceeding with caution is wise.

Do Your Sentences Have Strong, Active Verbs?

Strong, active verbs make your writing lively and vivid. By contrast, *to be* verbs (*is, was, were, has been,* and so on) and other **linking verbs** (*feels, became, seems, appears*), which connect a noun or pronoun to words that describe it, can make your writing sound dull. Often, these verbs contribute little meaning to a sentence. Whenever possible, use stronger, more active verbs.

TO BE VERB	The puppy *was* afraid of thunder.
ACTION VERBS	The puppy *whimpered* and *quivered* during the thunderstorm.
LINKING VERB	The child *looked* frightened as she boarded the bus for her first day of kindergarten.
ACTION VERBS	The child *trembled* and *clung* to her sister as she boarded the bus for her first day of kindergarten.

To strengthen your writing, try to use active verbs rather than passive verbs as much as possible. A **passive verb** is a form of the verb to be combined with a past participle (*walked, drank, shouted*). In a sentence with a passive verb, the subject is acted on and does not perform the action. By contrast, in a sentence with an **active verb**, the subject performs the action.

PASSIVE	It *was claimed* by the cyclist that the motorist failed to yield the right of way.
ACTIVE	The cyclist *claimed* that the motorist failed to yield the right of way.

Notice that the first sentence emphasizes the claim, not the person who made the claim. In the second sentence, the person who made the claim is the subject, and the verb is active.

Unless you decide deliberately to deemphasize the subject, try to avoid using passive verbs. On occasion, you may need to use passive verbs, however, to emphasize the object or person receiving the action.

▶ The Johnsons' house *was destroyed* by the flood.

Passive verbs may also be appropriate if you do not know or choose not to reveal who performed an action. Journalists often use passive verbs for this reason.

▶ It *was confirmed* late Tuesday that Senator Kraemer *is resigning*.

EXERCISE 7.5

Edit the following sentences by changing passive verbs to active ones, adding a subject when necessary.

1. Songs about peace were composed by folk singers in the 1960s.
2. The exam was thought to be difficult because it covered thirteen chapters.
3. For water conservation, it is recommended that low-water-consumption dishwashers be purchased.
4. The new satellite center was opened by the university so that students could attend classes nearer their homes.
5. In aggressive telemarketing sales calls, the consumer is urged by the caller to make an immediate decision before prices change.

ESSAY IN PROGRESS 1

For your essay in progress (the one you worked on in Chapters 5 and 6) or any essay you are working on, evaluate and edit your sentences.

ANALYZING YOUR WORD CHOICE

Each word you select contributes to the meaning of your essay. Consequently, when you are revising, be sure to analyze your word choice, or **diction**. The words you choose should suit your purpose, audience, and tone. This section describes four aspects of word choice to consider as you evaluate and revise your essay.

- Tone and level of diction
- Word connotations
- Concrete and specific language
- Figures of speech

Are Your Tone and Level of Diction Appropriate?

Imagine that as a technician at a computer software company you discover a time-saving shortcut for installing the company's best-selling software program. Your supervisor asks you to write two memos describing your discovery and how it works—one for your fellow technicians at the company and the other for customers who might purchase the program. Would both memos say the same thing in the same way? Definitely not. The two memos would differ not only in content but also in tone and level of diction. The memo addressed to the other technicians would be technical and concise, explaining how to use the shortcut and why it works. The memo directed to customers would praise the discovery, mention the time customers will save, and explain in nontechnical terms how to use the shortcut.

Tone refers to how you sound to your readers and how you feel about your topic. Your word choice should be consistent with your tone. Your memo to the technicians would have a direct, no-nonsense tone. Your memo to the customers would be enthusiastic.

There are three common **levels of diction**—formal, popular, and informal. The **formal** level of diction is serious and dignified. Think of it as the kind of language that judges use in interpreting laws, presidents employ when greeting foreign dignitaries, or speakers choose for commencement addresses. Formal diction is often written in the third person, tends to include long sentences and multisyllabic words, and contains no slang or contractions. It has a slow, rhythmic flow and an authoritative, distant, and impersonal tone. Here is an example taken from *The Federalist, No. 51,* a political tract written by James Madison in 1788 to explain constitutional theory.

> It is of great importance in a republic, not only to guard the society against the oppression of its rulers, but to guard one part of the society against the injustice of the other part. Different interests necessarily exist in different classes of citizens. If a majority be united by a common interest, the rights of the minority will be insecure.

Formal diction is also used in scholarly publications, in operation manuals, and in most academic fields. Notice in the following excerpt from a chemistry textbook that the language is concise, exact, and marked by specialized terms, called *jargon,* used within the particular field of study. The examples of jargon are in italics.

> A *catalyst* is classified as *homogeneous* if it is present in the same *phase* as that of the *reactants.* For reactants that are *gases,* a *homogeneous catalyst* is also a *gas.*
> ATKINS AND PERKINS, *Chemistry: Molecules, Matter, and Change*

Popular or casual diction is common in magazines and newspapers. It sounds more conversational and personal than formal diction. Contractions may be used, and sentences tend to be shorter and less varied than in formal diction. The first person (*I, me, mine, we*) or second person (*you, your*) may be used. Consider this example taken from a popular newsmagazine, *Newsweek.*

Pop quiz: What percentage of 18- to 25-year-olds can correctly identify the vice president? The answer, according to a Pew survey released last week, is 51 percent. (Older Americans do about 15 points better.) Maybe Dick Cheney should come out of hiding after all.

Jonathan Alter, "Give the Pols a Gold Star"

In this excerpt, the writer conveys a light, casual tone.

Informal diction, also known as *colloquial language,* is the language of everyday speech and conversation. It is friendly and casual. Contractions (*wasn't, I'll*), slang expressions (*cops, chill out,* "What up?"), sentence fragments, and first-person and second-person pronouns are all common in informal diction. This level of diction should not be used in essays and academic writing, except when it is part of a quotation or a block of dialogue. Here is an example of informal diction.

This guy in my history class is a psycho. He doesn't let anybody talk but him. I mean, this guy interrupts all the time. Never raises his hand. He drives us nuts—what a loser.

Notice the use of the first person, slang expressions, and a loose sentence structure.

EXERCISE 7.6

Revise the following informal statement by giving it a more formal level of diction.

It hadn't occurred to me that I might be exercising wrong, though I suppose the signs were there. I would drag myself to the gym semi-regularly and go through the motions of walking (sometimes jogging) on the treadmill and doing light weight training. But I rarely broke a sweat. I just didn't have the energy. "Just doing it" wasn't cutting it. My body wasn't improving. In fact, certain areas were getting bigger, overly muscular. I needed someone to kick my butt—and reduce it too.

Wendy Schmid, "Roped In," *Vogue*

Do You Use Words with Appropriate Connotations?

Many words have two levels of meaning—a denotative meaning and a connotative meaning. A word's **denotation** is its precise dictionary definition. For example, the denotative meaning of the word *mother* is "female parent." A word's **connotation** is the collection of feelings and attitudes the word evokes, its emotional colorings or shades of meaning. A word's connotation may vary, of course, from one person to another. One common connotation of *mother* is a warm, caring person. Some people, however, may think of a mother as someone with strong authoritarian control. Similarly, the phrase *horror films* may conjure up memories of scary but fun-filled evenings for some people and terrifying experiences for others.

Since the connotations of words can elicit a wide range of responses, be sure the words you choose convey only the meanings you intend. In each pair of words that follows, notice that the two words have a similar denotation but different connotations.

> artificial/ fake
> firm/stubborn
> lasting/endless

EXERCISE 7.7

Describe the different connotations of the three words in each group of words.

1. crowd/mob/gathering
2. proverb/motto/saying
3. prudent/penny-pinching/frugal
4. token/gift/keepsake
5. display/show/expose

Do You Use Concrete Language?

Specific words convey much more information than general words. The following examples show how you might move from general to specific word choices.

General	*Less General*	*More Specific*	*Specific*
store	department store	Sears	Sears at the Galleria Mall
music	popular music	country and western music	Garth Brooks's "Friends in Low Places"

Concrete words add life and meaning to your writing. In each of the following sentence pairs, notice how the underlined words in the first sentence provide little information, whereas the underlined words in the second sentence provide interesting details and add meaning.

GENERAL	Our <u>vacation</u> was <u>great fun</u>.
CONCRETE	Our <u>rafting trip</u> was filled with <u>adventure</u>.

GENERAL	The <u>red flowers</u> were blooming in our yard.
CONCRETE	<u>Crimson and white petunias</u> were blooming in our yard.

Suppose you are writing about a shopping mall that has outlived its usefulness. Instead of saying "a number of stores were unoccupied, and those that were still in business were shabby," you could describe the mall in concrete, specific terms that would enable your readers to visualize it.

The vacant storefronts with "For Rent" signs plastered across the glass, the half-empty racks in the stores that were still open, and the empty corridors suggested that the mall was soon to close.

EXERCISE 7.8

Revise the following sentences by adding concrete, specific details.

1. The book I took on vacation was exciting reading.
2. The students watched as the instructor entered the lecture hall.
3. The vase in the museum was an antique.
4. At the crime scene, the reporter questioned the witnesses.
5. Although the shop was closed, we expected someone to return at any moment.

Do You Use Fresh, Appropriate Figures of Speech?

A **figure of speech** is a comparison that makes sense imaginatively or creatively, but not literally. For example, if you say "the movie was *a roller coaster ride,*" you do not mean the movie was an actual ride. Rather, you mean the movie was thrilling, just like a ride on a roller coaster. This figure of speech, like all others, compares two seemingly unlike objects or situations by finding one point of similarity.

Fresh and imaginative figures of speech can help you create vivid images for your readers. However, overused figures of speech can detract from your essay. Be sure to avoid common **clichés** (trite or overused expressions) such as *blind as a bat, green with envy, bite the bullet,* or *sick as a dog.*

Although there are many kinds of figures of speech, the most useful types are simile, metaphor, and personification. In a **simile,** the word *like* or *as* is used to make a direct comparison of two unlike things.

> The child acts *like a tiger.*
>
> The noise in a crowded high school cafeteria is as deafening *as a caucus of crows.*

A **metaphor** also makes a comparison of unlike things, but does not use the word *like* or *as.* Instead, the comparison is implied.

> That child is a tiger.
>
> If you're born in America with black skin, you're born in prison.
> MALCOLM X, "Interview"

Personification describes an idea or object by giving it human qualities or characteristics.

> A sailboat, or any other pleasure vehicle, devours money.

In this example, the ability to eat is ascribed to an inanimate object, the sailboat.

When you edit an essay, look for and eliminate overused figures of speech, replacing them with creative, fresh images. If you have not used any figures of speech, look for descriptions that could be improved by using a simile, a metaphor, or personification.

EXERCISE 7.9

Invent fresh figures of speech for two items in the following list.

1. Parents of a newborn baby
2. A lengthy supermarket line or a traffic jam
3. A relative's old refrigerator
4. A man and woman obviously in love
5. Your team's star quarterback or important player

For more on figures of speech, see Chapter 9, p. 261.

Evaluating Your Word Choice

Use Figure 7.2 on page 192 to help you evaluate your word choice. If you have difficulty identifying which words to revise, ask a classmate or friend to read and evaluate your essay by using the flowchart as a guide and marking any words that may need revision.

A word-processing program is a useful editing tool. For example, you might experiment with several different word choices in a paragraph, print out all versions, and make comparisons. Because it is difficult to spot ineffective word choices on a computer screen, print a copy of your essay and work with the print copy, circling words or phrases that may need revision.

ESSAY IN PROGRESS 2

For the essay you worked on in Essay in Progress 1, use Figure 7.2 to evaluate and edit your word choice.

SUGGESTIONS FOR PROOFREADING

Once you are satisfied with your sentences and words and your edited essay as a whole, you are ready for the final step of the writing process — *proofreading*. When you proofread, you make sure your essay is error-free and is presented in acceptable manuscript format. Your goals are to catch and correct surface errors — such as errors in grammar, punctuation, spelling, and mechanics — as well as keyboarding or typographical errors. Making sure your essay is free of surface errors will help

For information on manuscript format, see Chapter 20, p. 712.

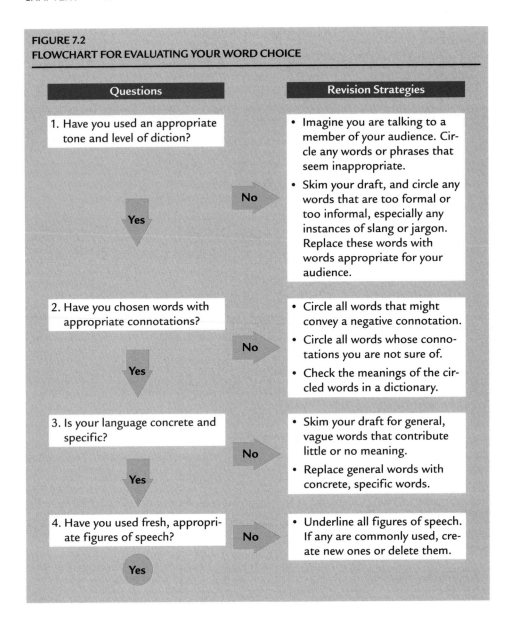

FIGURE 7.2
FLOWCHART FOR EVALUATING YOUR WORD CHOICE

Questions	Revision Strategies
1. Have you used an appropriate tone and level of diction?	• Imagine you are talking to a member of your audience. Circle any words or phrases that seem inappropriate. • Skim your draft, and circle any words that are too formal or too informal, especially any instances of slang or jargon. Replace these words with words appropriate for your audience.
2. Have you chosen words with appropriate connotations?	• Circle all words that might convey a negative connotation. • Circle all words whose connotations you are not sure of. • Check the meanings of the circled words in a dictionary.
3. Is your language concrete and specific?	• Skim your draft for general, vague words that contribute little or no meaning. • Replace general words with concrete, specific words.
4. Have you used fresh, appropriate figures of speech?	• Underline all figures of speech. If any are commonly used, create new ones or delete them.

create a favorable impression in readers — of both the essay and of you as its writer. Careless proofreading is a sign of a careless writer, and if you are writing for a class, careless mistakes will cause your instructor to give you a lower grade. The guidelines in this section will help you become a careful proofreader.

If you are using a computer, print out a clean copy of your essay for proofreading. Do not attempt to work with a previously marked-up copy or on a computer screen. Spotting errors in grammar, spelling, punctuation, and mechanics is easier when you work with a clean printed copy. Be sure to double-space the copy to allow room for you to mark corrections between lines.

Use the following suggestions to produce an error-free essay.

1. **Review your paper once for each type of error.** Because it is difficult to spot all types of surface errors simultaneously during a single proofreading, you should read your essay several times, each time focusing on *one* error type—errors in spelling, punctuation, grammar, mechanics, and so on.

2. **Read your essay backward, from the last sentence to the first.** Reading in this way will help you concentrate on spotting errors without being distracted by the flow of ideas.

3. **Use the spell-check and grammar-check functions cautiously.** If you are working with a word processor or computer, the spell-check function can help you spot some spelling and keyboarding errors, but you cannot rely on it to catch all spelling errors. A spell-check program can detect misspelled words, but it cannot detect the difference in meaning between *there* and *their* or *to* and *too,* for example. Similarly, the grammar-check function can identify only certain kinds of errors and is not a reliable substitute for a careful proofreading.

4. **Read your essay aloud.** By reading aloud slowly and deliberately, you can catch certain errors that sound awkward, such as missing words, errors in verb tense, and errors in the singular or plural forms of nouns.

5. **Ask a classmate to proofread your paper.** Another reader may spot errors you have overlooked.

Keeping an Error Log

You may find it helpful to keep an error log as part of your writing journal. Start by recording errors from several graded or peer-reviewed papers in the log. Then look for patterns in the types of errors you tend to make. Once you identify these types of errors, you can proofread your essays specifically for them.

In the sample error log in Figure 7.3, notice that the student kept track of five types of errors in three writing assignments. By doing so, she discovered that most of her errors fell into the categories of subject-verb agreement, spelling, and verb tense. She was then able to proofread for those errors specifically. The error log also allowed the student to keep track of her progress in avoiding these types of errors over time.

ESSAY IN PROGRESS 3

For the essay you edited in Essay in Progress 2, use one or more of the proofreading tips on page 191 to catch and correct errors in spelling, punctuation, grammar, and mechanics.

FIGURE 7.3
SAMPLE ERROR LOG

Type of Error	Assignment 1	Assignment 2	Assignment 3
Subject-verb agreement	X	XX	XX
Spelling	XXXX	XXX	XXX
Verb tense	XX	XX	XXX
Word choice	X		X
Parallelism			X

STUDENTS WRITE

Recall that Christine Lee's essay, "A Trend Taken Too Far: The Reality of Real TV," was developed, drafted, and revised in the Students Write sections of Chapters 4 to 6. Printed here are the first two paragraphs of Lee's essay with Lee's final editing and proofreading changes. Each revision has been numbered. The list following the excerpt explains the reason for each change. The final draft of Lee's essay, with these changes incorporated into it, appears in Chapter 6, on pages 168–71.

A Trend Taken Too Far: The Reality of Real TV

1 Do you remember life before the reality TV craze?

Before reality TV, television viewers seemed interested
①
only in the fictional lives of characters in situational

comedies and serial dramas. Characters were played by
②
professional actors, and the shows were written by profes-

sional writers. Except for a few early reality type

shows such as <u>Cops</u> and <u>Candid Camera</u>, this simple for-

mula was what network television offered. Then came MTV's

<u>The Real World</u> in 1992. The high ratings that this cable

show garnered made network executives take notice of the genre. Eventually <u>Survivor</u> debuted in the summer of 2000. *When* <u>Survivor</u> caught the attention of even more viewers/ and **③** dominated television ratings/, ~~Television~~ *television* networks changed **④** their programming. It seemed that every network acted as though it had to become "real" to compete with <u>Survivor</u> and maintain viewer interest. The problem with networks trying to copy <u>Survivor</u> is that the original <u>Survivor</u> offered more interesting elements to its audience than any reality TV show modeled after it. <u>Survivor</u> was engaging and dramatic, but the shows that followed it were less interesting and less tasteful, lacking drama and relying on gimmicks.

<u>Survivor</u> captured the interest of a wide viewing   2 audience because it was fresh and ~~provocative~~ *entertaining*. <u>Survivor</u> **⑤** *introduced* **⑥** *in* *they* **⑦** ~~had~~ real participants/ ~~There was~~ a contest where ~~contestants~~ competed against each other in an exotic location. The participants on <u>Survivor</u> were ethnically and socially diverse and represented a variety of ages including younger, middle aged and older adults. The location for *a* **⑧** <u>Survivor</u> was fascinating/; ~~A~~ South Pacific island was more interesting than any house full of people on a sitcom. However, the most unique feature of <u>Survivor</u> was to make the participants compete for a million dollar prize. Contestants were divided into two camps that had to compete

```
to win everyday supplies, like food and shelter. At the

end of each episode, players voted, and one of them was
                            and lost his or her chance for ⑨
kicked off the show,/ losing the million dollars. The
                ^
last contestant on the island wins. To win the game,
                            manipulated ⑩
contestants created alliances and messed with other con-
                        ⑪ drew television viewers back each week.
testants. All of these unique elements kept viewers glued
                                        ^
to their sets.
```

Notice that in editing and proofreading these paragraphs, Lee improved the clarity and variety of her sentences; chose clearer, more specific words; and corrected errors in punctuation.

1. A comma was needed to separate the opening phrase from the rest of the sentence.

2. A comma was needed between two independent clauses joined by *and*.

3. *Viewers* is a plural noun but is not possessive. The apostrophe should not follow the word.

4. Lee combined the two sentences to emphasize the cause-and-effect relationship between the two ideas. (For more on combining sentences and sentence variety, see p. 177.)

5. The word *provocative* suggests something that arouses or stimulates. This connotation was not intended nor supported in the paragraph, so Lee changed the word to *entertaining*. (For more on connotation of words, see p. 188.)

6. Lee replaced the verb *had* with *introduced* because the latter is more descriptive. (For more on using descriptive verbs, see p. 185.)

7. A *contest* with *contestants* is redundant, so Lee eliminated the redundancy. (For more on redundancy, see p. 175.)

8. Lee combined the two sentences to tie the two ideas more closely together and to indicate that the second idea more fully explains the first. (For more on varying sentence patterns, see p. 177.)

9. Lee clarified that the contestant lost the *chance* to win the million dollars.

10. Lee replaced the slang term *messed with* with more acceptable language. (For more on slang, see p. 187.)

11. Lee eliminated the cliché *glued to their sets* and replaced it with a fresher expression. (For more on clichés and figures of speech, see p. 190.)

PART 3

Patterns of
Development

Narration: Recounting Events

CHAPTER QUICK START

Homelessness is a serious national problem with many possible causes. The photograph on the opposite page shows a homeless family. Imagine the series of events that might have caused this particular family to become homeless. Did the parents lose their jobs? If so, how? Did they spend their entire savings on life-saving surgery for one of the children? Did a fire destroy their home?

Writing Quick Start

Working by yourself or with a classmate, construct a series of events that may have caused the family in the photograph to become homeless. Write a brief summary of the events you imagined.

WRITING A NARRATIVE

As you imagined this family's path to homelessness, you constructed the beginnings of a narrative. You began to describe a series of events or turning points, and you probably wrote them in the order in which they occurred. In this chapter you will learn how to write narrative essays as well as how to use narratives in essays that rely on one or more other patterns of development.

WHAT IS NARRATION?

A narrative relates a series of events, real or imaginary, in an organized sequence. It is a story, but it is *a story that makes a point*. You probably exchange family stories, tell jokes, read biographies or novels, and watch television situation comedies or dramas—all of which are examples of the narrative form. In addition, narratives are an important part of the writing you will do in college and in your career, as the examples in the accompanying box illustrate.

Narratives provide human interest, spark our curiosity, and draw us close to the storyteller. In addition, narratives can do the following.

- *Create a sense of shared history,* linking people together. The members of a culture share certain stories and events, true or untrue, that unite them. Examples of American stories include the Boston Tea Party and the first Thanksgiving.

- *Provide entertainment.* Most people enjoy a thrilling movie or an intriguing book.

SCENES FROM COLLEGE AND THE WORKPLACE

- Each student in your *business law course* must attend a court trial and complete the following written assignment: Describe what happened and what the proceedings illustrated about the judicial process.

- In a *sociology* course, your class is scheduled to discuss the nature and types of authority figures in U.S. society. Your instructor begins by asking class members to describe situations in which they found themselves in conflict with an authority figure.

- Your job in *sales* involves frequent business travel, and your company requires you to submit a report for each trip. You are expected to recount the meetings you attended, your contacts with current clients, and new sales leads.

- *Offer instruction.* Children learn about good and bad behavior and moral and immoral actions through stories. "Pinocchio" teaches children not to tell lies, and "The Boy Who Cried Wolf" admonishes them not to raise false alarms.

- *Provide insight.* Stories can help you discover values, explore options, and examine motives. By reading a story, you can think through a dilemma without actually experiencing it.

The following narrative relates the author's experience with racial profiling. As you read, notice how the narrative makes a point by presenting a series of events that build to a climax.

Right Place, Wrong Face
Alton Fitzgerald White

This narrative was first published in The Nation *in October 1999. Alton Fitzgerald White is an actor, singer, and dancer and has appeared in several Broadway shows. He is the author of* Uncovering the Heart Light (1999), *a collection of poems and short stories.*

As the youngest of five girls and two boys growing up in Cincinnati, I was raised to believe that if I worked hard, was a good person, and always told the truth, the world would be my oyster. I was raised to be a gentleman and learned that these qualities would bring me respect.

While one has to earn respect, consideration is something owed to every human being. On Friday, June 16, 1999, when I was wrongfully arrested at my Harlem apartment building, my perception of everything I had learned as a young man was forever changed — not only because I wasn't given even a second to use the manners my parents taught me, but mostly because the police, whom I'd always naively thought were supposed to serve and protect me, were actually hunting me.

I had planned a pleasant day. The night before was a payday, plus I had received a standing ovation after portraying the starring role of Coalhouse Walker Jr. in the Broadway musical *Ragtime*. It is a role that requires not only talent but also an honest emotional investment of the morals and lessons I learned as a child.

Coalhouse Walker Jr. is a victim (an often misused word, but in this case true) of overt racism. His story is every black man's nightmare. He is hardworking, successful, talented, charismatic, friendly, and polite. Perfect prey for someone with authority and not even a fraction of those qualities. On that Friday afternoon, I became a real-life Coalhouse Walker. Nothing could have prepared me for it. Not even stories told to me by other black men who had suffered similar injustices.

5   Friday for me usually means a trip to the bank, errands, the gym, dinner, and then off to the theater. On this particular day, I decided to break my pattern of getting up and running right out of the house. Instead, I took my time, slowed my pace, and splurged by making strawberry pancakes. Before I knew it, it was 2:45; my bank closes at 3:30, leaving me less than 45 minutes to get to midtown Manhattan on the train. I was pressed for time but in a relaxed, blessed state of mind. When I walked through the lobby of my building, I noticed two light-skinned Hispanic men I'd never seen before. Not thinking much of it, I continued on to the vestibule, which is separated from the lobby by a locked door.

6   As I approached the exit, I saw people in uniforms rushing toward the door. I sped up to open it for them. I thought they might be paramedics, since many of the building's occupants are elderly. It wasn't until I had opened the door and greeted them that I recognized that they were police officers. Within seconds, I was told to "hold it"; they had received a call about young Hispanics with guns. I was told to get against the wall. I was searched, stripped of my backpack, put on my knees, handcuffed, and told to be quiet when I tried to ask questions.

7   With me were three other innocent black men who had been on their way to their U-Haul. They were moving into the apartment beneath mine, and I had just bragged to them about how safe the building was. One of these gentlemen got off his knees, still handcuffed, and unlocked the door for the officers to get into the lobby where the two strangers were standing. Instead of thanking or even acknowledging us, they led us out the door past our neighbors, who were all but begging the police in our defense.

8   The four of us were put into cars with the two strangers and taken to the precinct station at 165th and Amsterdam. The police automatically linked us, with no questions and no regard for our character or our lives. No consideration was given to where we were going or why. Suppose an ailing relative was waiting upstairs, while I ran out for her medication? Or young children, who'd been told that Daddy was running to the corner store for milk and would be right back? My new neighbors weren't even allowed to lock their apartment or check on the U-Haul.

9   After we were lined up in the station, the younger of the two Hispanic men was identified as an experienced criminal, and drug residue was found in a pocket of the other. I now realize how naive I was to think that the police would then uncuff me, apologize for their mistake, and let me go. Instead, they continued to search my backpack, questioned me, and put me in jail with the criminals.

The rest of the nearly five-hour ordeal was like a horrible dream. 　10
I was handcuffed, strip-searched, taken in and out for questioning.
The officers told me that they knew exactly who I was, knew I was in
Ragtime, and that in fact they already had the men they wanted.

How then could they keep me there, or have brought me there in 　11
the first place? I was told it was standard procedure. As if the average
law-abiding citizen knows what that is and can dispute it. From what
I now know, "standard procedure" is something that every citizen,
black and white, needs to learn, and fast.

I felt completely powerless. Why, do you think? Here I was, 　12
young, pleasant, and successful, in good physical shape, dressed in
clean athletic attire. I was carrying a backpack containing a substantial paycheck and a deposit slip, on my way to the bank. Yet after
hours and hours I was sitting at a desk with two officers who not
only couldn't tell me why I was there but seemed determined to find
something on me, to the point of making me miss my performance.

It was because I am a black man! 　13

I sat in that cell crying silent tears of disappointment and injus- 　14
tice with the realization of how many innocent black men are convicted for no reason. When I was handcuffed, my first instinct had
been to pull away out of pure insult and violation as a human being.
Thank God I was calm enough to do what they said. When I was
thrown in jail with the criminals and strip-searched, I somehow knew
to put my pride aside, be quiet, and do exactly what I was told, hating
it but coming to terms with the fact that in this situation I was a
victim. They had guns!

Before I was finally let go, exhausted, humiliated, embarrassed, 　15
and still in shock, I was led to a room and given a pseudo-apology. I
was told that I was at the wrong place at the wrong time. My reply?
"I was where I live."

Everything I learned growing up in Cincinnati has been shat- 　16
tered. Life will never be the same. 　　　　　　　　　　■

Characteristics of a Narrative

As you can see from "Right Place, Wrong Face," a narrative does not merely report
events; a narrative is *not* a transcript of a conversation or a news report. Although
it does include events, conversations, and vivid descriptions, a narrative is a story
that conveys a particular meaning. It presents actions and details that build toward a climax, the point at which the conflict of the narrative is resolved. Most
narratives use dialogue to present selected portions of conversations that move the
story along.

Narratives Make a Point

A narrative makes a point or supports a thesis by telling readers about an event or a series of events. The point may be to describe the significance of the event or events, make an observation, or present new information. Often a writer will state the point directly, using an explicit thesis statement. Other times a writer may leave the main point unstated, using an implied thesis. Either way, the point should always be clear to your readers. The point also determines the details the writer selects and the way they are presented.

The following excerpt from a brief narrative written by a student is based on the photo at the start of this chapter. After imagining the series of events that might have brought the family to homelessness, the student wrote this final paragraph.

> Jack and Melissa are kind, patient people who want nothing more than to live in a house or an apartment instead of camping out on a street curb. Unfortunately, their unhappy story and circumstances are not uncommon. Thousands of Americans, through no fault of their own, share their hopeless plight. The homeless can be found on street corners, in parks, and under bridges in the coldest months of winter. Too often, passersby shun them and their need for a helping hand. They either look away, repulsed by the conditions in which the homeless live, and assume they live this way out of choice rather than necessity, or they gaze at them with disapproving looks, walk away, and wonder why such people do not want to work.

Notice that the writer makes a point about the homeless and about people's attitudes toward them directly. Note, too, how the details support the writer's point.

Narratives Convey Action and Detail

A narrative presents a detailed account of an event or a series of events. In other words, a narrative is like a camera lens that zooms in on an event and makes readers feel like they can see the details and experience the action.

For more on descriptive writing, see Chapter 9.

Writers of narratives can involve readers in several ways — through *dialogue,* with *physical description,* and by *recounting action.* In "Right Place, Wrong Face" both physical description and the recounting of events help build suspense and make the story come alive. Readers can visualize easily the scene at White's apartment building and the scene at the police station.

Narratives Present a Conflict and Create Tension

An effective narrative presents a **conflict** — such as a struggle, question, or problem — and works toward its resolution. The conflict can be between participants or between a participant and some external force, such as a law, value, moral, or act of nature. **Tension** is the suspense created as the story unfolds and as the reader wonders how the conflict will be resolved. In "Right Place, Wrong Face," for example, tension is first suggested in the third paragraph: "I had planned a pleasant day," suggesting that what was planned did not materialize. The tension becomes evident in paragraphs 7 to 14, and the conflict is resolved in paragraph 15, when White is released. The point just before the conflict is resolved is called the **climax**. The main point of the story—how White's life is changed by the incident of racial profiling—concludes the narrative.

EXERCISE 8.1

Working alone or with a classmate, complete each of the following statements by setting up a conflict. Then for one of the completed statements, write three to four sentences that build tension through action or dialogue (or both).

1. You are ready to leave the house when . . .
2. You have just turned in your math exam when you realize that . . .
3. You recently moved to a new town when your spouse suddenly becomes seriously ill . . .
4. Your child just told you that . . .
5. Your best friend phones you in the middle of the night to tell you . . .

Narratives Sequence Events

The events in a narrative must be arranged in an order that is easy for readers to follow. Often but not always, a narrative presents events in chronological order—the order in which they happened. "Right Place, Wrong Face," for example, uses this straightforward sequence. At other times writers may use the techniques of flashback and foreshadowing to make their point more effectively. A **flashback** returns the reader to events that took place in the past, whereas **foreshadowing** hints at events in the future. Both of these techniques are used frequently in drama, fiction, and film. A soap opera, for instance, might open with a scene showing a woman lying in a hospital bed, flash back to a scene showing the accident that put her there, and then return to the scene in the hospital. A television show might foreshadow what is to come by beginning with a wedding that is the result of events and conflicts that the program then proceeds to dramatize. When used sparingly, these techniques can build interest and add variety to a narrative, especially a lengthy chronological account.

Narratives Use Dialogue

Just as people reveal much about themselves by what they say and how they say it, dialogue can reveal much about the characters in a narrative. Dialogue is often used to dramatize the action, emphasize the conflict, and reveal the personalities or motives of the key participants in a narrative. Keep in mind that dialogue should resemble everyday speech; it should sound natural, not forced or formal. Consider these examples.

FORCED DIALOGUE	Maria confided to her grandfather, "I enjoy talking with you. I especially like hearing you tell of your life in Mexico long ago. I wish I could visit there with you."
NATURAL	Maria confided to her grandfather, "Your stories about Mexico when you were a kid are great. I'd like to go there with you."

EXERCISE 8.2

For one of the following situations, imagine what the person might say and how he or she would say it. Then write five or six sentences of natural-sounding dialogue. If your dialogue sounds forced or too formal, try saying it out loud into a tape recorder.

1. An assistant manager is trying to explain to a supervisor that an employee offends customers.
2. A man or a woman has just discovered that he or she and a best friend are dating the same person.
3. A babysitter is disciplining an eight-year-old girl for pouring chocolate syrup on her brother's head.

Narratives Are Told from a Particular Point of View

Many narratives use the first-person point of view, in which the key participant speaks directly to the reader ("*I* first realized the problem when . . ."). Other narratives use the third-person point of view, in which an unknown storyteller describes what happens to the key participants ("The problem began when Saul Overtone . . ."). The first person is used in "Right Place, Wrong Face."

Both the first person and third person offer a distinct set of advantages. The first person allows you to assume a personal tone and to speak directly to your audience. You can easily express your attitudes and feelings and offer your interpretation and commentary. When you narrate an event that occurred in your own life, for example, the first person is probably your best choice. In "Right Place, Wrong Face" the first person allows White to express directly his anger, humiliation, and outrage.

One drawback to using the first person, however, is that you cannot easily convey the inner thoughts of other participants unless they are shared with you. The third-person point of view gives the narrator more distance from the action and often provides a broader, more objective perspective than the first-person point of view.

EXERCISE 8.3

For each of the following situations, decide which point of view would work best. Discuss with your classmates the advantages and disadvantages of using the first- and third-person points of view for each example.

1. The day you and several friends played a practical joke on another friend
2. An incident of sexual or racial discrimination that happened to you or someone you know
3. An incident at work that a coworker told you about

Visualizing a Narrative: A Graphic Organizer

Whether or not you are a spatial learner, it is often helpful to see the content and organization of an essay in simplified, visual form. The graphic organizer shown in Figure 8.1 is a visual diagram of the basic structure of a narrative. A graphic organizer can help you structure your writing, analyze a reading, and recall key events as you generate ideas for an essay.

For more on graphic organizers, see Chapter 2, p. 34.

FIGURE 8.1
GRAPHIC ORGANIZER FOR A NARRATIVE ESSAY

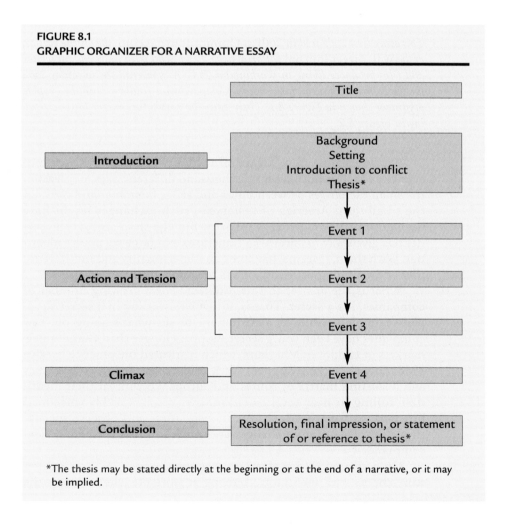

*The thesis may be stated directly at the beginning or at the end of a narrative, or it may be implied.

Use Figure 8.1 as a basic model. However, keep in mind that narrative essays vary in organization and may lack one or more of the elements included in the model. When you incorporate narration into an essay in which you also use other patterns of development, you will probably need to condense or eliminate some of the elements shown in Figure 8.1. Whether you write a narrative essay or incorporate narration in a different kind of essay, use a graphic organizer to help you visualize the structure of your essay.

The following selection, "Selling Civility," is an example of a narrative. Read it first, and then study the graphic organizer for it in Figure 8.2 (on p. 210).

Selling Civility
Peter Scott

This essay first appeared in 2001 at OpinionJournal.com, *the online edition of the* Wall Street Journal *editorial page. Peter Scott is an independent writer and film producer living in Washington, D.C. As you read the selection, look for the elements of a narrative essay. Compare your findings with the graphic organizer shown in Figure 8.1. Then study the graphic organizer for this reading in Figure 8.2.*

1   For some time now, a general incivility has made its way into everyday life. It is noticeable in a thousand different ways, not least in the small exchanges between buyer and seller, customer and clerk. In the small-town America of yesteryear, such exchanges might have been governed by a genial familiarity. But the shop around the corner has given way to sprawling franchises and large corporate identities. With them, it seems, has come an impersonality and indifference that adds stinging little indignities to simple transactions.

2   What is the answer to this problem? For a growing number of companies, it's a secret. That is, it involves sending in a secret shopper—a "mole" posing as a customer—to see what's going on. Few companies have been using secret shoppers longer than Giant Supermarkets of Landover, Maryland, which instituted the practice back in 1958. Giant's secret shoppers work undercover, using code names and a shifting matrix of routes and "drops" to conceal their identities. Toiling in near total isolation, they receive weekly voice-mail instructions from headquarters to visit stores and observe specific employees. Last-minute changes are communicated through a field commander.

3   On a steamy Friday afternoon, secret shopper "N" sets out on store checks with me in tow. Arriving at store 215, she evaluates the

parcel-pickup area even before killing the ignition of her battered minivan. While there is plenty of hustle, a bagboy named Ryan is wearing his hat backward, one of several offenses for which he'll later be written up. Seconds later, a more serious 10-point "courtesy error" is assessed against Caprice from the produce department when we "hover" near her and she fails to greet us.

At a service counter, N spots a woman chewing gum, a definite   4
no-no. Attempting to read her nametag, we sprint to the hydroponic tomatoes for a better view. Sorry, Tanita, you're busted. These and other scores will be delivered to the store manager in the next 10 days, a time lag designed to protect the shopper's identity.

As we shop, N describes her favorite tactics. In addition to   5
"hovering" to see if she'll be greeted, N likes to watch the deli and service counters. After Bobby from the meat department practically bowls us over ("no acknowledgement"), we ask Gerald about shrimp for an imaginary party ("no closing") and see Valentina about special-ordering an ice-cream cake ("customer had to ask for assistance").

Exiting checkout, N asks if I noticed anything unusual about our   6
cashier's performance. I don't. N calmly shares her findings, later written up as "no greeting"; "does not keep bills separate/sideways"; and an "incorrect price code." The store earns a respectable final score, but "nobody went the extra mile," N notes.

Ten days later, I arrange a parking lot rendezvous with "P," a fit   7
and energetic 68-year-old now in his eighth year as a Giant secret shopper. "I think of it very much as a mission," says the former nuclear-sub commander. Laughing, he concedes that his former career "kind of prepared me in a lot of respects for this job."

P buzzes through each store like an efficiency expert conducting   8
a time-and-motion study. He gathers duplicate orders so he can check two different cashiers without leaving the store. Leaving cart number two in the calm of the pet-food aisle, we march to checkout, where the cashier spots our "cashier challenge," a bottle of spring water we've stashed under the cart, a signature secret-shopper move.

The cashiers fare admirably, but the big winner is Chris, an eager   9
produce clerk who practically carries us to the California avocados. Later, P will nominate him for a commendation and possible cash reward. He'll phone in his findings and, leaving nothing to chance, spell the young man's name using naval phonetics: Charlie, Hotel, Romeo, India, Sierra. For P, today's mission ended in victory.

In such a way, modern commerce — whether Giant or just   10
gigantic — can police itself into the conscientiousness and civility of mom-and-pop stores.   ■

FIGURE 8.2
GRAPHIC ORGANIZER FOR "SELLING CIVILITY"

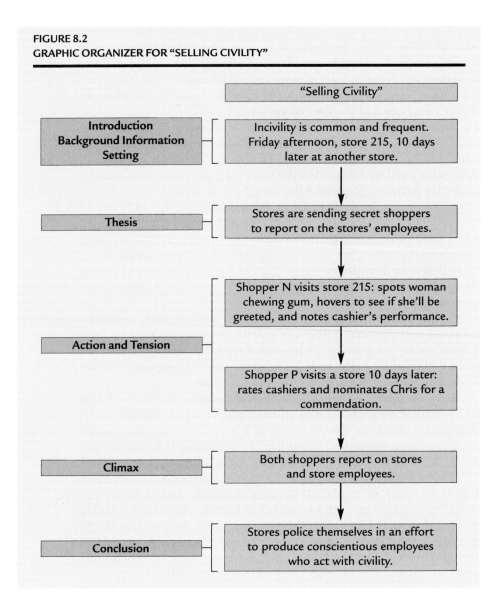

To draw detailed graphic
organizers using a com-
puter, visit www
.bedfordstmartins.com
/successfulwriting.

EXERCISE 8.4

Using the graphic organizers in Figures 8.1 and 8.2 as models, draw a graphic organizer
for "Right Place, Wrong Face" (pp. 201–03).

INTEGRATING A NARRATIVE INTO AN ESSAY

In many of your essays, you will want to use a narrative along with one or more other patterns of development to support your thesis effectively. In much of the writing you encounter in newspapers, magazines, and textbooks, the patterns of development often mix and overlap. Similarly, although "Right Place, Wrong Face" is primarily a narrative, it also uses cause and effect to explain why White was detained despite evidence that he was a respectable, law-abiding citizen. "Selling Civility" is a narrative that contains descriptions of grocery store employees.

For more on description and cause and effect, see Chapters 9 and 15.

Although most of your college essays will not be primarily narrative, you can often use stories to illustrate a point, clarify an idea, support an argument, or capture readers' interest in essays that rely on another pattern of development or on several patterns. Here are a few suggestions for using narration effectively in the essays you write.

1. **Be sure that your story illustrates your point accurately and well.** Don't include a story just because it's funny or interesting. It must support your thesis.

2. **Keep the narrative short.** Include only relevant details, those facts that are necessary to help your reader understand the events you are describing.

3. **Introduce the story with a transitional sentence or clause that indicates you are about to shift to a narrative.** Otherwise, your readers may wonder, "What's this story doing here?" Your transition should also make clear the connection between the story and the point it illustrates.

4. **Use descriptive language, dialogue, and action.** These elements make narratives vivid, lively, and interesting in any essay.

In "Another Mother's Child: A Letter to a Murdered Son" on page 233, Norma Molen incorporates narration into a persuasive essay.

A GUIDED WRITING ASSIGNMENT

Learning Style Options

The following guide will lead you through the process of writing a narrative essay. Although your essay will be primarily a narrative, you may choose to use one or more other patterns of development as well. Depending on your learning style, you might decide to start at various points and move back and forth within the process. If you are a spatial learner, for example, you might begin by visualizing and sketching the details of your narrative. If you are a social learner, you might prefer to start out by evaluating your audience.

The Assignment

Write a narrative essay about an experience in your life that had a significant effect on you or that changed your views in some important way. Choose one of the following topics or one that you think of on your own. The readers of your campus newspaper are your audience.

1. An experience that caused you to learn something about yourself
2. An incident that revealed the true character of someone you knew
3. An experience that helped you discover a principle to live by
4. An experience that explains the personal significance of a particular object
5. An incident that has become a family legend, perhaps one that reveals the character of a family member or illustrates a clash of generations or cultures
6. An incident that has allowed you to develop an appreciation or awareness of your ethnic identity

For more on description and comparison and contrast, see Chapters 9 and 12.

As you develop your narrative essay, be sure to consider using one or more of the other patterns of development. You might use description to present details about a family member's appearance, for example, or comparison and contrast to compare your attitudes or ideas to those of a parent or child.

Generating Ideas

Use the following steps to help you choose a topic and generate ideas about the experience or incident you decide to write about.

Choosing an Experience or Incident That Leads to a Working Thesis

Be sure that the experience you write about is memorable and vivid and that you are comfortable writing about it. No student wants to discover, when a draft is nearly completed, that he or she cannot remember important details about an experience or that it does not fulfill the requirements of the assignment.

The following suggestions will help you choose an experience. Experiment and use whatever suggestions prove helpful to you. After you have chosen one, make sure that you can develop it by formulating a working thesis.

For more on formulating a working thesis, see Chapter 4, p. 89.

Learning Style Options

For more on prewriting strategies, see Chapter 3.

1. You can probably eliminate one or more broad topic choices right away. List those that remain across the top of a piece of paper or on your computer screen — for example, *Learn about Self, A Principle to Live By,* and *Family Legend.* Then brainstorm about significant experiences or incidents in your life, and write each one you think of beneath the appropriate heading.

2. Brainstorm with another student, discussing and describing experiences or incidents that fit one or more of the suggested topics.

3. Flip through a family photo album, or page through a scrapbook, diary, or yearbook. Your search will remind you of people and events from the past.

4. Work backward. Think of a principle you live by, an object you value, or a family legend. How did it become so?

5. Using freewriting or another prewriting technique, write down any experiences or incidents that come to mind. The memory of one incident will trigger memories of other incidents. Then sort your list to see if any of these experiences or incidents fulfill the assignment.

│ ESSAY IN PROGRESS 1
│
│ For the assignment given on page 212, use one or more of the preceding sugges-
│ tions to choose an experience or incident to write about and formulate a work-
│ ing thesis for your choice.

Considering Your Purpose, Audience, and Point of View

Once you have chosen an experience or incident to write about, the next step is to consider your purpose, audience, and point of view. Recall from Chapter 3 that most essays have one of three possible purposes — to inform, to express thoughts or feelings, or to persuade.

For more on purpose, audience, and point of view, see Chapter 3, pp. 65–69.

Thinking about your audience may help you clarify your purpose and decide what to include in your essay. For this Guided Writing Assignment, your audience is readers of your campus newspaper. In an essay about a dispute at a basketball game, for example, you would need to explain the relevant plays, rules, and penalties because not all readers of the campus newspaper could be expected to know those details. However, if your audience consisted solely of basketball players, they would be familiar with the rules, and you could omit these explanations.

At this stage of planning your narrative essay, you should also decide on a point of view. If the basketball narrative was written to express your feelings about the incident, it would probably be most effective in the first person. But if the narrative's purpose was instead to inform readers about what happened at the game, the third person would be appropriate. Consider the pros and cons of using each point of view for your narrative. In most cases, you will use the first person to relate a personal experience.

Gathering Details about the Experience or Incident

This step involves recollecting as many details about the experience or incident as possible and recording them on paper or in a computer file. Reenact the story, sketching the scene or scenes in your mind. Identify key actions, describe key participants, and describe your feelings. Here are a few ways to generate ideas.

Learning Style Options

1. Replay the experience or incident in your mind. If you have a strong visual memory, close your eyes, and imagine the incident or experience taking place. Jot down what you see, hear, smell, and feel — colors, dialogue, sounds, odors, and sensations — and how these details make you feel.

2. Write the following headings on a piece of paper, or type them on your computer screen: *Scene, Key Actions, Key Participants, Key Lines of Dialogue,* and *Feelings.* Then list ideas under each heading.

3. Describe the incident or experience to a friend. Have your friend ask you questions as you retell the story. Jot down the details that the retelling and questioning help you recall.

4. Consider different aspects of the incident or experience by asking *who, what, when, where, how,* and *why* questions. Record your answers.

In addition, as you gather details for your narrative, be sure to include the types of details that are essential to an effective narrative.

- *Scene:* **Choose relevant sensory details.** Include enough detail about the place where the experience occurred to allow your readers to feel as if they are there. Details that appeal to the senses work best. Also try to recall important details that direct your readers' attention to the main points of the narrative, and avoid irrelevant details that distract readers from the main point.

For more on sensory details, see Chapter 9, p. 242.

- *Key actions:* **Choose actions that create tension, build it to a climax, and resolve it.** Be sure to gather details about the conflict of your narrative. Answer the following questions.

  Why did the experience or incident occur?
  What events led up to it?
  How was it resolved?
  What were its short- and long-term outcomes?
  What is its significance now?

- *Key participants:* **Concentrate only on the appearance and actions of those people who were directly involved.** People who were present but not part of the incident or experience need not be described in detail or perhaps even included.

- *Key lines of dialogue:* **Include dialogue that is interesting, revealing, and related to the main point of the story.** To make sure the dialogue sounds natural, read the lines aloud, or ask a friend to do so.

- *Feelings:* **Record your feelings before, during, and after the experience or incident.** Did you reveal your feelings then? If so, how? How did others react to you? How do you feel about the experience or incident now? What have you learned from it?

ESSAY IN PROGRESS 2

For the experience or incident you chose in Essay in Progress 1 (p. 213), use one or more of the preceding suggestions to generate details.

Evaluating Your Ideas

Evaluate the ideas you have gathered about your topic before you begin drafting your narrative. You want to make sure you have enough details to describe the experience or incident vividly and meaningfully.

Begin by rereading everything you have written with a critical eye. As you do, add dialogue, descriptions of actions, or striking details as they come to mind. Highlight the most relevant material, and cross out any material that does not directly support your main point. You might use a two-color highlighting system—one color for key actions and dialogue, and another color for key details about the experience or incident. Some students find it helpful to read their notes aloud. If you are working on a computer, highlight usable ideas by making them bold or moving them to a separate page or document for easy access when drafting.

> TRYING OUT YOUR IDEAS ON OTHERS
>
> Once you are satisfied with the details you have generated about your incident or experience, you are ready to discuss your ideas with others. Working in a group of two or three students, each student should narrate his or her experience and state the main point of the narrative. Then work together to answer the following questions about the narrative.
>
> 1. What more do you need to know about the experience or incident?
> 2. What is your reaction to the story?
> 3. How do the events of the narrative support or not support the main point?

ESSAY IN PROGRESS 3

Gather your prewriting and any comments you have received from your classmates or instructor, and evaluate the details you have developed so far. Based on your findings, generate additional details. Highlight the most useful details and omit those that do not support the main point.

Developing Your Thesis

For more on thesis statements, see Chapter 4, p. 89.

Your thesis should make clear the main point of your narrative. You should already have a working thesis in mind. Now is the time to focus it. For example, a student who brainstormed a list of ideas and decided to write about her family's antique silver platter wrote the following focused thesis statement for her narrative.

> The silver serving platter, originally owned by my great-grandmother, became our most prized family heirloom after a robbery terrorized our family.

Notice that the thesis identifies the object, introduces the experience that made the object a valuable family possession, and expresses the main point of the narrative.

A thesis statement may be placed at the beginning of a narrative essay. In "Right Place, Wrong Face" (p. 201), for example, the thesis appears near the beginning of the essay. A thesis may also be placed at the end of a narrative, as in "Selling in Minnesota" (p. 228).

ESSAY IN PROGRESS 4

Develop a thesis statement for the narrative you worked on in Essays in Progress 1–3. Make sure the thesis expresses the main point of the incident or experience you have chosen to write about.

Once you have a thesis, you may need to do some additional prewriting to collect evidence for the thesis, including dialogue, action, and details. Your prewriting at this stage may involve elaborating on some of the details you've already collected. Be sure your events and details contribute to the tension or suspense of the narrative.

See Chapter 4, p. 95, for more on supporting a thesis with evidence.

Organizing and Drafting

Once you are satisfied with your thesis and your support for it, you are ready to organize your ideas and write your first draft. Use the following suggestions for organizing and drafting your narrative.

For more on drafting an essay, see Chapter 5.

Choosing a Narrative Sequence

As noted earlier in the chapter, all of the events of a narrative may follow a chronological order from beginning to end, or some events may be presented as flashbacks or foreshadowing for dramatic effect. Consider, for example, the options available to the student writing about her family's antique silver platter. Chronological order could be used to describe the events of the robbery in the order they happened. Or the writer could start with her sister's discovery of the platter in the bushes and then flash back to tell how it got there. Another option would be to foreshadow the robbery by describing a relevant scene from the past, such as when she polished the platter and wondered why her family valued the antique.

The following strategies will help you determine the best sequence for your narrative.

1. Write a brief description of each event on an index card. Be sure to highlight the card that contains the climax. Experiment with various

Learning Style Options

ways of arranging your details by rearranging the cards. When you have chosen a sequence, prepare an outline of your narrative.

2. Draw a graphic organizer of the experience or incident (see p. 207).

3. Use a word-processing program to create a list of the events. Rearrange the events using the cut-and-paste function, experimenting with different sequences.

ESSAY IN PROGRESS 5

Using one or more of the preceding suggestions, plan the order of the events for your narrative essay.

Drafting the Narrative Essay

Now that you've determined your narrative sequence, you are ready to begin drafting your essay. As you write, use the following guidelines to help keep your narrative on track.

For more on writing effective paragraphs, including introductions and conclusions, see Chapter 5.

The introduction.   Your essay's introduction should catch your reader's attention, provide useful background information, and set up the sequence of events. Your introduction may also contain your thesis, if you have decided to place it at the beginning of the essay.

The story.   The story should build tension and follow a clear order of progression. As you draft your narrative, be conscious of your paragraphing, devoting a separate paragraph to each major action or distinct part of the story. Use transitional words and phrases such as *during, after,* and *finally* to connect events and guide readers along.

For more on transitions, see Chapter 5, p. 128.

In addition, be consistent in your use of verb tense. Most narratives are told in the past tense ("Yolanda discovered the platter . . ."). Fast-paced, short narratives, however, are sometimes related in the present tense ("Yolanda discovers the platter . . ."). Avoid switching between the past and present tenses unless the context of the narrative clearly requires it.

The ending.   Your final paragraph should conclude the essay in a satisfying manner. A summary is usually unnecessary and may detract from the impact of the narrative. Instead, try ending in one of the following ways.

• **Make a final observation about the experience or incident.** For an essay on part-time jobs in fast-food restaurants, a writer could conclude by writing: "Overall, I learned a lot more about getting along with people than I did about operating a franchise."

- **Ask a probing question.** For an essay on adventure travel, a writer could conclude with a question: "Although the visit to Nepal was enlightening for me, do the native people really want or need us there?"

- **Suggest a new but related direction of thought.** For an essay on racial profiling, for example, a writer could conclude by suggesting that police sensitivity training might have changed the outcome of the situation.

- **Refer back to the beginning,** as White does in the final paragraph of "Right Place, Wrong Face" (p. 203).

- **Restate the thesis in different words.**

ESSAY IN PROGRESS 6

Using the narrative sequence you developed in Essay in Progress 5 and the preceding guidelines for drafting, write a first draft of your narrative essay.

Analyzing and Revising

If possible, set your draft aside for a day or two before rereading and revising it. As you reread your draft, focus on improving the overall effectiveness of your narrative. Will it interest readers and make them want to know what happens next? Does it make your point clear? To discover weaknesses in your draft, try the following strategies.

1. Reread your paper aloud or ask a friend to do so as you listen. Hearing your essay read out loud may help you identify parts in need of revision.

2. Write an outline or draw a graphic organizer or review the one you created earlier. Does your narrative follow the intended sequence?

Learning Style Options

As you analyze your narrative, be on the lookout for dialogue that doesn't support your thesis, events that need further explanation or description, and details that contribute nothing to the overall impression you want to convey. Use Figure 8.3 on page 220 to help you discover the strengths and weaknesses of your narrative. You might also ask a classmate to review your essay. Your reviewer's comments and impressions may reveal strengths and weaknesses in the narrative that you overlooked.

For more on the benefits of peer review, see Chapter 6, p. 155.

ESSAY IN PROGRESS 7

Revise your narrative essay, using Figure 8.3 on page 220 and the suggestions of your classmates to guide you.

FIGURE 8.3
FLOWCHART FOR REVISING A NARRATIVE ESSAY

Questions		Revision Strategies
1. Highlight the sentence(s) that expresses the main point of your narrative. Is the main point of the story clear?	**No**	• Rework your thesis to make it more explicit.
Yes		
2. At the bottom of your paper, *write* a brief sentence that summarizes the conflict of your narrative. Does the narrative present a clear *conflict*? Is it directly related to the main point?	**No**	• Add events and dialogue specific to the conflict. • Rework your thesis to make it better relate to the conflict.
Yes		
3. Place an *X* by each important scene, person, or action. Is it clear how each important scene, person, and action relates to both the main point and *conflict*?	**No**	• Delete extraneous scenes, persons, or events.
Yes		
4. Place a checkmark ✔ by each descriptive word or phrase. Is each important scene, person, or action vividly described?	**No**	• Brainstorm to discover more vivid details. • Consider adding dialogue to bring people and events to life.
Yes		

(Continued on next page)

FIGURE 8.3 *(Continued)*

Questions	Revision Strategies

5. In the margins of your paper, *number* the sequence of major events in chronological order. Is the sequence of events clear? If you use foreshadowing or flashbacks, is it clear where you do so?

No

- Look for gaps in the narrative, and add any missing events.
- Consider rearranging the events.
- Use transitions to clarify the sequence of events.

Yes

6. Underline the topic sentence of each paragraph. Is each paragraph focused on a separate part of the action?

No

- Be sure each paragraph has a topic sentence and supporting details. (See Chapter 5.)
- Consider combining closely related paragraphs.
- Split paragraphs that cover more than one event.

Yes

7. Wavy underline the dialogue. Is it realistic when you say it aloud? Does it directly relate to the *conflict*?

No

- Revise by telling someone what you want your dialogue to express. Record what you say.
- Eliminate dialogue that does not add anything to the story.

Yes

8. Circle each personal pronoun and each verb. Do you use a consistent point of view and verb tense?

No

- Reconsider your point of view and verb tense.
- Check for places where the tense changes for no reason and revise it to make it consistent.

Yes

(Continued on next page)

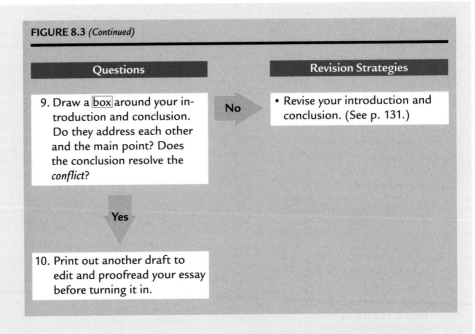

FIGURE 8.3 *(Continued)*

Questions		Revision Strategies
9. Draw a box around your introduction and conclusion. Do they address each other and the main point? Does the conclusion resolve the *conflict?*	**No** →	• Revise your introduction and conclusion. (See p. 131.)

Yes ↓

10. Print out another draft to edit and proofread your essay before turning it in.

Editing and Proofreading

The last step is to check your revised narrative essay for errors in grammar, spelling, punctuation, and mechanics. Be sure to look for the types of errors that you tend to make. (Refer to your error log.)

For more on keeping an error log, see Chapter 7, p. 193

For narrative essays, pay particular attention to the following kinds of sentence problems.

For more on varying sentence structure, see Chapter 7, p. 177.

1. **Make certain that your sentences vary in structure.** A string of sentences that are similar in length and structure is tedious to read.

   ▶ The Ding Darling National Wildlife Preserve is located on Sanibel Island,

   Florida, It was established in 1945 as the Sanibel Refuge. Its name was

   changed in 1967 to honor the man who helped found it.

2. **Be sure to punctuate dialogue correctly.** Use commas to separate the quotation from the phrase that introduces it, unless the quotation is integrated into your sentence. If your sentence ends with a quotation, the period should be inside the quotation marks.

▶ The wildlife refuge guide noted, "American crocodiles are an endangered species and must be protected."

▶ The wildlife refuge guide noted that/ "American crocodiles are an endangered species and must be protected."

ESSAY IN PROGRESS 8

Edit and proofread your narrative essay, remembering to vary sentence patterns and punctuate dialogue correctly. Don't forget to look for the types of errors you tend to make.

STUDENTS WRITE

Aphonetip Vasavong is a native of Laos who was a nursing student at Niagara University when she wrote this essay. She wrote it in response to an assignment given by her first-year writing instructor to describe an event that changed her life. As you read the essay, notice how Vasavong's narrative creates conflict and tension and builds to a climax and resolution. Highlight the sections where you think the tension is particularly intense.

```
              You Can Count on Miracles
                  Aphonetip Vasavong
       Most of us have experienced unusual coincidences        1
at least once in our lives--ones that are so unusual
and meaningful that they could not have happened by
chance alone. Many events that seem coincidental often
have simple explanations; however, some of these inci-
dents have no simple explanations. I had such an experi-
ence when I was eight years old and lost in the woods.
Strange as it may seem, a rabbit led me to safety. I
would not be here today if it were not for that rabbit.
       Until I was eight, my family lived in Laos. In         2
1986, however, my family and I left Laos to prevent the
Communists from capturing my father. He is an educated
```

man, and at that time the Communist government wanted to imprison educated people. The government was placing such people in concentration camps, similar to those used in Germany and Eastern Europe during World War II, to prevent them from forming a party that might overthrow the Communists. To protect my father from being captured and imprisoned in Laos, my family decided to immigrate to America.

3   We had to leave Laos quickly and secretively. In order to prevent suspicion, we told our neighbors that we were taking a two-week family vacation to see our grandfather. Instead, we stayed with our grandmother for two days, until we were able to find someone willing to escort us across the river to Thailand. On the second night, we planned to board a boat that would take us to a small town where we could spend the night. I remember it was around 2 a.m. when my father woke us up. He divided the ten of us into two groups of five because it was too risky to walk to the river as a large group; people would be more likely to notice us and report us to the Communist soldiers. We were not allowed to speak or make any noise at all because we might have awakened people or disturbed their dogs. My father instructed us carefully: "Hold on to each other's jackets and stay in line. Move carefully and quietly, and we'll all be safe soon."

4   In a group with my brothers, my sister, and an escort lady, I was the last person in line. On the way to the river, everyone else was walking fast through a dark, wooded area, and I could not keep up with them. Somehow I accidentally let go of my sister's jacket and got left behind in the woods. I was alone in the middle of what seemed like nowhere. It was so dark I could not see anything or anyone. As I waited in terror for the escort lady to come back to look for me, I started to cry. I waited a while longer, and still no one came back for me.

Suddenly, something ran out of the bushes onto a   5
nearby path. I could see that it was a rabbit. It was
beautiful and bright, like a light. It came back toward
me and stood in front of me. I reached out to pet it,
but it ran toward the same path that it had come from a
moment ago. I decided to follow the rabbit along the
path. As I did, I was able to see my way through the
woods because the rabbit and the path were bright, while
the trees and the dense groundcover remained dark. I
continued to follow the rabbit along the path until it
disappeared into the darkness. I looked around for the
rabbit, and what I saw instead was my family getting
into the canoes. I turned back once more to look for the
rabbit, but it was gone. When I got on the canoe, I was
relieved and overjoyed to see my family again. My father
pulled me close to him and whispered, "We thought you
were lost forever. How did you find us?"

Unusual experiences such as mine occur to people   6
everywhere, but most people do not take the time to
think about their meaning. Some critics argue that these
occurrences are merely coincidental. My experience leads
me to believe otherwise. Being lost in the woods and
having a brightly lit rabbit lead me safely to my family
cannot be attributed to chance alone.

Analyzing the Essay

1. Evaluate the effectiveness of Vasavong's thesis.
2. What ideas do you think should be expanded? That is, where did you find yourself wanting or needing more detail?
3. How effectively does Vasavong establish conflict and create tension?
4. Where does Vasavong use foreshadowing? Explain its effectiveness.
5. Evaluate the title, introduction, and conclusion of the essay.

Reacting to the Essay: Discussion and Journal Writing

1. Vasavong's family held a "trust no one" attitude. Why was that necessary? In what situation today, if any, would such an attitude be necessary?

2. Vasavong's father escaped Laos to avoid persecution because of his education. Where does persecution still exist today? Why does it occur?

3. Vasavong believes that the appearance of the rabbit did not happen by chance. Do you agree? Why or why not?

4. Write a journal entry describing your interpretation of an unusual coincidence or a memorable event from your childhood.

READING A NARRATIVE

The following section provides advice for reading narratives. Two model essays illustrate the characteristics of narrative writing covered in this chapter and provide opportunities to examine, analyze, and react to the writer's ideas. The second essay uses a narrative to support an argument.

WORKING WITH TEXT: READING NARRATIVES

For more on previewing an essay and other reading strategies, see Chapter 2.

It is usually a good idea to read a narrative essay several times before you attempt to discuss or write about it. Preview the essay first to get an overview of its content and organization. Then read it through to familiarize yourself with the events and action, noting also who did what, when, where, and how. Finally, reread the narrative, this time concentrating on its meaning.

What to Look For, Highlight, and Annotate

1. **Narrative elements.** When reading a narrative, it is easy to become immersed in the story and to overlook its importance or significance. Therefore, as you read, look for the answers to the following questions. Highlight those sections of the essay that reveal or suggest the answers.

- What is the writer's thesis? Is it stated directly or implied?
- What is the role of each participant in the story?
- What does the dialogue reveal about or contribute to the main point?
- What is the conflict?
- How does the writer create tension?

- What is the climax?
- How is the conflict resolved?

2. Sequence of events. Especially for lengthy or complex narratives and for those that flash back and forward among events, it is helpful to draw a graphic organizer or number the sequence of events in the margins. Doing so will help you establish the sequence of key events.

3. Keys to meaning. The following questions will help you evaluate the reading and discover its main point.

- What is the author's purpose in writing this narrative?
- For what audience is it intended?
- What is the lasting value or merit of this essay? What does it tell me about life, people, jobs, or friendships, for example?
- What techniques does the writer use to try to achieve his or her purpose? Is the writer successful?

4. Reactions. As you read, write down your reactions to and feelings about the events, participants, and outcome of the narrative. Include both positive and negative reactions; do not hesitate to challenge participants, their actions, and their motives.

How to Find Ideas to Write About

Since you may be asked to write a response to a narrative, keep an eye out for ideas to write about *as you read.* Pay particular attention to the issue, struggle, or dilemma at hand. Try to discover what broader issue the essay is concerned with. For example, in a story about children who dislike eating vegetables, the larger issue might be food preferences, nutrition, or parental control. Once you've identified the larger issue, you can develop your own ideas about it by relating it to your own experience.

For more about discovering ideas for a response paper, see Chapter 2.

THINKING CRITICALLY ABOUT NARRATION

A nonfiction narrative is often one writer's highly personal, subjective account of an event or a series of events. Unless you have reason to believe otherwise, assume that the writer is honest — that he or she does not lie or purposely distort the version of the experiences or incidents presented in the essay. You should also assume, however, that the writer chooses details selectively — to advance his or her narrative point. Use the following questions to think critically about the narratives you read.

Is the Writer Subjective?

Because a narrative is often highly personal, a critical reader must recognize that the information it contains is probably influenced by the author's values, beliefs, and attitudes. In "Right Place, Wrong Face," for example, the police officers are presented as uncaring and insensitive, but imagine how the police would describe the same incident. Two writers, then, may present two very different versions of a single incident. For example, suppose two observers—one with pro-life views, the other pro-choice—watched a protest in front of an abortion clinic. The pro-life observer would tell a quite different story about the protesters than would the pro-choice observer. Each would make a different narrative point.

What Is the Author's Tone?

Tone refers to how the author sounds to his or her readers or how he or she feels about the topic. Writers establish tone through word choice, sentence structure, and formality or informality. An author's tone can reflect many emotions—such as anger, joy, or fear. The tone of an essay narrating an event in the American war in Iraq might be serious, frightening, or alarming, whereas an essay narrating the activities of a procrastinating, well-meaning friend or relative might be light or humorous. The author's tone affects the reader's attitude toward the topic.

NARRATIVE ESSAY

As you read the following essay by Barbara Ehrenreich, consider how the writer uses the elements of narrative discussed in this chapter.

Selling in Minnesota
Barbara Ehrenreich

Barbara Ehrenreich is an award-winning political essayist, columnist, and social critic. Her works have appeared in Time *magazine, the* Nation, Harper's, *and the* Atlantic Monthly. *Ehrenreich is the author of numerous books, including the essay collection* The Worst Years of Our Lives *(1990),* Fear of Falling *(1989),* Blood Rites *(1997), and* Nickel and Dimed: On (Not) Getting by in America *(2001), from which this essay is adapted. In this selection, Ehrenreich poses as a minimum wage worker to discover the working conditions of low-paying jobs in the United States. As you read it, highlight or annotate each narrative element in the essay.*

In my second week [of working at Wal-Mart], two things change.   1
My shift changes from 10:00–6:00 to 2:00–11:00, the so-called closing
shift, although the store remains open 24/7. No one tells me this; I
find it out by studying the schedules that are posted, under glass, on
the wall outside the break room. Now I have nine hours instead of
eight, and my two fifteen-minute breaks, which seemed almost superfluous on the 10:00–6:00 shift, now become a matter of urgent calculation. Do I take both before dinner, which is usually about 7:30,
leaving an unbroken two-and-a-half-hour stretch when I'm weariest,
between 8:30 and 11:00? Or do I try to go two and a half hours without a break in the afternoon, followed by a nearly three-hour
marathon before I can get away for dinner? Then there's the question
of how to make the best use of a fifteen-minute break when you have
three or more urgent, simultaneous needs—to pee, to drink something, to get outside the neon and into the natural light, and most of
all, to sit down. I save about a minute by engaging in a little time theft
and stopping at the rest room before I punch out for the break. From
the time clock it's a seventy-five second walk to the store exit; if I stop
at the Radio Grill, I could end up wasting a full four minutes waiting
in line, not to mention the fifty-nine cents for a small-sized iced tea.
So if I treat myself to an outing in the tiny fenced-off area beside the
store, I get about nine minutes off my feet.

The other thing that happens is that the post–Memorial Day   2
weekend lull definitely comes to an end. Now there are always a
dozen or more shoppers rooting around in ladies'. New tasks arise,
such as bunching up the carts left behind by customers and steering
them to their place in the front of the store every half hour or so.
Now I am picking up not only dropped clothes but all the odd items
customers carry off from foreign departments and decide to leave
with us in ladies'—pillows, upholstery hooks, Pokémon cards, ear-
rings, sunglasses, stuffed animals, even a package of cinnamon buns.
And always there are the returns, augmented now by the huge volume
of items that have been tossed on the floor or carried fecklessly to
inappropriate sites. If I pick up misplaced items as quickly as I
replace the returns, my cart never empties and things back up dan-
gerously at the fitting room, where Rhoda or her nighttime replace-
ment is likely to hiss: "You've got three carts waiting, Barb. What's
the *problem*?"

Still, for the first half of my shift, I am the very picture of good-   3
natured helpfulness. Amazingly, I get praised by Isabelle, the thin
little seventyish lady who seems to be Ellie's adjutant: I am doing
"wonderfully," she tells me, and—even better—am "great to work
with." But then, somewhere around 6:00 or 7:00, when the desire to

sit down becomes a serious craving, a Dr. Jekyll/Mr. Hyde transformation sets in. I cannot ignore the fact that it's the customers' sloppiness and idle whims that make me bend and crouch and run. They are the shoppers, I am the antishopper, whose goal is to make it look as if they'd never been in the store. At this point, "aggressive hospitality" gives way to aggressive hostility. Their carts bang into mine, their children run amok.

4   It's the clothes I relate to, not the customers. And now a funny thing happens to me here on my new shift: I start thinking they're mine, not mine to take home and wear, because I have no such designs on them, just mine to organize and rule over. Same with ladies' wear as a whole. I patrol the perimeter with my cart, darting in to pick up misplaced and fallen items, making everything look spiffy from the outside. I don't fondle the clothes, the way customers do; I slap them into place, commanding them to hang straight, at attention, or lie subdued on the shelves in perfect order. In this frame of mind, the last thing I want to see is a customer riffling around, disturbing the place. In fact, I hate the idea of things being sold—uprooted from their natural homes, whisked off to some closet that's in God-knows-what state of disorder. I want ladies' wear sealed off in a plastic bubble and trucked away to some place of safety, some museum of retail history.

5   One night I come back bone-tired from my last break and am distressed to find a new person folding T-shirts in the [turtlenecks] area, *my* [turtlenecks] area. It's already been a vexing evening. Earlier, when I'd returned from dinner, the evening fitting room lady upbraided me for being late—which I actually wasn't—and said that if Howard knew, he probably wouldn't yell at me this time because I'm still pretty new, but if it happened again. . . . And I'd snapped back that I could care less if Howard yelled at me. So I'm a little wary with this intruder in [turtlenecks], and, sure enough, after our minimal introductions, she turns on me.

6   "Did you put anything away here today?" she demands.

7   "Well, yes, sure." In fact I've put something away everywhere today, as I do on every other day.

8   "Because this is not in the right place. See the fabric—it's different," and she thrusts the errant item up toward my chest.

9   True, I can see that this olive-green shirt is slightly ribbed while the others are smooth. "You've *got* to put them in their right places," she continues. "Are you checking the UPC numbers?"

10   Of course I am not checking the ten or more digit UPC numbers, which lie just under the bar codes—nobody does. What does she think this is, the National Academy of Sciences? I'm not sure what kind of deference, if any, is due here: Is she my supervisor now? But I

don't care, she's messing with my stuff. So I say, only without the numerals or the forbidden curse word, that (1) plenty of other people work here during the day, not to mention all the customers coming through, so why is she blaming me? (2) it's after 10:00 and I've got another cart full of returns to go, and wouldn't it make more sense if we both worked on the carts, instead of zoning the goddamn T-shirts?

To which she responds huffily, "I don't *do* returns. My job is to *fold.*" 　11

I leave that night shaken by my response to the intruder. If she's 　12 a supervisor, I could be written up for what I said, but even worse is what I thought. Am I turning mean here, and is that a normal response to the end of a nine-hour shift? There was another outbreak of mental wickedness that night. I'd gone back to the counter by the fitting room to pick up the next cart full of returns and found the guy who answers the phone at the counter at night, a pensive young fellow in a wheelchair, staring into space, looking even sadder than usual. And my uncensored thought was, At least you get to sit down.

This is not me, at least not any version of me I'd like to spend 　13 much time with. What I have to face is that "Barb," the name on my ID tag, is not exactly the same person as Barbara. "Barb" is what I was called as a child, and still am by my siblings, and I sense that at some level I'm regressing. Take away the career and the higher education, and maybe what you're left with is this original Barb, the one who might have ended up working at Wal-Mart for real if her father hadn't managed to climb out of the mines. So it's interesting, and more than a little disturbing, to see how Barb turned out—that she's meaner and slyer than I am, more cherishing of grudges, and not quite as smart as I'd hoped. ■

Examining the Reading

1. Describe the working conditions at Wal-Mart as experienced by the author.

2. What sort of tasks do the Wal-Mart employees perform? Provide details.

3. How and why does the author's attitude toward her job change as the essay progresses?

4. What details or sections of the essay identify Ehrenreich as a well-educated journalist rather than a low-wage worker?

5. Explain the meaning of each of the following words as used in the reading: *superfluous* (para. 1), *fecklessly* (2), *adjutant* (3), *errant* (8), and *regressing* (13). Refer to your dictionary as needed.

MAKING CONNECTIONS: Consumers and Workers

Both "Selling Civility" (pp. 208–09) and "Selling in Minnesota" (pp. 228–31) focus on employment and the services that workers provide to consumers. Each writer has a unique point to make about the relationship between consumers and workers.

Analyzing the Readings

1. Who is Ehrenreich's audience, and who is Scott's audience? What details do both authors use that would appeal to their respective audiences?
2. Ehrenreich conceals from her coworkers and employers that she intends to write about her experiences working in retail, and Scott conceals from the workers at the supermarket that they are being reviewed. What benefits does this concealment provide for each author? Do you agree with this approach to gathering information for an article? Why or why not?

Essay Idea

Write an essay about a particular experience that you had either as a worker or as a consumer that helped you better understand the relationship between consumer and worker. Cite both essays as examples.

Analyzing the Reading

1. Identify the writer's thesis. Is it implied or directly stated?
2. Describe the tone of Ehrenreich's essay. Highlight key phrases that reveal her attitude toward working at Wal-Mart.
3. The writer has to decide how to fit in her various breaks. Why does Ehrenreich include these details? What is she trying to convey about her job?
4. What other patterns of development does the author use? Provide examples of two and explain how they contribute to the narrative.
5. Does Ehrenreich present an objective or a subjective view of a Wal-Mart worker? Explain your answer.

Reacting to the Reading: Discussion and Journal Writing

1. Compare the author's portrayal of a retail store worker with your experiences as a shopper. Are her descriptions consistent with what you have experienced or observed?

2. Discuss whether this essay will affect the way you treat retail store employees. What adjustments might you make to your behavior in light of the conditions under which they work?

3. Ehrenreich makes a distinction between "Barb" and "Barbara," suggesting two different people, yet they merge as one. In what ways are you more than one person? Write a journal entry exploring this question.

NARRATION COMBINED WITH OTHER PATTERNS

In the following selection, Norma Molen uses a narrative within an essay that presents an argument.

For more on reading and writing arguments, see Chapters 16 and 17.

Another Mother's Child: A Letter to a Murdered Son
Norma Molen

Norma Molen read this letter on the steps of the Lincoln Memorial in Washington, D.C., during a Mother's Day rally against gun violence in 1992. The letter was later published in Catalyst, *a Salt Lake City alternative magazine, in 1993. Molen begins with the narrative, capturing her readers' attention and preparing them for her argument in favor of handgun restriction. As you read, notice how Molen integrates the narrative within her essay and makes it clear how the story illustrates her message.*

Dear Steven,

We find it difficult to speak of your terrible tragedy, yet we feel 1 we must. You told us at Christmas break you were dating a beautiful graduate student, Susan Clements, who lived in the women's wing of your dormitory. And just before you returned to school, you casually mentioned that Susan had received threatening phone calls from an ex-boyfriend, a graduate student at Stanford. You said there was nothing to worry about, that he was all bluff, but that he was causing Susan a great deal of distress. We were not too concerned because he was 3,000 miles away, yet we warned you not to get involved. You insisted you could handle it.

On April 23, Andreas Drexler, the ex-boyfriend, appeared in the 2 dormitory hall, just as Susan was unlocking the door to her room. Drexler shot once and missed. You ran to Susan's defense, and he shot you in the stomach, then ran down the hall and shot Susan three times in the face. Susan died immediately, you lived five days on machines before you were pronounced dead, and Drexler, despairing over his unspeakable crime, shot himself with the same gun. An unimaginable nightmare.

3   Three talented students dead. And for what purpose? A moment of passion from which there was no return.

4   We are sorry we brought you up in this violent land. Other advanced nations are ten to fifty times safer from gun violence than the United States. You would still be alive if you had been born in England, France, Germany, or Japan. We are a free people, but with this freedom we kill a staggering number with handguns. We have learned to accept the intolerable.

5   There is no legitimate need for a handgun in a civilized society, a technology designed specifically for killing, a weapon for the coward. And we, like most Americans, were lethargic about this grotesque carnage until you became a victim, not in a drug war, but on the 14th floor of the graduate dormitory at Indiana University. The killing is everywhere: 25,000 last year. And more people arm themselves each day because we have allowed the gun industry to promote a solution of complete madness.

6   Drexler, ironically a German, could never have committed this crime in his own country because he couldn't have purchased a gun. In civilized countries people don't buy handguns. The only exception in European countries is for members of target shooting societies, but the gun is never taken from the target range.

7   The immense tragedy that can never change is that we lost you, our poet and writer, our scholar. You disdained material things, always wore shorts and rode a bicycle, even in winter. You even refused to have a driver's license. And every time we go to an outdoor restaurant, for a bike ride, or a walk up the canyon, there will be an empty place. You were cheated of a career already begun. You were a published writer at age 22 with a short story in a collection called *Flash Fiction*. Who knows what you might have contributed? Several literature professors said you were the brightest student they ever had. They also spoke of Susan in superlatives.

8   We think a wall like the Vietnam Memorial should be built in front of the Capitol building, except this time it should record the names of the victims killed in their own land because their senators and representatives did not have the integrity and common sense to establish laws that would protect the public. It would be a daily reminder that your blood, Susan's blood, and the blood of thousands of other victims stains the flag.

9   After you died, artist Randall Lake called to remind us of the portrait of you he'd begun to paint. We were thrilled to see it. He caught your intelligent eyes, firm chin, and high cheekbones, your full, thick hair, and he captured your stance. Yet it was not finished. An unfin-

ished portrait is a perfect metaphor for your life. And Susan's. And all the others. ■

Examining the Reading

1. What main issue does Molen's essay address?
2. What is Molen's position on the issue? What reasons does she offer in support of her position?
3. Explain the meaning of each of the following words as it is used in the reading: *grotesque* (para. 5), *carnage* (5), *ironically* (6), *disdained* (7), and *superlatives* (7). Refer to your dictionary as needed.

Analyzing the Reading

1. What is Molen's thesis? (It is presented after the narrative.) Is its placement effective? Why or why not?
2. Describe the tone of Molen's essay. Give several examples of words and phrases that reveal her tone.
3. Explain how the narrative creates tension and builds to a climax.
4. Highlight several words or phrases that reveal Molen's subjective viewpoint.
5. Who is Molen's intended audience?

Reacting to the Reading: Discussion and Journal Writing

1. Do you think the letter format is effective? Why or why not?
2. Does Molen seriously advocate a wall similar to the Vietnam Memorial? What, if anything, do you think should be done to commemorate handgun victims?
3. Write a journal entry exploring or explaining your position on handgun ownership.

APPLYING YOUR SKILLS: ADDITIONAL ESSAY ASSIGNMENTS

Write a narrative on one of the following topics, using the elements and techniques of narration you learned in this chapter. Depending on the topic you choose, you may need to do library or Internet research to gather enough support for your ideas.

For more on locating and documenting sources, see Part 5.

To Express Your Ideas

1. Write a narrative about an incident or experience from the past that you see differently now than you did then.

2. In "Right Place, Wrong Face," White says he always believed that the police "were supposed to serve and protect" him. Through the incident he describes in the essay, White learns otherwise. Write a narrative describing an incident involving police officers or law enforcement agents that you may have experienced, observed, or read about. Did the incident change your attitude about police or law enforcement or confirm opinions you already held?

To Inform Your Reader

3. Write an essay informing your reader about the characteristics of a strong (or weak) relationship, the habits of successful (or unsuccessful) students, or the ways of keeping (or losing) a job. Use a narrative to support one or more of your main points.

To Persuade Your Reader

4. "Selling Civility" is concerned with improving the quality of service that customers receive. Have you been treated very poorly or particularly well by a clerk? Do you think that store employees are civil and polite or uncivil? Or can little more be expected of them given the nature of the job and the pay? Are improvements or changes needed? Write an essay taking a position on this issue. Support your position using a narrative of your experience with clerks or employees.

5. "Another Mother's Child" is a persuasive essay that uses narration to support the writer's position on gun control. Write an essay persuading your reader to take a particular stand on an issue of your choosing. Use a narrative to support your position on the issue or tell how you arrived at it.

Cases Using Narration

6. Write a paper on the advantages of an urban or a suburban lifestyle for a sociology course. Support some of your main points with events and examples from your own experiences.

7. Write a draft of the presentation you will give as the new personnel director of a nursing care facility in charge of training new employees. You plan to hold

your first orientation session next week, and you want to emphasize the importance of teamwork and communication by telling related stories from your previous job experiences.

EVALUATING YOUR PROGRESS
Part A: Using Narration

Write a paragraph that evaluates your use of narration. Be sure to

- Identify topics or situations in which narration will be useful.
- Explain what narration adds to an essay (how it strengthens it).
- Evaluate how effectively you provided background information, built action and tension, and presented the climax of your narrative.
- Identify any problems or trouble spots you experienced in using narration and explain how you dealt with them.

Part B: Analyzing Narrative Readings

The readings in this chapter are models of narration. Make a list of what you learned about writing (either about narration specifically or about writing in general) from each of the narrative essays you were assigned.

Part C: Proofreading and Editing

List the errors your instructor identified in your narrative essay(s). For more help with these problems, refer to Exercise Central (www.bedfordstmartins.com/successfulwriting).

Description: Portraying People, Places, and Things

Suppose you are volunteering at the Second Chance shelter for homeless dogs; you are asked to write a description to accompany the photograph for the weekly "Available for Adoption" column in a community newspaper. The following description was run for several weeks but received no response.

> *This one-year-old mixed breed black male (neutered) needs a new home. The adoption fee of $75 includes his first vet visit. Call 555-2298.*

You decide to write a more appealing description of the dog that will encourage people to consider adoption.

Writing Quick Start

Rewrite the advertisement, describing the dog in a way that will help convince readers to adopt him.

WRITING A DESCRIPTION

In rewriting the description, did you describe how the dog looks, feels, responds, or behaves? Did you choose details that emphasize its playfulness or willingness to interact with people? If so, you just wrote a successful description. In this chapter, you will learn how to write descriptions and how to use description to support and develop your ideas.

WHAT IS DESCRIPTION?

Description presents information in a way that appeals to one or more of the five senses—sight, sound, smell, taste, and touch—usually creating an overall impression or feeling. You use description every day, to describe a pair of shoes you bought, a flavor of ice cream you tasted, or a concert you recently attended.

Description is an important and useful communication skill. If you were an eyewitness to a car theft, for example, the detective investigating the crime would ask you to describe what you saw. You will also use description in many situations in college and on the job, as the examples in the accompanying box show.

Writers rely on description to present detailed information about people, places, and things and to grasp and sustain their readers' interest. When you write vivid descriptions, you not only make your writing more lively and interesting but also indicate your attitude toward the subject through your choice of words and details.

In the following lively description of a sensory experience of taste, you will feel as if you, too, are eating chilli peppers.

SCENES FROM COLLEGE AND THE WORKPLACE

- For a *chemistry* lab report, you are asked to describe the odor and appearance of a substance made by combining two chemicals.

- In an *art history* class, your instructor asks you to visit a local gallery, choose a particular painting, and describe in a two-page paper the artist's use of line or color.

- As a *nurse* at a local burn treatment center, one of your responsibilities is to record on each patient's chart the overall appearance of and change in second- and third-degree burns.

Eating Chilli Peppers
Jeremy MacClancy

Jeremy MacClancy is an anthropologist and tutor at Oxford University in England who has written several scholarly works in the field of anthropology. This essay is taken from his book Consuming Culture: Why You Eat What You Eat *(1993). As you read the selection, underline or highlight the descriptive words and phrases that convey what it's like to eat chilli peppers.*

How come over half of the world's population have made a powerful chemical irritant the center of their gastronomic lives? How can so many millions stomach chillies?

Biting into a tabasco pepper is like aiming a flame-thrower at your parted lips. There might be little reaction at first, but then the burn starts to grow. A few seconds later the chilli mush in your mouth reaches critical mass and your palate prepares for liftoff. The message spreads. The sweat glands open, your eyes stream, your nose runs, your stomach warms up, your heart accelerates, and your lungs breathe faster. All this is normal. But bite off more than your body can take, and you will be left coughing, sneezing, and spitting. Tears stripe your cheeks, and your mouth belches fire like a dragon celebrating its return to life. Eater beware!

As a general stimulant, chilli is similar to amphetamines — only quicker, cheaper, non-addictive, and beneficial to boot. Employees at the tabasco plant in Louisiana rarely complain of coughs, hay fever, or sinusitis. (Recent evidence, however, suggests that too many chillies can bring on stomach cancer.) Over the centuries, people have used hot peppers as a folk medicine to treat sore throats or inflamed gums, to relieve respiratory distress, and to ease gastritis induced by alcoholism. For aching muscles and tendons, a chilli plaster is more effective than one of mustard, with the added advantage that it does not blister the skin. But people do not eat tabasco, jalapeno, or cayenne peppers because of their pharmacological side-effects. They eat them for the taste — different varieties have different flavors — and for the fire they give off. In other words, they go for the burn.

Eating chillies makes for exciting times: the thrill of anticipation, the extremity of the flames, and then the slow descent back to normality. This is a benign form of masochism, like going to a horror movie, riding a roller coaster, or stepping into a cold bath after a sauna. The body flashes danger signals, but the brain knows the threat is not too great. Aficionados, self-absorbed in their burning passion, know exactly how to pace their whole chilli eating so that the flames are maintained at a steady maximum. Wrenched out of normal routines by the continuing assault on their mouths, they concentrate on the sensation and ignore almost everything else. They play with fire and just ride the burn, like experienced surfers cresting along a wave. For them, without hot peppers, food would lose its zest and their days would seem too dull. A cheap, legal thrill, chilli is the spice of their life.

5   In the rural areas of Mexico, men can turn their chilli habit into a contest of strength by seeing who can stomach the most hot peppers in a set time. This gastronomic test, however, is not used as a way to prove one's machismo, for women can play the game as well. In this context, chillies are a non-sexist form of acquired love for those with strong hearts and fiery passions—a steady source of hot sauce for their lives.

6   The enjoyable sensations of a running nose, crying eyes, and dragon-like mouth belching flames are clearly not for the timorous.

7   More tabasco, anyone?   ■

Characteristics of Descriptive Writing

Successful descriptions offer readers more than just a list of sensory details or a catalog of characteristics. In a good description, the details work together to create a dominant effect or impression. Writers often use comparison to help readers experience what they are writing about.

Description Uses Sensory Details

Sensory details appeal to one or more of the five senses—sight, sound, smell, taste, and touch. For example, in the second paragraph of "Eating Chilli Peppers" (p. 241), MacClancy describes the physical sensations that chilli peppers create. The third paragraph focuses on their druglike effects, and the fourth and fifth paragraphs emphasize their psychological effects. Throughout the essay the writer uses vivid language. Can you almost feel a chilli pepper burning in your mouth? MacClancy achieves this effect by using words that appeal to the senses of sight and taste. By appealing to the senses in your writing, you too can help your readers experience the object, sensation, event, or person you aim to describe.

Sight.   When you describe what something looks like, you help your reader create a mental picture of the subject. In the following excerpt, notice how Loren Eiseley uses visual detail to describe what he comes across in a field.

One day as I cut across the field which at that time extended on one side of our suburban shopping center, I found a giant slug feeding from a funnel of pink ice cream in an abandoned Dixie cup. I could see his eyes telescope and protrude in a kind of dim, uncertain ecstasy as his dark body bunched and elongated in the curve of the cup.

LOREN EISELEY, "The Brown Wasps"

The description allows the reader to imagine the slug eating the ice cream in a way that a bare statement of the facts — "On my way to the mall, I saw a slug in a paper cup" — would not do. Eiseley describes shape ("funnel of pink ice cream"), action ("bunched and elongated"), color ("pink funnel," "dark body"), and size ("giant"). Notice also how Eiseley includes specific details ("suburban shopping center," "Dixie cup") to help readers visualize the scene.

Sound. Sound can also be a powerful descriptive tool. Can you "hear" the engines in the following description?

They were one-cylinder and two-cylinder engines, and some were make-and-break and some were jump-spark, but they all made a sleepy sound across the lake. The one-lungers throbbed and fluttered, and the twin-cylinder ones purred and purred, and that was a quiet sound too. But now the campers all had outboards. In the daytime, in the hot mornings, these motors made a petulant, irritable sound; at night, in the still evening when the afterglow lit the water, they whined about one's ears like mosquitoes.

E. B. WHITE, "Once More to the Lake"

White conveys the sounds of the engines by using active verbs ("throbbed and fluttered," "purred and purred," "whined"), descriptive adjectives ("sleepy," "petulant," "irritable"), and a comparison ("whined about one's ears like mosquitoes").

Writers of description also use *onomatopoeia,* words that approximate the sounds they describe. The words *hiss, whine, spurt,* and *sizzle* are common examples.

Smell. Smells are sometimes difficult to describe, partly because we do not have as many adjectives for smells as we do for sights and sounds. Smell can be an effective descriptive device, however, as shown here.

Driving through farm country at summer sunset provides a cavalcade of smells: manure, cut grass, honeysuckle, spearmint, wheat chaff, scallions, chicory, tar from the macadam road.

DIANE ACKERMAN, *A Natural History of the Senses*

Notice how Ackerman lists nouns that evoke distinct odors and leaves it to the reader to imagine how they smell.

Taste. Words that evoke the sense of taste can make descriptions lively, as in "Eating Chilli Peppers." Consider also this restaurant critic's description of Vietnamese cuisine.

In addition to balancing the primary flavors—the sweet, sour, bitter, salty and peppery tastes whose sensations are, in the ancient Chinese system, directly related to physical and spiritual health—medicinal herbs were used in most dishes. . . . For instance, the orange-red annatto seed is used for its "cooling" effect as well as for the mildly tangy flavor it lends and the orange color it imparts.

MOLLY O'NEILL, "Vietnam's Cuisine: Echoes of Empires"

Notice that O'Neill describes the variety of flavors ("sweet, sour, bitter, salty and peppery") in Vietnamese cuisine.

Touch.   Descriptions of texture, temperature, and weight allow a reader not only to visualize but almost to experience an object or scene. In the excerpt that follows, Annie Dillard describes the experience of holding a Polyphemus moth cocoon.

We passed the cocoon around; it was heavy. As we held it in our hands, the creature within warmed and squirmed. We were delighted, and wrapped it tighter in our fists. The pupa began to jerk violently, in heart-stopping knocks. Who's there? I can still feel those thumps, urgent through a muffling of spun silk and leaf, urgent through the swaddling of many years, against the curve of my palm. We kept passing it around. When it came to me again it was hot as a bun; it jumped half out of my hand. The teacher intervened. She put it, still heaving and banging, in the ubiquitous Mason jar.

ANNIE DILLARD, *Pilgrim at Tinker Creek*

Dillard describes the texture of the cocoon ("a muffling of spun silk and leaf"), its temperature ("hot as a bun"), and its weight ("heavy") to give readers an accurate sense of what it felt like to hold it.

Description Uses Active Verbs and Varied Sentences

Sensory details are often best presented through active, vivid verbs and varied sentences. Look, for instance, at the active verbs in this sentence from paragraph 2 of MacClancy's essay.

The sweat glands *open,* your eyes *stream,* your nose *runs,* your stomach *warms up,* your heart *accelerates,* and your lungs *breathe* faster.

In fact, active verbs are often more effective than adverbs in creating striking and lasting impressions, as the following example demonstrates.

ORIGINAL   The team captain *proudly* accepted the award.

REVISED   The team captain *marched* to the podium, grasped the trophy, and gestured toward his teammates.

For more on varying sentence patterns and using active verbs, see Chapter 7, pp. 177 and 185.   Using varied sentences also contributes to the effective expression of sensory details. Be sure to use different types and patterns of sentences and to vary their lengths. Look again at the second paragraph in MacClancy's essay. Note how he varies his sentences to make the description interesting. Avoid wordy or repetitive sentences, especially those with strings of mediocre adjectives or adverbs (*pretty, really, very*), which tend to detract from the impression you are trying to create.

EXERCISE 9.1

Using **sensory details, active verbs,** and **varied sentences,** describe one of the common objects in the following list or one of your own choosing. Do not name the object in your description. Exchange papers with a classmate. Your reader should be able to guess the item you are describing from the details you provide.

1. A piece of clothing
2. A food item
3. An appliance
4. A machine
5. A computer keyboard

Description Creates a Dominant Impression

An effective description leaves the reader with a **dominant impression** — an overall attitude, mood, or feeling about the subject. The impression may be awe, inspiration, anger, or distaste, for example.

Let's suppose you are writing about an old storage box you found in your parents' attic and that the aspect of the box you want to emphasize (your slant) is *memories of childhood*. Given this slant or angle, you might describe the box in several ways, each of which would convey a different dominant impression.

For more on thesis statements, see Chapter 4, p. 89.

- "A box filled with treasures from my childhood brought back memories of long, sunny afternoons playing in our backyard."
- "Opening the box was like lifting the lid of a time machine, revealing toys and games from another era."
- "When I opened the box, I was eight years old again, fighting over my favorite doll with my twin sister, Erica."

Notice that each example provides a different impression of the contents of the storage box and would require a different type of support. That is, only selected objects from within the box would be relevant to each impression. Note, too, that in all of these examples, the dominant impression is stated directly rather than implied. Many times writers rely on descriptive language to imply a dominant impression.

In "Eating Chilli Peppers," notice how all the details evoke the thrill of eating the peppers for those who love them; as MacClancy says, "they go for the burn." The first two sentences of the essay pose the questions that the remaining paragraphs answer. The answer is the dominant impression: Eating chilli peppers is thrilling. To write an effective description, you need to select details carefully, including only those that contribute to the dominant impression you are trying to create. Notice that MacClancy does not clutter his description by describing the size, shape, texture, or color of chilli peppers. Instead he focuses on their thrilling, fiery hotness and the side effects they cause.

EXERCISE 9.2

Read the following paragraph and cross out details that do not contribute to the dominant impression.

> All morning I had had some vague sense that something untoward was about to happen. I suspected bad news was on its way. As I stepped outside, the heat of the summer sun, unusually oppressive for ten o'clock, seemed to sear right through me. In fact, now that I think about it, everything seemed slightly out of kilter that morning. The car, which had been newly painted the week before, had stalled several times. The flowers in the garden, planted for me by my husband, purchased from a nursery down the road, were drooping. It was as though they were wilting before they even had a chance to grow. Even my two cats, who look like furry puffballs, moved listlessly across the room, ignoring my invitation to play. It was then that I received the phone call from the emergency room telling me about my son's accident.

Description Uses Connotative Language Effectively

As noted in Chapter 7, most words have two levels of meaning—*denotative* and *connotative*. The denotation of a word is its precise dictionary meaning. For instance, the denotation of the word *flag* is "a piece of cloth used as a national emblem." Usually, however, feelings and attitudes are also associated with a word—emotional colorings or shades of meaning. These are the word's connotations. A common connotation of *flag* is patriotism—love and respect for one's country. As you write, be careful about the connotations of the words you choose. Select words that strengthen the dominant impression you are creating.

Description Uses Comparisons

For more on similes, metaphors, and personification, see Chapter 7, p. 190.

When describing a person or an object, you can help your readers by comparing it to something with which they are familiar. Several types of comparison are used in descriptive writing—similes, metaphors, personification, and analogies. In a **simile** the comparison is direct and is introduced by the word *like* or *as*. MacClancy uses a number of telling similes in "Eating Chilli Peppers."

- "Biting into a tabasco pepper is like aiming a flame-thrower at your parted lips."
- Eating chillies is "like going to a horror movie, riding a roller coaster, or stepping into a cold bath after a sauna."

A **metaphor** is indirect, implying the comparison by describing one thing as if it were another. Instead of the similes listed above, MacClancy could have used metaphors to describe the experience of eating chillies.

- Eating chilli peppers is a descent into a fiery hell.
- To eat chilli peppers is to ride the crest of a wave, waiting for the thrill.

Personification is a figure of speech in which an object is given human qualities or characteristics. "The television screen stared back at me" is an example. An **analogy** is an extended comparison in which one subject, often a more familiar one, is used to explain another. Like similes and metaphors, analogies add interest to your writing while making your ideas more real and accessible.

EXERCISE 9.3

Write a paragraph describing a food you enjoy. Focus on one sense, as MacClancy does, or appeal to several senses. If possible draw a comparison using a simile or metaphor.

Description Assumes a Vantage Point

A **vantage point** is the point or position from which you write a description. You can use either a fixed or a moving vantage point. With a *fixed vantage point,* you describe what you see from a particular position. With a *moving vantage point,* you describe your subject from different positions. A fixed vantage point is like a stationary camera trained on a subject from one direction. A moving vantage point is like a hand-held camera that captures the subject from many directions.

In "Eating Chilli Peppers," MacClancy uses a moving vantage point; he first reports sensations within the mouth and then moves on to other body parts. When you use a moving vantage point, be sure to alert your readers when you change positions. MacClancy gives his readers clues that his vantage point is changing. For example, in paragraph 2 he states, "the message spreads" to indicate that he is moving from the palate to sweat glands, eyes, and so forth.

Description Follows a Method of Organization

Effective descriptions must follow a clear method of organization. Three common methods of organization used in descriptive writing are spatial order, chronological order, and most-to-least or least-to-most order.

For more on these methods of organization, see Chapter 5, p. 110.

- When you use spatial order, you describe a subject from top to bottom, from inside to outside, or from near to far away. Or you may start from a central focal point and then describe the objects that surround it. For example, if you are describing a college campus, you might start by describing a building at the center of the campus—the library, perhaps. You would then describe the buildings that are near the library, and conclude by describing anything on the outskirts of the campus.

- Chronological order works well when you need to describe events or changes that occur in objects or places over a period of time. You might use chronological order to describe the changes in a puppy's behavior as it grows or to relate changing patterns of light and shadow as the sun sets.
- You might use least-to-most or most-to-least order to describe the smells in a flower garden or the sounds of an orchestra tuning up for a concert.

Visualizing a Description: A Graphic Organizer

For more on graphic organizers, see Chapter 2, p. 34.

The graphic organizer shown in Figure 9.1 will help you visualize the elements of a description. When you write an essay in which your primary purpose is to describe something, you'll need to follow the standard essay format—title, intro-

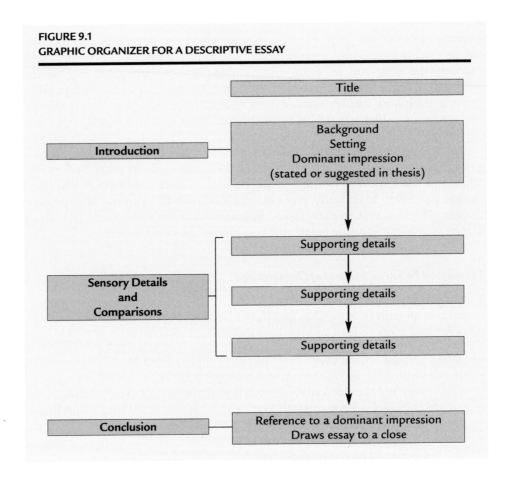

FIGURE 9.1
GRAPHIC ORGANIZER FOR A DESCRIPTIVE ESSAY

Title

Introduction —— Background / Setting / Dominant impression / (stated or suggested in thesis)

Sensory Details and Comparisons —— Supporting details → Supporting details → Supporting details

Conclusion —— Reference to a dominant impression / Draws essay to a close

duction, body, and conclusion—with slight adaptations and adjustments. In a descriptive essay, the introduction provides a context for the description and presents the thesis statement, which states or suggests the dominant impression. The body of the essay presents sensory details that support the dominant impression. The conclusion draws the description to a close and makes a final reference to the dominant impression. It may offer a final detail or make a closing statement.

When you incorporate a description into an essay in which you also use other patterns of development, you will probably need to condense or eliminate one or more of these elements of a description essay.

The following essay, "The Sweat Bath Ritual," is a good example of description. Read the essay and then study the graphic organizer for it in Figure 9.2 (p. 252).

The Sweat Bath Ritual
Mary Brave Bird

Mary Brave Bird, also known as Mary Crow Dog, is a political activist and writer from the Rosebud Reservation in South Dakota. She has written two memoirs, Lakota Woman *(1990) and* Ohitika Woman *(1993), about her life on the reservation and her participation with the American Indian Movement. This essay is taken from* Lakota Woman, *for which she won a National Book Award in 1991. As you read the selection, highlight the sensory details and other details that contribute to the writer's dominant impression.*

Some of our medicine men always say that one must view the world through the eye in one's heart rather than just trust the eyes in one's head. "Look at the real reality beneath the sham realities of things and gadgets," Leonard always tells me. "Look through the eye in your heart. That's the meaning of Indian religion." 1

The eye of my heart was still blind when I joined Leonard to become his wife. I knew little of traditional ways. I had been to a few peyote meetings without really understanding them. I had watched one Sun Dance, and later the Ghost Dance held at Wounded Knee, like a spectator—an emotional spectator, maybe, but no different from white friends watching these dances. They, too, felt emotion. Like myself they did not penetrate through symbolism to the real meaning. I had not yet participated in many ancient rituals of our tribe—the sweat bath, the vision quest, yuwipi, the making of relatives, the soul keeping. I did not even know that these ceremonies 2 were still being performed. There were some rituals I did not even know existed.

3   I had to learn about the sweat bath, because it precedes all sacred ceremonies, and is at the same time a ceremony all by itself. It is probably the oldest of all our rituals because it is connected with the glowing stones, evoking thoughts of Tunka, the rock, our oldest god. Our family's sweat lodge, our oinikaga tipi, is near the river which flows through Crow Dog's land. That is good. Pure, flowing water plays a great part during a sweat. Always at the lodge we can hear the river's voice, the murmur of its waters. Along its banks grows washte wikcemna, a sweet-smelling aromatic herb — Indian perfume.

4   The lodge is made of sixteen willow sticks, tough but resilient and easy to bend. They are formed into a beehive-shaped dome. The sweat lodges vary in size. They can accommodate anywhere from eight to twenty-four people. The bent willow sticks are fastened together with strips of red trade cloth. Sometimes offerings of Bull Durham tobacco are tied to the frame, which is then covered with blankets or a tarp. In the old days buffalo skins were used for the covering, but these are hard to come by now. The floor of the little lodge is covered with sage. In the center is a circular pit to receive the heated rocks. In building a lodge, people should forget old quarrels and have only good thoughts.

5   Outside the lodge, wood is piled up in a certain manner to make the fire in which the rocks will be heated — peta owihankeshni — the "fire without end" which is passed on from generation to generation. After it has blazed for a while, white limestone rocks are placed in its center. These rocks do not crack apart in the heat. They come from the hills. Some of them are covered with a spidery network of green moss. This is supposed by some to represent secret spirit writing.

6   The scooped-out earth from the firepit inside the lodge is formed up into a little path leading from the lodge entrance and ending in a small mound. It represents Unci — Grandmother Earth. A prayer is said when this mound is made. A man is then chosen to take care of the fire, to bring the hot rocks to the lodge, often on a pitchfork, and to handle the entrance flap.

7   In some places men and women sweat together. We do not do this. Among us, men and women do their sweat separately. Those taking part in a sweat strip, and wrapped in their towels, crawl into the little lodge, entering clockwise. In the darkness inside they take their towels off and hunker down naked. I was astounded to see how

many people could be swallowed up by this small, waist-high, igloo-shaped hut. The rocks are then passed into the lodge, one by one. Each stone is touched with the pipe bowl as, resting in the fork of a deer antler, it is put into the center pit. The leader goes in first, sitting down near the entrance on the right side. Opposite him, at the other side of the entrance sits his helper. The leader has near him a pail full of cold, pure water and a ladle. Green cedar is sprinkled over the hot rocks, filling the air with its aromatic odor. Outside the entrance flap is a buffalo-skull altar. Tobacco ties are fastened to its horns. There is also a rack for the pipe to rest on.

Anywhere from twelve to sixty rocks can be used in this cere- 8 mony. The more rocks, the hotter it will be. Once the rocks have been passed into the lodge, the flap is closed. Inside it is dark except for the red glow of the rocks in the pit. Now the purification begins. As sage or cedar is sprinkled on the rocks, the men or women participating catch the sacred smoke with their hands, inhaling it, rubbing it all over their face and body. Then cold water is poured on the rocks. The rising cloud of white steam, "grandfather's breath," fills the lodge. A sweat has four "doors," meaning that the flap is opened four times during the purification to let some cool outside air in, bringing relief to the participants.

Everybody has the privilege to pray or speak of sacred things dur- 9 ing the ceremony. It is important that all take part in the ritual with their hearts, souls, and minds. When women have their sweats, a medicine man runs them—which is all right because it is so dark inside that he cannot see you.

The first time I was inside the oinikaga tipi, the sweat lodge, 10 when water was poured over the rocks and the hot steam got to me, I thought that I could not endure it. The heat was beyond anything I had imagined. I thought I would not be able to breathe because it was like inhaling liquid fire. With my cupped hands I created a slightly cooler space over my eyes and mouth. After a while I noticed that the heat which had hurt me at first became soothing, penetrating to the center of my body, going into my bones, giving me a wonderful feeling. If the heat is more than a person can stand, he or she can call out "Mitakuye oyasin!"—All my relatives!—and the flap will be opened to let the inside cool off a bit. I was proud not to have cried out. After the sweat I really felt newly born. My pores were opened and so was my mind. My body tingled. I felt as if I had never experienced pain. I was deliciously light-headed, elated, drunk with the spirit. Soon I began looking forward to a good sweat. ■

FIGURE 9.2
GRAPHIC ORGANIZER FOR "THE SWEAT BATH RITUAL"

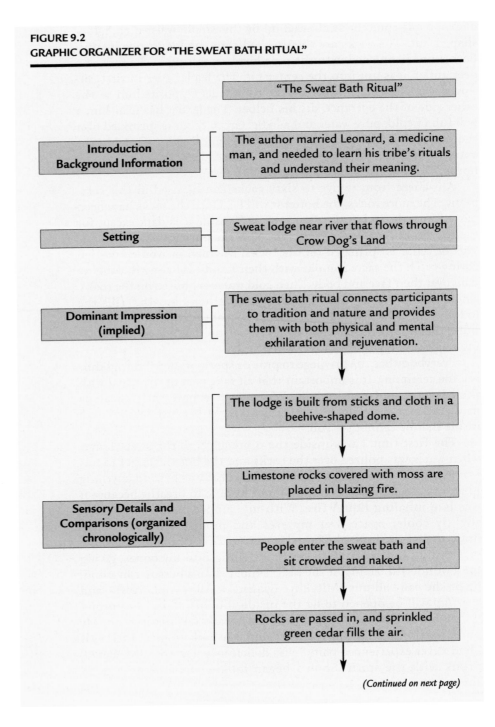

"The Sweat Bath Ritual"

Introduction
Background Information

The author married Leonard, a medicine man, and needed to learn his tribe's rituals and understand their meaning.

Setting

Sweat lodge near river that flows through Crow Dog's Land

Dominant Impression
(implied)

The sweat bath ritual connects participants to tradition and nature and provides them with both physical and mental exhilaration and rejuvenation.

Sensory Details and
Comparisons (organized
chronologically)

The lodge is built from sticks and cloth in a beehive-shaped dome.

Limestone rocks covered with moss are placed in blazing fire.

People enter the sweat bath and sit crowded and naked.

Rocks are passed in, and sprinkled green cedar fills the air.

(Continued on next page)

FIGURE 9.2 (*Continued*)

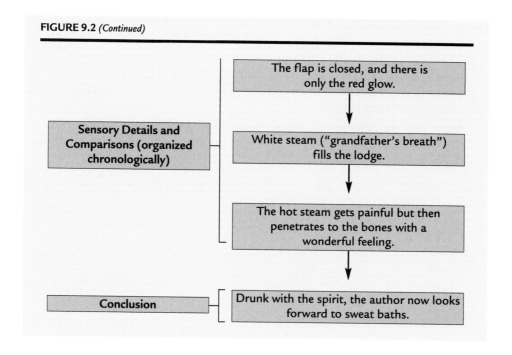

EXERCISE 9.4

After examining each part of MacClancy's "Eating Chilli Peppers" (pp. 241–42), draw a graphic organizer that shows how this essay is constructed.

To draw detailed graphic organizers using a computer, visit www .bedfordstmartins.com /successfulwriting.

INTEGRATING DESCRIPTION INTO AN ESSAY

Sometimes description alone fulfills the purpose of an essay. In most cases, however, you will use descriptions in other types of essays. For instance, in a narrative essay, description plays an important role in helping readers experience events, reconstruct scenes, and visualize action. Similarly, you would use descriptions to explain the causes or effects of a phenomenon, to compare or contrast animal species, and to provide examples of defensive behavior in children (illustration). Writers use description to keep their readers interested in the material. Description, then, is essential to many types of academic and business writing.

Use the following guidelines to build effective descriptions into the essays you write.

1. **Include only relevant details.** Whether you describe an event, a person, or a scene, the sensory details you choose should enhance the reader's understanding of your subject.

2. **Keep the description focused.** Select enough details to make your essential points and dominant impression clear. Readers may become impatient if you include too many details.

3. **Make sure the description fits the essay's tone and point of view.** A personal description, for example, is not appropriate in an essay explaining a technical process.

In "Sunday!" on page 275, Clay Risen incorporates description into a cause-and-effect essay.

A GUIDED WRITING ASSIGNMENT

The following guide will lead you through the process of writing an essay that uses description. You may choose to write a descriptive essay or to employ description within an essay that relies on another pattern of development. Depending on your learning style, you may choose to work through this Guided Writing Assignment in various ways. If you are an abstract learner, for example, you might begin by brainstorming about the general subject. If you are a concrete learner, you might prefer to begin by freewriting specific details. If you are a pragmatic learner, you might start by thinking about how to organize your description.

Learning Style Options

The Assignment

Write a descriptive essay using one of the following topics or one that you think of on your own. Your classmates are your audience.

1. An adult toy, such as a camera, DVD player, computer, golf clubs, cooking gadget, and so on
2. A hobby, sport, or activity, one that you enjoy either engaging in or observing others doing on campus, in your neighborhood, or on television
3. An annoying or obnoxious person or a pleasant, courteous one

As you develop your description, consider using other patterns of development. For example, you might compare and contrast an unfamiliar activity to one you engage in regularly, or you might narrate an incident that reveals a person's positive or negative qualities.

For more on comparison and contrast, see Chapter 12. For more on narration, see Chapter 8.

Generating Ideas and Details

Use the following steps to help you choose a topic and generate ideas.

Choosing a Topic

To write an effective description, you must be familiar with the subject or have the opportunity to observe the subject directly. Never try to describe the campus computer lab without visiting it or the pizza served in the snack bar without tasting it.

For more on conducting observations, see Chapter 19, p. 69.

For more on prewriting strategies, see Chapter 3.

Use the following suggestions to choose an appropriate topic.

1. Once you have selected a topic, use freewriting, mapping, group brainstorming, or another prewriting technique to generate a list of specific objects, activities, or people that fit the assignment.

2. Look over your list of possible topics. Identify the one or two subjects that you find most interesting and that you can describe in detail.

3. Make sure your subject is one you are familiar with or one you can readily observe. You may need to observe the object, activity, or person several times as you work through your essay.

ESSAY IN PROGRESS 1

Using the preceding suggestions, choose a topic to write about for the assignment option you selected on page 255.

Considering Your Purpose, Audience, and Point of View

For more on purpose, audience, and point of view, see Chapter 3.

A descriptive essay may be objective, subjective, or both, depending on the writer's purpose. In an *objective* essay, the writer's purpose is to inform — to present information or communicate ideas without obvious bias or emotion. All writers convey their feelings to some extent, but in an objective essay the writer strives to focus on giving information. For example, a geologist's description of a rock formation written for a scientific journal would be largely objective; its purpose would be to inform readers of the height of the formation, the type of rock it contains, and other characteristics of the subject. Objective essays are generally written in the third person.

In a *subjective* essay, which is often written in the first person, the writer's purpose is to create an emotional response. Whereas an objective essay describes only what the writer observes or experiences, a subjective essay describes both the observation or experience *and* the writer's feelings about it. Therefore, a rock climber's description of a rock formation would focus on the writer's impressions of and reactions to the experience of climbing it, such as the feeling of the smooth rock on a hot day and the exhilaration of reaching the top. But the rock climber's description might also include objective details about the height and composition of the rock formation to help readers see and feel what it's like to climb one.

Once you've chosen a subject and considered your purpose and point of view, think about your audience. For this assignment your audience is your classmates. How familiar are your classmates with your subject? If they are unfamiliar with the subject, you will need to provide a more thorough introduction and a greater amount of detail than if your audience has some knowledge of it.

Choosing an Aspect of Your Subject to Emphasize

Almost any subject you choose will be made up of many more details than you could possibly include in an essay. Start by selecting several possible slants or angles on your subject that you would like to emphasize. If your subject is a person, you might focus on a particular character trait, such as compulsiveness or sense of humor, and then generate a list of descriptive terms that illustrate the trait. To describe an object, you might emphasize its usefulness, value, or beauty.

In descriptive writing, choosing which aspect of your subject to emphasize is similar to narrowing a topic. To come up with an appropriate slant or angle on your subject, list several possible slants and then record details about each one as they come to mind. Choose the one slant that seems most promising and for which you generated plenty of sensory details.

For more on narrowing a topic, see Chapter 3, p. 63.

ESSAY IN PROGRESS 2

Using one or more prewriting techniques, come up with several possible slants on your subject and details to support them. Then choose the slant about which you can write the most effective description.

Collecting Details That Describe Your Subject

Once you've decided on a slant or angle to emphasize, you're ready for the next step—collecting and recording additional sensory details. The following suggestions will help you generate details.

Learning Style Options

For more on generating details, see Chapter 3, p. 69.

For more on prewriting strategies, see Chapter 3.

1. Brainstorm about your subject. Record any sensory details that support the slant or angle you have chosen.
2. Try describing your subject to a friend, concentrating on the slant you have chosen. You may discover that details come quickly during conversation. Make notes on what you said and on your friend's response.
3. Draw a quick sketch of your subject and label the parts. You may find yourself recalling additional details as you draw.
4. Divide a piece of paper or a computer file into five sections. Label the sections *sight, sound, taste, touch,* and *smell.* Consider the following characteristics in developing sensory details.

TABLE 9.1
CHARACTERISTICS TO CONSIDER IN DEVELOPING SENSORY DETAILS

Sight	Sound	Smell	Taste	Touch
Color	Volume	Agreeable/ disagreeable	Pleasant/ unpleasant	Texture
Pattern	Pitch	Strength	Salty, sweet, sour, bitter	Weight
Shape	Quality			Temperature
Size				

Finding Comparisons and Choosing a Vantage Point

Try to think of appropriate comparisons—similes, metaphors, or analogies—for as many details in your list as possible. Jot down your comparisons in the margin next to the relevant details in your list. Don't expect to find a comparison for each detail. Your goal is to discover one or two strong comparisons that you can use in your essay.

Next consider whether to use a fixed or moving vantage point. Think about the aspect of your subject you have chosen to emphasize and how it can best be communicated, from one or several locations. Ask yourself the following questions.

1. What vantage point(s) will provide the most useful information?
2. From which vantage point(s) can I provide the most revealing or striking details?

ESSAY IN PROGRESS 3

Use one or more of the preceding suggestions to develop details that support the aspect or slant of your subject that you are emphasizing. Then find comparisons and decide on a vantage point.

Evaluating Your Details

Evaluate the details you have collected to determine which ones you can use in your essay. Begin by rereading all of your notes with a critical eye. Highlight vivid, concrete details that will create pictures in your reader's mind. Eliminate vague details as well as those that do not support your slant on the subject. If you are working on a computer, highlight usable ideas by making them bold or moving them to a separate page or document for easy access when drafting.

> ### TRYING OUT YOUR IDEAS ON OTHERS
> Working in a group of two or three students, discuss your ideas and details for this chapter's assignment. Each writer should explain his or her slant on the subject and provide a list of the details collected for the subject. Then as a group evaluate the writer's details and suggest improvements.

ESSAY IN PROGRESS 4

Use your notes and the comments of your classmates to evaluate the details you have collected so far. Omit irrelevant and vague details and add more vivid and concrete details if they are needed.

Creating a Dominant Impression

As noted earlier, think of the dominant impression as a thesis that conveys your main point and holds the rest of your essay together. The dominant impression also creates a mood or feeling about the subject, which all other details in your essay explain or support.

The dominant impression you decide on should be the one about which you feel most knowledgeable and confident. It should also appeal to your audience, offer an unusual perspective, and provide new insights on your subject. Finally, keep in mind that you may need to do additional prewriting to gather support for your dominant impression. This step is similar to collecting evidence for a thesis (see Chapter 4), except the "evidence" for a descriptive essay consists of sensory details. Therefore, before you begin drafting your essay, check to see if you have enough sensory details to support your dominant impression.

ESSAY IN PROGRESS 5

Using the preceding guidelines, select the dominant impression you want to convey about your subject and do additional prewriting, if necessary, to gather enough details to support it.

Organizing and Drafting

For more on drafting an essay, see Chapter 5.

Once you are satisfied with your dominant impression and your support for it, you are ready to organize your ideas and draft your essay.

Choosing a Method of Organization

Select the method of organization that will best support your dominant impression. For example, if you have chosen to focus on a person's slovenly appearance, then a spatial (top to bottom, left to right) organization may be effective. If you are describing a scary visit to a wildlife preserve, then chronological order would be a useful method of organization. A most-to-least or least-to-most arrangement might work best for a description of the symptoms of pneumonia. Also consider organizing your details by the five senses. For instance, to describe a chocolate-chip cookie, you could give details about how it looks, how it smells, how it tastes, and how it feels in your mouth.

If you are working on a computer, use your word-processing program's cut-and-paste function to try different methods of organization.

For a list of transitions, see Chapter 5, p. 129.

Regardless of which method you choose for organizing your details, be sure to connect your ideas and guide your reader with transitional words and phrases.

Drafting the Description

For more on writing effective paragraphs, including introductions and conclusions, see Chapter 5.

As you draft your essay, remember that all of your details must support your dominant impression. Other details, no matter how interesting or important they may seem, should not be included. For example, if you are describing the way apes in a zoo imitate one another and humans, only details about how the apes mimic people and other apes should be included. Other details, such as the condition of the apes' environment and types of animals nearby, do not belong in the essay. Be careful as well about the *number* of details you include. Too many details will tire your readers, but an insufficient number will leave your readers unconvinced of your main point. Select striking sensory details that make your point effectively; leave out details that tell the reader little or nothing.

Try also to include one or two telling metaphors or similes. If you cannot think of any, however, don't stretch to construct them. Effective comparisons usually come to mind as you examine your subject. Contrived comparisons will only lessen the impact of your essay.

As you write your description, remember that the sensory language you use should enable your readers to re-create the person, object, or scene in their minds. Keep the following three guidelines in mind as you write.

1. Create images that appeal to the five senses. As noted earlier, your descriptions should appeal to one or more of the senses. See pages 242–44 for examples of ways to engage each of the five senses.

2. Avoid vague, general descriptions. Use specific, not vague, language to describe your subject. Notice the differences between the following descriptions.

VAGUE   The pizza was cheaply prepared.

CONCRETE   The supposedly "large" pizza was miniature, with a nearly imperceptible layer of sauce, a light dusting of cheese, a few paper-thin slices of pepperoni, and one or two stray mushroom slices.

Vivid descriptions hold your readers' interest and give them a more complete picture of your subject. For example, notice how the list below becomes increasingly more concrete.

Animal → dog → golden retriever → male golden retriever → six-month-old male golden retriever puppy → Ivan, my six-month-old male golden retriever puppy

You can create a similar progression of descriptive words for any person, object, or place that you want to describe.

3. Use figures of speech and analogies effectively. Figures of speech (similes, metaphors) and analogies create memorable images that enliven your writing and capture your readers' attention. Here are some tips for using figurative language in your writing.

- Choose fresh, surprising images. Avoid overused clichés such as *cold as ice* and *it's a hop, skip, and a jump away.*

- Make sure the similarity between the two items being compared is apparent. If you write *"Peter* looked like an *unpeeled tangerine,"* your reader will not be able to guess what characteristics Peter shares with the tangerine. "Peter's *skin* was as dimpled as a *tangerine peel"* gives the reader a clearer idea of what Peter looks like.

- Don't mix or combine figures of speech. Such expressions, called **mixed metaphors,** are confusing and often unintentionally humorous. For example, the following sentence mixes images of a hawk and a wolf.

The fighter jet was a hawk soaring into the clouds, growling as it sought its prey.

ESSAY IN PROGRESS 6

Draft your essay. Use the preceding suggestions to organize your details and support your dominant impression. Even if your essay is primarily descriptive, consider incorporating a narrative, an illustration, or a comparison (or another pattern of development) to strengthen the dominant impression.

Analyzing and Revising

If possible, set your draft aside for a day or two before rereading and revising it. As you reread your draft, focus on its overall effectiveness, not on grammar and mechanics. To analyze your draft, use one or more of the following strategies.

Learning Style Options

1. Reread your paper aloud or ask a friend to do so as you listen. You may "hear" parts that seem contrived or skimpy or notice descriptions that do not work.
2. Ask a classmate to read your draft and describe the dominant impression, comparing his or her version to the one you intended. Note ideas that your reader overlooked or misinterpreted.
3. Write an outline or draw a graphic organizer (using the format shown on p. 248), or update the outline or graphic organizer you prepared earlier. Look for ideas that do not seem to fit or that lack supporting details and for places where your organization needs tightening.

For more on the benefits of peer review, see Chapter 6, p. 158.

Use Figure 9.3 to help you discover the strengths and weaknesses of your descriptive essay. You might also ask a classmate to review your essay using the questions in the flowchart. For each answer that refers you to the right column of the chart, ask your reviewer to explain why he or she answered in that way.

ESSAY IN PROGRESS 7

Using Figure 9.3 as a guide, as well as suggestions made by your classmates, revise your essay.

Editing and Proofreading

For more on keeping an error log, see Chapter 7, p. 193.

The last step is to check your revised essay for errors in grammar, spelling, punctuation, and mechanics. Be sure to look for the types of errors you tend to make. (Refer to your error log.)

FIGURE 9.3
FLOWCHART FOR REVISING A DESCRIPTIVE ESSAY

Questions	Revision Strategies
1. Without looking at your essay, *write* a sentence that states the dominant impression your essay is to convey. Next, highlight the sentences in your essay that express the *dominant impression*. Compare the two statements. Are they similar?	• Reread your essay. Make a list of the different impressions it conveys. • Choose one impression that you have the most to say about, and brainstorm to develop additional details that support it.

No

Yes

| 2. Place a checkmark ✔ by each sensory detail. Does each detail support your *dominant impression?* Are your connotations appropriate? | • Eliminate irrelevant sensory details.
• For any words with inappropriate connotations, substitute words that better support your dominant impression. |

No

Yes

| 3. Review the sensory details you have ✔ checkmarked. Have you used vivid language? Have you included enough to help your reader visualize the topic? | • Brainstorm to discover additional sensory details.
• Replace passive verbs with active ones. Vary your sentences. |

No

Yes

| 4. Place [brackets] around each comparison—simile, metaphor, and analogy. Is each fresh and effective? | • Look for and eliminate clichés.
• Brainstorm to find fresh comparisons.
• Instead of writing, try speaking to a friend. |

No

Yes

(Continued on next page)

FIGURE 9.3 *(Continued)*

Questions	Revision Strategies
5. *Write* a sentence describing the point of view that you used. Does it give the clearest possible view of your subject? **No →**	• Consider other points of view. Would these make your essay more interesting? • If your essay seems too busy or unfocused, consider switching to a different point of view.

Yes ↓

Questions	Revision Strategies
6. In the margin next to each paragraph, *write* the specific part of the description on which it focuses. Is each paragraph well developed and focused on a separate part of the description? **No →**	• Consider combining closely related paragraphs. • Split paragraphs that cover more than one part of the description.

Yes ↓

Questions	Revision Strategies
7. *Write* a brief outline depicting how you have organized your details. Is it clear from your essay how the details are organized? **No →**	• Arrange your details using a different order — spatial, chronological, or most-to-least or least-to-most order. • Experiment with several arrangements to see which works best. • Add transitions where necessary to connect your ideas.

Yes ↓

Questions	Revision Strategies
8. Underline the topic sentence of each paragraph. Compare the sensory details (✔) to the topic sentence. Does the topic sentence make clear what is being described? **No →**	• Revise so that each paragraph has a topic sentence and supporting details.

Yes ↓

(Continued on next page)

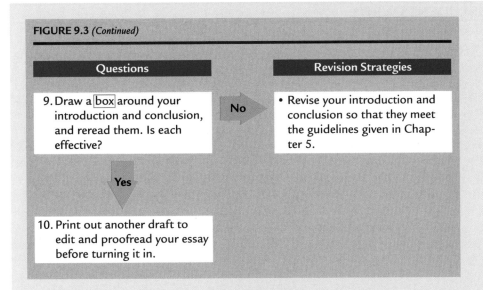

FIGURE 9.3 *(Continued)*

For descriptive writing, pay particular attention to the punctuation of adjectives. Keep the following rules in mind.

1. Use a comma between coordinate adjectives that are not joined by *and*.

   ▶ Singh was a confident, skilled pianist.

The order of coordinate adjectives can be scrambled (*skilled, confident pianist* or *confident, skilled pianist*).

2. Do not use commas between cumulative adjectives.

   ▶ *Two frightened brown* eyes peered at us from under the sofa.

You would not write *frightened two brown eyes*.

3. Use a hyphen to connect two words that work together as an adjective before a noun. Here are a few examples.

   ▶ *well-used* book

   ▶ *perfect-fitting* shoes

   ▶ *foil-wrapped* pizza

ESSAY IN PROGRESS 8

Edit and proofread your essay, paying particular attention to the use and punctuation of adjectives and to the errors listed in your error log.

STUDENTS WRITE

Maria Rodriguez, a twenty-five-year-old returning student, wrote the following essay in response to an assignment for a writing class. She was asked to describe a rewarding or frustrating experience. As you read, highlight words, phrases, and sentences that have sensory appeal and that help you see and hear what the writer experienced.

Health Clubs: Only for the Beautiful and the Fit

Maria Rodriguez

1   If you are like the average sedentary adult who enjoys a fair amount of junk food, who is slightly but not noticeably overweight, and whose exercise threshold is such that 15 minutes on the stationary bicycle at level zero leaves you wondering whether you should dial 911, do not join a health club to get physically fit. You will feel like a failure before you have begun.

2   Going to the gym where my first aerobics class was held was like being thrown into a glitzy, overdecorated, migraine-inducing discotheque with a bunch of adult-sized cheerleaders, each of whom had a cute name like "Mimi" or "Didi" or "Gigi." Little did I know when I put on my tattered gray sweats and my discount sneakers that I would be expected to conform to a rigid dress code: a spandex outfit with a matching headband. The "beautiful people," who arrived for class already physically fit, with hair sprayed and makeup intact, looked at me as though I had just landed from Jupiter. Pretending not to notice their haughty stares, I decided to participate actively in the class. "Why yes, this could be fun," I thought, and it might have been, too, except that everyone was doing some sort of complicated dance that involved simultaneously jumping, turning, counting, and applauding--all to extremely loud-pitched, fast-paced, ear-aching music. Most disturbingly, they were doing this

dance gleefully, as if they enjoyed it. And while I know that it shouldn't have, all this cheerful jumping and happy clapping really got on my normally inactive nerves.

Feeling defeated both in appearance and performance, 3 I decided to leave the aerobics class and head for the weight room. Now, if you have never been to a weight room, the one piece of information you need to know before you go is that these people, mostly men with huge, hard muscles, take weight lifting very seriously. They grunt and groan and gyrate while lifting metal bars weighing several hundred pounds above their heads. Then they bring this heavy metal object down to their slim, oil-slicked waists and then down to their feet. Finally, they drop the metal on the ground with a thunderous thud and a gut-wrenching moan. They look up at themselves in a mirror and stare purposefully at their overdeveloped bodies with a sober "I look very healthy" look. It's not clear to me why the mirror is there in the first place, nor why they would want to look at themselves with pained facial expressions, oozing oil all over a shiny metal dumbbell and contemplating how many more times they should repeat this bizarre ritual. However, unlike the aerobics enthusiasts, who at least give the impression of being jolly, these weight-lifting zealots are evidently an unhappy lot--so much so that when I attempted to have a conversation with one of them, he growled.

Having lost all hope of ever fitting in with the 4 somber weight-lifting crowd, I chose to walk on the track. While I walked, I overheard parts of other walk- ers' conversations. These were not particularly interest- ing conversations, but I hoped they might be at least somewhat instructive on the subject of fitness. Although I listened intently, I had difficulty following the conversations because they were peppered with health- club jargon completely foreign to the unfit and not-so- beautiful. Words like "abs" and "pecs" kept creeping into the conversation. I kept hearing the terms "carbs" and "crunches," the latter term evidently denoting some sort of exercise as well.

5   Later, in the dressing room, it occurred to me that walking in the mall is cheaper than a fitness center, and it doesn't require wearing spandex, being maniacally cheerful, acting morosely serious, or learning a new language. In fact, mall walking is the perfect solution to my fitting-in-while-getting-fit problem. Also, there is an additional advantage to walking the mall. I will be forced to pass a candy shop while walking. I can get good nutrition and exercise at the same time. After all, I don't want to get totally fit; then I would have to join a health club.

Analyzing the Essay

1. Describe the writer's dominant impression about health clubs. Is it stated explicitly or implied?

2. To which senses does the writer appeal? Cite several examples from the essay.

3. Which descriptions do you find particularly strong? What makes them effective? Which, if any, are weak, and how can they be improved?

4. In addition to description, what other patterns of development does the writer use? How do these patterns make the description more effective?

Reacting to the Essay: Discussion and Journal Writing

1. Explain why you agree or disagree with the writer's attitude toward aerobics and weight lifting.

2. Body image is important to many people who belong to health clubs. How important is body image to Rodriguez? How important is it to your friends and family?

3. Exercise has grown in popularity in recent years. To what factors do you attribute its increased popularity? Write an entry about these factors in your journal.

READING A DESCRIPTION

The following section provides advice for reading descriptive essays. Two model essays illustrate the characteristics of description covered in this chapter and provide opportunities to examine, analyze, and react to the writer's ideas. The second essay uses a description as part of a cause-and-effect essay.

WORKING WITH TEXT: READING DESCRIPTIVE ESSAYS

When you read descriptive essays, you are more concerned with impressions and images than you are with the logical progression of ideas. To get the full benefit of descriptive writing, you need to connect what you are reading to your own senses of sight, sound, smell, touch, and taste. Here are some guidelines for reading descriptive essays.

For more on reading strategies, see Chapter 2.

What to Look For, Highlight, and Annotate

1. Plan on reading the essay more than once. Read it a first time to get a general sense of what's going on in the essay. Then reread it, this time paying attention to sensory details.
2. Be alert for the dominant impression as you read. If it is not directly stated, ask yourself this question: "How does the author want me to feel about the subject?" Your answer will be the dominant impression the writer wants to convey.
3. Highlight particularly striking details and images that you may want to refer to again or that may help you analyze the essay's effectiveness.
4. Identify the author's vantage point and method of organization.
5. Analyze each paragraph and decide how it contributes to the dominant impression. In a marginal annotation, summarize your analysis.
6. Observe how the author uses language to achieve his or her effect; notice types of images, sentence structure, and placement of adjectives and adverbs.
7. Study the introduction and conclusion. What is the purpose of each?
8. Evaluate the title. What meaning does it contribute to the essay?
9. Use marginal annotations or your journal to record the thoughts and feelings the essay evokes in you. Try to answer these questions: "What did I feel as I read? How did I respond? What feelings was I left with after reading the essay?"

How to Find Ideas to Write About

For more on discovering ideas for a response paper, see Chapter 2.

Since you may be asked to write a response to a descriptive essay, keep an eye out for ideas to write about as you read. Try to think of parallel situations that evoked similar images and feelings in you. For example, for an essay describing the peace and serenity the author experienced while sitting beside a remote lake in a forest, try to think of situations in which you felt peace and serenity or your feelings when you visited a national park or wilderness area. Perhaps you had negative feelings, such as anxiety about being in a remote spot. Such negative feelings may be worth exploring as well.

THINKING CRITICALLY ABOUT DESCRIPTION

Words are powerful. They can create lasting impressions, shape attitudes, and evoke responses. The words a writer chooses to describe a subject, then, can largely determine how readers view and respond to that subject. For example, suppose you want to describe a person's physical appearance. You can make the person seem attractive and appealing or ugly and repellent, depending on the details you choose and the meanings of the words you select.

APPEALING   The stranger had an impish, childlike grin, a smooth complexion with high cheekbones, and strong yet gentle hands.

REPELLENT   The stranger had limp blond hair, cold vacant eyes, and teeth stained by tobacco.

Writers use details and word connotations to shape their essays and affect their readers' response. Use the following questions to think critically about the descriptions you read.

What Details Does the Writer Omit?

As you read an essay, ask yourself: "What hasn't the writer told me?" or "What else would I like to know about the subject?" As you have seen, writers often omit details because they are not relevant; they may also omit details that contradict the dominant impression they intend to convey.

To be sure you are getting a complete and fairly objective picture of a subject, consult more than one source of information. You have probably noticed that each television news program you watch usually has a slightly different slant on a news event; each offers different details or film footage. Once you view several versions of the same event, you eventually form your own impression of it by combining and synthesizing the various reports. Often, you must do the same thing when reading descriptions. Pull together information from several sources and form your own impression.

How Does the Writer Use Connotative Language?

The sensory details writers choose often reveal their feelings and attitudes toward the subject and convey the dominant impression. If a writer describes a car as "fast and sleek," the wording suggests approval, whereas if the writer describes it as "bold and glitzy," the wording suggests a less favorable attitude.

As you read, pay particular attention to connotations; they are often used intentionally to create a particular emotional response. Get in the habit of highlighting words with strong connotations or annotating them in the margin. As you write, you can and should use connotative language. Recognize, however, that you are nudging your reader in a particular direction by doing so.

DESCRIPTIVE ESSAY

As you read the following essay by Amy Tan, consider how she uses the characteristics of description discussed in this chapter.

Inferior Decorating
Amy Tan

Amy Tan is based in San Francisco and New York and was born into a traditional Chinese home in Oakland, California. Her writing has explored assimilation, culture clashes, and generation gaps. She is best known for her novels, such as The Joy Luck Club *(1989), which was made into a movie in 1993;* The Kitchen God's Wife *(1991); and* The Bonesetter's Daughter *(2000). She has also written two children's books—* The Chinese Siamese Cat *(1994) and* The Moon Lady *(1992). The following reading is taken from her most recent essay collection,* The Opposite of Fate *(2003). As you read, highlight the details that help you visualize Tan's home.*

I am not overly superstitious. But then again, I am not one to take unnecessary chances. 1

Why risk displeasing the gods (or God, the Buddha, and the muses) when a subtle sprinkling of good-luck charms and a few tasteful signs of respect can make heaven smile down on earth? (Speaking of the elevated perspective of holy ones: My mother told me I should hang my inscribed Chinese banners *upside down* so that 2 those on high can read them more easily. Nothing more annoying to deities than to have to cock their sacred heads to read a mere mortal's plea suspended hundreds of miles below.)

3   If you were to enter my home, you probably wouldn't see any obvious signs that I place my life in the hands of divine intervention, or, for that matter, in the hands of an interior decorator. The first impression is, I hope, one of a cozy abode: unpretentious and intelligently appointed to accommodate the fur balls of a cat. But if you stayed for tea, you might begin to notice what my husband refers to as "kitsch," or "clutter," or sometimes "Amy's junk."

4   These are my good-luck charms, and they come mostly in the form of dragons, fish, strategically placed mirrors, and heaven forgive me, New Age crystals. (As to the cultural deviation of the last, there's nothing mystical about their inclusion. I just happen to agree with what my niece Melissa once told me — that it warms the heart to see "Mr. Sun playing with Mrs. Glass.")

5   In the foyer at the top of the stairs is a rosewood chair, a bit of Chinese gothic whimsy from the 1920s. The arch of the back and the hand rests are carved with dragons, their piercing inlaid-ivory eyes guarding over its owner, me, another dragon. Next to the chair is a bamboo-and-wire birdcage. This houses only lucky turquoise and copper Chinese coins. Meanwhile, the birds (plastic and made in Taiwan), sit outside the cage and chirp warnings whenever the cage of money is disturbed. On a carved stand opposite the birdcage sits a porcelain vase big enough for me to climb into. If you were to look inside the vase, you'd see painted there a lionhead goldfish swimming about, which, along with an electronic alarm system, is excellent for chasing off devilish spirits and thieves. Above the vase is a mirror with a nineteenth-century dragon carving as its frame.

6   A word about mirrors: They can supposedly repel bad luck or attract good. I'm not sure about which laws of physics apply. All I know is that I once had a neighbor whose nightly hammering nearly drove my husband and me up the wall; after we aimed a curved mirror in his direction — *total silence*. In my current home, the dragon mirror is directed at a nice neighbor who has a surfeit of parking spaces in his garage. I have no garage, but I'm usually lucky enough to find a space in front of my door.

7   My study is where I've applied most of my decorating skills. Scattered about are chimes, banners with lucky sayings, and wooden fish — as well as a stuffed piranha for fighting off heavy-duty distractions from writing.

8   And the location of my study is particularly auspicious, according to Chinese principles of *feng shui* ("wind and water"). Its three bay

windows overlook neighborhood rooftops and face north toward water and mountains. In terms of San Francisco real estate principles, it means I have a knockout view of the Presidio's eucalyptus forest, the Golden Gate Bridge, San Francisco Bay, Angel Island, the Marin Headlands, and Tiburon. But here's where the Chinese gods and literary muses come into conflict; the muses have decreed that I hang shades in front of the view, the better to concentrate on the computer screen, rather than on sailboats, mating pigeons, and cable TV repair people shimmying across the slanted roofs.

While I'm on the subject of computer screens, some years ago, while writing my first book, I stuck a Dymo-tape message across the top of my monitor that read: "Call Your Guardian Angel." This was my reminder to think about my sources of inspiration. One day my mother saw the reminder, sat down at my desk, and proceeded to have a "chat" with my computer, thinking that this was where her mother, whom she considered my muse, now resided in motherboard sartorial splendor. Well, just in case a hundred-year-old spirit really is my muse, I've placed three bamboo calligraphy brushes below the monitor, as well as copper clappers from Tibet.

By far my best and favorite lucky charm sits in a corner of my office. It, or rather *she*, is an exquisitely painted Chinese porcelain statue about twelve inches tall. I've grown up seeing statues in Chinese restaurants and stores. They're usually kept in miniature temples and given offerings of tea and oranges. Shopowners tend to pick a god or goddess who corresponds to the kind of luck they wish to have flowing through their doors, say the God of Money for a constantly ringing cash register, or the God of War for aggressive business deals.

I chose an unnamed goddess while writing my then untitled second book. I didn't think it was good manners to ask her for anything as crass as good reviews and placement on bestseller lists. And anyway, if she was anything like my mother, my goddess had never even heard of the *New York Times*. In the end, I asked only that I be able to write the best book I could, and that no matter what happened to it, I would have no regrets, no sorrows. I called my statue Lady Sorrowfree and titled the last chapter after her. I titled the book *The Kitchen God's Wife*, which was how she was known, as the wronged spouse of a wandering husband. I gave her offerings of airline mini-bottles of Jack Daniel's.

Do these things really work? All I know is this: I have been incredibly lucky these past few years. What I may lack in terms of sense of style, I more than make up for by giving myself a sense of luck.

And if my Chinese luck runs out, not to worry. I have the standard American charms as well: insurance and lawyers.   ∎

MAKING CONNECTIONS: Tradition and Culture

Both "The Sweat Bath Ritual" (pp. 249–51) and "Inferior Decorating" (pp. 271–73) describe cultural traditions and reveal the importance of these traditions to the authors.

Analyzing the Readings

1. What does each author assume her audience understands about the culture she is writing about? How does each use sensory details to explain her culture?
2. Explain each author's attitude toward her cultural traditions and the way she integrates them into her modern lifestyle. What details in each essay make the author's attitude apparent?

Essay Idea

Write an essay in which you describe a cultural or family tradition other than your own. For example, you could describe a religious holiday or a vegetarian's Thanksgiving. What aspects of that tradition are similar to your own? What aspects make it different?

Examining the Reading

1. What do we learn about Tan's living space? What details about her home does Tan omit that you think would be interesting or revealing?
2. Why does the author have good-luck symbols in her home?
3. How does Tan regard her talent for writing?
4. What does the author mean in the last paragraph when she states that she has "insurance and lawyers?"
5. Explain the meaning of each of the following words as used in the reading: *kitsch* (para. 3), *deviation* (4), *surfeit* (6), *auspicious* (8), and *sartorial* (9). Refer to your dictionary as needed.

Analyzing the Reading

1. What dominant impression does Tan convey in this essay? Is it stated or implied? Explain your answers.
2. What is the significance of this essay's title?
3. Evaluate Tan's use of detail. What types of sensory detail does she use, and how do these details contribute to the overall meaning of the essay?

4. How does Tan use humor in her writing? Why is this particularly appropriate in this work?

5. Highlight several examples of how Tan uses connotative language to create a favorable impression of her home.

Reacting to the Reading: Discussion and Journal Writing

1. Discuss the process of creative pursuits. Where do people find inspiration to write, draw, paint, compose, and so forth?

2. Do you own good-luck charms or perform particular actions to bring good luck? If so, discuss their effectiveness.

3. Write a journal entry explaining whether you hold superstitions.

DESCRIPTION COMBINED WITH OTHER PATTERNS

As you read the following essay by Clay Risen, notice how he uses description within an essay that traces a cause-and-effect relationship.

Sunday!
Clay Risen

Clay Risen is based in Washington, D.C., and has been an assistant editor at the New Republic *since January 2003. He is also an associate editor of* Flak Magazine, *an online periodical devoted to critical reviews of art and media. His work has appeared in many publications, including the* American Prospect, Foreign Policy, Metropolis, *the* New York Times, *and the* New York Observer. *The following essay appeared in the* Atlantic Monthly *in 2004. As you read, highlight the descriptions you find most striking, and note what they add to the essay.*

Above everything else, a Monster Truck rally is about the smell. Long before Bigfoot and Grave Digger hit the arena floor, the scent of racing fuel seeps up through the stands. Suffused with sulfur, it has an odor akin to rotten eggs — though die-hard fans will tell you it's better than roses. By the end of the rally, exhaust fumes hover over the crowds like cumulus clouds, giving everyone a slight headache. 1

Then there's the overpowering, high-pitched noise of the trucks themselves. Imagine a dental drill held up to a microphone. Next, add a tuba for counterpoint. Now imagine that sound in stereo, as 2 two or more trucks often appear at the same time. If you forgot to bring earplugs, you could lose your hearing. The piercing roar sends an inexplicable twinge of fear through your lower chest; sitting there, it's easy to understand why dive-bomber pilots used to attach whistles to their planes' wings. Suddenly, you're not in a sports arena, but along the Western Front. Welcome to America, where thousands of people pay $20 to get high on fuel exhaust and tempt shell shock, all to watch outsized trucks demolish late-model sedans.

3   I grew up in Nashville, and practically every other month one of several itinerant Monster Truck tours would invade our local fairgrounds. It was, for a still-slumbering town like Nashville circa 1987, a big deal. But, for some reason, despite the incessant Saturday-morning ads reminding me that on *Sunday! Sunday! Sunday!* my city would be overrun by the likes of Black Stallion, Reptoid, and Godzilla, I never made it to a rally. So, when a friend called recently to tell me the Monster Jam Series 2004 was coming to Baltimore's 1st Mariner Arena and asked if I wanted to go, I didn't think twice.

4   At a typical rally, eight trucks will compete in two events. At our rally, this meant a sort of long jump followed by a "freestyle," in which trucks received points for how creatively they could destroy a pile of cars. That night, the trucks included Little Tiger, Eradicator, and Grave Digger, the reigning king of the Monster Truck world and the center of its marketing offensive. (For an extra $20, fans could buy plastic boomerangs complete with Grave Digger "flame stripes.") An emcee gave a running profile of each truck—where it was built, which rallies it had won. (As in horseracing, the vehicles far outshine their drivers, who come across as little more than appendages to the machines that carry them to victory.) There's not much precision to the competition—it was never clear to me, for instance, whether the long jump was judged by hang time or distance or height. But, then, a Monster Truck rally isn't really a competition. It's a celebration. It's pure fantasy, the annihilation of the everyday—in this case, old Fords and Chevys—by overpowering technology.

5   The friend who invited me, John, is a political science graduate student at Johns Hopkins and an Irish national. Which means that, like many Europeans living in the United States, he is also an anthropologist of Americana. He has seen the world's largest ball of twine, and he has eaten turducken.[1] He has made the pilgrimage to Graceland. But, until recently, he'd yet to attend a Monster Truck rally. Along with us came two German exchange students from John's pro-

---

[1] A boneless chicken stuffed inside a boneless duck stuffed inside a boneless turkey.

gram who, like him, had seen Monster Trucks on cable television as children and were eager to experience the real thing.

They loved it. They loved it for the smells and the noise and the destruction. They loved it for the supersized nature of everything in the arena, from the two-pint cups of beer to the overweight fans to the tons of dirt that had been spread over the arena floor, which the trucks kicked up in mighty sprays each time they jumped a ramp. They loved the oddly sexual undertones of it all, like the emcee's repeated promise that the trucks could "go full throttle all night long." They loved it for the pro-wrestling faux-dramas that the pro-moters inserted between events — such as an ongoing tête-à-tête between the emcee and "Hot Rod," an impish redneck who rode around the arena in a garishly painted pint-sized truck of his own. But, above all else, they loved it for what it said to them about Amer-ica. The rally was concentrated red state, the kind of experience you can't get from grad-student seminars or Ph.D. dissertations. "Mon-ster Truck rallies," John told me later, "account for a thousandth of a percent of what Europeans get of American culture, yet I think we had a suspicion that this is where America's heart is, that these are the Americans who count, who vote, and on whose behalf the coun-try is directed." 6

The rally, he said, was about waste — and waste of a sort that only Americans could conceive of. The narrow version of the American Dream is no longer unique to America: You can live in the suburbs and eat at McDonald's not only in Dublin or Berlin, but in Mumbai or Guangzhou. But the larger promise of America — that there is so much of everything that we can spend it and waste it and destroy it for our own amusement — is still alien to most of the world. This is particularly true in Europe, where the ups and downs of the twenti-eth century taught that stability, prudence, and conservation are to be valued above all. No wonder my friends loved it. 7

That night in Baltimore was an exercise in what the rest of the world would likely deem a parody of this country's excessiveness. And yet it seemed, as we left the arena, that the crowd had taken in everything they saw without a single grain of salt. Which didn't mean they thought a real competition had just taken place — far from it. Rather, they took it in because, like John and Co., they loved what the Monster Trucks told them about America. But, in their case, it com-municated not excess, but strength, transmitted in its most tactile, overpowering form. Maybe they were just high on exhaust fumes, but it seemed that for them — and millions of other Monster Truck fans — as long as Grave Digger reigns supreme, America would be all right. ■ 8

Examining the Reading

1. Explain Americans' attraction to and fascination with monster trucks.

2. How do non-Americans perceive the monster truck rally?

3. Why is Risen optimistic about America?

4. What details about the truck rally did the author not present but might provide a different impression of the event?

5. Explain the meaning of each of the following words as used in the reading: *suffused* (para. 1), *itinerant* (3), *appendages* (4), *annihilation* (4), and *prudence* (7). Refer to your dictionary as needed.

Analyzing the Reading

1. Express the essay's dominant impression in your own words.

2. Highlight examples of particularly effective sensory details. How do these contribute to the essay?

3. Evaluate the placement of the thesis statement at the end of the essay. How would the essay be changed if the thesis were placed at the beginning?

4. Highlight several examples of connotative language that create a positive impression of the event.

5. What patterns other than description does Risen use in the essay? What do they contribute to the essay?

Reacting to the Reading: Discussion and Journal Writing

1. The monster truck rally can be described as a spectacle. What other spectacles do Americans enjoy?

2. Do you agree that Americans are wasteful and excessive? Give examples to support your answer.

3. Write a journal entry about a recent public event you attended. Create a dominant impression and describe the event's appeal.

APPLYING YOUR SKILLS: ADDITIONAL ESSAY ASSIGNMENTS

For more on locating and documenting sources, see Part 5.

Write a descriptive essay on one of the following topics, using what you learned about description in this chapter. Depending on the topic you choose, you may need to conduct library or Internet research.

To Express Your Ideas

1. Suppose a famous person, living or dead, visited your house for dinner. Write an essay describing the person and the evening and expressing your feelings about the occasion.

2. In "Eating Chilli Peppers" the author describes the love that some people have for eating peppers. Write an essay for your classmates describing a food that a family member or close friend enjoys but that you dislike.

To Inform Your Reader

3. Write an essay describing destruction or devastation you have observed as a result of a natural disaster (hurricane, flood), an accident, or a form of violence.

4. Write a report for your local newspaper on a local sporting event you recently observed or participated in.

To Persuade Your Reader

5. Suppose you want to persuade your parents to loan you money. The loan may be to purchase a used car or to rent a more expensive apartment, for example. Write a letter to them persuading them to make the loan. Include a description of your current car or apartment.

6. "The Sweat Bath Ritual" describes the author's first sweat bath. Write a letter describing to a classmate an experience or activity that you thought you would dislike but then enjoyed. In your letter, try to persuade your classmate to participate in the same activity.

Cases Using Description

7. Imagine that you are a product buyer for a cosmetics distributor, a food company, or a furniture dealership. Write a descriptive review of a product recommending to the board of directors whether or not to distribute it. Use something that you are familiar with or come up with your own product (such as an electronic gadget, an advice book on parenting, or a new cosmetic). Describe the product in a way that will help convince the company to accept your recommendation.

8. Write a brief description of your ideal internship. Then write an essay to accompany your application for your ideal summer internship. The sponsoring agency requires every applicant to submit an essay that describes the

knowledge and experience the applicant can bring to the internship and the ways that the position would benefit the applicant personally and professionally.

EVALUATING YOUR PROGRESS
Part A: Using Description

Write a paragraph that evaluates your use of description. Be sure to

- Identify one everyday, one academic, and one workplace situation in which description would be useful.
- For which of the five senses was it easiest to write sensory details? For which was it most difficult?
- Which method(s) of organization did you use? What other methods could you have used?
- Identify any problems or trouble spots you experienced in using description, and explain how you dealt with them.

Part B: Analyzing Descriptive Readings

For each reading you were assigned, evaluate the writer's use of descriptive details. Which senses were strongly represented? Were some omitted? How would the essay change if all descriptive details were omitted?

Part C: Proofreading and Editing

List the errors your instructor identified in your descriptive essay(s). For more help with these problems, refer to Exercise Central (www .bedfordstmartins.com/successfulwriting).

Illustration: Explaining with Examples

CHAPTER QUICK START

In a social problems class, the instructor projects the photograph shown on the opposite page onto a screen. The instructor makes the following statement: "Environmental pollution is a growing national problem." She asks the class to think of several examples of situations similar to the one shown in the photograph that confirm this view.

Writing Quick Start

Using the instructor's statement as your topic sentence, write a paragraph that supports this statement with examples of different types of environmental pollution that you have either observed or read about.

WRITING AN ILLUSTRATION ESSAY

The sentences you have just written could be part of an illustration essay. Your essay might explain specific situations that illustrate your thesis about pollution and the environment. When writers use illustration, they support their points with clear, specific examples. This chapter will show you how to write an essay that uses illustration as the primary method of development, as well as how to use illustration in other types of essays.

WHAT IS ILLUSTRATION?

Illustration is a means of using specific situations to reveal the essential characteristics of a topic or to reinforce a thesis. By providing examples to make abstract ideas concrete, you often can connect them to situations within the reader's experience. Unfamiliar terms also can become clear once examples are provided. Most textbooks are filled with examples for this reason. Writers in academic and work situations commonly use illustration as well (see the accompanying box for examples).

In the following illustration essay, "Rambos of the Road," Martin Gottfried uses examples to support a thesis.

SCENES FROM COLLEGE AND THE WORKPLACE

- For a *literature* class, you are assigned to write an analysis of the poet Emily Dickinson's use of metaphor and simile. To explain your point about her use of animals in metaphors, you provide specific examples from several of her poems.

- You are studying sexual dimorphism—differences in appearance between the sexes—for a *biology* course. The following question appears on an exam: "Define sexual dimorphism, and illustrate its occurrence in several different species." In your answer, you give examples of peacocks, geese, and chickens, explaining how the males and females in each species differ in physical appearance.

- You are an *elementary school reading teacher* and have been asked by your principal to write a justification to the school board for the new computer software you have requested. You decide to give several examples of how the software will benefit particular types of students.

Rambos of the Road
Martin Gottfried

Martin Gottfried has been a drama critic for such publications as the New York Post, *the* Saturday Review, *and* New York. *Currently he is a senior editor for* American School Board Journal. *He has also written several books, including* In Person: The Great Entertainers *(1985),* All His Jazz: The Life and Death of Bob Fosse *(1990),* George Burns and the Hundred-Year Dash *(1996), and* Balancing Act: The Authorized Biography of Angela Lansbury *(1998). This essay was first published in* Newsweek, *the weekly news magazine, in 1986. As you read the selection, notice where Gottfried employs compelling examples to support his thesis and highlight those you find particularly striking.*

1   The car pulled up and its driver glared at us with such sullen intensity, such hatred, that I was truly afraid for our lives. Except for the Mohawk haircut he didn't have, he looked like Robert De Niro in *Taxi Driver,* the sort of young man who, delirious for notoriety, might kill a president.

2   He was glaring because we had passed him and for that affront he pursued us to the next stoplight so as to express his indignation and affirm his masculinity. I was with two women and, believe it, was afraid for all three of us. It was nearly midnight and we were in a small, sleeping town with no other cars on the road.

3   When the light turned green, I raced ahead, knowing it was foolish and that I was not in a movie. He didn't merely follow, he chased, and with his headlights turned off. No matter what sudden turn I took, he followed. My passengers were silent. I knew they were alarmed, and I prayed that I wouldn't be called upon to protect them. In that cheerful frame of mind, I turned off my own lights so I couldn't be followed. It was lunacy. I was responding to a crazy *as* a crazy.

4   "I'll just drive to the police station," I finally said, and as if those were the magic words, he disappeared.

5   It seems to me that there has recently been an epidemic of auto macho — a competition perceived and expressed in driving. People fight it out over parking spaces. They bully into line at the gas pump. A toll booth becomes a signal for elbowing fenders. And beetle-eyed drivers hunch over their steering wheels, squeezing the rims, glowering, preparing the excuse of not having seen you as they muscle you off the road. Approaching a highway on an entrance ramp recently, I was strong-armed by a trailer truck, so immense that its driver all but

blew me away by blasting his horn. The behemoth was just inches from my hopelessly mismatched coupe when I fled for the safety of the shoulder.

6   And this is happening on city streets, too. A New York taxi driver told me that "intimidation is the name of the game. Drive as if you're deaf and blind. You don't hear the other guy's horn and you sure as hell don't see him."

7   The odd thing is that long before I was even able to drive, it seemed to me that people were at their finest and most civilized when in their cars. They seemed so orderly and considerate, so reasonable, staying in the right-hand lane unless passing, signaling all intentions. In those days you really eased into highway traffic, and the long, neat rows of cars seemed mobile testimony to the sanity of most people. Perhaps memory fails, perhaps there were always testy drivers, perhaps — but everyone didn't give you the finger.

8   A most amazing example of driver rage occurred recently at the Manhattan end of the Lincoln Tunnel. We were four cars abreast, stopped at a traffic light. And there was no moving even when the light had changed. A bus had stopped in the cross traffic, blocking our paths: it was a normal-for-New-York-City gridlock. Perhaps impatient, perhaps late for important appointments, three of us nonetheless accepted what, after all, we could not alter. One, however, would not. He would not be helpless. He would go where he was going even if he couldn't get there. A Wall Street type in suit and tie, he got out of his car and strode toward the bus, rapping smartly on its doors. When they opened, he exchanged words with the driver. The doors folded shut. He then stepped in front of the bus, took hold of one of its large windshield wipers and broke it.

9   The bus doors reopened and the driver appeared, apparently giving the fellow a good piece of his mind. If so, the lecture was wasted, for the man started his car and proceeded to drive directly *into the bus*. He rammed it. Even though the point at which he struck the bus, the folding doors, was its most vulnerable point, ramming the side of a bus with your car has to rank very high on a futility index. My first thought was that it had to be a rental car.

10   To tell the truth, I could not believe my eyes. The bus driver opened his doors as much as they could be opened and he stepped directly onto the hood of the attacking car, jumping up and down with both his feet. He then retreated into the bus, closing the doors behind him. Obviously a man of action, the car driver backed up and rammed the bus again. How this exercise in absurdity would have been resolved none of us will ever know for at that point the traffic unclogged and the bus moved on. And the rest of us, we passives of

the world, proceeded, our cars crossing a field of battle as if nothing untoward had happened.

It is tempting to blame such belligerent, uncivil and even neu- 11
rotic behavior on the nuts of the world, but in our cars we all become a little crazy. How many of us speed up when a driver signals his intention of pulling in front of us? Are we resentful and anxious to pass him? How many of us try to squeeze in, or race along the shoulder of a lane merger? We may not jump on hoods, but driving the gantlet, we seethe, cursing not so silently in the safety of our steel bodies on wheels — fortresses for cowards.

What is it within us that gives birth to such antisocial behavior 12
and why, all of a sudden, have so many drivers gone around the bend? My friend Joel Katz, a Manhattan psychiatrist, calls it "a Rambo pattern. People are running around thinking the American way is to take the law into your own hands when anyone does anything wrong. And what constitutes 'wrong'? Anything that cramps your style."

It seems to me that it is a new America we see on the road now. It 13
has the mentality of a hoodlum and the backbone of a coward. The car is its weapon and hiding place, and it is still a symbol even in this. Road Rambos no longer bespeak a self-reliant, civil people tooling around in family cruisers. In fact, there aren't families in these machines that charge headlong with their brights on in broad daylight, demanding we get out of their way. Bullies are loners, and they have perverted our liberty of the open road into drivers' license. They represent an America that derides the values of decency and good manners, then roam the highways riding shotgun and shrieking freedom. By allowing this to happen, the rest of us approve.   ■

Characteristics of Illustration Essays

Effective illustration essays support a generalization with specific, pertinent examples that maintain readers' interest and help fulfill the author's purpose. Because an illustration essay needs to be more than a list of examples, a well-thought-out organization is essential.

Illustration Uses Examples to Support Generalizations

Examples are an effective way to support generalizations. A **generalization** is a broad statement about a topic. Often, the thesis of an essay contains a generalization. In "Rambos of the Road" Gottfried's thesis contains a generalization about "an epidemic of auto macho" behavior.

The following statements are generalizations because they make assertions about an entire group or category.

- Most college students are energetic, ambitious, and eager to get ahead in life.
- Gestures play an important role in nonverbal communication.
- Boys are more willing to participate in class discussions than are girls.

To explain and support any one of these generalizations, you would need to provide specific examples to show how or why the statement is accurate. For instance, you could support the first generalization about college students by describing several students who demonstrate energy and ambition. However, because this general statement says "*Most* college students are energetic . . . ," other types of support would need to accompany the examples of individual college students. Relevant facts, statistics, expert opinions, anecdotes, personal observations, or descriptions could be used to show that the generalization applies to the majority of college students.

EXERCISE 10.1

Using one or more prewriting strategies for generating ideas, think of at least one example that supports each general statement.

1. Television offers some programs with educational or social value.
2. Today's parents are not strict enough with their children.
3. The favorite pastime of most men is watching sports on television.

Illustration Uses Examples to Explain or Clarify

Examples are also useful when you need to explain an unfamiliar topic, a difficult concept, or an abstract term for your readers.

Unfamiliar topics.   When your audience has little or no knowledge of your topic, consider using examples to help your readers understand it. In "Rambos of the Road," Gottfried uses an extended example of real-life road rage to help his readers understand that topic.

Difficult concepts.   Many concepts are difficult for readers to grasp by definition alone. For instance, a reader might guess that the term *urbanization,* a key concept in sociology, has something to do with cities. Defining the concept as, say, "the process by which an area becomes part of a city" would give the reader more to go on. But examples of formerly suburban areas that have become urban would make the concept immediately understandable.

Abstract terms.   Abstract terms refer to ideas, rather than to people or to concrete things you can see and touch. Terms such as *truth* and *justice* are abstract. Because abstractions are difficult to understand, examples help clarify them.

In other cases, however, abstract terms mean different things to different people. Here you give examples to clarify what *you* mean by an abstract term. Suppose you use the term *unfair* to describe your employer's treatment of employees. Readers might have different ideas of fairness. Providing examples of the employer's unfair treatment would make your meaning clear.

EXERCISE 10.2

The following list contains a mix of unfamiliar topics, difficult concepts, and abstract terms. Choose three items from the list, and think of examples that illustrate their meanings.

1. Phobia
2. Conformity
3. Gender role
4. Self-fulfilling prophecy
5. Sexual harassment

Illustration Maintains Readers' Interest

Examples that give readers a glimpse of an event or a circumstance and that allow them to imagine themselves there also help maintain readers' interest. In "Rambos of the Road" we can visualize Gottfried's example of a bus driver leaping out of the bus and stamping on the hood of the car. Similarly, Gottfried's opening example of being followed by an angry driver creates tension; we want to keep reading to learn the outcome.

Illustration Takes Purpose and Audience into Account

A successful illustration essay uses either a series of related examples or one extended example to support its thesis. The number and type of examples to include will depend on your purpose and audience. In an essay arguing that one car is a better buy than another, you would need to give a series of examples to show the various models, years, and options available to potential car buyers. But in an essay written for an audience of high school students about the consequences of dropping out of school, a single poignant example would be appropriate.

Your audience also plays a role in deciding what type of examples to include in an essay. At times, technical examples may be appropriate; at other times, more personal or nontechnical ones are effective. For instance, suppose you want to persuade readers that the Food and Drug Administration should approve a new cancer drug. If your audience is composed of doctors, your examples would include statistical studies and technical explanations of the drug's effectiveness. But if your audience is the general public, you would include personal anecdotes about lives being saved and nontechnical examples of the drug's safety. In addition, try to choose examples that represent different aspects of or viewpoints on your topic. In writing about the new drug, for instance, you might include expert opinion from researchers as well as the views of doctors, patients, and a representative of the company that manufactures the drug.

EXERCISE 10.3

For one of the following topics, suggest examples that would suit the different audiences listed.

1. Your college's policy on academic dismissal
   a. First-year students attending a college orientation session
   b. Students facing academic dismissal
   c. Parents or spouses of students who have been dismissed for academic reasons
2. A proposal recommending that drivers over the age of sixty-five undergo periodic assessment of their ability to operate a motor vehicle safely
   a. Senior citizens
   b. State senators
   c. Adult children of elderly drivers

Illustration Uses Carefully Selected Examples

The examples you use to explain your thesis should be carefully chosen. Select examples that are relevant, representative, accurate, and striking. *Relevant* examples have a direct and clear relationship to your thesis. If your essay advocates publicly funded and operated preschool programs, support your case with examples of successful publicly funded programs, not privately operated ones.

An example is *representative* when it shows a typical or real-life situation, not a rare or unusual one. In many cases, you will need to give several representative examples. For instance, in an essay arguing that preschool programs advance children's reading skills, one example of an all-day, year-round preschool would not be representative of all or most other programs.

Be sure the examples you include are *accurate.* Report statistics objectively, and provide readers with enough information so that they can evaluate the reliability of the data. Notice how the second example provides better detail for the reader.

EXAMPLE LACKING DETAIL AND ACCURACY	Most students in preschool programs have better language skills than children who don't attend such programs.
ACCURATE EXAMPLE	According to an independent evaluator, 73 percent of children who attended the Head Start program in Clearwater, after one year of attendance, had better language skills than students who did not attend the program.

Finally, choose examples that are *striking and dramatic* and that will make a strong, lasting impression on your readers.

ORDINARY EXAMPLE	On his first day of preschool, Damon was frightened and withdrawn, but after the first week, he learned important social skills.
STRIKING EXAMPLE	On his first day of preschool, Damon refused to speak to anyone and communicated only by nodding his head because he was scared. However, by the end of the first week, he was comfortably playing with new preschool friends.

At times, it may be necessary to conduct research to find examples outside of your knowledge and experience. For the essay on preschool programs, you would need to do library or Internet research to obtain statistical information. You might also interview a preschool administrator or teacher to gather firsthand anecdotes and opinions or visit a preschool classroom to observe the program in action.

Illustration Organizes Details Effectively

When you use examples to support a thesis, you need to decide how to organize both the examples and the details that accompany them. Often one of the methods of organization discussed in Chapter 6 will be useful—most-to-least, least-to-most, chronological, or spatial order. For example, in an essay explaining why people wear unconventional dress, the examples might be arranged spatially, starting with outlandish footwear and continuing upward to headgear. In some instances you may want to organize your examples according to another pattern of development, such as comparison and contrast or cause and effect. To support the thesis that a local department store needs to improve its customer services, you might begin by contrasting the department store with several computer stores that do have better customer services and offering examples of the services provided by each.

Visualizing an Illustration Essay: A Graphic Organizer

The graphic organizer shown in Figure 10.1 will help you visualize the components of an illustration essay. As you can see, the structure is straightforward: The introduction contains background information and usually includes the thesis, the body paragraphs give one or more related examples, and the conclusion presents a final statement. For an essay using one extended example—such as a highly descriptive account of an auto accident intended to persuade readers to wear seat belts—the body of the essay would focus on the details of that one example.

For more on graphic organizers, see Chapter 2, p. 34.

When you incorporate examples into an essay that uses other patterns of development, you might develop an example over several paragraphs or include a brief, one-paragraph example to illustrate a point.

The following essay, "A Dash of Comma Sense," is an illustration essay. Read the essay, and then study the graphic organizer for it in Figure 10.2 (on p. 295).

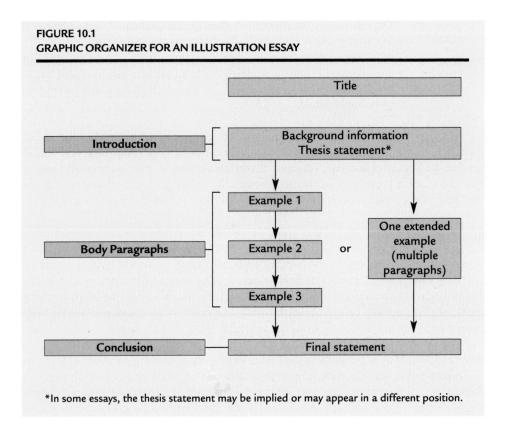

FIGURE 10.1
GRAPHIC ORGANIZER FOR AN ILLUSTRATION ESSAY

*In some essays, the thesis statement may be implied or may appear in a different position.

A Dash of Comma Sense
George F. Will

George F. Will is a well-known political commentator. He writes regular columns for the Washington Post *and* Newsweek *and has appeared on* World News Tonight *and other television news programs. His books include collections of essays and columns such as* The Leveling Wind: Politics, the Culture, and Other News, 1990–1994 *(1995) and* With a Happy Eye But . . . : America and the World 1997–2002 *(2002), as well as two books on baseball. Will won the Pulitzer Prize for commentary in 1977. The following essay was published in the* Washington Post *on May 21, 2004. As you read, note how Will uses one or more examples to support each of his main points.*

The actress Margaret Anglin left this note in the dressing room 1
of another actress: "Margaret Anglin says Mrs. Fiske is the best
actress in America." Mrs. Fiske added two commas and returned
the note: "Margaret Anglin, says Mrs. Fiske, is the best actress in
America."

Little things mean a lot. That is the thesis of a wise and witty wee 2
book, *Eats, Shoots and Leaves,* just published by Lynne Truss, a British
writer and broadcaster. She knows that proper punctuation, "the
basting that holds the fabric of language in shape," is "both the sign
and the cause of clear thinking." The book's title comes from a joke:
A panda enters a cafe, orders a sandwich, eats, draws a pistol, fires a
few shots, then heads for the door. Asked by a waiter to explain his
behavior, he hands the waiter a badly punctuated wildlife manual
and says: "I'm a panda. Look it up." The waiter reads the relevant
entry: "Panda: large black-and-white bear-like mammal. Eats, shoots
and leaves."

Behold the magical comma. It can turn an unjust aspersion 3
against an entire species ("No dogs please") into a reasonable request
("No dogs, please"), or it can turn a lilting lyric into a banal inquiry
("What is this thing called, love?"). The Christmas carol actually is
"God rest ye merry, gentlemen," not "God rest ye, merry gentlemen."

Huge doctrinal consequences flow from the placing of a comma 4
in what Jesus, when on the cross, said to the thief: "Verily, I say unto
thee, This day thou shalt be with me in Paradise" or "Verily, I say unto
thee this day, Thou shalt be with me in Paradise." The former leaves
little room for Purgatory.

Combined with a colon, a comma can fuel sexual warfare: "A 5
woman without her man is nothing" becomes "A woman: without
her, man is nothing." But a colon in place of a comma can subtly emit
a certain bark.

"President Bush said, 'Get Bob Woodward.'"

"President Bush said: 'Get Bob Woodward.'"

But beware the derangement known as commaphilia, which 6
results in the promiscuous cluttering of sentences with superfluous
signals. A reader once asked James Thurber why he had put a comma
after the word *dinner* in this sentence: "After dinner, the men went
into the living room." Thurber, a comma minimalist, blamed the
New Yorker's commaphilic editor, Harold Ross: "This particular
comma was Ross' way of giving the men time to push back their
chairs and stand up."

Truss, a punctuation vigilante, says punctuation marks are traf- 7
fic signals telling readers to slow down, pause, notice something,
take a detour, stop. Punctuation, she says, "directs you how to read,

in the same way musical notation directs a musician how to play" with attention to the composer's intentions regarding rhythm, pitch, tone and flow.

8   The almost-always-ghastly exclamation point has been rightly compared to canned laughter. F. Scott Fitzgerald said it was like laughing at your own joke. But not always. Victor Hugo, wondering how his *Les Miserables* was selling, sent this telegram to his publisher: "?" The publisher wired back: "!"

9   The dash can be, among other things, droll, as Byron understood:

> *He learned the arts of riding, fencing, gunnery,*
> *And how to scale a fortress — or a nunnery.*

Or:

> *A little still she strove, and much repented,*
> *And whispering "I will ne'er consent"—consented.*

10   The humble hyphen performs heroic services, making possible compounds that would otherwise be unsightly (*de-ice* rather than *deice; shell-like* rather than *shelllike*). And a hyphen can rescue meaning. As Truss says, "A cross-section of the public is quite different from a cross section of the public." If you are a pickled-herring merchant, you will not want to be called a pickled herring merchant. The difference between extra-marital sex and extra marital sex is not to be sneezed at.

11   The connection between the words *punctilious,* which means "attentive to formality or etiquette," and *punctuation* is instructive. Careful punctuation expresses a writer's solicitude for the reader. Of course punctuation, like most other forms of good manners, may yet entirely disappear, another victim of progress, this time in the form of e-mail, cell-phone text messages and the like. Neither the elegant semicolon nor the dashing dash is of use to people whose preferred literary style is "CU B4 8?" and whose idea of Edwardian prolixity is: "Saw Jim — he looks gr8 — have you seen him — what time is the thing 2morrow." Oh, for the era when a journalist telephoned from Moscow to London to add a semicolon to his story!   ■

EXERCISE 10.4

Draw a graphic organizer for "Rambos of the Road" (pp. 285–87).

FIGURE 10.2
GRAPHIC ORGANIZER FOR "A DASH OF COMMA SENSE"

To draw detailed graphic organizers using a computer, visit www .bedfordstmartins.com /successfulwriting.

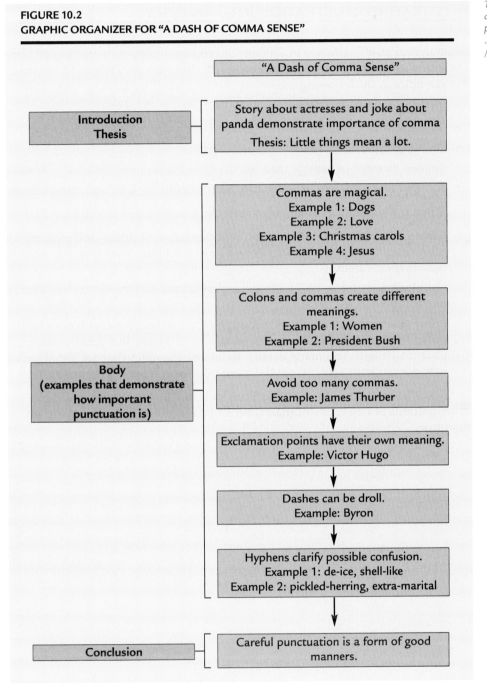

INTEGRATING ILLUSTRATION INTO AN ESSAY

Examples are an effective way to explain concepts or to support a thesis in an essay that relies on one or more other patterns of development. You might, for instance, use examples in the following ways.

- To *define* a particular advertising ploy
- To *compare* two types of small businesses
- To *classify* types of movies
- To *show the effects* of aerobic exercise
- To *argue* that junk food is unhealthy because of its high fat and salt content

  When using examples in an essay, keep the following tips in mind.

1. **Choose examples that are relevant, representative, accurate, and striking.** In most cases, you will include only one or two examples. Therefore, you need to choose them carefully.

2. **Use clear transitions.** Be sure to use a clear transition to make it clear that an example is to follow.

3. **Limit descriptive detail.** Provide enough details so that your reader can understand how an example illustrates your generalization but don't overwhelm your reader with too many details. Extended examples that are too detailed may distract your reader from the main point you are trying to make.

In "Words That Wound" (p. 317), Kathleen Vail uses illustration along with several other patterns of development (narration and description) to make a point about road rage.

A GUIDED WRITING ASSIGNMENT

The following guide will lead you through the process of writing an illustration essay. You will use examples to support your thesis, but you may need to use one or more of the other patterns of development to organize your examples or relate them to one another. Depending on your learning style, you may choose to work through this Guided Writing Assignment in different ways.

The Assignment

Write an illustration essay. Select one of the following topics or one that you think of on your own. Your audience consists of readers of your campus newspaper.

1. The connection between clothing and personality
2. The long-term benefits of a part-time job
3. The idea that you are what you eat
4. The problems of balancing school, job, and a family
5. Controlling or eliminating stress
6. Decision-making techniques
7. Effective (or ineffective) parenting
8. The popularity of a particular sport, television show, or hobby

As you develop your essay, consider using one or more of the other patterns of development. For example, you might use narration to present an extended example that illustrates the difficulties of balancing schoolwork with a job and family. You might compare decision-making techniques. Or you might describe your favorite television show.

For more on narration, description, and comparison and contrast, see Chapters 8, 9, and 12.

Generating Ideas

Use the following guidelines to help you narrow a topic and generate ideas.

Narrowing Your Topic

Once you have chosen an assignment topic, your first step is to narrow it so that it becomes a manageable topic for your essay. Use a prewriting technique to discover possible narrowed topics.

For more on prewriting strategies, see Chapter 3.

After prewriting, review your work and select a narrowed topic that can be supported by one or more examples. For instance, suppose you have come up with two manageable topics about anxiety. One is to discuss the effects of test anxiety; another is to discuss methods for controlling test anxiety. If you decide to write about the effects of test anxiety, you would need to provide several examples of test situations in which individuals "freeze" or "go blank." For the second narrowed topic, methods for controlling test anxiety, you would need to explain a process. You might use an extended example to show how one person overcame test anxiety.

Considering Your Purpose, Audience, and Point of View

For more on purpose, audience, and point of view, see Chapter 3.

Your purpose and audience will affect the type and number of examples you include. If you are writing a persuasive essay, you may need several examples to provide sufficient evidence. However, if you are writing an informative essay in which you explain how to select educational toys, one extended example may be sufficient.

Consider your audience in deciding what kinds of examples to include. For this assignment, your audience is made up of the readers of your campus newspaper. Think about whether this audience is interested in and familiar with your topic. If your audience is familiar with your topic, you may want to use complex examples. However, simple, straightforward examples would be appropriate for an audience unfamiliar with your topic.

You also need to consider which point of view to use. In most illustration essays, the emphasis is on the examples. For this reason, illustration is often written in the third person, as in "Goin' Gangsta, Choosin' Cholita: Claiming Identity" (p. 311). When personal examples are used, however, writers may use the first person, as in "Rambos of the Road" (p. 285).

Developing Your Thesis

For more on thesis statements, see Chapter 4, p. 89.

Your next step is to develop a working thesis about your narrowed topic. The thesis in an illustration essay is the idea that all of the examples support. To write an effective thesis statement, use the following guidelines.

- Identify the narrowed topic of your essay.
- Make a generalization about your narrowed topic that you will support with examples.

You can develop a thesis statement in several ways, depending on your learning style. For instance, a concrete learner writing about the effects of absent fathers on families may begin by listing the problems and behaviors that children in such single-parent families exhibit. An abstract learner, in contrast, might write the thesis first and then generate examples that support the generalization.

Once you are satisfied with your thesis statement, use the following suggestions to help you think of examples that illustrate it. As you brainstorm examples, you may think of situations that illustrate a different or more interesting thesis. Don't hesitate to revise or change your thesis as you discover more about your topic.

For more on prewriting strategies, see Chapter 3.

Learning Style Options

1. Jot down all of the instances or situations you can think of that illustrate your thesis.

2. Close your eyes and visualize situations that relate to your thesis.

3. Systematically review your life—year by year, place by place, or job by job—to recall situations that illustrate your thesis.

4. Discuss your thesis with a classmate. Try to match or better each other's examples.

5. Create two columns on a piece of paper or in a computer file. In the first column, type a list of words describing how you feel about your narrowed topic. (For example, the topic *cheating on college exams* might generate such feelings as anger, surprise, and confusion.) In the second column, elaborate on these feelings by adding details about specific situations. (For example, you might write about how surprised you were to discover your best friend had cheated on an exam.)

6. Research your topic in the library or on the Internet to uncover examples outside your own experience.

For more on library and Internet research, see Chapter 19.

ESSAY IN PROGRESS 1

Using the preceding guidelines, choose and narrow your topic. Then develop a working thesis statement and brainstorm examples that illustrate the thesis.

Choosing and Evaluating Your Examples

Brainstorming will lead you to discover a wealth of examples—many more than you could possibly use in your essay. Your task, then, is to select the examples that will best support your thesis. Use the following criteria in choosing examples.

1. **Choose relevant examples.** The examples you choose must clearly demonstrate the point or idea you want to illustrate. To support the thesis that high schools do not provide students with the instruction and training in physical education necessary to maintain a healthy lifestyle, you would not use as an example a student who is underweight because of a recent illness. Since lack of preparation in high school is not responsible for this student's problem, the case would be irrelevant to your thesis.

2. **Choose a variety of useful examples.** If you are using more than one example, choose examples that reveal different aspects of your topic. In writing about students who lack physical education skills, you would need to provide examples of students who lack different kinds of skills—strength, agility, and so forth. You can also add variety by using expert opinion, quotations, observations, or statistics to illustrate your thesis.

3. **Choose representative examples.** Choose typical cases, not rare or unusual ones. To continue with the thesis about physical education, a high school all-star football player who lacks adequate strength or muscular control would be an exceptional case. A high school graduate who did not learn to play a sport and failed to develop a habit of regular exercise would be a more representative example.

4. **Choose striking examples.** Include examples that capture your readers' attention and make a vivid impression. In "Rambos of the Road" (p. 285), Gottfried's example of the car-and-bus confrontation is a striking illustration of road rage.

5. **Choose accurate examples.** Be sure the examples you include are accurate. They should be neither exaggerated nor understated. For the thesis about high school students, for example, you would lose credibility if you exaggerated the students' physical condition.

6. **Choose examples that appeal to your audience.** Some examples will appeal to one type of audience more than to another type. If you want to illustrate high school graduates' lack of training in physical education for an audience of high school seniors, examples involving actual students may be most appealing, whereas for an audience of parents, expert opinion and statistics would be appropriate.

 If you are working on a computer, highlight strong examples by making them bold or moving them to a separate page or document for easy access when drafting.

TRYING OUT YOUR IDEAS ON OTHERS

Working in a group of two or three students, discuss your thesis and supporting examples for this chapter's assignment. Use the list of criteria on pages 299–300 to guide the discussion and to make suggestions for improving each student's thesis and examples.

ESSAY IN PROGRESS 2

Using the preceding suggestions and the feedback you have received from classmates, evaluate your examples, and decide which ones you will include in your essay.

Organizing and Drafting

Once you are satisfied with your thesis and the examples you have chosen to illustrate it, you are ready to organize your ideas and write your draft essay.

For more on drafting an essay, see Chapter 5.

Choosing a Method of Organization

Use the following guidelines to organize your essay.

1. **If you are using a single, extended example, relate events in the order in which they happened or choose another method of organization.** If the example is not made up of events, you might use most-to-least, least-to-most, or spatial organization. For instance, if you want to use in-line skating as an example of the importance of protective athletic gear, you might arrange the details spatially, describing the skater's head gear first, then the elbow and wrist pads, and then the knee protection.

For more on chronological organization, see Chapter 8.

2. **If you are using several examples, decide how you will order them.** Many illustration essays order examples in terms of their importance, from most to least or from least to most important. However, other arrangements are possible. Examples of childhood memories, for instance, could follow chronological order.

3. **If you have many examples, consider grouping them in categories.** For instance, in an essay about the use of slang words, you might classify examples according to how they are used by teenagers, by adults, and by other groups.

For more on classification and division, see Chapter 13.

ESSAY IN PROGRESS 3

Using the preceding suggestions, choose a method for organizing your examples. Then draw a graphic organizer, or write an outline of your essay.

Drafting the Illustration Essay

Once you have decided on a method of organization, your next step is to write a first draft. Here are some tips for drafting an illustration essay.

1. **Each paragraph should express one key idea; the example or examples in that paragraph should illustrate that key idea.** Develop your body paragraphs so that each one presents a single example or group of closely related examples.

2. **Use the topic sentence in each paragraph to make clear the particular idea that each example or set of examples illustrates.** Each topic sentence should focus the readers' attention and explain how the examples in the paragraph support the thesis.

3. **Provide sufficient detail about each example.** Explain each example using vivid descriptive language. Your goal is to make your readers feel as if they are experiencing or observing the situation.

4. **Use transitions to move your readers from one example to another.** Without transitions, your essay will seem choppy and disconnected. Use transitions such as *for example* and *in particular* to keep your readers on track.

5. **Begin with a clear introduction.** In most illustration essays, the thesis is stated at the outset. Your introduction should also spark readers' interest and include background information about the topic.

6. **End with an effective conclusion.** Your essay should not end with your last example. Instead it should conclude with a final statement that pulls together your ideas and reminds readers of your thesis.

For more on description, see Chapter 9. For more on using sufficient detail, see Chapter 5, p. 126.

For more on transitions, see Chapter 5, p. 128.

For more on writing effective paragraphs, including introductions and conclusions, see Chapter 5.

ESSAY IN PROGRESS 4

Using the preceding guidelines, write a first draft of your illustration essay.

Analyzing and Revising

If possible, set aside your draft for a day or two before rereading and revising it. As you reread and review your draft, concentrate on its organization, level of detail, and overall effectiveness, not on grammar or mechanics. To evaluate and revise your draft, use the following strategies.

Learning Style Options

For more on the benefits of peer review, see Chapter 6, p. 158.

1. Reread your paper aloud, or ask a friend to do so as you listen.
2. Write an outline, draw a graphic organizer, or update the outline or organizer that you created earlier. Look for weaknesses in how examples are organized.

Use Figure 10.3 to help you discover the strengths and weaknesses of your illustration essay. You might also ask a classmate to review your essay using the questions in the flowchart. For each answer that refers you to the right column of the chart, ask your reviewer to explain why he or she answered in that way.

ESSAY IN PROGRESS 5

Revise your draft using Figure 10.3 and any comments you have received from peer reviewers.

Editing and Proofreading

The last step is to check your revised essay for errors in grammar, spelling, punctuation, and mechanics. Look for the types of errors you commonly make. (Refer to your error log.)

For more on keeping an error log, see Chapter 7, p. 193.

For illustration essays, pay particular attention to the following common errors.

1. **Inconsistent verb tense** Be consistent in the verb tense that you use in your extended examples. When citing an event from the past as an example, always use the past tense to describe it.

   ▶ Special events *are* an important part of children's lives. Parent visitation day at school *was* an event my daughter talked about for an entire week. Children *are* also excited by . . .

2. **Inconsistent use of first, second, or third person** Be sure to use the first person (*I, me*), the second person (*you*), or the third person (*he, she, it, him, her, they, them*) consistently throughout your essay.

   ▶ I visited my daughter's first-grade classroom during parents' week last

   month. Each parent was invited to read a story to the class, and ~~you~~ *we* were

   encouraged to ask the children questions afterward.

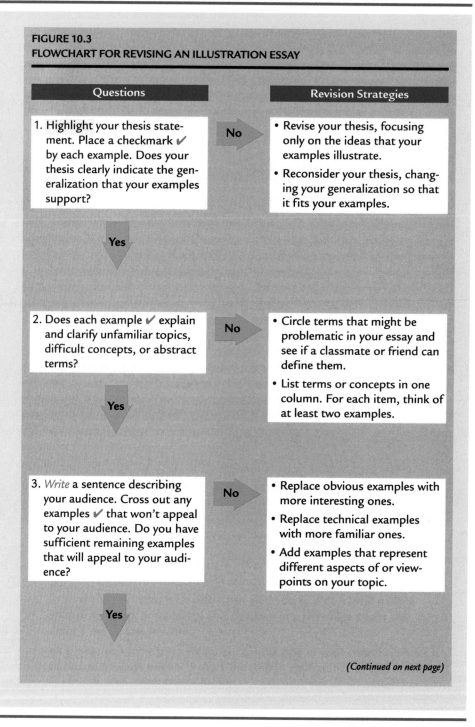

FIGURE 10.3
FLOWCHART FOR REVISING AN ILLUSTRATION ESSAY

Questions	Revision Strategies
1. Highlight your thesis statement. Place a checkmark ✔ by each example. Does your thesis clearly indicate the generalization that your examples support?	• Revise your thesis, focusing only on the ideas that your examples illustrate. • Reconsider your thesis, changing your generalization so that it fits your examples.

Yes

| 2. Does each example ✔ explain and clarify unfamiliar topics, difficult concepts, or abstract terms? | • Circle terms that might be problematic in your essay and see if a classmate or friend can define them.
• List terms or concepts in one column. For each item, think of at least two examples. |

Yes

| 3. *Write* a sentence describing your audience. Cross out any examples ✔ that won't appeal to your audience. Do you have sufficient remaining examples that will appeal to your audience? | • Replace obvious examples with more interesting ones.
• Replace technical examples with more familiar ones.
• Add examples that represent different aspects of or viewpoints on your topic. |

Yes

(Continued on next page)

FIGURE 10.3 *(Continued)*

Questions	Revision Strategies
4. *Write* a sentence stating the purpose of your essay. Cross out any examples ✔ that don't fulfill your purpose. Do you have sufficient remaining examples?	**No** → • Brainstorm examples that are more appropriate to your subject. • Consider using more than one example or cutting back and using one extended example.

Yes ↓

5. Reread each example ✔ you checked in question 1. Are your examples relevant, varied, striking, representative, and appealing?	**No** → • Eliminate examples that do not illustrate your thesis. • Brainstorm or conduct research to discover relevant or more striking examples. • Expand your examples to include more details. • Consider adding other kinds of examples (such as expert opinion and statistics).

Yes ↓

6. Underline the topic sentence of each paragraph. Does each clearly make a point that the example(s) ✔ illustrate?	**No** → • Add topic sentences that clearly indicate the point each example or group of examples illustrates. • Reorganize your essay according to the idea the examples illustrate.

Yes ↓

(Continued on next page)

FIGURE 10.3 *(Continued)*

Questions		Revision Strategies
7. *Write* a brief outline detailing your method of organization. Draw [brackets] around each transitional word and phrase. Is your method of organization clear and effective?	**No** →	• Review the methods of organization discussed in Chapter 5. • Consider using a different organizing strategy. • Add transitions if your essay sounds choppy.

Yes ↓

| 8. Draw a box around your introduction and conclusion. Is each effective? | **No** → | • Revise your introduction and conclusion so that they meet the guidelines discussed in Chapter 5. |

Yes ↓

9. Print out another draft to edit and proofread your essay before turning it in.

3. **Sentence fragments** When introducing examples, be sure to avoid sentence fragments; each sentence must have both a subject and a verb.

▶ Technology is becoming part of teenagers' daily lives. ~~For example, high~~ *High*

school students who carry pagers. *are an example.*

ESSAY IN PROGRESS 6

Edit and proofread your illustration essay, paying particular attention to consistent use of verb tense and point of view. Don't forget to look for the types of errors you tend to make.

STUDENTS WRITE

Michael Jacobsohn originally wrote the following essay as part of his application to Harvard University. It was later published as "The Harmony of Life" in *Harvard Magazine* in 1996. As you read the illustration essay, highlight the examples that best convey the writer's love of musicals.

The Harmony of Life

Michael Jacobsohn

I am first in my class, an all-state football player, weigh 220 pounds, and can lift up small cars, yet I have a secret that I have kept hidden for years. It rages within me, yearning to break free and reveal itself in both shame and splendor. I can contain it no longer. I must shed my inhibitions and proclaim aloud, "So help me, God, I love musicals!"   1

Until now, only my family and those who have had the experience of calling my house in the midst of one of my renditions of the confrontation scene between Javert and Valjean from <u>Les Misérables</u> knew about my passion for musical theater. For years I have endured ridicule from my sisters and their friends who have overheard me belting out the lyrics to "Sunrise, Sunset" from <u>Fiddler on the Roof</u> while in the shower. Ever since my first musical, <u>Jesus Christ Superstar</u>, seven years ago, I have been obsessed with the telling of stories through melody and verse. My heart leaps when I see that <u>Phantom of the Opera</u> is coming to the local theater or when <u>Guys and Dolls</u> is appearing on television at one in the morning.   2

Music is the most beautiful and powerful way to relate emotion. Thus, the entire structure of a story is enhanced by presenting action and dialogue through song. The topic of a story can deal with anything from religion, such as <u>Godspell</u>, to a ravenous man-eating plant (Audrey II in <u>Little Shop of Horrors</u>), but no matter which, music brings to life a story line and places a   3 production forever in one's head by providing a harmony to be continually associated with it.

4   Musicals also provide me with an emotional outlet. When enthralled by a member of the opposite sex, I am wont to burst into a performance of "Maria" from West Side Story. After an exhaustive football practice, my lips chant "I'm Free" from the rock opera Tommy; and at my desk, feeling haughty after getting the highest grade on a calculus test, I sing quietly, "I am the very model of a modern Major-General," from The Pirates of Penzance. I can delve into the recesses of my mind and produce a piece fitting for any occasion, and I take pride in this ability.

5   While preparing this confession, a less musically inclined friend of mine happened upon a rough draft of the revelation. As he heartily laughed at me, he asked, "Can this be? Can the fact that Michael Jacobsohn is both an academic and football colossus and a lover of musicals be reconciled?" I replied, "The bald, fat Marlon Brando of Apocalypse Now is the same Marlon Brando in Guys and Dolls. Just as Kurtz and Sky Masterson* are one and the same, so does my love for musicals reconcile itself with the other facets of my personality. It is unwise to stereotype, just as it is unwise to typecast." Inside, I shall sing forever.

Kurtz and Sky Masterson: Kurtz is a character played by Marlon Brando in the film *Apocalypse Now* (1979). Sky Masterson is the male lead in the musical *Guys and Dolls* and was played by Brando in the 1955 movie version.

Analyzing the Essay

1. What is Jacobsohn's thesis, and what does it tell us about him?
2. How does Jacobsohn's introduction capture your interest?
3. Evaluate the quantity and types of examples the writer provides.

4. How are the details in the essay organized? Is the organization effective?

5. Evaluate paragraph 3. What suggested revisions would you offer the writer?

Reacting to the Essay: Discussion and Journal Writing

1. Jacobsohn says that musicals provide an emotional outlet for him. Discuss whether other art forms can serve the same function.

2. Discuss the meaning and effectiveness of the essay's title.

3. Jacobsohn claims that his love of musicals is his hidden secret, a passion that is known to few people. What interests or hobbies do you have that do not fit the image others hold of you? Write a journal entry describing such an interest and the way that it is unlike your other interests and talents.

READING AN ILLUSTRATION ESSAY

The following section provides advice for reading illustration essays. Two exemplify the characteristics of illustration covered in this chapter and provide opportunities to examine, analyze, and react to the writer's ideas. The second essay uses illustration along with other methods of development.

WORKING WITH TEXT: READING ILLUSTRATION ESSAYS

Examples are dramatic, real, and concrete, and it is easy to pay too much attention to them. Be sure to focus on the key points the examples illustrate. Here are some suggestions for reading illustration essays with a focused eye.

For more on reading strategies, see Chapter 2.

What to Look For, Highlight, and Annotate

1. Read the essay more than once. Read the essay once to grasp its basic ideas; reread it to analyze its structure and content.

2. Begin by identifying and highlighting the thesis statement. If the thesis is not directly stated, ask yourself this question: "What one major point do all of the examples illustrate?"

3. Study and highlight the examples. Note in the margin the characteristics or aspects of the thesis each example illustrates.

4. Record your response to each example, either by using annotations or by writing in a journal. Try to answer these questions: "How well do the examples explain or clarify the thesis? Do I feel convinced of the writer's thesis after reading the essay? Would more or different examples have been more effective?"

5. Notice how the examples are organized. Are they organized in order of importance, in chronological order, in spatial order, or by some other method?

6. Note how the examples fit with any other patterns of development used in the essay.

How to Find Ideas to Write About

For more on discovering ideas for a response paper, see Chapter 2.

When you are asked to write a response to an illustration essay, keep an eye out for ideas to write about as you read. Try to think of similar or related examples from your personal experience. While reading "Rambos of the Road," for instance, you might have thought about driving behaviors you have observed. You might have recalled other examples of drivers who exhibit road rage, who are oblivious to those around them, who are reckless, or who are careful and considerate. Each of these examples could lead you to a thesis and ideas for writing.

THINKING CRITICALLY ABOUT ILLUSTRATION

When you read text that uses illustration to support generalizations, read with a critical eye. Study the examples and how they are used in the essay. Use the following questions to think critically about the examples you read.

What Is the Emotional Impact of the Examples?

For more on emotional appeals, see Chapter 16, p. 575

Examples are primarily a means of explaining or persuading, but they can also be used to evoke emotional responses. A description of a tiger pacing in a small zoo enclosure, rubbing its body against a fence, and scratching an open sore would provide a vivid example of the behavior exhibited by some wild animals in captivity. Such an example can evoke feelings of pity, sympathy, or even outrage.

Writers often choose examples with emotional appeal to manipulate their readers' feelings, especially in persuasive writing. Although it is not necessarily wrong for a writer to use examples that evoke emotional responses, as a critical reader you should be aware of their use so that you can avoid being manipulated. When you encounter an example that evokes an emotional response, try to set your emotions aside and look at the example objectively. In the case of the essay about the tiger, for instance, you might ask, "Why are animals held in captivity? What are the benefits of zoos?"

Are the Examples Representative?

Not all writers choose examples that convey a full picture of the subject. In the example about zoos, you might ask if the animals in all zoos are confined in small enclosures. Especially when you read persuasive writing, attempt to confirm through other sources that the writer's examples are fair and representative, and try to think of examples that might contradict the writer's point.

Is the Generalization Supported?

Evaluate whether the writer provides enough relevant examples to support the generalization and lead you to accept the thesis. Study each example closely: Is it clear and fully explained? Does it illustrate the thesis? What other types of examples, such as statistics or expert opinion, might strengthen the essay? In the hypothetical essay about the tiger, for instance, the expert opinion of zoologists would support the generalization that the primary function of a zoo should be to preserve animal species. Similarly, statistics on the number of species preserved in zoos would be relevant.

ILLUSTRATION ESSAY

As you read the following essay by Nell Bernstein, consider how the author uses the elements of illustration discussed in this chapter.

Goin' Gangsta, Choosin' Cholita: Claiming Identity
Nell Bernstein

Nell Bernstein is a San Francisco journalist who writes about current issues and is the editor of YO! (Youth Outlook). *The following excerpt from an essay originally appeared in 1994 in* West *magazine, the Sunday supplement to the* San Jose Mercury News. *It describes several California teenagers and their viewpoints on ethnic and racial identity. As you read the selection, highlight the statements and examples that reveal the teenagers' views.*

1   Her lipstick is dark, the lip liner even darker, nearly black. In baggy pants, a blue plaid Pendleton, her bangs pulled back tight off her forehead, 15-year-old April is a perfect cholita, a Mexican gangsta girl.

2   But April Miller is Anglo. "And I don't like it!" she complains. "I'd rather be Mexican."

3   April's father wanders into the family room of their home in San Leandro, California, a suburb near Oakland. "Hey, cholita," he teases. "Go get a suntan. We'll put you in a barrio and see how much you like it."

4   A large, sandy-haired man with "April" tattooed on one arm and "Kelly" — the name of his older daughter — on the other, Miller spent 21 years working in a San Leandro glass factory that shut down and moved to Mexico a couple of years ago. He recently got a job in another factory, but he expects NAFTA* to swallow that one, too.

5   "Sooner or later we'll all get nailed," he says. "Just another stab in the back of the American middle class."

6   Later, April gets her revenge: "Hey, Mr. White Man's Last Stand," she teases. "Wait till you see how well I manage my welfare check. You'll be asking me for money."

7   A once almost exclusively white, now increasingly Latin and black working-class suburb, San Leandro borders on predominantly black East Oakland. For decades, the boundary was strictly policed and practically impermeable. In 1970 April Miller's hometown was 97 percent white. By 1990 San Leandro was 65 percent white, 6 percent black, 15 percent Hispanic, and 13 percent Asian or Pacific Islander. With minorities moving into suburbs in growing numbers and cities becoming ever more diverse, the boundary between city and suburb is dissolving, and suburban teenagers are changing with the times.

8   In April's bedroom, her past and present selves lie in layers, the pink walls of girlhood almost obscured, Guns N' Roses and Pearl Jam posters overlaid by rappers Paris and Ice Cube. "I don't have a big enough attitude to be a black girl," says April, explaining her current choice of ethnic identification.

9   What matters is that she thinks the choice is hers. For April and her friends, identity is not a matter of where you come from, what you were born into, what color your skin is. It's what you wear, the music you listen to, the words you use — everything to which you pledge allegiance, no matter how fleetingly.

10   The hybridization of American teens has become talk show fodder, with "wiggers" — white kids who dress and talk "black" — appear-

---

NAFTA (North American Free Trade Agreement): An agreement among North American countries to ease restrictions on the exchange of goods and services.

ing on TV in full gangsta regalia. In Indiana a group of white high school girls raised a national stir when they triggered an imitation race war at their virtually all white high school last fall simply by dressing "black."

In many parts of the country, it's television and radio, not neigh- 11
bors, that introduce teens to the allure of ethnic difference. But in California, which demographers predict will be the first state with no racial majority by the year 2000, the influences are more immediate. The California public schools are the most diverse in the country: 42 percent white, 36 percent Hispanic, 9 percent black, 8 percent Asian.

Sometimes young people fight over their differences. Students at 12
virtually any school in the Bay Area can recount the details of at least one "race riot" in which a conflict between individuals escalated into a battle between their clans. More often, though, teens would rather join than fight. Adolescence, after all, is the period when you're most inclined to mimic the power closest at hand, from stealing your older sister's clothes to copying the ruling clique at school.

White skaters and Mexican would-be gangbangers listen to gang- 13
sta rap and call each other "nigga" as a term of endearment; white girls sometimes affect Spanish accents; blond cheerleaders claim Cherokee ancestors.

"Claiming" is the central concept here. A Vietnamese teen in Hay- 14
ward, another Oakland suburb, "claims" Oakland—and by implication blackness—because he lived there as a child. A law-abiding white kid "claims" a Mexican gang he says he hangs with. A brown-skinned girl with a Mexican father and a white mother "claims" her Mexican side, while her fair-skinned sister "claims" white. The word comes up over and over, as if identity were territory, the self a kind of turf.

Will Mosley says he and his friends listen to rap groups like 15
Compton's Most Wanted, NWA, and Above the Law because they "sing about life" . . . that is, what happens in Oakland, Los Angeles, anyplace but where Will is sitting today, an empty Round Table Pizza in a minimall.

"No matter what race you are," Will says, "if you live like we do, 16
then that's the kind of music you like."

And how do they live? 17

"We don't live bad or anything," Will admits. "We live in a pretty 18
good neighborhood, there's no violence or crime. I was just . . . we're just city people, I guess."

Will and his friend Adolfo Garcia, 16, say they've outgrown try- 19
ing to be something they're not. "When I was 11 or 12," Will says, "I thought I was becoming a big gangsta and stuff. Because I liked that music, and thought it was the coolest, I wanted to become that. I

wore big clothes, like you wear in jail. But then I kind of woke up. I looked at myself and thought, 'Who am I trying to be?'"

20   They may have outgrown blatant mimicry, but Will and his friends remain convinced that they can live in a suburban tract house with a well-kept lawn on a tree-lined street in "not a bad neighborhood" and still call themselves "city" people on the basis of musical tastes. "City" for these young people means crime, graffiti, drugs. The kids are law-abiding, but these activities connote what Will admiringly calls "action." With pride in his voice, Will predicts that "in a couple of years, Hayward will be like Oakland. It's starting to get more known, because of crime and things. I think it'll be bigger, more things happening, more crime, more graffiti, stealing cars."

21   "That's good," chimes in 15-year-old Matt Jenkins, whose new beeper — an item that once connoted gangsta chic but now means little more than an active social life — goes off periodically. "More fun."

22   The three young men imagine with disdain life in a gangsta-free zone. "Too bland, too boring," Adolfo says. "You have to have something going on. You can't just have everyday life."

23   "Mowing your lawn," Matt sneers.

24   "Like Beaver Cleaver's house," Adolfo adds. "It's too clean out here."

25   Not only white kids believe that identity is a matter of choice or taste or that the power of "claiming" can transcend ethnicity. The Manor Park Locos — a group of mostly Mexican-Americans who hang out in San Leandro's Manor Park — say they descend from the Manor Lords, tough white guys who ruled the neighborhood a generation ago.

26   Not every young Californian embraces the new racial hybridism. Andrea Jones, 20, an African-American who grew up in the Bay Area suburbs of Union City and Hayward, is unimpressed by what she sees mainly as shallow mimicry. "It's full of posers out here," she says. "When Boyz N the Hood came out on video, it was sold out for weeks. The boys all wanna be black, the girls all wanna be Mexican. It's the glamour."

27   Driving down the quiet, shaded streets of her old neighborhood in Union City, Andrea spots two white preteen boys in Raiders jackets and hugely baggy pants strutting erratically down the empty sidewalk. "Look at them," she says. "Dislocated."

28   She knows why. "In a lot of these schools out here, it's hard being white," she says. "I don't think these kids were prepared for the backlash that is going on, all the pride now in people of color's ethnicity, and our boldness with it. They have nothing like that, no identity, nothing they can say they're proud of.

"So they latch onto their great-grandmother who's a Cherokee, 29
or they take on the most stereotypical aspects of being black or
Mexican. It's beautiful to appreciate different aspects of other
people's culture—that's like the dream of what the 21st century
should be. But to garnish yourself with pop culture stereotypes just
to blend—that's really sad."

Those who dismiss the gangsta and cholo styles as affectations 30
can point to the fact that several companies market overpriced
knockoffs of "ghetto wear" targeted at teens.

But there's also something going on out here that transcends 31
adolescent faddishness and pop culture exoticism. When white
kids call their parents "racist" for nagging them about their baggy
pants; when they learn Spanish to talk to their boyfriends; when
Mexican-American boys feel themselves descended in spirit from
white "uncles"; when children of mixed marriages insist that they
are whatever race they say they are, all of them are more than just
confused.

They're inching toward what Andrea Jones calls "the dream of 32
what the 21st century should be." In the ever more diverse communities of Northern California, they're also facing the complicated
reality of what their 21st century will be.

Meanwhile, in the living room of the Miller family's San Leandro 33
home, the argument continues unabated. "You don't know what you
are," April's father has told her more than once. But she just keeps on
telling him he doesn't know what time it is.   ■

Examining the Reading

1. What does racial or ethnic identity mean to April Miller? According to Bernstein, by what standards does she define herself?

2. What does Bernstein mean by "the complicated reality" of the twenty-first century (para. 32)?

3. Explain the meaning of "claiming" (para. 14) as it is used in this essay.

4. What possible causes does Bernstein offer to explain why the California
   teenagers developed such attitudes about their racial and ethnic identity?

5. Explain the meaning of each of the following words as it is used in the reading: *impermeable* (para. 7), *hybridization* (10), *connoted* (21), and *affectations* (30).
   Refer to your dictionary as needed.

MAKING CONNECTIONS: Culture and Choosing Who You Are

Both "Goin' Gangsta, Choosin' Cholita: Claiming Identity" (pp. 311–15) and "Spanglish," which appears in Chapter 14 (pp. 473–75), describe how aspects of a culture—manner of dress and music—can be exchanged and combined into a new cultural fusion that people can identify with and participate in.

Analyzing the Readings

1. What do the readings express about how people identify themselves? What differences do you see in the points they make?

2. Write a journal entry illustrating how one or more cultures or sub-cultures influence your style, tastes, or interests. (*Subcultures* are groups that share parts of a dominant culture but have their own unique customs, lifestyle, or values. Vegetarians, jazz musicians, college football players, and medical doctors each form a subculture, for example.)

Essay Idea

Write an essay in which you explore how aspects of cultures or subcultures intersect and combine. How are you exposed to different cultures or sub-cultures?

Analyzing the Reading

1. What generalization does Bernstein make? How effectively is the generalization supported in this essay?

2. The writer uses the example involving April Miller in the introduction and conclusion. Do you find this strategy effective? Why or why not?

3. Evaluate Bernstein's use of illustration: Are the examples relevant and representative? Does Bernstein include enough examples? Explain your responses.

4. *Identity* is an abstract term. How does Bernstein make this term real and understandable?

5. What impact do Bernstein's examples have? How might various readers (white teenagers, members of the group being imitated, parents of teenagers) react differently to these examples?

Reacting to the Reading: Discussion and Journal Writing

1. Discuss why you agree or disagree with this statement: Teenagers who establish their identities by copying members of racial or ethnic groups strengthen unwanted stereotypes.

2. Have you observed teenagers claiming an ethnic or a racial identity? How do they look and behave? What seems to motivate them?

3. What factors most contribute to your sense of identity? Write a journal entry describing who you are and how you define yourself. Include examples.

ILLUSTRATION COMBINED WITH OTHER PATTERNS

As you read the following essay by Kathleen Vail, notice how she uses examples along with other patterns of development to support her main point.

Words That Wound
Kathleen Vail

Kathleen Vail is an associate editor and frequent contributor to the American School Board Journal, *which covers school management, educational policy and law, school achievement, and research. The following selection appeared in* American School Board Journal *in 1999. As you read the selection, look for and highlight the examples Vail uses to support her thesis.*

Brian Head saw only one way out. On the final day of his life, during economics class, the 15-year-old stood up and pointed a semi-automatic handgun at himself. Before he pulled the trigger, he said his last words: "I can't take this anymore." 1

Brian's father, William Head, has no doubt why his only child chose to take his life in front of a classroom full of students five years ago. Brian wanted everyone to know the source of his pain, the suffering he could no longer endure. The Woodstock, Ga., teen, overweight with thick glasses, had been systematically abused by school bullies since elementary school. Death was the only relief he could imagine. "Children can't vote or organize, leave or run away," says Head. "They are trapped." 2

For many students, school is a torture chamber from which there is no escape. Every day, 160,000 children stay home from school because they are afraid of being bullied, according to the National 3

Association of School Psychologists. In a study of junior high and high school students from small Midwestern towns, nearly 77 percent of the students reported they'd been victims of bullies at school — 14 percent saying they'd experienced severe reactions to the abuse. "Bullying is a crime of violence," says June Arnette, associate director of the National School Safety Center. "It's an imbalance of power, sustained over a period of time."

4   Yet even in the face of this suffering, even after Brian Head's suicide five years ago, even after it was revealed this past spring that a culture of bullying might have played a part in the Columbine High School shootings, bullying remains for the most part unacknowledged, underreported, and minimized by schools. Adults are unaware of the extent and nature of the problem, says Nancy Mullin-Rindler, associate director of the Project on Teasing and Bullying in the Elementary Grades at Wellesley College Center for Research on Women. "They underestimate the import. They feel it's a normal part of growing up, that it's character-building."

5   After his son's death, William Head became a crusader against bullying, founding an effort called Kids Hope to prevent others from suffering as Brian had. Unfortunately, bullying claimed another victim in the small town of Woodstock: 13-year-old Josh Belluardo. Last November, on the bus ride home from school, Josh's neighbor, 15-year-old Jonathan Miller, taunted him and threw wads of paper at him. He followed Josh off the school bus, hit the younger boy in the back of the head, and kicked him in the stomach. Josh spent the last two days of his life in a coma before dying of his injuries. Miller, it turns out, had been suspended nearly 20 times for offenses such as pushing and taunting other students and cursing at a teacher. He's now serving a life sentence for felony murder while his case is on appeal.

6   Bullying doesn't have to result in death to be harmful. Bullying and harassment are major distractions from learning, according to the National School Safety Center. Victims' grades suffer, and fear can lead to chronic absenteeism, truancy, or dropping out. Bullies also affect children who aren't victimized: Bystanders feel guilty and helpless for not standing up to the bully. They feel unsafe, unable to take action. They also can be drawn into bullying behavior by peer pressure. "Any time there is a climate of fear, the learning process will be compromised," says Arnette.

7   A full 70 percent of children believe teachers handle episodes of bullying "poorly," according to a study by John Hoover at the University of North Dakota at Grand Forks. It's no wonder kids are reluctant to tell adults about bullying incidents. "Children feel no one will take them seriously," says Robin Kowalski, professor of psychology at

Western Carolina University, Cullowhee, N.C., who's done research on teasing behavior.

Martha Rizzo, who lives in a suburb of Cincinnati, calls bullying   8
the "dirty little secret" of her school district. Both her son and daughter were teased in school. Two boys in her son's sixth-grade class began taunting him because he wore sweatpants instead of jeans. They began to intimidate him during class. Once they knocked the pencil out of his hand during a spelling test when the teacher's back was turned. He failed the test. Rizzo made an appointment with the school counselor. The counselor told her he could do nothing about the behavior of the bullies and suggested she get counseling for her son instead. "Schools say they do something, but they don't, and it continues," says Rizzo. "We go in with the same problem over and over again."

Anna Billoit of Louisiana went to her son's middle school teach-   9
ers when her son, who had asthma and was overweight, was being bullied by his classmates. Some of the teachers made the situation worse, she says. One male teacher suggested to her that the teasing would help her son mature. "His attitude was 'Suck it up, take it like a man,'" says Billoit.

Much bullying goes on in so-called transition areas where there   10
is little or no adult supervision: hallways, locker rooms, restrooms, cafeterias, playgrounds, buses, and bus stops. When abuse happens away from adult eyes, it's hard to prove that the abuse occurred. Often, though, bullies harass their victims in the open, in full view of teachers and other adults. Some teachers will ignore the behavior, silently condoning it. But even when adults try to deal with the problem, they sometimes make things worse for the victim by not handling the situation properly. Confronting bullies in front of their peers only enhances the bullies' prestige and power. And bullies often step up the abuse after being disciplined. "People know it happens, but there's no structured way to deal with it," says Mullin-Rindler. "There's lots of confusion about what to do and what is the best approach."

Societal expectations play a part in adult reactions to childhood   11
bullying. Many teachers and administrators buy into a widespread belief that bullying is a normal part of childhood and that children are better off working out such problems on their own. But this belief sends a dangerous message to children, says Head. Telling victims they must protect themselves from bullies shows children that adults can't and won't protect them. And, he points out, it's an attitude adults would never tolerate themselves. "If you go to work and get slapped on the back of the head, you wouldn't expect your supervisor

to say, 'It's your problem—you need to learn to deal with it yourself,' " says Head. "It's a human-rights issue."

12   Ignoring bullying is only part of the problem. Some teachers go further by blaming the victims for their abuse by letting their own dislike for the victimized child show. "There's a lot of secret admiration for the strong kids," says Eileen Faucette of Augusta, Ga. Her daughter was teased so badly in the classroom that she was afraid to go to the blackboard or raise her hand to answer a question. The abuse happened in front of her teacher, who did nothing to stop it.

13   Head also encountered a blame-the-victim attitude toward his son. Brian would get into trouble for fighting at school, but when Head and his wife investigated what happened, they usually found that Brian had been attacked by other students. The school, Head said, wanted to punish Brian along with his attackers. "The school calls it fighting," Head says. "But it's actually assault and battery."

14   And changes are coming. This past April, five months after Josh Belluardo's death, the Georgia State Legislature passed an anti-bullying law. The law defines bullying as "any willful attempt or threat to inflict injury on another person when accompanied by an apparent present ability to do so" or "any intentional display of force such as would give the victim reason to fear or expect immediate bodily harm." Schools are required to send students to an alternative school if they commit a third act of bullying in a school year. The law also requires school systems to adopt anti-bullying policies and to post the policies in middle and high schools.

15   Head was consulted by the state representatives who sponsored the bill, but he believes the measures don't go far enough. He urges schools to treat bullying behavior as a violation of the state criminal law against assault, stalking, and threatening, and to call the police when the law is broken.

16   He knows it's too late for Brian, too late for Josh, too late for the teens who died in Littleton. But he continues to work, to educate and lobby on the devastating effects of bullying so that his son's death will not have been in vain.

17   "We should come clean and say what we've done in the past is wrong," says Head. "Now we will guarantee we'll protect the rights of students." ∎

Examining the Reading

1. How does Vail present bullying as both a general and a specific problem?

2. Why does bullying persist in school settings? Whom does the author blame?

3. How does bullying affect children who are not bullied?

4. Explain the statement that bullying is "an imbalance of power, sustained over a period of time" (para. 3).

5. Explain the meaning of each of the following words as it is used in the reading: *sustained* (3), *crusader* (5), *compromised* (6), *condoning* (10), and *lobby* (16).

Analyzing the Reading

1. Does Vail provide a sufficient number of examples to support her thesis?

2. In addition to illustration, what other patterns of development does the writer use to support her thesis? Give examples from the reading.

3. Examine the examples that are included in Vail's essay. What is the emotional impact of her examples?

4. Are the examples that Vail uses fair and representative of the situation in today's public schools?

5. What audience is Vail addressing? How do Vail's examples address her audience and purpose?

Reacting to the Reading: Discussion and Journal Writing

1. Discuss whether bullying occurs among adults in more subtle ways.

2. What rules or policies could schools establish that would reduce bullying?

3. Write a journal entry exploring actions that would encourage more states to enact antibullying laws.

APPLYING YOUR SKILLS: ADDITIONAL ESSAY ASSIGNMENTS

Write an illustration essay on one of the following topics, using what you learned about illustration in this chapter. Depending on the topic you choose, you may need to conduct library or Internet research.

For more on locating and documenting sources, see Part 5.

To Express Your Ideas

1. In an article for the campus newspaper, explain what you consider to be the three most important qualities of a college instructor. Support your opinion with vivid examples from your experience.

2. Explain to a general audience the role played by grandparents within a family, citing examples from your family.

To Inform Your Reader

3. In "Rambos of the Road" Martin Gottfried explains the concept of "auto macho," also known as "road rage," using examples from his own experience. Explain the concept of *peer pressure,* using examples from your experience.

4. Describe to an audience of college students the qualities or achievements you think should be emphasized during job interviews. Give examples that show why the qualities or achievements you choose are important to potential employers.

To Persuade Your Reader

5. Argue for or against an increased emphasis on physical education in public schools. Your audience is your local school committee.

6. In a letter to the editor of a local newspaper, argue for or against the establishment of a neighborhood watch group.

Cases Using Illustration

7. Prepare the oral presentation you will give to your local town board to convince them to lower the speed limit on your street. Use examples as well as other types of evidence.

8. Write a letter to the parents of three-year-old children who will begin attending your day-care center this year, explaining how the parents can prepare their children for the day-care experience. Support your advice with brief but relevant examples.

EVALUATING YOUR PROGRESS
Part A: Using Illustration

Write a paragraph that evaluates your use of illustration. Be sure to

- Identify topics or situations in which illustration will be useful. Are there topics or audiences for which illustration would not be the most effective method of development?
- Explain what factors you considered in choosing examples to include in an illustration essay.
- Identify any problems or trouble spots you experienced in using illustration and explain how you dealt with them.

Part B: Analyzing Illustration Readings

How does illustration compare to other methods of development that you have learned? What are its advantages and disadvantages?

Part C: Proofreading and Editing

List the errors your instructor identified in your illustration essay(s). For more help with these problems, refer to Exercise Central (www .bedfordstmartins.com/successfulwriting).

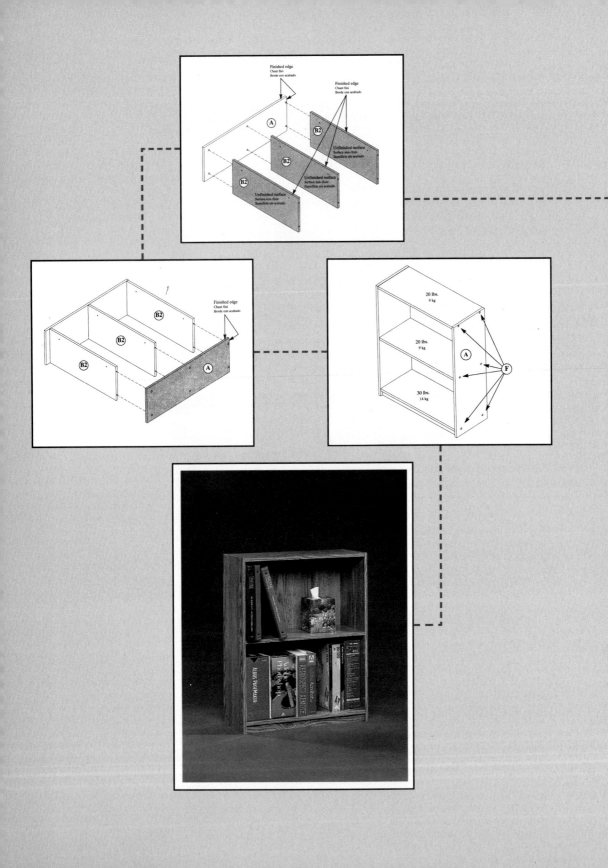

CHAPTER QUICK START

Suppose you are a technical writer and have been asked to write the instructions that will accompany this diagram for assembling a bookshelf.

Writing Quick Start

Write a brief paragraph describing how to perform the steps shown in the diagram. Your audience consists of people who have bought the materials to assemble the bookshelf.

Process Analysis: Explaining How Something Works or Is Done

WRITING A PROCESS ANALYSIS

To describe the steps involved in assembling a bookshelf, you had to explain a process. You use process analysis whenever you explain how something is done or how it works—how to make lasagna, how to change a flat tire, or how a bill becomes law. This chapter will show you how to write a well-organized, easy-to-understand process analysis essay and how to incorporate process analysis into essays that use other patterns of development.

WHAT IS PROCESS ANALYSIS?

A **process analysis** explains in step-by-step fashion how something works or how something is done or made. Process analyses provide people with practical information—directions for assembling equipment, instructions for registering for classes, and directions for using a search engine on the Internet. Sometimes, process analyses inform people about things that affect their lives, such as an explanation of how a medication works or how a child learns to read. Whatever the purpose, the information in a process analysis must be accurate, clear, and easy to follow.

Process analysis is a common type of writing in college and on the job (see the accompanying box for a few examples). Whether you are writing for a college course or for your colleagues at work, two types of writing situations call for the use of process analysis:

- To explain how something works or is done to readers *who want or need to perform the process*
- To explain how something works or is done to readers *who want to understand the process but not actually perform it*

SCENES FROM COLLEGE AND THE WORKPLACE

- For a *child development* course, your assignment is to visit a day-care center, choose one confrontation between a child and a teacher, and explain how the teacher resolved the conflict.
- As part of a *chemistry* lab report, you are asked to summarize the procedure you followed in preparing a solution or conducting an experiment.
- While working as an *engineer* at a water treatment plant, you are asked by your supervisor to write a description of how the city's drinking water is tested and treated for contamination.

The first type, a *how-to essay,* may explain how to teach a child the alphabet, for instance. Your primary purpose in writing a how-to essay is to present the steps in the process clearly and completely so that your readers can perform the task you describe. For the second type of process analysis, a *how-it-works essay,* you might explain how a popular radio talk show screens its callers. Your primary purpose in writing a how-it-works essay is to present the steps in the process clearly enough so that your readers can fully understand it. At times, you may read or write essays that contain elements of both types of process analysis. In writing about how a car alarm system works, for example, you might find it necessary to explain how to activate and deactivate the system as well as how it works.

The following essay exemplifies a how-to process analysis essay.

Fender Benders: Legal Do's and Don'ts
Armond D. Budish

Armond D. Budish is an attorney and a consumer-law journalist. He is also the author of Avoiding the Medicaid Trap: How to Beat the Cata-strophic Costs of Nursing Home Care *(1989) and writes columns for the* Cleveland Plain Dealer *and* Family Circle, *from which the following essay, published in 1994, is excerpted. The article is written in journalistic style, using headings and numbered lists, and it does not have a conclusion. As you read, highlight the thesis and notice the trouble spots in the process that Budish anticipates for his readers.*

The car ahead of you stops suddenly. You hit the brakes, but you just can't stop in time. Your front bumper meets the rear end of the other car. Ouch! 1

There doesn't seem to be any damage, and it must be your lucky day because the driver you hit agrees that it's not worth hassling with insurance claims and risking a premium increase. So after exchanging addresses, you go your separate ways. 2

Imagine your surprise when you open the mail a few weeks later only to discover a letter from your "victim's" lawyer demanding $10,000 to cover car repairs, pain and suffering. Apparently the agreeable gentleman decided to disagree, then went ahead and filed a police report blaming you for the incident and for his damages. 3

When automobiles meet by accident, do you know how to respond? Here are 10 practical tips that can help you avoid costly legal and insurance hassles. 4

1. STOP! IT'S THE LAW.

5   No matter how serious or minor the accident, stop immediately. If possible, don't move your car—especially if someone has been injured. Leaving the cars as they were when the accident occurred helps the police determine what happened. Of course, if your car is blocking traffic or will cause another accident where it is, then move it to the nearest safe location.

6   For every rule there are exceptions, though. If, for example, you are rear-ended at night in an unsafe area, it's wisest to keep on going and notify the police later. There have been cases in which people were robbed or assaulted when they got out of their cars.

2. ZIP LOOSE LIPS.

7   Watch what you say after an accident. Although this may sound harsh, even an innocent "I'm sorry" could later be construed as an admission of fault. Also be sure not to accuse the other driver of causing the accident. Since you don't know how a stranger will react to your remarks, you run the risk of making a bad situation worse.

8   Remember, you are not the judge or jury; it's not up to you to decide who is or is not at fault. Even if you think you caused the accident, you might be wrong. For example: Assume you were driving 15 miles over the speed limit. What you probably were not aware of is that the other driver's blood-alcohol level exceeded the legal limits, so he was at least equally at fault.

3. PROVIDE REQUIRED INFORMATION.

9   If you are involved in an accident, you are required in most states to give your name, address and car registration number to any person injured in the accident; the owner, driver or passenger in any car that was damaged in the accident; a police officer on the scene. If you don't own the car (say it belongs to a friend or your parents), you should provide the name and address of the owner.

10   You must produce this information even if there are no apparent injuries or damages and even if you didn't cause the accident. Most states don't require you to provide the name of your insurance company, although it's usually a good idea to do so. However, don't discuss the amount of your coverage—that might inspire the other person to "realize" his injuries are more serious than he originally thought.

What should you do if you hit a parked car and the owner is not   11
around? The law requires you to leave a note with your name, and the
other identifying information previously mentioned, in a secure
place on the car (such as under the windshield wiper).

4. GET REQUIRED INFORMATION.

You should obtain from the others involved in the accident the   12
same information that you provide them with. However, if the other
driver refuses to cooperate, at least get the license number and the
make and model of the car to help police track down the owner.

5. CALL THE POLICE.

It's obvious that if it's a serious accident in which someone is   13
injured, the police should be called immediately. That's both the law
and common sense. But what if the accident seems minor? Say you're
stopped, [and] another car taps you in the rear. If it's absolutely clear
to both drivers that there is no damage or injury, you each can go
your merry way. But that's the exception.

Normally, you should call the police to substantiate what   14
occurred. In most cities police officers will come to the scene, even
for minor accidents, but if they won't, you and the other driver
should go to the station (of the city where the accident occurred) to
file a report. Ask to have an officer check out both cars.

If you are not at fault, be wary of accepting the other driver's   15
suggestion that you leave the police out of it and arrange a private
settlement. When you submit your $500 car-repair estimate several
weeks later, you could discover that the other driver has developed
"amnesia" and denies being anywhere near the accident. If the police
weren't present on the scene, you may not have a legal leg to stand on.

Even if you are at fault, it's a good idea to involve the police. Why?   16
Because a police officer will note the extent of the other driver's damages in his or her report, limiting your liability. Without police presence the other driver can easily inflate the amount of the damages.

6. IDENTIFY WITNESSES.

Get the names and addresses of any witnesses, in case there's a   17
legal battle some time in the future. Ask bystanders or other
motorists who stop whether they saw the accident; if they answer
"yes," get their identifying information. It is also helpful to note the
names and badge numbers of all police officers on the scene.

7. Go to the Hospital.

18   If there's a chance that you've been injured, go directly to a hospital emergency room or to your doctor. The longer you wait, the more you may jeopardize your health and the more difficult it may be to get reimbursed for your injuries if they turn out to be serious.

8. File a Report.

19   Every driver who is involved in an automobile incident in which injuries occur must fill out an accident report. Even if the property damage is only in the range of $200 to $1,000, most states require that an accident report be filed. You must do this fairly quickly, usually in 1 to 30 days. Forms may be obtained and filed with the local motor vehicle department or police station in the city where the accident occurred.

9. Consider Filing an Insurance Claim.

20   Talk with your insurance agent as soon as possible after an accident. He or she can help you decide if you should file an insurance claim or pay out of your own pocket.

21   For example, let's say you caused an accident and the damages totaled $800. You carry a $250 deductible, leaving you with a possible $550 insurance claim. If you do submit a claim, your insurance rates are likely to go up, an increase that will probably continue for about three years. You should compare that figure to the $550 claim to determine whether to file a claim or to pay the cost yourself. (Also keep in mind that multiple claims sometimes make it harder to renew your coverage.)

10. Don't Be Too Quick to Accept a Settlement.

22   If the other driver is at fault and there's any chance you've been injured, don't rush to accept a settlement from that person's insurance company. You may not know the extent of your injuries for some time, and once you accept a settlement, it's difficult to get an "upgrade." Before settling, consult with a lawyer who handles personal injury cases.

23   When you haven't been injured and you receive a fair offer to cover the damage to your car, you can go ahead and accept it.   ■

Characteristics of Process Analysis Essays

A process analysis essay should include everything your reader needs to know to understand or perform the process. In addition to presenting an explicit thesis, the essay should provide a clear, step-by-step description of the process, define key terms, give any necessary background information, describe any equipment needed to perform the process, supply an adequate amount of detail, and, for a how-to essay, anticipate and offer help with potential problems.

Process Analysis Usually Includes an Explicit Thesis Statement

A process analysis usually contains a clear thesis that identifies the process to be discussed and suggests the writer's attitude or approach toward it. The thesis statement tells why the process is important or useful to the reader. In "Fender Benders: Legal Do's and Don'ts," for instance, Budish states: "Here are 10 practical tips that can help you avoid costly legal and insurance hassles."

Here are two examples of thesis statements for how-to process analyses that suggest the usefulness or importance of the process.

> Switching to a low-fat diet, a recent nutritional trend, can improve weight control dramatically.

> By carefully preparing for a vacation in a foreign country, you can save time and prevent hassles.

In a how-it-works essay, the writer either reveals why the information is worth knowing or makes an assertion about the nature of the process itself. Here are two examples of thesis statements for how-it-works essays.

> Although understanding the grieving process will not lessen the grief that you experience after the death of a loved one, knowing that your experiences are normal does provide some comfort.

> Advertisers often appeal to the emotions of the audience for whom a product is targeted; some of these appeals may be unethical.

Process Analysis Is Organized Chronologically

The steps or events in a process analysis are usually organized in chronological order—that is, the order in which the steps are normally completed. In "Fender Benders: Legal Do's and Don'ts" Budish uses a numbered list to show the chronological organization of his advice, from the moment that an accident occurs to the point when an insurance settlement is accepted. For essays that explain lengthy processes, the steps may be grouped into categories to make the process easier to understand.

On occasion, the steps of a process may not have to occur in any particular order. For example, in an essay on how to resolve a dispute between two coworkers, the order of the recommended actions may depend on the nature of the dispute. In this situation, some logical progression of recommended actions should be used, such as starting with informal or simple steps and progressing to more formal or complex ones.

EXERCISE 11.1

Choose one of the following processes. It should be one you are familiar with and are able to explain to others. Draft a working thesis statement and a chronological list of the steps or stages of the process.

1. How to use a computer program
2. How to study for an exam
3. How to perform a task at work
4. How to operate a machine
5. How to complete an application (such as for college, a job, or a credit card)

Process Analysis Defines Technical Terms

For more on defining terms, see Chapter 14, p. 468.

In most cases, you should assume that your audience is not familiar with the technical terms associated with the process you are describing. In a process essay, be sure to define specialized terms for your readers. In describing how cardiopulmonary resuscitation (CPR) works, for instance, you would need to explain the meanings of such terms as *airway, sternum,* and *cardiac compression.*

EXERCISE 11.2

Choose one of the following processes that you are familiar with and are able to explain to others. For the process you choose, list the technical terms and definitions that you need to use to explain the process.

1. How to perform a task at home or at work (such as changing the oil in a car or taking notes during a court hearing)
2. How a piece of equipment or a machine works (such as a treadmill or a lawn mower)
3. How to repair an object (such as restringing a tennis racket or a violin)

Process Analysis Provides Background Information

In some process analysis essays, readers may need background information to understand the process. For example, in an explanation of how CPR works, general readers might need information on how the heart functions to understand how pressing down on a person's breastbone propels blood into the arteries. In "Fender Benders: Legal Do's and Don'ts," Budish opens with a scenario that illustrates why his essay is important to drivers involved in accidents.

Process Analysis Describes Necessary Equipment

When special equipment is needed to perform the process, you should describe the equipment for readers. For example, in an essay explaining how to use a computer system to readers unfamiliar with computers, you would describe the keyboard, monitor, printer, and so forth. If necessary, you should also explain where to obtain it.

EXERCISE 11.3

For the process you selected in Exercise 11.2 (p. 332), consider what background information and equipment are needed to understand and perform the process.

Process Analysis Provides an Appropriate Level of Detail

In deciding the level of detail to include in a process analysis essay, you should be careful not to overwhelm your readers with too many technical details. An essay about how to perform CPR written by and for physicians would be highly technical, but it would be much less so if written for a friend who is considering whether to enroll in a CPR course. However, you would need to include enough detail to show your readers how to perform the steps of the CPR process.

In "Fender Benders: Legal Do's and Don'ts" Budish is writing for a general audience. He is careful to provide details about legal implications because he assumes that his audience is unfamiliar with legal matters.

Keep in mind that when you write essays explaining technical or scientific processes, you can use sensory details and figures of speech to make your writing lively and interesting. Rather than giving dry technical details, try using descriptive language.

For a process involving many complex steps or highly specialized equipment, consider using a drawing or schematic diagram to help your readers visualize the steps they need to follow or understand. For example, in an essay explaining how to detect a wiring problem in an electric stove, you might include a diagram of the stove's circuitry.

Process Analysis Anticipates Trouble Spots and Offers Solutions

Especially in a how-to essay, you need to anticipate potential trouble spots or areas of confusion and offer advice to the reader on how to avoid or resolve them. In an essay explaining how to apply for a mortgage, for instance, you would need to anticipate the difficulty of finding a cosigner and give advice on how to resolve that problem.

A how-to process analysis essay should also warn readers of any difficult, complicated, or critical steps, encouraging them to pay special attention to a difficult step or to take extra care in performing a critical one. In "Fender Benders: Legal Do's and Don'ts," Budish warns readers about the possible results of not calling the police to the scene of an accident. You should also warn readers of any steps in the process that they may have trouble completing. For instance, in a how-to essay on hanging wallpaper, you would warn readers about the difficulties of handling sheets of wallpaper and suggest folding the sheets to make them easier to work with.

EXERCISE 11.4

For one of the processes listed in Exercise 11.1 or Exercise 11.2, identify potential trouble spots in the process and describe how to avoid or resolve them.

Visualizing a Process Analysis Essay: A Graphic Organizer

For more on graphic organizers, see Chapter 2, p. 34.

The graphic organizer in Figure 11.1 shows the basic organization of a process analysis essay. When your main purpose is to explain a process, you should follow this standard format, including a title, an introduction, body paragraphs, and a

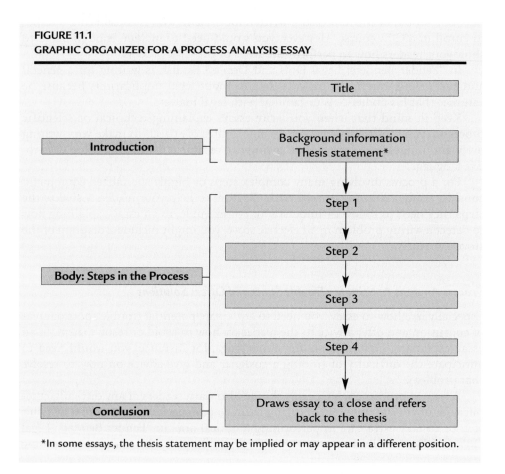

FIGURE 11.1
GRAPHIC ORGANIZER FOR A PROCESS ANALYSIS ESSAY

Title

Introduction — Background information / Thesis statement*

Step 1

Step 2

Body: Steps in the Process

Step 3

Step 4

Conclusion — Draws essay to a close and refers back to the thesis

*In some essays, the thesis statement may be implied or may appear in a different position.

conclusion. Your introduction should include any necessary background information and present your thesis statement. Your body paragraphs should explain the steps of the process in chronological order. Your conclusion should draw the essay to a satisfying close and refer back to the thesis.

When you incorporate process analysis into an essay using one or more other patterns of development, briefly introduce the process and then move directly to the steps involved. If the process is complex, you may want to add a brief summary of it before the transition back to the main topic of the essay.

Read the following how-it-works essay, "How the Oscars Work," and then study the graphic organizer for it in Figure 11.2 (on p. 339).

How the Oscars Work
Melissa Russell-Ausley and Tom Harris

Melissa Russell-Ausley has worked as a staff writer for the informational Web site HowStuffWorks.com, where this reading first appeared. Tom Harris, who has also served as a staff writer for the site, is currently its editorial director. HowStuffWorks.com, started in North Carolina by a computer science teacher, tries "to clearly explain technology, biology, and the world in a way that is interesting and accessible to anyone who wants to learn." As you read, notice how the authors break down the category of "the Oscars" into increasingly smaller, more manageable sections, such as the organization of the Academy of Motion Picture Arts and Sciences and the history of the awards ceremony.

Every spring, the movie industry gears up for its biggest celebra-   1
tion: the Academy Awards, more commonly known as the Oscars. There is extensive press coverage of the event, even down to the arrival of the stars; flashbulbs and microphones abound as the nominees and other famous, well-dressed guests make their way down the red carpet, flanked by cheering onlookers. The Oscars aren't just for Hollywood's most powerful and glamorous, though: millions of people tune in every year to root for their favorite movies and actors, check out the incredible clothing on display, or maybe just catch any embarrassing podium mishaps as they happen. Let's take a look at the organization behind the Oscars, see what the Academy actually is, and learn how the Oscars are awarded.

THE ACADEMY

So many Oscar winners gush "l would like to thank the Acad-   2
emy" that it's become a cliché. But what is the Academy, anyway? And

why should it be thanked? The Academy, in this case, is the Academy of Motion Picture Arts and Sciences, a professional honorary society formed in 1927. In spirit, the Academy is something like the Phi Beta Kappa Society or National Honor Society. It's an organization dedicated to promoting excellence in a particular field (filmmaking). Just like similar organizations, it has many members connected to that field (more than 5,000 filmmaking professionals).

3   You must be invited by the Academy to become a member. Different branches of the Academy (focusing on different aspects of the filmmaking world) have their own standards of eligibility for potential members. The Academy is involved in a lot of different projects—from film preservation to developing new film technology—but it's best known for its yearly awards ceremony.

4   The purpose of the Academy Awards is to promote excellence in filmmaking by honoring extraordinary achievements from the previous year. Members of the Academy, including actors, producers, directors, and a variety of other film craftsmen, choose who will receive the awards that year by casting ballots. So when a winner thanks the Academy, he or she is really thanking all their professional peers who collectively decided to bestow the honor. They're also thanking the organization as a whole, which decided to hand out awards in the first place.

ALL ABOUT OSCAR

5   We generally think of the entire Academy Awards ceremony as "the Oscars," but Oscar is really just a nickname for the actual award statuettes and their image. When MGM art director Cedric Gibbons and sculptor George Stanley created the statuette in 1928, the Academy referred to it as the Academy Award of Merit. It didn't take on the name Oscar until the 1930s. There are several stories about the nickname's origin, and nobody is completely sure of the truth. The Academy supports this version: In the early '30s, an Academy librarian named Margaret Herrick remarked that the statue looked like her Uncle Oscar. The name stuck, and the Academy staff began referring to the statue as "Oscar." In 1934, Sidney Skolsky mentioned the nickname in a column on Katharine Hepburn's first best actress win. The name caught on, and the Academy officially adopted it in 1939.

PICKING THE WINNERS

6   The first stage in selecting Oscar winners is narrowing all the possible honorees in a given year down to five nominees for each

award category. To be eligible for nominations in any of the feature film categories, a movie must meet these basic requirements:

- It must be more than 40 minutes long.
- Its public premiere must have been in a movie theater, during the appropriate calendar year.
- It must have premiered in 35 mm or 70 mm film format or in 24-frame, progressive-scan digital format.
- It must have played in an L.A. County theater, for paid admission, for seven consecutive days, beginning in the appropriate calendar year.

If producers or distributors would like their eligible film to be 7 considered for an Oscar nomination, they must submit an Official Screen Credits form. This form lists the production credits for all related Oscar categories. The Academy collects these forms and lists the submitted films in the "Reminder List of Eligible Releases." In January, the Academy mails a nomination ballot and a copy of the "Reminder List" to each Academy member.

For most of the award categories, only Academy members in that 8 particular field are allowed to vote for nominees (that is, only directors submit nominations for best director and only editors submit nominations for best editor). Foreign film and documentary nominees are chosen by special screening groups made up of Academy members from all branches, and everybody gets to select best picture nominees. Foreign film nominees are selected from a list of films submitted by other nations. Each other country can submit only one film per year.

An Academy member can select five nominees per category, 9 ranked in order of preference. For most categories, voters write in only the film title. For acting categories, the voters pick specific actors. It's up to the individual Academy voters to decide whether an actor should be nominated for a leading role or supporting role. An actor can't be nominated for both categories for a single performance, however. The Academy assigns the nominee to whichever category the nominee qualifies for first. Producers often take out ads in *Variety* and other major movie industry magazines to suggest nominees for particular categories.

Academy members typically have a couple of weeks to submit 10 their choices for nominees. Once the ballots are in, the accounting firm PricewaterhouseCoopers tabulates the nominee ballot votes in secrecy. Soon after, the Academy announces the nominees in an early morning press conference at the Samuel Goldwyn Theatre in Beverly Hills. A week or so later, the Academy mails final ballots to all Academy members. Members have two weeks to return the ballots, and then the "polls" are closed. PricewaterhouseCoopers tabulates the votes in absolute secrecy and seals the results.

11   While all this is going on, production companies are sinking considerable funds into campaigning for their contenders. The Academy condones any efforts to get Academy members to see the films, but restricts production companies from mailing out inappropriate incentives. Production companies are allowed to send Academy members video copies of contender films and to organize special screenings of their films.

12   After all the ballots are in and the votes are counted, it all comes down to the big night itself. Oscar night honors big-budget entertainment, and, appropriately, it is a big-budget entertainment event itself. Every year, hundreds of workers, including carpenters, artists, musicians, cameramen, and chefs, work days on end preparing for the big show. The result, in a good year, is a vibrant, glamorous celebration of all things Hollywood.   ■

To draw detailed graphic organizers using a computer, visit www .bedfordstmartins.com /successfulwriting.

| **EXERCISE 11.5**

Draw a graphic organizer for "Fender Benders: Legal Do's and Don'ts" (pp. 327–30).

INTEGRATING PROCESS ANALYSIS INTO AN ESSAY

While some essays you write will focus solely on explaining a process, other essays will incorporate an explanation of a process into a discussion that relies on a different pattern of development, such as description or narration. Let's suppose, for instance, that you are writing a descriptive essay about an alcohol abuse program for high school students. Although description is your primary pattern of development, you decide to include a brief process analysis of how alcohol impairs mental functioning.

Use the following tips to incorporate process analysis into essays based on other patterns of development.

1. **Provide a brief summary or overview of the process rather than a detailed step-by-step explanation.** Too much detail will divert your readers from the primary focus of your essay. Consider explaining only the major steps in the process rather than every step in detail.

2. **Make it clear *why* the process analysis is included.** Use a transitional sentence to alert readers that a process analysis will follow and to suggest why it is

FIGURE 11.2
GRAPHIC ORGANIZER FOR "HOW THE OSCARS WORK"

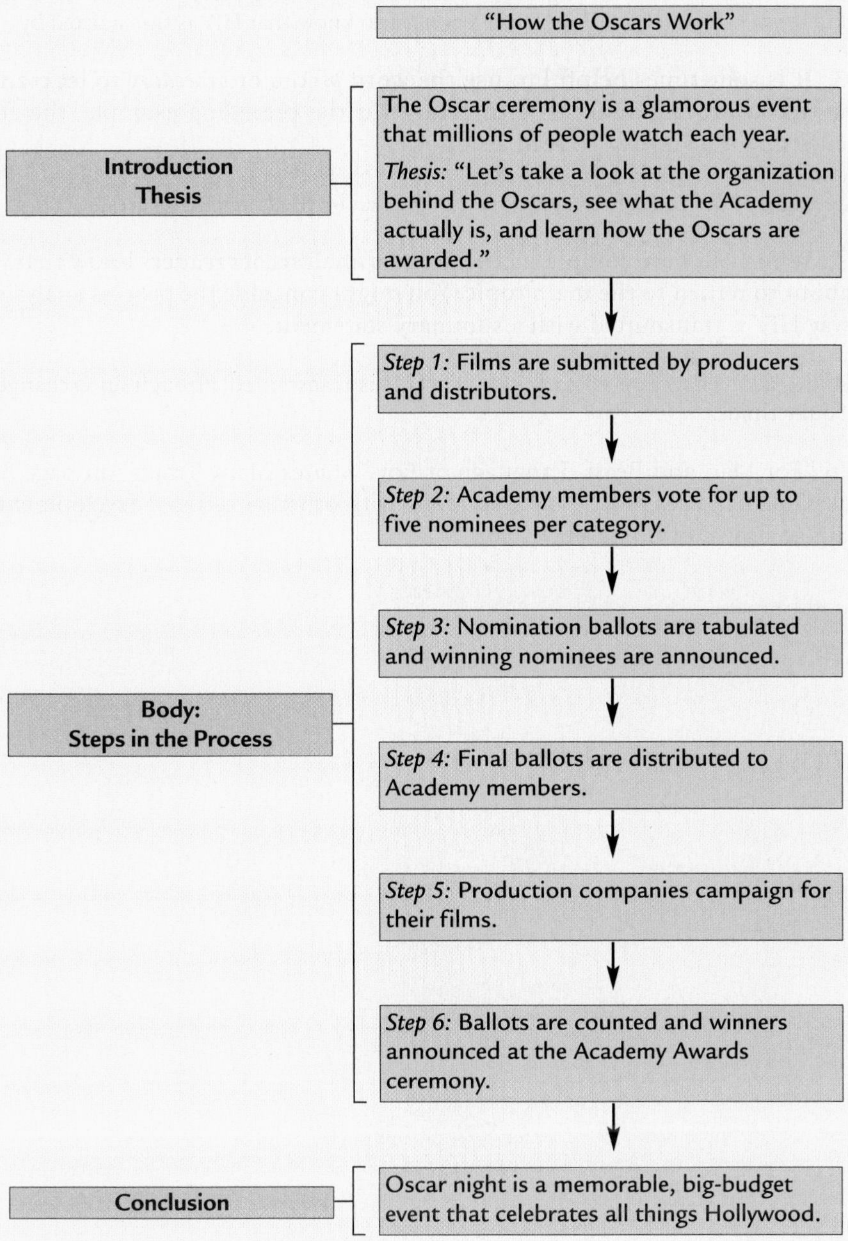

"How the Oscars Work"

Introduction
Thesis

The Oscar ceremony is a glamorous event that millions of people watch each year.
Thesis: "Let's take a look at the organization behind the Oscars, see what the Academy actually is, and learn how the Oscars are awarded."

Step 1: Films are submitted by producers and distributors.

Step 2: Academy members vote for up to five nominees per category.

Step 3: Nomination ballots are tabulated and winning nominees are announced.

Body:
Steps in the Process

Step 4: Final ballots are distributed to Academy members.

Step 5: Production companies campaign for their films.

Step 6: Ballots are counted and winners announced at the Academy Awards ceremony.

Conclusion

Oscar night is a memorable, big-budget event that celebrates all things Hollywood.

included. For example, here is how you might introduce a brief summary of the process by which AIDS is spread through HIV (human immunodeficiency virus).

> Before you explain to teenagers *how* to avoid contracting HIV, you need to let them know *what* they are avoiding. Teenagers need to know that HIV is transmitted by . . .

3. It is sometimes helpful to use the word *process* **or** *procedure* **to let readers know that a process analysis is to follow.** In the preceding example, the final sentence might be revised to read as follows.

> Teenagers need to know that HIV is transmitted by the following process.

4. When you have completed the process analysis, let readers know that you are about to return to the main topic. You might conclude the process analysis of the way HIV is transmitted with a summary statement.

> Above all, teenagers need to know that HIV is transmitted through an exchange of bodily fluids.

In "For Man and Beast, Language of Love Shares Many Traits" on page 363, Daniel Goleman uses process analysis along with other patterns of development to explain an aspect of human behavior.

A GUIDED WRITING ASSIGNMENT

The following guide will help you write a process analysis e
a how-to or a how-it-works essay. Although you will fo
analysis, you may need to integrate one or more other pa
opment in your essay.

The Assignment

Write a process analysis essay on one of the following topics or one that
you choose on your own. Be sure the process you choose is one that you
know enough about to explain to others or can learn about through observation or research. Your audience consists of readers who are unfamiliar
with the process, including your classmates.

How-to Essay Topics

1. How to improve _____ (your study habits, your wardrobe,
   your batting average)
2. How to be a successful _____ (diver, parent, gardener)
3. How to make or buy _____ (an object for personal use or
   enjoyment)
4. How to prepare for _____ (a test, a job interview, an oral
   presentation)

How-It-Works Essay Topics

1. How your college _____ (spends tuition revenues, hires
   professors, raises money)
2. How _____ works (an answering machine, a generator,
   email, or a search engine)
3. How a decision is made to _____ (accept a student at a
   college, add or eliminate a local or state agency)
4. How _____ is put together (a quilt, a news broadcast, a
   football team, a Web site)

As you develop your process analysis essay, you will probably use narrative strategies, description (for example, to describe equipment or
objects), or illustration (such as to show an example of part of the process).

*For more on narration,
description, and illustration, see Chapters 8–10.*

Selecting a Process

The following guidelines will help you select a process to write about. You may want to use one of the prewriting techniques discussed in Chapter 3. Consider your learning style when you select a prewriting technique. You might try questioning, group brainstorming, or sketching a diagram of a process. Be sure to keep the following tips in mind.

- For a how-to essay, choose a process that you can visualize or perform as you write. Keep the equipment nearby for easy reference. In explaining how to scuba dive, for example, it may be helpful to have your scuba equipment in front of you.

- For a how-it-works essay, choose a topic about which you have background knowledge or for which you can find information. Unless you are experienced in woodworking, for example, do not try to explain how stains produce different effects on different kinds of wood.

- Choose a topic that is useful and interesting to your readers. Unless you can find a way to make an essay about how to do the laundry interesting, do not write about it.

ESSAY IN PROGRESS 1

Using the preceding suggestions, choose a process to write about from the list of essay topics on page 341, or choose a topic of your own.

Considering Your Purpose, Audience, and Point of View

Once you choose a process to write about, consider your purpose and audience. How-to and how-it-works essays can be informative, persuasive, or both. Your main aim is always to inform readers, but you may want to persuade readers that they should try the process (how-to) or that the process is beneficial or should be changed (how-it-works).

For this Guided Writing Assignment, your audience consists of general readers, including your classmates, who are unfamiliar with the process that you are going to analyze. As you develop your essay, think about what your audience wants and needs to know about the process. Keep the following questions about your audience in mind.

1. What background information does my audience need?
2. What terms should I define?
3. What equipment should I describe?

4. How much detail does my audience need?

5. What trouble spots require special attention and explanation?

When considering your audience, you also need to think about point of view. Writers of how-to essays commonly use the second person, addressing the reader directly as *you*. The second-person point of view is informal and draws the reader in, as in Budish's essay on "Fender Benders: Legal Do's and Don'ts." For how-it-works essays, the third person (*he, she, it*) is commonly used, as in "How the Oscars Work."

For more on purpose, audience, and point of view, see Chapter 3, p. 65.

ESSAY IN PROGRESS 2

For the process you selected in Essay in Progress 1, use the preceding guidelines to consider your purpose, the needs of your audience, and your point of view.

Developing Your Thesis

For more on thesis statements, see Chapter 4.

Once you have chosen a process to write about and carefully considered your purpose, audience, and point of view, your next step is to develop a working thesis. As noted earlier, the thesis of a process analysis essay tells readers *why* the process is important, beneficial, or relevant to them (see p. 331). In a how-to essay on jogging, for instance, your thesis might state the benefits of the activity.

Considering your audience is especially important in developing a thesis for a process analysis, since what may be of interest or importance to one audience may be of little interest to another audience.

ESSAY IN PROGRESS 3

Write a working thesis statement that tells readers why the process you have chosen for your essay is important, beneficial, or relevant to them.

Listing the Steps and Gathering Details

Once you are satisfied with your working thesis statement, your next task is to list the steps in the process and to gather appropriate and interesting details. You may need to do additional prewriting to generate details that will help you explain the process. Use the following suggestions.

For more on prewriting strategies, see Chapter 3.

Learning Style Options

1. On paper or on your computer, list the steps in the process as they occur to you, keeping these questions in mind.

   • What separate actions are involved?

   • What steps are obvious to me but may not be obvious to someone unfamiliar with the process?

   • What steps, if omitted, will lead to problems or failure?

2. Discuss your process with classmates to see what kinds of details they need to know about your topic.

For more on library and Internet research, see Chapter 19.

3. Once you have a list of steps, generate details by doing additional prewriting or doing research in the library or on the Internet. First, add the details that readers need to understand the process itself. You might include sensory details about the process. (Check the five questions on pages 342–43 to make sure you have sufficient detail.)

ESSAY IN PROGRESS 4

Using the preceding guidelines, brainstorm a list of the steps involved in the process. Then add details that will help you explain the steps. If necessary, interview someone knowledgeable about the process, or do library or Internet research to gather more details.

Evaluating Your Ideas and Thesis

Take a few minutes to evaluate the process you have chosen and determine whether your analysis of it is meaningful, worthwhile, and relevant to your audience. Start by rereading everything you have written with a critical eye.

TRYING OUT YOUR IDEAS ON OTHERS

Working in a group of two or three students, discuss your ideas and thesis for this chapter's assignment. Each writer should state his or her topic and thesis and describe the steps in the process. Then, as a group, evaluate each writer's work. Group members should answer the following questions.

1. How familiar are you with the process the writer has chosen?
2. Is the writer's explanation of the process detailed and complete?
3. What additional information do you need to understand or perform the process?
4. What unanswered questions do you have about the process?

Highlight usable details; cross out any that seem unnecessary or repetitious. As you review your work, add steps, details, definitions, and background information where they are needed.

ESSAY IN PROGRESS 5

Using the preceding suggestions and the feedback you have received from classmates, evaluate your thesis and your steps and decide whether you need to add details.

Organizing and Drafting

Once you have gathered enough details to explain the steps in the process, developed your thesis statement, and considered the advice of peer reviewers, you are ready to organize your ideas and draft your essay.

For more on drafting an essay, see Chapter 5.

Organizing the Steps in the Process

For a process that involves fewer than ten steps, you can usually arrange the steps chronologically, devoting one paragraph to each step. However, for a more complex process with ten or more steps, group the steps into related categories to avoid overwhelming your reader. Divide the steps of a complex process into three or four major groups, devoting one paragraph to each group of steps.

Try experimenting with different orders and groupings. Using a computer's cut-and-paste function will make it easy to rearrange your groupings. For an essay on how to run a successful garage sale, the steps might be organized into these main groups.

Group 1: Locating and collecting merchandise
Group 2: Advertising
Group 3: Pricing and setting up
Group 4: Conducting the sale

Below each main group, you would list the steps related to it.

Group 1: Steps for Locating and Collecting Merchandise

1. Clean out your closets, basement, and attic.
2. Offer to clear out the closets, attics, and basements of friends and relatives.
3. Pick up merchandise discarded at the town dump.

After a one-paragraph introduction to the essay, devote one paragraph to each group of steps. A topic sentence introduces the group, and the rest of the paragraph explains the individual steps involved. For example, in the essay about the garage sale, the paragraph devoted to group 1 would include a topic sentence about locating and collecting merchandise and a discussion of the three steps related to this task.

ESSAY IN PROGRESS 6

Review the list of steps you generated in Essay in Progress 5. If your process involves ten or more steps, use the preceding guidelines to group the steps into related categories. Write an outline or draw a graphic organizer to ensure that your steps are in chronological sequence.

Drafting the Process Analysis Essay

Once you have organized the steps of the process, your next task is to write a first draft. Use the following guidelines to draft your essay.

1. **Include reasons for the steps.** Unless the reason is obvious, explain why each step or group of steps is important and necessary. Locating merchandise is an important step in running a successful garage sale and does not need justification, but the importance of other details about conducting the sale may not be as apparent. For instance, your readers may not realize that robberies often occur during garage sales. If you mention this issue in your paragraph on your fourth major step, conducting the sale, then readers will be more likely to take the precautions you suggest, such as locking the house and wearing a waist-wallet.

2. **Consider using graphics and headings.** A drawing or diagram is sometimes necessary to make your steps easier to understand. Suppose you are explaining how automobile seat belts protect passengers from injury. Readers would benefit from studying a diagram that illustrates how sudden deceleration of an automobile causes a pendulum to activate a locking device that prevents passengers from pitching forward. Remember, however, that a graphic is not a substitute for a clearly written explanation.

When using a graphic, be sure to introduce it in your essay and refer to it by its title. If you are including more than one graphic, assign a number to each one (*Figure 1, Figure 2*) and include the number in your text reference.

When writing about a lengthy or complicated process, consider adding headings to divide the body of your essay into manageable segments. Headings also call attention to your main topics and signal changes in topic. Budish uses headings in "Fender Benders: Legal Do's and Don'ts" to identify steps in the process he describes.

3. Use transitions. To avoid writing a process analysis that sounds monotonous, use transitions such as *before, next,* and *finally.*

For more on transitions, see Chapter 5, p. 128.

4. Write an effective introduction. The introduction usually presents your thesis statement and includes necessary background information. It should also capture your readers' interest and focus their attention on the process. Notice how Budish starts "Fender Benders: Legal Do's and Don'ts" with an anecdote about a traffic accident and its unexpected consequences — an outcome that readers can avoid by following the process he presents. For some essays, you may want to explain that the process you are describing is related to other processes and ideas. For a lengthy or complex process, consider including an overview of the steps or providing a brief introductory list.

For more on writing effective paragraphs, including introductions and conclusions, see Chapter 5.

5. Use an appropriate tone. By the time your readers move from your introduction to the body of your essay, they should have a good idea of the tone of your essay. Recall from "Fender Benders: Legal Do's and Don'ts" how Budish establishes a direct yet friendly tone in his introductory paragraphs by choosing words and phrases such as "Ouch!" and "Imagine your surprise." The tone you choose should be appropriate for your audience and purpose. In some situations, a matter-of-fact tone is appropriate; other times, an emotional or humorous tone may be suitable.

For more on tone, see Chapter 7, p. 187.

6. Write a satisfying conclusion. An essay that ends with the final step in the process may sound incomplete to your readers. Especially in a how-it-works essay, readers appreciate a satisfying conclusion. In your conclusion, you might emphasize the value or importance of the process, describe particular situations in which it is useful, or offer a final amusing or emphatic comment or anecdote.

ESSAY IN PROGRESS 7

Draft your process essay, using the organization you developed in Essay in Progress 6 and the preceding guidelines for drafting.

Analyzing and Revising

If possible, wait at least a day before rereading and revising your draft. As you reread your draft, concentrate on the organization and your ideas, not on grammar or mechanics. Use one or more of the following suggestions to analyze your draft.

Learning Style Options

1. Read your essay aloud to one or two friends or classmates. Ask them to interrupt you if they have questions or if a step is unclear.

2. For a how-to essay, evaluate by visualizing the steps or following them exactly. Be careful to complete only the steps included in your essay. Following your directions to the letter will help you discover gaps and identify sections that are unclear.

3. Update the graphic organizer or outline you prepared earlier. Look to see if the steps are sequenced correctly and if each step is covered in enough detail.

Use Figure 11.3 to guide your analysis. You might also ask a classmate to review your draft essay using the questions in the flowchart. For each answer that refers you to the right column of the chart, ask your reviewer to explain why he or she answered in that way. For a how-to essay, ask your reviewer to try out the process, if possible, or to imagine himself or herself doing so. Encourage your reader to ask questions wherever necessary. These questions will help you discover where and what to add or revise. For a how-it-works essay, ask your reviewer to describe the process to you. As you listen to the explanation, you may discover sections in which your information is incomplete or unclear.

For more on the benefits of peer review, see Chapter 6, p. 158.

ESSAY IN PROGRESS 8

Revise your draft using Figure 11.3 and any comments you received from peer reviewers.

Editing and Proofreading

The last step is to check your revised essay for errors in grammar, spelling, punctuation, and mechanics. Be sure to look for errors that you tend to make. (Refer to your error log.)

For more on keeping an error log, see Chapter 7, p. 193.

As you edit and proofread your process analysis essay, watch out for two grammatical errors in particular—comma splices and shifts in verb mood.

1. Avoid comma splices. A comma splice occurs when two independent clauses are joined only by a comma. To correct a comma splice, add a coordinating conjunction (*and, but, for, nor, or, so,* or *yet*), change the comma to a semicolon, or divide the sentence into two sentences. You can also subordinate one clause to the other.

FIGURE 11.3
FLOWCHART FOR REVISING A PROCESS ANALYSIS

Questions		Revision Strategies

1. Highlight your thesis statement. Does it make clear the importance of the process you are discussing?

No →
- Ask yourself: "Why do I need to know this process? Why is it important?" Incorporate the answers into your thesis statement.

↓ **Yes**

2. *Number* the steps or groups of your process in the margin of your paper. Are they organized in chronological order (or in some other logical progression)?

No →
- Visualize or actually complete the process to discover the best order in which to do it.
- Study your graphic organizer or outline to determine if any steps are out of order.

↓ **Yes**

3. Place an *X* beside any technical terms you have used. Is each unfamiliar term defined?

No →
- Define technical terms for your readers.
- Ask a classmate to read definitions of unfamiliar terms.

↓ **Yes**

4. Place [brackets] around any background information you have provided in your introduction. Is it sufficient? Have you provided an overview of the process, if needed?

No →
- Give an example of a situation in which the process might be used.
- Explain that related processes and ideas depend on the process you are describing.

↓ **Yes**

(Continued on next page)

FIGURE 11.3 (*Continued*)

Questions		Revision Strategies
5. Draw a (circle) around any equipment you have mentioned. Have you included all necessary equipment?	**No** →	• Describe equipment you have overlooked. • Describe equipment that might be unfamiliar to readers.

Yes ↓

| 6. Place checkmarks ✔ beside key details of the process. Have you included an appropriate level of detail for your readers? | **No** → | • Add or delete background information in your introduction.
• Add or delete definitions of technical terms.
• Add or delete detail. |

Yes ↓

| 7. For a how-to essay, <u>double underline</u> sections where you have anticipated problems and difficulties for your readers. Are these sections clear and reassuring? | **No** → | • Add more detail about critical steps.
• Warn your readers about confusing or difficult steps.
• Offer advice on what to do if things go wrong. |

Yes ↓

| 8. Underline the topic sentence of each paragraph. Does each paragraph contain a topic sentence that focuses the paragraph on a separate step or group of steps? | **No** → | • Revise so that each paragraph has a topic sentence and supporting details.
• Ask a classmate whether more or less detail is needed for each step. |

Yes ↓

(Continued on next page)

FIGURE 11.3 (*Continued*)

Questions		Revision Strategies
9. Draw a box around and reread your introduction and conclusion. Is each effective?	**No** →	Revise your introduction and conclusion so that they meet the guidelines in Chapter 5.

Yes

10. Print out another draft to edit and proofread before turning in your essay.

▶ The first step in creating a flower arrangement is to choose an attractive

　　　　but

container, the container should not be the focal point of the arrangement.

▶ Following signs is one way to navigate a busy airport, looking for a map is
another.

▶ To place a long-distance call using a credit card, first dial 0 and the 10 digit

　　　　. Next

number, next punch in your credit card number and PIN.

　After you have placed

▶ Place the pill on the cat's tongue, hold its mouth closed, rubbing its chin
until it swallows the pill.

   2. Avoid shifts in verb mood. A verb can have three *moods* — indicative, imperative, and subjunctive. The **indicative mood** is used to express ordinary statements and to ask questions.

▶ The modem is built into the computer.

   The **imperative mood** is used for giving orders, advice, and directions. The subject of a verb in the imperative mood is understood to be *you*, but it is not expressed.

▶ (You) Plant your feet firmly before swinging the club.

The **subjunctive mood** is used for making statements contrary to fact or for wishes and recommendations.

▶ I suggest that a new phone line be installed.

When writing a process analysis, be sure to use a consistent mood throughout your essay.

▶ The firefighters told the third-grade class the procedures to follow if a fire

occurred in their school. They emphasized that children should leave the

they should
building quickly. Also, move at least 100 feet away from the building.
^

ESSAY IN PROGRESS 9

Edit and proofread your essay, paying particular attention to avoiding comma splices and shifts in verb mood.

STUDENTS WRITE

Kyle Mares was a student at Crafton Hills Community College in California when he wrote the following essay. He was asked to write an essay explaining a process that he had mastered. As you read, consider if the steps outlined in the essay clearly explain the process of creating a Web site.

Creating Your Own Web Site

Kyle Mares

1   Despite the challenges involved, there are many
advantages to publishing your own Web site on the Internet. For example, having your résumé available online for
potential employers to view can showcase your technical
savvy, and a Web site built around your personal interests and concerns can connect you to any like-minded
person with Internet access. To create your own Web site

and reap the benefits associated with having one, you
need to follow a five-step process that includes planning, designing, creating content, testing and reviewing,
and finally publishing and promoting your Web site.

    To start, you will need to plan your Web site by
considering where to publish it, how to build it, and
what it will contain. You first need to consider where
you will publish it because each option offers different
benefits and drawbacks. The first option is to use free
Web publishing through an Internet service provider like
AOL or Earthlink. Even though these hosting services are
free, they provide limited storage space for your files,
and they insert advertisements into your Web pages,
affecting your layout. The second option is a fee-based,
or dedicated, hosting service like DreamHost or Yahoo
Geocities. These offer more storage space, professional
design advice, and a greater degree of freedom and flexibility, but there is a cost to use these services. The
third option is to purchase your own Web server, but
although this gives you ultimate control over your site,
a server is expensive and requires a constant connection
to the Internet. For beginners, the best option is to
publish through one of the free hosting services that
offers the most server space and the fewest restrictions.
Many colleges also host their students' personal Web
pages for free without inserting advertisements, so be
sure to check with your school first to see if this is
an option.

    After determining where to publish your site, you
need to plan how you will build it. There are two
ways to build a Web site: You can create code in HTML
(hypertext markup language), or you can use an authoring
program. HTML is the computer language designers use
to create Web sites. When Web browsers read a Web page,
they convert the HTML coding into the page you see.
Learning to write HTML is challenging, but it is a useful and marketable skill. However, if learning HTML seems

too difficult, you can use an authoring program like FrontPage or Dreamweaver. Because these computer programs work like word-processing programs, they allow you to build a Web page without knowing how to use HTML and are often the easiest way for beginners to build their site.

4   The last step in planning your Web site is to create a site map--a diagram of all the pages on the site. You can use a word-processing program to create your diagram or merely sketch it out on paper. Like a roadmap, a site map shows the basic structure of your site, allowing you to follow it when implementing design and content.

5   Once you have a site map, you are ready to begin designing the site. The design of your Web site is crucial because a poorly designed site discourages people from visiting it. A good design should attract and capture your audience's attention. There are a wide variety of design details to consider, such as use of navigation bars, color, font, visuals, and links. To keep your reader oriented, make sure that the overall design is consistent from page to page. You can achieve this through the use of repeated headers, footers, and sidebars. Before you begin, it is a good idea to spend some time visiting other sites on the Web, noting both good and poor applications of design elements and creating a list of what design features might work on your site. When designing your site, check each page thoroughly to ensure that the layout, colors, navigation tools, links, and other design elements are clear and easy to follow. Problems like unclearly labeled links may require changes to fix them, but it is much better to catch a mistake and correct it early in the design process than to publish a flawed Web site and receive a torrent of complaint emails.

6   Once you have a basic design in place, you are ready to create content. Content is the material on the Web site, the unique text and graphics for every page.

Keep your users interested by offering compelling information in a wide variety of formats, such as figures,
visuals, sound and video clips, and articles and analysis
that they may not find anywhere else. However, even the
fanciest graphics and images won't hold someone's attention if there is no significant content, so be sure to
invest just as much time developing the words for your
site as you did planning and designing it. To keep your
site fresh and to keep people returning to it, you may
need to update it regularly with new text and data. Your
topic will determine how often to update your site. For
example, if your site deals with an upcoming election,
you should update whenever new information becomes available. You will have to check the entire site every time
you update it, but you will keep the content relevant,
fresh, and interesting for your audience.

The final step before launching your Web site is to   7
test and review all aspects of the site to ensure that
everything performs as it should. In doing so, you may
find that certain elements and features do not work as
intended and that you need to find creative solutions.
It is a good idea to have a friend review your site to
see if he or she has any difficulty navigating the
pages. Test all details on your pages to make them as
user-friendly as possible, and don't be afraid to visit
other sites to see how they handle various problems and
obstacles.

Once you are satisfied with your Web site, you are   8
ready to publish and promote it. To launch the site,
follow your hosting service's instructions for publishing. To make others aware of your site's existence, you
can publicize your Web site by submitting it to search
engines and Web rings, online links of similar Web
sites. Offer to exchange links with people who run similar pages so that readers from the community you are
trying to reach learn of your Web site. Depending on the
subject of your site, consider posting its address, or

URL (uniform resource locator), on related message boards
and newsgroups to create interest or even placing an ad
for it in your college newspaper. This extra effort will
help ensure that others will visit and make use of your
site.

9   Although a lot of time and effort are necessary to
build your own Web site, the creative process is richly
rewarding. In the Information Age, Web expertise is a
valuable skill, and each step in designing Web pages
will teach you new techniques and skills that can be
used in a wide variety of careers. There are incredible
opportunities for people who take a hands-on approach to
the Internet, and by publishing your own pages you'll
gain valuable experience that will benefit you in your
future endeavors.

Analyzing the Essay

1. Evaluate the writer's thesis statement and introduction. Do they suggest why making a Web site might be useful and important to readers? Explain.

2. What are the potential trouble spots in the process that Mares identifies?

3. Does the introduction provide enough background information, or do you wish the writer had included more information? Explain.

4. Evaluate the essay's level of detail. Do you think you could create a Web site using Mares's instructions? If not, where is additional detail needed?

5. Does Mares's conclusion bring his essay to a satisfying close? Why or why not?

Reacting to the Essay: Discussion and Journal Writing

1. Mares states that Web expertise is a valuable skill and that it can be useful in a variety of careers. What other skills do you think that employers would find desirable? What skills do you hope to acquire to prepare you for employment?

2. Discuss both the benefits and drawbacks of having your own Web site.

3. Mares says that it takes a great deal of time to create a Web site. Write a journal entry explaining why such an investment of time might be worthwhile for this project or for another project you hope to accomplish in the next year.

READING A PROCESS ANALYSIS

The following section provides advice for reading a process analysis. Two model essays illustrate the characteristics of process analysis covered in this chapter and provide opportunities to examine, analyze, and react to the writer's ideas. The second essay uses process analysis along with other methods of development.

WORKING WITH TEXT: READING PROCESS ANALYSIS ESSAYS

Process analysis is a common method of explaining; it is often used in textbooks, including this one, and in other forms of academic writing. To read a process analysis effectively, use the following suggestions.

For more on reading strategies, see Chapter 2.

What to Look For, Highlight, and Annotate

1. Look for and highlight the thesis statement. Try to discover why the writer believes the process is important or useful.

2. For a how-to essay, look for difficulties you might experience in the process or questions you may need to ask about it.

3. Highlight or underline each step or grouping of steps. Using a different colored highlighter or an asterisk (*), mark steps that the author warns are difficult or troublesome.

4. For a complex or especially important process (such as one you will need to apply on an exam), outline or draw a graphic organizer of the steps. Try explaining each step in your own words without referring to the text.

5. For a how-to essay, imagine yourself carrying out the process as you read.

6. Highlight or use a symbol to mark new terms as they are introduced.

7. Annotate the sections that summarize complex steps.

How to Find Ideas to Write About

Look for ideas to write about *as you read.* Record your ideas and impressions as marginal annotations. Think about why *you* want or need to understand the process. Think of situations in which you can use or apply the information. Also try to think of processes similar to the one described in the essay. If you think of metaphors or analogies, make a note of them. Consider how other processes are the same and how they are different from the one in the essay.

For more on discovering ideas for a response paper, see Chapter 2.

THINKING CRITICALLY ABOUT PROCESS ANALYSIS

Although most process analyses are straightforward and informative, you should still consider the author's motives for writing and knowledge of the topic. Use the following questions to think critically about the process analyses you read.

What Are the Writer's Motives?

As you read, ask yourself, "Why does the writer want me to understand or carry out this process? What is his or her motive?" At times, an author may have a hidden motive for explaining a process. For example, a writer opposed to the death penalty may use graphic details about the process of executions to shock readers and persuade them to oppose the death penalty. Because writers do not always state the purpose of their essays, it is your job as a critical reader to detect any hidden motives. Even a how-to article on a noncontroversial topic can have a hidden agenda, such as one entitled "How to Lose Ten Pounds" that was written by the owner of a weight-loss clinic.

Is the Writer Knowledgeable and Experienced?

When you read process analyses, always consider whether the writer has sufficient knowledge about or experience with the process. This step is especially important if you intend to perform the task. Following the advice of someone who is not qualified to give it can be a waste of time or even dangerous. For scholarly, academic, popular, and most other types of writers, it is possible to check credentials and determine whether the writer is considered an expert in the field. An article about a new treatment for asthma by an author who has no credentials in medicine would not be a reliable source of information on that topic. In addition to checking the writer's credentials, consider whether he or she supports assertions with outside sources, expert opinion, and quotes from authorities.

PROCESS ANALYSIS ESSAY

As you read the following essay, notice how the author uses the elements of process analysis discussed in this chapter.

Remote Control: How to Raise a Media Skeptic
Susan Douglas

Susan Douglas is a media critic for The Progressive *and a lecturer on media literacy. She has written the book* Where the Girls Are: Growing Up Female with the Mass Media *(1994) and contributed articles to such periodicals as the* Village Voice, The Nation, *and the* Journal of American History. *The following selection—a how-to essay—is from a 1997 issue of* Utne Reader, *a periodical that publishes articles from specialized magazines known as alternative media. As you read the selection, highlight the steps that Douglas outlines, and consider the order in which she presents them.*

1   "Mommy, Mommy, come here now! Hurry, you're gonna miss it. It's Barbie's High-Steppin' Pony, and its legs really move! Hurreeeeey!"

2   "No!" I bark, as I'm wiping the dog barf up from the carpet, stirring the onions again so they don't burn, and slamming the phone down on a caller from Citibank who wants to know how I'm doin' today. It is 5:56 p.m., and I'm in no mood. "I don't come for commercials, and besides, the horse doesn't really move—they just make it look that way."

3   "Oh yeah?" demands my daughter, sounding like a federal prosecutor. "It can too. It's not like those old ones where you told me they faked it—this one really does move."

4   So now I have to go see and, indeed, the sucker takes batteries, and the stupid horse moves—sort of. "See, Mommy, the commercials don't always lie."

5   Moments like this prompt me to wonder whether I'm a weak-kneed, lazy slug or, dare I say it, a hypocrite. See, I teach media studies, and, even worse, I go around the country lecturing about the importance of media literacy. One of my talking points is how network children's programming is, ideologically, a toxic waste dump. Yet here I am, just like millions of parents during that portion of the day rightly known as hell hour—dinnertime—shoving my kid in front of Nickelodeon so my husband and I can get dinner on the table while we whisper sweet nothings like "It's your turn to take her to Brownies tomorrow" and "Oh, I forgot to tell you that your mother called three days ago with an urgent message."

6   We let her watch Nickelodeon, but I still pop in to ridicule Kool-Aid commercials or to ask her why Clarissa's parents (on *Clarissa Explains It All*) are so dopey. I am trying to have it both ways: to let

television distract her, which I desperately need, and to help her see through its lies and banalities. I am very good at rationalizing this approach, but I also think it isn't a bad compromise for overworked parents who believe Barbie is the anti-Christ* yet still need to wash out grotty lunch boxes and zap leftovers at the end of the day.

7   It's best to be honest up front: My house is not media proofed. I am not one of those virtuous, haloed parents who has banished the box from the home. I actually believe that there are interesting, fun shows for my daughter to watch on TV. (And I'm not about to give up *ER*.)

8   But I'm also convinced that knowing about television, and growing up with it, provides my daughter with a form of cultural literacy that she will need, that will tie her to her friends and her generation and help her understand her place in the world. So instead of killing my TV, I've tried to show my daughter basic nonsense-detecting techniques. Don't think your choices are either no TV or a zombified kid. Studies show that the simple act of intervening — of talking to your child about what's on television and why it's on there — is one of the most important factors in helping children understand and distance themselves from some of the box's more repugnant imagery.

9   I recommend the quick surgical strike, between throwing the laundry in and picking up the Legos. Watch a few commercials with them and point out that commercials lie about the toys they show, making them look much better than they are in real life. Count how many male and female characters there are in a particular show or commercial and talk about what we see boys doing and what we see girls doing. Why, you might ask, do we always see girls playing with makeup kits and boys playing with little Johnny Exocet missiles? Real-life dads change diapers, push strollers, and feed kids, but you never see boys doing this with dolls on commercials. Ask where the Asian and African-American kids are. Point out how most of the parents in shows geared to kids are much more stupid than real-life parents. (By the way, children report that TV shows encourage them to talk back to their folks.) Tell them that all those cereals advertised with cartoon characters and rap music (like Cocoa Puffs and Trix) will put giant black holes in their teeth that only a dentist with a drill the size of the space shuttle can fix.

10   One of the best words to use when you're watching TV with your kids is *stupid,* as in "Aren't Barbie's feet — the way she's always forced

---

*Anti-Christ: In the Christian religion, the evil person who will appear in the days before Christ returns.

to walk on her tiptoes—really stupid?" or "Isn't it stupid that Lassie is smarter than the mom on this show?" (My favorite Barbie exercise: Put your kitchen timer on for a minute and make your daughter walk around on her tiptoes just like Barbie; she'll get the point real fast.) *Cool*—a word that never seems to go out of style—is also helpful, as in "Isn't it cool that on *Legends of the Hidden Temple* (a game show on Nickelodeon) the girls are as strong and as fast as the boys?" Pointing out what's good on TV is important too.

See, I think complete media-proofing is impossible, because the   11
shallow, consumerist, anti-intellectual values of the mass media permeate our culture. And we parents shouldn't beat ourselves up for failing to quarantine our kids. But we can inoculate them—which means exposing them to the virus and showing them how to build up a few antibodies. So don't feel so guilty about letting them watch TV. Instead, have fun teaching them how to talk back to it rather than to you. ■

Examining the Reading

1. What is the author's view of children's television programming and of commercial advertisements? What, in particular, does she dislike?

2. What techniques does Douglas use to teach her daughter to be critical of what she views on television?

3. What benefits does Douglas claim that her daughter receives from television?

4. Explain the meaning of each of the following words as it is used in the reading: *hypocrite* (para. 5), *ideologically* (5), *banalities* (6), *rationalizing* (6), and *permeate* (11). Refer to your dictionary as needed.

Analyzing the Reading

1. Identify Douglas's thesis statement. What background information does she provide to support the thesis?

2. Discuss how Douglas's use of exaggeration supports her purpose in writing this essay.

3. Where does Douglas anticipate trouble spots in the process and offer solutions? In what places, if any, would more advice have been helpful to you?

4. Where does Douglas provide adequate detail? Identify those sections as well as any places where you think more detail is needed.

> ## MAKING CONNECTIONS: Parents and Children
>
> Both "Remote Control: How to Raise a Media Skeptic" (pp. 359–61) and "Bringing Out Your Child's Gifts" (pp. 419–22) guide parents in the difficult tasks of parenting.
>
> ### Analyzing the Readings
>
> 1. Both essays are written for parents and people interested in child development. What details convey this? Evaluate the level of detail each essay uses.
> 2. These two readings describe how parents should help their children become better critical thinkers and strengthen their children's natural talents. Write a journal entry describing which method of parental instruction—White's or Douglas's—you think is better. Why? Be sure to use specific details.
>
> ### Essay Idea
>
> What anxieties or fears do you think new parents face today? Do you think new parents today will have a tougher job than parents a generation ago? If so, why? If not, why?

5. Does Douglas appear to be knowledgeable about her subject? Support your answer with evidence.

Reacting to the Reading: Discussion and Journal Writing

1. Explain why you agree or disagree with the writer's critical views of the "shallow, consumerist, anti-intellectual values of the mass media" (para. 11).
2. Look for misleading images or stereotypes in the television programs you watch. Then write a journal entry describing one such image or stereotype.

PROCESS ANALYSIS COMBINED WITH OTHER PATTERNS

As you read the following essay by Daniel Goleman, notice how he combines process analysis with other patterns of development.

For Man and Beast, Language of Love Shares Many Traits

Daniel Goleman

Daniel Goleman holds a Ph.D. in behavioral and brain sciences and has pub-lished several books on psychology, including Emotional Intelligence *(1995),* Working with Emotional Intelligence *(1998),* The Emotionally Intelligent Workplace: How to Select For, Measure, and Improve Emotional Intelligence in Individuals, Groups, and Organizations *(2001), and* Destructive Emotions: A Scientific Dialogue with the Dalai Lama *(2003). He has taught at Harvard University and has been a sen-ior editor at* Psychology Today. *This essay appeared in the* New York Times *in February 1995. As you read the selection, highlight the thesis and the steps in the process.*

1   With the same ethological methods they have long used in stud-ies of animals, scientists are turning their attention to the nuances of human courtship rituals — otherwise known as flirting.

2   By turning the ethologist's lens on human courtship, scientists are finding striking similarities with other species, suggesting that the nonverbal template used by *Homo sapiens* for attracting and approaching a prospective mate is to some extent part of a larger, shared animal heritage.

3   A woman parades past a crowded bar to the women's room, hips swaying, eyes resting momentarily on a likely man and then coyly looking away just as she notices his look. This scenario exemplifies a standard opening move in courtship, getting attention, said Dr. David Givens, an anthropologist in Washington who is writing a book about evolution and behavior. "In the first phase of courting, humans broadcast widely a nonverbal message that amounts to 'notice me,'" said Dr. Givens. "They do it through movement, through their dress, through gesture."

4   From hundreds of hours of observations in bars and at parties, Dr. Givens discovered that women, more than men, tend to prome-nade, making numerous trips to the women's room, for instance, both to scout and to be seen.

5   A second nonverbal message in this earliest stage is "I am harm-less," Dr. Givens has found. The gestures and postures humans use to send this message are shared with other mammals, particularly pri-mates. Charles Darwin, who noted the same gestures in his 1859

book, *The Expressions of the Emotions in Man and Animals,* called them "submissive displays."

6   Perhaps the first serious study of flirting was done in the 1960's by Dr. Irenaus Eibl-Eibesfeldt, an eminent ethologist at the Max Planck Institute in Germany. Dr. Eibl-Eibesfeldt traveled to cultures around the world with a camera that took pictures from the side so he could stand near couples and take their pictures without their realizing they were being observed. In research in Samoa, Brazil, Paris, Sydney, and New York, Dr. Eibl-Eibesfeldt discovered an apparently universal nonverbal human vocabulary for flirting and courtship.

7   In humans, one such gesture is a palm-up placement of the hand, whether on a table or a knee, a reassuring sign of harmlessness. Another submissive display is the shoulder shrug, which, ethologists suggest, derives from an ancient vertebrate reflex, a posture signifying helplessness. A posture combining the partly shrugged shoulder and a tilted head — which displays the vulnerability of the neck — is commonly seen when two people who are sexually drawn to each other are having their first conversation, Dr. Givens said.

8   Being playful and childish is another way potential lovers often communicate harmlessness. "You see the same thing in the gray wolf," said Dr. Givens.

9   When wolves encounter each other, they usually give a show of dominance, keeping their distance. But in a sexual encounter, they become playful and frisky, "like puppies," said Dr. Givens, "so they can accept closeness." The next step is a mutual show of submission, all of which paves the way for physical intimacy.

10   "We still go through the ritual of courtship much like our mammalian ancestors," said Dr. Givens. "These gestures are subcortical, regulated by the more primitive part of our brain. They have nothing to do with the intellect, with our great neocortex."

11   The nonverbal repertoire for flirting is "part of a natural sequence for courtship worldwide," said Dr. Helen Fisher, an anthropologist at Rutgers University in New Brunswick, N.J., and author of *The Anatomy of Love* (Fawcett, 1993). "Mothers don't teach this to their daughters."

12   "In evolutionary terms, the payoff for each sex in parental investment differs: to produce a child a woman has an obligatory nine-month commitment, while for a man it's just one sexual act," said Dr. David Buss, a psychologist at the University of Michigan in Ann Arbor and author of *The Evolution of Desire* (Basic Books, 1994). "For men in evolutionary terms what pays is sexual access to a wide variety of women, while for women it's having a man who will commit time and resources to helping raise children."

From this view, the coyness of courtship is a way to "test a prospective partner for commitment," said Dr. Jane Lancaster, an anthropologist at the University of New Mexico in Albuquerque. "Women, in particular, need to be sure they're not going to be deserted."

Coyness is not seen in species where the female does not need the sustained help or resources of a male to raise her young, said Dr. Lancaster. In species where a single act of copulation is the only contact a female requires with the father of her young, "there's a direct assertion of sexual interest by the female," said Dr. Lancaster.

But in species where two parents appreciably enhance the survival of offspring, "females don't want to mate with a male who will abandon them," said Dr. Lancaster. In such species, "the courtship dances are coy, a test to see if the male is willing to persist and pursue or simply wants a momentary dalliance," he said. "Instead of the female simply getting in a posture for mating, she repeats a promise-withdraw sequence, getting in the mating posture and then moving away."

In humans, flirtatious looks imitate this sequence. The coy look a woman gives a man is the beginning of a continuing series of approach-withdraw strategies that will unfold over the course of their courtship. These feminine stratagems signal the man, "I'm so hard to win that if you do win me you won't have to worry about me getting pregnant by another male," said Dr. Lancaster.

A taxonomy of 52 "nonverbal solicitation behaviors" observed in flirting women has been garnered by Dr. Monica Moore, a psychologist at Webster University in St. Louis. In her research, conducted in singles bars, shopping malls, and other places young people go to meet those of the opposite sex, Dr. Moore has found that the women who send flirtatious signals most frequently are most likely to be approached by men—even more so than are women who are rated as more attractive.

"It's not who's most physically appealing," said Dr. Moore, "but the woman who's signaling availability that men approach."

Flirting is the opening gambit in a continuing series of negotiations at every step of the way in courtship. Indeed, the first major negotiation point is signaled by the flirtatious look itself.

"When a man is looking at a woman and she senses it, her first decision is, 'Do I have further interest in him?'" said Dr. Beverly Palmer, a psychologist at California State University in Dominguez Hills who has studied flirting. "If so, by flirting she sends the next signal: 'I'm interested in you, and yes, you can approach me.'"

Once the first conversation begins, there is "a major escalation point," said Dr. Fisher.

"The woman has a whole new basis for judging the man," she said. "A large number of prospective pickups end here."

23   Though men may say they are well aware of the tentativeness of flirting, Dr. Buss's findings suggest a male tendency—at least among college-age men—toward wishful thinking in interpreting flirtatious looks. In settings where men and women go to meet someone of the opposite sex, Dr. Buss said, "we find that when you ask men what it means for a woman to smile at them, they interpret it as a sexual invitation."

24   "But when you ask women what it means," he continued, "they'll say it just indicates she wants to get to know him better."

25   In interviews with 208 college-age men and women published this month in the *Journal of Sex Research,* Dr. Buss and colleagues found that when it comes to seduction, "the sexual signals that work for a woman backfire for men."

26   "There's a huge sex difference in how effective different tactics are," he added.

27   Perhaps not surprisingly, the research showed that for women, direct sexual approaches—dressing seductively, dancing close, staring into a man's eyes—worked well in leading to sexual contact. But for men similar direct strategies were failures.

28   Instead, for men the less overtly seductive tried-and-true romantic stratagems fared best. "For men the most effective approaches are displays of love and commitment," said Dr. Buss. "Telling her he really loves her, that he cares and is committed."   ■

Examining the Reading

1. What is Goleman's purpose?
2. In what courtship behaviors are humans and animals similar?
3. According to Goleman, how do male and female flirting behaviors differ?
4. Explain the meaning of each of the following words as it is used in the reading: *ethological* (para. 1), *template* (2), *mammalian* (10), *repertoire* (11), *evolutionary* (12), and *escalation* (21). Refer to your dictionary as needed.

Analyzing the Reading

1. Goleman uses process analysis to explain how human courtship works. What other patterns of development does the writer use in the essay? Choose one pattern, and explain how Goleman uses it to develop his thesis.
2. What technical terms does Goleman explain? What other terms, if any, do you think he should have explained?
3. What method of organization does this essay follow? Give examples from the reading to support your answer.

4. Evaluate Goleman's use of detail. Why does he explain some steps in the courtship process in greater detail than other steps?

5. Explain why Goleman is qualified to write this essay.

Reacting to the Reading: Discussion and Journal Writing

1. Discuss why you agree or disagree with Goleman's description of flirtatious behavior in humans.

2. Observe couples in a public place, such as in restaurants or on campus. What flirtatious behaviors do you notice? Are the behaviors consistent with Goleman's description? Why or why not?

3. In a journal entry, discuss why you agree or disagree with Goleman that women and men flirt for different reasons.

APPLYING YOUR SKILLS: ADDITIONAL ESSAY ASSIGNMENTS

Write a process analysis essay on one of the following topics. Depending on the topic you choose, you may need to conduct library or Internet research.

For more on locating and documenting sources, see Part 5.

To Express Your Ideas

1. How children manage their parents
2. How to relax and do nothing
3. How to find enough time for your children

To Inform Your Reader

4. How to avoid or speed up red-tape procedures
5. How a particular type of sports equipment protects an athlete
6. How to remain calm while giving a speech

To Persuade Your Reader

7. How important it is to vote in a presidential election
8. How important it is to select the right courses in order to graduate on time
9. How important it is to exercise every day

Cases Using Process Analysis

10. In your communication course, you are studying friendship development and the strategies that people use to meet others. Write an essay describing the strategies people use to meet new people and develop friendships.

11. You are employed by a toy manufacturer and have been asked to write a brochure that encourages children to use toys safely. Prepare a brochure that describes at least three steps children can follow to avoid injury.

EVALUATING YOUR PROGRESS
Part A: Using Process Analysis

Write a paragraph that evaluates your use of process analysis. Be sure to

- Identify situations in which process analysis will be useful.
- How did you adapt your process essay to suit your audience? How would your essay change if you were writing for an audience either more or less familiar with your topic?
- Identify any problems or trouble spots you experienced in using process analysis and explain how you dealt with them.

Part B: Analyzing Process Analysis Readings

For each reading you were assigned, identify at least one writing strategy (either about process specifically or about writing in general) that you can or did use in your own writing. How could the writer(s) have made the process(es) more understandable?

Part C: Proofreading and Editing

List the errors your instructor identified in your process analysis essay(s). For more help with these problems, refer to Exercise Central (www.bedfordstmartins.com/successfulwriting).

Comparison and Contrast: Showing Similarities and Differences

CHAPTER QUICK START

The two photographs on the opposite page were taken at wedding ceremonies. Study the photographs and make two lists — a list of the ways the two wedding scenes are similar and a list of the ways the wedding scenes are different. Include details that you notice about the people and setting, such as clothing, facial expressions, and background details.

Writing Quick Start

Write a paragraph about the photos that answers these questions: How are these two wedding scenes the same, and how are they different?

WRITING A COMPARISON OR CONTRAST ESSAY

Your paragraph about the wedding ceremonies is an example of comparison and contrast writing. In it you probably wrote about similarities and differences in dress, location of the ceremony, and so forth. In addition, you probably organized your paragraph in one of two ways: (1) by writing about one wedding and then the other or (2) by alternating back and forth between the two weddings as you discussed each point of similarity or difference. This chapter will show you how to write effective comparison or contrast essays as well as how to incorporate comparison and contrast into essays using other patterns of development.

WHAT ARE COMPARISON AND CONTRAST?

Using **comparison and contrast** involves looking at both similarities and differences. Analyzing similarities and differences is a common and useful decision-making skill that you use daily. You make comparisons when you shop for a pair of jeans, select a sandwich in the cafeteria, or choose a television program to watch. You also compare options and alternatives when you make important decisions about which college to attend, which field to major in, and which person to date.

You will find many occasions to use comparison and contrast in the writing you do in college and on the job (see the accompanying box for a few examples). In addition, in most essays of this type you will use one of two primary methods of organization, as the following two readings illustrate. The first essay, "An Amazing

---

SCENES FROM COLLEGE AND THE WORKPLACE

- For a course in *criminal justice,* your instructor asks you to participate in a panel discussion comparing organized crime in three societies — Italy, Japan, and Russia.

- For a *journalism* course, you are assigned to interview two local television news reporters and write a paper contrasting their views on journalistic responsibility.

- As a *computer technician* for a pharmaceutical firm, you are asked to compare and contrast several models of notebook computers and recommend the one the company should purchase for its salespeople.

Journey: 100 Years in America" by Roger Simon and Angie Cannon, uses a **point-by-point organization.** The writers move back and forth between their two subjects (life in a neighborhood in the New York City of 1900 and the New York City of 2000), comparing them on the basis of several key points or characteristics. The second essay, Ian Frazier's "Dearly Disconnected," uses a **subject-by-subject organization.** Here the author describes the key points or characteristics of one subject (pay phones) before moving on to those of his other subject (cell phones).

POINT-BY-POINT ORGANIZATION

An Amazing Journey: 100 Years in America
Roger Simon and Angie Cannon

Roger Simon is chief political correspondent for U.S. News & World Report. *He has been an investigative reporter and columnist for the* Chicago Sun Times, Chicago Tribune, *and* Baltimore Sun. *Simon has also written several books on American politics, including* Road Show *(1990) and* Show Time *(1998). Angie Cannon is a staff writer for the Washington bureau of Knight Ridder, a newspaper and journalism syndicate. Her articles appear in print and online in numerous publications. She is the author of* 23 Days of Terror: The Compelling True Story of the Hunt and Capture of the Beltway Snipers *(2003). This article appeared in* U.S. News & World Report *in 2001. As you read this selection, underline or highlight each point of comparison.*

To understand who we are — how life in America has changed and how it has remained the same — *U.S. News* compared the story of one family who lived at a New York address in 1900 with those who live there today and tracked the changes recorded by the U.S. census. The picture that emerges is one of a nation that continues to be defined, in many ways, by its immigrants, even though today's are of decidedly different origin from those of a century ago. America is more diverse, with nearly 7 million people saying they belong to more than one race. Most of us live in metropolitan areas today, not in the countryside. Far more of us own our own homes today, but families are smaller, if we have them at all. We are putting off marriage and kids. More of us, straight and gay, are simply living together. The number of single parents, both fathers and mothers, is on the rise. Millions are living alone. We earn vastly more money and are better educated. We are healthier and live longer. And most of us who work work less.

2   Julius Streicher, who came to America from Germany in 1885, was what the census of 1900 called a "provisions dealer," which meant a food wholesaler or grocer with his own store. His job wouldn't necessarily have made him wealthy, but he would have had, as he walked down the five front steps of his building, a nickel in his pocket or, better yet, "two nickels to rub together."

3   When the Streichers lived at 253 East 10th Street, the area was the northern fringes of the Lower East Side. Today, it's the artsy, bohemian East Village. In the 1970s the streets were teeming with heroin junkies. Many buildings were abandoned. Even as recently as 1991, it was front-page news when cops rousted about 200 home-less people from a tent city in nearby Tompkins Square Park. Today, that's changed. Over the past decade, the East Village has gotten more gentrified. The public elementary school, which used to be mostly Hispanic and black, now is increasingly white. Small shops of trendy clothing designers dot the same streets that pushcarts lined 100 years ago. The gentrification upsets Dudley Sabo, 87, who has lived at 253 East 10th for 30 years. "People with money moved in, and they weren't as friendly as before," complains Sabo, now retired from teaching art at the Brooklyn Museum. "There's no community. There's rich people on one side and other people on the other."

4   Still, Julius Streicher would recognize some things about his old neighborhood. Ukrainian and Russian immigrants today cram for language tests at concrete tables in Tompkins Square Park. Streicher's census form, filled out in the spidery script of Census Enumerator August Scheufeh, records that while Julius could speak English, his wife could not. Their daughter, the form notes, was in school, and so she probably spoke both languages.

5   Today, some of the windows at 253 East 10th Street have bars on them, which would have been unlikely 100 years ago. There are four apartments to a floor — 20 in all. But it's no longer a building of immigrants. For almost $900 a month, Harvey Weissman, 30, who grew up in Connecticut, has a small one-bedroom apartment in the building without central air but with great views of majestic sky-scrapers. At first, Weissman didn't feel he fit into the neighborhood. With an economics and Spanish degree from Clark University, he pursued a career as an accountant. But he decided that wasn't who he really was. Eventually, he chucked the corporate job. Today, he's trying to build an acting career. "Now I feel very happy to be here; the creative energy is very strong," he says. "It gives me courage to see other people doing it."

We don't know exactly where Julius Streicher's grocery was   6
located, but it is unlikely that it was very far from his building. Virtually everything one needed in life could be found in the neighborhood. But as Streicher walked through the streets, he probably wouldn't even have noted what a visitor today would: the smell. True, the streets were lined with pushcarts selling all manner of fragrant foodstuffs — America could produce virtually every edible grain, fruit, and vegetable on the planet — but the nation's cities smelled like stables. The automobile had already been invented, but horseless carriages were still novelty items. (There were only about 8,000 cars in the entire country, though they had already accounted for 36 traffic fatalities.) So it was the horse that made the cities move, and it was calculated (the census created in ordinary Americans a mania for statistics) that the horses of New York City dumped 2.5 million pounds of manure and 60,000 gallons of urine on the streets each day.

Streicher would not have cared. Without horses, food didn't   7
move in America, and moving food was his business. You could debate whether 1900 was a simpler time than now — nobody had to worry about global warming, violence in the movies (there were no movies), or computer viruses back then. But they did have to worry about their horses dying. The animal epidemic of 1872 killed a quarter of all the horses in America, helped bring on the Panic of 1873, and created scenes reminiscent of the Dark Ages. "In many cities, teams of men pulled carts, and wagons," Thomas J. Schlereth wrote in *Victorian America*, "as homes went without fuel deliveries, fires blazed unfought, and garbage remained uncollected." Only winter, which killed off the mosquitoes that carried the disease, saved the day and the horses.

They made an enormous clatter on the streets all around Julius   8
Streicher, the steel rims of the wooden carriage wheels banging over the rough-hewn granite paving stones called Belgian blocks that formed 10th Street. (Asphalt, considerably less attractive, but easier on the backside if one was riding in a carriage, was already being poured on other New York streets.) Everything, from the loud crying of the pushcart peddlers, to the shouting children darting everywhere, to the squeal of the elevated train, gave New York the same feel that it has today: a city on the move, on the make, a place of velocity. And in 1900, people loved velocity. After seven years of depression, the economy had begun booming in 1898. Though the country was still very young — the grandparents of people alive in 1900 had fought under Gen. George Washington at the Battle of Yorktown, and there were still parts of the country where white men had yet to set foot — America was now well on its way to dominating the world.   ■

SUBJECT-BY-SUBJECT ORGANIZATION

Dearly Disconnected

Ian Frazier

Ian Frazier has published several books, including Great Plains *(2001),* Family *(2002), and the humor collections* Dating Your Mom *(1986) and* Coyote vs. Acme *(2002), and he has edited the well-known compilations* The Best American Essays 1997 *and* The Best American Travel Writing 2003. *A former staff writer for the* New Yorker, *he still contributes to the magazine frequently. His most recent book is a collection of his* New Yorker *columns about New York City titled* Gone to New York *(2005). The following essay was adapted from a column that appeared in* Mother Jones Wire *magazine in February 2000. As you read, highlight the key points Frazier makes about pay phones and cell phones and his attitudes toward each.*

1   Before I got married I was living by myself in an A-frame cabin in northwestern Montana. The cabin's interior was a single high-ceilinged room, and at the center of the room, mounted on the rough-hewn log that held up the ceiling beam, was a telephone. The woman I would marry was living in Sarasota, Florida, and the distance between us suggests how well we were getting along at the time. We had not been in touch for several months; she had no phone. One day she decided to call me from a pay phone. We talked for a while, and after her coins ran out I jotted the number on the wood beside my phone and called her back. A day or two later, thinking about the call, I wanted to talk to her again. The only number I had for her was the pay phone number I'd written down.

2   The pay phone was on the street some blocks from the apartment where she stayed. As it happened, though, she had just stepped out to do some errands a few minutes before I called, and she was passing by on the sidewalk when the phone rang. She had no reason to think that a public phone ringing on a busy street would be for her. She stopped, listened to it ring again, and picked up the receiver. Love is pure luck; somehow I had known she would answer, and she had known it would be me.

3   Long afterwards, on a trip to Disney World in Orlando with our two kids, then aged six and two, we made a special detour to Sarasota to show them the pay phone. It didn't impress them much. It's just a nondescript Bell Atlantic pay phone on the cement wall of a building, by the vestibule. But its ordinariness and even boringness only make me like it more; ordinary places where extraordinary events have

occurred are my favorite kind. On my mental map of Florida that pay phone is a landmark looming above the city it occupies, and a notable, if private, historic site.

I'm interested in pay phones in general these days, especially when I get the feeling that they are about to go away. Technology, in the form of sleek little phones in our pockets, has swept on by them and made them begin to seem antique. My lifelong entanglement with pay phones dates me; when I was young they were just there, a given, often as stubborn and uncongenial as the curbstone underfoot. They were instruments of torture sometimes. You had to feed them fistfuls of change in those pre-phone-card days, and the operator was a real person who stood maddeningly between you and whomever you were trying to call. And when the call went wrong, as communication often does, the pay phone gave you a focus for your rage. Pay phones were always getting smashed up, the receivers shattered to bits against the booth, the coin slots jammed with chewing gum, the cords yanked out and unraveled to the floor.

There was always a touch of seediness and sadness to pay phones, and a sense of transience. Drug dealers made calls from them, and shady types who did not want their whereabouts known, and otherwise respectable people planning assignations, and people too poor to have phones of their own. In the movies, any character who used a pay phone was either in trouble or contemplating a crime. Mostly, pay phones evoked the mundane: "Honey, I'm just leaving. I'll be there soon." But you could tell that a lot of undifferentiated humanity had flowed through these places, and that in the muteness of each pay phone's little space, wild emotion had howled.

The phone on the wall of the concession stand at Redwood Pool, where I used to stand dripping and call my mom to come and pick me up; the sweaty phones used almost only by men in the hallway outside the maternity ward at Lenox Hill Hospital in New York; the phone in the old wood-paneled phone booth with leaded glass windows in the drugstore in my Ohio hometown — each one is as specific as a birthmark, a point on earth unlike any other. Recently I went back to New York City after a long absence and tried to find a working pay phone. I picked up one receiver after the next without success. Meanwhile, as I scanned down the long block, I counted half a dozen or more pedestrians talking on their cell phones.

It's the cell phone, of course, that's putting the pay phone out of business. The pay phone is to the cell phone as the troubled and difficult older sibling is to the cherished newborn. You sometimes hear people yelling on their cell phones, but almost never yelling at them. Cell phones are toylike, nearly magic, and we get a huge kick out of them, as often happens with technological advances until the new wears off. When I see a cell-phone user gently push the little antenna and fit the phone back into its brushed-vinyl carrying case and tuck the case inside his jacket beside his heart, I feel sorry for the beat-up pay phone standing in the rain.

8   People almost always talk on cell phones while in motion — driving, walking down the street, riding on a commuter train. The cell phone took the transience the pay phone implied and turned it into VIP-style mobility and speed. Even sitting in a restaurant, the person on a cell phone seems importantly busy and on the move. Cell-phone conversations seem to be unlimited by ordinary constraints of place and time, as if they represent an almost-perfect form of communication whose perfect state would be telepathy.

9   And yet no matter how we factor the world away, it remains. I think this is what drives me so nuts when a person sitting next to me on a bus makes a call from her cell phone. Yes, this busy and important caller is at no fixed point in space, but nevertheless I happen to be beside her. The job of providing physical context falls on me; I become her call's surroundings, as if I'm the phone booth wall. For me to lean over and comment on her cell-phone conversation would be as unseemly and unexpected as if I were in fact a wall; and yet I have no choice, as a sentient person, but to hear what my chatty fellow traveler has to say.

10   I don't think that pay phones will completely disappear. Probably they will survive for a long while as clumsy old technology still of some use to those lagging behind, and as a backup if ever the superior systems should temporarily fail. Before pay phones became endangered I never thought of them as public spaces, which of course they are. They suggested a human average; they belonged to anybody who had a couple of coins. Now I see that, like public schools and public transportation, pay phones belong to a former commonality our culture is no longer quite so sure it needs.

11   I have a weakness for places — for old battlefields, car-crash sites, houses where famous authors lived. Bygone passions should always have an address, it seems to me. Ideally, the world would be covered with plaques and markers listing the notable events that occurred at each particular spot. A sign on every pay phone would describe how a woman broke up with her fiancé here, how a young ballplayer learned that he had made the team. Unfortunately, the world itself is fluid, and changes out from under us. Eventually pay phones will become relics of an almost-vanished landscape, and of a time when there were fewer of us and our stories were on an earlier page. Romantics like me will have to reimagine our passions as they are — unmoored to earth, like an infinitude of cell-phone messages flying through the atmosphere. ∎

Characteristics of Comparison or Contrast Essays

When writers use comparison and contrast, they consider subjects with characteristics in common, examining similarities, differences, or both. Whether used as the primary pattern of development or alongside another pattern, comparison and contrast can help writers achieve their purpose and make a point about their subjects.

Comparison or Contrast Has a Clear Purpose

A comparison and contrast essay usually has one of three purposes: *to express ideas, to inform,* or *to persuade.* In an essay about the two weddings shown in the chapter-opening photographs, the purpose could be to express ideas about unconventional weddings by showing how they are similar to and different from traditional American weddings. The purpose also could be to inform readers about variations in wedding ceremonies. Finally, the purpose could be to persuade readers that one wedding is more formal or more bound in tradition. Whatever the purpose of a comparison and contrast essay, it should be made clear to readers. In "An Amazing Journey: 100 Years in America" (p. 373), for example, it's clear that the authors intend to compare and contrast life in New York City in 1900 and in 2000.

Comparison or Contrast Considers Shared Characteristics

The familiar expression "You can't compare apples and oranges" makes a useful point about comparisons: You cannot compare two unlike things unless they have something in common. Apples and oranges can be compared if they share at least one characteristic—nutritional value, for instance.

When making a comparison, then, a writer needs to choose a **basis of comparison**—a common characteristic on which to base the essay. Baseball and football might be compared on the basis of their entertainment value or the types of athletic skill they require. The basis of comparison determines the type of details the essay should include. In an essay about the value of baseball and football as forms of entertainment, for example, the number of people who watch the Superbowl versus the World Series on television would be relevant, whereas the types of equipment used by the players of each sport would not be relevant.

EXERCISE 12.1

For three items in the following list, identify two possible bases of comparison you could use to compare each pair of topics.

1. Two means of travel or transportation
2. Two means of communication (emails, telephone calls, postal letters, telephone text messages)
3. Two pieces of equipment

4. Two magazines or books
5. Two types of television programming

A Comparison or Contrast Essay Fairly Examines Similarities, Differences, or Both

Depending on their purpose, writers using comparison and contrast may focus on similarities, differences, or both. In an essay intended to *persuade* readers that performers Britney Spears and Jennifer Lopez have much in common in terms of talent and cultural influence, the writer would focus on similarities — hit records, millions of fans, and parts in movies. However, an essay intended to *inform* readers about the singers would probably cover both similarities and differences, discussing the singers' different childhoods or singing styles.

An essay focusing on similarities often mentions a few differences, usually in the introduction, to let readers know the writer is aware of the differences. Conversely, an essay that focuses on differences might mention a few similarities. In "An Amazing Journey: 100 Years in America" Simon and Cannon mention a similarity (the importance of immigrants at the end of two centuries) before describing the differences in living conditions in 1900 and 2000.

Whether you cover similarities, differences, or both in an essay, you should strive to treat your subjects fairly. Relevant information should not be purposely omitted to show one subject in a more favorable light. In an essay about Britney Spears and Jennifer Lopez, for instance, you would not leave out information about Spears's charity work in an effort to make Lopez appear to be a nicer person. In "Dearly Disconnected," Frazier regrets the demise of the pay phone but feels that cell phones are "toylike, nearly magic."

Comparison or Contrast Makes a Point

Whatever the purpose of a comparison or contrast essay, its main point about its subjects should spark readers' interest rather than bore them with a mechanical listing of similarities or differences. This main point can serve as the thesis for the essay, or the thesis can be implied in the writer's choice of details. In "An Amazing Journey: 100 Years in America," for example, the authors state their main point and thesis explicitly in the first sentence of paragraph 1, where they explain their intent to compare the lives of people living in 1900 and in 2000.

An explicit thesis has three functions.

1. It identifies the *subjects* being compared or contrasted.
2. It suggests whether the focus is on *similarities, differences,* or *both.*
3. It states the *main point* of the comparison or contrast.

Notice how the following three sample theses meet the above criteria. Note, too, that each thesis suggests why the comparison or contrast is meaningful and worth reading about.

——— similarities ———   *——— subjects ———*
Similar appeals in commercials for three popular breakfast cereals reveal
——— main point ———
America's obsession with fitness and health.

——— difference ——— *——— subjects ———* *——— similarities ———*
Although different in purpose, weddings and funerals each draw families
——— main point ———
together and confirm family values.

——— subjects ———
The two cities Niagara Falls, Ontario, and Niagara Falls, New York, demonstrate
——— differences ——— *——— main point ———*
two different approaches to appreciating nature and preserving the environment.

EXERCISE 12.2

For one of the topic pairs you worked on in Exercise 12.1 (p. 379), select the basis of comparison that seems most promising. Then write a thesis statement that identifies the subjects, the focus (similarities, differences, or both), and the main point.

Comparison or Contrast Considers a Sufficient Number of Significant Characteristics and Details

A comparison or contrast essay considers characteristics that are significant as well as relevant to the essay's purpose and thesis. In "An Amazing Journey: 100 Years in America," for example, Simon and Cannon consider several significant characteristics of lifestyle, including work patterns, neighborhood characteristics, languages of residents, features of the building, and so forth.

Although the number of details can vary by topic, usually at least three or four significant characteristics are needed to support a thesis. Each characteristic should be fully described or explained so readers can grasp the main point of the comparison or contrast. A writer may use sensory details, dialogue, examples, expert testimony, and other kinds of detail in a comparison or contrast essay. In "Dearly Disconnected," Frazier supports his points by using anecdotes and vivid descriptions.

Visualizing a Comparison or Contrast Essay: Two Graphic Organizers

Suppose you want to compare two houses (house A and house B) built by the same architect for the purpose of evaluating how the architect's style has changed over time. After brainstorming ideas, you decide to base your essay on these points of comparison — layout, size, building materials, and landscaping. You could organize your essay in one of two ways — point by point or subject by subject.

For more on graphic organizers, see Chapter 2, p. 34.

Point-by-Point Organization

In a *point-by-point organization,* you would go back and forth between the two houses, noting similarities and differences between them on each of the four points of comparison, as shown in the graphic organizer in Figure 12.1.

FIGURE 12.1
GRAPHIC ORGANIZER FOR A POINT-BY-POINT COMPARISON AND CONTRAST ESSAY

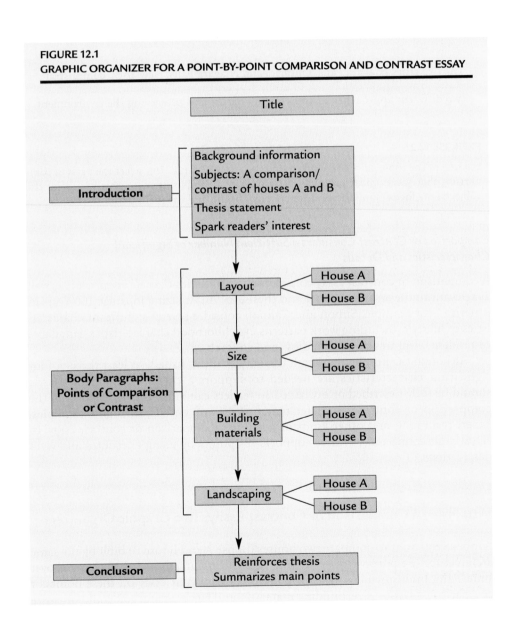

Subject-by-Subject Organization

In a *subject-by-subject organization,* you would first discuss all points about house A—its layout, size, building materials, and landscaping. Then you would do the same for house B. This pattern is shown in the graphic organizer in Figure 12.2.

FIGURE 12.2
GRAPHIC ORGANIZER FOR A SUBJECT-BY-SUBJECT
COMPARISON AND CONTRAST ESSAY

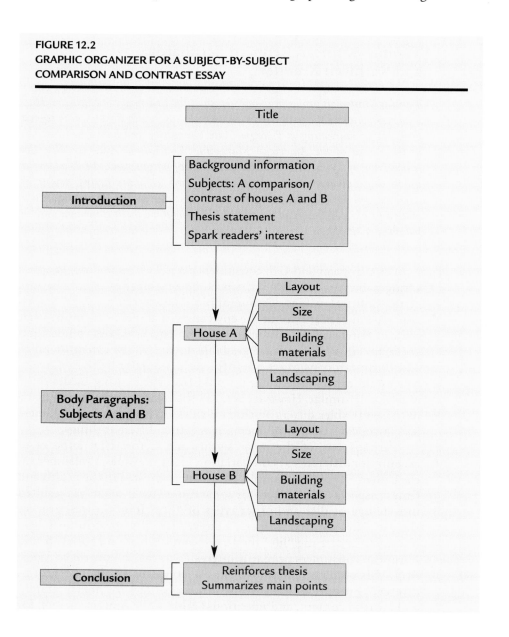

The following essay uses a point-by-point organization. Read the essay, and then study the graphic organizer for it in Figure 12.3 on page 386.

Who's Eating What, and Why, in the United States and Europe?

Thomas Kinnear, Kenneth Bernhardt, and Kathleen Krentler

Thomas Kinnear is professor of marketing at the University of Michigan. He is a former editor of the Journal of Marketing. *Kenneth Bernhardt is regents professor of marketing at Georgia State University and has served as chair of the Board of the American Marketing Association. Kathleen Krentler is professor of marketing and vice president of programs at the Academy of Marketing Science. This essay first appeared as a marketing profile in Kinnear and Bernhardt's college textbook,* Principles of Marketing, *fourth edition (1995). As you read the selection, highlight the thesis statement and the points of comparison.*

1   Do European and U.S. consumers eat alike? Yes and no. People's eating habits are strongly influenced by a number of factors besides taste. Cultural values, demographic characteristics, personal finances, and concern about the environment all help determine what you eat. Furthermore, advances in technology, laws, and competition are factors in what foods are available to you. To the extent that U.S. and European consumers are influenced similarly by these factors, you would expect and, indeed, would find their eating habits to be remarkably similar. However, because the relative influence of many of these variables differs on the two sides of the Atlantic, U.S. diners and Europeans often find themselves eating different things.

2   Perhaps one of the most significant factors that appears to account for differences is the variation in social values. Consumers in the United States, for example, have been interested in the health and fitness aspects of their food for some time. This interest has resulted in a deluge of diet and other types of "lite" food on U.S. grocery shelves. European consumers, however, are just beginning to get interested in diet and "lite" foods. A recent study found both U.S. and European consumers primarily interested in the fat content of foods. After this commonality, however, the concerns of the two groups diverged. Europeans want (in descending order) freshness, vitamin and mineral content, and nutritional value while Americans look for foods low in salt, cholesterol, and sugar.

Ironically, as European interest in diet and "lite" goods is increasing, many U.S. consumers appear to be switching back to what has been called real food. Increasingly, healthy eating in the U.S. alternates with the consumption of heartier fare. Like other food producers, McDonald's appears to be responding to this move by downplaying its reduced-fat McLean Deluxe Burger (dubbed the McFlopper by some cynics) and introducing the Mega Mac, a half-pound hamburger patty.

Recent statistics reveal a demographic difference that may also account for variation in eating habits. A study found that 44 percent of Western European women reported being homemakers and only 33 percent said they worked outside the home. This is approximately the reverse of U.S. statistics on these same factors. Marketers realize that the presence of a full-time homemaker in a home is likely to account for different shopping, cooking, and eating habits for the entire family.

Economic and ecological factors can also help shape our eating habits. Consumers in the United States have traditionally been concerned with price. In the last few years, European consumers have become increasingly cost-conscious as well, due in large part to a recessionary economy throughout the early 1990s. Consumers with less money to spend and less optimism about the economy are likely to eat differently. Consumers on both sides of the Atlantic are also increasingly concerned about the environment. Marketers have found themselves having to respond to demands for reductions in excessive packaging, for example.

Advances in technology mean changes in what consumers eat. The introduction of the microwave oven, for example, has affected what's for dinner in U.S. households for the last twenty years. Microwavable food is a relatively new phenomenon in Europe, however.

Traditionally, European consumers have claimed that having a wide variety is much less important to them than it is to residents of the United States. However, increased competition from popular private-label products is pushing producers in industries like breakfast cereals to introduce more products into the European market. Time will tell whether European consumers will become more like U.S. consumers and respond to broader product offerings or whether they reject the strategy.

The changes in the European market brought on by economic, competitive, and social upheaval [are] providing opportunities for marketers who respond appropriately. Pepsico Corporation, for example, entered the Polish market in 1993 with "3-in-1" outlets combining Pizza Hut, Taco Bell, and KFC. The outlets have been very successful.

FIGURE 12.3
GRAPHIC ORGANIZER FOR "WHO'S EATING WHAT, AND WHY, IN THE UNITED STATES AND EUROPE?"

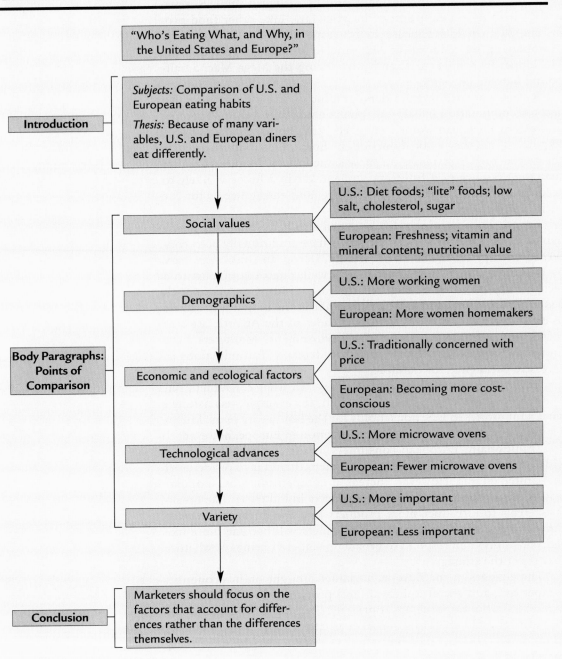

Smart marketers should be less concerned with whether U.S. and   9
European consumers are alike and more concerned with monitoring
the variety of factors that account for potential similarities and differences. Attention to the dynamic nature of those factors will produce opportunities for the alert marketer.   ■

To draw detailed graphic organizers using a computer, visit www.bedfordstmartins.com/successfulwriting.

| **EXERCISE 12.3**

Draw a graphic organizer for "An Amazing Journey: 100 Years in America" (p. 373) or "Dearly Disconnected" (p. 376).

INTEGRATING COMPARISON AND CONTRAST INTO AN ESSAY

Although you will write some essays using comparison and contrast as the primary pattern of development, in most cases you will integrate comparisons or contrasts into essays that rely on other patterns, such as description, process analysis, or argument. Comparisons or contrasts can be particularly effective in persuasive essays.

Use the following tips to incorporate comparison or contrast into essays based on other patterns of development.

1. **Determine the purpose of the comparison or contrast.** What will it contribute to your essay?

2. **Introduce the comparison or contrast clearly.** Tell your readers how it supports the main point of the essay. Do not leave it to them to figure out why the comparison is included.

3. **Keep the comparison or contrast short and to the point.** An extended comparison will distract readers from the overall point of your essay.

4. **Organize the points of the comparison or contrast.** Even though it is part of a larger essay, the comparison or contrast should follow a point-by-point or subject-by-subject organization.

5. **Use transitions.** Transitional words and expressions are especially important in easing the flow into the comparison or contrast and then back to the essay's primary pattern of development.

In "Defining a Doctor, with a Tear, a Shrug, and a Schedule" on page 410, Abigail Zuger uses comparison and contrast along with other patterns of development.

A GUIDED WRITING ASSIGNMENT

The following guide will lead you through the process of writing a comparison or contrast essay. Although you will focus on comparing or contrasting your subjects, you may need to integrate one or more other patterns of development in your essay.

The Assignment

Write a comparison or contrast essay on one of the following topic pairs or one of your own choice. Depending on the topic pair you choose, you may need to use Internet or library sources to develop and support your ideas about the subjects. Your audience is your classmates.

1. Two public figures
2. Two forms of entertainment (such as movies, concerts, radio, music videos) or one form of entertainment as it is used today and as it was used ten or more years ago
3. Two styles of communication, dress, or teaching
4. The right and wrong ways of doing something
5. Your views versus your parents' or grandparents' views on an issue
6. Two different cultures' approaches to a rite of passage, such as birth, puberty, marriage, or death
7. Two different cultures' views on the roles that should be played by men and women in society
8. Two products from two different eras

As you develop your comparison or contrast essay, consider using one or more other patterns of development. For example, you might use process analysis to explain the right and wrong ways of doing something or cause and effect to show the results of two teaching styles on learners.

For more on process analysis, see Chapter 11. For more on cause and effect, see Chapter 15.

Generating Ideas

Generating ideas involves choosing subjects to compare and prewriting to discover similarities, differences, and other details about the subjects.

Choosing Subjects to Compare

Take your time in selecting the assignment option and in identifying specific subjects for it. Use the following guidelines to get started.

For more on prewriting strategies, see Chapter 3.

Learning Style Options

1. Some of the options listed on page 388 are concrete (comparing two public figures); others are more abstract (comparing communication styles or views on an issue). Consider your learning style and choose the option with which you are most comfortable.

2. If you are a social learner, choose subjects that your classmates are familiar with so you can discuss your subjects with them. Try group brainstorming about various possible subjects.

3. Choose subjects with which you have some firsthand experience or that you are willing to research. You might try questioning or writing assertions to help you generate ideas.

4. Choose subjects that interest you. You will have more fun writing about them, and your enthusiasm will enliven your essay. Try mapping or sketching to come up with interesting subjects.

ESSAY IN PROGRESS 1

Using the preceding suggestions, choose an assignment option from the list on page 388 or an option you think of on your own. Then do some prewriting to help you select two specific subjects for your comparison or contrast essay.

Choosing a Basis of Comparison and a Purpose

Suppose you want to compare or contrast two well-known football players—a quarterback and a linebacker. If you merely present various similarities and differences about the two players, your essay will lack direction. To avoid this problem, you need to choose a basis of comparison and a purpose for writing. You could compare the players on the basis of the positions they play, describing the skills and training needed for each position. Your purpose would be to *inform* readers about the two positions. Alternatively, you could base your comparison on their performances on the field; in this case, your purpose might be to *persuade* readers to accept your evaluation of both players. Other bases of comparison might be the players' media images, contributions to their teams, or service to the community.

Once you have a basis of comparison and a purpose in mind, try to state them clearly in a few sentences. Refer to these sentences as you work to keep your essay on track.

ESSAY IN PROGRESS 2

For the assignment option and subjects you selected in Essay in Progress 1, decide on a basis of comparison and a purpose for your essay. Describe both clearly in a few sentences. Keep in mind that you may revise your basis of comparison and purpose as your essay develops.

Considering Your Audience and Point of View

For more on audience and point of view, see Chapter 3, p. 65.

As you develop your comparison or contrast essay, keep your audience in mind. Choose points of comparison that will interest your readers. For example, if you are evaluating two local summer recreation programs for children, an audience of parents would be interested in the details of the programs' operations, such as costs, hours, activities, and supervision. However, an audience of elementary school principals might be more interested in the programs' goals and objectives and how the programs are administered and funded. For this chapter's assignment, your audience is made up of your classmates. Keep them in mind as you develop your essay.

When considering your audience, you also need to think about point of view or how you should address your readers. Most comparison or contrast essays are written in the third person. However, the first person may be appropriate when you use comparison and contrast to express personal thoughts or feelings.

Discovering Similarities and Differences and Generating Details

Your next step is to discover how your two subjects are similar, how they are different, or both. Depending on your learning style, you can approach this task in a number of different ways.

Learning Style Options

1. On paper or on your computer, create a two-column list of similarities and differences. Jot down ideas in the appropriate column.

2. Ask a classmate to help you brainstorm aloud by mentioning only similarities; then counter each similarity with a difference. Write notes on the brainstorming.

3. For concrete subjects, try visualizing them. Take notes on what you see, or draw a sketch of your subjects.

4. Create a scenario in which your subjects interact. For example, if your topic is automobiles of the 1920s and 1990s, imagine taking your great-grandfather, who owned a Model T Ford, for a drive in a 2002 luxury car. How would he react? What would he say?

5. Do research on your two subjects at the library or on the Internet.

Keep in mind that your readers will need plenty of details to grasp the similarities and differences between your subjects. Description, examples, and facts will make your subjects seem real to your readers. Recall the amount of descriptive detail Frazier uses in "Dearly Disconnected" to explain his attachment toward pay phones.

For more on description, see Chapter 9.

To maintain an even balance between your two subjects, do some brainstorming, freewriting, or research to gather roughly the same amount of detail for each. This guideline is especially important if your purpose is to demonstrate that subject A is preferable to or better than subject B. Your readers will become suspicious if you provide plenty of detail for subject A and only sketchy information about subject B.

For more on library and Internet research, see Chapter 19.

ESSAY IN PROGRESS 3

Use the preceding suggestions and one or more prewriting strategies to discover similarities and differences and to generate details about your two subjects.

Developing Your Thesis

The thesis statement for a comparison or contrast essay needs to fulfill the three criteria noted earlier: It should identify the subjects; suggest whether you will focus on similarities, differences, or both; and state your main point. In addition, your thesis should tell readers why your comparison or contrast of the two subjects is important or useful to them. Look at the following sample thesis statements.

For more on thesis statements, see Chapter 4, p. 89.

WEAK   The books by Robert Parker and Sue Grafton are similar.

REVISED   The novels of Robert Parker and Sue Grafton are popular because readers are fascinated by the intrigues of witty, independent private detectives.

The first thesis is weak because it presents the two subjects in isolation, without placing the comparison within a context or giving the reader a reason to care about it. The second thesis is more detailed and specific. It provides a basis for comparison and indicates why the similarity is worth reading about. As you develop your thesis, think about what your comparison says about people, life, or behavior. In "Who's Eating What, and Why, in the United States and Europe?" for example, the authors' thesis claims that technology, laws, and culture can affect something as commonplace as what we eat.

| ESSAY IN PROGRESS 4

| Using the preceding suggestions, write a thesis statement for this chapter's essay
| assignment. The thesis should identify the two subjects of your comparison; tell
| whether you will focus on similarities, differences, or both; and convey your main
| point to readers.

Evaluating Your Ideas and Thesis

Your prewriting should have yielded numerous ideas and details about the
subjects of your comparison. Your next steps are to evaluate your ideas and
thesis and to choose the points and details of comparison to include in
your essay.

Selecting Points of Comparison

With your thesis in mind, review your prewriting by underlining or highlighting ideas that pertain to your thesis and eliminating those that do
not. If you are working on a computer, highlight these key ideas in bold
type or move them to a separate file, using the cut-and-paste function of
your word-processing program. Try to identify the points or characteristics by which you can best compare your subjects. For example, if your
thesis is about evaluating the performance of two football players, you
would probably select various facts and details about their training, the
plays they make, and their records.

Think of points of comparison as the main similarities or differences
that support your thesis. In "An Amazing Journey: 100 Years in America,"
Simon and Cannon discuss several important differences between the
beginning and end of the twentieth century—work habits, neighborhood
characteristics, and residents' languages—but omit minor points that
could sidetrack readers and weaken the effect of their essay.

Take a few minutes to evaluate your ideas and thesis. Make sure you
have enough points of comparison to support your thesis and enough
details to develop those points. If necessary, do additional prewriting to
generate sufficient support for your thesis.

| ESSAY IN PROGRESS 5

| Using the preceding suggestions and comments from your classmates, list the
| points of comparison you plan to use in your essay and evaluate your ideas and
| thesis. Refer to the list of characteristics on pages 379–81 to help you with your
| evaluation.

TRYING OUT YOUR IDEAS ON OTHERS

Working in a group of two or three students, discuss your ideas and thesis for this chapter's assignment. Each writer should state his or her topic, thesis, and points of comparison. Then, as a group, evaluate each writer's work.

Organizing and Drafting

Once you have evaluated your thesis, points of comparison, and details, you are ready to organize your ideas and draft your essay.

For more on drafting an essay, see Chapter 5.

Choosing a Method of Organization

Before you begin writing, decide whether you will use a point-by-point or a subject-by-subject organization (review Figures 12.1 and 12.2). To select a method of organization, consider the complexity of your subjects and the length of your essay. You may also need to experiment with the two approaches to see which works better. It is a good idea to make an outline or draw a graphic organizer at this stage.

Here are a few other guidelines to consider.

1. The subject-by-subject method tends to emphasize the larger picture, whereas the point-by-point method emphasizes details and specifics.
2. The point-by-point method often works better for lengthy essays because it keeps both subjects current in your reader's mind.
3. The point-by-point method is often preferable for complicated or technical subjects. For example, if you compare two computer systems, it would be easier to explain the function of a memory card once and then describe the memory cards in each of the two systems.

ESSAY IN PROGRESS 6

Choose a method of organization—point by point or subject by subject—and organize the points of comparison you generated in Essay in Progress 5.

Drafting the Comparison or Contrast Essay

Now that you know how to organize your essay, your next step is to write a first draft. Use the following guidelines.

1. If you are drafting a point-by-point essay, keep the following suggestions in mind.

- Work back and forth between your two subjects, generally mentioning the subjects in the same order. If both subjects share a particular characteristic (as they do in para. 8 of Simon and Cannon's essay on page 375), then you may want to mention the two subjects together.

- Arrange your points of comparison carefully; start with the clearest, simplest points and then move on to more complex ones.

2. If you are drafting a subject-by-subject essay, keep the following suggestions in mind.

- Be sure to cover the same points for both subjects.

- Cover the points of comparison in the same order in both halves of your essay.

- Write a clear statement of transition wherever you switch from one subject to the other.

3. Use analogies. An **analogy**, or *extended metaphor,* is a special type of comparison that uses a familiar subject to explain a less familiar one. For example, a writer could explain the evolution of the universe by comparing it to the stages of a human's life. In this sense, analogies differ from similes and metaphors (see p. 190), which make comparisons based on a single shared point. You can use an analogy as part of a comparison and contrast essay or as a way to make comparisons within an essay that relies on some other pattern of development.

For more on transitions, see Chapter 5, p. 128.

4. Use transitions. Transitions are especially important in helping readers follow the points you make in a comparison or contrast essay. Transitions alert readers to shifts between subjects or to new points of comparison. An essay that lacks transitions sounds choppy and unconnected. Use transitional words and phrases such as *similarly, in contrast, on the one hand, on the other hand,* and *not only . . . but also.*

For more on writing effective paragraphs, including introductions and conclusions, see Chapter 5.

5. Write an effective introduction. Although Frazier's "Dearly Disconnected" is effective without an introduction, most of the comparison or contrast essays you write should have a clear introduction that sparks your readers' interest, presents your subjects, states your thesis, and includes any background information your readers may need.

6. Write a satisfying conclusion. Your conclusion should offer a final comment on your comparison or contrast, reminding readers of your thesis. For a lengthy or complex essay, you might want to summarize your main points as well.

ESSAY IN PROGRESS 7

Using the organization you developed in Essay in Progress 6 and the preceding guidelines for drafting, write a first draft of your comparison or contrast essay.

Analyzing and Revising

If possible, set your draft aside for a day or two before rereading and revising it. As you reread your draft, concentrate on your ideas and not on grammar or mechanics. Use one or more of the following suggestions to analyze your draft.

1. Reread your essay aloud, or ask a friend or classmate to do so as you listen.

   Learning Style Options

2. Draw a graphic organizer, make an outline, or update the organizer or outline you prepared earlier. A graphic organizer or outline will indicate whether your organization contains inconsistencies or gaps.

3. Read each paragraph with this question in mind: "So what?" If any paragraph does not answer that question, revise or delete it.

Use Figure 12.4 to guide your analysis of the strengths and weaknesses in your draft essay. You might also ask a classmate to review your draft essay using the questions in the flowchart. Encourage your reader to ask questions wherever necessary about the purpose of the essay and the major points of comparison or contrast and to give you feedback on any parts that are unclear. Your reviewer should consider each question listed in the flowchart, explaining each "No" answer.

For more on the benefits of peer review, see Chapter 6, p. 158.

ESSAY IN PROGRESS 8

Revise your draft using Figure 12.4 and any comments you received from peer reviewers.

Editing and Proofreading

The last step is to check your revised essay for errors in grammar, spelling, punctuation, and mechanics. Be sure to check your error log for the types of errors you tend to make.

For more on keeping an error log, see Chapter 7, p. 193.

FIGURE 12.4
FLOWCHART FOR REVISING A COMPARISON OR CONTRAST ESSAY

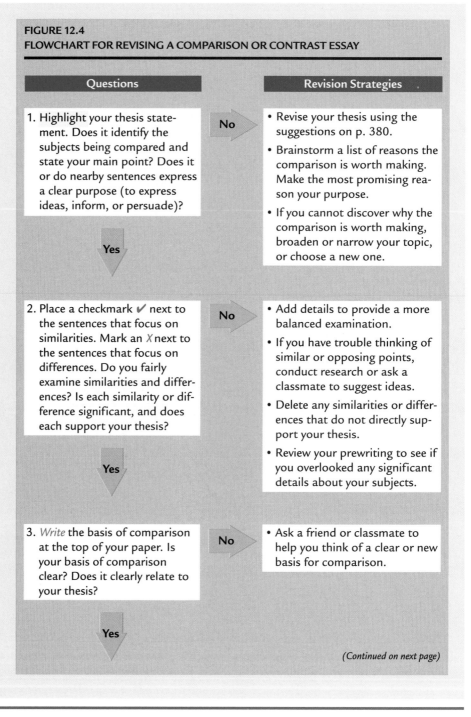

Questions		Revision Strategies
1. Highlight your thesis statement. Does it identify the subjects being compared and state your main point? Does it or do nearby sentences express a clear purpose (to express ideas, inform, or persuade)?	No	• Revise your thesis using the suggestions on p. 380. • Brainstorm a list of reasons the comparison is worth making. Make the most promising reason your purpose. • If you cannot discover why the comparison is worth making, broaden or narrow your topic, or choose a new one.

Yes

| 2. Place a checkmark ✔ next to the sentences that focus on similarities. Mark an *X* next to the sentences that focus on differences. Do you fairly examine similarities and differences? Is each similarity or difference significant, and does each support your thesis? | No | • Add details to provide a more balanced examination.
 • If you have trouble thinking of similar or opposing points, conduct research or ask a classmate to suggest ideas.
 • Delete any similarities or differences that do not directly support your thesis.
 • Review your prewriting to see if you overlooked any significant details about your subjects. |

Yes

| 3. *Write* the basis of comparison at the top of your paper. Is your basis of comparison clear? Does it clearly relate to your thesis? | No | • Ask a friend or classmate to help you think of a clear or new basis for comparison. |

Yes

(Continued on next page)

FIGURE 12.4 *(Continued)*

Questions	Revision Strategies
4. Draw a (circle) around the shared characteristics on which you base your essay. Do you include at least one characteristic for each paragraph?	**No** → • Use *who, what, where, when,* and *how* to generate characteristics about your subjects or to find those common to both.

Yes ↓

| 5. Underline the topic sentence of each paragraph. Does each paragraph have a topic sentence? Is each paragraph focused on a separate point or shared characteristic? | **No** → • Follow the guidelines for writing clear topic sentences (p. 118).
• Split paragraphs that focus on more than one point or characteristic.
• Consider combining closely related paragraphs. |

Yes ↓

| 6. Draw a wavy underline under the concrete details in each paragraph. Do you include enough details to make your comparisons vivid and interesting? Do all of your details relate to your topic sentences and shared characteristics? | **No** → • Add or delete details as necessary.
• Review your prewriting to see if you overlooked any significant points or details about your subjects.
• Research your subjects to come up with additional details or examples. (See Chapters 18 and 19.) |

Yes ↓

(Continued on next page)

FIGURE 12.4 *(Continued)*

Questions		Revision Strategies
7. *Draw* a brief diagram of the organization of your essay. Did you use either point-by-point or subject-by-subject organization throughout the essay? Is that clear to your reader?	**No** →	• Study your diagram to find inconsistencies or gaps. • Reorganize your essay using only one method of organization consistently.

Yes ↓

| 8. Draw a box around your introduction and conclusion. Does the introduction provide a context for your comparison? Is the conclusion satisfying and relevant to the comparison? | **No** → | • Revise your introduction to meet the guidelines in Chapter 5, p. 132.
• Review what the comparison suggests; then revise your conclusion.
• Propose an action or way of thinking that is appropriate in light of the comparison.
• Revise your conclusion to meet the guidelines in Chapter 5, p. 135. |

Yes ↓

| 9. Print out another draft to edit and proofread your essay before turning your essay in. | | |

As you edit and proofread your comparison or contrast essay, watch out for the following types of errors.

1. Look at adjectives and adverbs and their degrees of comparison — *positive, comparative,* and *superlative.* Make sure you change the form of adjectives and adverbs when you compare two items (comparative) and when you compare three or more items (superlative). The following examples show how adjectives and adverbs change forms.

	Adjectives	**Adverbs**
Positive	sharp	early
Comparative	sharper	earlier
Superlative	sharpest	earliest

▶ Both *The Others* and *Hannibal* were suspenseful, but I liked *The Others* ~~best.~~ *better.*

▶ George, Casey, and Bob all play basketball badly, but Bob's game is ~~worse.~~ *worst.*

2. Make sure that items in a pair linked by correlative conjunctions (*either . . . or, neither . . . nor, not only . . . but also*) are in the same grammatical form.

▶ The Grand Canyon is not only a spectacular tourist attraction, but also ~~scientists consider it~~ a useful geological record. *for scientists.*

ESSAY IN PROGRESS 9
Edit and proofread your essay, paying particular attention to adjectives and adverbs used to compare and to items linked by correlative conjunctions.

STUDENTS WRITE

Heather Gianakos was a first-year student when she wrote the following comparison and contrast essay for her composition course. Although she has always enjoyed both styles of cooking that she discusses, she needed to do some research in the library and on the Internet to learn more about their history. As you read the essay, highlight the writer's thesis and points of comparison.

Border Bites
Heather Gianakos

Chili peppers, tortillas, tacos: All these foods   1
belong to the styles of cooking known as Mexican, Tex-
Mex, and Southwestern. These internationally popular
styles often overlap; sometimes it can be hard to tell

which style a particular dish belongs to. Two particular traditions of cooking, however, play an especially important role in the kitchens of Mexico and the American Southwest: native-derived Mexican cooking ("Mexican"), and Anglo-influenced Southwestern cooking, particularly from Texas ("Southwestern"). The different traditions and geographic locations of the inhabitants of Mexico and of the Anglo-American settlers in the Southwest have resulted in subtle, flavorful differences between the foods featured in Mexican and Southwestern cuisine.

2   Many of the traditions of Southwestern cooking grew out of difficult situations--cowboys and ranchers cooking over open fires, for example. Chili, which can contain beans, beef, tomatoes, corn, and many other ingredients, was a good dish to cook over a campfire because everything could be combined in one pot. Dry foods, such as beef jerky, were a convenient way to solve food storage problems and could be easily tucked into saddlebags. In Mexico, by contrast, fresh fruits and vegetables such as avocados and tomatoes were widely available and did not need to be dried or stored. They could be made into spicy salsa and guacamole. Mexicans living in coastal areas could also enjoy fish and lobster dishes (Jamison and Jamison 5).

3   Corn has been a staple in the American Southwest and Mexico since the time of the Aztecs, who made tortillas (flat, unleavened bread, originally made from stone-ground corn and water) similar to the ones served in Mexico today (Jamison and Jamison 5). Southwesterners, often of European descent, adopted the tortilla but often prepared it with wheat flour, which was easily available to them. Wheat-flour tortillas can now be found in both Mexican and Southwestern cooking, but corn is usually the primary grain in dishes with precolonial origins. Tamales (whose name derives from a word in Nahuatl, the Aztec group of languages) are a delicious example: A hunk of cornmeal dough, sometimes combined with ground meat, is wrapped in corn husks and steamed. In Southwestern cook-

ing, corn is often used for leavened corn bread, which is made with corn flour rather than cornmeal and can be flavored with jalapeños or back bacon.

Meat of various kinds is often the centerpiece of both Mexican and Southwestern tables. However, although beef, pork, and chicken are staples in both traditions, they are often prepared quite differently. Fried chicken rolled in flour and dunked into sizzling oil or fat is a popular dish throughout the American Southwest. In traditional Mexican cooking, however, chicken is often cooked more slowly, in stews or baked dishes, with a variety of seasonings, including ancho chiles, garlic, and onions. 4

Ever since Southwestern cattle farming began with the early Spanish missions in Texas, beef has been eaten both north and south of the border. In Southwestern cooking, steak--flank, rib eye, or sirloin--grilled quickly and served rare is often a chef's crowning glory. In Mexican cooking, beef may be combined with vegetables and spices and rolled into a fajita or served ground in a taco. For a Mexican food purist, in fact, the only true fajita is made from skirt steak, although Mexican food as it is served in the United States often features chicken fajitas. 5

In Texas and the Southwest United States, barbecued pork ribs are often prepared in barbecue cookoffs, similar to chili-cooking competitions. Such competitions have strict rules for the preparation and presentation of the food and for sanitation (Central Texas Barbecue Association). However, while the BBQ is seen as a Southwestern specialty, barbecue ribs as they are served in Southwestern-themed restaurants today actually come from a Hispanic and Southwest Mexican tradition dating from the days before refrigeration: Since pork fat, unlike beef fat, has a tendency to become rancid, pork ribs were often marinated in vinegar and spices and then hung to dry. Later the ribs were basted with the same sauce and grilled (Campa 278). The resulting dish has become a favorite both north and south of the border, although in 6

Mexican cooking, where beef is somewhat less important than in Southwestern cooking, pork is equally popular in many other forms, such as chorizo sausage.

7   Cooks in San Antonio or Albuquerque would probably tell you that the food they cook is as much Mexican as it is Southwestern. Regional cuisines in such areas of the Southwest as New Mexico, southern California, and Arizona feature elements of both traditions; Chimichangas, deep-fried burritos, actually originated in Arizona (Jamison and Jamison 11). Food lovers who sample regional specialties, however, will note, and savor, the contrast between the spicy, fried or grilled, beef-heavy style of Southwestern food and the richly seasoned, corn- and tomato-heavy style of Mexican food.

Works Cited

Campa, Arthur L. Hispanic Culture in the Southwest. Norman: U of Oklahoma P, 1979.

Central Texas Barbecue Association. "CTBA Rules." 16 Aug. 2004. 6 May 2005. <http://www.vvm.com/ctba-bbq/>.

Jamison, Cheryl Alters, and Bill Jamison. The Border Cookbook. Boston: Harvard Common, 1995.

Analyzing the Essay

1. Evaluate Gianakos's title and introduction. Do they provide the reader with enough background on her topic?
2. What method of organization does Gianakos use in her essay?
3. Identify Gianakos's points of comparison.
4. How does Gianakos's use of sources contribute to her essay?

Reacting to the Essay: Discussion and Journal Writing

1. Gianakos compares the cuisines of the American Southwest and Mexico. Suggest several other possible bases of comparison that could be used to compare these geographic regions.

2. What other regional cuisines might make effective topics for a comparison and contrast essay?

3. Write a journal entry describing your reaction to Southwestern and Mexican foods or two other regional cuisines.

READING COMPARISON AND CONTRAST

The following section provides advice for reading comparison and contrast essays. Two model essays illustrate the characteristics of comparison and contrast covered in this chapter and provide opportunities to examine, analyze, and react to the writer's ideas. The second essay uses comparison and contrast along with other methods of development.

WORKING WITH TEXT: READING COMPARISON OR CONTRAST ESSAYS

Reading a comparison and contrast essay is somewhat different from reading other kinds of essays. First, the essay contains two or more subjects instead of just one. Second, the subjects are being compared, contrasted, or both, so you must follow the author's points of comparison between or among them. Use the following guidelines to read comparison and contrast essays effectively.

For more on reading strategies, see Chapter 2.

What to Look For, Highlight, and Annotate

1. As you preview the essay, determine whether it uses the point-by-point or subject-by-subject organization. Knowing the method of organization will help you move through the essay more easily.

For more on previewing, see Chapter 2, p. 24.

2. Identify and highlight the thesis statement, if it is stated explicitly. What does it tell you about the essay's purpose, direction, and organization?

3. Read the essay once to get an overall sense of how it develops. As you read, highlight each point of comparison the writer makes.

4. Review the essay by drawing a graphic organizer (see Figures 12.1 and 12.2). Doing so will help you learn and recall the key points of the essay.

How to Find Ideas to Write About

To respond to or write about a comparison and contrast essay, consider the following strategies.

For more on discovering ideas for a response paper, see Chapter 2

- Compare the subjects using a different basis of comparison. If, for example, an essay compares or contrasts athletes in various sports on the basis of salary, you could compare them according to the training required for each sport.
- For an essay that emphasizes differences, consider writing about similarities, and vice versa.
- To write an essay that looks at one point of comparison in more depth, you might do research or interview an expert on the topic.

THINKING CRITICALLY ABOUT COMPARISON AND CONTRAST

Is the Author Biased?

Bias refers to a writer's own views about a topic. Some writers express their prejudices and preferences clearly, while others do so subtly. A biased piece of writing is not necessarily unreliable, but by being aware of an author's bias, readers can find sources that present other sides of an issue. To recognize bias, pay close attention to the language being used. Does the author use words with double meanings or offensive connotations? Also consider the overall tone. Ask yourself, "Is a particular slant taken toward the subject?"

COMPARISON AND CONTRAST ESSAY

As you read the following essay by psychologist Daniel Goleman, notice how the writer uses the elements of comparison and contrast discussed in this chapter.

His Marriage and Hers: Childhood Roots
Daniel Goleman

Daniel Goleman holds a Ph.D. in behavioral and brain sciences and has published a number of books on psychology, including Vital Lies, Simple Truths *(1985),* The Meditative Mind *(1988),* Working with Emotional Intelligence *(1998),* The Emotionally Intelligent Workplace: How to Select For, Measure, and Improve Emotional Intelligence in Individuals, Groups, and Organizations *(2001), and* Destructive Emotions: A Scientific Dialogue with the Dalai Lama *(2003), and as coauthor,* The Creative Spirit *(1992) and* Primal Leadership: Realizing the Powers of Emotional Intelligence *(2002). In his book* Emotional Intelligence *(1995), from which the following selection was taken, Goleman asserts that daily living requires skill in handling emotions. He describes the skill and explains how to develop it. As you read the selection, notice how the writer uses comparison and contrast to explore his subject—differences between the sexes—and highlight his key points of comparison.*

As I was entering a restaurant on a recent evening, a young man stalked out the door, his face set in an expression both stony and sullen. Close on his heels a young woman came running, her fists desperately pummeling his back while she yelled, "Goddamn you! Come back here and be nice to me!" That poignant, impossibly self-contradictory plea aimed at a retreating back epitomizes the pattern most commonly seen in couples whose relationship is distressed: She seeks to engage, he withdraws. Marital therapists have long noted that by the time a couple finds their way to the therapy office, they are in this pattern of engage-withdraw, with his complaint about her "unreasonable" demands and outbursts, and her lamenting his indifference to what she is saying.

This marital endgame reflects the fact that there are, in effect, two emotional realities in a couple, his and hers. The roots of these emotional differences, while they may be partly biological, also can be traced back to childhood and to the separate emotional worlds boys and girls inhabit while growing up. There is a vast amount of research on these separate worlds, their barriers reinforced not just by the different games boys and girls prefer but by young children's fear of being teased for having a "girlfriend" or "boyfriend."[1] One study of children's friendships found that three-year-olds say about half their friends are of the opposite sex; for five-year-olds it's about 20 percent, and by age seven almost no boys or girls say they have a best friend of the opposite sex.[2] These separate social universes intersect little until teenagers start dating.

Meanwhile, boys and girls are taught very different lessons about handling emotions. Parents, in general, discuss emotions—with the exception of anger—more with their daughters than their sons.[3] Girls are exposed to more information about emotions than are boys: when parents make up stories to tell their preschool children, they use more emotion words when talking to daughters than to sons; when mothers play with their infants, they display a wider range of emotions to daughters than to sons; when mothers talk to daughters about feelings, they discuss in more detail the emotional state itself than they do with their sons—though with the sons they go into more detail about the causes and consequences of emotions like anger (probably as a cautionary tale).

Leslie Brody and Judith Hall, who have summarized the research on differences in emotions between the sexes, propose that because girls develop facility with language more quickly than do boys, this leads them to be more experienced at articulating their feelings and more skilled than boys at using words to explore and substitute for emotional reactions such as physical fights; in contrast, they note, "boys, for whom the verbalization of affects is de-emphasized, may become largely unconscious of their emotional states, both in themselves and others."[4]

5   At age ten, roughly the same percent of girls as boys are overtly aggressive, given to open confrontation when angered. But by age thirteen, a telling difference between the sexes emerges: Girls become more adept than boys at artful aggressive tactics like ostracism, vicious gossip, and indirect vendettas. Boys, by and large, simply continue being confrontational when angered, oblivious to these more covert strategies.[5] This is just one of many ways that boys — and later, men — are less sophisticated than the opposite sex in the byways of emotional life.

6   When girls play together, they do so in small, intimate groups, with an emphasis on minimizing hostility and maximizing cooperation, while boys' games are in larger groups, with an emphasis on competition. One key difference can be seen in what happens when games boys or girls are playing get disrupted by someone getting hurt. If a boy who has gotten hurt gets upset, he is expected to get out of the way and stop crying so the game can go on. If the same happens among a group of girls who are playing, the game stops while everyone gathers around to help the girl who is crying. This difference between boys and girls at play epitomizes what Harvard's Carol Gilligan points to as a key disparity between the sexes: boys take pride in a lone, tough-minded independence and autonomy, while girls see themselves as part of a web of connectedness. Thus boys are threatened by anything that might challenge their independence, while girls are more threatened by a rupture in their relationships. And, as Deborah Tannen has pointed out in her book *You Just Don't Understand*, these differing perspectives mean that men and women want and expect very different things out of a conversation, with men content to talk about "things," while women seek emotional connection.

7   In short, these contrasts in schooling in the emotions foster very different skills, with girls becoming "adept at reading both verbal and nonverbal emotional signals, at expressing and communicating their feelings," and boys becoming adept at "minimizing emotions having to do with vulnerability, guilt, fear, and hurt."[6] Evidence for these different stances is very strong in the scientific literature. Hundreds of studies have found, for example, that on average women are more empathic than men, at least as measured by the ability to read

someone else's unstated feelings from facial expression, tone of voice, and other nonverbal cues. Likewise, it is generally easier to read feelings from a woman's face than a man's; while there is no difference in facial expressiveness among very young boys and girls, as they go through the elementary-school grades boys become less expressive, girls more so. This may partly reflect another key difference: women, on average, experience the entire range of emotions with greater intensity and more volatility than men—in this sense, women are more "emotional" than men.[7]

All of this means that, in general, women come into a marriage   8
groomed for the role of emotional manager, while men arrive with much less appreciation of the importance of this task for helping a relationship survive. Indeed, the most important element for women—but not for men—in satisfaction with their relationship reported in a study of 264 couples was the sense that the couple has "good communication."[8] Ted Huston, a psychologist at the University of Texas who has studied couples in depth, observes, "For the wives, intimacy means talking things over, especially talking about the relationship itself. The men, by and large, don't understand what the wives want from them. They say, 'I want to do things with her, and all she wants to do is talk.'" During courtship, Huston found, men were much more willing to spend time talking in ways that suited the wish for intimacy of their wives-to-be. But once married, as time went on the men—especially in more traditional couples—spent less and less time talking in this way with their wives, finding a sense of closeness simply in doing things like gardening together rather than talking things over.

This growing silence on the part of husbands may be partly due   9
to the fact that, if anything, men are a bit Pollyannaish about the state of their marriage, while their wives are attuned to the trouble spots: in one study of marriages, men had a rosier view than their wives of just about everything in their relationship—lovemaking, finances, ties with in-laws, how well they listened to each other, how much their flaws mattered.[9] Wives, in general, are more vocal about their complaints than are their husbands, particularly among unhappy couples. Combine men's rosy view of marriage with their aversion to emotional confrontations, and it is clear why wives so often complain that their husbands try to wiggle out of discussing the troubling things about their relationship. (Of course this gender difference is a generalization and is not true in every case; a psychiatrist friend complained that in his marriage his wife is reluctant to discuss emotional matters between them and he is the one who is left to bring them up.)

10   The slowness of men to bring up problems in a relationship is no doubt compounded by their relative lack of skill when it comes to reading facial expressions of emotions. Women, for example, are more sensitive to a sad expression on a man's face than are men in detecting sadness from a woman's expression.[10] Thus a woman has to be all the sadder for a man to notice her feelings in the first place, let alone for him to raise the question of what is making her so sad.

11   Consider the implications of this emotional gender gap for how couples handle the grievances and disagreements that any intimate relationship inevitably spawns. In fact, specific issues such as how often a couple has sex, how to discipline the children, or how much debt and savings a couple feels comfortable with are not what make or break a marriage. Rather, it is how a couple discusses such sore points that matters more for the fate of their marriage. Simply having reached an agreement about how to disagree is key to marital survival; men and women have to overcome the innate gender differences in approaching rocky emotions. Failing this, couples are vulnerable to emotional rifts that eventually can tear their relationship apart. . . . [T]hese rifts are far more likely to develop if one or both partners have certain deficits in emotional intelligence.   ■

NOTES

1. The separate worlds of boys and girls: Eleanor Maccoby and C. N. Jacklin, "Gender Segregation in Childhood," in H. Reese, ed., *Advances in Child Development and Behavior* (New York: Academic Press, 1987).
2. Same-sex playmates: John Gottman, "Same and Cross Sex Friendship in Young Children," in J. Gottman and J. Parker, eds., *Conversation of Friends* (New York: Cambridge University Press, 1986).
3. This and the following summary of sex differences in socialization of emotions are based on the excellent review in Leslie R. Brody and Judith A. Hall, "Gender and Emotion," in Michael Lewis and Jeannette Haviland, eds., *Handbook of Emotions* (New York: Guilford Press, 1993).
4. Brody and Hall, "Gender and Emotion," p. 456.
5. Girls and the arts of aggression: Robert B. Cairns and Beverley D. Cairns, *Lifelines and Risks* (New York: Cambridge University Press, 1994).
6. Brody and Hall, "Gender and Emotion," p. 454.
7. The findings about gender differences in emotion are reviewed in Brody and Hall, "Gender and Emotion."
8. The importance of good communication for women was reported in Mark H. Davis and H. Alan Oathout, "Maintenance of Satisfaction in Romantic Relationships: Empathy and Relational Competence," *Journal of Personality and Social Psychology* 53, 2 (1987), pp. 397–410.
9. The study of husbands' and wives' complaints: Robert J. Sternberg, "Triangulating Love," in Robert Sternberg and Michael Barnes, eds., *The Psychology of Love* (New Haven: Yale University Press, 1988).

10. Reading sad faces: The research is by Dr. Ruben C. Gur at the University of Pennsylvania School of Medicine.

Examining the Reading

1. Summarize the differences that Goleman claims exist between men's and women's ways of expressing emotion.

2. According to Goleman, what are the root causes of the differences between how men and women express emotion?

3. How can the emotional differences between spouses cause marital difficulties, according to the writer?

4. Explain how boys and girls play differently, according to Goleman.

5. Explain the meaning of each of the following words as they are used in the reading: *epitomizes* (para. 1), *articulating* (4), *ostracism* (5), *vendettas* (5), *disparity* (6), and *empathic* (7). Refer to your dictionary as needed.

Analyzing the Reading

1. What is Goleman's thesis?

2. Identify the purpose of the essay and list the points of comparison.

3. For each point of comparison, evaluate the evidence Goleman offers to substantiate his findings. Do you find the evidence sufficient and convincing? Why or why not? What other information might the writer have included?

4. What types of details does Goleman provide to explain each point of comparison?

5. Do you think Goleman maintains an objective stance on the issue, despite his gender?

Reacting to the Reading: Discussion and Journal Writing

1. Do you think any of Goleman's generalizations about men and women are inaccurate? Discuss the evidence, if any, that would prove Goleman wrong.

2. Discuss a situation from your experience that either confirms or contradicts one of Goleman's generalizations.

3. Make a list of the emotional differences and resulting behavioral conflicts between men and women that you have observed. Decide which differences are explained by Goleman. Write a journal entry describing your findings.

MAKING CONNECTIONS: Women and Men

In "For Man and Beast, Language of Love Shares Many Traits" (Chapter 11, pp. 363–65) and "His Marriage and Hers: Childhood Roots" (pp. 404–08), Daniel Goleman explores the differences between women and men and their relationships.

Analyzing the Readings

1. What are the different points that each reading makes? Are Goleman's ideas consistent with each other?
2. Watch a television program, and then write a journal entry analyzing the interactions between men and women as revealed in the program. How closely do the characters' actions and words match Goleman's observations, if at all?

Essay Idea

Write an essay analyzing a significant relationship between a male and a female you know. Use Goleman's essays as examples. How closely, if at all, does the relationship match Goleman's observations?

COMPARISON AND CONTRAST COMBINED WITH OTHER PATTERNS

In the following reading, notice how Abigail Zuger uses comparison and contrast to explain a change that is occurring in the training of doctors and in expectations for medical students' behavior.

Defining a Doctor, with a Tear, a Shrug, and a Schedule
Abigail Zuger

Abigail Zuger is a physician at Bellevue Hospital in New York City who specializes in HIV/AIDS. Her experiences working in the early years of the AIDS epidemic led her to write Strong Shadows: Scenes from an Inner City AIDS Clinic *(1995). The following essay, published in November 2004, is among the many articles she has contributed to the* New York Times.

I had two interns to supervise that month, and the minute they sat down for our first meeting, I sensed how the month would unfold.

The man's white coat was immaculate, its pockets empty save for a sleek Palm Pilot that contained his list of patients. The woman used a large loose-leaf notebook instead, every dog-eared page full of lists of things to do and check, consultants to call, questions to ask. Her pockets were stuffed, and whenever she sat down, little handbooks of drug doses, wadded phone messages, pens, highlighters, and tourniquets spilled onto the floor.

The man worked the hours legally mandated by the state, not a minute more, and sometimes considerably less. He was seldom in the hospital before 8 in the morning and left by 5 unless he was on call. He ate a leisurely lunch every day and was never late for rounds. The woman got to the hospital around dawn and was on the move for the rest of the day. Sometimes she went home when she was supposed to, but sometimes, if one of her patients was particularly sick, she would sign out to the covering intern and keep working, often talking to patients' relatives long into the night. "I am now breaking the law," she would announce cheerfully to no one in particular, then trot off to do just a few final chores.

The man had a strict definition of what it meant to be a doctor. He did not, for instance, "do nurses' work" (his phrase). When one of his patients needed a specimen sent to the lab and the nurse didn't get around to it, neither did he. No matter how important the job was, no matter how hard I pressed him, he never gave in. If I spoke sternly to him, he would turn around and speak just as sternly to the nurse. The woman did everyone's work. She would weigh her patients if necessary (nurses' work), feed them (aides' work), find salt-free pickles for them (dietitians' work), and wheel them to X-ray (transporters' work).

The man was cheerful, serene, and well rested. The woman was overtired, hyperemotional, and constantly late. The man was interested in his patients, but they never kept him up at night. The woman occasionally called the hospital from home to check on hers. The man played tennis on his days off. The woman read medical articles. At least, she read the beginnings; she tended to fall asleep halfway through.

I felt as if I was in a medieval morality play[1] that month, living with two costumed symbols of opposing philosophies in medical

---

[1]*morality play:* a play performed in the Middle Ages in which characters represent abstractions (love, death, peace, and so on); its purpose is to teach a lesson about right and wrong.

education. The woman was working the way interns used to: total immersion seasoned with exhaustion and adrenaline. As far as she was concerned, her patients were her exclusive responsibility. The man was an intern of the new millennium. His hours and duties were delimited; he saw himself as part of a health care team, and his patients' welfare as a shared responsibility.

7   This new model of medical internship got some important validation in the *New England Journal of Medicine* last week, when Harvard researchers reported the effects of reducing interns' work hours to 60 per week from 80 (now the mandated national maximum). The shorter workweek required a larger staff of interns to spell one another at more frequent intervals. With shorter hours, the interns got more sleep at home, dozed off less at work, and made considerably fewer bad mistakes in patient care.

8   Why should such an obvious finding need an elaborate controlled study to establish? Why should it generate not only two long articles in the world's most prestigious medical journal but also three long, passionate editorials? Because the issue here is bigger than just scheduling and manpower.

9   The progressive shortening of residents' work hours spells nothing less than a change in the ethos of medicine itself. It means the end of Dr. Kildare, Superstar—that lone, heroic healer, omniscient, omnipotent, and ever-present. It means a revolution in the complex medical hierarchy that sustained him. Willy-nilly, medicine is becoming democratized, a team sport.

10   We can only hope the revolution will be bloodless. Everything will have to change. Doctors will have to learn to work well with others. They will have to learn to write and speak with enough clarity and precision so that the patient's story remains accurate as care passes from hand to hand. They will have to stop saying "my patient" and begin to say "our patient" instead.

11   It may be, when the dust settles, that the system will be more functional, less error-prone. It may be that we will simply have substituted one set of problems for another. We may even find that nothing much has changed. Even in the Harvard data, there was an impressive range in the hours that the interns under study worked. Some logged in over 90 hours in their 80-hour workweek. Some put in 75 instead. Medicine has always attracted a wide spectrum of individuals, from the lazy and disaffected to the deeply committed. Even draconian scheduling policies may not change basic personality traits or the kind of doctors that interns grow up to be.

12   My month with the intern of the past and the intern of the future certainly argues for the power of the individual work ethic. Try as I might, it was not within my power to modify the way either of them

functioned. The woman cared too much. The man cared too little. She worked too hard, and he could not be prodded into working hard enough. They both made careless mistakes. When patients died, the man shrugged and the woman cried. If for no other reason than that one, let us hope that the medicine of the future still has room for people like her. ∎

Examining the Reading

1. How do the two interns differ in their approach to medicine?
2. What different philosophies of medicine do the two interns represent?
3. Describe the working conditions of interns.
4. What do we learn about the author and her philosophy of medical practice?
5. Explain the meaning of each of the following words as used in the reading: *delimited* (para. 6), *ethos* (9), *omniscient* (9), *omnipotent* (9), and *draconian* (11). Refer to your dictionary as needed.

Analyzing the Reading

1. Highlight Zuger's thesis and evaluate its placement.
2. Identify the points of comparison on which the essay is based.
3. What other patterns of development does the author use? Give one example and explain how it contributes to the essay.
4. Evaluate the effectiveness of the point-by-point organization. How would the essay differ if it had been written using a subject-by-subject organization?
5. Evaluate the essay's conclusion. How does it reflect the thesis and organization of the essay?

Reacting to the Reading: Discussion and Journal Writing

1. Discuss an experience of visiting a doctor or hospital. Within which philosophy of medical care did your treatment fall?
2. Discuss the training and education you will need for a career you are interested in pursuing. What knowledge and skills will you need to succeed in the field, and how will the training provide them?
3. Write a journal entry exploring whether medical care has become depersonalized. Give examples from your experience.

APPLYING YOUR SKILLS: ADDITIONAL ESSAY ASSIGNMENTS

Write a comparison or contrast essay on one of the following topics, using what you have learned in this chapter. Depending on the topic you choose, you may need to conduct library or Internet research.

For more on locating and documenting sources, see Part 5.

To Express Your Ideas

1. Compare two families that you know or are part of. Include points of comparison that reveal what is valuable and important in family life.

2. Compare your values and priorities today to those you held when you were in high school.

3. Compare your lifestyle today to the lifestyle you intend to follow after you graduate from college.

To Inform Your Reader

4. Compare library resources to those available on the Internet.

5. Compare something from the past with its counterpart in the present, as Simon and Cannon do in "An Amazing Journey: 100 Years in America" (p. 373).

To Persuade Your Reader

6. Choose a technological change that has occurred in recent years, as Frazier does in "Dearly Disconnected" (p. 376), and argue either that it is beneficial or that its drawbacks outweigh its usefulness compared with the old technology.

7. Compare two views on a controversial issue, arguing in favor of one of them.

8. Compare two methods of doing something (such as disciplining a child or training a pet), arguing that one method is more effective than the other.

Cases Using Comparison and Contrast

9. You are taking a course in photography and have been asked to write a paper comparing and contrasting the advantages and uses of black-and-white versus color film. Your instructor is your audience.

10. You are working in the advertising department of a company that manufactures in-line skates. Your manager has asked you to evaluate two periodicals and recommend which one the company should use to run its advertisements.

EVALUATING YOUR PROGRESS
Part A: Using Comparison and Contrast

Write a paragraph that evaluates your use of comparison and contrast. Be sure to

- Identify one everyday, one academic, and one workplace situation in which comparison and contrast would be a useful method for organizing information.
- What method of organization did you use in your comparison and contrast essay(s)? Did you discover any disadvantages or limitations of the method? How would your essay(s) have changed if you had used a different method of organization?
- Identify any problems or trouble spots you experienced in using comparison and contrast, and explain how you dealt with them.

Part B: Analyzing Comparison and Contrast Readings

The readings in this chapter are models of essays using comparison and contrast. Some use a subject-by-subject organization; others use a point-by-point organization. What do you perceive to be the strengths of each method?

Part C: Proofreading and Editing

List the errors your instructor identified in your comparison and contrast essay(s). For more help with these problems, refer to Exercise Central (www.bedfordstmartins.com/successfulwriting).

"SWISS ARMY" PERSONALITY

Rini

Classification and Division: Explaining Categories and Parts

The cartoon on the opposite page depicts the personality types of a single person. Take a few minutes to think about your own personality and the various personality types that either you or people you know have.

Come up with a name for each personality type you can think of or that is shown in the cartoon, then make a list of people you know who fit each category. To test whether this system works, consider whether you know people who would fit into more than one category.

WRITING A CLASSIFICATION OR DIVISION ESSAY

In categorizing the types of personalities, you used a process called *classification;* you grouped people you know into categories based on specific characteristics. This chapter will show you how to write effective classification and division essays as well as how to incorporate classification and division into essays using other patterns of development.

WHAT ARE CLASSIFICATION AND DIVISION?

You use classification to organize things and ideas daily. Your dresser drawers are probably organized by categories, with socks and sweatshirts in different drawers. Grocery stores, phone directories, libraries, and even restaurant menus arrange items in groups according to similar characteristics.

Classification, then, is a process of sorting people, things, or ideas into groups or categories to help make them more understandable. For example, your college catalog classifies its course offerings by schools, divisions, and departments. Think how difficult it would be to find courses in the catalog if it were arranged alphabetically instead of by categories.

Division, similar to classification, begins with *one* item and breaks it down into parts. Thus, for example, the humanities department at your college may be divided into English, modern languages, and philosophy, and the modern language courses might be further divided into Spanish, French, Chinese, and Russian. Division is closely related to process analysis, which is covered in Chapter 11.

A classification or division essay explains a topic by describing types or parts. For example, a classification essay might explore types of advertising—direct mail, radio, television, newspaper, and so forth. A division essay might describe the parts of an art museum—exhibit areas, museum store, visitor services desk, and the like.

SCENES FROM COLLEGE AND THE WORKPLACE

- For a course in *anatomy and physiology,* you are asked to study the structure and parts of the human ear by identifying the function of each part.

- As part of a *business management* report, you need to consider how debt liability differs for three types of businesses—a single proprietorship, a partnership, and a corporation.

- While working as a *facilities planner,* you are asked to conduct a feasibility study of several new sites. You begin by sorting the sites into three categories: within state, out of state, and out of country.

You will find many occasions to use classification and division in the writing you do in college and the workplace (see the accompanying box for a few examples). In the following essay, Paula M. White classifies the kinds of intelligence found in children. An example of a division essay, "A Brush with Reality: Surprises in the Tube" by David Bodanis, appears on page 426.

Bringing Out Your Child's Gifts
Paula M. White

Paula M. White is an editor and the author of numerous articles published in Essence *and* Black Enterprise *magazines. This essay is from the September 1997 issue of* Essence, *a periodical for African American women. White describes seven types of intelligence a child may demonstrate. As you read the selection, highlight the types of intelligence and their key characteristics.*

As a child, I loved books so much that I would get a flashlight and try to read under the covers after my parents had put me to bed at night. I also kept a journal, wrote and produced plays for family and friends, and composed stories using my friends as the characters. Because of my natural verbal skills, I did well on standardized tests and was always near the top of my class.

My brother, Keith, on the other hand, was good at making friends. He never met a stranger, and whenever someone needed a helping hand, he was there. He was always lending his video games and designer clothes, and when he began driving, he frequently volunteered to shuttle his friends around. Keith was also an active member of numerous community-service clubs. But rarely did his good deeds and unselfish works translate into a stellar report card.

Keith and I were very different kids who learned in very different ways. And like most folks, we grew up in a household where a premium was placed on education. Good grades were rewarded and bad grades meant grief. Yet, despite our mother's high expectations, she always gave us the freedom to learn in our own way. When we weren't doing homework, Mom was shuttling us to street festivals and puppet shows, animal farms and children's museums. Keith played soccer and the clarinet; I took tap and ballet classes (to tame my wayward feet). We explored worlds that we were good—and not so good—at. And we grew.

Although she didn't know it then, my mother was a proponent of the theory of multiple intelligences. According to this theory, everyone has talents or gifts in many areas, and when we play to our strongest suits, the most effective learning usually occurs. Sometimes, however, these strong suits aren't where parents want them to be.

5   "If we look at children only in traditional ways, and the child doesn't have 'schoolhouse' intelligence [is strong in linguistics or math], parents will figure they don't have a promising child," says psychologist Thomas Armstrong of Sonoma County, California. "However, by considering multiple intelligences, parents can look deeper and see talents they may have neglected."

6   Ellen Winner, a professor of psychology at Boston College and the author of *Gifted Children: Myths and Realities,* explains that if you want to identify where your child's potential lies, simply take note of the activities she naturally gravitates toward. Winner says she believes that if parents recognize and nurture a child's inborn abilities, the child will be able to build her confidence and self-esteem much more than any IQ or other standardized-test result ever could.

7   "IQ tests are very limited," says Winner. "They're pretty good for predicting how well your child will do in school because they test subject matter that schools value. But they don't predict how well your child is going to do in life."

MULTIPLE INTELLIGENCES MADE SIMPLE

8   Uncovering your child's strengths and providing opportunities for him to develop do not have to be complicated or costly. In his books *Awakening Your Child's Natural Genius* and *In Their Own Way: Discovering and Encouraging Your Child's Personal Learning Style,* Armstrong offers these guidelines for recognizing and cultivating the seven intelligences in your child.

9   A **verbal-linguistic child** speaks and/or reads at an early age; enjoys writing; spins tall tales or tells jokes and stories; has a good memory for names, places, dates, or trivia; enjoys reading in her spare time; spells words easily; appreciates nonsense rhymes and tongue twisters; likes doing crossword puzzles.

10   *How they learn:* These kids learn best by saying, hearing, and seeing words.

11   *How to nurture them:* Provide them with books, records, and tapes of the spoken word; create opportunities for writing; engage them in discussions; give them access to such tools as a tape recorder, a typewriter, and a computer for word making; read books together; have evenings of storytelling; take them places where words are important, including bookstores and libraries; play games such as *Black Heritage Brain Quest, Scrabble, Trivial Pursuit, Boggle, Jeopardy* or *Wheel of Fortune.*

12   A **logical-mathematical child** computes arithmetic problems quickly in his head; enjoys using computers; asks questions like "Where does the universe end?" "What happens after we die?" and "When did time begin?"; plays chess, checkers, or other strategy

games and wins; enjoys brainteasers, logical puzzles; devises experiments to test things he doesn't understand; likes patterns.

How they learn: These children think in terms of concepts and look for abstract patterns and relationships.

How to nurture them: Provide them with materials they can experiment with, such as science resources. Visit science museums, computer fairs and electronics exhibitions. They enjoy logical puzzles and games like backgammon, *Clue,* dominoes, *Mastermind, Monopoly,* and *Othello.*

A **visual-spatial child** spends free time drawing, designing things, or building articles with Lego blocks; reports clear visual images when thinking; easily reads maps, charts, and diagrams; likes it when you show movies, slides, or photographs; enjoys doing jigsaw puzzles or mazes; daydreams a lot; is fascinated with machines and contraptions and sometimes comes up with her own inventions.

How they learn: These youngsters usually learn visually and need to be taught through images, pictures, metaphor, and color.

How to nurture them: Use films, slides, diagrams, maps, charts, art activities, construction kits, visualization exercises, and vivid stories. Visit architectural landmarks, planetariums, and art museums. Play games such as checkers, chess, *Classic Concentration, Connect Four, Pictionary,* and ticktacktoe.

A **musical child** frequently sings, hums, or whistles quietly to himself; has strong opinions about the music you play on the radio or stereo; is sensitive to nonverbal sounds in the environment, such as crickets chirping, distant bells ringing; remembers melodies of songs; tells you when a musical note is off-key; needs music to study; collects records or tapes.

How they learn: These children learn best through rhythm and melody. They can learn almost anything more easily if it's sung, tapped, or whistled.

How to nurture them: Provide music lessons (if the child wants them), play different types of music around the house, involve them in rhythmic activities and sing-along time. Use percussion instruments or metronomes to help them learn rote material. Good games include *Encore, NoteAbility, Hot Potato, Simon,* and *Song Burst.*

A **bodily-kinesthetic child** does well in competitive sports; moves, twitches, taps, or fidgets while sitting in a chair; enjoys physical activities like swimming, biking, hiking, or skateboarding; needs to touch people when talking to them; enjoys scary amusement rides; demonstrates skill in a craft like woodworking, sewing, or carving; cleverly mimics other people's gestures, mannerisms, or behaviors; communicates well through body language.

How they learn: These kids learn best by moving their bodies and working with their hands.

23   *How to nurture them:* Provide them with access to playgrounds, swimming pools, and gyms. Let them fix machines, build models, and care for small animals. Play games like *Twister,* jacks, *Jenga, Pick-Up Sticks, Operation,* and charades.

24   An **interpersonal child** enjoys socializing; knows everybody's business, such as who has a crush on whom, who's mad at whom, and where the fight is going to be after school; serves as mediator when disputes arise; seems particularly streetsmart; gets involved in after-school group activities; has empathy for others' feelings.

25   *How they learn:* These children learn best by relating to and cooperating with people.

26   *How to nurture them:* Let them teach other kids; get them involved in community projects, school clubs, and volunteer organizations where they can learn by interacting with others; have family discussions and problem-solving sessions. Play games like *LifeStories* and *Therapy: The Game.*

27   An **intrapersonal child** shies away from group activities; keeps a diary or has ongoing projects and hobbies that are semisecretive in nature; displays a sense of independence or strong will; seems to live in her own private, inner world; likes to play alone; seems to have a deep sense of self-confidence; often is labeled eccentric; is self-motivated.

28   *How they learn:* These kids frequently learn best when they're left to themselves.

29   *How to nurture them:* Give them a chance to pursue independent study and individualized projects or games. Respect their privacy; let them know it's okay to be independent. Play games like *Scruples* and *The Ungame.*

Caveat Emptor

30   "It's wisest to look at all your child's abilities and foster each of them," Armstrong says. He warns against simply finding the greatest strength and teaching everything through that one entry point; you run the risk of pigeonholing your youngster, and your child also misses out on the chance to develop in other areas.

31   "The most important thing is for parents to be balanced and take it a step at a time," Armstrong concludes. "Parents shouldn't make it a job to develop their child's intelligences."

32   My brother Keith is now a teacher. I'm a writer and editor. We ultimately ended up in professions that matched our natural-born gifts. I suppose my mom knew without knowing that nurturing our strengths and working with us on our weaknesses was the way to get us to the other side of childhood, well-adjusted, productive and confident. I pray that I can follow her lead and do the same for my kids. ∎

Characteristics of Classification and Division Essays

A successful classification or division essay is meaningful to its audience. The writer uses one principle of classification or division, with exclusive categories or parts that are broad enough to include all of the members of the group.

Classification Groups and Division Divides Ideas According to One Principle

To sort items into groups, a writer needs to decide how to categorize them. For example, birds could be classified in terms of their size, habitat, or diet. For a division essay, the writer must decide into what parts to divide the topic. A journalist writing about a new aquarium could divide the topic according to type of fish displayed, suitability for children of different ages, or the quality of the exhibits.

To develop an effective set of categories or parts, a writer needs to choose one principle of classification or division and use it consistently throughout the essay or within a particular section of the essay. In "Bringing Out Your Child's Gifts," White uses the principle of types of intelligence to categorize children's gifts throughout her essay.

Once a writer chooses a principle of classification or division, the next step is to identify a manageable number of categories or parts. An essay classifying birds according to diet, for example, might use five or six types of diet, not twenty.

Classification and Division Are Meaningful to an Audience

Because several different principles can be used to categorize any group, the writer's purpose will determine the principle of classification. The personnel director of a college might classify professors by age in preparing a financial report that projects upcoming retirements, whereas a student writing a paper about teaching methods might categorize professors by teaching style.

To develop a meaningful classification, therefore, focus on both your readers and your purpose. Choose a principle of classification that will interest your readers. If, for instance, you want to inform parents about the types of day-care facilities in your town, you could classify day-care centers according to the services they offer because your readers would be looking for that information.

Division essays, too, are guided by purpose and audience. For example, the journalist who divides the aquarium exhibits according to their suitability for children of different ages might be writing to persuade readers of the leisure section of his newspaper that the aquarium is designed for children.

EXERCISE 13.1

Brainstorm three different principles of classification or division you could use for each of the following topics.

1. Sports teams
2. Fast-food restaurants

3. Convenience stores
4. Academic subjects
5. Novels

Classification Uses Categories and Division Uses Parts That Are Exclusive and Comprehensive

The categories or parts you choose should not overlap. In other words, a particular item or person should fit in no more than one category. A familiar example is age: The categories *25 to 30* and *30 to 35* are not mutually exclusive since someone who is thirty would fit in both. The second category should be changed to *31 to 35*. In an essay about the nutritional value of pizza, you could divide your topic into carbohydrates, proteins, and fats, but you would not add a separate category for saturated fat, since saturated fat is already contained in the fats category.

The categories or parts you choose should also be comprehensive. In a division essay, all the major parts of an item should be included. In a classification essay, each member of the group should fit into one category or another. For example, an essay categorizing fast-food restaurants according to the type of food they serve would have to include a category for pizza.

EXERCISE 13.2

Choose a principle of classification or division for two of the topics listed in Exercise 13.1. Then make a list of the categories in which each item could be included or parts into which each item could be divided.

Classification or Division Fully Explains Each Category or Part

A classification or division essay contains adequate detail so that each category or part can be understood by readers. In "Bringing Out Your Child's Gifts," White clearly describes each of the seven types of intelligence, using expert testimony, personal observation, and other kinds of details. Details such as these enable readers to "see" the writer's categories or parts in a classification or division essay.

Classification or Division Develops a Thesis

The thesis statement in a classification or division essay identifies the topic and may reveal the principle used to classify or divide the topic. In most cases it also suggests why the classification or division is relevant or important. In "Bringing Out Your Child's Gifts," for example, the thesis is that "everyone has talents or gifts in many areas, and when we play to our strongest suits, the most effective learning usually occurs" (para. 4).

Here are a few other examples of thesis statements.

Most people consider videos a form of entertainment; however, videos can also serve educational, commercial, and political functions.

The Grand Canyon is divided into two distinct geographical areas, the North Rim and the South Rim; each offers different views, facilities, and climatic conditions.

Visualizing a Classification or Division Essay: A Graphic Organizer

The graphic organizer shown in Figure 13.1 outlines the basic organization of a classification or division essay. The introduction announces the topic, gives

For more on graphic organizers, see Chapter 2, p. 34.

FIGURE 13.1
GRAPHIC ORGANIZER FOR A CLASSIFICATION OR DIVISION ESSAY

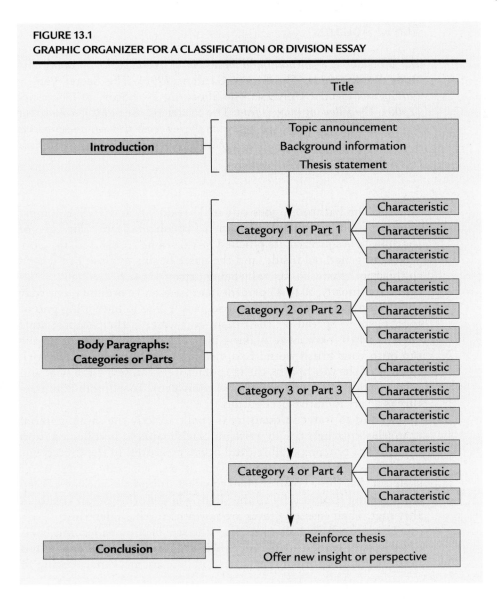

background information, and states the thesis. The body paragraphs explain the categories or parts and their characteristics. The conclusion brings the essay to a satisfying close by reinforcing the thesis and offering a new insight on the topic.

Read the following division essay and then study the graphic organizer for it in Figure 13.2 (on p. 429).

A Brush with Reality: Surprises in the Tube
David Bodanis

David Bodanis is a journalist and the author of several books, including The Body Book *(1984),* The Secret Garden *(1992),* The Secret Family *(1997), and* Electric Universe: The Shocking True Story of Electricity *(2005). The following essay is from* The Secret House *(1986), a book that traces a family of five through a day, analyzing foods they eat and products they use. As you read the selection, highlight the writer's thesis and the sections where he divides his topic into parts.*

1   Into the bathroom goes our male resident, and after the most pressing need is satisfied, it's time to brush the teeth. The tube of toothpaste is squeezed, its pinched metal seams are splayed, pressure waves are generated inside, and the paste begins to flow. But what's in this toothpaste, so carefully being extruded out?

2   Water mostly, 30 to 45 percent in most brands: ordinary, everyday simple tap water. It's there because people like to have a big gob of toothpaste to spread on the brush, and water is the cheapest stuff there is when it comes to making big gobs. Dripping a bit from the tap onto your brush would cost virtually nothing; whipped in with the rest of the toothpaste, the manufacturers can sell it at a neat and accountant-pleasing $2 per pound equivalent. Toothpaste manufacture is a very lucrative occupation.

3   Second to water in quantity is chalk: exactly the same material that schoolteachers use to write on blackboards. It is collected from the crushed remains of long-dead ocean creatures. In the Cretaceous seas chalk particles served as part of the wickedly sharp outer skeleton that these creatures had to wrap around themselves to keep from getting chomped by all the slightly larger other ocean creatures they met. Their massed graves are our present chalk deposits.

4   The individual chalk particles — the size of the smallest mud particles in your garden — have kept their toughness over the aeons, and now on the toothbrush they'll need it. The enamel outer coating of

the tooth they'll have to face is the hardest substance in the body—tougher than skull, or bone, or nail. Only the chalk particles in toothpaste can successfully grind into the teeth during brushing, ripping off the surface layers like an abrading wheel grinding down a boulder in a quarry.

The craters, slashes, and channels that the chalk tears into the teeth will also remove a certain amount of built-up yellow in the carnage, and it is for that polishing function that it's there. A certain amount of unduly enlarged extra-abrasive chalk fragments tear such cavernous pits into the teeth that future decay bacteria will be able to bunker down there and thrive; the quality control people find it almost impossible to screen out these errant super-chalk pieces, and government regulations allow them to stay in.

In case even the gouging doesn't get all the yellow off, another substance is worked into the toothpaste cream. This is titanium dioxide. It comes in tiny spheres, and it's the stuff bobbing around in white wall paint to make it come out white. Splashed around onto your teeth during the brushing it coats much of the yellow that remains. Being water soluble it leaks off in the next few hours and is swallowed, but at least for the quick glance up in the mirror after finishing it will make the user think his teeth are truly white. Some manufacturers add optical whitening dyes—the stuff more commonly found in washing machine bleach—to make extra sure that that glance in the mirror shows reassuring white.

These ingredients alone would not make a very attractive concoction. They would stick in the tube like a sloppy white plastic lump, hard to squeeze out as well as revolting to the touch. Few consumers would savor rubbing in a mixture of water, ground-up blackboard chalk, and the whitener from latex paint first thing in the morning. To get around that finicky distaste the manufacturers have mixed in a host of other goodies.

To keep the glop from drying out, a mixture including glycerine glycol—related to the most common car antifreeze ingredient—is whipped in with the chalk and water, and to give that concoction a bit of substance (all we really have so far is wet colored chalk), a large helping is added of gummy molecules from the seaweed *Chondrus crispus*. This seaweed ooze spreads in among the chalk, paint, and antifreeze, then stretches itself in all directions to hold the whole mass together. A bit of paraffin oil (the fuel that flickers in camping lamps) is pumped in with it to help the moss ooze keep the whole substance smooth.

With the glycol, ooze, and paraffin we're almost there. Only two major chemicals are left to make the refreshing, cleansing substance we know as toothpaste. The ingredients so far are fine for cleaning, but they wouldn't make much of the satisfying foam we have come to expect in the morning brushing.

10   To remedy that, every toothpaste on the market has a big dollop of detergent added too. You've seen the suds detergent will make in a washing machine. The same substance added here will duplicate that inside the mouth. It's not particularly necessary, but it sells.

11   The only problem is that by itself this ingredient tastes, well, too like detergent. It's horribly bitter and harsh. The chalk put in toothpaste is pretty foul-tasting too, for that matter. It's to get around that gustatory discomfort that the manufacturers put in the ingredient they tout perhaps the most of all. This is the flavoring, and it has to be strong. Double rectified peppermint oil is used — a flavorer so powerful that chemists know better than to sniff it in the raw state in the laboratory. Menthol crystals and saccharin or other sugar simulators are added to complete the camouflage operation.

12   Is that it? Chalk, water, paint, seaweed, antifreeze, paraffin oil, detergent, and peppermint? Not quite. A mix like that would be irresistible to the hundreds of thousands of individual bacteria lying on the surface of even an immaculately cleaned bathroom sink. They would get in, float in the water bubbles, ingest the ooze and paraffin, maybe even spray out enzymes to break down the chalk. The result would be an uninviting mess. The way manufacturers avoid that final obstacle is by putting something in to kill the bacteria. Something good and strong is needed, something that will zap any accidentally intrudant bacteria into oblivion. And that something is formaldehyde — the disinfectant used in anatomy labs.

13   So it's chalk, water, paint, seaweed, antifreeze, paraffin oil, detergent, peppermint, formaldehyde, and fluoride (which can go some way towards preserving children's teeth) — that's the usual mixture raised to the mouth on the toothbrush for a fresh morning's clean. If it sounds too unfortunate, take heart. Studies show that thorough brushing with just plain water will often do as good a job. ■

To draw detailed graphic organizers using a computer, visit www .bedfordstmartins.com /successfulwriting.

EXERCISE 13.3

Draw a graphic organizer for "Bringing Out Your Child's Gifts" (p. 419).

INTEGRATING CLASSIFICATION OR DIVISION INTO AN ESSAY

Classification or division is often used along with one or more other patterns of development. For example, an essay that argues for stricter gun control may categorize guns in terms of their firepower, use, or availability. A narrative about a

FIGURE 13.2
GRAPHIC ORGANIZER FOR "A BRUSH WITH REALITY: SURPRISES IN THE TUBE"

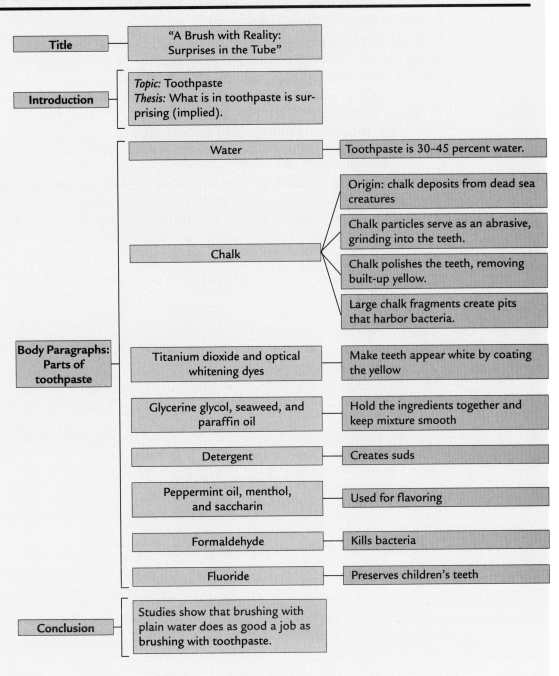

writer's frustrating experiences in a crowded international airport terminal may describe the different parts or areas of the airport.

Use the following tips to incorporate classification or division into an essay based on another pattern of development.

1. **Avoid focusing on why the classification or division is meaningful.** When used as a secondary pattern, its significance should be clear from the context in which the classification or division is presented.

2. **State the principle of classification.** Do so briefly but make sure it is clear to your readers.

3. **Name the categories or parts.** In the sentence that introduces the classification or division, name the categories or parts to focus your readers' attention on the explanation that follows.

4. **Make the classification or division comprehensive and exclusive.** The categories or parts should be complete and should not overlap.

5. **Include both classification and division or more than one system of classification, if necessary.** Keep in mind that when you use two or more systems of classification or division, it must be clear that each system is separate.

In "The Men We Carry in Our Minds" on page 454, Scott Russell Sanders uses classification along with other patterns of development to develop his thesis about the lives of men.

A GUIDED WRITING ASSIGNMENT

The following guide will lead you through the process of writing a classification or division essay. Note that you may need to integrate one or more other patterns of development in your essay to develop your thesis or make a point. Depending on your learning style, you may choose various ways of generating and organizing ideas.

The Assignment

Write a classification or division essay on a topic in one of the following lists or on a topic you choose on your own. Depending on the topic you select, you may need to use Internet or library sources to develop and support your ideas about it. You may also need to narrow the topic. Your audience consists of readers of your local newspaper.

Classification

1. Types of pets
2. Types of sports fans
3. Types of movies
4. Types of classmates
5. Types of shoppers
6. Types of television dramas

Division

1. Your family
2. A machine or piece of equipment
3. An organization
4. A sports team or extracurricular club
5. A public place (a building, stadium, department store, or theme park)
6. Your college

As you develop your classification or division essay, consider using one or more other patterns of development. For example, in a classification essay, you might compare and contrast types of sports fans or give examples of types of movies. In a division essay, you might describe the parts of a theme park or other public place.

For more on description, illustration, and comparison and contrast, see Chapters 9, 10, and 12.

Generating Ideas

There are two primary methods for generating ideas and for classifying or dividing those ideas. With method 1, you first generate details and then group the details into categories or parts. With method 2, you first generate categories or parts and then generate details that support them. Here is how both methods apply to classification essays and division essays:

Classification

Method 1: Think of details that describe the group and then use the details to categorize group members.

Method 2: Identify categories and then think of details that fit each category.

Division

Method 1: Brainstorm details about your topic and then group the details into parts or sections.

Method 2: Think about how your topic can be divided into easy-to-understand parts.

Considering Your Purpose, Audience, and Point of View

For more on purpose, audience, and point of view, see Chapter 3, p. 65.

Your principle of classification or division, your categories or parts, and your details must all fit your purpose, audience, and point of view. If your purpose is to inform novice computer users about the components of a personal computer (PC), your parts and details must be straightforward and nontechnical. However, if your purpose is to persuade computer technicians to purchase a particular kind of PC, your parts and details would be more technical. For this Guided Writing Assignment, your audience is the readers of your local newspaper.

As you work on your classification or division essay, ask yourself the following questions.

- Do my details and categories advance the purpose of the essay?
- Will my readers understand the categories or parts?
- Is my principle of classification or division appropriate for my purpose and audience?
- What point of view will best suit my purpose and audience — first, second, or third person?

You are now ready to try method 1 or method 2 for generating ideas.

Method 1: Generating Details and Grouping Them into Categories or Parts

To use method 1, try the following techniques for generating details, deciding on a principle of classification or division, and choosing categories or parts.

Generating details.   Begin with one or more of the following strategies.

For more on prewriting strategies, see Chapter 3.

Learning Style Options

1. Visit a place where you can observe your topic or the people associated with it. For example, to generate details about pets, visit a pet store or an animal shelter. Make notes on what you see and hear. Record conversations, physical characteristics, behaviors, and so forth.

For more on observation, see Chapter 19, p. 691.

2. Discuss your topic with a classmate or friend. Focus your talk on the qualities and characteristics of your topic.

3. Brainstorm a list of all the features or characteristics of your topic that come to mind.

4. Draw a map or diagram that illustrates your topic's features and characteristics.

5. Conduct library or Internet research to discover facts, examples, and other details about your topic.

Choosing a principle of classification or division.   Your next task is to decide which principle or basis you will use to classify or divide your subject. Read through your details, looking for shared features or characteristics. Your principle of classification or division should be interesting and meaningful to your audience. It should also enable you to make a worthwhile point. For an essay on highway drivers, you might classify drivers according to their driving habits, focusing on annoying or unsafe habits that you have observed. Experiment with several principles of classification or division until you find one that fits your purpose and audience.

For more on library and Internet research, see Chapter 19.

Choosing categories or parts.   With your principle of classification or division in mind, use the following suggestions to determine your categories or parts.

1. *In a classification essay,* make sure most or all members of the group fit into one of your categories. For example, in an essay about unsafe driving habits, you would include every bad habit. *In a division essay,* no

essential parts should be left out. For example, in an essay about parts of a baseball stadium, you would not exclude the infield or bleachers.

2. *In a classification essay,* be sure the categories are exclusive; each group member should fit into one category only. In the essay about unsafe driving habits, the categories of reckless drivers and aggressive drivers would overlap, so exclusive categories should be used instead. *In a division essay,* make sure the parts do not overlap. In the essay about the parts of a baseball stadium, the parts "playing field" and "infield" would overlap, so it would be better to use three distinct parts of the field — infield, outfield, and foul-ball area.

3. Create specific categories or parts that will engage your readers. *In a classification essay,* categorizing drivers by their annoying driving habits would be more interesting than simply distinguishing between "good" and "bad" drivers. *A division essay* on players' facilities in a baseball stadium — dugout, locker room, and bullpen — would be more interesting to sports fans than an essay describing different seating sections of the stadium.

4. Once you establish your categories or parts, you may need to do additional prewriting to come up with enough details (examples, facts, anecdotes, and observations) to explain each category or part adequately.

5. Choose descriptive names that emphasize the distinguishing feature of the category or part. *In a classification essay,* you might categorize highway drivers as "I-own-the-road" drivers, "I'm-in-no-hurry" drivers, and "I'm-daydreaming" drivers. *In a division essay* about the parts of a baseball stadium, you might use "homerun heaven" to name one part.

Method 1 is effective when you approach the classification or division from part to whole — identifying details and then grouping the details. Depending on your learning style and your topic, it may be easier to start by creating categories or parts and then filling in details about each one. In this case, use method 2.

Method 2: Generating Categories or Parts and Supplying Details

When you are familiar with your topic, you can begin by finding categories into which items may be sorted (or parts into which something can be divided). Once you have a tentative list of categories or parts, you can generate details and examples relevant to each one. To use method 2, try the following techniques.

Choosing categories or parts.   Try one or more of the following strategies.

Learning Style Options

1. Discuss your topic with a classmate or friend. Question each other about how the topic can be categorized or divided.

2. Visit a place where you can observe your topic or the people associated with it. Make notes on what you see and hear.

3. Brainstorm principles of classification or division. Then test the effectiveness of each principle by quickly listing the categories or parts into which the topic may be divided.

4. Draw graphic organizers, experimenting with several different categories or parts into which your topic may be classified or divided (see Figures 13.1 and 13.2 for examples of graphic organizers).

5. Conduct library or Internet research. Try to discover information that will help you classify or divide your topic.

Before moving on to the next step, make sure your categories or parts meet the criteria discussed earlier in the chapter (see pp. 423–25).

Identifying the key features of each category or part.   Once you have a workable list of categories or parts, the next step is to identify key features. These are the features that you will use to explain and differentiate each category or part for your readers. Recall how White, in "Bringing Out Your Child's Gifts," clearly describes the major characteristics of each type of intelligence that children exhibit.

Consider again the three categories of annoying highway drivers. You might distinguish each type of driver by the key characteristics listed here.

1. "I-Own-the-Road" Drivers
   • Are inconsiderate of other drivers
   • Weave in and out of traffic
   • Honk horns or flash lights to intimidate others into letting them pass

2. "I'm-in-No-Hurry" Drivers
   • Drive below the speed limit
   • Cause other drivers to become impatient
   • Drive in the left lane

3. "I'm-Daydreaming" Drivers
   • Fail to observe other drivers
   • Fail to signal when changing lanes
   • Wander over the dividing line or onto the shoulder of the road

As you identify characteristics for each category, you may find that two categories or parts overlap or that a category or part is too broad. Do not hesitate to create, combine, or eliminate categories or parts.

Generating details. For each category or part, you need to supply specific details that will make it clear and understandable to your readers. As you work on your essay, then, write down examples, situations, or sensory details that illustrate each category or part. In "Bringing Out Your Child's Gifts," for example, White explains each category of intelligence and then describes how each type of child can learn and be nurtured.

ESSAY IN PROGRESS 1

Choose a topic for your classification or division essay from the list of assignment options on page 431, or choose one on your own. Then use the preceding guidelines for method 1 *or* method 2 to generate details about your topic, choose a principle of classification or division, and devise a set of categories or parts. Whatever method you use, list the examples, situations, or other details that you will use to describe each category or part. You might try drawing a graphic organizer.

Developing Your Thesis

For more on thesis statements, see Chapter 4, p. 89.

Once you choose categories or parts and are satisfied with your details, you are ready to develop a thesis for your essay. Remember that your thesis statement should identify your topic and reveal your principle of division or classification. In most cases, it should also suggest why your classification or division is useful or important. Notice how the following weak theses have been strengthened by showing both what the categories are and why they are important.

WEAK	There are four types of insurance that most people can purchase.
REVISED	If you understand the four common types of insurance, you will be able to make sure that you, your family members, and your property are protected.
WEAK	Conventional stores are only one type of retailing; other types are becoming more popular.
REVISED	Although conventional stores are still where most people purchase products, three new types of shopping are becoming

increasingly popular—face-to-face sales conducted in a home, sales via telephone or computer, and sales from automatic vending machines.

Draft your thesis and then check your prewriting to make sure you have enough details to support the thesis. If necessary, do some additional prewriting. In addition, keep in mind that a lengthy or complex topic may require a more elaborate thesis and introduction. You may need to provide more detailed information about your principle of classification or division or its importance.

⸾ ESSAY IN PROGRESS 2
⸾
⸾ Using the preceding guidelines, develop a thesis for your classification or divi-
⸾ sion essay.

Evaluating Your Ideas and Thesis

Take a few minutes to evaluate your ideas and thesis. Start by rereading everything you have written with a critical eye. Highlight the most useful details and delete those that are repetitious or irrelevant. If you are working on a computer, highlight useful details in bold type or move them to a separate file. As you review your work, add useful ideas that come to mind.

┌───┐
  TRYING OUT YOUR IDEAS ON OTHERS

  Working in a group of two or three students, discuss your ideas and thesis
  for this chapter's assignment. Each writer should describe to the group his
  or her topic, principle of classification or division, and categories or parts.
  Then, as a group, evaluate each writer's work and suggest recommendations
  for improvement.
└───┘

⸾ ESSAY IN PROGRESS 3
⸾
⸾ Using the preceding suggestions and comments from your classmates, evaluate
⸾ your thesis, your categories or parts, and the details you plan to use in your essay.
⸾ Refer to the list of characteristics on pages 423–25 to help you with your evalua-
⸾ tion.

Organizing and Drafting

For more on drafting an essay, see Chapter 5.

Once you have evaluated your categories or parts, reviewed your thesis, and considered the advice of your classmates, you are ready to organize your ideas and draft your essay.

Choosing a Method of Organization

For more on methods of organization, see Chapter 5, p. 110.

Choose the method of organization that best suits your purpose. One method that works well in classification essays is the least-to-most arrangement. You might arrange your categories in increasing order of importance or from least to most common, difficult, or frequent. Other possible sequences include chronological order (when one category occurs or is observable before another) or spatial order (when you classify physical objects).

Spatial order often works well in division essays, as does order of importance. In describing the parts of a baseball stadium, you might move from stands to playing field (spatial order). In writing about the parts of a hospital, you might describe the most important areas first (operating rooms and emergency room) and then move to less important facilities (waiting rooms and visitor cafeteria).

 To experiment with different methods of organization, create a new computer file for each possible method and try out each one.

Drafting the Classification or Division Essay

Once you decide how to organize your categories or parts, your next step is to write a first draft. Use the following guidelines to draft your essay.

1. **Explain each category or part.** Begin by defining each category or part, taking into account the complexity of your topic and the background knowledge of your audience. For example, if you classify types of behavioral disorders in an essay written for a general audience, you would need to define such terms as *schizophrenic* and *delusional*.

2. **Provide details that describe each category or part.** Be sure to show how each category or part is distinct from the others. Include a wide range of details—sensory details, personal experiences, examples, and comparisons and contrasts.

3. **Generally, allow one or more paragraphs for each category or part.**

4. **Use transitions.** Your reader needs transitions to keep on track as you move from one category or part to another. In addition, transitions help distinguish key features between and within categories or parts.

For more on transitions, see Chapter 5, p. 128.

5. **Provide roughly the same amount and kind of detail and description for each of your categories or parts.** For instance, if you give an example of one type of mental disorder, you should give an example for every other type discussed in the essay.

6. **Consider adding headings or lists.** Presenting the parts or categories within a numbered list or in sections with headings can help make them clear and distinct. Headings or lists can be especially useful when you have a large number of categories or parts.

7. **Consider adding a visual such as a diagram or flowchart.** Diagrams, flowcharts, or other visuals can make your system of classification or division clearer for your readers. Graphics software, available with some word-processing programs, can help you produce professional-looking charts and diagrams.

8. **Write an effective introduction.** Your introduction usually includes your thesis statement. It also should provide background information and explain further, if needed, your principle of classification or division. It might suggest why the classification or division is useful.

For more on writing effective paragraphs, including introductions and conclusions, see Chapter 5.

9. **Write a satisfying conclusion.** Your conclusion should bring your essay to a satisfying close, reemphasizing your thesis or offering a new insight or perspective on the topic. A classification essay on types of mental disorders might emphasize the need for improved treatment programs.

   If you have trouble finding an appropriate way to conclude your essay, return to your statement about why the classification or division is useful and important and try to extend or elaborate on that statement.

ESSAY IN PROGRESS 4

Draft your classification or division essay, using an appropriate method of organization and the preceding guidelines for drafting.

Analyzing and Revising

If possible, set aside your draft for a day or two before rereading and revising it. As you review your draft, remember that your goal is to revise your classification or division essay to make it clearer and more effective. Focus

Learning Style Options

on content and ideas and not on grammar, punctuation, or mechanics. Use one or more of the following strategies to analyze your draft.

1. Reread your essay aloud. You may "hear" parts that need revision.

2. Ask a friend or classmate to read your draft and to give you his or her impression of your categories of classification or division. Compare your reader's impressions with what you intend to convey and revise your draft accordingly.

3. Draw a graphic organizer, make an outline, or update the organizer or outline you drew or made earlier. In particular, look for any categories or parts that lack sufficient details and revise to include them.

For more on the benefits of peer review, see Chapter 6, p. 158.

Use Figure 13.3 to guide your analysis of the strengths and weaknesses in your draft essay. You might also ask a classmate to review your draft using the questions in the flowchart. For each "No" response, ask your reviewer to explain his or her answer.

ESSAY IN PROGRESS 5

Revise your draft using Figure 13.3 and any comments you received from peer reviewers.

Editing and Proofreading

The last step is to check your revised essay for errors in grammar, spelling, punctuation, and mechanics. Watch for the types of errors you tend to make (refer to your error log).

For more on keeping an error log, see Chapter 7, p. 193.

When editing a classification or division essay, pay specific attention to two particular kinds of grammatical error — choppy sentences and omitted commas following introductory elements.

For more on combining sentences and varying sentence patterns, see Chapter 7.

1. Avoid short, choppy sentences, which can make a classification or division sound dull and mechanical. Try combining a series of short sentences and varying sentence patterns and lengths.

▶ Working dogs are another one of the American Kennel Club's breed *, such as German shepherds and sheep-herding dogs,* categories. ~~These include German shepherds and sheep-herding dogs.~~

▶ *The fountain pen, one* ~~One~~ standard type of writing instrument, ~~is the fountain pen.~~ It is sometimes messy and inconvenient to use.

FIGURE 13.3
FLOWCHART FOR REVISING A CLASSIFICATION AND DIVISION ESSAY

Questions		Revision Strategies

1. Highlight your thesis statement. Does it, along with your introduction, explain your principle of classification or division and suggest why it is important?

No →

- Revise your thesis to make your justification stronger or more apparent.
- Add explanatory information to your introduction.

Yes ↓

2. *Write* the principle of classification you used at the top of your paper. Do you use one principle of classification or division consistently throughout the essay or throughout a particular section? Does it clearly relate to your thesis?

No →

- Review your categories or parts, choose the principle that best fits your purpose, and rethink your categories or parts.
- Rewrite your thesis to reflect your principle of classification.

Yes ↓

3. *Number* each category or part in the margin of your paper. Do you have a manageable number?

No →

- For a classification essay, narrow your topic to a smaller, more manageable group.
- For a division essay, divide your topic into fewer parts.

Yes ↓

(Continued on next page)

FIGURE 13.3 *(Continued)*

Questions		Revision Strategies

4. *Write* a list of categories or parts. Do your categories or parts cover all or most members of the group or parts of the topic?

No →

- Revise your categories or parts so that each item fits into one group only.
- Brainstorm or do research to add categories or parts.

Yes ↓

5. Place checkmarks ✔ beside the details that explain each category or part. Does your essay fully explain each category or part? (If it reads like a list, answer "No.")

No →

- Brainstorm or do research to discover more details.
- Add examples, definitions, facts, and expert testimony to improve your explanations.

Yes ↓

6. *Sketch* a brief outline of the organization you used to structure your essay. Is the organization clear? Are the categories or parts organized in a way that suits your purpose?

No →

- Draw a graphic organizer to evaluate your present organization.
- Refer to Chapter 5 to discover an organizing plan.

Yes ↓

(Continued on next page)

FIGURE 13.3 *(Continued)*

Questions	Revision Strategies
7. Underline the topic sentence of each paragraph. Is each paragraph focused on a separate category or part?	**No** → • Consider combining closely related paragraphs. • Split paragraphs that cover more than one category or part.

Yes ↓

Questions	Revision Strategies
8. Draw a box around your conclusion. Does it offer a new insight or perspective on the topic?	**No** → • Ask yourself: "So what? What does this mean?" Build your answers into the conclusion.

Yes ↓

9. Print out another draft to edit and proofread your essay before turning it in.

---

2. Add a comma after opening phrases or clauses that are longer than four words.

▶ When describing types of college students, be sure to consider variations in age.

▶ Although there are many types of cameras, most are easy to operate.

ESSAY IN PROGRESS 6

Edit and proofread your essay, paying particular attention to sentence variety and length and comma usage.

STUDENTS WRITE

Ryan Porter was a first-year student when he wrote the following essay in response to an assignment for his writing course. He is an avid reader of car magazines and enjoys antique cars, especially cars of the 1950s. As you read the essay, identify the basis of classification and the categories he uses, and annotate your reactions to Porter's details.

Motor Heads

Ryan Porter

1   As you probably realize, we live in an automobile-oriented society; car culture is everywhere. Can you really say that you don't care about cars or that you are not a car lover on some level? Although your interest may be merely practical, there are multitudes of people who are car nuts to some degree.

2   You see them on Sundays in spring, gathered around the glittering external exhaust pipes of a classic Duesenberg dual-cowl phaeton parked on the fairway at an antique auto show or on Saturday nights in summer in a fast-food parking lot, jostling each other to peek at the chromed engine bay of a chopped and channeled '56 Chevy Bel Air. You see them bunched up at the parts counter at Pep Boys or poring over the car magazines at Borders Books. These are the motor heads or the car nuts. Like all nuts, they come in many varieties. You can tell the type of car nut by the kind of car the nut worships.

3   The first variety, the aficionado, is usually wealthy or has pretensions of wealth. Aficionados own classic cars from the 1920s and 1930s, such as the fabled Duesenberg, Hispano-Suiza, Packard, or Bentley. If they own more than one, you might hear them talk of the cars in their "stable," as if these machines were thoroughbred horses. These autos are extremely valuable-- often selling at auction for hundreds of thousands of dollars--and can be considered part of their investment

portfolios. Because of this, aficionados rarely, if ever, drive their cars, preferring instead to have the vehicles trailered to shows. Aficionados never actually put a wrench to any lug nut on one of their classic cars; instead they hire a mechanic who specializes in maintaining antiques and classics. Aficionados treat their classic cars like fine crystal. Maybe they should collect crystal instead; it takes up less room and is a lot easier to maintain.

The second type of car nut, the gear head, can be seen sporting grease-smeared T-shirts with faded Camaro, Mustang, or Corvette logos. Unlike the aficionados, the gear heads are ready, willing, and able to thrust a wrench-wielding hand into the engines of their Camaros, Mustangs, or Corvettes. They can disassemble a turbo hydramatic transmission and then reassemble it at a moment's notice. They have wrenches in their jeans pocket. Gear heads seem to have ESP when it comes to automobile engines. A gear head can pop open the hood of your car, listen with head cocked and eyes closed for a second or two, and tell you that you have nine hundred miles left on your timing belt. You say, "Sure I do, buddy." Five weeks later you're stranded on the side of the road as a friendly police officer observes, "Sounds like the timing belt is gone." When most people think of a car nut, it is the gear head who comes to mind. Hollywood has been using the gear head in movies and television shows for decades: James Dean in the 1950s, the Fonz in the 1970s, and Tim Allen in <u>Home Improvement</u> in the 1990s. On a practical level, you may not ever want to be a gear head, but you'd want your brother-in-law to be one. 4

On a more specialized level, there is the make-specific car nut. This is not your uncle Walter, who always drove Fords and swore by them. The make-specific car nuts go far beyond that, knowing every detail about every model of one specific brand of automobile. They 5 might love Porsches, for instance, rattling off observations like, "The '96 Turbo's machined rather than cast cylinder fins dissipate hot air better than those of the Carrera 2." Make-specific car nuts bore their friends to tears with descriptions of the differences between the drip-rail moldings on the 1959 versus 1960 Oldsmobile Super 88 Vista Cruiser sedans. Upon spotting two old Woodstock-era Volkswagen (VW) Beetles putt-putting down the road, the make-specific car nut will handily determine the year they were made. It's eerie; everyone knows you can't tell one year's vintage VW from another. Make-specific car nuts dress like you and me, except they wear accessories--tie clips, cuff links, pens, and dress shirts--adorned with their favorite car's logo. Will coffee served in a Firebird mug stay warm longer?

6   Orphan-make hoarders are the twin of make-specific car nuts, except orphan-make hoarders love only the cars manufactured by companies no longer in business. They are determined to collect every model of every Packard or Kaiser-Frazer ever produced. Usually residing in rural areas, the hoarder often owns a thirty-acre parcel of land upon which are parked a hundred or more examples of the make in various stages of decomposition, not one of which is drivable. Do you need the horn-ring for a 1951 Studebaker President Land Cruiser? The orphan-make hoarder has fourteen of them.

7   Finally, closer in orbit to our own planet, we have the wishful thinkers. They read Road & Track, Car and Driver, and Automobile every month and dream of someday owning a Ferrari Testarossa or Porsche 911 Turbo. Wishful thinkers drag their families or friends to car shows, auto races, and antique auto events. You find them in auto showrooms whenever a new model is introduced, demanding to road-test the new BMW roadster or Mustang GT that they have no intention of buying. The salespeople call them "tire-kickers." The wishful thinker owns a five-year-old Honda Civic sedan.

As you can see, car nuts cross all social and eco-   8
nomic levels, reflecting the diversity of our society.
You probably know a car nut or may be one yourself.
America is a nation in love with the automobile. Whatever their variety, car nuts take that love to the next
level: obsession.

Analyzing the Essay

1. Identify Porter's thesis.
2. How does the writer establish the importance or meaningfulness of his classification?
3. Identify Porter's principle of classification and the categories he establishes.
4. What other patterns of development does Porter use to develop each category?
5. Evaluate the title, introduction, and conclusion.
6. Consider Porter's tone. What kind of audience does he address?

Reacting to the Essay: Discussion and Journal Writing

1. Evaluate the categories Porter establishes. Are they realistic? Describe someone you know who fits into one of the categories.
2. Discuss other principles that might be used in a classification essay about automobiles.
3. Write a journal entry describing what you sense is Porter's attitude toward three or more of his categories of "car nuts."

READING A CLASSIFICATION OR DIVISION ESSAY

The following section provides advice for reading classification or division as well as two model essays. The first essay illustrates the characteristics of classification covered in this chapter. The second essay uses classification along with other methods of development. Both essays provide opportunities to examine, analyze, and react to the writers' ideas.

WORKING WITH TEXT: READING CLASSIFICATION OR DIVISION

For more on reading strategies, see Chapter 2.

A classification or division essay is usually tightly organized and relatively easy to follow. Use the following suggestions to read classification essays, division essays, or any writing that uses classification or division.

What to Look For, Highlight, and Annotate

1. Highlight the thesis statement, principle of classification, and the name or title of each category or part.
2. Use a different color highlighter (or another marking method, such as asterisks or numbers) to identify the key features of each category. In a textbook reading, for example, the characteristics of each category are what you are expected to learn.
3. Mark important definitions and vivid examples for later reference.
4. Add annotations indicating where you find a category or part confusing or where you think more detail is needed.

How to Find Ideas to Write About

For more on discovering ideas for a response paper, see Chapter 2.

To gain a different perspective on the reading, think of other ways of classifying or dividing the topic. For example, consider an essay that classifies types of exercise programs at health clubs according to the benefits they offer for cardiovascular health. Such exercise programs could also be classified according to their cost, degree of strenuousness, type of exercise, and so forth.

A classification or division provides the reader with one particular viewpoint on the subject. Be sure to keep in mind that it is *only* one viewpoint. Once you identify alternative viewpoints, choose one to write about.

THINKING CRITICALLY ABOUT CLASSIFICATION AND DIVISION

How Does the Principle of Classification or Division Serve the Writer's Purpose?

The writer's purpose often shapes the nature of a classification or division essay. It is your job as a critical reader to determine how the writer's purpose affects the principle of classification or division used in an essay as well as the overall impression conveyed about the topic. For example, a writer who wants to give adult readers an unfavorable impression of high school students might classify—and thereby emphasize—students' leisure-time activities. By contrast, a writer who instead categorizes the part-time jobs students hold or the contributions students make to family life could give adult readers a favorable impression of high school students.

As a critical reader, then, keep the following questions in mind.

- What effect does the classification or division have on the reader's attitude toward and impression of the topic being classified or divided?

- What alternative classifications or divisions would give the reader a different viewpoint?

CLASSIFICATION ESSAY

As you read the following selection by Joseph A. DeVito, consider how the writer employs the elements of classification or division discussed in this chapter.

Territoriality
Joseph A. DeVito

Joseph A. DeVito holds a Ph.D. from the University of Illinois and is a professor of communication at Hunter College. He is also the author of numerous college textbooks, including Messages: Building Interpersonal Communication, *sixth edition (2004),* Essentials of Human Communication, *fifth edition (2004), and* Human Communication, *ninth edition (2003), from which this excerpt is taken. As you read the selection, highlight the categories the writer uses to explain the territoriality of human behavior.*

One of the most interesting concepts in ethology (the study of animals in their natural surroundings) is territoriality. For example, male animals will stake out a particular territory and consider it their own. They will allow prospective mates to enter but will defend it against entrance by others, especially other males of the same species. Among deer, the size of the territory signifies the power of the buck, which in turn determines how many females he will mate with. Less powerful bucks will be able to control only small parcels of land and so will mate with only one or two females. This is a particularly adaptive measure, since it ensures that the stronger members will produce most of the offspring. When the "landowner" takes possession of an area—either because it is vacant or because he gains it through battle—he marks it, for example, by urinating around the boundaries. The size of the animal's territory indicates the status of the animal within the herd.

2   The size and location of human territory also say something about status (Mehrabian, 1976; Sommer, 1969). An apartment or office in midtown Manhattan or downtown Tokyo, for example, indicates extremely high status. The cost of the territory restricts it to those who have lots of money.

3   Status is also signaled by the unwritten law granting the right of invasion. Higher-status individuals have more of a right to invade the territory of others than vice versa. The boss of a large company, for example, can invade the territory of a junior executive by barging into her or his office, but the reverse would be unthinkable.

4   Some researchers claim that territoriality is innate and demonstrates the innate aggressiveness of humans. Others claim that territoriality is learned behavior and is culturally based. Most, however, agree that a great deal of human behavior can be understood and described as territorial, regardless of its origin.

TYPES OF TERRITORIES

5   *Primary territory.*   Primary territories are your exclusive preserve: your desk, room, house, or backyard, for example. In these areas you are in control. It's similar to the home field advantage that a sports team has when playing in its own ballpark. When you are in these primary areas, you generally have greater influence over others than you would in someone else's territory. For example, when in their own home or office people take on a kind of leadership role; they initiate conversations, fill in silences, assume relaxed and comfortable postures, and maintain their positions with greater conviction. Because the territorial owner is dominant, you stand a better chance of getting your raise, your point accepted, and the contract resolved in your favor if you are in your own primary territory (Marsh, 1988).

6   *Secondary territory.*   Secondary territories, although they do not belong to you, are associated with you perhaps because you have occupied them for a long period of time or they have been assigned to you. For example, your desk in a classroom may be a secondary territory if it was assigned to you or if you have regularly occupied it and others treat it as yours. Your neighborhood turf, a cafeteria table that you regularly occupy, or a favorite corner of a local coffee shop may be secondary territories. You feel a certain "ownership-like" attachment to the place although it is really not yours in any legal sense.

Public territory.   Public territories are those areas that are open to all   7
people: a park, movie house, restaurant, or beach, for example. The
European café, the food court in a suburban mall, and the public
spaces in large city office buildings are public spaces that, although
established for eating, also serve to bring people together and to
stimulate communication. The electronic revolution, however, may
well change the role of public space in stimulating communication
(Drucker & Gumpert, 1991; Gumpert & Drucker, 1995). For example,
home shopping clubs make it less necessary for people to go shopping "downtown" or to the mall, and consequently they have less
opportunity to run into other people and to talk and to exchange
news. Similarly, electronic mail permits communication without
talking and without even going out of one's home to mail a letter.
Perhaps the greatest change is telecommuting (Giordano 1989),
which allows people to work without even leaving their homes. The
face-to-face communication that normally takes place in an office is
replaced by communication via computer.

Tᴇʀʀɪᴛᴏʀɪᴀʟ Eɴᴄʀᴏᴀᴄʜᴍᴇɴᴛ

Look around your home. You probably see certain territories that   8
different people have staked out and where invasions are cause for at
least mildly defensive action. This is perhaps seen most clearly with
siblings who each have (or "own") a specific chair, room, radio, and
so on. Father has his chair and Mother has her chair.

In classrooms where seats are not assigned, territoriality can also   9
be observed. When a student sits in a seat that has normally been
occupied by another student, the regular occupant will often become
disturbed and resentful.

Following Lyman and Scott (1967; DeVito & Hecht, 1990),   10
Table [1] identifies the three major types of territorial encroachment:
violation, invasion, and contamination.

You can react to encroachment in several ways (Lyman & Scott,   11
1967; DeVito & Hecht, 1990). The most extreme form is *turf defense.*
When you cannot tolerate the intruders, you may choose to defend
the territory against them and try to expel them. This is the method
of gangs that defend "their" streets and neighborhoods by fighting
off members of rival gangs (intruders) who enter the territory.

A less extreme defense is *insulation,* a tactic in which you erect   12
some sort of barrier between yourself and the invaders. Some people
do this by wearing sunglasses to avoid eye contact. Others erect
fences to let others know that they do not welcome interpersonal
interaction.

TABLE [1]
THREE TYPES OF TERRITORIAL ENCROACHMENT

Name	Definition	Example
Violation	Unwarranted use of another's territory and thereby changing the meaning of that territory	Entering another's office or home without permission
Invasion	Entering the territory of another and thereby changing the meaning of that territory	Parents entering a teen's social group
Contamination	Rendering a territory impure	Smoking a cigar in a kitchen

13　　*Linguistic collusion,* another method of separating yourself from unwanted invaders, involves speaking in a language unknown to these outsiders. Or you might use professional jargon to which they are not privy. Linguistic collusion groups together those who speak that language and excludes those who do not know the linguistic code. Still another type of response is *withdrawal;* you leave the territory altogether.

MARKERS

14　　Much as animals mark their territory, humans mark theirs with three types of markers: central, boundary, and earmarkers (Hickson & Stacks, 1993). *Central markers* are items you place in a territory to reserve it. For example, you place a drink at the bar, books on your desk, and a sweater over the chair to let others know that this territory belongs to you.

15　　*Boundary markers* set boundaries that divide your territory from "theirs." In the supermarket checkout line, the bar placed between your groceries and those of the person behind you is a boundary marker. Similarly, the armrests separating seats in movie theaters and the rises on each side of the molded plastic seats on a bus or train are boundary markers.

16　　*Earmarkers*—a term taken from the practice of branding animals on their ears—are those identifying marks that indicate your possession of a territory or object. Trademarks, nameplates, and initials on a shirt or attaché case are all examples of earmarkers. ■

References

DeVito, J. A., & Hecht, M. L. (Eds.). (1990). *The nonverbal communication reader.* Prospect Heights, IL: Waveland.

Drucker, S. J., & Gumpert, G. (1991). Public space and communication: The zoning of public interaction. *Communication Theory, 1* (November), 294–310.

Giordano, J. (1989). *Telecommuting and organizational culture: A study of corporate consciousness and identification.* Unpublished doctoral dissertation, University of Massachusetts, Amherst, MA.

Gumpert, G., & Drucker, S. J. (1995). Place as medium: Exegesis of the café drinking coffee, the art of watching others, civil conversation—with excursions into the effects of architecture and interior design. *The Speech Communication Annual, 9* (Spring), 7–32.

Hickson, M. L., & Stacks, D. W. (1993). *NVC: Nonverbal communication: Studies and applications,* 3rd ed. Dubuque, IA: Wm. C. Brown.

Lyman, S. M., & Scott, M. B. (1967). Territoriality: A neglected sociological dimension. *Social Problems, 15,* 236–249.

Marsh, P. (1988). *Eye to eye: How people interact.* Topsfield, MA: Salem House.

Mehrabian, A. (1976). *Public places and private spaces.* New York: Basic Books.

Sommer, R. (1969). *Personal space: The behavioral basis of design.* Upper Saddle River, NJ: Prentice-Hall/Spectrum.

Examining the Reading

1. Describe the three types of territories that DeVito identifies in his classification.

2. According to the writer, in what ways do humans react to territorial encroachment?

3. Describe the three types of territorial markers that DeVito discusses and classifies.

4. Define each of the following words as it is used in the reading: *innate* (para. 4), *dominant* (5), *encroachment* (10), *expel* (11), and *collusion* (13). Refer to your dictionary as needed.

Analyzing the Reading

1. What is DeVito's thesis?

2. What principle of classification does the writer use to establish the three types of territories? Does he employ the same principle or a different one in his classifications of encroachment and markers?

3. What other patterns of development does DeVito use to explain his classification of territoriality, encroachment, and markers?

4. Evaluate the introduction. What methods are employed to spark readers' interest in the topic of territoriality?

Reacting to the Reading: Discussion and Journal Writing

1. Discuss examples of secondary territoriality that you have observed or experienced.

2. Discuss other possible principles of classification that might be used to classify human territories.

3. Write a journal entry describing how you dealt with a situation involving territorial encroachment.

CLASSIFICATION COMBINED WITH OTHER PATTERNS

In the following essay, Scott Russell Sanders combines classification with other patterns of development to support a thesis about types of men.

The Men We Carry in Our Minds
Scott Russell Sanders

Scott Russell Sanders is a professor of English at Indiana University. He is also the author of numerous works of fiction, including two novels, Terrarium *(1985) and* The Invisible Company *(1989); several short-story collections; and two children's books,* Aurora Means Dawn *(1989) and* Here Comes the Mystery Man *(1993). His other works include* Staying Put: Making a Home in a Restless World *(1993),* Writing from the Center *(1995),* Hunting for Hope: A Father's Journey *(1998),* The Force of Spirit *(2000), and* Bloomington Past and Present *(2002), and articles published in* Harper's, *the* New York Times, *and the* Georgia Review. *This essay was originally published in 1984 in the* Milkweed Chronicle, *a journal of literature and the arts. As you read the selection, notice that Sanders uses classification as well as description and illustration to develop his ideas. Highlight the categories that the writer establishes.*

1   The first men, besides my father, I remember seeing were black convicts and white guards, in the cottonfield across the road from our farm on the outskirts of Memphis. I must have been three or

four. The prisoners wore dingy gray-and-black zebra suits, heavy as canvas, sodden with sweat. Hatless, stooped, they chopped weeds in the fierce heat, row after row, breathing the acrid dust of boll-weevil poison. The overseers wore dazzling white shirts and broad shadowy hats. The oiled barrels of their shotguns flashed in the sunlight. Their faces in memory are utterly blank. Of course those men, white and black, have become for me an emblem of racial hatred. But they have also come to stand for the twin poles of my early vision of manhood — the brute toiling animal and the boss.

When I was a boy, the men I knew labored with their bodies. They 2 were marginal farmers, just scraping by, or welders, steel workers, carpenters; they swept floors, dug ditches, mined coal, or drove trucks, their forearms ropy with muscle; they trained horses, stoked furnaces, built tires, stood on assembly lines wrestling parts onto cars and refrigerators. They got up before light, worked all day long whatever the weather, and when they came home at night they looked as though somebody had been whipping them. In the evenings and on weekends they worked on their own places, tilling gardens that were lumpy with clay, fixing broken-down cars, hammering on houses that were always too drafty, too leaky, too small.

The bodies of the men I knew were twisted and maimed in ways 3 visible and invisible. The nails of their hands were black and split, the hands tattooed with scars. Some had lost fingers. Heavy lifting had given many of them finicky backs and guts weak from hernias. Racing against conveyor belts had given them ulcers. Their ankles and knees ached from years of standing on concrete. Anyone who had worked for long around machines was hard of hearing. They squinted, and the skin of their faces was creased like the leather of old work gloves. There were times, studying them, when I dreaded growing up. Most of them coughed, from dust or cigarettes, and most of them drank cheap wine or whiskey, so their eyes looked bloodshot and bruised. The fathers of my friends always seemed older than the mothers. Men wore out sooner. Only women lived into old age.

As a boy I also knew another sort of men, who did not sweat and 4 break down like mules. They were soldiers, and so far as I could tell they scarcely worked at all. During my early school years we lived on a military base, an arsenal in Ohio, and every day I saw GIs in the guardshacks, on the stoops of barracks, at the wheels of olive drab Chevrolets. The chief fact of their lives was boredom. Long after I left the arsenal I came to recognize the sour smell the soldiers gave off as that of souls in limbo. They were all waiting — for wars, for transfers, for leaves, for promotions, for the end of their hitch — like so many braves waiting for the hunt to begin. Unlike the warriors of older tribes, however, they would have no say about when the battle would start or how it would be waged. Their waiting was broken only when they practiced for war. They fired guns at targets, drove tanks across the churned-up fields of the military reservation, set off bombs in the wrecks of old fighter planes. I knew this was all play. But I also felt certain that when the hour for killing arrived, they would kill. When the real shooting started, many of them would die. This was what soldiers were for, just as a hammer was for driving nails.

5   Warriors and toilers: those seemed, in my boyhood vision, to be the chief destinies for men. They weren't the only destinies, as I learned from having a few male teachers, from reading books, and from watching television. But the men on television — the politicians, the astronauts, the generals, the savvy lawyers, the philosophical doctors, the bosses who gave orders to both soldiers and laborers — seemed as remote and unreal to me as the figures in tapestries. I could no more imagine growing up to become one of these cool, potent creatures than I could imagine becoming a prince.

6   A nearer and more hopeful example was that of my father, who had escaped from a red-dirt farm to a tire factory, and from the assembly line to the front office. Eventually he dressed in a white shirt and tie. He carried himself as if he had been born to work with his mind. But his body, remembering the earlier years of slogging work, began to give out on him in his fifties, and it quit on him entirely before he turned sixty-five. Even such a partial escape from man's fate as he had accomplished did not seem possible for most of the boys I knew. They joined the Army, stood in line for jobs in the smoky plants, helped build highways. They were bound to work as their fathers had worked, killing themselves or preparing to kill others.

7   A scholarship enabled me not only to attend college, a rare enough feat in my circle, but even to study in a university meant for the children of the rich. Here I met for the first time young men who had assumed from birth that they would lead lives of comfort and power. And for the first time I met women who told me that men were guilty of having kept all the joys and privileges of the earth for themselves. I was baffled. What privileges? What joys? I thought about the maimed, dismal lives of most of the men back home. What had they stolen from their wives and daughters? The right to go five days a week, twelve months a year, for thirty or forty years to a steel mill or a coal mine? The right to drop bombs and die in war? The right to feel every leak in the roof, every gap in the fence, every cough in the engine, as a wound they must mend? The right to feel, when the lay-off comes or the plant shuts down, not only afraid but ashamed?

8   I was slow to understand the deep grievances of women. This was because, as a boy, I had envied them. Before college, the only people I had ever known who were interested in art or music or literature, the

only ones who read books, the only ones who ever seemed to enjoy a sense of ease and grace were the mothers and daughters. Like the menfolk, they fretted about money, they scrimped and made-do. But, when the pay stopped coming in, they were not the ones who had failed. Nor did they have to go to war, and that seemed to me a blessed fact. By comparison with the narrow, ironclad days of fathers, there was an expansiveness, I thought, in the days of mothers. They went to see neighbors, to shop in town, to run errands at school, at the library, at church. No doubt, had I looked harder at their lives, I would have envied them less. It was not my fate to become a woman, so it was easier for me to see the graces. Few of them held jobs outside the home, and those who did filled thankless roles as clerks and waitresses. I didn't see, then, what a prison a house could be, since houses seemed to me brighter, handsomer places than any factory. I did not realize — because such things were never spoken of — how often women suffered from men's bullying. I did learn about the wretchedness of abandoned wives, single mothers, widows; but I also learned about the wretchedness of lone men. Even then I could see how exhausting it was for a mother to cater all day to the needs of young children. But if I had been asked, as a boy, to choose between tending a baby and tending a machine, I think I would have chosen the baby. (Having now tended both, I know I would choose the baby.)

So I was baffled when the women at college accused me and my   9
sex of having cornered the world's pleasures. I think something like my bafflement has been felt by other boys (and by girls as well) who grew up in dirt-poor farm country, in mining country, in black ghettos, in Hispanic barrios, in the shadows of factories, in Third World nations — any place where the fate of men is as grim and bleak as the fate of women. Toilers and warriors. I realize now how ancient these identities are, how deep the tug they exert on men, the undertow of a thousand generations. The miseries I saw, as a boy, in the lives of nearly all men I continue to see in the lives of many — the body-breaking toil, the tedium, the call to be tough, the humiliating powerlessness, the battle for a living and for territory.

When the women I met at college thought about the joys and   10
privileges of men, they did not carry in their minds the sort of men I had known in my childhood. They thought of their fathers, who were bankers, physicians, architects, stockbrokers, the big wheels of the big cities. These fathers rode the train to work or drove cars that cost more than any of my childhood houses. They were attended from morning to night by female helpers, wives and nurses and secretaries. They were never laid off, never short of cash at month's end, never lined up for welfare. These fathers made decisions that mattered. They ran the world.

11   The daughters of such men wanted to share in this power, this glory. So did I. They yearned for a say over their future, for jobs worthy of their abilities, for the right to live at peace, unmolested, whole. Yes, I thought, yes yes. The difference between me and these daughters was that they saw me, because of my sex, as destined from birth to become like their fathers, and therefore as an enemy to their desires. But I knew better. I wasn't an enemy, in fact or in feeling. I was an ally. If I had known, then, how to tell them so, would they have believed me? Would they now?   ■

Examining the Reading

1. Identify the categories of men that Sanders establishes.
2. Why, as a boy, did Sanders envy women?
3. How did Sanders's view of women change while he was in college?

MAKING CONNECTIONS: Fathers and Husbands

Both "The Men We Carry in Our Minds" (pp. 454–58) and "Life without Father" (pp. 497–500) examine the roles of men and ask questions about what it means to be a man and a father. As you answer the following questions, keep in mind that Sanders is relating his experience growing up in the 1950s, whereas Blankenhorn is describing a problem in the United States of the 1990s and today.

Analyzing the Readings

1. What problems do the men of Sanders's youth face? What role does Sanders's father play in his life? How does that relate to Blankenhorn's thesis regarding the youth of today?
2. Write a journal entry explaining whether you agree with Blankenhorn's statement that "men are not ideally suited to responsible fatherhood." How does Blankenhorn support this statement? How do you think Sanders would respond to this statement?

Essay Ideas

Write an essay in which you explore the pressures men face in contemporary society. How are these pressures similar to or different from those felt by women?

4. Explain the meaning of each of the following words as it is used in the reading: *emblem* (para. 1), *limbo* (4), *expansiveness* (8), *undertow* (9), and *tedium* (9). Refer to your dictionary as needed.

Analyzing the Reading

1. Identify Sanders's thesis statement.
2. What principle does the writer use to establish his categories of men?
3. Sanders makes numerous comparisons in the essay. Identify two comparisons that you think are particularly effective. Give reasons to support your choices.
4. Identify several descriptions and examples that Sanders uses to explain his views of men and women.
5. What is the meaning of the essay's title?

Reacting to the Reading: Discussion and Journal Writing

1. Discuss alternative principles that could be used to classify men.
2. Discuss whether Sanders's views of men and women are applicable today.
3. Write a journal entry explaining how you think Sanders would answer the two questions he poses in the conclusion.

APPLYING YOUR SKILLS: ADDITIONAL ESSAY ASSIGNMENTS

Write a classification or division essay on one of the following topics, using what you learned about classification and division in this chapter. Depending on the topic you choose, you may need to conduct library or Internet research.

For more on locating and documenting sources, see Part 5.

To Express Your Ideas

1. Explain whether you are proud of or frustrated with your ability to budget money. For example, you might classify budget categories that are easy to master versus those that cause problems.
2. Explain why you chose your career or major. Categorize the job opportunities or benefits of your chosen field and indicate why they are important to you.

3. Divide a store, such as a media shop, department store, or grocery store, into departments. Describe where you are most and least tempted to over-spend.

To Inform Your Reader

4. Write an essay for the readers of your college newspaper classifying college instructors' teaching styles.

5. Explain the parts of a ceremony or event you have attended or participated in.

6. Divide a familiar substance into its components, as Bodanis does in "A Brush with Reality: Surprises in the Tube" (p. 425).

To Persuade Your Reader

7. Categorize types of television violence to develop the argument that violence on television is harmful to children.

8. In an essay that categorizes types of parenting skills and demonstrates how they are learned, develop the argument that effective parenting skills can be acquired through practice, training, or observation.

9. Classify the men and women you have known. Use your classification to support a thesis about men and women in general, as Sanders does in "The Men We Carry in Our Minds" (p. 454).

Cases Using Classification or Division

10. Write an essay for an introductory education class, identifying a problem you have experienced or observed in the public education system. Divide public education into parts to better explain your problem.

11. You oversee the development of the annual catalog for a large community college, including the section describing the services offered to students. Decide how that section of the catalog should be organized and then list the categories it should include. Finally, write a description of the services in one category.

EVALUATING YOUR PROGRESS
Part A: Using Classification and Division

Write a paragraph that evaluates your use of classification or division. Be sure to

- Identify situations in which classification or division will be useful. What topics are best suited to classification and which seem more appropriate for division?
- What principle of classification did you use in your essay(s)? How did you choose it?
- To what extent did your principle of classification shape your essay(s)? How would your essay(s) have changed if you had used a different principle?
- Identify any problems or trouble spots you experienced in using classification or division, and explain how you dealt with them.

Part B: Analyzing Classification and Division Readings

The readings in this chapter are models of essays using classification and division. Analyze the point of view used in the readings you were assigned. What advantages and disadvantages does each point of view offer?

Part C: Proofreading and Editing

List the errors your instructor identified in your classification and division essay(s). For more help with these problems, refer to Exercise Central (www.bedfordstmartins.com/successfulwriting).

Definition: Explaining What You Mean

Study the photograph on the opposite page. How might you explain the relationship between and among the people in the photograph?

Write a paragraph naming and explaining the relationship between and among the people in the photograph. Include the name of the relationship and explain its characteristics.

WRITING A DEFINITION

In your paragraph, you named and described the relationship illustrated in the photo, perhaps including one or more characteristics that distinguish it from other relationships. In other words, you have just written a definition. This chapter will show you how to write effective definitions, how to explore and explain a topic using an extended definition, and how to incorporate definition into essays using other patterns of development.

WHAT IS A DEFINITION?

A **definition** is a way of explaining what a term means or which meaning is intended when a word has a number of different meanings. Often a definition is intended for someone who is unfamiliar with the thing or idea being defined. You might define *slicing* to someone unfamiliar with golf or explain the term *koi* to a person unfamiliar with tropical fish.

You use definitions every day in a variety of situations. You might explain the term *CD-ROM drive* to someone unfamiliar with personal computers. If you call a friend a *nonconformist,* she might ask you exactly what you mean, or you and a friend might disagree over what constitutes *feminism.*

When a group shares a set of terms with commonly understood meanings, communication is simplified. For example, many sports and hobbies have their own language. Hockey fans know terms such as *high-sticking, icing, puck,* and *blueline;* photographers speak of *f-stop, ASA,* and *sky filters.* Professions and academic fields of study also have their own specialized terminology. A surgeon, for example, does not need to ask the surgical nurse for the small, straight knife with the thin, sharp blade; he or she asks for a *scalpel.* Many other academic and work situations

SCENES FROM COLLEGE AND THE WORKPLACE

- On an exam for a *health and fitness course,* the following short-answer question appears: "Define the term *wellness.*"
- Your *philosophy* instructor asks you to write a paper exploring the ethics of mercy killing; as part of the essay, you need to define the concepts *terminal illness* and *chronic condition.*
- As a *chemical engineer* responsible for your department's compliance with the company's standards for *safety* and *work efficiency,* you write a brief memo to your staff defining each term.

require that you write or learn definitions, as the examples in the box on page 464 indicate.

The essay that follows is an example of a definition of a Hispanic tradition, cracking *cascarones.*

Cracking Cascarones
Yleana Martinez

Yleana Martinez's essay first appeared in 1996 in Hispanic, *a magazine that covers social and cultural issues but also includes current information on a wide range of subjects. Martinez has written numerous other articles for* Hispanic *magazine on such topics as AIDS, education, and Hispanic traditions. As you read the selection, pay particular attention to how Martinez defines* cascarones. *Highlight the characteristics of the tradition of cracking* cascarones *that the writer identifies.*

This April 7, on Easter Sunday morning, many Hispanic families will celebrate the religious holiday by attending Mass. And for some, the solemnity of observing Christ's resurrection will give way to the mischievous fun of cracking confetti-filled *cascarones,* or eggshells, on unsuspecting heads.   1

Eggs have had symbolic meaning for centuries. They were used in ancient fertility rites to ensure a bountiful harvest or that a marriage produced a child. These rituals were held at the start of the spring season. Easter, with its message of renewal and hope, is celebrated on the first Sunday after the full moon of the vernal equinox. The Easter of modern times shares with its pre-Christian counterparts the fertility symbols of rabbits and eggs. My own memories of this holiday, however, barely contain a religious aspect and instead, concentrate on the fun and excitement of *cascarones.*   2

Growing up in South Texas, my siblings and I awakened on warm spring mornings for the egg hunt. Barefooted and in pajamas, we'd race outside, first to search for the basket left by *La Coneja,*[1] then to collect the *cascarones* we decorated in the days leading up to Easter. The basket always had foil-wrapped chocolate eggs and rabbits as well as hideously sweet neon-pink and yellow marshmallow chicks.   3

We'd hold up the hems of our pajama tops to carry the *cascarones*—a delicate task since we also lugged our basket of candy treasures with the same hand. We'd use our free hand to scoop the   4

---

[1]*La Coneja:* The Easter bunny.

eggs from their hiding places. Woe to the child who carelessly smashed some of his or her precious arsenal, for that was how we regarded our *cascarones.*

5   After Mass, the family would drive to a ranch for a reunion and the traditional *carne asada.*[2] Just before sundown, we'd get the signal from a grownup that the moment had arrived. All manners and civility were lost as everyone chased each other around, smashing dozens of painted eggshells on delicate craniums.

6   The *cascarón* activity may seem irreverent, but it has a respectable tradition. Along the Mexico border, *cascarones* have long been a part of the Easter tradition. References to the craft have been documented as early as 1897, when the Folklore Society of London published a catalogue with illustrations of elaborate eggshell figures and decorated eggs from all over Mexico. The Mexican tradition of painting eggs and filling them with colored bits of paper is practiced in the U.S. Southwest from California to Texas. The popularity of this tradition may stem from the view that *cascarones* are more fun to decorate than hard-boiled eggs because you're not stuck with having to eat them all.

7   *Cascarones* are found in some Hispanic communities throughout the year. In cities from Tucson to San Antonio, they can be purchased in folk art shops and at fiestas and church festivals. They're cheap and easy to make and can bring a nice profit to those who make them. Some people along the border have even turned *cascarones* into beautiful art.

8   Consider Doña Gloria Moroyoqui, a half-Mayo, half-Yaquí Indian who lives in Nogales, Sonora, Mexico. Her creations go beyond the typical painted egg with a tissue paper "hat." Moroyoqui, who is recognized mainly for her skill at making paper flowers and *piñatas,*[3] constructs elaborate human figures with painted eggshell heads. She often demonstrates her craft at the Tumacacori National Historical Park in Arizona. Her *cascarones* are often described as "phenomenal."

9   Dr. Jim Griffith, coordinator at the University of Arizona Libraries Southwest Folklore Center, says he has seen a "*cascarón* revolution" in the past two decades. Because the eggshells are used for any festive occasion, many women who decorate them professionally are able to support their families, he says. According to Griffith, the *cascarón*-makers of southern Arizona's Santa Clara Valley favor putting cone-shaped "hats," sometimes almost a foot tall, over the egg's

---

[2]*carne asada:* Grilled meat, barbecue.
[3]*piñatas:* Containers, usually made of papier-mâché, that are filled with treats and hung from the ceiling.

opening. They then add strips of fringed *papel de china*[4] in alternating layers, like streamers. The eggs are adorned with glitter, feathers, and other material. He's seen the eggs painted with human faces, as well as animals like cows and penguins. "They've gone visually wild," Griffith says. "*Cascarones* are no longer just eggshells with different colors painted on them and paper glued on them to keep the confetti in. They're very, very elaborate. Until you've seen them, it's hard to know what they look like."

In Laredo, Texas, Maria Villarreal uses felt-tip markers to paint 10 more than 3,000 eggs a year. Villarreal, a homemaker, was never enamored of the single-colored, water-dipped eggs, so she started painting the eggs with markers during her free time. She lets her imagination take over as she holds the eggshell over her finger, rotating it to paint clowns, cartoon characters, flowerbeds, and other fanciful images. Some of her Easter eggs have complex scenes that need to be viewed from all sides to fully appreciate them. One features a desert scene with cactus, jackrabbits, and snakes; another depicts an underwater scene with brilliant tropical fish skirting among the kelp.

Villarreal, who has seven grandchildren, sells her eggs to friends 11 and co-workers referred by her family. She charges $1.25 a dozen. Her children collect the eggs year-round for her, and weeks before Easter, she begins to get orders from people who want to buy them. "I've been doing this twenty years. It's my hobby," Villarreal says. "But now I do it all year long. It's become a habit for my children to bring me the empty eggshells."

Like so many other customs, *cascarones* involve days, sometimes 12 weeks, of preparation and constitute a fun family project. *Cascarón*-making starts in the kitchen. The family's chief cook takes special care to crack open the eggs at one end. The eggs are drained into a bowl; then the shells are carefully rinsed out and left to dry. When a sufficient number have been collected, all the artist needs is egg dye, glue, tissue paper, and confetti. After the eggs are dry, they are filled with confetti. The artist cuts circles from tissue paper (or forms cones), then pastes them over the opening.

Cascarones are usually stored in egg cartons and left within easy 13 reach of the Easter Bunny, who magically hides them outside before the kids wake up on Easter Sunday (remember, *cascarones* are for cracking on the hardest part of the body — the crown of the head — and not for throwing). Huge quantities of confetti and eggshells will fly all over the place, so it's best to perform the ceremony outdoors. *Cascarones* do make a mess, but considering the fun and laughter they produce, you'll find they are worth it. ■

---

[4]*papel de china:* Crepe paper; crinkled tissue paper.

Characteristics of Extended Definitions

When you suspect your reader may not understand a key term, offer a brief definition. Often, however, a standard definition will not be sufficient to explain the meaning of a complex idea or concept. At times you may need an entire essay to define a term. For example, if you were asked to define the term *happiness,* you would probably have trouble coming up with a brief definition because the emotion is experienced in a variety of situations. However, you could explore the term in an essay and explain all that it means to you. Such a lengthy, detailed definition is called an **extended definition.**

Extended definitions are particularly useful in exploring a topic — in examining its various meanings and applications. In some instances, an extended definition may begin with a standard definition that anchors the essay's thesis statement. At other times, an extended definition may begin by introducing a new way of thinking about the term. Whatever approach is used, the remainder of the definition then clarifies the term by using one or more other patterns of development.

An Extended Definition Often Includes a Brief Explanation of the Term

In an essay that provides an extended definition of a **term,** readers will find it useful to have a brief definition to help them begin to grasp the concept. A brief or standard definition is the kind found in a dictionary and consists of three parts:

- The *term* itself
- The *class* to which the term belongs
- The *characteristics* that distinguish the term from all others in its class

For example, a wedding band is a piece of jewelry. "Jewelry" is the **class** or group of objects that includes wedding bands. To show how a wedding band differs from other members of that class, you would need to define its **distinguishing characteristics** — the details that make it different from other types of jewelry: it is a ring, often made of gold, that the groom gives to the bride or the bride gives to the groom during a marriage ceremony.

Here are a few more examples of this three-part structure.

Term	*Class*	*Distinguishing Characteristics*
fork	utensil	Two or more prongs
		Used for eating or serving food
Dalmatian	breed of dog	Originated in Dalmatia
		Has short, smooth coat with black or dark brown spots

To write a standard definition, use the following guidelines.

1. **Describe the class as specifically as possible.** This will make it easier for your reader to understand the term you define. In the preceding example, notice that for *Dalmatian* the class is not *animal* or *mammal*, but a *breed of dog*.

2. **Do not use the term (or forms of the term) as part of your definition.** Do not write, "*Mastery* means that one has *mastered* a skill." In place of *mastered*, you could use *learned*, for example.

3. **Include enough distinguishing characteristics so that your readers will not mistake the term for something similar within the class.** If you define *answering machine* as "a machine that records messages," your definition would be incomplete because computers also record messages.

4. **Do not limit the definition so much that it becomes inaccurate.** Defining *bacon* as "a smoked, salted meat from a pig that is served at breakfast" would be too limited because bacon is also served at other meals.

Look at the following definition of the term *bully*, taken from a magazine article on the topic. As you read it, study the highlighting and marginal notes.

Term

The term *bully* does not have a standard definition, but Dan Olweus, professor of psychology at the University of Bergen, has honed the definition to three

Three characteristics — core elements—bullying involves a pattern of *repeated aggressive behavior* with *negative intent* directed from one child to another where there is a *power difference*. Either a larger child or several children pick on one child, or one child is clearly more dominant than the others. Bullying is not the same as garden-variety aggression; although aggression may involve similar acts, it happens between two people of equal status. By definition, the bully's target has difficulty defending him- or herself, and the bully's aggressive behavior is intended to cause distress.

Example of power difference

Distinguishes this term from similar — terms

HARA ESTROFF MARANO, "Big. Bad. Bully."

EXERCISE 14.1

Write a standard definition for two of the following terms.

1. hero
2. giraffe
3. science fiction
4. ATM
5. friendship

An Extended Definition Is Specific and Focused

An extended definition focuses on a specific term and discusses it in detail. In "Cracking *Cascarones*," Martinez concentrates on a specific Hispanic tradition. She recalls childhood memories of cracking *cascarones,* relates the history of the tradition, describes their preparation, and introduces some people who make them. Although *cascarones* are only one part of her family's traditional Easter celebration, Martinez focuses solely on that part.

An Extended Definition Makes a Point

The thesis of an extended definition essay often includes a brief standard definition of the term and tells why it is worth reading about. In "Cracking *Cascarones*," Martinez includes a brief definition of the term in her thesis and tells readers that cracking *cascarones* is "mischievous fun" (para. 1).

The following thesis statements include a brief definition and make a point about the term.

> Produced by the body, hormones are chemicals that are important to physical as well as emotional development.

> Euthanasia, the act of ending the life of someone suffering from a terminal illness, is an issue that should not be legislated; rather, it should be a matter of personal choice.

An Extended Definition Uses Other Patterns of Development

To explain the meaning of a term, writers usually integrate one or more other patterns of development. Here are some examples of how other patterns might be used in an extended definition.

- *Narrate* a term's history (or etymology) or a story that demonstrates its use (Chapter 8).
- *Describe* the item a term stands for (Chapter 9).
- Offer *examples* of how a term is used (Chapter 10).
- Explain how something works, its *process* (Chapter 11).
- *Compare* or *contrast* a term to similar terms (Chapter 12).
- *Classify* a term within a category or *divide* it into its parts (Chapter 13).
- Examine the *causes* and *effects* of a term (Chapter 15).
- *Argue* in favor of a particular definition of a term (Chapter 17).

In "Cracking *Cascarones*," for example, Martinez relies on several patterns of development. She uses narration to present the history of *cascarones,* includes examples of *cascarones* as artwork, describes the *cascarones* made by several artists, and presents the process by which *cascarones* are made.

EXERCISE 14.2

For one of the terms listed in Exercise 14.1 (p. 469), describe how you might use two or three patterns of development in an extended definition of the term.

An Extended Definition Includes Sufficient Distinguishing Characteristics and Details

An extended definition includes enough distinguishing characteristics and details so that readers can fully understand the term. In "Cracking *Cascarones*," Martinez gives vivid descriptions of numerous characteristics of *cascarones,* allowing her readers to visualize both the *cascarones* and the celebration in which they are used.

EXERCISE 14.3

For one of the terms listed in Exercise 14.1 (p. 469), list the distinguishing characteristics that you might use in building an extended definition.

An Extended Definition May Use Negation and Address Misconceptions

A writer may use **negation** — explaining what a term *is not* as well as what *it is* — to show how the term is different from the other terms in the same class. For example, in an essay defining *rollerblading,* you might clarify how it is unlike *rollerskating,* which uses a different type of wheeled boot that allows different kinds of motions. You can also use negation to clarify personal meanings. In defining what you mean by *relaxing vacation,* you might include examples of what is not relaxing — the pressure to see something new every day, long lines, crowded scenic areas, and many hours in a car each day.

In addition, an extended definition may need to address popular misconceptions about the term being defined. In an essay defining *plagiarism,* for instance, you might correct the mistaken idea that plagiarism is only passing off another's paper as your own, while it actually also includes using other writers' quotes or general phrases and not giving them credit.

EXERCISE 14.4

For two of the following broad topics, select a narrowed term and develop a standard definition of it. Then, for each term, consider how you could address misconceptions and use negation in an extended definition of the term.

1. A type of dance
2. A play, call, or player position in a sport
3. A piece of clothing (hat, jacket, or jeans)
4. A term related to a course you are taking
5. A type of business

Visualizing an Extended Definition Essay: A Graphic Organizer

For more on graphic organizers, see Chapter 2, p. 34.

The graphic organizer in Figure 14.1 shows the basic organization of an extended definition essay. The introduction announces the term, provides background information, and usually includes the thesis statement (which briefly defines the term and indicates its significance to readers). The body paragraphs, which are organized using one or more patterns of development, present the term's distinguishing characteristics along with supporting details. The conclusion refers back to the thesis and brings the essay to a satisfying close.

As you read the following essay, "Spanglish," look for the elements illustrated in the basic graphic organizer for an extended definition. Then study the graphic organizer for the essay in Figure 14.2.

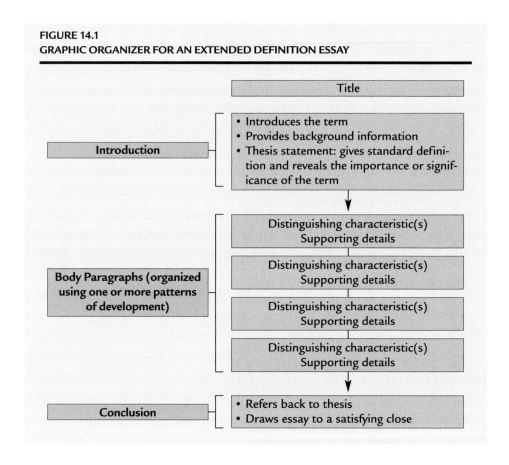

FIGURE 14.1
GRAPHIC ORGANIZER FOR AN EXTENDED DEFINITION ESSAY

Title

Introduction
• Introduces the term
• Provides background information
• Thesis statement: gives standard definition and reveals the importance or significance of the term

Body Paragraphs (organized using one or more patterns of development)

Distinguishing characteristic(s)
Supporting details

Distinguishing characteristic(s)
Supporting details

Distinguishing characteristic(s)
Supporting details

Distinguishing characteristic(s)
Supporting details

Conclusion
• Refers back to thesis
• Draws essay to a satisfying close

Spanglish

Janice Castro, Dan Cook, and Christina Garcia

Janice Castro is senior health-care correspondent for Time *magazine. She published* The American Way of Health: How Medicine Is Changing and What It Means to You *(1994). This article appeared as a collaboration with Dan Cook and Christina Garcia in a special* Time *feature on Latinos. As you read the selection, underline or highlight the thesis, the standard definition, and the distinguishing characteristics of* Spanglish.

In Manhattan a first-grader greets her visiting grandparents, happily exclaiming, "Come here, *siéntate!*" Her bemused grandfather, who does not speak Spanish, nevertheless knows she is asking him to sit down. A Miami personnel officer understands what a job applicant means when he says, "*Quiero un* part time." Nor do drivers miss a beat reading a billboard alongside a Los Angeles street advertising CERVEZA—SIX PACK!

This free-form blend of Spanish and English, known as Spanglish, is common linguistic currency wherever concentrations of Hispanic Americans are found in the U.S. In Los Angeles, where 55% of the city's 3 million inhabitants speak Spanish, Spanglish is as much a part of daily life as sunglasses. Unlike the broken-English efforts of earlier immigrants from Europe, Asia, and other regions, Spanglish has become a widely accepted conversational mode used casually—even playfully—by Spanish-speaking immigrants and native-born Americans alike.

Consisting of one part Hispanicized English, one part Americanized Spanish, and more than a little fractured syntax, Spanglish is a bit like a Robin Williams comedy routine: a cracking line of cross-cultural patter straight from the melting pot. Often it enters Anglo homes and families through children, who pick it up at school or at play with their young Hispanic contemporaries. In other cases, it comes from watching TV; many an Anglo child watching *Sesame Street* has learned *uno dos tres* almost as quickly as one two three.

Spanglish takes a variety of forms, from the Southern California Anglos who bid farewell with the utterly silly "*hasta la* bye-bye" to the Cuban-American drivers in Miami who *parquean* their *carros*. Some Spanglish sentences are mostly Spanish, with a quick detour for an English word or two. A Latino friend may cut short a conversation by glancing at his watch and excusing himself with the explanation he must "*ir al* supermarket."

5   Many of the English words transplanted in this way are simply handier than their Spanish counterparts. No matter how distasteful the subject, for example, it is still easier to say "income tax" than *impuesto sobre la renta.* At the same time, many Spanish-speaking immigrants have adopted such terms as VCR, microwave, and dishwasher for what they view as largely American phenomena. Still other English words convey a cultural context that is not implicit in the Spanish. A friend who invites you to *lonche* most likely has in mind the brisk American custom of "doing lunch" rather than the languorous afternoon break traditionally implied by *almuerzo.*

6   Mainstream Americans exposed to similar hybrids of German, Chinese, or Hindu might be mystified. But even Anglos who speak little or no Spanish are somewhat familiar with Spanglish. Living among them, for one thing, are 19 million Hispanics. In addition, more American high school and university students sign up for Spanish than any other foreign language.

7   Only in the past ten years, though, has Spanglish begun to turn into a national slang. Its popularity has grown with the explosive increases in U.S. immigration from Latin American countries. English has increasingly collided with Spanish in retail stores, offices, and classrooms, in pop music, and on street corners. Anglos whose ancestors picked up such Spanish words as *rancho, bronco, tornado,* and *incommunicado,* for instance, now freely use such Spanish words as *gracias, bueno, amigo,* and *por favor.*

8   Among Latinos, Spanglish conversations often flow more easily from Spanish into several sentences of English and back.

9   Spanglish is a sort of code for Latinos: the speakers know Spanish, but their hybrid language reflects the American culture in which they live. Many lean to shorter, clipped phrases in place of the longer, more graceful expressions their parents used. Says Leonel de la Cuesta, an assistant professor of modern languages at Florida International University in Miami: "In the U.S., time is money, and that is showing up in Spanglish as an economy of language." Conversational examples: *taipiar* (type) and *winshi-wiper* (windshield wiper) replace *escribir a máquina* and *limpiaparabrisas.*

10   Major advertisers, eager to tap the estimated $134 billion in spending power wielded by Spanish-speaking Americans, have ventured into Spanglish to promote their products. In some cases, attempts to sprinkle Spanglish through commercials have produced embarrassing gaffes. A Braniff airlines ad that sought to tell Spanish-speaking audiences they could settle back *en* (in) luxuriant *cuero* (leather) seats, for example, inadvertently said they could fly without clothes (*encuero*). A fractured translation of the Miller Lite slogan

told readers the beer was "Filling, and less delicious." Similar blunders are often made by Anglos trying to impress Spanish-speaking pals. But if Latinos are amused by mangled Spanglish, they also recognize these goofs as a sort of friendly acceptance. As they might put it, *no problema.* ■

EXERCISE 14.5

Draw a graphic organizer for "Cracking *Cascarones*" on page 465.

To draw detailed graphic organizers using a computer, visit www .bedfordstmartins.com /successfulwriting.

INTEGRATING DEFINITIONS INTO AN ESSAY

You will often need to include either standard or extended definitions in your writing. College exams may ask you to write a definition in response to a short-answer question or an essay question. Definitions are also useful for explaining unfamiliar terms in any type of essay. Whatever the type of essay, the following kinds of terms usually require definition.

- **Define judgmental terms.** Judgmental terms mean different things to different people. If you describe a policy as "fiscally unsound," you would need to define your use of *fiscally unsound.*

- **Define technical terms.** Technical terms are used in a particular field or discipline. In the field of law, for example, such terms as *writ, deposition, hearing,* and *plea* have very specific meanings. Especially when writing for an audience that is unfamiliar with your topic, be sure to define technical terms.

- **Define abstract terms.** Abstract terms refer to ideas or concepts rather than physical objects. Examples are *happiness, heroism,* and *conformity.* Because abstract terms refer to ideas, they often need explanation and definition.

- **Define controversial terms.** Because they evoke strong emotions, controversial terms — such as *politically correct, affirmative action,* and *chemical warfare* — are often subject to several interpretations. When writing about controversial subjects, define exactly how you use each related term in an essay.

In general, if you are not sure whether a term needs a definition, you usually should include a brief definition to avoid any confusion or misunderstanding. Definitions can be added to an essay in several different ways. At times you may want to offer a standard definition in a separate sentence. At other times a brief definition or synonym can be incorporated into a sentence. In this case, you use commas, dashes, or parentheses to set off the definition.

FIGURE 14.2
GRAPHIC ORGANIZER FOR "SPANGLISH"

Title	"Spanglish"

Introduction

Introduces Spanglish through examples of first-grader, job applicant, and sign on the highway.
Thesis: Spanglish is a free-form blend of Spanish and English and is common wherever concentrations of Hispanic Americans are found in the United States.

Body Paragraphs (distinguishing characteristics)

Spanglish is a blend of Hispanicized English and Americanized Spanish, with incorrect syntax; it enters the home through children or television.

Spanglish can take a variety of forms; it is often Spanish with a few English words.

English words are used because they are handier than similar Spanish words.

Anglos who know little or no Spanish can understand Spanglish.

Spanglish has become a national slang.

Spanglish may alternate between Spanish and English sentences.

Spanglish is an identity code for some Latinos; it reflects their knowledge of American culture.

Advertisers have made humorous blunders attempting to use Spanglish.

Conclusion

Latinos accept blunders as friendly recognition and acceptance of Spanglish: "No problema."

Implicit memory, the nonconscious retention of information about prior experiences, is important in eyewitness accounts of crimes.

Empathy—a shared feeling of joy for people who are happy or distress for people who are in pain—explains the success of many popular films.

In "Life without Father" (p. 497), David Blankenhorn uses definition within an essay that mixes several other methods of development.

A GUIDED WRITING ASSIGNMENT

The following guide will lead you through the process of writing an extended definition essay. Although you will focus on definition, you will need to integrate one or more other patterns of development to develop your essay.

The Assignment

Write an extended definition essay on one of the following topics or one that you choose on your own. You will need to narrow one of these general topics to a more specific term for your definition essay. Your audience is made up of your classmates.

1. A type of music (rock, jazz, classical)
2. Charisma
3. A type of television show
4. A social problem
5. Leisure time
6. Rudeness or politeness

For more on using examples or comparison and contrast, see Chapters 10 and 12.

As you develop your extended definition essay, consider using one or more other patterns of development. For example, you might include several examples to illustrate charisma, or you might explain R&B music by comparing it to and contrasting it with rock music. For more on patterns of development, see page 470.

Generating Ideas

The following guidelines will help you narrow your general topic and identify distinguishing characteristics.

Narrowing the General Topic to a Specific Term

For more on narrowing a topic, see Chapter 3, p. 63.

Your first step is to narrow the broad topic you have selected to a more specific term. For example, the term *celebrity* is probably too broad a topic for a brief essay, but the topic can be narrowed to a particular type of celebrity, such as a *sports celebrity, Hollywood celebrity, local celebrity,* or *political celebrity.* You might then focus your definition on sports celebrities, using Payton

Manning and Serena Williams as examples to illustrate the characteristics of sports celebrities.

Use the following suggestions for finding a suitable narrowed term for your definition essay.

For more on prewriting strategies, see Chapter 3.

1. Use a branching diagram or clustering to classify the general topic into specific categories. Choose the category that you are especially interested in or familiar with.

Learning Style Options

For more on classification and division, see Chapter 13.

2. Think of someone who might serve as an example of the general topic and consider focusing your definition essay on that person.

3. Discuss your general topic with a classmate to come up with specific terms related to it.

ESSAY IN PROGRESS 1

For the assignment option you chose on page 478 or on your own, narrow your general term into several specific categories of terms. Then choose one narrowed term for your extended definition essay.

Considering Your Purpose, Audience, and Point of View

Carefully consider your purpose and audience before you develop details for your essay. The purpose of a definition essay can be expressive, informative, or persuasive. You might, for example, write an essay that defines *search engines* and that expresses your frustration or success with using them to locate information on the Internet. Or you might write an informative essay on search engines in which you discuss the most popular ones. Finally, you might write a persuasive essay in which you argue that one search engine is superior to all others.

For more on purpose, audience, and point of view, see Chapter 3, p. 65.

When your audience is unfamiliar with a term, you will need to present detailed background information and define all specialized terms that you use. Your audience for this Guided Writing Assignment is your classmates. As you develop your essay, keep the following questions in mind.

1. What, if anything, can I assume my audience already knows?

2. What does my audience need to know to understand or accept my definition?

In addition, consider which point of view will be most effective for your essay. Most definition essays are written in the third person, while the first person is used occasionally, as in "Cracking *Cascarones*."

Identifying Distinguishing Characteristics and Supporting Details

The following suggestions will help you identify distinguishing characteristics and supporting details for the specific term you intend to define in your essay.

Learning Style Options

1. Discuss the term with a classmate, making notes as you talk.
2. Brainstorm a list of (a) words that describe your term, (b) people and actions that might serve as examples of the term, and (c) everything a person would need to know to understand the term.

For more on observation, see Chapter 19, p. 691.

3. Observe a person who is associated with the term or who performs some aspect of it. Take notes on your observations.
4. Look up the term's *etymology*, or origin, in the *Oxford English Dictionary*, *A Dictionary of American English*, or *A Dictionary of Americanisms*, all of which are available in the reference section of your library. Take notes; the word's etymology will give you some of its characteristics and details and might give you ideas on how to organize your essay.
5. Think of incidents or situations that reveal the meaning of the term.
6. Think of similar and different terms with which your reader is likely to be more familiar.

For more on Internet research, see Chapter 19, p. 673.

7. Do a search on the Internet for the term. Visit three or four Web sites and take notes on or print out what you discover at each site.

ESSAY IN PROGRESS 2

For the narrowed term you selected in Essay in Progress 1, use the preceding suggestions to generate a list of distinguishing characteristics and supporting details.

Developing Your Thesis

For more on thesis statements, see Chapter 4, p. 89.

Once you have gathered the distinguishing characteristics and supporting details for your term, you are ready to develop your thesis. It is a good idea to include a brief standard definition within your thesis and an explanation of why your extended definition of the term might be useful, interesting, or important to readers.

Notice how the following weak thesis statement can be revised to reveal the writer's main point.

> **WEAK**   Wireless cable is a means of transmitting television signals through the air by microwave.

REVISED   The future of wireless cable, a method of transmitting television
                signals through the air using microwaves, is uncertain.

ESSAY IN PROGRESS 3

Write a working thesis statement that briefly defines your term and tells readers
why understanding it might be useful or important to them.

Evaluating Your Ideas and Thesis

Take a few minutes to evaluate your ideas and thesis. Highlight details that
best help your readers distinguish your term from other similar terms. If
you are writing on a computer, highlight key information in bold type or
move it to a separate file. Also check your prewriting to see if you have
enough details — examples, facts, descriptions, expert testimony, and so
forth. If you find that your characteristics or details are skimpy, choose a
different method from the list on page 480 to generate additional material. If you find you still need more details, research the term in the library
or on the Internet.

> ### TRYING OUT YOUR IDEAS ON OTHERS
>
> Working in a group of two or three students, discuss your ideas and thesis
> for this chapter's assignment. Each writer should state his or her term, the-
> sis, distinguishing characteristics, and supporting details. Then, as a group,
> evaluate each writer's work and offer suggestions for improvement.

ESSAY IN PROGRESS 4

Using the preceding suggestions and comments from your classmates, evaluate
your thesis, distinguishing characteristics, and details. Refer to the list of characteristics on pages 468–71 to help you with your evaluation.

Organizing and Drafting

Once you have evaluated your distinguishing characteristics, supporting
details, and thesis and considered the advice of your classmates, you are
ready to organize your ideas and draft your essay.

*For more on drafting an
essay, see Chapter 5.*

Choosing Other Patterns of Development

To a considerable extent, the organization of an extended definition essay depends on the patterns of development you decide to use. Try to choose the patterns before you begin drafting your essay.

Suppose you want to define the term *lurking* as it is used in the context of the Internet, where it usually means reading newsgroup or listserv messages without directly participating in the ongoing discussion. You could develop and expand the essay by using one or more other patterns of development as noted in the following list.

Pattern of Development	*Defining the Term* **Lurking**
Narration (Chapter 8)	Relate a story about learning something important by lurking.
Description (Chapter 9)	Describe the experience of lurking.
Illustration (Chapter 10)	Give examples of typical situations involving lurking.
Process analysis (Chapter 11)	Explain how to lurk in an Internet chatroom.
Comparison and contrast (Chapter 12)	Compare and contrast lurking to other forms of observation.
Classification and division (Chapter 13)	Classify the reasons people lurk — for information, entertainment, and so on.
Cause and effect (Chapter 15)	Explain the benefits or outcomes of lurking.
Argument (Chapters 16 and 17)	Argue that lurking is an ethical or unethical practice.

You would use the pattern or patterns that suit your audience and purpose as well as the term. For instance, narrating a story about lurking might capture the interest of an audience unfamiliar with the Internet, whereas classifying different types of people who lurk might be of interest to an audience familiar with online environments.

For more on organizing an essay, see Chapter 5.

With your pattern(s) firmly in mind, think about how to organize your characteristics and details. An essay classifying different types of people who lurk would probably follow a least-to-most or most-to-least arrangement. An essay incorporating several patterns of development might use a number of arrangements. At this stage, it is a good idea to make an outline or draw a graphic organizer. To experiment with different organizational plans, create a computer file for each possibility.

ESSAY IN PROGRESS 5

For the thesis you wrote in Essay in Progress 3, decide which pattern(s) of development you will use to develop your characteristics and details. Draw a graphic organizer or write an outline to help you see how each pattern will work.

Drafting an Extended Definition Essay

Use the following guidelines to draft your essay.

1. **Include enough details.** Be sure you include sufficient information to enable your reader to understand each characteristic.

2. **Consider including the history or etymology of the term.** You might include a brief history of your term in the introduction or in some other part of your essay to capture your readers' interest.

3. **Use transitions.** As you move from characteristic to characteristic, be sure to use a transitional word or phrase to signal each change and guide your readers along. The transitions *another, also,* and *in addition* are especially useful in extended definitions.

   For more on transitions, see Chapter 5, p. 128.

4. **Write an effective introduction and a satisfying conclusion.** As noted earlier, your introduction should introduce the term, provide any needed background information, and state your thesis (which includes a standard definition as well as your main point). Also, when introducing your term, it may be helpful to use negation, explaining what the term is and what it is not. Alternatively, you might use your introduction to justify the importance of your topic, as the authors of "Spanglish" do in the second paragraph.

   For more on writing effective paragraphs, including introductions and conclusions, see Chapter 5.

   Your conclusion should reinforce your thesis and draw the essay to a satisfying close, as Martinez's conclusion does in "Cracking Cascarones."

ESSAY IN PROGRESS 6

Draft your extended definition essay, using the pattern(s) of development you selected in Essay in Progress 5 and the preceding guidelines for drafting.

Analyzing and Revising

If possible, set your draft aside for a day or two before rereading and revising it. As you review your draft, concentrate on your ideas and organization, not on grammar or mechanics. Use one or more of the following suggestions to analyze your draft.

Learning Style Options

1. Delete or make unreadable the title and all mentions of the term, and then ask a classmate to read your essay. Alternatively, you could read your essay aloud, substituting "Term X" each time the term occurs. Then ask your classmate to identify the term you are defining. If your reader or listener cannot come up with the term or a synonym for it, you probably need to make your distinguishing characteristics more specific or add details.

2. Test your definition by trying to think of exceptions to it as well as other terms that might be defined in the same way.

   • *Exceptions.* Try to identify exceptions to your distinguishing characteristics. Suppose, for example, you define *sports stars* as people who exemplify sportsmanlike behavior. Since most people can name current sports stars who indulge in unsportsmanlike behavior, this distinguishing characteristic needs to be modified or deleted.

   • *Other terms that fit all of your characteristics.* For example, in defining the term *bulletproof vest,* you would explain that it is a piece of clothing worn by law-enforcement officers, among others, to protect them from bullets and other life-threatening blows. Another kind of protective clothing—a helmet—would also fit your description, however. You would need to add information about *where* on the body a bulletproof vest is worn.

3. To see if your essay follows the organization you intend, draw a graphic organizer or make an outline (or update the organizer or outline you made earlier).

For more on the benefits of peer review, see Chapter 6, p. 155.

Use Figure 14.3 to guide your analysis. You might also ask a classmate to review your draft using the questions in the flowchart. For each "No" answer, ask your reviewer to explain his or her answer. In addition, ask your reviewer to describe his or her impressions of your main point and distinguishing characteristics. Your reviewer's comments will help you identify the parts of your essay that need revision.

ESSAY IN PROGRESS 7

Revise your draft using Figure 14.3 and any comments you received from peer reviewers.

FIGURE 14.3
FLOWCHART FOR REVISING AN EXTENDED DEFINITION ESSAY

Questions	Revision Strategies

1. Highlight your thesis statement. Does it include a brief definition of the term? Does it indicate why your extended definition is useful, interesting, or important?

No →

- Use the guidelines on pages 468–72 to identify the class and distinguishing characteristics of your term.
- Incorporate a standard definition into your thesis.
- Ask yourself, "Why is this definition worth reading about?" Add your answer to your thesis.

↓ **Yes**

2. *Number* the parts of your extended definition in the margin. Do these parts make your definition specific and focused?

No →

- Delete any details that do not help define your term.
- Narrow your term further.

↓ **Yes**

3. Place checkmarks ✔ beside the distinguishing characteristics of your definition. Do they make your term distinct from similar terms?

No →

- Do additional research or prewriting to discover more characteristics and details.

↓ **Yes**

(Continued on next page)

FIGURE 14.3 *(Continued)*

Questions	Revision Strategies

4. *Write* the name of the pattern(s) of development you used in your essay. Does it connect your details and help explain the distinguishing characteristics of your term?

No →
- Review the list of patterns on pages 470–71 and consider using one or more of them to enhance your definition.

Yes ↓

5. Draw [brackets] around sections where you use negation or address misconceptions. Does each section eliminate possible misunderstandings?

No →
- Revise your explanation of what your term is not.
- Add facts or expert opinion to correct readers' mistaken notions about the term.

Yes ↓

6. Underline the topic sentence of each paragraph. Does each paragraph focus on a particular characteristic? Is each paragraph well developed?

- Consider combining closely related paragraphs.
- Split paragraphs that cover more than one characteristic.
- Be sure each body paragraph has a topic sentence and supporting details (see Chapter 5).

Yes ↓

(Continued on next page)

FIGURE 14.3 *(Continued)*

Questions		Revision Strategies
7. Draw a box around your introduction and conclusion. Does the introduction provide necessary background information? Does your conclusion bring the essay to a satisfying close?	**No** →	• Add background information that sets a context for the term you are defining. • Revise your introduction and conclusion so that they meet the guidelines presented in Chapter 5 (pp. 131–36).

Yes ↓

8. Print out another draft to edit and proofread your essay before turning it in.

Editing and Proofreading

The final step is to check your revised essay for errors in grammar, spelling, punctuation, and mechanics. Be sure to check your error log for the types of errors you commonly make.

For more on keeping an error log, see Chapter 7, p. 193.

As you edit and proofread your extended definition essay, watch out for the following types of errors commonly found in this type of writing.

1. Make sure you avoid the awkward expressions *is when* or *is where* in defining your term. Instead, name the class to which the term belongs.

▶ Early bird specials ~~is when~~ restaurants ~~offer reduced-price dinners~~ *are reduced-priced dinners served in* late in the afternoon and early in the evening.

▶ A rollover is ~~where~~ *a transaction in which* an employee transfers money from one retirement account to another.

2. Make sure subjects and verbs agree in number. When two subjects are joined by *and,* the verb should be plural.

> ▶ Taken together, the military and Medicare ~~costs~~ *cost* U.S. taxpayers an enormous amount of money.

When two nouns are joined by *or,* the verb should agree with the noun closest to it.

> ▶ For most birds, the markings or wing span ~~are~~ *is* easily observed with a pair of good binoculars.

When the subject and verb are separated by a prepositional phrase, the verb should agree with the subject of the sentence, not with the noun in the phrase.

> ▶ The features of a hot-air balloon ~~is~~ *are* best learned by studying the attached diagram.

ESSAY IN PROGRESS 8

Edit and proofread your essay, paying particular attention to avoiding *is when* or *is where* expressions and correcting errors in subject-verb agreement.

STUDENTS WRITE

David Harris was a student at the State University of New York at Geneseo when he wrote the following essay. The assignment was to write an extended definition of a specialized term related to one of his areas of interest. Being a sports fan, Harris chose the salary cap that was instituted in the National Football League in the 1990s. As you read, note in the margins where Harris uses other patterns of development—such as narration, comparison and contrast, and cause and effect—to define the salary cap as an innovation that has been beneficial to the league.

Leveling the Playing Field: The NFL Salary Cap

David Harris

1   In the 1990s, professional sports salaries, including those for football players, increased at record-breaking rates. Previously, players had been "owned" by a specific team, and when their contracts ran out, they needed permission to negotiate with other teams. With the

arrival of free agency in the 1970s and 1980s, players became free to negotiate with any team after a contract expired. This freedom caused bidding wars, which eventually raised salaries dramatically. To control the expense of these rising salaries, the National Football League (NFL) instituted a salary cap in 1994. In general, a salary cap in sports is a limit on the amount of money a team can spend on player salaries, either per-player or as a total limit for the team's roster ("Salary Cap"). The salary cap has given every team, regardless of revenue, a chance to compete for the NFL championship.

The National Football League owners had searched for ways to increase profitability by limiting ballooning player salaries. As a result of collective bargaining with the NFL players' union during 1993, a salary cap was arrived at as a way of controlling salaries and of leveling the competitive playing field across the league. The players' association was granted a form of free agency that would allow players to market themselves to other teams after a certain number of years of service. In exchange for this limited free agency, the owners were granted the salary cap.

The NFL salary cap is a total team limit salary cap; in 2004 the NFL salary cap was $80.6 million (Pasquarelli). Each NFL team had to bring down its total of salaries paid to this $80.6 million mark. However, a player's salary is not always the same as his value according to the salary cap. A player's value under the cap equals his salary for a given year plus the portion of his signing bonus he receives that year. Signing bonuses can be distributed over the length of a contract unevenly, if the team chooses to do so. As a result, many teams run into huge salary cap problems because of back-loaded contracts. A team that wins the Super Bowl one year could have to cut many of its star players to remain under the salary cap the next year. A rookie's contract typically is much smaller than that of a proven player. So replacing a high-priced veteran, who may have a heavily back-loaded contract, with a low-cost rookie is an excellent way to manage a cap and translates into more money for players at other positions. Therefore, continued success in the NFL is a product of good management and good scouting, which can help teams stay under their caps.

4   The NFL salary cap is absolute, but it does change from year to year. In 2003 the NFL salary cap was $75 million, but it increased by 6.6 percent to $80.6 million dollars in 2004 (ESPN.com). The salary cap is not randomly set but is derived from league revenues. It is a calculation of a percentage of combined revenue of all teams divided by the thirty-two teams in the NFL. This salary cap is in effect for the whole season. The cap is a "hard" cap; no team can exceed it without penalty. If a team exceeds the salary cap at any point in the season, the NFL has the right to cut any player, starting from the lowest salary, until the team is below the set cap. Cutting a player from a team eliminates him from the team's payroll, but any other team can acquire him at his current contracted rate. This provides a huge incentive for teams to carefully manage their cap numbers throughout the season. Furthermore, teams that violate this cap may be made to forfeit upcoming draft picks or can be fined up to $1 million per day they remain in violation. Recently, both the Pittsburgh Steelers and the San Francisco 49ers were penalized draft picks, and the 49ers were fined for violation of this policy.

5   The salary cap has the added benefit of keeping smaller-city teams, such as the Buffalo Bills, in contention with the larger-city teams. Since the NFL salary cap was instituted in 1994, no team has won more than two Super Bowls. Only the 1998 and 1999 Denver Broncos won consecutive Super Bowls, and since 1994 the most appearances in the Super Bowl by one team has been three ("Super Bowl Recaps"), by the New England Patriots.

6   Sports without salary caps have had trouble keeping the level of competition equal. In Major League Baseball, for example, the largest baseball markets dominate, and teams in smaller cities cannot compete. The New York

Yankees' team salary has been the highest in the league
since 1996, and since then they have made a total of six
appearances in the World Series, have won four times,
and have finished first in their division every year
(MLB.com). No team can come even close to this kind of
dominance in the NFL due to the salary cap.

The NFL and the players have benefited greatly from   7
the addition of the salary cap. Under the salary cap,
fan interest has grown to record levels, and professional
football has become the most financially successful of
American sports leagues. And this wealth has been shared:
as the teams' revenues have increased, so have the athletes' salaries. The salary cap has had a tremendous
impact on the game of football, the fans of football,
and the owners of football teams. The cap keeps all
teams in contention. For that, the fans are grateful.

Works Cited

ESPN.com. 2005. 28 April 2005 <http://sports.espn.go.com>.

MLB.com. 2005. MLB Advanced Media. 5 May 2005
    <http://www.mlb.com>.

Pasquarelli, Len. "High Cap Will Be Good News for Strapped
    Teams." ESPN.com. 2005. 28 April 2005 <http://
    sports.espn.go.com/nfl/columns/story?columnist
    =pasquarelli_len&id=1738866>.

"Salary Cap." WordIQ.com. 2004. 25 April 2005 <http://
    www.wordiq.com/definition/Salary_cap>.

"Super Bowl Recaps." SuperBowl.com. 2005. NFL Enterprises.
    5 May 2005 <http://www.superbowl.com/history/recaps>.

Analyzing the Essay

1. Identify Harris's thesis. Where does he suggest the topic's importance?
2. Evaluate the background information Harris provides. Is it sufficient for readers who are unfamiliar with the topic?
3. What patterns of development does Harris use to define the NFL salary cap?
4. Identify the distinguishing characteristics Harris uses.
5. Evaluate the effectiveness of his title, introduction, and conclusion.

Reacting to the Essay: Discussion and Journal Writing

1. Discuss whether the salaries of professional football players are commensurate or out of proportion with the risk and skill involved in the game.

2. Discuss whether salary caps should be instituted for other professional teams.

3. Write a journal entry exploring the impact of professional football (or another professional sport you are familiar with) on our society.

READING DEFINITIONS

The following section provides advice for reading definitions as well as two model essays. The first essay illustrates the characteristics of an extended definition covered in this chapter. The second essay uses definition along with other methods of development. Both essays provide opportunities to examine, analyze, and react to the writers' ideas.

WORKING WITH TEXT: READING DEFINITIONS

For more on reading strategies, see Chapter 2.

As you encounter new fields of study throughout college, you will be asked to learn sets of terms that are specific to academic disciplines. Articles in academic journals, as well as most textbooks, contain many new terms.

If you need to learn a large number of specialized terms, try the index-card system. Using three- by five-inch cards, write a word on the front of each card, and on its back write the word's meaning, pronunciation, and any details or examples that will help you remember it. Be sure to write the definition in your own words; don't copy the author's definition. To study, test yourself by reading the front of the cards and trying to recall the definition on the back of the cards. Then reverse the process. Shuffle the pack of cards to avoid learning terms in a particular order.

What to Look For, Highlight, and Annotate

1. As you read a definition, whether in a textbook or an essay, identify the class and highlight or underline the distinguishing characteristics. Mark any that are unclear or for which you need further information.

2. Make sure you understand how the term differs from similar terms, especially those presented in the same article or chapter. If a textbook or article does not explain sufficiently how two or more terms differ, check a standard dictionary. Each academic field of study also has its own dictionaries that list terms specific

to the discipline. Examples include *Music Index, Taber's Cyclopedic Medical Dictionary,* and *A Dictionary of Economics.*

3. Many students find it useful to highlight definitions using a special color of pen or highlighter or to designate them using annotations. You might use *V* for vocabulary, *Def.* for definition, or some other annotation.

How to Find Ideas to Write About

As you read an extended definition or an article containing brief definitions, jot down any additional characteristics or examples that come to mind. When you respond to the article, you might write about how the definition could be expanded to include these. You might also try the following strategies.

For more on discovering ideas for a response paper, see Chapter 2.

- Think of other terms in the same class that you might write about.
- Try to relate the definitions to your own experience. Where or when have you observed the characteristics described? Your personal experiences might be used in an essay in which you agree with or challenge the writer's definitions.
- If the writer has not already done so, you might use negation to expand the meaning of the term or you might explore the word's etymology.

THINKING CRITICALLY ABOUT DEFINITION

Some definitions are more straightforward and factual than others. Standard definitions of terms such as *calendar, automobile,* or *taxes* are not likely to be disputed by most readers. At other times, however, definitions can reflect bias, hide unpleasantness, and evoke conflicting reactions and emotions in readers. Use the following questions to think critically about the definitions you read.

Are the Writer's Definitions Objective?

Especially in persuasive essays, definitions are sometimes expressed in subjective, emotional language that is intended to influence the reader. For example, a writer who defines a *liberal* as "someone who wants to allow criminals to run free on the streets while sacrificing the rights of innocent victims" reveals a negative bias toward liberals and intends to make the reader dislike them. When reading definitions, think critically. Ask yourself the following questions.

1. Do I agree with the writer's definition of this term?
2. Do I think these characteristics apply to all members of this group?
3. Is the writer's language meant to inflame my emotions?

Are the Writer's Definitions Evasive?

A **euphemism** is a word or phrase that is used in place of an unpleasant or objectionable word. For example, the phrase *suffers occasional irregularity* is a euphemism for *constipation,* while *passed away* is often used instead of *died.* At times, a writer may offer a euphemism as a synonym. For example, in describing a military action in which innocent civilians were killed, a writer may characterize the killings as "collateral damage." Be alert to the use of euphemisms. Like persuasive definitions, they are intended to shape your thinking.

EXTENDED DEFINITION ESSAY

Dude, Do You Know What You Just Said?
Mike Crissey

Mike Crissey is a staff writer for the Associated Press. The following article, which appeared in the Pittsburgh Post-Gazette *on December 8, 2004, is based on research done by Scott Kiesling, a professor of linguistics at the University of Pittsburgh. Kiesling's work focuses on the relationship between language and identity, particularly in the contexts of gender, ethnicity, and class. As you read, notice how the writer uses a combination of expert testimony, anecdotal evidence, and personal observations to support his main point.*

1   Dude, you've got to read this. A University of Pittsburgh linguist has published a scholarly paper deconstructing and deciphering *dude,* the bane of parents and teachers, which has become as universal as *like* and another vulgar four-letter favorite. In his paper in the fall edition of the journal *American Speech,* Scott Kiesling says *dude* is much more than a greeting or catchall for lazy, inarticulate, and inexpressive (and mostly male) surfers, skaters, slackers, druggies, or teenagers. "Without context there is no single meaning that dude encodes and it can be used, it seems, in almost any kind of situation. But we should not confuse flexibility with meaninglessness," Kiesling said.

2   Originally meaning "old rags," a "dudesman" was a scarecrow. In the late 1800s, a "dude" was akin to a dandy, a meticulously dressed man, especially in the western United States. *Dude* became a slang term in the 1930s and 1940s among black zoot suiters and Mexican American pachuchos. The term began its rise in the teenage lexicon with the 1982 movie *Fast Times at Ridgemont High.* Around the same time, it became an exclamation as well as a noun. Pronunciation

purists say it should sound like "duhd"; "dood" is an alternative, but it is considered "uncool" or old.

To decode *dude*, Kiesling listened to conversations with fraternity members he taped in 1993 and had undergraduate students in socio-linguistics classes in 2001 and 2002 write down the first twenty times they heard *dude* and who said it during a three-day period. He's also a lapsed *dude*-user who during his college years tried to talk like Jeff Spicoli, the slacker surfer "dude" from *Fast Times at Ridgemont High.*

According to Kiesling, *dude* has many uses: an exclamation ("Dude!" and "Whoa, Dude!"); to one-up someone ("That's so lame, dude."); to disarm confrontation ("Dude, this is so boring."), or simply to agree ("Dude."). It's inclusive or exclusive, ironic or sincere.

Kiesling says *dude* derives its power from something he calls cool solidarity: an effortless or seemingly lazy kinship that's not too intimate; close, dude, but not that close. *Dude* "carries . . . both solidarity (camaraderie) and distance (non-intimacy) and can be deployed to create both of these kinds of stance, separately or together," Kiesling wrote. Kiesling, whose research focuses on language and masculinity, said that cool solidarity is especially important to young men — anecdotally the predominant *dude*-users — who are under social pressure to be close with other young men but not enough to be suspected as gay. "It's like *man* or *buddy*. There is often this male-male addressed term that says, 'I'm your friend but not much more than your friend,'" Kiesling said. Aside from its duality, *dude* also taps into nonconformity, despite everyone using it, and a new American image of leisurely success, he said.

The nonchalant attitude of *dude* also means that women sometimes call each other *dudes*. And less frequently, men will call women *dudes* and vice versa, Kiesling said. But that comes with some rules, according to self-reporting from students in a 2002 language and gender class at the University of Pittsburgh included in his paper. "Men report that they use *dude* with women with whom they are close friends, but not with women with whom they are intimate," according to his study.

His students also reported that they were least likely to use the word with parents, bosses, and professors. "It is not who they are but what your relationship is with them. With your parents, you likely have a close relationship, but unless you're Bart Simpson, you're not going to call your parent *dude*," Kiesling said. "There are a couple of young professors here in their thirties and every once in a while we use *dude*. Professors are dudes, but most of the time they are not."

And *dude* shows no signs of disappearing. "More and more our culture is becoming youth centered. In southern California, youth is valued to the point that even active seniors are dressing young and talking youth," said Mary Bucholtz, an associate professor of linguistics at the University of California, Santa Barbara. "I have seen middle-aged men using *dude* with each other."

9   So what's the point, dude? Kiesling and linguists argue that language and how we use it is important. "These things that seem frivolous are serious because we are always doing it. We need to understand language because it is what makes us human. That's my defense of studying *dude*," Kiesling said.   ■

Examining the Reading

1. What are some of the uses of the word *dude*?
2. Who uses the word *dude* and when?
3. What is the history of the word *dude*?
4. Explain what is meant by "cool solidarity."
5. Explain the meaning of each of the following words as used in the reading: *catchall* (para. 1), *meticulously* (2), *lexicon* (2), and *sociolinguistics* (3). Refer to your dictionary as needed.

Analyzing the Reading

1. Identify the thesis statement of this essay.
2. Why does the author include what the word does not mean and to whom people do not say it?
3. What are the distinguishing characteristics of the term *dude*?
4. Evaluate the introduction. How does it capture readers' interest?
5. Could the term *dude* be considered a euphemism? If so, what words or phrases does it replace?

Reacting to the Reading: Discussion and Journal Writing

1. Discuss the uses and users of the word *dude* that you have observed. Do your observations conform with those identified in the essay?
2. Linguist Kiesling is an "admitted *dude*-user" (3). Do you think this affects his ability to study and research its use?
3. Choose a slang or informal word or phrase that is used on your campus or among your friends. Write a journal entry defining the term and explaining its uses.

MAKING CONNECTIONS: Language

Both "Spanglish" (pp. 473–75) and "Dude, Do You Know What You Just Said?" (pp. 494–96) discuss language change and evolution.

Analyzing the Readings

1. In what way does each essay make a point about language change and evolution?
2. Write a journal entry exploring this question: Why do various groups or cultures use words and phrases that are unique to that particular group or culture?

Essay Idea

Write an essay in which you explore language change and evolution among college students. Give examples of new words and phrases that have recently entered your speaking vocabulary.

DEFINITION COMBINED WITH OTHER PATTERNS

In the following selection, David Blankenhorn uses an extended definition as part of an argument.

Life without Father
David Blankenhorn

David Blankenhorn is the author of Fatherless America: Confronting Our Most Urgent Social Problem *(1995), from which this selection is taken. Blankenhorn is the editor of several other nonfiction works and has published articles in the* New Republic, Washington Post, *and* Journal of Marriage and Family. *As you read the selection, notice how Blankenhorn defines the concept of fatherhood and highlight the terms he introduces and defines.*

The United States is becoming an increasingly fatherless society. 1
A generation ago, a child could reasonably expect to grow up with his or her father. Today, a child can reasonably expect not to. Fatherlessness is approaching a rough parity with fatherhood as a defining feature of childhood.

2   This astonishing fact is reflected in many statistics, but here are the two most important: Tonight, about 40 percent of U.S. children will go to sleep in homes in which their fathers do not live. More than half of our children are likely to spend a significant portion of childhood living apart from their fathers. Never before in this country have so many children been voluntarily abandoned by their fathers. Never before have so many children grown up without knowing what it means to have a father.

3   Fatherlessness is the most harmful demographic trend of this generation. It is the leading cause of the decline in the well-being of children. It is also the engine driving our most urgent social problems, from crime to adolescent pregnancy to domestic violence. Yet, despite its scale and social consequences, fatherlessness is frequently ignored or denied. Especially within our elite discourse, it remains a problem with no name.

4   Surely a crisis of this scale merits a name — and a response. At a minimum, it requires a serious debate: Why is fatherhood declining? What can be done about it? Can our society find ways to invigorate effective fatherhood as a norm of male behavior? Yet, to date, our public discussion has been remarkably weak and defeatist. There is a prevailing belief that not much can or even should be done to reverse the trend.

5   As a society, we are changing our minds about men's role in family life. Our inherited understanding of fatherhood is under siege. Men are increasingly viewed as superfluous to family life: either expendable or part of the problem. Masculinity itself often is treated with suspicion, and even hostility, in our cultural discourse. Consequently, our society is unable to sustain fatherhood as a distinctive domain of male activity.

6   The core question is simple: Does every child need a father? Increasingly, our society's answer is "no." Few idea shifts in this century are as consequential as this one. At stake is nothing less than what it means to be a man, who our children will be and what kind of society we will become.

7   My . . . criticism [is] not simply of fatherlessness but of a *culture* of fatherlessness. For, in addition to fathers, we are losing something larger: our idea of fatherhood. Unlike earlier periods of father absence in our history, such as wartime, we now face more than a physical loss affecting some homes. The 1940s child could say: My father had to leave for a while to do something important. The '90s child must say: My father left me permanently because he wanted to.

8   This is a cultural criticism because fatherhood, much more than motherhood, is a cultural invention. Its meaning is shaped less by

biology than by a cultural script, a societal code that guides — and at times pressures — a man into certain ways of acting and understanding himself.

Like motherhood, fatherhood is made up of both a biological 9
and a social dimension. Yet, across the world, mothers are far more successful than fathers at fusing these dimensions into a coherent identity. Is the nursing mother playing a biological or a social role? Feeding or bonding? We can hardly separate the two, so seamlessly are they woven together. But fatherhood is a different matter. A father makes his sole biological contribution at the moment of conception, nine months before the infant enters the world. Because social paternity is linked only indirectly to biological paternity, a connection cannot be assumed. The phrase "to father a child" usually refers only to the act of insemination, not the responsibility for raising the child. What fathers contribute after conception is largely a matter of cultural devising.

Moreover, despite their other virtues, men are not ideally suited 10
to responsible fatherhood. Men are inclined to sexual promiscuity and paternal waywardness. Anthropologically, fatherhood constitutes what might be termed a necessary problem. It is necessary because child well-being and societal success hinge largely on a high level of paternal investment: men's willingness to devote energy and resources to the care of their offspring. It is a problem because men frequently are unwilling or unable to make that vital investment.

Because fatherhood is universally problematic, cultures must 11
mobilize to enforce the father role, guiding men with legal and extralegal pressures that require them to maintain a close alliance with their children's mother and invest in their children. Because men don't volunteer for fatherhood as much as they are conscripted into it by the surrounding culture, only an authoritative cultural commitment to fatherhood can fuse biological and social paternity into a coherent male identity. For exactly this reason, anthropologist Margaret Mead and others have observed that the supreme test of any civilization is whether it can socialize men by teaching them to nurture their offspring.

The stakes could hardly be higher. Our society's conspicuous failure to sustain norms of fatherhood reveals a failure of collective 12
memory and a collapse of moral imagination. It undermines families, neglects children, causes or aggravates our worst social problems, and makes individual adult happiness, both female and male, harder to achieve.

Ultimately, this failure reflects nothing less than a culture gone 13
awry, unable to establish the boundaries and erect the signposts that

can harmonize individual happiness with collective well-being. In short, it reflects a culture that fails to "enculture" individual men and women, mothers and fathers.

14   In personal terms, the main result of this failure is the spread of a me-first egotism hostile to all except the most puerile understandings of personal happiness. In social terms, the results are a decline in children's well-being and a rise in male violence, especially against women. The most significant result is our society's steady fragmentation into atomized individuals, isolated from one another and estranged from the aspirations and realities of common membership in a family, a community, a nation, bound by mutual commitment and shared memory.

15   Many voices today, including many expert voices, urge us to accept the decline of fatherhood with equanimity. Be realistic, they tell us. Divorce and out-of-wedlock childbearing are here to stay. Growing numbers of children will not have fathers. Nothing can be done to reverse the trend itself. The only solution is to remedy some of its consequences: More help for poor children. More sympathy for single mothers. Better divorce. More child-support payments. More prisons. More programs aimed at substituting for fathers.

16   Yet what Abraham Lincoln called the better angels of our nature always have guided us in the opposite direction. Passivity in the face of crisis is inconsistent with the American tradition. Managing decline never has been the hallmark of American expertise. In the inevitable and valuable tension between conditions and aspirations — between the social "is" and the moral "ought" — our birthright as Americans always has been our confidence that we can change for the better.

17   Does every child need a father? Our current answer hovers between "not necessarily" and "no." But we need not make permanent the lowering of our standards. We can change our minds. We can change our minds without passing new laws, spending more tax dollars, or empaneling more expert commissions. Once we change our philosophy, we might well decide to pass laws, create programs, or commission research. But the first and most important thing to change is not policies but ideas.

18   Our essential goal must be the rediscovery of the fatherhood idea: For every child, a legally and morally responsible man.

19   If my goal could be distilled into one sentence, it would be this: A good society celebrates the ideal of the man who puts his family first. Because our society is lurching in the opposite direction, I see the Good Family Man as the principal casualty of today's weakening focus on fatherhood. Yet I cannot imagine a good society without him.   ∎

Examining the Reading

1. Why is fatherhood a "cultural invention" (para. 8), according to Blankenhorn?
2. According to the author, why are men not ideally suited to fatherhood?
3. What are the effects of fatherlessness?
4. What solutions to the problem of fatherless families does Blankenhorn offer?
5. Explain the meaning of each of the following words as it is used in the reading: *demographic* (3), *conscripted* (11), *collective* (12, 13), *puerile* (14), and *equanimity* (15). Refer to your dictionary as needed.

Analyzing the Reading

1. Identify Blankenhorn's thesis statement.
2. What characteristics of fatherlessness does Blankenhorn include in his essay?
3. What patterns of development, in addition to definition, does Blankenhorn employ?
4. Evaluate the essay's introduction and conclusion.
5. Is Blankenhorn's definition of fatherlessness primarily objective or subjective?

Reacting to the Reading: Discussion and Journal Writing

1. What problems have you observed or experienced in fatherless families?
2. Discuss actions that can be taken to encourage responsible fatherhood.
3. Write a journal entry agreeing or disagreeing with Blankenhorn's statement that "Men are not ideally suited to responsible fatherhood" (para. 10).

APPLYING YOUR SKILLS: ADDITIONAL ESSAY ASSIGNMENTS

Write an extended definition essay on one of the following topics, using what you learned about definition in this chapter. Depending on the topic you choose, you may need to conduct library or Internet research.

For more on locating and documenting sources, see Chapters 19 and 20.

To Express Your Ideas

Choose a specific audience and write an essay defining and expressing your views on one of the following terms.

1. Parenting
2. Assertiveness
3. Sexual harassment

To Inform Your Reader

4. Write an essay defining a term from a sport, hobby, or form of entertainment. Your audience is a classmate who is unfamiliar with the sport, hobby, or pastime.

5. Write an essay defining the characteristics of the "perfect job" you hope to hold after graduation. Your audience is your instructor.

6. Write an essay defining an important concept in a field of study, perhaps from one of your other courses. Your audience is other students not enrolled in the course.

To Persuade Your Reader

As Blankenhorn does (p. 497), write an essay defining a term and demonstrating that the issue is either increasing or decreasing in your community. Your audience is readers of your local newspaper. Choose a term from the following list.

7. Racism or ethnic stereotyping
8. Sexual discrimination
9. Age discrimination

Cases Using Definition

10. You are a fifth-grade teacher and are working on a lesson plan entitled "What Is American Democracy?" How will you limit the term *American democracy* to define it for your audience? What characteristics and details will you include?

11. Write a press release for a new menu item as part of your job as public relations manager for a restaurant chain. First, choose the new menu item, and then define the item and describe its characteristics using sensory details.

EVALUATING YOUR PROGRESS
Part A: Using Definition

Write a paragraph that evaluates your use of definition. Be sure to

- Identify topics or situations in which definition will be useful.
- Did you use negation, address misconceptions, or use other patterns of development? If so, evaluate their effectiveness.
- To what extent did your principle of classification shape your essay(s)? How would your essay(s) have changed if you had used a different principle?
- Identify any problems or trouble spots you experienced in using definition and explain how you dealt with them.

Part B: Analyzing Definition Readings

The readings in this chapter are models of essays using definition. Write a paragraph explaining how the essays you read served as models for your own writing. In other words, what features of the essays helped you write your essay(s)?

Part C: Proofreading and Editing

List the errors your instructor identified in your definition essay(s). For more help with these problems, refer to Exercise Central (www.bedfordstmartins.com/successfulwriting).

Cause and Effect: Using Reasons and Results to Explain

Assume you are a journalist for your local newspaper reporting on a natural disaster that has occurred in a nearby town. Your immediate task is to write a story to accompany the photograph shown on the opposite page.

Writing Quick Start

Write a paragraph telling your readers why the disaster occurred and what happened as a result of it. For the purpose of this activity, you should make up a plausible account of the event you see in the photograph.

WRITING A CAUSE-AND-EFFECT ESSAY

Your paragraph is an example of cause-and-effect writing. By describing why the disaster happened, you explained *causes*. By explaining what happened as a result of the disaster, you explained *effects*. This chapter will show you how to write strong causal analyses as well as how to incorporate cause and effect into essays using other patterns of development.

WHAT ARE CAUSES AND EFFECTS?

A **cause-and-effect essay,** also called a *causal analysis,* analyzes (1) *causes* (why an event or phenomenon happens), (2) *effects* (what happens because of the event or phenomenon), or (3) both causes and effects. The essay generally shows how one event or phenomenon brings about another: Losing your car keys (the *cause*) leads you to be late for class (the *effect*).

Almost everything you do has a cause and produces an effect. If you skip lunch because you need to study for a test, you feel hungry. If you drop a glass because it is slippery, it breaks. Young children attempting to discover and make sense of the complex world around them continually ask "Why?" Adults also think about and govern their lives in terms of causes and effects: "What would happen if I dropped a class or turned a paper in late?" or "Why did that happen?" (for example, "Why wouldn't my car start this morning?" or "Why does the wind pick up before a storm?"). Many academic disciplines also focus on why questions: Psychologists are concerned with *why* people behave as they do; biologists study *why* the human body functions and reacts as it does; historians consider *why* historical events occurred.

Many everyday occasions require you to use causal analyses. If your child is hurt in an accident, the doctor may ask you to describe the accident and its effects on your child. You will also find many occasions to use causal analysis in the writing you do in college and on the job (see the accompanying box for examples).

SCENES FROM COLLEGE AND THE WORKPLACE

- For an essay exam in your *twentieth-century history* course, you are required to discuss the causes of U.S. involvement in the Korean conflict.

- For a *health and nutrition* course, you decide to write a paper on the relationship between diet and heart disease.

- For your job as an *investment analyst,* you need to explain why a certain company is going to be profitable in the next year.

In the following essay, "Bad Conduct, by the Numbers," Jennifer Jacobson examines the effects of monitoring athletes' incidents of poor sportsmanship.

Bad Conduct, by the Numbers
Jennifer Jacobson

Jennifer Jacobson is a regular contributor to the Chronicle of Higher Education, *in which the following essay appeared in May 2004. As you read the selection, highlight and label the chain of effects that resulted from one college athletic conference's decision to monitor unsportsmanlike conduct among students who play soccer.*

Rudeness, taunting, and viciousness have become more prevalent 1 at all levels of athletics. Gyrating in the end zone after touchdowns, hanging onto the rim after slam dunks, yelling at referees, and intentionally fouling opponents are largely accepted as the norm in professional sports, and such behaviors are seeping into college athletics as well. In addition to the general incivility of poor sportsmanship, educators say athletes are losing sight of the ideals of athletics: fair play, honesty, and mutual respect. "We have an overemphasis of 'win at all costs' that begins at the peewee level," says Todd S. Hutton, president of Utica College. "We place so much emphasis on winning and not enough emphasis on sportsmanship. We're swimming against the tide here."

Utica's athletics conference, hardly immune to these problems, 2 is taking steps to fix them. Having seen promising early results, it is trying to spread its program to the rest of Division III of the National Collegiate Athletic Association and, possibly, the rest of college sports. The Empire 8 Conference, a group of small colleges in upstate New York, monitors unsportsmanlike conduct among its athletes and coaches by tracking the personal-conduct fouls they commit during each game and reporting the numbers to college officials. "Sportsmanship is an important value of our membership," says Chuck Mitrano, commissioner of the conference, who came up with the idea. Tracking fouls is "something we felt we needed to do."

After Mr. Mitrano took office in August 2001, he noticed athletes 3 questioning officials' calls and using vulgar language. So he proposed to the conference's presidents, athletics directors, and coaches that teams record each time a player received a personal-conduct foul—yellow and red cards in soccer and lacrosse, for example—and send him the information within two business days. By tracking fouls, athletics directors, coaches, and presidents are more aware of such violations and are talking to athletes about their behavior in an effort to head off problems before they start, Mr. Mitrano says.

TRACKING RED CARDS

4   The conference started tracking red cards in men's and women's soccer in the fall of 2002, and in the fall of 2003 began to track all personal-conduct fouls for the sports that recognize them — basketball, soccer, field hockey, football, lacrosse, and volleyball. In August 2003, the conference also decided that if athletes or coaches were ejected from a game, they would have to sit out the next one, and that Mr. Mitrano would notify the president of that player's or coach's college of the violation. "Student-athletes, coaches, and athletic teams in general, they're representing the institution," he says. "Anytime anyone's ejected from a contest, that's obviously not the best representation," and presidents "want to be aware of it as soon as possible."

5   The emphasis on sportsmanship appears to have paid off: Most Empire 8 teams have reduced their personal-conduct fouls over the past couple of years. For instance, men's basketball teams, including coaches, received 37 technical fouls in the 2002–3 academic year and 23 in 2003–4, while women's basketball squads received 8 technical fouls in 2002–3 and 4 in 2003–4. Men's soccer teams received 103 yellow cards and 5 red cards in 2002; in 2003, the totals fell to 86 and 4, respectively. But the numbers for women's soccer teams increased, from 10 yellow and no red cards in 2002 to 16 yellow and 2 red in 2003. Mr. Mitrano notes that only two of the yellow cards handed out to the women's teams in 2003 were awarded for specifically unsportsmanlike conduct, and that the two red cards were given to players who had touched the ball with their hands near the goal, an automatic penalty.

6   "Because of the success we had in our program and casual conversations with colleagues, I felt our program would be good to bring to the entire division," the commissioner says. So, after getting an $11,000 grant from the NCAA, he asked conference commissioners in all of Division III last summer to begin tracking their athletes' personal-conduct fouls and submit the totals to him. He told them that he would keep information about individual institutions confidential.

7   Of the 26 Division III conferences with football teams, 21 responded to Mr. Mitrano's request, as did 33 of the 37 conferences with men's soccer teams and 34 of the 39 conferences with women's soccer teams. He found that football players in the Empire 8 committed 48 personal-conduct penalties, while other conferences' players committed as few as 21 and as many as 190. Among men's soccer

teams in Division III, the Empire 8 had the third-fewest number of yellow cards and the second-fewest number of red cards. Among women's soccer teams, the conference compiled the seventh-fewest number of yellow cards.

"Clearly in Division III we are not immune to sportsmanship concerns," says Daniel C. Dutcher, Division III's chief of staff, even though member-college officials may sometimes think they are immune because in the small colleges of Division III, "transgressions may not receive as much attention as in other divisions," he says.

8

Mr. Dutcher says he cannot know for sure whether good sportsmanship is on the decline in the division, and he applauds the commissioner's attempts to find out. "Without data, we really don't know," he says. "It's all kind of anecdotal. One of the important things that Chuck's program does is help us to start establishing a baseline."

9

As successful as the Empire 8's program may be, no one is calling it a panacea. During a February men's basketball game between Nazareth College of Rochester and St. John Fisher College, one player threw a punch at an opponent, prompting a bench-clearing brawl. A handful of players were suspended from subsequent games and required by their colleges to perform community service.

10

"One of the things you're trying to instill in Division III is life skills," says Mike Daley, head basketball coach at Nazareth. The idea, he says, is to "teach young men how to deal with adversity as well as success, the calls you may not agree with, the contact that takes place."

11

"If you have an argument with your boss, are you going to reach across the desk and pop him?" he says. Teaching students how to handle stress in the right way is not new, says Mr. Daley, who has coached at Nazareth for 18 years. But the lesson has become harder for students to learn as professional athletes continue to get away with foul language and taunting. "Kids are seeing this and get the impression that is what you have to do to get an edge on your opponent," the coach says. Seeing coaches and professional athletes behave badly during games—not just intentionally fouling opponents but challenging referees and trash-talking—sends the wrong message, he says.

12

Mike DeBlois, a sophomore and reserve guard for Nazareth, agrees that professional athletes sometimes set bad examples. He remembers seeing Joe Horn, a receiver for the NFL's New Orleans Saints, retrieve a hidden cellphone in the end zone and pretend to make a call after scoring a touchdown in a game last season.

13

"People need to realize it's a game," says Mr. DeBlois. "To compete as hard as they can but in a friendly way." ∎

14

Characteristics of Cause-and-Effect Essays

As you can see from Jacobson's essay on monitoring unsportsmanlike behavior, a causal analysis has a clear purpose: to explain causes or effects or both. In addition, a cause-and-effect essay includes a thesis, follows a logical organizational plan, develops each cause or effect fully, and may recognize or dispel readers' assumptions about the topic.

Causal Analysis Focuses on Causes, Effects, or Both

In deciding whether to consider causes, effects, or both, it is important to distinguish the causes from the effects. Some are relatively easy to identify.

Cause	*Effect*
You get a flat tire. ⟶	You are late for work.
You forget to mail a loan payment. ⟶	You receive a past-due notification.
There is a power failure. ⟶	You lose changes made to a computer file.

In complex situations, however, the causes and effects are less clear, and causes may not always be clearly separable from effects. For example, some people have an obsession with dieting (*effect*) because they have a poor body image (*cause*). Yet an obsession with dieting (*cause*) can lead to a poor body image (*effect*).

To identify causes and effects, think of causes as the *reasons that something happened* and effects as the *results of the thing that happened*.

Cause	*Effect*
Event *X* happened because . . . ◀——EVENT *X*——▶	The result of event *X* was . . .

EXERCISE 15.1

Working either alone or with a classmate, list one or more possible causes for each of the following events or phenomena.

1. You observe a peacock strutting down a city street.
2. You are notified by the airline that the flight you had planned to take tonight has been canceled.
3. Your phone frequently rings once and then stops ringing.
4. Your town decides to fund a new public park.
5. Your best friend keeps saying, "I'm too busy to get together with you."

EXERCISE 15.2

Working either alone or with a classmate, list one or more possible effects for each of the following events.

1. You leave your backpack containing your wallet on the bus.
2. You decide to change your major.
3. Your spouse is offered a job in a city five hundred miles away from where you live now.
4. You volunteer as a Big Brother or Big Sister.
5. A close relative becomes very ill.

Multiple causes and effects.   Causal analysis can be complex when it deals with an event or phenomenon that has multiple causes, effects, or both.

1. Several causes may produce a single effect. For example, you probably chose the college you attend now (*one effect*) for a number of reasons, including the availability of courses in your major, the cost of tuition, the reputation of the school, and its distance from your home (*multiple causes*).

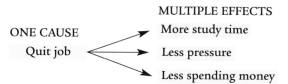

MULTIPLE CAUSES

Courses available
Cost
Reputation
Distance

ONE EFFECT
College attended

2. One cause may have several effects. For instance, your decision to quit your part-time job (*one cause*) will result in more study time, less pressure, and less spending money (*multiple effects*).

MULTIPLE EFFECTS

ONE CAUSE
Quit job

More study time
Less pressure
Less spending money

3. Related events or phenomena may have both multiple causes and multiple effects. For instance, an increase in the number of police officers patrolling the street in urban areas along with the formation of citizen watch groups (*multiple causes*) will result in less street crime and more small businesses (*multiple effects*).

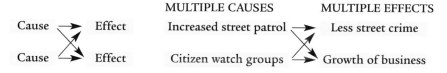

MULTIPLE CAUSES   MULTIPLE EFFECTS

Cause → Effect

Cause → Effect

Increased street patrol → Less street crime

Citizen watch groups → Growth of business

Chains of events.   In some cases a series of events forms a chain in which each event is both the effect of what happened before it and the cause of the next event. In other words, a simple event can produce a chain of consequences.

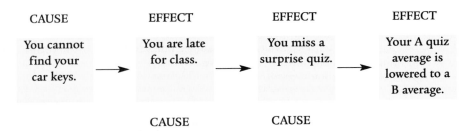

Once you clearly separate causes and effects, you can decide whether to focus on causes, effects, or both.

Causal Analysis Has a Clear Purpose

A cause-and-effect essay may be expressive, but more often it is informative, persuasive, or both. In an essay about the effects of the death of a close relative, for example, you would express your feelings about the person by showing how the loss affected you. An essay describing the sources (*causes*) of the pollution of a local river could be primarily informative, or it could be informative and persuasive if it also discussed the positive results (*effects*) of enforcing antipollution laws.

Some cause-and-effect essays have more than one purpose. For example, an essay may examine the causes of academic cheating (informative) and propose policies that could help alleviate the problem (persuasive). In "Bad Conduct, by the Numbers," Jacobson aims to inform readers about the effects of monitoring and reporting unsportsmanlike conduct as well as to suggest that unsportsmanlike behavior diminishes the benefits that players and fans derive from sports (para. 1).

EXERCISE 15.3

In a small group or with a classmate as a partner, choose two topics from the following list. Then, for each topic, consider how you would write a causal analysis with (a) an informative purpose and (b) a persuasive purpose.

1. Changes in airline safety standards
2. Rapid changes in computer hardware
3. Sexual harassment in the workplace
4. The popularity of health clubs and fitness centers
5. The increasing number of unsolicited Internet advertisements

---

Causal Analysis Includes a Clear Thesis Statement

Most cause-and-effect essays have a clear thesis statement that identifies the topic, makes an assertion about that topic, and suggests whether the essay focuses on causes, effects, or both. In "Bad Conduct, by the Numbers," Jacobson makes it clear to readers that her focus is unsportsmanlike conduct. The writer also makes an assertion about her topic: "By tracking fouls, athletics directors, coaches, and presidents are more aware of such violations and are talking to athletes about their behavior in an effort to head off problems before they start" (para. 3).

The following sample thesis statements show two other ways of approaching an essay about unsportsmanlike conduct. One emphasizes causes, the other emphasizes causes and effects, and both make assertions about the topic.

CAUSES	The root causes of unsportsmanlike behavior lie in how society regards athletes, elevating them to positions of fame and heroism and thereby making them unaccountable for their behavior.
CAUSES AND EFFECTS	Unsportsmanlike behavior has numerous deep-rooted causes, and regardless of its origin, it produces negative effects on fans, other players, and the institutions they represent.

Causal Analysis Follows a Logical Organization

A cause-and-effect essay is organized logically and systematically. It may present causes or effects in chronological order—the order in which they happened. In "Bad Conduct, by the Numbers," Jacobson uses chronological order, beginning with the Empire 8 Conference's decision to monitor bad conduct in men's and women's soccer, the extension of this policy to all sports, and the extension of the policy to the entire division. Alternatively, a most-to-least or least-to-most order may be used to sequence the causes or effects according to their importance. An essay about increased immigration to the United States might begin with the most important causes and progress to lesser ones.

Causal Analysis Explains Each Cause or Effect Fully

A causal analysis essay presents each cause or effect in a detailed and understandable way. Examples, facts, descriptions, comparisons, statistics, and anecdotes may be used to explain causes or effects. Jacobson uses several of these elements to make her essay interesting and understandable. She uses examples to demonstrate unsportsmanlike behavior: players "gyrating in the end zone" and "yelling at referees" (para. 1). She uses statistics to report the success of the monitoring program (paras. 5 and 7) and includes a brief anecdote about a player who made a cell-phone call from the end zone after a touchdown (para. 13).

For most cause-and-effect essays, you will need to research your topic to locate evidence that supports your thesis. In an essay about the effects on children of viewing violence on television, for instance, you might need to locate research or statistics that document changes in children's behavior after watching violent programs. In addition to statistical data, expert opinion is often used as evidence. For example, in "Bad Conduct, by the Numbers," Jacobson includes the expert opinion of the president of Utica College to suggest that winning is being overemphasized and a quotation from the head basketball coach of Nazareth College to emphasize the value of stress management.

Causal Analysis May Affirm or Dispel Readers' Assumptions

Some cause-and-effect essays affirm or dispel popular ideas that readers may assume to be true. An essay on the effects of capital punishment might attempt to dispel the notion that it is a deterrent to crime. Similarly, in "Bad Conduct, by the Numbers," Jacobson begins by criticizing the currently popular notion that it is important to "win at all costs."

Dealing with the causes or effects that readers assume to be primary is an effective strategy, whether the purpose of the essay is informative or persuasive. In an informative essay, you create a sense of completeness or the impression that nothing has been overlooked. In a persuasive essay, you assure readers that other viewpoints have been recognized.

Visualizing Cause-and-Effect Essays: Three Graphic Organizers

For more on graphic organizers, see Chapter 2, p. 34.

The graphic organizers in Figures 15.1 through 15.3 show the basic organization of three types of causal-analysis essays. Figure 15.1 shows the organization of an

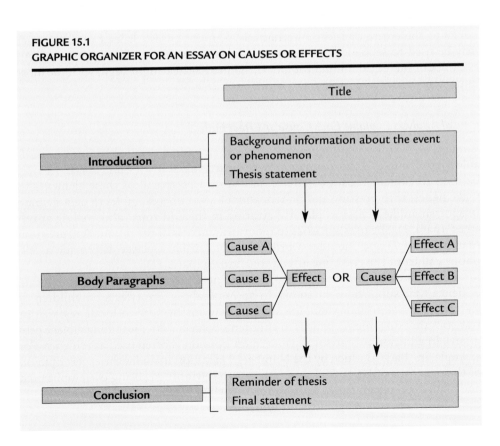

FIGURE 15.1
GRAPHIC ORGANIZER FOR AN ESSAY ON CAUSES OR EFFECTS

essay that examines either causes *or* effects. Figure 15.2 shows the organization of an essay that examines a chain of causes and effects, while Figure 15.3 shows two possible arrangements for an essay that focuses on multiple causes and effects. All three types of causal analyses include an introduction (which identifies the event, provides background information, and states a thesis) as well as a conclusion. Notice in Figures 15.2 and 15.3 that causes are presented before effects. Although this is the typical arrangement, writers sometimes reverse it by discussing effects first and then causes to create a sense of drama or surprise.

When you incorporate causes, effects, or both into an essay that is not primarily a causal analysis, you can adapt one of these organizational plans to suit your purpose.

FIGURE 15.2
GRAPHIC ORGANIZER FOR AN ESSAY ON A CHAIN OF CAUSES AND EFFECTS

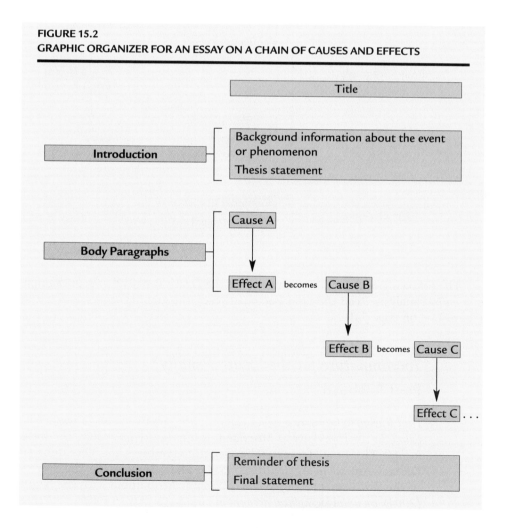

FIGURE 15.3
GRAPHIC ORGANIZER FOR AN ESSAY ON MULTIPLE CAUSES AND EFFECTS

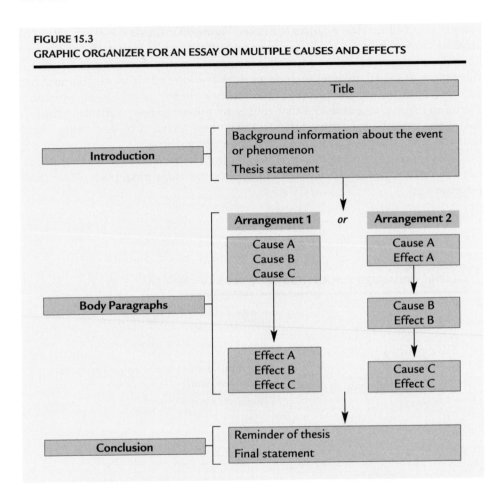

The following essay — "Too Immature for the Death Penalty?" — is an example of a causal analysis. Read the essay and then study the graphic organizer for it in Figure 15.4 on page 521.

Too Immature for the Death Penalty?
Paul Raeburn

Paul Raeburn, formerly a senior editor at BusinessWeek *and a journalism fellow at the University of Maryland, is a freelance journalist. His books include* The Last Harvest: The Genetic Gamble That Threatens to Destroy American Agriculture *(1996),* Mars: Uncovering the Secrets of the Red Planet *(2000), and most recently* Acquainted with the Night *(2004), an autobiographical account of his struggle with his children's depres-*

sion and bipolar disorder. As you read, highlight the multiple biological reasons Raeburn cites in his argument that adolescents are less able than adults to control their behavior.

Just after 2 a.m. on Sept. 9, 1993, Christopher Simmons, 17, and   1
Charles Benjamin, 15, broke into a trailer south of Fenton, Mo., just outside St. Louis. They woke Shirley Ann Crook, a 46-year-old truck driver who was inside, and proceeded to tie her up and cover her eyes and mouth with silver duct tape. They then put her in the back of her minivan, drove her to a railroad bridge and pushed her into the river below, where her body was found the next day. Simmons and Benjamin later confessed to the abduction and murder, which had netted them $6. Police called it "a cheap price for a life."

The two were convicted. Benjamin was sentenced to life in prison,   2
and Simmons was given the death penalty. The Missouri Supreme Court overturned Simmons's sentence last year, and the case is now before the U.S. Supreme Court, which recently heard arguments on the constitutionality of the death penalty for those who are 16 or 17 when they commit their crimes. (The court has already ruled against execution of anyone under 16.)

Unlike other death-penalty cases, this one has drawn intense   3
interest from the American Medical Association, the nation's psychiatrists and psychologists and other health and research groups. They've filed briefs with the court making a novel scientific argument—that juveniles should not be executed because their brains are still developing. In other words, teenagers cannot be held fully responsible for their actions because all the wiring to allow adult decision making isn't completed yet. As Stephen K. Harper, a professor of juvenile justice at the University of Miami School of Law, puts it, "Adolescents are far less culpable than we knew."

The briefs in the Simmons case are based on research that shows   4
that the human brain, once thought to be fully wired by about age 12, continues to grow and mature into the early or mid-20's. And the last part to mature is the frontal lobes, or prefrontal cortex, responsible for all the hallmarks of adult behavior—impulse control, the regulation of emotions, and moral reasoning. "Scientists can now demonstrate that adolescents are immature not only to the observer's naked eye but in the very fibers of their brains," says the brief by the A.M.A. and the psychiatrists. "Normal adolescents cannot be expected to operate with the level of maturity, judgment, risk aversion or impulse control of an adult."

Parents of teenagers might greet this news by asking what,   5
exactly, we are paying our scientists to do. We don't need a neuroscientist to tell us that adolescents sometimes make dumb decisions.

That has been clear since the first protohuman teen defied his parents' orders to get back to the cave before dark. The question is: Why do they act that way?

6   "The old idea was that adolescence was a social phenomenon, not biological," says Dr. Jay Giedd, a psychiatrist and the chief of brain imaging in the child psychiatry branch at the National Institute of Mental Health. Teenage turmoils were thought to be shaped by the instruction we received from parents and peers in the arts of growing up. Giedd was one of the first to provide a visual demonstration that "maybe it's not social, maybe there is actual biology to explain why a lot of cultures have put age limits on things." He made images of children's and teenagers' brains with an M.R.I. scanner, repeating the scans every two years for more than a decade, to see how the brain changed. The images showed that the brain continues to develop until the mid-20's, and it does so in an unexpected way.

7   The amount of gray matter—made up of brain cells and their connections—increases until the brain has more than it needs. This occurs in different parts of the brain at different ages; in the frontal lobes, the growth continues until about age 11 in girls and 12½ in boys. Then the brain begins to "prune" that excess gray matter, severing some of the connections. At the same time, it reinforces other connections, wrapping them with white matter, a heavier layer of insulation also known as myelin. This pruning and reinforcement represents the maturing of the brain. The process continues into the mid-20's.

8   All the while, the brain is adapting to its environment. A teenager who studies the piano, for example, will strengthen connections in the auditory part of the brain. Another who studies drawing will do the same in the visual cortex. And all of us who fail to learn a foreign language before our early teenage years will prune the connections we used to learn our own language—and condemn ourselves to years of struggling with French verbs.

9   Nobody is arguing that teenagers deserve a pass; the new brain science is not a get-out-of-jail-free card. Sometimes adolescents do appear to act like adults—but the point is that they can't do so consistently. And even when they seem to be acting like adults, they are using their brains in a different way. Adolescents, unlike adults, often operate from a more instinctual, reflexive part of the brain.

10   Abigail Baird, a developmental neuroscientist at Dartmouth, asked teenagers ages 12 to 18 to identify emotions on faces in photographs. She monitored their brains with a functional M.R.I. scanner, which shows which parts are active during a specific task. When adults see faces, the amygdala kicks in to say "this is something important." Then the frontal lobes make an assessment, check with

memory and other parts of the brain and coordinate a response ("It's my wife and she doesn't look happy. Better run out for flowers"). Almost all the time, adults get the emotions right.

When Baird scanned teenagers, however, she found that they often misidentified the emotions in the pictures. When shown a face expressing fear, for example, they would identify it as surprise, or even happiness. "The finding was that the alarm system — the amygdala — was ready to go," she said. "But the interpreter — the prefrontal cortex — doesn't care, and they don't seem to be able to make it care." The amygdala zeroed in on the faces as something important, but the frontal lobes couldn't focus enough to get the identification right.

Teenagers in stressful situations — under the influence of peer pressure or, like Simmons and Benjamin, in the midst of committing a burglary — are not going to act like adults. Their brains can't handle it. Beatriz Luna, a neuroscientist at the University of Pittsburgh, has compared the brains of adults and teenagers doing a task in which they must resist the instinctive tendency to gaze at a dot of light on a computer screen. As in Baird's experiments, adults recruit various parts of the brain to help. But teenagers don't seem to do that. "It takes them an extreme effort," says Luna. "When everything is perfect, they can act like adults. But you add a little bit of stress, and that can break down."

The lesson applies widely. "This is why kids who are good kids, who know right from wrong, sometimes do stupid things," says Dr. David Fassler, a psychiatrist in Burlington, Vt., and a spokesman for the American Psychiatric Association on this issue. "They act on impulse." How, then, do most teenagers survive adolescence without harming themselves or winding up in jail? Good parenting is one reason, Baird says. "The people around you are like an external frontal cortex," she says.

None of this means that Simmons should be absolved of his repugnant crime on the grounds that his amygdala made him do it. The question is whether he, and others who are 16 or 17 when they commit their crimes, should be held to the same standard as adults. "There's no question that the new science is changing the debate," says Laurence Steinberg, a psychologist at Temple University and the director of the MacArthur Foundation Research Network on Adolescent Development and Juvenile Justice. In 2002, the Supreme Court ruled that mentally retarded criminals are exempt from the death penalty because of "disabilities in areas of reasoning, judgment and control of their impulses." The scientific evidence suggests that 16- and 17-year olds share similar "disabilities" in reasoning and judgment.

15   The Missouri attorney general, in his petition to the Supreme Court, argues that the court should not ban the juvenile death penalty until there is a national consensus supporting a ban. A consensus may be forming—seven states, not counting Missouri, have eliminated the juvenile death penalty since 1989, some by getting rid of executions altogether. So has the federal government. But 19 states still allow such executions.

16   In an interview with the *St. Louis Post-Dispatch* two years ago, Simmons, then 26, said he broke into Crook's house to get money for drugs. How did that lead to murder? "I ask myself why, and I don't understand why," he said. "We just lost all sense of stealing things."

17   Was Simmons thinking and acting like an adult when he murdered Shirley Ann Crook? That's a question science can't answer. As the A.M.A. and the psychiatrists write in their brief, scientists can "shed light on certain measurable attributes" related to teenagers' culpability. But "science cannot, of course, gauge moral culpability." That is what the Supreme Court must do. ■

EXERCISE 15.4

To draw detailed graphic organizers using a computer, visit www .bedfordstmartins.com /successfulwriting.

Draw a graphic organizer for "Bad Conduct, by the Numbers" on page 507.

INTEGRATING CAUSE AND EFFECT INTO AN ESSAY

While some essays you write will focus solely on causal analysis, other essays will include cause and effect with other patterns. In an essay comparing two popular magazines that have different journalistic styles, for example, you might explain the effects of each style on readers' attitudes.

Use the following tips to integrate causal analyses into essays that rely on other patterns of development.

1. **Use transitions to announce shifts to a causal explanation.** If your readers do not expect a causal explanation, launching into consideration of causes or effects without a transition may confuse them or cause them to misinterpret your message. In writing about your college president's decision to expand the Career Planning Center, for example, you might introduce your discussion of causes by writing "The three primary factors responsible for her decision are. . . ."

2. **Keep the causal explanation direct and simple.** Since your overall purpose is not to explore causal relationships, an in-depth analysis of causes and

FIGURE 15.4
GRAPHIC ORGANIZER FOR "TOO IMMATURE FOR THE DEATH PENALTY?"

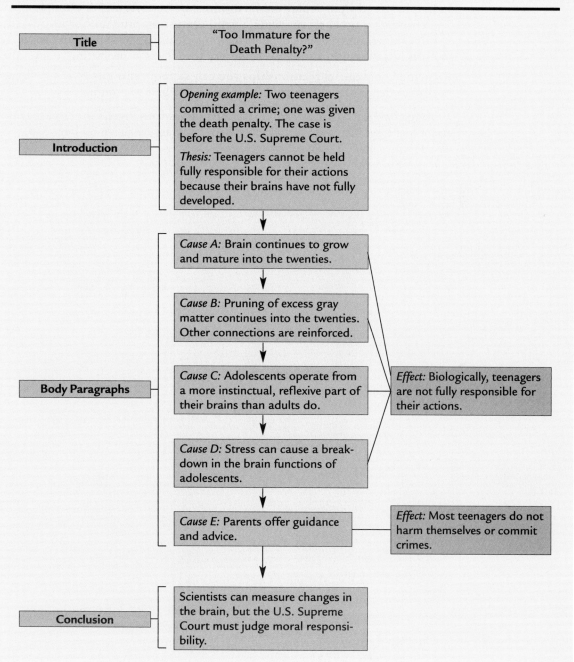

effects will distract your readers from your main point. Therefore, focus on the most important causes and effects.

3. **Emphasize why particular points or ideas are important.** For example, if you are writing a tip sheet on using a word-processing program for an audience of beginners and include an instruction that users should save material frequently, you should warn your readers of the effects of neglecting to save copy.

4. **Include only causal relationships you can support and justify.** If you do not have evidence to support a cause or effect, it is best to omit it.

To read an essay that integrates causal analysis with several other patterns of development, see "Hitting the 'Granite Wall'" by Gary M. Stern on page 545.

A GUIDED WRITING ASSIGNMENT

The following guide will lead you through the process of writing a cause-and-effect essay. Although you will focus primarily on causal analysis, you will probably need to integrate one or more other patterns of development in your essay. Depending on your learning style, you may work through this assignment in different ways. This Guided Writing Assignment will provide you with alternatives.

The Assignment

Write a cause-and-effect essay on one of the following topics or one that you choose on your own. Your essay may consider causes, effects, or both. Your audience consists of your classmates or members of the community in which you live.

1. The popularity (or lack of popularity) of a public figure
2. Cheating on college exams
3. Rising college costs
4. A current trend or fad
5. A major change or decision in your life
6. A problem on campus or in the community
7. A major national or international event

As you develop your causal-analysis essay, consider how you can use one or more other patterns of development. For example, you might use narration to help explain the effects of a particular community problem. In an essay about the causes of a current fad, you might compare the fad to one that is obsolete. Or you might classify rising college costs in an essay covering the causes and effects of that phenomenon.

For more on narration, see Chapter 8. For more on comparison and contrast, see Chapter 12. For more on classification, see Chapter 13.

Generating Ideas

When selecting an event or phenomenon to write about, be sure to choose one with which you are familiar or about which you can find information in the library or on the Internet.

Considering Your Purpose, Audience, and Point of View

For more on purpose, audience, and point of view, see Chapter 3, p. 65.

Once you choose a topic, your next step is to decide whether you want your essay to be informative, persuasive, or a mixture of both. Depending on your purpose, you may decide to explain why something occurred (*causes*), what happened as a result of an occurrence (*effects*), or both. Keep the length of your essay in mind as you think about these issues. It would be unrealistic, for example, to try to discuss both the causes and effects of child abuse in a five-page paper.

As you generate ideas, keep your audience in mind as well. For this Guided Writing Assignment, your audience consists of your classmates or members of your community. If they are unfamiliar with the topic you are writing about or if your topic is complex, consider limiting your essay to primary causes or effects (those that are obvious and easily understood). If your audience is generally familiar with your topic, then you can deal with secondary causes or effects.

The level of technical detail you include should also be determined by your audience. Suppose you are writing to explain the climatic conditions that cause hurricanes and your audience is your classmates. For this audience, you would provide far fewer technical details than you would for an audience of environmental science majors.

The point of view you choose should suit your audience and purpose. Although academic writing usually uses the third person, the first person may be used to relate relevant personal experiences.

Discovering Causes and Effects

For more on prewriting strategies, see Chapter 3.

After considering your purpose, audience, and point of view, use the following suggestions to help you discover causes, effects, or both.

Learning Style Options

1. Write your topic in the middle of the page or at the top of your computer screen. Brainstorm all possible causes and effects, writing causes on the left and effects on the right.

2. Replay the event in your mind. Ask yourself, "Why did the event happen?" and "What happened as a result of it?" Make notes on the answers.

3. Try asking questions and writing assertions about the problem or phenomenon. Did a chain of events cause the phenomenon? What effects are not obvious?

4. Discuss your topic with a classmate or friend. Ask his or her opinion on the topic's causes, effects, or both.

5. Research your topic in the library or on the Internet. You might begin by entering a keyword about the topic into an Internet search engine. Make notes on possible causes and effects or print out copies of the relevant Web pages you discover.

For more on library and Internet research, see Chapter 19.

6. Ask a friend or classmate to interview you about your topic. Try to explain causes, effects, or both as clearly as possible.

ESSAY IN PROGRESS 1

For the assignment option you chose on page 523 or on your own, use the preceding suggestions to generate a list of causes, effects, or both for your topic.

Identifying Primary Causes and Effects

Once you have a list of causes or effects (or both), your next task is to sort through them and decide which causes or effects are *primary,* or most important. For example, if your topic is the possible effects of television violence on young viewers, two primary effects might be an increase in aggressive behavior and a willingness to accept violence as normal. Less important, or *secondary,* effects might include learning inappropriate or offensive words. In essays about controversial issues, primary causes or effects may differ depending on the writer.

Use the following questions to help you decide which causes and effects are most important.

Causes

What are the most obvious and immediate causes?
What cause(s), if eliminated, would drastically change the event, problem, or phenomenon?

Effects

What are the obvious effects of the event, problem, or phenomenon?
Which effects have the most serious consequences? For whom?

ESSAY IN PROGRESS 2

Review the list you prepared in Essay in Progress 1. Separate primary causes and primary effects from secondary ones.

Checking for Hidden Causes, Effects, and Errors in Reasoning

Once you identify primary and secondary causes and effects, examine them to be sure you have not overlooked any causes and effects and have avoided common reasoning errors.

Hidden causes and effects.   Be on the alert for the hidden causes or effects that may underlie a causal relationship. For example, if a child often reports to the nurse's office complaining of a stomachache, a parent may reason that the child has digestive problems. However, a closer study of the behavior may reveal that the stomachaches are the result of stress and anxiety. To avoid overlooking hidden causes or effects, be sure to examine a causal relationship closely. Do not assume the most obvious or simplest explanation is the only one.

Mistaking chronology for causation.   Avoid the *post hoc, ergo propter hoc* ("after this, therefore because of this") fallacy—the assumption that because event *B* followed event *A* in time, *A* caused *B* to occur. For example, suppose you decide against having a cup of coffee one morning, and later the same day you score higher than ever before on a political science exam. Although one event followed the other in time, you cannot assume that reducing your coffee intake caused the high grade.

To avoid the *post hoc* fallacy, look for evidence that one event did indeed cause the other. Plausible evidence might include testimony from others who experienced the same sequence of events or documentation proving a causal relationship between the events.

Mistaking correlation for causation.   Just because two events occur at about the same time does not mean they are causally related. For example, suppose sales of snow shovels in a city increased at the same time sales of gloves and mittens increased. The fact that the two events occurred simultaneously does not mean that snow shoveling causes people to buy more mittens and gloves. Most likely, a period of cold, snowy weather caused the increased sales of these items. Again, remember that evidence is needed to verify that the two events are related and that a causal relationship exists.

Unsupported assumptions.   Assumptions are ideas or generalizations that you or your readers accept as truths without questioning their validity. Although assumptions can be true, in many cases people make sweeping generalizations that are untrue. For instance, it is untrue to say that all senior citizens are nonproductive members of society because the evidence suggests that many seniors continue to work or contribute to their communities in other ways. Many assumptions are based on *stereotypes* — generalizations about the characteristics or behaviors of an entire group of people or things based on the characteristics or behavior of some members of the group. Because unsupported assumptions can interfere with your reasoning and lead to erroneous statements of cause and effect, examine your ideas carefully to be sure you avoid making this error.

For more on errors in reasoning, see Chapter 16, p. 573.

Gathering Evidence

A convincing cause-and-effect essay must give a complete explanation of each primary cause or effect that you include. To explain your causes and effects, you'll probably use one or more other patterns of development. For example, you may need to narrate events, present descriptive details, define important terms, explain processes unfamiliar to the reader, include examples that illustrate a cause or an effect, or make comparisons to explain unfamiliar concepts.

At this point, it is a good idea to do some additional prewriting to gather evidence to support your causes, effects, or both. You may also want to search on the Web to obtain more specific information or pay a visit to your college library. Whatever approach you take, try to discover several types of evidence, including facts, expert opinion, personal observation, quotations, and statistics.

Developing Your Thesis

Once you are satisfied with your causes and effects and the evidence you have generated to support them, your next step is to develop a working thesis. As noted earlier, the thesis for a causal analysis identifies the topic, makes an assertion about the topic, and tells whether the essay focuses on causes, effects, or both.

For more on thesis statements, see Chapter 4, p. 89.

Use the following tips to write a clear thesis statement.

1. State the cause-and-effect relationship. Do not leave it to your reader to figure out the causal relationship. In the following example, note that the original thesis is weak and vague, whereas the revision clearly states the causal relationship.

▶ Breathing paint fumes in a closed environment can be dangerous./~~People~~ *for people*
because their lungs are especially sensitive to irritants.
suffering from asthma and emphysema ~~are particularly vulnerable.~~

The revised thesis makes the cause-and-effect connection explicit by using the word *because* and by including necessary information about the problem.

2. Avoid overly broad or absolute assertions. They are difficult or impossible to support.

a major
▶ Drugs are ~~the root~~ cause of inner-city crime.

The revised thesis acknowledges drugs as one cause of crime but does not claim that drugs are the only cause.

3. Use qualifying words. Unless a cause-and-effect relationship is well established and accepted, qualify your thesis statement.

may be
▶ Overemphasizing competitive sports is harmful to the psychological development of young children.

Changing the verb from *is* to *may be* qualifies the statement, allowing room for doubt.

4. Avoid an overly assertive or a dogmatic tone. The tone of your essay, including your thesis, should be confident but not overbearing.

Substantial evidence suggests
▶ ~~There is no question~~ that American youths have changed in response to the culture in which they live.

The phrase *Substantial evidence suggests* creates a less dogmatic tone than *There is no question.*

ESSAY IN PROGRESS 3

Using the preceding guidelines, study your list of causes, effects, or both; gather evidence; and develop a working thesis for your essay.

Evaluating Your Ideas and Thesis

Take a few minutes to evaluate the causal relationship you have chosen and determine whether your analysis of the relationship is meaningful, worthwhile, and relevant to your audience. Start by rereading everything you have written with a critical eye. Highlight causes, effects, and evidence that seem usable; cross out items that are unnecessary or repetitious or that don't support your thesis. If you are working on a computer, highlight useful material in bold type or move it to a separate file. If you find that your evidence is skimpy, do additional research or prewriting to generate more information. Also think about how you can use other patterns of development (such as comparison or illustration) to further support your thesis.

TRYING OUT YOUR IDEAS ON OTHERS

Working in a group of two or three students, discuss your ideas and thesis for this chapter's assignment. Each writer should describe his or her topic (the event, problem, or phenomenon), thesis, causes or effects (or both), and supporting evidence. Then, as a group, evaluate each writer's work and causal analysis, pointing out any errors in reasoning and suggesting additional causes, effects, or evidence.

ESSAY IN PROGRESS 4

Using the preceding suggestions and your classmates' comments, evaluate your thesis and the evidence you have gathered to support it. Refer to the characteristics of cause-and-effect essays discussed on pages 510–14 to help you with this step.

Organizing and Drafting

Once you have evaluated your cause-and-effect relationship and thesis and considered the advice of your classmates, you are ready to organize your ideas and draft your essay.

For more on drafting an essay, see Chapter 5.

Choosing a Method of Organization

Review Figures 15.1, 15.2, and 15.3 to find the graphic organizer that is closest to your essay's basic structure. Then choose a method of organization that will help you present your ideas effectively. Chronological order works well when there is a clear sequence of events. In explaining why an entrepreneur was successful in opening a small business, for example, you might trace the causes in the order they occurred. However, if a key decision was crucial to the entrepreneur's success (such as the decision to advertise on a local television station), you might decide to focus on that cause first. In this case, the causes would be arranged from most to least important. Use a word-processing program to experiment with different methods of organizing your ideas.

Drafting the Cause-and-Effect Essay

After deciding how to organize the essay, your next step is to write a first draft. Use the following guidelines to draft your essay.

1. **Provide well-developed explanations.** Be sure that you provide sufficient evidence that the causal relationship exists. Offer a number of reasons and choose a variety of types of evidence (examples, statistics, expert opinion, and so on) to demonstrate that you correctly perceived the relationship between causes and effects. Try to develop each cause or effect into a detailed paragraph with a clear topic sentence.

2. **Use strong transitions.** Use a transition each time you move from an explanation of one cause or effect to an explanation of another. When you move from discussing causes to discussing effects (or vice versa) or when you shift to a different pattern of development, use strong transitional sentences to alert your reader to the shift. Transitional words and phrases that are useful in cause-and-effect essays include *because, since, as a result,* and *therefore.*

3. **Avoid overstating causal relationships.** When writing about causes and effects, avoid words and phrases that overstate the causal relationship, such as *it is obvious, without doubt, always,* and *never.* These words and phrases wrongly suggest that a causal relationship is absolute and without exception. Instead, use words and phrases that qualify, such as *it is possible, it is likely,* and *most likely.*

4. **Write an effective introduction.** Your introduction should identify the topic and causal relationship as well as draw your reader into the essay.

5. **Write a satisfying conclusion.** Your conclusion may remind readers of your thesis and should draw your essay to a satisfying close.

For more on transitions, see Chapter 5, p. 128.

For more on writing effective paragraphs, including introductions and conclusions, see Chapter 5.

ESSAY IN PROGRESS 5

Draft your cause-and-effect essay, using an appropriate method of organization and the preceding guidelines for drafting.

Analyzing and Revising

If possible, set your draft aside for a day or two before rereading and revising it. As you review your draft, concentrate on how you organize and present your ideas, not on grammar, punctuation, or mechanics. Use one or more of the following suggestions to analyze your draft.

Learning Style Options

1. Reread your essay aloud or ask a friend to do so as you listen. You may "hear" sections that are unclear or that require more evidence.

2. Draw a graphic organizer or update the one you drew earlier, using Figure 15.1, 15.2, or 15.3 as a model. Then study the visual organization of your ideas. Do they proceed logically? Do you see a way to organize your ideas more effectively for your readers? As an alternative, outline your essay or update an outline you made earlier to analyze your essay's structure.

3. Evaluate a chain of events essay by visualizing each step in the chain (review Figure 15.2). Does each effect become the next cause? Follow the chain exactly to identify any sections that are unclear.

Regardless of the technique you use, look for unsupported assumptions, errors in reasoning, and primary or hidden causes or effects you may have overlooked.

Use Figure 15.5 to guide your analysis of the strengths and weaknesses of your draft. You might also ask a classmate to read your paper and then summarize the primary causes, effects, or both that your paper discusses. If he or she misses or misinterprets any causes or effects, focus your revision on strengthening your explanation of the material that confused your reader. Also ask your classmate to use Figure 15.5 to react to and critique your essay. Your reviewer should consider each question listed in the flowchart and, for each "No" response, try to explain his or her answer.

For more on the benefits of peer review, see Chapter 6, p. 155.

ESSAY IN PROGRESS 6

Revise your draft using Figure 15.5 and any comments you received from peer reviewers.

Editing and Proofreading

The final step is to check your revised essay for errors in grammar, spelling, punctuation, and mechanics. Be sure to check your error log for the types of errors you commonly make.

For more on keeping an error log, see Chapter 7, p. 193.

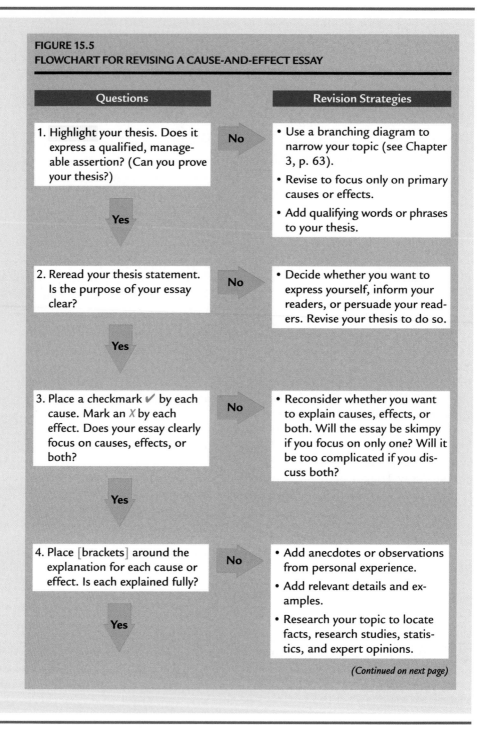

FIGURE 15.5
FLOWCHART FOR REVISING A CAUSE-AND-EFFECT ESSAY

Questions		Revision Strategies
1. Highlight your thesis. Does it express a qualified, manageable assertion? (Can you prove your thesis?)	**No** →	• Use a branching diagram to narrow your topic (see Chapter 3, p. 63). • Revise to focus only on primary causes or effects. • Add qualifying words or phrases to your thesis.
↓ **Yes**		
2. Reread your thesis statement. Is the purpose of your essay clear?	**No** →	• Decide whether you want to express yourself, inform your readers, or persuade your readers. Revise your thesis to do so.
↓ **Yes**		
3. Place a checkmark ✔ by each cause. Mark an X by each effect. Does your essay clearly focus on causes, effects, or both?	**No** →	• Reconsider whether you want to explain causes, effects, or both. Will the essay be skimpy if you focus on only one? Will it be too complicated if you discuss both?
↓ **Yes**		
4. Place [brackets] around the explanation for each cause or effect. Is each explained fully?	**No** →	• Add anecdotes or observations from personal experience. • Add relevant details and examples. • Research your topic to locate facts, research studies, statistics, and expert opinions.
↓ **Yes**		

(Continued on next page)

FIGURE 15.5 *(Continued)*

Questions		Revision Strategies
5. *Draw* a graphic organizer or *write* a brief outline of your major topics. Do your ideas progress logically?	**No**	• Compare your organizer or outline to the graphic organizers in Figures 15.1, 15.2, and 15.3. Look for places where you can rearrange causes, effects, or both.
Yes		
6. *Write* the order of presentation (chronological, least-to-most, or most-to-least) you used at the top of your essay. Is it clear and effective?	**No**	• Choose a different order and rearrange your draft.
Yes		
7. Circle sections where you have recognized readers' assumptions and either supported or challenged them. Are these sections complete and effective?	**No**	• Discuss popular ideas readers might assume about your topic and either support or challenge them.
Yes		
8. Underline each topic sentence. Is each paragraph focused on a separate cause or effect?	**No**	• Be sure each paragraph has a topic sentence and supporting details (see Chapter 5). • Consider combining closely related paragraphs. • Split paragraphs that cover more than one cause or effect.
Yes		

(Continued on next page)

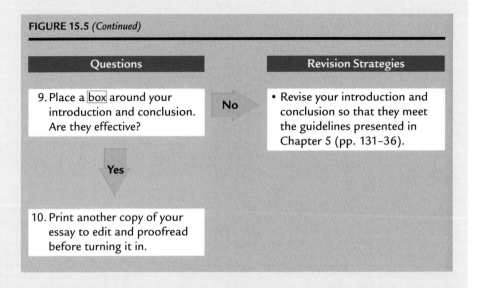

FIGURE 15.5 *(Continued)*

Questions		Revision Strategies
9. Place a box around your introduction and conclusion. Are they effective?	**No**	• Revise your introduction and conclusion so that they meet the guidelines presented in Chapter 5 (pp. 131–36).
Yes		
10. Print another copy of your essay to edit and proofread before turning it in.		

As you edit and proofread your causal-analysis essay, watch out for two types of errors commonly found in this type of writing—wordy sentences and mixed constructions.

1. Look for and revise wordy sentences. When explaining causal relationships, writers often use complex and compound-complex sentences. These sentences can sometimes become wordy and confusing. Look for ways to eliminate empty phrases and simplify your wording.

▶ ~~As you are already well aware,~~ viruses *Certain types of computer* ~~of certain types in a computer~~ file often create errors that you cannot explain ~~in documents~~ and may eventually result in lost data.

2. Revise to eliminate mixed constructions. A mixed construction happens when a writer connects phrases, clauses, or both that do not work together in a sentence.

▶ ~~Samantha, although~~ *Although* she was late for work, ~~but~~ was not reprimanded by her boss. *Samantha*

Using both *although* and *but* makes this a mixed sentence. To avoid mixed constructions, check words that join your phrases and clauses. Pay attention to prepositions and conjunctions. Also, check to be sure that the subjects of your sentences can perform the actions described by the verbs. If not, revise the sentence to supply the appropriate verb.

▶ Higher academic standards ~~ignore~~ *discourage* gifted but underprepared athletes who are motivated to improve their academic skills.

ESSAY IN PROGRESS 7

Edit and proofread your essay, paying particular attention to eliminating wordiness and mixed constructions.

STUDENTS WRITE

Harley Tong was a first-year liberal arts major at Niagara County Community College when he wrote this essay in response to an assignment for his writing class. He was asked to write a cause-and-effect essay explaining why and how he took action to correct a frustrating or unpleasant situation or resolve a problem he faced. As you read the essay, notice how Tong carefully presents the causes of his early departure from high school. Highlight the causes he cites and indicate which causes are primary.

An Early Start

Harley Tong

For many students, high school is a place to enjoy   1
the company of friends while getting an education. For
some, it's a challenge to keep up with course work while
participating in clubs, organizations, and sports. For a
few others, though, it seems a waste of time and a
struggle to remain interested in schoolwork.

A year ago, I was a sophomore in high school and an   2
honor roll student with an average in the nineties, but
all of the courses I took seemed uninteresting. I felt
that high school was not the place for me. The combination of the unchallenging course work, hostile fellow
students, mediocre faculty, and unfair school policies

led me to make the decision to go directly to college after my sophomore year.

3   First of all, the courses I was taking in high school presented no challenge for me. Many of them were at the Regents level rather than at the higher levels like honors or advanced placement. Even though I had been moved ahead in my science and language classes, I was never placed into honors-level classes. I wanted to stay ahead and be challenged by my course work, but there wasn't much work to do. I became bored because the classes moved so slowly and became repetitive in certain areas.

4   The way I was treated by other students also played an important part in my decision. In high school, I never seemed to fit in with anyone. A lot of students belonged to their own groups of friends. These groups discriminated against anyone who didn't fit in. They often made me feel out of place. Many students verbally assaulted me in the halls and during homeroom. Some students also started fights with me, and as a result, I was suspended frequently.

5   In addition, I wanted to leave high school because I felt that many of my teachers and counselors were uninspiring and unsupportive. Many teachers were incapable of doing their jobs or just did them poorly. Most teachers taught by having us copy notes from the overhead projector or chalkboard, or they simply handed us our notes. Students were not introduced to computers unless they were taking computer classes and were not taught the use of calculators for complicated mathematics. I received little support from my counselor or any of the other faculty members in my attempt to leave high school early. My counselor thought that I wasn't mature enough to handle the college workload or the atmosphere. My global studies teacher, who had talked to my counselor and learned that I wanted to leave school early, told me how she felt about the idea in front of the

entire class. She also told me that our principal would never approve of "such a stupid idea."

School policies were another major factor in my decision to leave high school. The administration's views on students' rights and how they should be interpreted were very unfair. Free speech was almost totally banned and other basic rights were denied to students. Students were not allowed to voice opinions about teachers and their teaching styles or actions in class. There were no teacher evaluation forms for students to fill out. Policies concerning fighting, harassment, and skipping class could be lightly or heavily enforced depending on whether or not you were a favorite of the teachers. My suspensions resulted from the school's policy regarding fighting: Even though I was attacked and did not do anything to defend myself, I was still punished for being involved. These suspension policies, which were allegedly designed by administrators to protect students, actually prevented students from keeping up with class work and maintaining good grades.

6

During my sophomore year, I came up with a plan that would allow me to attend the local community college instead of taking my junior and senior years at the high school. I would take equivalent course material at the college and transfer the grades and credits back to the high school. While I took the courses required for high school graduation, I would also be completing requirements for my graduation from college. As the year drew to a close, I arranged for a meeting between the principal and my father. My father gave his permission and the school finally agreed to my plan.

7

All of the things that made high school so miserable for me that year finally seemed unimportant because I was on my way to a better education. Over the summer, I held three jobs to earn money for tuition and then started to work for a local construction company, which I still work for. During my first semester, I took the

8

maximum of eighteen credit hours and worked full time to raise money for the spring semester. I also worked at the college radio station and was given my own show for the spring semester. I worked hard over the semester and got good grades as a result.

9   My experiences since I left high school have been great. I have made many new friends, enjoyed all of my professors, and have joined a few clubs. Everyone at college thinks my leaving high school early is an incredible opportunity and they are all very supportive. This was probably one of the best things I have ever done, and I hope I can keep on being successful not only in school but also in other aspects of life. I have no regrets about leaving high school and hope that what I did will make it easier for students in similar situations to realize that they can live up to their potential.

Analyzing the Essay

1. Identify Tong's thesis statement.
2. Describe Tong's audience and purpose.
3. Why did Tong leave high school early? Identify his primary and secondary causes.
4. What patterns of development does the writer use to support his thesis and maintain readers' interest?
5. Evaluate the introduction and conclusion.

Reacting to the Essay: Discussion and Journal Writing

1. How does your high school experience compare to Tong's? Did you experience or observe any similar problems? Were there benefits to your high school experience that were missing from Tong's?
2. Tong mentions several grievances he had with his high school. Evaluate your high school experience. How would you grade your counselors, teachers, and peers? Be sure to support your grades with specific examples.
3. Tong devised an unconventional plan to solve a problem. Write a journal entry describing an unconventional step you either took or considered taking to solve a problem you faced.

READING CAUSE-AND-EFFECT ESSAYS

The following section provides advice for reading causal analyses. Two model essays illustrate the characteristics of causal analysis covered in this chapter and provide opportunities to examine, analyze, and react to the writer's ideas. The second essay uses causal analysis with other patterns of development.

WORKING WITH TEXT: READING CAUSAL ANALYSES

Reading cause-and-effect essays requires critical thinking and analysis as well as close attention to detail. The overall questions to keep in mind are these: What is the relationship between the events or phenomena the writer is describing and the proposed causes or effects? Has the writer perceived this relationship accurately and completely?

For more on reading strategies, see Chapter 2.

Use the following suggestions when reading text that deals with causes and effects.

What to Look For, Highlight, and Annotate

1. Identify the author's thesis. Look for evidence that suggests a causal relationship actually exists.
2. Make a specific effort to distinguish between causes and effects. Mark or highlight causes in one color and effects in another.
3. Annotate causes or effects that are unclear or that are not supported by sufficient evidence.
4. Distinguish between primary and secondary causes or effects, especially in a lengthy or complex essay. Mark primary causes *PC* and secondary causes *SC*.
5. Be alert for key words that signal a causal relationship. A writer may not always use obvious transitional words and phrases. Notice how each of the following examples suggests a cause or effect connection.

   CAUSES

   One *source* of confusion on the issue of gun control is . . .
   A court's decision *is motivated by* . . .

   EFFECTS

   One *impact* of the Supreme Court decision was . . .
   One *result* of a change in favored-nation status may be . . .

6. As you read, fill in a graphic organizer to map a complex causal relationship, sorting causes from effects (see Figures 15.1, 15.2, and 15.3).

7. Establish the sequence of events for an essay that is not organized chronologically. Some authors may discuss effects before presenting causes. Other authors may not mention the key events in a complex series of events in the order they occurred. Use your computer to draw a timeline or write a list of the events in chronological order.

How to Find Ideas to Write About

For more on discovering ideas for a response paper, see Chapter 2.

To respond to or write about a cause-and-effect essay, consider the following strategies.

- If the essay discusses the causes of an event, a phenomenon, or a problem, consider writing about the effects or vice versa.
- Think of and write about other possible causes or effects.
- For a chain of events essay, write about what might have happened if the chain had been broken at some point.
- Write about the secondary causes or effects the writer does not mention.
- Write about a cause-and-effect relationship from your own life that is similar to one in the essay.

THINKING CRITICALLY ABOUT CAUSE AND EFFECT

Reading and evaluating causal relationships involves close analysis and may require that you do research to verify a writer's assertions. Use the following questions to think critically about the causal analyses you read.

What Is the Writer's Purpose?

Consider how the writer is describing certain effects and how this description advances his or her purpose, such as to persuade readers to accept a particular position on an issue. A graphic description of the physical effects of an experimental drug on laboratory animals, for example, may strengthen a writer's argument against the use of animals in medical research.

Does the Writer Cover All Major Causes or Effects?

Consider whether the writer presents a fair description of all major causes or effects. For example, a writer who favors using animals for medical research might fail to mention the painful effects of testing on laboratory animals. Conversely, a writer who opposes using animals for medical research might fail to mention that several human diseases are now controllable as a result of tests performed on animals. In either case, the writer does not offer a complete, objective account.

Does the Writer Provide Sufficient Evidence for the Causal Relationship?

Look for whether the writer provides *sufficient* supporting evidence to prove the existence of a causal relationship between the events or phenomena. For example, suppose a writer makes this assertion: "Medical doctors waste the resources of health insurance companies by ordering unnecessary medical tests." For support the writer relies on one example involving a grandparent who was required to undergo twenty-two tests and procedures before being approved for minor outpatient surgery. This anecdote is relevant to the writer's assertion, but one person's experience is not enough to prove a causal relationship. Consider whether the writer might have provided the additional support (such as statistics and expert opinion) or whether adequate support could not be found for the assertion.

CAUSAL-ANALYSIS ESSAY

The following essay by Laurence Steinberg reports the results of his research into the causal relationship between students' part-time employment and diminished achievement in school.

Part-Time Employment Undermines Students' Commitment to School

Laurence Steinberg

Laurence Steinberg holds a Ph.D. in psychology and is professor of psychology at Temple University. His books include Adolescence *(seventh edition, 2005);* When Teenagers Work *(1986);* Beyond the Classroom: Why School Reform Has Failed and What Parents Need to Do *(1996), from which this essay is taken; and* The Ten Basic Principles of Good Parenting *(2004). Steinberg reports the results of research he and his colleagues conducted on high school students. As you read the selection, highlight the causes and effects Steinberg discusses.*

There are a variety of barometers by which one can measure the   1
impact of employment on student achievement, and we used several
in our research. We compared the grades of students who work a

great deal with those who work in limited amounts or not at all. We also contrasted workers with nonworkers, and those who work a lot with those who work a little, on different indicators of their commitment to education, such as how much time they spend on homework, how often they cut classes, or how far they want to go in school. And finally, we looked at the impact of employment on various measures of student engagement, such as how hard students try and how steadily they pay attention in class.

2   All in all, our research shows that heavy commitment to a part-time job during the school year — say, working 20 hours per week or more — significantly interferes with youngsters' school achievement and scholastic commitment. Students who work a lot perform worse in school, are less committed to their education, and are less engaged in class than their classmates who work less or not at all. For example, in our study, students who were working more than 20 hours weekly were earning lower grades, spending less time on homework, cutting class more often, and cheating more frequently, and they reported lower levels of commitment to school and more modest educational aspirations.

3   It has become clear from our research, as well as a host of other studies, that the key issue is not whether a student works, but how much time he or she devotes to a job. Working for more than 20 hours per week is likely to be harmful, but working for less than 10 hours per week does not seem to take a consistent toll on school performance. Most probably, the effects of working for between 10 and 20 hours weekly vary from student to student — some can handle it, while others can't. We should keep in mind, however, that half of all employed seniors, about one-third of all juniors, and about one-fifth of all sophomores work above the 20-hour threshold — indicating that large numbers of students are at risk of compromising their school careers by their part-time jobs. These findings suggest that one reason for widespread student disengagement is the fact that so many students are working at part-time jobs.

4   In our study, we were able to examine whether working long hours lessens youngsters' commitment to school or, alternatively, whether disengagement from school leads students to work. We did this by following students over time, as they increased or decreased their work hours, and studying how different patterns of employment affected school performance and engagement. When students increase their work hours, does their commitment to school decline as a result? When students cut back on their employment, does their school performance improve?

5   The answer to both of these questions is yes. While it is true that the more disengaged students are more likely to work long hours to

begin with, it appears that working makes a bad situation worse. In other words, over time, the more students work, the less committed to school they become, even if they begin work with a more negative attitude toward school. (Working long hours also adversely affects students who enter the workplace with positive attitudes toward school.) When students withdraw from the labor force, however, or cut back on their work hours, their interest in school rises. The good news, then, is that the negative effects of working on schooling are reversible.

There are several explanations for the negative effects of working on students' engagement in school. First, when students work many hours each week, they have less time to devote to school assignments. According to our studies, one common response to this time pressure is for working students to cut corners by taking easier classes, copying assignments from other students, cutting class, or refusing to do work that is assigned by their teachers. Over time, as these become established practices, students' commitment to school is eroded bit by bit. About one-third of the students in our study said they take easier classes because of their jobs.

Second, in order to work 20 or more hours each week, many students must work on weekday evenings. Evening work may interfere not only with doing homework but with both sleep and diet—studies show that working teenagers get less rest and eat less healthy meals than nonworking teenagers—and burning the midnight oil may make working teenagers more tired in school. Teachers frequently complain about working students falling asleep in class. Nearly a third of the students in our study said they were frequently too tired from work to do their homework.

Third, it appears that the excitement of earning large amounts of spending money may itself make school seem less rewarding and interesting. Although mind-wandering during school is considered a hallmark of adolescence, working students report significantly more of it than nonworkers. Indeed, the "rush" from earning and spending money may be so strong that students who have a history of prolonged intensive employment—those who, for example, have been working long hours since their sophomore year—are actually at greater risk than their classmates of dropping out before graduating.

Finally, working long hours is associated with increased alcohol and drug use. Students who work long hours use drugs and alcohol about 33 percent more often than students who do not work. Alcohol and drug use, in turn, are linked to disengagement from school, so any activity that leads adolescents to drink or experiment with drugs is likely to depress their school performance. Interestingly enough, our longitudinal studies show that working long hours leads to increased alcohol and marijuana use. Teenagers with between $200 and $300 of discretionary income per month have a lot more money to spend on drugs and alcohol than their peers, and this is one of the things they spend their earnings on.

10   Given the widespread belief that employment during adolescence is supposed to be character-building, it no doubt will come as a surprise to many readers to hear that working at a part-time job diminishes students' engagement in school and increases their drug and alcohol use. But studies of how student workers actually spend their time on the job suggest that the real surprise is that we've held on to the myth of the benefits of adolescent work experience for as long as we have.   ■

Examining the Reading

1. What measures does Steinberg use to assess the effects of employment on students' academic performance?

2. Does Steinberg's study conclude that working long hours is a cause of students' disinterest in school, an effect of their disinterest, or both?

3. According to Steinberg, what negative effects does employment have on academic performance?

4. According to Steinberg's study, what happens when students stop working twenty or more hours per week?

5. Explain the meaning of each of the following words as it is used in the reading: *barometers* (para. 1), *engaged* (2), *toll* (3), *eroded* (6), and *longitudinal* (9). Refer to your dictionary as needed.

Analyzing the Reading

1. Identify Steinberg's thesis.

2. What is the writer's purpose?

3. Does the essay focus on causes, effects, or both? What type of evidence does Steinberg use? Is it sufficient?

4. Describe the overall organization of the essay. Can you identify a chain of events anywhere in the essay? If so, draw a graphic organizer of it.

5. Highlight the transitional words and phrases Steinberg uses to guide readers through the essay.

6. Evaluate the conclusion. How does Steinberg draw the essay to a close?

Reacting to the Reading: Discussion and Journal Writing

1. Steinberg's research study involved high school students. Would you expect similar findings in a study of the effects of employment on the academic performance of college students? Explain your reasons.

2. Steinberg seems to overlook the fact that some high school students must work because their families need the money. Do you think Steinberg is unfair to students who must work?

3. Steinberg cites four negative effects of employment on the academic performance of high school students. Write a journal entry explaining which effect you find most (or least) compelling. Can you think of additional effects? Use your experiences with work and school to support your answer.

PATTERNS COMBINED

In the following essay, Gary M. Stern uses cause and effect as well as other patterns to support his assertion about hidden obstacles to Latinos' career advancement in U.S. workplaces.

Hitting the "Granite Wall"
Gary M. Stern

Gary M. Stern is a New York–based freelance author who has written for the Wall Street Journal, Reuters, *Investor's Business Daily, Vanity Fair,* Woman's World, American Way, *and* USA Weekend. *He served as ghost-writer for* Garden of Dreams, *a 2004 book about the history of Madison Square Garden, and has written nonfiction children's books, including a biography of Andre Agassi and a book on Congress. He has profiled Eddie Murphy, Rob Reiner, Spike Lee, and Sissy Spacek. As you read, highlight the causes Stern cites for the "granite wall" Latinos face in the workplace.*

Most corporations point to their finely crafted diversity mission statements, diversity councils filled with multicultural staff, and inclusion on lists of "Best Companies for Minorities" as proof of their diversity progress. Yet experts say that few companies succeed at promoting minority employees to high levels of Corporate America. Many accomplish little in diversity except window dressing, promote few Latinos to senior positions, and cause many talented Latinos and blacks to flee corporate careers. Since most employees, consultants, and even publications in search of ads don't want to "burn bridges" and alienate the company endorsing their checks, rarely does anyone criticize a corporation's diversity efforts.

2   Yet most companies "talk the talk but don't walk the walk. When you peel back the onion, there are few minorities in positions of power. There are hundreds of minorities at the junior level, but they don't advance. Many of these diversity initiatives are marketing campaigns to get consumer dollars," says Kenneth Arroyo Roldan, the CEO of Wesley, Brown, Bartle & Roldan, one of the country's largest minority executive recruiting firms, based in New York. Out of frustration with observing diversity obstacles, Roldan has decided to speak out.

3   Many companies have done an effective job of recruiting and hiring talented minorities and adding to their minority suppliers, he acknowledges. But many minority employees in the fifth to seventh year stagnate in their job and become frustrated, watching their white non-Hispanic colleagues advance in the corporation. "Most minorities find the glass ceiling and hit a granite wall," he says. Stuck in their jobs, "many minorities leave the corporation out of frustration and become entrepreneurial," says Roldan.

4   But Roldan also faults Latinos themselves for not understanding "how the dance is played." Too many Latinos gravitate toward non-revenue-producing specialties such as public relations and ethnic marketing and fail to get on the fast track. "It's not your dad's Chevrolet. Many Hispanics have cultural inhibitions to jumping jobs," he says. Moreover, Latinos tend to network with each other in Hispanic organizations, which leads to "talking with each other" but not advancing their careers, he says.

5   Companies aren't explicitly discriminating or trying to inhibit Latino advancement. "It's not intentional; it's educational. Most companies don't have the skills to advance talented minorities. They may not have the architecture in place to have certain programs or mentors," Roldan says. Corporations offer sensitivity training and minority internship programs, but until corporations open the executive suites and corporate boards to Latinos and African Americans, real progress won't happen, he says.

6   A study by Donna María Blancero and Robert G. Del Campo for *Hispanic MBA Magazine* affirms Roldan's point that Latinos have been kept out of the corporate power structure. Though Latinos account for 10 percent of the workforce, they number 4.5 percent of managers. Since serving as a CEO or senior officer is often a prerequisite for being named to a company's influential board of directors, Hispanics rarely are named to a board. Only 1.7 percent of board members are Hispanics.

7   Why do so few talented and educated Latinos advance beyond a certain plateau? Blancero, an associate professor of business administration at Touro University International in Cypress, California,

attributes it to a combination of factors including an inability to identify a mentor. "Mentors only select people they think will be successful and often that's not a racial or ethnic minority. If you're a Hispanic woman in an organization, how many senior Hispanic women can you find who will mentor you?" she asks rhetorically. Furthermore, "most Latinos are the first ones in their family with a college degree. We haven't learned how to play golf at a country club. We have networks that look like ourselves," she says.

But the corporate culture often discourages Latino advancement. "Corporate culture is [still] dominated by white male America," says Alfonso Martínez, the president of the Hispanic Association on Corporate Responsibility (HACR), a Washington, D.C.-based nonprofit that advocates for Hispanic inclusion in Corporate America and has signed partnership agreements with twenty-seven *Fortune* 500 companies. "The formal and informal networks established by the dominant culture have not been sufficiently flexible. People who don't fit the dominant culture are seen as different and therefore included at lesser rates," he adds. What specifically can companies do to create actual change and promote Latino advancement? Blancero would like to see managers held accountable for promoting talented minorities and for their ability to create a level playing field. Training managers to prevent them from excluding people from promotion based on stereotypes and preconceived notions would also help. Creating a mentoring system that gives Latinos access to people in power that can groom them for future positions is critical.

The few Latinos who manage to surmount the obstacles must do more to change the dominant culture, adds Martínez. He points to Jim Padilla, chief operating officer at Ford Motor Company, who in 2003 spearheaded a Multicultural Alliance, which brings together ten divisions at Ford to collaborate on multicultural efforts. Suggestions from the Multicultural Alliance contributed to Ford's naming Latina Kim Casiano as a member of its board of directors, creating a Multicultural Affairs public affairs officer, and "making everyone at Ford aware that recruiting and developing minorities is a priority," explains Blanca Fauble, director of its Multicultural Alliance, based in Dearborn, Michigan.

Some companies are using their board of directors to make a real difference in diversity, Martínez says. For example, MGM Mirage in 2002 established a board diversity committee, chaired by Alexis M. Herman, the former U.S. Secretary of Labor and board member, which has the same status as the compensation and audit committees. This sends the message that "diversity at MGM Mirage is a critical business priority," notes Punam Mathur, its senior vice president in charge of Corporate Diversity and Community Affairs, based in Las Vegas, Nevada. Since 53 percent of its 42,000 employees at its ten hotel and casinos are minorities, the company is committed to establishing a level playing field. Though 9.4 percent of its managerial staff is Latino, the committee is trying to increase that number to reflect its 25 percent Latino staff. Accomplishments of the diversity committee include establishing a $500,000 recruitment/scholarship at the University of Nevada–Las Vegas Hotel School to attract more minorities to the school (students are 9 percent Latino and 2 percent African American) and provide paid summer internships at MGM Mirage and mentors at the hotel.

11   For one longtime corporate worker, finding the right mentor and taking risks were keys to his success. Carlos Linares, who was born in Cuba and immigrated to the United States at age four, started as an AT&T account executive, selling long-distance services to small businesses in San Francisco in 1984. Over an eighteen-year career, he made several job changes including a stint in human resources but then, guided by a mentor, became a sales manager for Latin America for AT&T Network Systems in Miami in 1993. He ultimately managed a staff of 6,000 people, overseeing sales in the Caribbean and parts of South America.

12   How was Linares able to surmount the hurdles that thwart so many other Latinos? Art Medieros, a senior manager, mentored Linares at Lucent Technologies (a spinoff of AT&T) and "taught me a lot about being an executive and running a large, complex operation," he says. Medieros promoted Linares twice and upon his retirement recommended Linares for regional president, which helped secure the position. As regional president, Linares helped grow Lucent's business in Latin America from $185 million to $1 billion from 1997 through 1999. "I advanced because of my work ethic, results, the fact that I could lead people and work effectively in the corporation across several organizations," says Linares, who is based in Davie, Florida. In 2002, he left Lucent (which slashed two-thirds of its staff) and is now seeking a CEO position. His advice: avoid dead-end staff jobs and get involved in profit-and-loss responsibilities, where producing profits leads to promotions.

13   What will it take for Latinos to gain access to actual power at *Fortune* 500 companies? Roldan replies, "We need to develop future leaders. There's no feeder pool. Hispanics are an increasingly larger group with more buying power, but too often diversity means African Americans." Blancero adds, "There has to be an accountable culture that does not discriminate. Organizations are filled with micro-inequities. Accountable managers must be rewarded."

HACR's Martínez encourages Latinos to take control of their   14
own careers, without blaming corporate culture. Hispanics have to
rid themselves of feeling victimized and must "gain advanced
degrees, find their own individual advocacy voice, and know that
with success comes responsibility," he says.   ■

Examining the Reading

1. According to Stern, why are Latinos failing to move up the corporate ladder?
2. How does the corporate culture discourage Latino advancement?
3. According to Stern, how can Latinos move forward in the business world?
4. What can companies do to promote the advancement of Latinos?
5. Explain the meaning of each of the following words as used in the reading: *stagnate* (para. 3), *entrepreneurial* (3), *prerequisite* (6), *surmount* (9), and *micro- inequities* (13). Refer to your dictionary as needed.

Analyzing the Reading

1. Identify Stern's thesis statement.
2. What does Stern hope to accomplish by writing this essay?
3. Why does the author include the personal story of Carlo Linares? What causes and effects of Linares's life are relevant to the essay?
4. Evaluate Stern's comparisons of Latinos to African Americans. Why does he include these?
5. Evaluate the evidence that Stern provides to support the reasons he offers for Latinos' lack of advancement. What other kinds of evidence would strengthen the essay?

Reacting to the Reading: Discussion and Journal Writing

1. Discuss the issue of discrimination in the workplace. How widespread is it, and where do you see it?
2. What factors, other than those addressed by Stern, might contribute to Latinos' "hitting the granite wall"?
3. Write a journal entry exploring the value of a mentor. What opportunities, insights, or advantages does mentorship offer?

MAKING CONNECTIONS: Racial Discrimination

Both "Hitting the Granite Wall" (pp. 545–49) and "Right Place, Wrong Face" (pp. 201–03) deal with the effects of racial discrimination.

Analyzing the Readings

1. While both authors address racial discrimination, they use two very different approaches (one describes many incidents; the other focuses on a single incident). They also use two different points of view. Explain the advantages and disadvantages of each approach and point of view. To what type(s) of audience does each appeal?
2. Write a journal entry exploring whether you feel the incidents of discrimination in these two essays are typical and representative of racial discrimination in U.S. society.

Essay Idea

Write an essay in which you describe the effects of discrimination on a particular person or group with which you are familiar. Define what discrimination the group faces and propose solutions. (You need not limit yourself to racial discrimination; you might discuss age, sex, weight, or workplace discrimination, for example.)

APPLYING YOUR SKILLS: ADDITIONAL ESSAY ASSIGNMENTS

For more on locating and documenting sources, see Part 5.

Write a cause-and-effect essay on one of the following topics, using what you learned about causal analysis in this chapter. Depending on the topic you choose, you may need to conduct library or Internet research.

To Express Your Ideas

1. Write an essay explaining the causes of a "bad day" you recently experienced.

2. Suppose you or a friend or a relative won a large cash prize in a national contest. Write an essay about the effects of winning the prize.

To Inform Your Reader

3. Young children frequently ask the question "Why?" Choose a "Why" question you have been asked by a child or think of a "Why" question you have always wondered about (Examples: Why is the sky blue? Why are sunsets red? Why do parrots learn to talk?). Write an essay answering your question. Your audience is young children.
4. Write an essay explaining how you coped with a stressful situation.
5. Write a memo to your supervisor at work explaining the causes and effects of requiring employees to work overtime.

To Persuade Your Reader

6. Write a letter to the dean of academic affairs about a problem at your school. Discuss causes, effects, or both and propose a solution to the problem.
7. Write a letter to the editor of your local newspaper explaining the possible effects of a proposed change in your community and urging citizens to take action for or against it.
8. Write a letter to the sports editor of your city's newspaper. You are a fan of a professional sports team, and you just learned that the team was sold to new owners who may move the team to a different city. In your letter, explain the effects on the city and the fans if the team moves away.

Cases Using Cause and Effect

9. Your psychology professor invites you to participate in a panel discussion on the psychology of humor. You are required to research this question: "What makes a joke funny?" Conduct research on the topic and write a paper summarizing your findings for the panel discussion.
10. A scandal has arisen within a company. Employees have been using company computers to send each other email messages that contain ethnic and racial slurs. In a letter to the human resources manager, either defend the employees' freedom of speech or call for their censure or dismissal. Also explain the immediate and long-term consequences of their actions and give reasons to support your position.

EVALUATING YOUR PROGRESS
Part A: Using Cause and Effect

Write a paragraph that evaluates your use of cause and effect. Be sure to

- Identify topics or situations in which cause and effect will be useful.
- Explain whether you focused on causes, effects, or both.
- What method(s) of organization did you find particularly useful?
- Identify any problems or trouble spots you experienced in using cause and effect and explain how you dealt with them.

Part B: Analyzing Cause-and-Effect Readings

The readings in this chapter are models of essays using cause and effect. Write a paragraph explaining how the essays you read served as models for your own writing. In other words, what features of the essays helped you write your essay(s)?

Part C: Proofreading and Editing

List the errors your instructor identified in your cause-and-effect essay(s). For more help with these problems, refer to Exercise Central (www.bedfordstmartins.com/successfulwriting).

Reading and Writing Arguments

Reading Arguments

Suppose you work for an advertising agency and need to write ad copy for a new model of car. Study the ad on the opposite page as an example of how to appeal to car buyers. Note that the purpose of the advertisement is to convince readers to buy the car.

Working alone or with one or two classmates, describe the appeal the advertisement makes and to whom the appeal is directed. Then describe how the ad might be revised to appeal to a different audience. Consider the visual as well as the written features of the advertisement.

The print advertisement you just evaluated is an example of a brief argument. An **argument** makes a claim and offers reasons and evidence in support of the claim. You evaluate arguments at home, work, and school every day. A friend may try to convince you to share an apartment, or your parents may urge you to save more. Many arguments, including print advertisements and television commercials, require you to analyze visual as well as verbal messages. In your college courses and at work, you often need to judge the claims and weigh the evidence of arguments (see the accompanying box for a few examples).

In this chapter, you will learn how to read, analyze, and evaluate arguments. In Chapter 17, you will learn strategies for writing effective argument essays.

THE BASIC PARTS OF AN ARGUMENT

In everyday conversation, an argument can be a heated exchange of ideas between two people. College roommates might argue over who should clean the sink or who left the door unlocked last night. Colleagues in a company may argue over policies or procedures. An effective argument is a logical, well-thought-out presentation of ideas that makes a claim about an issue and supports that claim with evidence. An ineffective argument may be an irrational, emotional release of feelings and frustrations. Many sound arguments, however, combine emotion with logic. A casual conversation can also take the form of a reasoned argument, as in the following sample dialogue.

SCENES FROM COLLEGE AND THE WORKPLACE

- To prepare for a class discussion in a *sociology* course, you are asked to read and evaluate an essay proposing a solution to the decline of city centers in large urban areas.

- In a *mass communication* class, your instructor assigns three articles that take different positions on the issue of whether journalists should provide graphic coverage of accidents and other human tragedies. You are asked to articulate your own opinion on this issue.

- While working as a *purchasing agent* for a carpet manufacturer, you are listening to a sales pitch by a sales representative who is trying to convince you to purchase a new type of plastic wrapping that is used for shipping carpets.

DAMON: I've been called for jury duty. I don't want to go. They treat jurors so badly!

MARIA: Why? Everybody is supposed to do it.

DAMON: Have you ever done it? I have. First of all, they force us to serve, whether we want to or not. And then they treat us like criminals. Two years ago I had to sit all day in a hot, crowded room with other jurors while the TV was blaring. I couldn't read, study, or even think! No wonder people will do anything to get out of it.

Damon argues that jurors are treated badly. He offers two reasons to support his claim and uses his personal experiences to support the second reason (that jurors are treated "like criminals"), which also serves as an emotional appeal.

An effective argument must clearly state an *issue*, a *claim*, and *support*. In the preceding exchange between Damon and Maria, for instance, "fairness of jury duty" is the issue, "jury duty is unfair" is the claim, and Damon's two reasons are the support. In many cases an argument also recognizes or argues against opposing viewpoints, in which case it includes a *refutation*. Although this example does not include a refutation, consider how Damon might refute the opposing claim that jury duty gives citizens the privilege of participating in the justice system. Like most types of essays, an argument should end with a *conclusion* that sums up the main points and provides a memorable closing statement or idea.

As you read the following argument essay, note the issue, the writer's claim, and the support she offers. In addition, look for places where the writer recognizes or refutes opposing views.

When Volunteerism Isn't Noble

Lynn Steirer

Lynn Steirer was a student at Northampton County Area Community College when she wrote the following essay, which was published in the New York Times *in 1997. It appeared on the op-ed page, a forum for discussing current issues that appears opposite the editorial page.*

Engraved in stone over the front entrance to my old high school   1
is the statement, "No Man Is Free Who Is Not Master of Himself." No surprise for a school named Liberty.

Some time ago, the Bethlehem school board turned its back on   2
the principle for which my school was named when it began requiring students to perform community service or other volunteer work.

Students would have to show that they had done 60 hours of such service, or they would not receive their high school diploma.

3   That forced me to make a decision. Would I submit to the program even though I thought it was involuntary servitude, or would I stand against it on principle? I chose principle, and was denied a diploma.

4   Bethlehem is not alone in requiring students to do volunteer work to graduate. Other school districts around the country have adopted such policies, and in the state of Maryland, students must do volunteer work to graduate.

5   Volunteerism is a national preoccupation these days. It all began when Retired General Colin Powell, at President Clinton's request, led a three-day gathering in Philadelphia of political and business leaders and many others. General Powell called for more people to volunteer. That was a noble thought.

6   But what President Clinton had in mind goes far beyond volunteering. He called for high schools across the country to make community service mandatory for graduation. In other words, he wanted to *force* young people to do something that should be, by its very definition, voluntary.

7   That would destroy, not elevate, the American spirit of volunteerism. I saw firsthand how many of my classmates treated their required service as a joke, claiming credit for work they didn't do or exaggerating the time it actually took.

8   Volunteering has always been important to me. As a Meals on Wheels aide and a Girl Scout, I chose to give hundreds of hours to my community, at my own initiative.

9   While my family and I fought the school's mandatory service requirement, I continued my volunteering, but I would not submit my hours for credit. Two of my classmates joined me in this act of civil disobedience. At the same time, with the assistance of the Institute for Justice, a Washington legal-policy group, we sued the school board.

10   As graduation neared, a school official pulled me aside and said it was not too late to change my mind. That day, I really thought about giving in. Then he asked the question that settled it for me. "After all," he said, "what is more important, your values or your diploma?"

11   I chose to give up my diploma, eventually obtaining a graduate equivalency degree instead. The courts decided against us and, unfortunately, the Supreme Court declined to hear our case. The school has continued the program.

12   Volunteering is important. But in a country that values its liberty, we should make sure that student "service" is truly voluntary. ■

The Issue

An argument is concerned with an **issue** — a controversy, a problem, or an idea about which people hold different points of view. In "When Volunteerism Isn't Noble," the issue is mandatory community service for high school graduation.

The Claim

The **claim** is the point the writer tries to prove, usually the writer's view on the issue. Consider, for example, whether you think the death penalty is right or wrong. You could take one of three stands — or make one of three claims — on this issue.

> The death penalty is never right.
> The death penalty is always right.
> The death penalty is the right choice under certain circumstances.

The claim often appears as part of the thesis statement in an argument essay. In Steirer's argument about volunteerism, the claim is that forcing students to volunteer "will destroy, not elevate, the American spirit of volunteerism" (para. 7). In some essays, however, the claim is implied rather than stated directly.

There are three types of claims: *claims of fact, claims of value,* and *claims of policy.* A **claim of fact** can be proved or verified. A writer employing a claim of fact bases the claim on verifiable facts or data, as in the following example.

> **The greenhouse effect is likely to take a serious toll on the environment within the next decade.**

A **claim of value** focuses on showing how one thing or idea is better or more desirable than other things or ideas. Issues involving questions of right versus wrong or acceptable versus unacceptable often lead to claims of value. Such claims are subjective opinions or judgments that cannot be proved. In "When Volunteerism Isn't Noble," for instance, Steirer claims that community service should be "truly voluntary" (para. 12). Here is an example of a claim of value.

> **Doctor-assisted suicide is a violation of the Hippocratic oath and therefore should not be legalized.**

A **claim of policy** offers one or more solutions to a problem. Often the verbs *should, must,* or *ought* appear in the statement of the claim.

> **The motion picture industry must accept greater responsibility for the consequences of violent films.**

EXERCISE 16.1

Either on your own or with one or two classmates, choose two of the following issues and write two claims for each issue. Use different types of claims. For example, if one statement is a claim of value, the other should be a claim of policy or fact.

1. Legalization of drugs
2. Welfare reform
3. Television violence
4. Protection for endangered species
5. Mandatory public school uniforms

The Support

The **support** consists of the ideas and information intended to convince readers that the claim is sound or believable. Three common types of support are *reasons, evidence,* and *emotional appeals.*

Reasons

For more on reasons as support in an argument, see Chapter 17, p. 596.

When writers make claims about issues, they have reasons for doing so. In "When Volunteerism Isn't Noble," for example, Steirer's claim—that community service should not be mandatory for high school graduation—is supported by several reasons, including her observation that students treat the mandatory community service "as a joke" (para. 7). A **reason,** then, is a general statement that backs up a claim. It explains why the writer's view on an issue is reasonable or correct. However, reasons alone are not sufficient support for an argument. Each reason must be supported by evidence and, often, by emotional appeals.

Evidence

In an argument, evidence usually consists of facts, statistics, and expert opinion. Examples and observations from personal experience can also serve as evidence. The following examples show how different types of evidence may be used to support a claim about the value of reading to children.

CLAIM	Reading aloud to preschool and kindergarten children improves their chances of success in school.
FACTS	First-grade children who were read to as preschoolers learn to read earlier than children who were not read to.
STATISTICS	A 1998 study by Robbins and Ehri demonstrated that reading aloud to children produced a 16 percent improvement in the children's ability to recognize words used in a story.
EXPERT OPINION	Dr. Maria Morealle, a child psychologist, urges parents to read two or three books to their children daily (Pearson 52).

EXAMPLES	Stories about unfamiliar places or activities increase a child's vocabulary. For example, reading a story about a farm to a child who lives in a city apartment will acquaint the child with such new terms as *barn, silo,* and *tractor.*
PERSONAL EXPERIENCE	When I read to my three-year-old son, I notice that he points to and tries to repeat words.

In "When Volunteerism Isn't Noble," Steirer offers several examples of how high school students treat mandatory community service "as a joke": they claim credit unfairly and exaggerate their time spent doing volunteer work. The writer also uses her personal experience at Bethlehem High School to support her claim.

Emotional Appeals

Emotional appeals evoke the needs or values that readers care deeply about. For instance, a writer might appeal to readers' need for safety and security when urging them to install deadbolts on their apartment doors. You would appeal to the value that a sick friend places on your friendship if you urge him to visit a medical clinic by saying, "If you won't go for your own good, then do it for me."

Appealing to needs.   People have various **needs,** including physiological needs (food and drink, health, shelter, safety, sex) and psychological needs (a sense of belonging or accomplishment, self-esteem, recognition by others, or self-realization). Appeals to needs are used by your friends and family, by people who write letters to the editor, and by personnel directors who write job listings. Advertisements often appeal directly or indirectly to one or more various needs.

Appealing to values.   A **value** is a principle or quality that is judged to be important, worthwhile, or desirable, such as freedom, justice, loyalty, friendship, patriotism, duty, and equality. Values are difficult to define because not everyone considers the same principles or qualities important. Even when people agree on the importance of a value, they may not agree about what that value means. For example, although most people value honesty, some would say that white lies intended to protect a person's feelings are dishonest, while others would maintain that white lies are justified. Arguments often appeal to values that the writer assumes most readers will share. Steirer, in her essay on volunteerism, appeals to two widely held values—that it is worthy to stand up for one's own principles (para. 3) and that "No Man Is Free Who Is Not Master of Himself" (para. 1).

EXERCISE 16.2

As the director of a day-care center, you need to create a budget report for next year. The report will itemize purchases and expenses as well as justify the need for each purchase or expenditure. Choose two of the following items and write a justification (reasons) for their purchase, explaining why each item would be beneficial to the children (evidence).

1. VCR
2. Tropical fish tank
3. Answering machine
4. Read-along books with tapes
5. Set of Dr. Seuss books

The Refutation

The **refutation**, also called the *rebuttal,* recognizes and argues against opposing viewpoints. Suppose you want to argue that you deserve a raise at work (your claim). As support for your claim, you will remind your supervisor of the contributions and improvements you have made while you have been employed by the company, your length of employment, your conscientiousness, and your promptness. But you suspect that your supervisor may still turn you down, not because you don't deserve the raise but because other employees might demand a similar raise. By anticipating this potential objection, you can build into your argument the reasons that the objection is not valid. You may have more time invested with the company and more responsibilities than the other employees, for example. In doing so, you would be offering a refutation.

Basically, refutation involves finding a weakness in the opponent's argument, either by casting doubt on the opponent's reasons or by questioning the accuracy, relevancy, and sufficiency of the opponent's evidence.

For more on refutation, acknowledgment, and accommodation, see Chapter 17, p. 599.

Sometimes writers are unable to refute an opposing view or may choose not to, perhaps because the opposing view is weak. However, most writers of arguments acknowledge or accommodate the opposing viewpoint in some way if they cannot refute it. They **acknowledge** an opposing view by simply stating it. By **accommodating** an opposing view, they note that the view has merit and find a way of addressing it. In an argument opposing hunting, for example, a writer might simply *acknowledge* the view that hunting bans would cause a population explosion among wild animals. The writer might *accommodate* this opposing view by stating that if a population explosion were to occur, the problem could be solved by reintroducing natural predators into the area.

The Conclusion

The conclusion of an argument essay should leave you with a final impression of the argument. A conclusion may restate the thesis in a forceful way or make a final appeal to values. For example, in "When Volunteerism Isn't Noble," Steirer makes a final appeal to values by referring to "a country that values its liberty." In "Economic Affirmative Action," Koerth makes a final appeal by reiterating a key reason for abandoning racial affirmative action.

GENERAL STRATEGIES FOR READING ARGUMENTS

To understand the complex relationships among the ideas presented in an argument, you'll need to read it at least two times. Read it once to get an overview of the issue, claim, and support. Then reread it to identify the structure and evaluate the ideas and the relationships among them.

Because argument essays can be complex, you will find it helpful to annotate and summarize them. You may want to photocopy the essay before you begin reading, so that you can mark it up in the various ways suggested in this section. The following strategies, which you should use before and while reading, will help focus your attention on what is important and make the task of writing about what you have read easier.

For more on reading strategies, see Chapter 2.

Before You Read

Before you read an argument essay, look for information that will make your first reading more productive. Use the following strategies.

1. **Think about the title.** The title may suggest the focus of the essay in a direct statement or in a synopsis of the claim. Here are a few examples of titles.

   "In Defense of Voluntary Euthanasia"
   "The Case for Medicalizing Heroin"
   "Single-Sex Education Benefits Men, Too"

   You can tell from the titles that the first essay argues for euthanasia, the second supports the use of heroin for medical purposes, and the third argues for single-sex schools.

EXERCISE 16.3

For each of the following essay titles, predict the issue and the claim you would expect the author to make.

1. "The Drugs I Take Are None of Your Business"
2. "Watch That Leer and Stifle That Joke at the Water Cooler"
3. "Crazy in the Streets: A Call for Treatment of Street People"
4. "Penalize the Unwed Dad? Fat Chance"
5. "A Former Smoker Applauds New Laws"

---

2. **Check the author's name and credentials.** If you recognize the author's name, you may have some sense of what to expect or what not to expect in the essay. For example, an essay written by syndicated columnist Dave Barry, known for his humorous articles, would likely make a point through humor or sarcasm, whereas an essay by Martin Luther King Jr. would seriously address

an issue current during his lifetime—most likely, civil rights. You also want to determine whether the author is qualified to write on the issue at hand. Essays in newspapers, magazines, and academic journals often include a brief review of the author's credentials and experiences related to the issue. Books include biographical notes about authors. When an article lacks an author's name, which often happens in newspapers, you need to evaluate the reliability of the publication in which the article appears.

For more on evaluating sources, see Chapter 18, p. 648.

3. **Check the original source of publication.** If the essay does not appear in its original source, use the headnote, footnotes, or citations to determine where the essay was originally published. Some publications have a particular viewpoint. *Ms.* magazine, for instance, has a feminist slant. *Wired* generally favors advances in technology. If you are aware of the viewpoint that a publication advocates, you can sometimes predict the stand an essay will take on a particular issue. The publication's intended audience can also provide clues.

4. **Check the date of publication.** The date of publication provides a context for the essay and helps you evaluate it. The more recent an article is, the more likely it is to reflect current research or debate on an issue. For instance, an essay on the existence of life on other planets written in the 1980s would lack recent scientific findings that might confirm or discredit the supporting evidence. When obtaining information from the World Wide Web, you should be especially careful to check the date the article was posted or last updated.

5. **Preview the essay.** Read the opening paragraph, any headings, the first sentence of one or two paragraphs per page, and the last paragraph. Previewing may also help you determine the author's claim.

6. **Think about the issue before you read.** When you think about an argument before reading, you may be less influenced by the writer's appeals and more likely to maintain an objective, critical viewpoint. Write the issue at the top of a sheet of paper, in your journal, or in a word-processing document. Then create two columns for pros and cons, listing as many ideas as you can in each column.

Use the preceding six suggestions to *get ready* to read the following argument essay, "Economic Affirmative Action." Do *not* read the essay until you have worked through the next section, While You Read (p. 566).

Economic Affirmative Action
Ted Koerth

Ted Koerth was a first-year student at the University of Virginia when he wrote the following editorial for the campus newspaper, the Cavalier Daily. *At the time he wrote the article, he was planning to major in government and Spanish.*

Two words probably do not exist that can stir up more of a conversational frenzy than *affirmative action*. The debate surrounding
such policies presents itself daily in the media, a seemingly never-
ending saga destined to go back and forth forever.

Proponents of such policies argue that they not only give an
advantage to underrepresented minority groups, but they help to set-
tle some cosmic score that went askew during the first two hundred
years of American history. People who oppose affirmative action
measures argue that they encourage acceptance of underqualified
applicants and that sufficient reparation time has elapsed. A growing
majority of those opponents think that minorities do not deserve the
push they get; hence the rise in complaints of reverse discrimination.

Despite the deeply felt emotions both sides of the debate harbor,
a fair way to reform affirmative action's current state does exist.
Many of the qualms some have with affirmative action have to do
with the fact that it is based solely on race, for race is natural and
unintentional. None of us chooses our race. So to treat someone differently because of his or her race demonstrates a glaring ignorance
on the part of the prejudiced. We must consider, however, the opposite side of the coin, which often does not receive as much thought.

If we cannot judge people poorly because of their race, we cannot
judge them superior for the same reason, nor should we use race to
decide that a certain class of individuals needs a helping hand from
any other.

Here the affirmative action argument comes into play. The problem starts when race becomes the basis for giving out advantages
such as college admissions. Choosing minority groups for special
treatment in admissions implies that those groups lack the ability to
achieve those things on their own, a bigoted assumption totally without founding. Granted, simple demographics demonstrate that certain ethnic groups are more highly represented in certain classes, but
we cannot consider that an exclusive phenomenon, given that no
group of people has all the same characteristics. Therefore, a generalization implying that any certain number of racial groups needs
help lacks reason. For that reason, we need to fix affirmative action.

If two students have had the exact same opportunities during
their lives but one is an American Indian and the other Caucasian,
the American Indian will receive acceptance priority if her academic
achievements are similar, simply because she belongs to an underrepresented group. That implies that an American Indian who
achieves is out of the ordinary—a foolish assumption.

Take another example: Two students, one white and one Asian
American, score the same on standardized tests and are equally qualified for a job. The white student, however, comes from a lower class,

single-parent family, and the Asian student comes from the family of an affluent judge. If those two have equal academic achievements, affirmative action as it now exists would likely give a boost to the Asian student, though he has lived an easier life. The extra efforts the Caucasian student made go unnoticed, and he receives no boost.

8   For those reasons, America needs an affirmative action system that gives a boost not to members of groups that unfortunately suffered from past discrimination because the days of rampant discrimination in the United States have passed for the most part. Continuing to pay back groups who previously had to deal with prejudice unfairly punishes other racial majorities for the sins of their ancestors. Instead, we need a system that gives a boost to those who have had to overcome considerable financial, physical, or other obstacles to achieve what they have achieved. Such a policy would not shut any ethnic group out of the process; it would only include anyone who has succeeded without financial assistance. If it occurs that a majority of those who benefit from that system still come from minority groups, that is fine. At least they have benefited from a system that recognizes their situation, not just their skin color.

9   The affirmative action debate roars on in the United States, with animosity on both sides building constantly. Our current system supposes a certain inherent inferiority of minority groups who in the past have experienced discrimination — an inferiority that simply does not exist. If the government were to institute an equal opportunity system that tries to help those who have had to deal with financial and physical obstacles, we could ease tensions and deal more fairly with admissions policies. Until we can respect the abilities of all ethnic groups, our country will divide its people along racial lines, as the tension rises to a fever pitch. ■

While You Read

The following tips will help you read an argument essay carefully.

1. **Read first for an initial impression.** During your first reading, do not concentrate on specifics. Instead, read to get an overall impression of the argument and to identify the issue and the author's claim. Also try to get a general feel for the essay, the author, and the approach the author takes toward the topic. Do not judge or criticize; focus on what the author has to say.

2. **Read a second time with a pen in hand.** As you reread the essay, mark or highlight the claim, reasons, and key supporting evidence. Write annotations, not-

ing appeals to needs and values. Jot down ideas, questions, or challenges to the writer's argument as they come to mind. Summarize reasons and key supporting evidence as you encounter them. In an argument, one idea is often linked to the next. Consequently, readers often find it useful and necessary to reread earlier sections before moving ahead.

3. **Underline key terms or unfamiliar words.** Because an argument can depend on defining terms in a specific way, it is especially important to understand how the writer defines key terms and concepts. In arguments, precise definitions are crucial. If the author does not define terms precisely, look up their meanings in a dictionary. Jot down the definitions in the margins.

Using the preceding tips for reading arguments, turn back to page 564 and read "Economic Affirmative Action." Then read it again and answer the questions that follow.

1. What is Koerth's claim?
2. Is Koerth's claim one of fact, value, or policy?
3. What reasons and types of evidence does Koerth provide to support his claim?
4. What types of emotional appeals does Koerth make, if any?
5. Does Koerth recognize or refute the opposing viewpoint? If so, how?

STRATEGIES FOR FOLLOWING THE STRUCTURE OF AN ARGUMENT

In some ways, an argument resembles a building. The writer lays a foundation and then builds on that foundation. Reasons and evidence presented early in the essay often support ideas introduced later on, as the lower floors in a building support the higher ones. Once you recognize an argument's plan or overall structure, you are in a better position to understand it and evaluate its strengths and weaknesses. This section offers strategies for following the structure of an argument — including identifying key elements in a graphic organizer and writing a summary — that can help you analyze and evaluate an essay.

Using a Graphic Organizer

The graphic organizer shown in Figure 16.1 outlines the basic relationships among ideas in an argument essay. However, unlike the graphic organizers in Part 3 of this text, this organizer does not necessarily reflect the order in which the ideas are presented in an argument essay. Instead, Figure 16.1 provides a way for you, as a

FIGURE 16.1
GRAPHIC ORGANIZER FOR AN ARGUMENT ESSAY

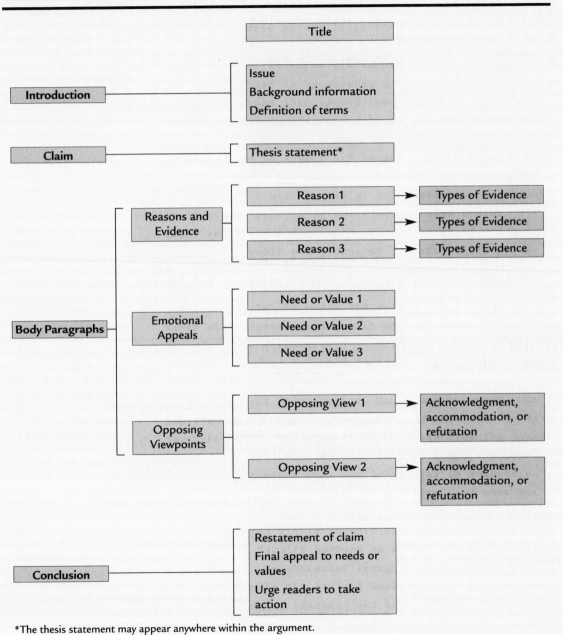

*The thesis statement may appear anywhere within the argument.

reader, to organize those ideas. That is, an argument does not necessarily state (or imply) the issue in the first paragraph, but the issue is the first thing you need to identify to follow the structure of an argument. Similarly, the claim may not appear in the first paragraph (though it is often stated early in the essay), and the evidence may be presented at various places within the essay. Regardless of the order a writer follows, his or her ideas can be shown in a graphic organizer like the one in Figure 16.1. To construct such an organizer, use the following suggestions.

1. You may find it helpful to read and highlight the essay before drawing a graphic organizer. Visual learners, however, may prefer to fill in the organizer as they read.

2. Record ideas in your own words, not in the author's words.

3. Reread difficult or confusing parts of the essay before filling in those sections of the organizer.

4. Try working through the graphic organizer with a classmate.

   Study the graphic organizer for "Economic Affirmative Action" in Figure 16.2.

Learning Style Options

See Chapter 19, p. 684, for suggestions on paraphrasing. For more on reading difficult material, see Chapter 2, p. 34.

To draw detailed graphic organizers using a computer, visit www .bedfordstmartins.com /successfulwriting.

EXERCISE 16.4

Draw a graphic organizer for "When Volunteerism Isn't Noble" on page 557.

Writing a Summary

Writing a summary of an argument is another useful way to study the structure of ideas in an essay. A summary eliminates detail; only the major supporting ideas remain. You can write a summary after you draw a graphic organizer or use a summary to uncover an argument's structure.

The following guidelines will lead you through the process of writing a summary. (When you draw a graphic organizer first, start with summary step 4.)

For more on summarizing, see Chapter 2, p. 42.

1. Read the essay two or more times before you attempt to summarize it.

2. Divide the argument into sections or parts, noting the function of each section in the margin. You might write "offers examples" or "provides statistical backup," for instance. Label the issue, the claim, sections offering reasons and evidence, opposing viewpoints, and the conclusion.

3. Write brief marginal notes stating the main point of each paragraph or each related group of paragraphs. It may be helpful to use one margin for a content summary and the other to indicate function. Study the accompanying sample annotated portion of "When Volunteerism Isn't Noble."

FIGURE 16.2
GRAPHIC ORGANIZER FOR "ECONOMIC AFFIRMATIVE ACTION"

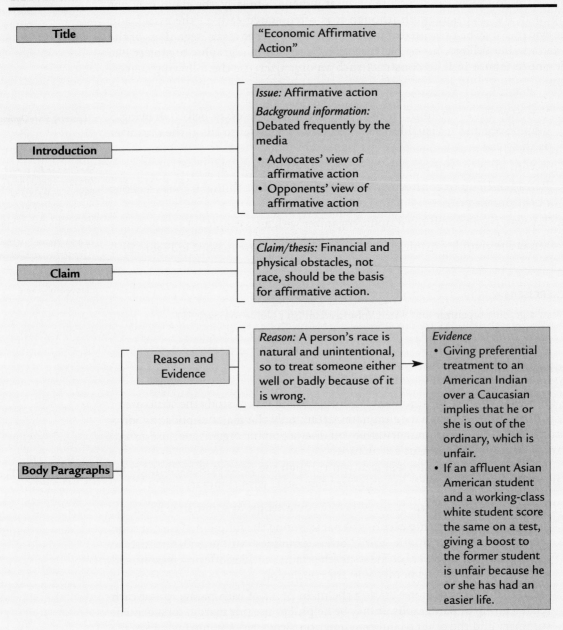

FIGURE 16.2 *(Continued)*

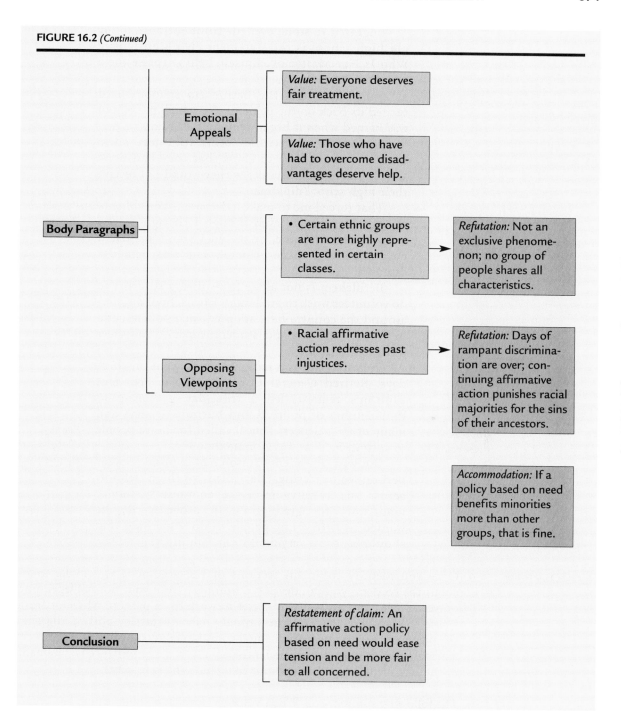

Engraved in stone over the front entrance to my old high school is the statement "No Man Is Free Who Is Not Master of Himself." No surprise for a school named Liberty.

background

Some time ago, the Bethlehem school board turned its back on the principle for which my school was named when it began requiring students to perform community service or other volunteer work. Students would have to show that they had done sixty hours of such service, or they would not receive their high school diploma.

mandatory policy

That forced me to make a decision. Would I submit to the program even though I thought it was involuntary servitude, or would I stand against it on principle? I chose principle and was denied a diploma.

writer's dilemma

Bethlehem is not alone in requiring students to do volunteer work to graduate. Other school districts around the country have adopted such policies, and in the state of Maryland, students must do volunteer work to graduate.

other schools have similar policy

Volunteerism is a national preoccupation these days. Retired General Colin Powell, at President Clinton's request, led a three-day gathering in Philadelphia of political and business leaders and many others. General Powell called for more people to volunteer. That was a noble thought.

opposing viewpoint

Powell & Clinton support

But what President Clinton had in mind goes far beyond volunteering. He called for high schools across the country to make community service mandatory for graduation. In other words, he wanted to *force* young people to do something that should be, by its very definition, voluntary.

forcing isn't voluntary

Learning Style Options

4. Once you identify the main sections of the argument and make notes about the content, you can develop a summary from your notes. Depending on your learning style, you may prefer to work from parts to whole or from whole to parts. Pragmatic learners often prefer to start by putting together the pieces of the argument (individual paragraphs) to see what they produce, whereas creative learners may prefer to begin with a one-sentence restatement of the argument and then expand it to include the key points.

The following summary of "When Volunteerism Isn't Noble" shows an acceptable level of detail.

SAMPLE SUMMARY

The Bethlehem school board required sixty hours of community service for high school graduation, but the writer refused to submit her community service hours (as a volunteer for Meals on Wheels and as a Girl Scout) and was denied a diploma. Other school districts in other states have similar requirements. In addition, General Powell favored volunteerism, and President Clinton called for a mandatory graduation requirement. Nevertheless, the writer maintains that making volunteerism mandatory destroys it. She cites the following personal observation as evidence: Her classmates treated the requirement as a joke and cheated in reporting their hours. The writer feels strongly that in a free society, community service should be voluntary. She gave up her diploma because of this conviction, though eventually she received a high school equivalency degree. She also sued the school board, but the U.S. Supreme Court refused to consider the case.

EXERCISE 16.5

Write a summary for "Economic Affirmative Action" on page 564.

STRATEGIES FOR ANALYZING AND EVALUATING AN ARGUMENT

The graphic organizer shown in Figure 16.1 provides you with an easy way to lay out the ideas in an argument essay. Once you are familiar with an essay's content and organization, the next step is to analyze and evaluate the argument, including the writer's claim and support for the claim.

Review the pro-and-con list you wrote before reading (see p. 564), noting the points covered as well as those not covered. Consider the ideas raised in the argument and write about them in your journal. Explore your overall reaction and raise questions. Talk back to the author. Compare your ideas on the issue with those of the author. You will then be ready to analyze the argument more systematically. (For a checklist covering all of these elements, see Figure 16.3 on p. 577.)

For more on raising questions about an essay, see Chapter 2.

Analyzing the Elements of and Reasoning in an Argument

To analyze an argument, you need to study closely the writer's purpose, audience, definitions of key terms in the claim, credibility, and support (reasons and evidence). You also need to evaluate his or her emotional appeals, treatment of opposing viewpoints, possibly faulty reasoning, and conclusion.

The Basic Components

As you read an argument, consider the following aspects of any persuasive writing.

- **The writer's purpose** Try to discover the writer's motive for writing. Ask yourself questions: "Why does the writer want to convince me of this? What does he or she stand to gain, if anything?" If a writer stands to profit personally from the acceptance of an argument, be especially careful to ask critical questions.

- **The intended audience** Writers often reveal the intended audience by the language they use and the familiarity or formality of the tone. Also look at the reasons and types of evidence offered, the emotional appeals and examples, and the comparisons the writer makes.

- **Definitions of key terms** Underline any terms in the statement of the claim that can have more than one meaning. Then read through the essay to see if these terms are clearly defined and used consistently throughout the argument.

- **The writer's credibility** As you read an argument, judge the writer's knowledge and trustworthiness. Ask yourself if the writer seems to have a thorough understanding of the issue, acknowledges opposing views and addresses them respectfully, and establishes common ground with the reader.

For more on evaluating evidence, see Chapter 4, p. 99.

- **Support: reasons and evidence** Does the writer supply sufficient reasons and evidence that are relevant to the claim and accurate? Facts offered as evidence should be accurate, complete, and taken from reputable sources. In particular, statistical evidence should be current and from reliable sources. The evidence should be typical, and any authorities cited should be experts in their field.

Emotional Appeals

As noted earlier in the chapter, writers of arguments appeal to or engage readers' emotions. Such appeals are a legitimate part of an argument. However, a writer should not attempt to manipulate readers' emotions to distract them from the issue and the evidence. Table 16.1 presents some common unfair emotional appeals.

Opposing Viewpoints

If an argument essay takes into account opposing viewpoints, you must evaluate these viewpoints and the way the writer deals with them. Ask yourself the following questions.

- **Does the author state the opposing viewpoint clearly?** Can you tell from the essay what the opposition says?

- **Does the author present the opposing viewpoint fairly and completely?** That is, does the author recognize the opposing viewpoint and treat it with respect, or does he or she attempt to discredit or demean people holding an opposing view? Does the author present all the major parts of the opposing viewpoint or only those parts that he or she is able to refute?

- **Does the author clearly show why the opposing viewpoint is considered wrong or inappropriate?** Does the author apply sound logic? Are reasons and evidence provided?
- **Does the author acknowledge or accommodate points that cannot be refuted?**

As you read, jot down clues or answers to these questions in the margins of the essay.

Faulty Reasoning

In an argument essay, a writer may inadvertently introduce **fallacies,** or errors in reasoning or thinking. Several types of fallacies can weaken an argument, undermine a writer's claim, and call into question the relevancy, believability, or consistency of supporting evidence. Following is a brief review of the most common types of faulty reasoning.

For more on reasoning, see Chapter 17, p. 596.

Circular reasoning. Also called **begging the question,** *circular reasoning* occurs when a writer uses the claim (or part of it) as evidence by simply repeating the claim in different words. The statement "*Cruel* and unusual experimentation on helpless animals is *inhumane*" is an example.

TABLE 16.1
COMMON UNFAIR EMOTIONAL APPEALS

Emotional Appeal	*Example*
Name-calling: using an emotionally loaded term to create a negative response	"That reporter is an *egotistical bully*."
Ad hominem: attacking the opponent rather than his or her position on the issue	"How could anyone who didn't fight in a war criticize the president's foreign policy?"
False authority: quoting the opinions of celebrities or public figures about topics on which they are not experts	"According to singer Jennifer Hope, welfare reform is America's most urgent social problem."
Plain folks: urging readers to accept an idea or take an action because it is suggested by someone who is just like they are	"Vote for me. I'm just a regular guy."
Appeal to pity: arousing sympathy by telling hard-luck or excessively sentimental stories	"Latchkey children come home to an empty house or apartment, a can of soup, and a note on the refrigerator."
Bandwagon: appealing to readers' desire to conform ("Everyone's doing it, so it must be right")	"It must be okay to exceed the speed limit, since so many people speed."

Hasty generalization.   A *hasty generalization* occurs when the writer draws a conclusion based on insufficient evidence or isolated examples. If you taste three pieces of chocolate cake and on the basis of that small sample conclude that all chocolate cakes are overly sweet, you would be making a hasty generalization.

Sweeping generalization.   When a writer claims that something applies to all situations and instances without exception, the claim is called a *sweeping generalization.* To claim that all computers are easy to use is a sweeping generalization because the writer is probably referring only to the models with which he or she is familiar.

False analogy.   When a writer compares two situations that are not sufficiently parallel or similar, the result is a *false analogy.* Just because two items or events are alike in some ways does not mean they are alike in all ways. If you wrote, "A human body needs rest after strenuous work, and a car needs rest after a long trip," you would falsely compare the human body with an automobile engine.

Non sequitur.   A *non sequitur* — which means "it does not follow" — occurs when no logical relationship exists between two or more ideas. For example, in the comment "Because my sister is financially independent, she will make a good parent," no logical relationship exists between financial independence and good parenting.

Red herring.   With a *red herring,* a writer attempts to distract readers from the main issue by raising an irrelevant point. For example, suppose you are arguing that television commercials for alcoholic beverages should be banned. To mention that some parents give sips of alcohol to their children distracts readers from the issue of television commercials.

For more on the post
hoc *fallacy, see Chapter
15, p. 526.*

Post hoc fallacy.   The *post hoc, ergo propter hoc* ("after this, therefore because of this") fallacy, or *post hoc* fallacy, occurs when a writer assumes that event A caused event B simply because B followed A. For example, the claim "Student enrollment fell dramatically this semester because of the recent appointment of the new college president" is a post hoc fallacy because other factors may have contributed to the decline in enrollment.

Either-or fallacy.   An *either-or* fallacy argues that there are only two sides to an issue and that only one of them is correct. For instance, on the issue of legalizing drugs, a writer may argue that all drugs must be *either* legalized *or* banned, ignoring other positions (such as legalizing marijuana use for cancer patients undergoing chemotherapy).

EXERCISE 16.6

Locate at least one brief argument essay or article and bring it to class. Working in a group of two or three students, analyze each argument using the preceding guidelines and the checklist in Figure 16.3.

FIGURE 16.3
CHECKLIST FOR ANALYZING AN ARGUMENT ESSAY

ELEMENT	*QUESTIONS*
1. The issue	• What is in dispute?
2. The claim	• Is the claim stated or implied?
	• Is it a claim of fact, value, or policy?
	• Does the author give reasons for making the claim?
3. The support	• What facts, statistics, expert opinions, examples, and personal experiences are presented?
	• Are appeals made to needs, values, or both?
4. The writer's purpose	• What is the author's purpose for writing the argument?
	• Why does the author want to convince readers to accept the claim?
	• What does the author stand to gain if the claim is accepted?
5. The intended audience	• Where is the argument essay published?
	• To whom do the reasons, evidence, and emotional appeals, examples, and comparisons seem targeted?
6. Definitions	• Are key terms in the author's claim clearly defined, especially terms that have ambiguous meanings?
7. The writer's credibility	• Is the author qualified, fair, and knowledgeable?
	• Does the author establish a common ground with readers?
8. The strength of the argument: reasons and evidence	• Does the author supply several reasons to back up the claim?
	• Is the evidence relevant, accurate, current, and typical?
	• Are the authorities cited reliable experts?
	• Are fallacies or unfair emotional appeals used?
9. Opposing viewpoints	• Does the author address opposing viewpoints clearly, fairly, and completely?
	• Does the author acknowledge, accommodate, or refute opposing viewpoints with logic and relevant evidence?
	• Does the author use emotional appeals appropriately?
	• Has the author used any logical fallacies?
10. The conclusion	• Does the author conclude the argument effectively?

THINKING CRITICALLY ABOUT ARGUMENT

Synthesizing Your Reading

In many academic situations, you will need to read and compare two or more sources on a given topic. This skill, called *synthesis*, involves drawing together two or more sets of ideas to discover similarities and differences and create new ideas and insights. You will synthesize sources — including books, articles and essays, textbook materials, and lecture notes — in writing research papers, preparing for class discussions, and studying for tests. Synthesis is especially important when you read two or more argument essays on one issue. Because each author is trying to show that his or her point of view is the correct one, you need to consider all sides of the issue carefully to develop your own position, especially if you intend to write your own argument about the topic. Use the following questions to guide your synthesis of arguments or any other sources.

- On what points do the sources agree?
- On what points do the sources disagree?
- How do the sources differ in viewpoint, approach, purpose, and type of support?
- What did I learn about this topic from the sources?
- What can I conclude about this topic based on what I read?
- With which sources do I agree?
- How can I support my views on this topic?

The pair of essays on organ donation in this chapter and the pair on sport utility vehicles in Chapter 17 provide you with two opportunities to practice your synthesizing skills.

APPLYING YOUR SKILLS: ADDITIONAL READINGS

The following essays take differing views on the issue of the sale of human organs. Use the checklist in Figure 16.3 and the strategies for reading arguments presented in this chapter to analyze and evaluate each essay.

How Much Is That Kidney in the Window?
Bruce Gottlieb

Bruce Gottlieb is a freelance writer who studied at Harvard Law School. He was a staff writer for Slate.com *and author of its Pundit Central and Explainer columns until 1999. This essay appeared in* The New Republic *in*

2000. As you read the selection, underline or highlight Gottlieb's claim and the reasons he gives to support it.

Eight years ago, an article appeared in an obscure Israeli medical journal, *Medicine and Law,* arguing that American citizens should be permitted to sell their kidneys. This would require changing federal law, which since 1984 has made selling any organ, even one's own, a felony punishable by up to five years in jail. The author of the article was a Michigan pathologist named Jack Kevorkian.

Kevorkian's argument was that the current system of accepting kidneys only from dead patients and Good Samaritan donors provides too few kidneys. While this was true even then, the situation is worse today. As of April 30, there were 44,989 people on the waiting list for a kidney transplant. About 2,300 of them will die this year while waiting. If kidney sales were permitted, Kevorkian argued, these lives would almost certainly be saved.

He may be right. In recent years, economists and economically minded lawyers at the University of Chicago and Yale Law School have made similar arguments. The idea was endorsed two years ago in the pages of *The Lancet* by a group of prominent transplant surgeons from Harvard Medical School and hospitals in Canada and England. Of course, legalizing kidney sales remains a fringe view, both within the medical profession and outside it. But that needs to change.

There are several familiar arguments against legalizing kidney sales, beginning with the idea that giving up a kidney is too dangerous for the donor. But, popular though this argument is, the statistics don't bear it out — at least relative to other risks people are legally permitted to assume. In terms of effect on life expectancy, donating one of your two kidneys is more or less equivalent to driving an additional 16 miles to work each day. No one objects to the fact that ordinary jobs — like construction or driving a delivery van — carry roughly similar risks.

Another common objection is that government ought to encourage altruism, not profit seeking. But from the perspective that matters — the recipient's — this distinction is irrelevant, so long as the donated kidney works. It's not as if the point of kidney transplants were to improve the donor's karma. Moreover, kidneys from cadavers function for eight years, on average, whereas those from live donors last 17 years. (The reason is that kidneys can be "harvested" from live donors in circumstances less hectic than death and that donors and recipients can be better matched.)

This brings us to the most powerful objection to the sale of kidneys — that, in practice, it would result in the poor selling parts of their bodies to the rich. But in today's health care economy that probably wouldn't be the case. For several decades, Congress has mandated that Medicare pay the medical bills of any patient—of any age—who requires dialysis. Transplant surgery and postsurgical drug treatment are expensive, yes, but they're nothing compared to dialysis, which costs about $40,000 per year. That's a savings of $40,000 per year for the 17 years or so during which a transplanted kidney will function. In other words, insurers and the federal government would probably be happy to buy a kidney for anyone who needs one. They'd even be willing to pay donors considerable sums—$50,000, $100,000, or more. (Indeed, according to one estimate, if kidneys could be found for all the patients now on dialysis, Medicare would break even after just two years.)

7   At these prices, there would be no shortage of sellers. The government could enforce price floors to keep competitive sellers from bidding down the going rate for kidneys. And given the amount of money involved, it seems downright contradictory to argue that the poor should be prevented from taking the deal on the grounds that poverty is unfair. The solution to poverty is anyone's guess, but restricting poor people's economic opportunities definitely isn't the answer. Nor is it enough to say that there are better and more humane ways of leveling the distribution of wealth than allowing kidney sales. To argue against kidney selling, one must provide a better practical way of helping the disadvantaged. It does a poor person who wishes to sell his kidney no favors to tell him instead to lobby Congress for an increase in the minimum wage or a more egalitarian tax code. Besides, the kidney waiting list contains a disproportionate share of minorities. Thirty-five percent of the people on the waiting list are black; twelve percent are Hispanic. If the point of the current law is to temper the effects of income inequality, asking racial minorities to shoulder an unequal share of the burden is surely a step in the wrong direction.

8   Sure, critics will say that allowing kidney sales is the beginning of a slippery slope towards selling other, more essential organs. This, of course, would be a moral disaster, since it would mean legalizing serious maiming (selling eyes) or even murder (selling hearts or lungs). But the very outrageousness of this will keep it from happening. A slippery-slope argument is convincing only when it shows that the slipping would be either inevitable (for example, that legalizing abortion when a condom breaks means people would be less careful about birth control, thereby increasing abortions) or unconscious (outlawing child porn would lead to outlawing *Lolita*, since bureaucrats can't tell the difference). But it's easy for legislators to draft a law that clearly allows kidney selling but forbids other forms of

organ selling. (Kidneys are fairly unique in that, while everybody has two, somebody with just one can lead an almost entirely normal life.) And it seems implausible that a member of Congress would mistake public approval of kidney sales for approval of economic transactions that leave sellers dead or partially blind.

Nicholas L. Tilney, a Harvard Medical School professor and transplant surgeon, wrote a paper in 1989 against kidney selling. He says this is still the view of "100 out of 100 transplant surgeons." But in 1998—as the kidney shortage became more acute—he coauthored, along with other surgeons, lawyers, and philosophers, the provocative *Lancet* paper that argued for legalizing kidney sales. "We debated this question for about two years before writing that piece," says Tilney. "All of us transplanters, and I'm sure the public, have this tremendous gut reaction against it. That was sort of our initial reaction. And then, when we all got around and really thought about this and talked about it, our thinking began to change."

The prospect of someone going under the knife to earn a down payment on a new house or to pay for college is far from pleasant. But neither is the reality of someone dying because a suitable kidney can't be found. The free market may be the worst way to allocate kidneys. The worst, that is, except for all the other alternatives. ■

Examining the Reading

1. Why does Gottlieb favor organ sales?

2. Summarize the opposing viewpoints to organ sales that Gottlieb refutes.

3. Why does Gottlieb feel that allowing the poor to sell their body parts is justifiable?

4. Explain the meaning of each of the following words as it is used in the reading: *fringe* (para. 3), *altruism* (5), *egalitarian* (7), *disproportionate* (7), and *provocative* (9).

Analyzing the Reading

1. What is Gottlieb's claim? Is it a claim of fact, value, or policy? Explain how you know.

2. In what order does Gottlieb arrange the opposing viewpoints he discusses?

3. How does Gottlieb use expert opinion in this essay?

4. Most of the essay is devoted to refuting opposing viewpoints, while very few reasons in support of organ sales are given directly. Is this an effective argument, despite the lack of reasons?

5. What types of emotional appeals does Gottlieb make? Explain each.

Reacting to the Reading: Discussion and Journal Writing

1. Explain the meaning of the essay's title. How does it relate to the essay's claim?

2. Does mention of Dr. Kevorkian help or hinder Gottlieb's argument? Explain your reasons.

3. Suppose you were offered $10,000 for one of your kidneys. It would be removed in a foreign country to avoid any legal problems in the United States. Write a journal entry explaining your response to the offer.

"Strip-Mining" the Dead: When Human Organs Are for Sale
Gilbert Meilaender

Gilbert Meilaender is professor of Christian ethics at Valparaiso University. An associate editor of the Journal of Religious Ethics, *Meilaender specializes in religious ethics and bioethics. His books include* Faith and Faithfulness: Basic Themes in Christian Ethics *(1994),* Bioethics: A Primer for Christians *(1997), and most recently* Working: Its Meaning and Its Limits *(2000). This essay originally appeared in the* National Review *in October 1999. As you read, highlight Meilaender's claim and the reason he gives to support it.*

1   Eliminate suffering and expand the range of human choice. That sentence expresses the moral wisdom toward which our society is moving, and it is very minimal wisdom indeed. We can observe this minimalism at work especially well in the realm of bioethics, where we seem unable to find any guidance other than (1) relieve suffering and (2) promote self-determination. In accordance with such wisdom, we have forged ahead in the use of new technologies at the beginning of life and—with constantly increasing pressure for assisted suicide—at the end of it.

2   Less noticed—and perhaps not quite as significant—is the continuing pressure to increase the supply of organs for transplant. For the past quarter-century, transplantation technology has made rapid progress, though the "success rates" given for transplants may often

conceal an enormous amount of suffering and frustration endured by those who accept a transplant as the price of possible survival. During this time, there has been continuing debate about what policies ought to govern the procurement of organs from the dead for transplant. Should we simply wait to see whether the dying person, or, after death, his family, decides to offer usable organs? Should we require, as some states now do, that medical caregivers request donation? Should we presume that organs for transplant may be salvaged from a corpse unless the deceased had explicitly rejected the possibility or the family rejects it later? Should we "buy" organs, using financial incentives to encourage people to sell what they had not thought or wanted to give? And if we did use financial inducements, could one also sell organs such as kidneys even before death?

What we think about such questions depends on why we think 3 some people might hesitate to give organs for transplant. If their refusal is a thoughtless act, perhaps we simply need greater public education and awareness to encourage more people to give. If their refusal is not just thoughtless but wrong, perhaps we should authorize medical professionals routinely to salvage cadaver organs for transplant. If their refusal is selfish or, at least, self-regarding, perhaps we should appeal to their self-regarding impulses with an offer of financial compensation.

Moreover, if it is, as we are so often told, a "tragedy" or a "catas- 4 trophe" that many die while waiting for an organ transplant, perhaps we need to be more daring in our public policy. That is the view of many who are in the transplant business and many who ponder transplantation as a public-policy issue. While these issues have been debated over the last several decades, our society has steadfastly refused to consider any form of payment for organs. "Giving" rather than "selling" has been the moral category governing organ procurement. Indeed, the National Organ Transplant Act of 1984 forbids "any person to knowingly acquire, receive, or otherwise transfer any human organ for valuable consideration for use in human transplantation, if the transfer affects interstate commerce."

It's not hard to understand our national reluctance to permit the 5 buying and selling of human organs for transplant, for it expresses a repugnance that is deeply rooted in important moral sentiments. In part, the very idea of organ transplantation—which is, after all, in Leon Kass's striking phrase, "a noble form of cannibalism"—is unsettling. If we cannot always articulate clearly the reasons that it troubles us, the sentiment is nonetheless powerful. To view the body—even the newly or nearly dead body—as simply a useful collection of organs requires that we stifle within ourselves a fundamental human response. "We do not," C. S. Lewis once wrote, "look at trees either as Dryads or as beautiful objects while we cut them into beams; the first man who did so may have felt the price keenly, and the bleeding trees in Virgil and Spenser may be far-off echos of that primeval sense of impiety." Far more powerful impulses must be overcome if we are to view the human form simply as a natural object available for our use. Perhaps we are right to view it as such when transplantation is truly lifesaving, but doing so exacts a cost. By insisting that organs must be given freely rather than bought and sold, we have tried to find a way to live with the cost. The "donated" organ—even separated from the body, objectified, and used—remains, in a sense, connected with the one who freely gave it, whose person we continue to respect. By contrast, buying and selling—even if it would provide more organs needed for transplant—would make of the body simply a natural object, at our disposal if the price is right.

6   Our repugnance is rooted also in the sense that some things are simply not for sale. As a medium of exchange, money makes possible advanced civilization, which depends on countless exchanges in which our interdependence is expressed. But if we allow ourselves to suppose that it is a universal medium of exchange, we are bound to lose our moral bearings. Although there is nothing degrading about buying and selling, since exchange binds us together and allows us to delight in the diversity of goods, commerce enhances human life only when that life itself is not also turned into a commodity. Hence, our society has over time had to make clear that certain things—ecclesiastical and public offices, criminal justice, human beings themselves—may not be bought and sold.

7   Discussing the limits to money as a medium of exchange, Michael Walzer recounts an instructive story from our own history. In 1863, during the Civil War, the Union enacted an Enrollment and Conscription Act, which was the first military draft at the national level in our history. But the act contained a provision that allowed any man whose name was drawn in the lottery to purchase an exemption by paying $300 for a substitute (which, in effect, also offered an incentive for others who wanted or needed $300, even at the risk of death). Anti-draft riots broke out in July 1863 after the first drawing of lots, and we have never since—at least in such overt, crass form—allowed citizens to buy their way out of military service. It is one of those things that should not be for sale, one instance in which money should not be allowed to serve as a medium of exchange, and so we block that exchange.

8   Similarly, we have decided to block exchanges for human organs, even though they do take place in some other countries. That decision has been under attack for some time. It has even been criticized by Thomas Peters, for example, as—behold here the degradation of our public moral discourse—"imposing" the value of altruistic

donation on those who do not appreciate such a value or "coercing" families "to accept concepts foreign to them at a time of great personal loss." But the first real crack in the public-policy dike appeared in May of 1999, when the state of Pennsylvania announced its intention to begin paying relatives of organ donors $300 toward funeral expenses of their deceased relative. (Clearly, $300 doesn't buy as much as it did in 1863.)

Pennsylvania's decision has been characterized by Charles   9
Krauthammer as "strip-mining" the dead—and this in an essay defending the decision. It would, Krauthammer asserts, violate human dignity to permit the living to sell organs, but the newly dead body may be treated as a commodity if doing so promises "to alleviate the catastrophic shortage of donated organs." (Note, again, the language of catastrophe. Just as many workers might not have known their labor was "alienated" until Marxists told them, so we might not have thought it "catastrophic" that we die rather than strip-mine the human body in order to stay alive until transplant technology began to tell us it was.) Indeed, Krauthammer quite reasonably claims that the Pennsylvania program is, if anything, far too timid. If the idea is to get more organs for transplant, he suggests that not $300 but $3000—paid directly to relatives rather than to funeral homes— might be more the ticket.

To the degree that he persuades us, however, we might well judge   10
that Krauthammer himself has been too timid. Pennsylvania's plan for compensation continues to operate within the organ-donation system currently in place. It aims simply to provide a somewhat greater incentive for people to donate organs. What it will not affect is the reluctance—based in sound moral sentiment—of medical caregivers to ask dying people or their families to consider organ donation. If we really face a tragedy of catastrophic proportions, we might do better to allow organ-procurement firms seeking a profit to be the middleman. (After all, a human kidney was recently offered for sale on the Internet auction site eBay—and the bidding reached $5.7 million before the company stopped it.) With profit to be made, firms would find ways to overcome our natural reluctance to ask others to strip-mine the dead body. We could deal not only with our reluctance to give organs but also with our reluctance to ask for them by letting the market do what it does best. That Krauthammer does not suggest this—even for organs from the dead—suggests to me that he finds more "dignity" than he thinks not only in still-living human beings but also in the newly dead body.

Or, again, if it is a catastrophe that we face, we might simply   11
abandon the claim that it is always necessary to wait for death before procuring organs for transplant. For example, as Robert Arnold and Stuart Youngner have noted, a ventilator-dependent patient could

request that life support be removed and that, eight or so hours before, he be taken to the operating room and anesthetized, to have his kidneys, liver, and pancreas taken out. Bleeding vessels could be tied off, and the patient's heart would stop only after the ventilator was removed later that day, well before the patient could die of renal, hepatic, or pancreatic failure. And, of course, if our moral wisdom is confined to relieving suffering and respecting autonomy, we may find ourselves very hard pressed to explain why this should not be done—especially in the face of a "catastrophic shortage" of organs.

12   One might ask, If my death is an evil, why not at least try to get some good for others out of it? If my corpse is no longer my person, as it surely is not, why not treat it as a commodity if doing so helps the living? Ah, but that corpse is my mortal remains. There is no way to think of my person apart from it and no way to gaze upon it without thinking of my person—which person is a whole web of human relations, not a thing or a commodity. A corpse is uncanny precisely because we cannot, without doing violence to our humanity, divorce it fully from the person. To treat those mortal remains with respect, to refuse to see them as merely in service of other goods, is our last chance to honor the "extraterritoriality" of each human life and to affirm that the human person is not simply a "part" of a human community. Perhaps, if we do so honor even the corpse, I or some others will not live as long as we might, but we will have taken at least a small step toward preserving the kind of society in which anyone might wish to live.

13   More than a quarter century ago, writing about "Attitudes toward the newly dead," William F. May called attention to one of the Grimm Brothers tales about a young man who is incapable of horror. He does not shrink back from a hanged man, and he attempts to play with a corpse. His behavior might seem childish, but it is in fact inhuman. And his father sends him away "to learn how to shudder"—that is, to become human. In our society—where we devote enormous energy and money to keeping human beings alive—perhaps we too, in the face of proposals to strip-mine the dead, should consider learning once again how to shudder.   ■

Examining the Reading

1. Summarize Meilaender's reasons for opposing human organ sales.
2. Explain the meaning of the quotation that transplantation is "a noble form of cannibalism" (para. 5).

3. Why does Meilaender oppose organ sales but seem to approve of organ donation?

4. Explain the meaning of each of the following words as it is used in the reading: *bioethics* (para. 1), *catastrophe* (4), *ecclesiastical* (6), *uncanny* (12), and *extraterritoriality* (12).

Analyzing the Reading

1. What is Meilaender's claim?

2. To what needs and values does Meilaender appeal?

3. Explain the analogy that Meilaender draws between the Civil War draft exemption and organ donation. Is this an effective analogy? Why?

4. What opposing viewpoints does Meilaender recognize? Does he refute them? If so, how?

5. The last paragraph includes a reference to a Grimm Brothers tale. Is this reference effective in concluding the essay?

Reacting to the Reading: Discussion and Journal Writing

1. Strip-mining usually refers to the practice of stripping away soil and land, usually to sell products. Discuss whether organ sales can be compared to strip-mining. What similarities or differences exist?

2. Do you agree or disagree that a still-living human and a newly dead body should be treated with the same degree of respect and dignity?

3. Meilaender suggests that part of being human is knowing how to shudder. Write a journal entry explaining whether you think the ability to shudder is a distinct and necessary human characteristic.

Integrating the Readings

1. Which writer's argument did you find more convincing? Why?

2. Compare how each writer introduces the issue. In what context does each writer frame the issue?

3. How do you think Gottlieb might respond to Meilaender's claim?

4. If you could seek further information from each author, what questions would you ask?

Address | http://www.populationinstitute.org/ ▼

 The
Population
Institute

The Issue
Who We Are
Programs
Publications
News
Public Policy Advocacy
Awards & Grants
Jobs & Fellowships
Events
Personality of
   the Week
Make a Donation
Contact Us
Related Links
Search
Action

Overpopulation is not a distant issue. Its overwhelming problems are upon us. Every member of every future generation will be directly affected by what you and The Population Institute do now.

Action | The Issue | Who We Are | Programs | Publications
Public Policy Advocacy | Awards & Grants | Jobs & Internships | Events
Personality of the Week | Make a Donation | Contact Us | Related Links | Search

Writing Arguments

CHAPTER QUICK START

Suppose you are doing research and you locate the Web site shown on the opposite page. Its home page presents a brief argument: It identifies an issue (overpopulation), makes a claim (overpopulation causes problems for present and future generations), and invites readers to enter the site to find out what they can do to help (take action).

Writing Quick Start

Working alone or with one or two classmates, rewrite the Web page as a brief argument of one to three paragraphs. The claim is your thesis. Add support of your own to strengthen the argument: evidence, emotional appeals, and so on. Also consider why some readers might disagree with the claim and offer reasons to refute this view. Conclude your brief argument with a convincing statement.

WRITING AN ARGUMENT

By following the steps in the Writing Quick Start, you successfully started to build an argument. You made a claim, supported it with evidence, and refuted opposing views. This chapter will show you how to write clear, effective arguments.

WHAT IS AN ARGUMENT?

You encounter arguments daily in casual conversations, in newspapers, in classrooms, and on the job. Of the many arguments we hear and read, however, relatively few are convincing. A **sound argument** makes a claim and offers reasons and evidence in support of that claim. A sound argument also anticipates opposing viewpoints and acknowledges, accommodates, and/or refutes them.

The ability to construct and write sound arguments is an important skill in many aspects of life. Many political, social, and economic issues, for instance, are resolved through public and private debate. Knowing how to construct a sound argument is also essential to success in college and on the job (see the accompanying box for a few examples).

The following essay argues in favor of abolishing the U.S. penny.

SCENES FROM COLLEGE AND THE WORKPLACE

- For a *health science* course, you are part of a group working on an argument essay claiming that the results of genetic testing, which can predict a person's likelihood of contracting serious diseases, should be kept confidential.

- As a student member of the *Affirmative Action Committee* on campus, you are asked to write a letter to the editor of the campus newspaper defending the committee's recently drafted affirmative action plan for minorities and women.

- As a *lawyer* representing a client whose hand was seriously injured on the job, you must argue to a jury that your client deserves compensation for the work-related injury.

Abolish the Penny
William Safire

William Safire, a former speechwriter for Richard Nixon and Spiro Agnew, was a longtime op-ed columnist for the New York Times. *He is best known for "On Language," his column on grammar, usage, and etymology in the weekly* New York Times Magazine, *and he has published many books, including* Lend Me Your Ears: Great Speeches in History *(1997),* The Right Word in the Right Place at the Right Time: Wit and Wisdom from the Popular Language Column in the *New York Times Magazine (2004), and* Before the Fall: An Inside View of the Pre-Watergate White House *(2005). He won the Pulitzer Prize for commentary in 1978. As you read the following June 2, 2004, essay, notice how Safire gives his own reasons for abolishing the penny and anticipates possible counterarguments.*

Because my staunch support of the war in Iraq has generated such overwhelming reader enthusiasm, it's time to re-establish my contrarian credentials. (Besides, I need a break.) Here's a crusade sure to infuriate the vast majority of penny-pinching traditionalists: The time has come to abolish the outdated, almost worthless, bothersome, and wasteful penny. Even President Lincoln, who distrusted the notion of paper money because he thought he would have to sign each greenback, would be ashamed to have his face on this specious specie.

That's because you can't buy anything with a penny any more. Penny candy? Not for sale at the five-and-dime (which is now a "dollar store"). Penny-ante poker? Pass the buck. Any vending machine? Put a penny in and it will sound an alarm. There is no escaping economic history: it takes nearly a dime today to buy what a penny bought back in 1950. Despite this, the U.S. Mint keeps churning out a billion pennies a month.

Where do they go? Two-thirds of them immediately drop out of circulation, into piggy banks or—as the *Times*'s John Tierney noted five years ago—behind chair cushions or at the back of sock drawers next to your old tin-foil ball. Quarters and dimes circulate; pennies disappear because they are literally more trouble than they are worth. The remaining 300 million or so—that's 10 million shiny new useless items punched out every day by government workers who could be more usefully employed tracking counterfeiters—go toward driving retailers crazy. They cost more in employee-hours—to wait for buyers to fish them out, then to count, pack up and take them to the bank—than it would cost to toss them out. That's why you see "penny cups" next to every cash register; they save the seller time and the buyer the inconvenience of lugging around loose change that tears holes in pockets and now sets off alarms at every frisking-place.

4   Why is the U.S. among the last of the industrialized nations to abolish the peskiest little bits of coinage? At the G-8 summit next week, the Brits and the French — even the French! — who dumped their low-denomination coins 30 years ago, will be laughing at our senseless jingling. The penny-pinching horde argues: those $9.98 price tags save the consumer 2 cents because if the penny was abolished, merchants would "round up" to the nearest dollar. That's pound-foolish: the idea behind the 98-cent (and I can't even find a cent symbol on my keyboard any more) price is to fool you into thinking that "it's less than 10 bucks." In truth, merchants would round down to $9.95, saving the consumer billions of paper dollars over the next century.

What's really behind America's clinging to the pesky penny? Nostalgia cannot be the answer; if we can give up the barbershop shave with its steam towels, we can give up anything. The answer, I think, has to do with zinc, which is what pennies are mostly made of; light copper plating turns them into red cents. The powerful, outsourcing zinc lobby — financed by Canadian mines as well as Alaskan — entices front groups to whip up a frenzy of save-the-penny mail to Congress when coin reform is proposed.

5   But when the penny is abolished, the nickel will boom. And what is a nickel made of? No, not the metallic element nickel; our 5-cent coin is mainly composed of copper. And where is most of America's copper mined? Arizona. If Senator John McCain would get off President Bush's back long enough to serve the economic interests of his Arizona constituents, we'd get some long-overdue coin reform.

6   What about Lincoln, who has had a century-long run on the penny? He's still honored on the $5 bill, and will be as long as the dollar sign remains above the 4 on keyboards. If this threatens coin reformers with the loss of Illinois votes, put Abe on the dime and bump F.D.R.[1]

7   What frazzled pollsters, surly op-ed[2] pages, snarling cable talk-fests, and issue-starved candidates for office need is a fresh source of hot-eyed national polarization. Coin reform can close the controversy gap and fill the vitriol void. Get out those bumper stickers: Abolish the penny!   ■

---

[1]*F.D.R.:* Franklin Delano Roosevelt, U.S. president from 1933 to 1945.
[2]*op-ed:* the opinion section of the newspaper that is opposite the editorial page.

Characteristics of Argument Essays

All arguments are concerned with issues. In developing an argument essay, you need to narrow or limit the issue, make a clear and specific claim about the issue, analyze your audience, and give reasons and evidence to support the claim. In addition, you should follow a logical line of reasoning, use emotional appeals appropriately, and acknowledge, accommodate, and/or refute opposing views.

An Argument Focuses on a Narrowed Issue

An **issue** is a controversy, problem, or idea about which people disagree. In choosing an issue, therefore, be sure it is arguable — one that people have differing opinions on. For example, arguing that education is important in today's job market is pointless because people generally agree on that issue.

Depending on the issue you choose and the audience you write for, a clear definition of the issue may be required. Well-known issues need little definition, but for less familiar issues, readers may need background information. In an argument about the awarding of organ transplants, for example, you would give readers information about the scarcity of organ donors versus the number of people who need transplants. Notice how Safire announces and defines the issue in "Abolish the Penny," paragraph 1.

In addition, the issue you choose should be narrow enough to deal with adequately in an essay-length argument. For an essay on organ transplants, for instance, you could limit your argument to transplants of a particular organ or to one aspect of the issue, such as who does and does not receive them. When you narrow your issue, your thesis will be more precise and your evidence more specific. You can also provide more effective arguments against an opposing viewpoint.

EXERCISE 17.1

Working alone or in a group of two or three students, choose two of the following issues. For each issue, consider ways to limit the topic and list the background information readers might need to understand the issue.

1. Moral implications of state-operated lotteries
2. Computer networks and the right to privacy
3. Speech codes on campus
4. Religious symbols on public property
5. Mandatory drug testing

An Argument States a Specific Claim in a Thesis

To build a convincing argument, you need to make a clear and specific **claim**, one that tells readers your position on the issue. If writing arguments is new to you, it

For more on types of claims, see Chapter 16, p. 559.

is usually best to state your claim in a strong thesis early in the essay. Doing so will help you keep your argument on track. As you gain experience in writing arguments, you can experiment with placing your thesis later in the essay. In "Abolish the Penny," Safire makes a clear, specific claim in his opening paragraph: "The time has come to abolish the outdated, almost worthless, bothersome, and wasteful penny."

Here are a few examples of how general claims can be narrowed into clear and specific thesis statements.

GENERAL	More standards are needed to protect children in day-care centers.
SPECIFIC	Statewide standards are needed to regulate the child-to-caregiver ratio and the qualifications of workers in day-care centers.
GENERAL	The use of animals in testing should be prohibited.
SPECIFIC	The testing of cosmetics and skin-care products on animals should be prohibited.

While all arguments make and support a claim, some also call for specific action to be taken. An essay opposing human cloning, for example, might argue for a ban on that practice as well as urge readers to voice their opinions in letters to congressional representatives. Claims of policy often include a call for action.

For more on claims of policy, see Chapter 16, p. 559.

Regardless of the argument, you need to be careful about the way you state your claim. Avoid a general or absolute statement; your claim will be more convincing if you qualify or limit it. For example, if a writer arguing in favor of single-sex education makes the claim "Single-sex educational institutions are *always* more beneficial to girls than are coeducational schools," then opponents could easily cite exceptions to the claim and thereby show weaknesses in the argument. However, if the claim is qualified—as in "Single-sex educational institutions are *often* more beneficial to girls than are coeducational schools"—then an exception would not necessarily weaken the argument.

EXERCISE 17.2

Choose two of the following issues. Then, for each issue, write two thesis statements—one that makes a claim and contains a qualifying term and another that makes a claim and calls for action.

1. Controlling pornography on the Internet
2. Limiting immigration
3. Limiting political campaign spending
4. Making computer literacy a graduation requirement
5. Promoting competitive sports for young children

An Argument Depends on Careful Audience Analysis

To build a convincing argument, you need to know your audience. Because an argument is intended to influence readers' thinking, begin by anticipating your readers' views. First determine how familiar your audience is with the issue. Then decide whether your audience agrees with your claim, is neutral about or wavering on the claim, or disagrees with the claim.

Agreeing audiences. When you write for an audience that agrees with your claim, the focus is usually on urging readers to take a specific action. Agreeing audiences are the easiest to write for because they already accept your claim. Instead of presenting large amounts of facts and statistics as evidence, you can concentrate on reinforcing your shared viewpoint and building emotional ties with your audience. By doing so, you encourage readers to act on their beliefs.

For more on emotional appeals, see Chapter 16, p. 574.

Neutral or wavering audiences. Audiences are neutral or wavering when they have not made up their minds about or given much thought to an issue. Although they may be somewhat familiar with the issue, they may have questions about, misunderstandings about, or no interest in the issue. In writing for a neutral or wavering audience, emphasize the importance of the issue and offer explanations that clear up misunderstandings readers may have about it. Your goals are to establish yourself as a knowledgeable and credible writer, engender readers' trust, and present solid evidence in support of your claim.

Disagreeing audiences. The most challenging type of audience is the disagreeing audience—one that holds viewpoints in opposition to yours. Such an audience may also be hostile to your claim and have strong feelings about the issue. Disagreeing audiences believe their position is correct and are not eager to accept your views. They may also distrust you because you don't share their views on something they care deeply about.

In writing for a disagreeing audience, your goal is to persuade readers to consider your views on the issue. Be sure to follow a logical line of reasoning. Rather than stating your claim early in the essay, for a disagreeing audience it may be more effective to build slowly to your thesis. First establish a **common ground**—a basis of trust and goodwill—with your readers by mentioning shared interests, concerns, experiences, and points in your argument. Then, when you state your claim, the audience may be more open to considering your argument.

In "Abolish the Penny," Safire writes for a disagreeing audience. In the opening paragraph, Safire recognizes that he is likely to infuriate "penny-pinching traditionalists." Safire openly acknowledges the opposing view in paragraph 4, where he summarizes the argument of the "penny-pinching horde." Safire establishes a common ground with his readers by mentioning shared concerns (about productivity of government workers and political lobbyists) and referring to well-respected historical figures such as Abraham Lincoln and Franklin Delano Roosevelt.

EXERCISE 17.3

For one of the following claims, discuss how you would argue in support of it for an agreeing audience, a neutral or wavering audience, and a disagreeing audience.

1. Public school sex education classes should be mandatory because they help students make important decisions about their lives.
2. Portraying the effects of violent crime realistically on television may help to reduce the crime rate.
3. Children who spend too much time interacting with a computer may fail to learn how to interact with people.

An Argument Presents Reasons Supported by Convincing Evidence

In developing an argument, you need to have reasons for making a claim. A **reason** is a general statement that backs up a claim; it answers the question, "Why do I have this opinion about the issue?" You also need to support each reason with evidence. Suppose, for example, you argue that high school uniforms should be mandatory for three reasons: The uniforms (1) reduce clothing costs for parents; (2) help eliminate distractions in the classroom; and (3) reduce peer pressure. Each of your reasons would need to be supported by evidence, facts, statistics, examples, personal experience, or expert testimony. Carefully linking your evidence to reasons helps readers to see how the evidence supports your claim.

Be sure to choose reasons and evidence that will appeal to your audience. In the argument about mandatory school uniforms, high school students would probably not be impressed by your first reason—reduced clothing costs for parents—but they might consider your second and third reasons if you cite evidence that appeals to them, such as personal anecdotes from students. For an audience of parents, facts and statistics about reduced clothing costs and improved academic performance would be appealing types of evidence. In "Abolish the Penny," Safire offers several reasons for his claim and supports them with examples. For instance, pennies drop out of circulation, fall behind chair cushions, or hide at the back of sock drawers.

An Argument Follows a Logical Line of Reasoning

The reasons and evidence in an argument should follow a logical line of reasoning. The most common types of reasoning are induction and deduction (see the diagrams on page 597). Whereas **inductive reasoning** begins with evidence and moves to a conclusion, **deductive reasoning** begins with a commonly accepted statement or premise and shows how a conclusion follows from it. You can use one or both types of reasoning to keep your argument on a logical path.

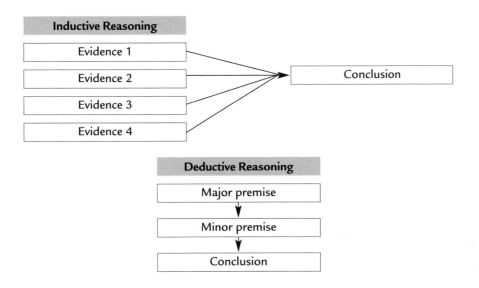

Inductive reasoning.   Inductive reasoning starts with specific evidence and moves to a generalization or conclusion. For example, suppose you go shopping for a new pair of sneakers. You try on one style of Nikes. It doesn't fit, so you try a different style. It doesn't fit either. You try two more styles, neither of which fits. Finally, because of your experience, you draw the conclusion that either you need to re-measure your feet or Nike does not make a sneaker that fits your feet. Think of inductive reasoning as a process of coming to a conclusion after observing a number of examples.

When you use inductive reasoning, you make an *inference* or guess about the cases that you have not experienced. In doing so, you run the risk of being wrong. Perhaps some other style of Nikes would have fit.

When building an inductive argument, be sure to consider all possible explanations for the cases you observe. In the shoe store, for example, perhaps the sales-person measured your foot incorrectly and brought you the wrong size sneakers. You also need to be sure that you have *sufficient* and *typical* evidence on which to base your conclusion. Suppose you observe one food stamp recipient selling food stamps for cash and another using them to buy candy bars. From these observations you conclude that the food stamp program should be abolished. Your reasoning is faulty, however, because these two cases are not typical of food stamp recipients and not sufficient for drawing a conclusion. You must scrutinize your evidence and make sure you have enough typical evidence to support your conclusion.

When you use inductive reasoning in an argument essay, the conclusion becomes the claim, and the specific pieces of evidence support your reasons for making the claim. For example, suppose you make a claim that Pat's Used Cars is unreliable. As support you might offer the following reasons and evidence.

REASON	Pat's Used Cars does not provide accurate information about its products.
EVIDENCE	My sister's car had its odometer reading tampered with. My best friend bought a car whose chassis had been damaged, yet the salesperson claimed the car had never been in an accident.
REASON	Pat's Used Cars doesn't honor its commitments to customers.
EVIDENCE	The dealership refused to honor the ninety-day guarantee for a car I purchased there. A local newspaper recently featured Pat's in a report on businesses that fail to honor guarantees.

Deductive reasoning.   Deductive reasoning begins with **premises**, statements that are generally accepted as true. Once the premises are accepted as true, then the conclusion must also be true. The most familiar deductive argument consists of two premises and a conclusion. The first statement, called a **major premise**, is a general statement about a group. The second statement, called a **minor premise**, is a statement about an individual belonging to that group. You have probably used this three-step reasoning, called a **syllogism**, without realizing it. For example, suppose you know that any food containing dairy products makes you ill. Because frozen yogurt contains dairy products, you conclude that frozen yogurt will make you ill.

When you use deductive reasoning, putting your argument in the form of a syllogism will help you write your claim and organize and evaluate your reasons and evidence. Suppose you want to support the claim that state funding for Kids First, an early childhood program, should remain intact. You might use the following syllogism to build your argument.

MAJOR PREMISE	State-funded early childhood programs have increased the readiness of at-risk children to attend school.
MINOR PREMISE	Kids First is a popular early childhood program in our state.
CONCLUSION	Kids First is likely to increase the readiness of at-risk children to attend school.

Your thesis statement would be "Because early childhood programs are likely to increase the readiness of at-risk children to attend school, state funding for Kids First should be continued." Your evidence would be the popularity and effectiveness of Kids First.

For more on fallacies, see Chapter 16, p. 576.

As you develop a logical argument, you also need to avoid introducing **fallacies,** or errors in reasoning.

An Argument Appeals to Readers' Needs and Values

For more on emotional appeals, see Chapter 16, p. 574.

Although an effective argument relies mainly on credible evidence and logical reasoning, emotional appeals can help support and enhance a sound argument.

Emotional appeals are directed toward readers' needs and values. **Needs** can be biological or psychological (food and drink, sex, a sense of belonging, and esteem, for example). **Values** are principles or qualities that readers consider important, worthwhile, or desirable. Examples include honesty, loyalty, privacy, and patriotism. In "Abolish the Penny," Safire appeals to the human need for efficiency to convince his readers to abolish outdated and worthless goods. Safire is also aware of the value of patriotism as he assures readers that presidential figures will remain on currency.

An Argument Recognizes Opposing Views

Recognizing or countering opposing arguments forces you to think hard about your own claims. When you listen to readers' objections, you may find reasons to adjust your own reasoning and develop a stronger argument. In addition, readers will be more willing to consider your claim if you take their point of view into account.

There are three methods of recognizing opposing views in an argument essay: *acknowledgment, accommodation,* and *refutation.*

1. When you **acknowledge** an opposing viewpoint, you admit that it exists and show that you have considered it. For example, readers opposed to mandatory high school uniforms may argue that a uniform requirement will not eliminate peer pressure because students will use other objects to gain status—such as backpacks, CDs, hairstyles, and cellular phones. You could acknowledge this viewpoint by admitting there is no way to stop teenagers from finding ways to compete for status.

2. When you **accommodate** an opposing viewpoint, you acknowledge readers' concerns, accept some of them, and incorporate them into your own argument. In arguing for mandatory high school uniforms, you might accommodate readers' view that uniforms will not eliminate peer pressure by arguing that the uniforms will eliminate one major and expensive means of competing for status.

3. When you **refute** an opposing viewpoint, you demonstrate the weakness of the opponent's argument. Safire refutes opposing views in his essay on abolishing the penny. He acknowledges that some people fear that abolishing the penny would encourage merchants to "round up" their prices to the next dollar. He refutes this fear by reassuring readers that merchants would more likely "round down" to a lower price.

EXERCISE 17.4

For the three claims listed in Exercise 17.3, identify opposing viewpoints and consider how you could acknowledge, accommodate, or refute them.

Visualizing an Argument Essay: A Graphic Organizer

The graphic organizer shown in Figure 17.1 will help you analyze arguments as well as plan those that you write. Unlike the graphic organizers in Part 3, this organizer does not necessarily show the order in which an argument may be presented. Some arguments, for example, may begin with a claim, whereas others may start with evidence or opposing viewpoints. Whatever your argument's sequence, you can adapt this organizer to fit your essay. Note, however, that not every element will appear in every argument.

Read the following essay by Rachel Jones and then study the graphic organizer for it in Figure 17.2 on page 604.

Not White, Just Right
Rachel Jones

Rachel Jones is a national correspondent for Knight-Ridder newspapers and president of the Journalism and Women Symposium. Her column in the Chicago Reporter, *a monthly newsletter focusing on race and policy issues, won the 1995 Unity in Media Award for Editorial Writing. This essay first appeared in* Newsweek, *a weekly newsmagazine, in 1997. As you read the selection, highlight Jones's claim, supporting evidence, and counter-arguments.*

1   In December of 1982, *Newsweek* published a My Turn column that launched my professional writing career and changed the course of my life. In that essay, entitled "What's Wrong with Black English," I argued that black youngsters need to become proficient in standard English. While the dialect known as black English is a valid part of our cultural history, I wrote, success in America requires a mastery of communications skills.

2   Fourteen years later, watching the increasingly heated debate over the use of black English in struggling minority urban school districts, I can't help but offer my own experience as proof that the premise is greatly flawed. My skill with standard English propelled me from a life of poverty and dead ends to a future I could have scarcely imagined. It has opened doors for me that might never have budged an inch for a poor black girl from Cairo, Illinois. It has empowered me in ways I can't begin to explain.

3   That empowerment still amazes me. The column, one that Ralph Waldo Emerson might have described as "a frank and hearty expres-

FIGURE 17.1
GRAPHIC ORGANIZER FOR AN ARGUMENT ESSAY

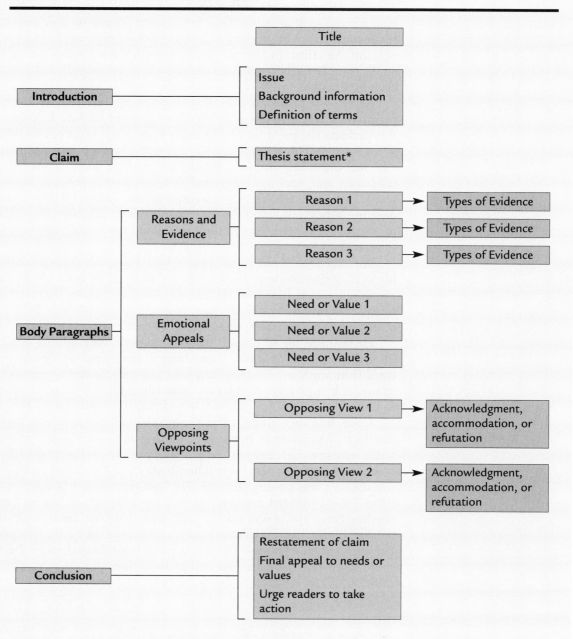

*The thesis statement may appear anywhere within the argument.

sion of what force and meaning is in me," has assumed an identity of its own, far beyond what I envisioned. It has been reprinted in at least 50 college English texts, anthologies, and writing course books. I still have a scrapbook of some of the letters that poured in from around the country, from blacks and whites, overwhelmingly applauding my opinion. An editor in Detroit said he recognized my name on a job-application letter because he'd clipped the column and used it in a class he'd taught.

4   Recently, a professor from Brigham Young University requested permission to record the material on a tape used for blind students. But perhaps the most humbling experience of all occurred in 1991, when I was on fellowship in Chicago and received a phone call from a 20-year-old college student. He had just read the essay in one of his textbooks and, on impulse, dialed directory assistance, seeking my name. Because the column was written in 1982, when I'd been a student in Carbondale — and Chicago wasn't my hometown — there was no reason for him to have found me; I could have been anywhere in the world.

5   We talked for about an hour that night. He thanked me profusely for writing that column. He was biracial and said that all his life his peers had teased him for "talking proper, for wishing [he] was *all* white." He said he was frustrated that so many black kids believed that speaking articulately was a white characteristic.

6   He thanked me so often it was almost unnerving. I hung up the phone in a sort of daze. Something I had written, communicated from my heart, had touched him so deeply he had to reach out to me. It brings tears to my eyes remembering it; I related to him so well.

7   I, too, had been ridiculed as a youth for my proper speech. But I had lots of support at home, and many poor urban black youths today may not share my advantages. Every afternoon my eight older brothers and sisters left their schoolbooks piled on every available surface, so I was poking through *The Canterbury Tales*[1] by age 8. My sister Julie corrected me every time I used "ain't" or "nope." My brother Peter was a star on the high-school debate team. And my mother, Eloise, has one of the clearest, most resonant speaking voices I've ever known. Though she was a poor housekeeper when I was growing up, she was articulate and plain-spoken.

---

[1]*The Canterbury Tales:* A collection of poems written by English author Geoffrey Chaucer (1340?–1400).

Knowing the price that was paid for me to develop my abilities, 8
it's infuriating to hear that some young blacks still perceive clear
speech as a Caucasian trait. Whether they know it or not, they're suc-
cumbing to a dangerous form of self-abnegation that rejects success
as a "white thing." In an age of backlash against affirmative action,
that's a truly frightening thought.

To me, this "whitewashing" is the crux of the problem. Don't 9
tell me that calling Ebonics[2] a "bridge" or an "attempt to reach
children where they are" will not deepen this perception in the
minds of disadvantaged young blacks. And though Oakland, California, school administrators[3] have amended their original position
on Ebonics, it still feels like a very pointed political statement to me,
one rooted in the ongoing discussions about socioeconomic justice
and educational equity for blacks. As much as I respect the cultural
foundations of Ebonics, I think Oakland trivializes these discussions and stokes the fires of racial misunderstanding. Senator Lauch
Faircloth may have been too hasty in calling the Oakland school
board's plan to introduce Ebonics "political correctness gone out
of control," but he's hardly to be condemned for raising the flag of
concern.

When immigrants worldwide fight to come to the United States, 10
many seeking to gain even the most basic English skills, claiming a
subset of language for black Americans is a damning commentary
on our history of inequity and lack of access to equal educational
opportunities in this country. Frankly, I'm still longing for a day
when more young blacks born in poverty will subscribe to my personal philosophy. After a lifetime of hard work to achieve my goal of
being a writer, of battling racism and forging my own path, I've
decided that I really don't care if people like me or not. But I demand
that they *understand* me, clearly, on my own terms. My mastery of
standard English gave me a power that no one can take away from
me, and it is important for any group of people hoping to succeed in
America. As a great-granddaughter of slaves, I believe success is my
birthright.

As I said back in December of 1982, I don't think I "talk white, I 11
think I talk right." That's not quite grammatically correct, but it's a
blessing to know the difference. ■

---

[2]*Ebonics:* The study of black English as a language.

[3]*Oakland School District:* The school board originally voted to treat African American
students as bilingual; the board modified this plan to focus on teaching proficiency in
standard English.

FIGURE 17.2
GRAPHIC ORGANIZER FOR "NOT WHITE, JUST RIGHT"

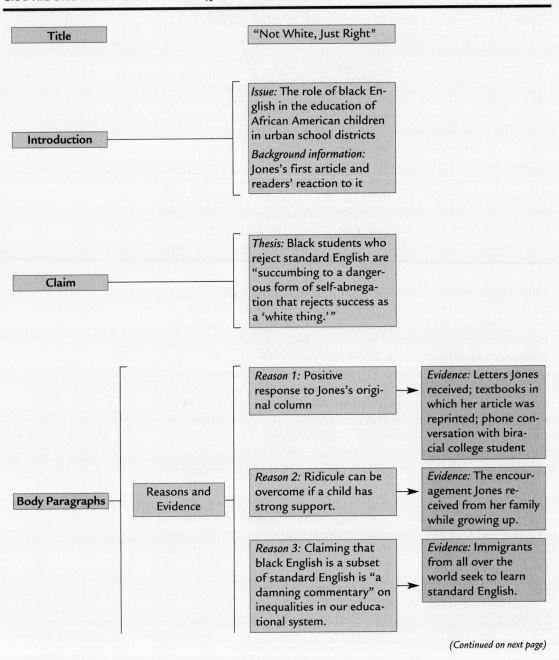

(Continued on next page)

FIGURE 17.2 *(Continued)*

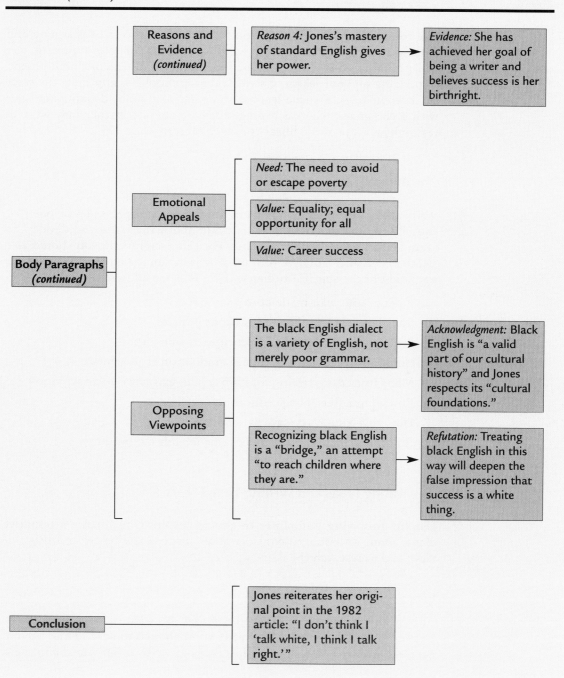

A GUIDED WRITING ASSIGNMENT

For more on the patterns of development, see Chapters 8–15.

The following guide will lead you through the process of planning and writing an argument essay. In presenting support for your argument, you will probably need to use one or more other patterns of development. Depending on your learning style, you may choose to approach the essay in different ways. A social learner may want to start by debating an issue with a classmate, whereas a pragmatic or concrete learner may want to research an issue in the library or on the Internet.

The Assignment

Write an argument essay on one of the following topic issues or one that you choose on your own. Make a claim about the issue and develop an argument in support of your claim. For this assignment, you should also select an audience. Analyze your readers' views on the issue and target your argument to the specific audience you choose to address.

1. Buying American-made products
2. Racial quotas in college admissions policies
3. Professional athletes and celebrities as role models
4. Community service as a college graduation requirement
5. Mandatory drug testing for high school extracurricular activities
6. Providing a free college education to prisoners
7. Donating kidneys to save lives of others
8. An environmental problem or issue in your community

Generating Ideas and Writing Your Thesis

Use the following guidelines to choose, explore, and make a tentative claim about an issue; to consider your purpose, audience, and point of view; and to research the issue.

Choosing and Exploring an Issue

Choose an issue that interests you and that you want to learn more about. Depending on how much you already know about a topic, you may need to conduct extensive research. For instance, to write an informed argument about mandatory drug testing for high school extracurricular activities, you would need to research existing laws, types of tests, and state and local policies. The issues listed in the assignment need to be narrowed. The issue about racial profiling in college admission policies, for instance, might be limited to private colleges in a particular geographic region.

If you have trouble choosing an issue, move to the next step and explore several promising issues until you can make a decision. Experiment with the following strategies to discover those that work for you and fit your learning style.

For more on prewriting strategies, see Chapter 3.

Learning Style Options

1. Brainstorm about different sides of the issue. Think of reasons and evidence that support various viewpoints.

2. Make a tentative claim and list reasons that support the claim. Then switch sides, state an opposing claim, and brainstorm to discover reasons and corresponding supporting evidence.

3. Draw a map of the issue, connecting ideas as they come to mind. Then narrow your issue: Start with one or two key ideas you generated and draw another map.

4. Conduct a mock argument with a classmate. Choose opposing views on the issue and defend your positions. Take notes on the argument. Notice the reasons and evidence you and your opponent use to support your positions.

5. Write the issue at the top of a piece of paper or in a computer file. Then divide the list into two columns, listing pros in one column and cons in the other.

6. Examine the issue by answering these key questions.

   - What is the issue? How can I best define it?
   - Is it an arguable issue?
   - What are some related issues?
   - How can I narrow the issue for an essay-length argument?
   - What are my views on the issue? How can I state my claim?
   - What evidence supports my claim?
   - Does my argument include a call for action? What do I want readers to do, if anything, about the issue?
   - Does the issue have a compromise position?

7. Talk with others who have experience with the issue or are experts. For example, if you argue for stricter laws to prevent child abuse, a case worker for a child welfare agency may be able to help you narrow the issue, gather evidence, and address opposing viewpoints. A friend who

For more on conducting an interview, see Chapter 19, p. 689.

experienced abuse as a child could provide another perspective. Keep in mind that sensitive topics should be approached tactfully and requests for confidentiality should be respected.

For more on Internet research, see Chapter 19, p. 673.

8. **Use the Internet.** Talk with others about the issue in a chatroom, newsgroup, or listserv. Use a search engine to locate discussion forums on your topic as well as Web sites that deal with the issue.

> **ESSAY IN PROGRESS 1**
>
> Use the preceding suggestions to choose an issue to write about (one from the list of assignments on page 606 or one you think of on your own) and to explore and narrow the issue.

Considering Your Purpose, Audience, and Point of View

Once you choose an issue and begin to explore it, consider carefully your purpose, audience, and point of view. Think about what you want to happen as a result of your argument: Do you want your readers to change their minds? Do you want them to feel more certain of their existing beliefs? Or would you have them take some specific action?

An effective argument is tailored to its audience. The reasons and the types of evidence you offer, the needs and values to which you appeal, and the common ground you establish all depend on your audience. Remember that for this Guided Writing Assignment, you select the audience for your essay. Use the following questions to analyze your audience.

1. What do my readers already know about the issue? What do they need to know?

2. How familiar are my readers with the issue? Do they have firsthand experience with it, or is their knowledge limited to what they've heard in the media and from other people?

3. Do my readers care about the issue? Why or why not?

4. Is my audience an agreeing, neutral or wavering, or disagreeing audience? How do their beliefs or values affect their views?

5. What shared views or concerns can I use to establish a common ground with my readers?

For more on purpose, audience, and point of view, see Chapter 3, p. 65.

In an argument essay, you can use the first-, second-, or third-person point of view, depending on the issue, your purpose for writing about it, and the reasons you offer in support of your claim. If it is important that your readers feel close to you and accept you or your experiences as part of your argument, the first person will help you achieve this closeness. In "Not White, Just Right," Jones uses the first person because she is offering her personal experiences as evidence. If you want to establish a familiarity with your audience, the second person may be most effective. The third person creates the most distance between you and your readers and works well when you want to establish an objective, impersonal tone.

Researching the Issue

Research is often an essential part of developing an argument. Reading what others have written on the issue helps you gather background information, reliable evidence, and alternative viewpoints.

You might begin by looking for essays in this book that are relevant to your issue. For example, if your issue is community service as a college graduation requirement, Steirer's "When Volunteerism Isn't Noble" (Chapter 16, p. 557) might be a good starting point.

You should also conduct library or Internet research to discover what others have written about the issue. Use the following guidelines to gather information on your topic.

For more on library and Internet research, see Chapter 19.

1. Skim through different library sources, including books, magazine and newspaper articles, encyclopedia entries, and textbooks on your topic. Look for relevant background information, evidence (such as facts, statistics, and examples), and opposing views.

2. Watch television or videotape documentaries on your topic or listen to debates on the radio. These sources can help you discover alternative viewpoints and expert testimony.

3. Research the issue on the World Wide Web. Use a search engine to locate Web sites with information on your topic.

4. Select several key sources for careful reading. Key sources include a representative sample of the different points of view on your issue, essays by experts in the field, and reports that provide useful and current statistical data.

For more on reading sources, see Chapter 18, p. 658.

5. Take notes as you read your key sources. Also add ideas to your brainstormed lists, notes, or maps. As you jot down notes, take steps to avoid inadvertently plagiarizing the words and ideas of other writers. Enclose direct quotations from sources in quotation marks, summarize and paraphrase information from sources carefully, and record all of the publication details you will need to cite your sources (author, title, publisher and site, publication date, page numbers, and so on).

For more on note-taking and on avoiding plagiarism, see Chapter 19, pp. 679 and 687. For more on documenting sources, see Chapter 20.

ESSAY IN PROGRESS 2

Using the preceding suggestions, consider your purpose, audience, and point of view. Be sure to answer the questions listed on page 608; your responses will help you tailor your argument, including your evidence and emotional appeals, to suit your intended audience.

Developing Your Thesis and Making a Claim

After doing research and reading what others have to say about the issue, your views on it may have softened, hardened, or changed in some other way. Before you develop a thesis and make a claim about the issue, consider your views on it in light of your research.

For more on thesis statements, see Chapter 4, p. 89.

As noted earlier in the chapter, the thesis for an argument essay makes a claim about the issue. As you draft your thesis, be careful to avoid general statements that are not arguable. Note the difference between a vague statement and a specific claim in the following examples.

> VAGUE   In recent years, U.S. citizens have experienced an increase in credit card fraud.
>
> SPECIFIC   Although the carelessness of merchants and electronic tampering contribute to the problem, U.S. consumers are largely to blame for the recent increase in credit card fraud.

The first example merely states a fact and is not a valid thesis for an argument. The second example makes a specific, arguable claim.

ESSAY IN PROGRESS 3

Using the preceding suggestions, write a working thesis that clearly expresses your claim about the issue.

Evaluating Your Ideas, Evidence, and Claim

To draw detailed graphic organizers using a computer, visit www.bedfordstmartins.com/successfulwriting.

Once you are satisfied with your working thesis, take a few minutes to evaluate the reasons and evidence you will use to support your claim. Begin by rereading everything you have written with a critical eye. Look for ways to organize your reasons (such as in the order of their strength or importance) and group your evidence for each reason. Draw a graphic organizer of your reasons and evidence, using Figure 17.1 as a model.

TRYING OUT YOUR IDEAS ON OTHERS

Working in a group of two or three students, discuss your claim, reasons, and evidence. Each writer should state his or her issue, claim, reasons, and evidence for this chapter's assignment. Then, as a group, evaluate each writer's work.

ESSAY IN PROGRESS 4

Using the list of the characteristics of argument essays on pages 593–99 and comments from your classmates, evaluate your claim and the reasons and evidence you have gathered to support it. (You might also use the questions in Figure 16.3, page 577, to help you evaluate your claim, reasons, and evidence.)

Considering Opposing Viewpoints

Once you evaluate the key elements in your argument, you are ready to consider opposing viewpoints and plan how to acknowledge, accommodate, and/or refute them. Your argument will be weak if you fail to at least acknowledge opposing viewpoints. Your readers may assume you did not think the issue through or that you dismissed alternative views without seriously considering them.

Create a pro-and-con list or review the one you made earlier. Then list all the possible objections to your argument. Try to group the objections to form two or more points of opposition.

To acknowledge an opposing viewpoint without refuting it, you can mention the opposition in your claim, as shown in this claim about enforcing speed limits.

▶ Although speed-limit laws are intended to save lives, the conditions that apply to specific highways should be taken into account in enforcing them.

The opposing viewpoint appears in a dependent clause attached to an independent clause that states the claim. By including the opposing viewpoint as part of the claim, you show that you take it seriously.

To accommodate an opposing viewpoint, find a portion of the opposing argument that you can build into your argument. One common way to accommodate objections is to suggest alternative causes for a particular situation. For example, suppose your argument defends the competency of most high school teachers. You suspect, however, that some readers think the quality of most high school instruction is poor and attribute it to teachers' laziness or lack of skill. You can accommodate this opposing view by suggesting that the poor instruction some schools provide may be due to a lack of instructional supplies rather than to teachers' incompetence.

If you choose to argue that an opposing view is not sound, you must refute it by pointing out problems or flaws in your opponent's reasoning or evidence. To refute an opponent's reasoning, check to see if your opponent uses faulty reasoning or fallacies. To refute an opponent's evidence, use one or more of the following guidelines.

For more on fallacies, see Chapter 16, p. 576.

1. **Give a counterexample** (one that is an exception to the opposing view). For instance, if the opponent argues that dogs are protective, give an example of a situation in which a dog did not protect its owner.

2. **Question the opponent's facts.** If an opponent claims that few professors give essay exams, present statistics demonstrating that a significant percentage of professors do give essay exams.

3. **Demonstrate that an example is not representative.** If an opponent argues that professional athletes are overpaid and cites the salaries of two famous quarterbacks, cite statistics that show that these salaries are not representative of all professional athletes.

4. **Demonstrate that the examples are insufficient.** If an opponent argues that horseback riding is a dangerous sport and offers two examples of riders who were seriously injured, point out that two examples are not sufficient proof.

5. **Question the credibility of an authority.** If an opponent quotes a television personality on welfare reform, point out that she is not a sociologist or public-policy expert and therefore is not an authority on welfare reform.

6. **Question outdated examples, facts, or statistics.** If your opponent presents evidence that is not recent on the need for more campus parking, you can argue that the situation has changed (enrollment has declined, bus service has increased).

7. **Present the full context of a quotation or group of statistical evidence.** If an opponent quotes an authority selectively or cites incomplete statistics from a research study on ozone depletion and its effects on skin cancer, the full context may show that your opponent has "edited" the evidence to suit his or her claim.

ESSAY IN PROGRESS 5

Write your claim on a piece of paper or in a computer file. Below it, list all possible opposing viewpoints. Then describe one or more strategies for acknowledging, accommodating, or refuting each opposing view.

TRYING OUT YOUR IDEAS ON OTHERS

Working in a group of two or three students, present your strategies for acknowledging, accommodating, or refuting opposing views. Critique each other's strategies and suggest others that each writer might use.

Organizing and Drafting

You are now ready to organize your ideas and draft your essay. You need to decide on a line of reasoning, choose a method of organization, and develop your essay accordingly.

Choosing a Line of Reasoning and a Method of Organization

To develop a method of organizing an argument, you might use *induction, deduction,* or both. Inductive reasoning begins with evidence and moves to a conclusion. Deductive reasoning starts with an observation that most people accept and shows how a certain conclusion follows from it. Whether you choose to use one or both lines of reasoning, this decision will influence how you organize your essay.

Here are four common ways to organize an argument.

Method I	*Method II*	*Method III*	*Method IV*
Claim/thesis	Claim/thesis	Support	Opposing viewpoints
Support	Opposing viewpoints	Opposing viewpoints	Support
Opposing viewpoints	Support	Claim/thesis	Claim/thesis

The method you choose depends on your audience, your purpose, and your issue. Depending on your issue and audience, it may be best to state your claim at the outset or at the end of your argument. You also need to decide whether to present your reasons and supporting evidence before or after you discuss opposing viewpoints. Finally, decide the order in which you will discuss your reasons and supporting evidence. Will you arrange them from strongest to weakest? Most to least obvious? Familiar to unfamiliar? In planning your organization, try drawing a graphic organizer or making an outline. Try different ways of organizing your essay on the computer, creating a document file for each alternative.

Drafting the Argument Essay

For more on drafting an essay, see Chapter 5.

Once you have chosen a method of organization for your argument, you are ready to write your first draft. Use the following guidelines to draft your essay.

For more on writing effective paragraphs, including introductions and conclusions, see Chapter 5.

1. **Write an effective introduction.** Your introduction should accomplish several things. It should *identify the issue* and *offer needed background information* based on your assessment of your audience's knowledge and experience. In addition, it should *define the terms* to be used in the argument. Most argument essays also include a thesis in the introduction, where you make your *claim*. The way you begin your essay will influence your readers' attitude toward you and your argument. Several strategies can help you to engage your readers right away.

   • Open by relating a personal experience, ideally one with which your readers can identify. (See, for example, "When Volunteerism Isn't Noble" by Lynn Steirer, p. 557.)
   • Open with an attention-getting remark. (See "Not White, Just Right" by Rachel Jones, p. 600.)
   • Open by recognizing a counterargument.

2. **Establish an appropriate tone.** The tone you adopt should depend on the issue and the type of claim you make as well as the audience to whom you write. For an argument on a serious issue such as the death penalty, you would probably use a serious, even somber tone. For a call-to-action argument, you might use an energetic, enthusiastic tone. For a disagreeing audience, you might use a friendly, nonthreatening tone. Be sure to avoid overly forceful or dogmatic language and statements that allow no room for opposing viewpoints (such as "It is obvious that . . ."). Also avoid language that may insult or alienate your reader ("Anybody who thinks . . . is . . .").

3. **State your reasons with your evidence.** Be sure to state clearly the reasons for your claim. Each reason can be used to anchor the evi-

dence that follows it. In an essay about mandatory high school uniforms, for example, you might use a reason (such as "Requiring high school uniforms will reduce clothing costs for parents") as a topic sentence for a paragraph. The rest of the paragraph would then consist of evidence supporting that particular reason.

4. **Cite the sources of your research.** As you present your evidence, be sure to include a citation for each quotation, summary, or paraphrase of ideas or information you borrow from sources. Even when you do not use an author's exact wording, you need to cite the original source.

For more on documenting sources, see Chapter 20.

5. **Use strong transitions.** Make sure you use transitions to move clearly from reason to reason in your argument, as in "*Also relevant* to the issue . . ." and "*Furthermore,* it is important to consider. . . ." Also be certain that you have distinguished your reasons and evidence from those of the opposition. Use a transitional sentence such as "Those opposed to the death penalty claim . . ." to indicate that you are about to introduce an opposing viewpoint. A transition such as "Contrary to what those in favor of the death penalty maintain . . ." can be used to signal a refutation.

For more on transitions, see Chapter 5, p. 128.

6. **Write a satisfying conclusion.** You can end an argument essay in a number of ways. Choose the strategy that will have the strongest impact on your audience.

   - Restate your thesis. (See "Not White, Just Right" by Rachel Jones, p. 608.)
   - Make a final appeal to values. (See "When Volunteerism Isn't Noble" by Lynn Steirer, p. 557.)
   - Project into the future. (See "Economic Affirmative Action" by Ted Koerth, p. 564.)
   - Urge readers to take a specific action.
   - Call for further study and research.

ESSAY IN PROGRESS 6

Using the preceding suggestions for organizing and drafting, choose the line of reasoning your argument will follow and a method of organization and write your first draft.

Analyzing and Revising

If possible, set your draft aside for a day or two before rereading and revising it. Then, as you review your draft, focus on discovering weak areas and on strengthening your overall argument, not on grammar or mechanics. Use one or more of the following suggestions to analyze your draft.

Learning Style Options

1. Read your draft essay, put it aside, and write one sentence that summarizes your argument. Compare your summary sentence and thesis (statement of claim) to see if they agree or disagree. If they do not agree, your argument needs a stronger focus.

2. Make an outline to help you see how your ideas fit together.

3. Read your essay aloud or ask a friend to do so as you listen. You may "hear" parts of your argument that do not seem to follow.

4. Draw a graphic organizer or update one you drew earlier, using Figure 17.1 as a model. Look to see if the graphic organizer reveals any weaknesses in your argument (for example, you don't have enough reasons to support your claim).

For more on the benefits of peer review, see Chapter 6, p. 155.

Use Figure 17.3 to guide your analysis. You might also ask a classmate to review your draft essay using the questions in the flowchart. For each "No" response, ask your reviewer to explain why he or she responded in that way.

ESSAY IN PROGRESS 7

Revise your draft using Figure 17.3 and any comments you received from peer reviewers.

Editing and Proofreading

For more on keeping an error log, see Chapter 7, p. 193.

The last step is to check your revised essay for errors in grammar, spelling, punctuation, and mechanics. Be sure to check your error log for the types of errors you tend to make. Look for the following two grammatical errors in particular.

1. Make sure that you use the subjunctive mood correctly. In an argument, you often write about what would or might happen in the future. When you use the verb *be* to speculate about conditions in the future, *were* is used in place of *was* to indicate a hypothetical situation.

   ▶ If all animal research ~~was~~ *were* outlawed, progress in the control of human diseases would be slowed dramatically.

FIGURE 17.3
FLOWCHART FOR REVISING AN ARGUMENT ESSAY

Questions		Revision Strategies

1. Draw a (circle) around the portion of your essay where you introduce the issue. Is the issue defined? Is enough information provided? Is the issue sufficiently narrow?

No →

- Ask a friend who is unfamiliar with the issue to ask you questions about it or to tell you what else he or she needs to know.
- Assume your reader has never heard of the issue. Write as if you are introducing the issue to the reader.
- Use a branching diagram or questions to limit your issue (see Chapter 3, p. 63).

↓ **Yes**

2. Highlight your thesis. Is your claim stated clearly and specifically in your thesis?

No →

- Without looking at your essay, write a one-sentence summary of what your essay is intended to prove.
- Try limiting the issue and claim to make them more specific.
- Add a qualifying word or phrase (*for example, may, possibly*) to your thesis.

↓ **Yes**

3. Who is your audience? *Write* a brief description of their characteristics. Is your essay targeted to the intended audience? Do you appeal to your readers' needs and values?

No →

- Examine each reason and piece of evidence. If it will not appeal to your audience, consider replacing it.
- Try to discover needs, values, and common experiences you share with your readers. Add appeals based on those needs, values, and experiences.
- If your audience is unfamiliar with the issue, add more background information.

↓ **Yes**

(Continued on next page)

FIGURE 17.3 *(Continued)*

Questions		Revision Strategies

4. Place a checkmark ✔ by each reason that supports your claim. Are your reasons and evidence convincing? Do they directly relate to your thesis?

No →

- State each reason clearly; then present evidence to support it.
- Brainstorm or conduct research to discover more reasons or stronger evidence.

↓ **Yes**

5. *Number* the margins of your paper to illustrate the progression of your argument. Does each step follow a logical progression? If your reasoning free of errors?

No →

- Check the progression of your argument and your use of inductive and deductive reasoning by creating an outline or graphic organizer.
- Check for and omit faulty reasoning and fallacies (see Chapter 16, p. 575).

↓ **Yes**

6. *Write* the method of organization you used. Is your method of organization clear? Is it effective for your argument?

No →

- Experiment with one or more other methods of organization (see p. 613).

↓ **Yes**

7. [Bracket] sections where you present opposing viewpoints. Do you acknowledge, accommodate, and/or refute opposing viewpoints?

No →

- Try acknowledging an opposing view in your statement of claim.
- Ask a classmate to help you find a portion of an opposing argument that you can build into your argument.
- Look for ways to refute an opponent's evidence (see Chapter 16, pp. 574–75).

↓ **Yes**

(Continued on next page)

FIGURE 17.3 *(Continued)*

Questions		Revision Strategies
8. Underline the topic sentence of each paragraph. Is each paragraph well developed and focused on a separate part of the argument?	**No** →	• Be sure each paragraph has a topic sentence and supporting evidence (see Chapter 6). • Consider combining closely related paragraphs. • Consider splitting a paragraph that covers more than one part of the argument.

Yes ↓

| 9. Draw a box around your introduction and conclusion. Are the introduction and conclusion effective? | **No** → | • Revise your introduction and conclusion so that they meet the guidelines on pages 614–15 and in Chapter 5 (pp. 131–36). |

Yes ↓

10. Print a copy of your essay to edit and proofread before turning it in.

---

2. Look for and correct ambiguous pronouns. A pronoun must refer to another noun or pronoun, called its *antecedent*. The pronoun's antecedent should be clearly named — not just implied.

▶ Children of divorced parents often are shuttled between two homes, and

this lack of stability
~~that~~ can be confusing and disturbing to them.
 ^

ESSAY IN PROGRESS 8

Edit and proofread your essay, paying particular attention to your use of the verb *be* in sentences that speculate about the future and to pronoun reference. Don't forget to look for errors you often make.

STUDENTS WRITE

Stanford DeWinter was a first-year student at Seattle Pacific University when he wrote the following essay arguing why today's college students should be concerned about the AIDS crisis. As you read the essay, note the patterns of development DeWinter uses to structure his argument. Also highlight the thesis and the reasons DeWinter gives to support it.

AIDS and You: A World Crisis and Its Local Effects

Stanford DeWinter

1   The world HIV/AIDS crisis poses one of the greatest health problems of all time. According to the World Health Organization (2005), across the planet, more than 60 million people have been infected with HIV; almost 20 million have died since the beginning of the epidemic, and more than 14,000 new infections occur each day. Many college students may not understand how directly this crisis affects them. However, today's students will be tomorrow's leaders, and the AIDS crisis will be even worse then. Therefore, all college students, no matter what their major fields of study, should learn about the impact that AIDS is having on the global economy, educational systems, and health-care structures so that they can face the challenges ahead. Students can apply their knowledge to action now that will give them preparation and experience for future careers and involvement.

2   Anyone interested in health care will have to address the HIV/AIDS issue in multiple ways. Doctors and nurses are on the front lines of the war against HIV/AIDS, both at home and abroad. Although great advances have been made in the treatment of HIV-positive patients, the disease remains a threat in the United States, where thousands of new cases are diagnosed each year. In addition, many countries currently have a shortage of qualified medical personnel. For example, in China, where about one million people are infected, only 200 doctors are trained to deal with HIV/AIDS; although

the United States cannot fill all the gaps, we can make
a huge difference in the quality and availability of
care (Chase 2004). Furthermore, this issue will affect
students who study biology and chemistry intending to go
into research. The race to find medications to treat,
cure, and vaccinate for HIV/AIDS involves many huge
biotech companies, pharmaceutical companies, and other
types of research institutions.

Much of this research into the causes of AIDS and   3
potential treatments is funded by the U.S. government and
privately run foundations, so college students considering a career in politics or the not-for-profit sector
will need to be informed about the disease. For example,
the National Institutes of Health (NIH), a government
institution, gave nearly $3 million for AIDS research
in 2004 (NIH 2004). In many cases, politicians must be
knowledgeable enough to make decisions about such uses of
tax dollars and explain them to constituents. Other funds
come from private foundations and not-for-profit organizations. The Gates Foundation alone has given over $1
billion in support of its HIV/AIDS, Tuberculosis, and
Reproductive Health Global Health Program since 1994
(Gates Foundation 2005). Students interested in fund-
raising, fund management, and development may find that
proposals dealing with HIV/AIDS research, education, and
treatment will come their way in large numbers.

Not only is the human cost in lives outrageous,   4
but the financial cost of HIV/AIDS is rising as local
economies fail. When local economies are unstable, the
world economy becomes more unstable. As explained in a
recent <u>Fortune</u> magazine article (Gunther 2004), as the
rates of infection in Russia, China, and India rise, the
damage to the world economy increases. One reason for
this is the huge amount of work American companies out-
source to these parts of the world. A study headed by
Sydney Rosen (2003) and published in the <u>Harvard Business
Review</u> states that "the epidemic both adds to companies'
labor costs and slows growth rates in many developing

economies" (82). This study explains in detail how expensive AIDS is for companies since they end up spending extra money on AIDS-related issues to conduct business both at home and abroad. The researchers claim that businesses should join the fight to prevent and cure AIDS to maintain financial health. Therefore, any student who is interested in business, finance, or economics will be dealing with this issue as a professional.

5   Teachers will have to present a great deal of information to their students as the epidemic becomes more and more serious. The HIV/AIDS issue will affect almost every subject area taught. One organization, the Association for Childhood Education International (ACEI), has already anticipated this need and has created an extensive list of resources for educators. This group states that "Children and young adolescents must have access to accurate medical information and services necessary to develop life skills, as they are the group most affected by the prevalence of HIV/AIDS" (ACEI 2002). Second, the ACEI recognizes that because many parents and teachers are dying from HIV/AIDS, children need a larger support system of schools, organizations, and individuals to raise them. Third, the group stresses that HIV/AIDS is a global problem and therefore deserves the attention of all people, "not just those that fail to bring the disease under control." This is a call to everyone, and perhaps especially to college students, who have the opportunity to explore a variety of approaches and solutions.

6   Some might say that we should focus only on our own nation and not get involved in the problems of other countries. However, HIV/AIDS is a problem that cuts across all lines: regional, social, economic, gender, sexual orientation, religion, and ethnicity. Because of the huge number of people worldwide who are affected and the severity of the disease, we must look beyond our own borders to help all those in need. College students are

progressing through an educational stage during which
they become less focused on themselves and more focused
on the world and their place in it. Part of this discovery will be the realization that the HIV/AIDS epidemic
is a crucial point of awareness. As a result, students,
no matter what their job plans, should be prepared to
work for employers that are becoming more globally aware
and are requiring that their employees become involved in
service projects. Students should thoroughly educate
themselves on this issue and become involved in some
way, not only to prepare themselves for their careers
but also to make a difference in the future of the human
race. What could be a better cause than one that affects
so many people at home and abroad? This disease has
ripped apart the fabric of many societies. Children are
being orphaned in staggering numbers. It is a basic
human right that people should not live in disease-
ravaged communities. In fact, it is amoral to ignore or
avoid the HIV/AIDS epidemic. We must be involved in
changing the course of this devastating disease. Start
now by investigating campus programs and other opportunities in your community. Go further into the international
scene by searching on the Internet for ways to unite
with people around the world joined in this fight to
save and improve lives.

Works Cited

Association for Childhood Education International. World
    AIDS Day 2003: Stigma and Discrimination. Nov. 2002.
    12 Apr. 2005. <http://www.udel.edu/bateman/acei/
    worldaids.htm>.
Chase, M. "Lack of AIDS Doctors in Poor Countries Stalls
    Treatment." Wall Street Journal 13 July 2004: B1.
Gates Foundation. Recent Global Health Grants. Jan. 2005.
    8 Apr. 2005. <http://www.gatesfoundation.org/
    GlobalHealth/Grants/default.htm?showYear=2004>.

Gunther, Marc. "A Crisis Business Can't Ignore." Fortune
    23 Aug. 2004: 72.

National Institutes of Health (2004). Fiscal Year 2005
    Plan for HIV-Related Research. Sept. 2003. 5 Apr.
    2005. <http://www.nih.gov/od/oar/public/pubs/
    fy2005/00_Overview_Plan2005.pdf>.

Rosen, Sydney, et al. "AIDS Is Your Business." Harvard
    Business Review 1 Feb. 2003: 80.

World Health Organization. WHO-UNAIDS HIV Vaccine
    Initiative. 2005. 14 Apr. 2005 <http://www.who.int/
    vaccine_research/diseases/hiv/en/>.

Analyzing the Essay

1. Highlight and evaluate DeWinter's thesis statement. How does it suggest the organization of the essay? How is it reinforced in the essay's conclusion?

2. What types of evidence does DeWinter offer to support his reasons?

3. Does DeWinter attempt to acknowledge opposing viewpoints? If so, how? Does he attempt to accommodate or refute them?

4. How does DeWinter attempt to establish common ground with his audience?

5. To what needs and values does DeWinter appeal?

Reacting to the Reading: Discussion and Journal Writing

1. Discuss how the HIV/AIDS crisis has affected your life or the lives of others you know.

2. In what ways is the HIV/AIDS crisis recognized on your campus or in your community? Does more need to be done to build awareness of the crisis?

3. Write a journal entry analyzing how your chosen career (or a career that you are considering) relates to and may be affected by the HIV/AIDS crisis.

READING AN ARGUMENT

The following section provides advice for reading an argument as well as two essays that take opposing views on a current issue—the increasing popularity of sport utility vehicles (SUVs). Each essay illustrates the characteristics of argument covered in this chapter and provides opportunities to examine, analyze, and react to the writer's ideas. For additional information on reading arguments critically, see Chapter 16, "Reading Arguments."

WORKING WITH TEXT: RESPONDING TO ARGUMENTS

Reading arguments requires careful attention and analysis: You must follow, analyze, and evaluate the writer's line of reasoning. Plan on reading an argument several times. Read it once to get an overview. Read it several times more to analyze and critique it. If you find an argument difficult to follow, fill in a graphic organizer (see p. 601) to help you as you read.

For more on reading arguments, see Chapter 16, especially the discussions of types of claims (p. 559) and types of evidence (p. 560).

What to Look For, Highlight, and Annotate

1. **The issue.** Identify and highlight the issue and notice how the writer introduces it and the background information he or she provides. Highlight definitions of key terms.

2. **The claim.** Identify and highlight the writer's statement of claim about the issue. Notice any qualifying or limiting words.

3. **Evidence and reasons.** Study and highlight the types of evidence the writer uses to support the claim—facts, statistics, expert opinion, examples, and personal experience. Is the evidence relevant, accurate, current, and typical? Does the writer state reasons before introducing evidence? Write annotations indicating your initial reactions to or questions about the reasons or evidence.

For more on annotating, see Chapter 2, p. 47, and Chapter 16, pp. 566 and 569.

4. **Emotional appeals.** Analyze the needs and values to which the writer appeals.

5. **Organization and reasoning.** Is the argument organized effectively? Does the writer follow a deductive or an inductive line of reasoning? Evaluate the writer's premises and conclusions and note whether any logical fallacies are made.

For more on needs and values, see Chapter 16, p. 561.

6. **Opposing viewpoints.** Does the writer acknowledge, accommodate, or refute opposing views? Highlight each instance.

How to Find Ideas to Write About

Since you may be asked to write a response to an argument, keep an eye out for ideas to write about as you read.

For more on discovering ideas for a response paper, see Chapter 2.

1. **Additional supporting evidence.** Use annotations to record additional examples, personal experiences, or other evidence that comes to mind in support of the claim. These ideas may be helpful in writing your own essay in support

of this writer's claim. They might also provide a start for a paper on one aspect of the writer's argument.

2. **Opposing viewpoints and evidence.** Note any opposing views that come to mind as you read. Record events or phenomena that do not support the claim or that contradict one of the author's reasons. Keep the following question in mind: "When would this not be true?" The ideas you generate may be useful in writing an essay in which you support an opposing claim.

3. **Related issues.** Think of issues that are similar to the one under discussion in the essay. You may notice, for example, that the line of reasoning applied to the issue of "riding the bus rather than driving" may in part be applicable to the issue of "walking rather than riding."

Keep these guidelines in mind as you read the following pair of essays by Andrew Simms and John Merline on the issue of SUVs.

Would You Buy a Car That Looked Like This?
Andrew Simms

Andrew Simms is policy director for the New Economics Foundation in England. He is also head of the Climate Change Programme and the Local Works Campaign. Simms's writing has appeared in the Guardian *and* Resurgence; *he is also the author of* An Environmental War Economy *(2001) and* The Health of the Planet and the Wealth of Nations: A Story of Ecological Debt *(2005). As you read, evaluate the evidence Simms uses to support his argument against SUVs.*

1   They clog the streets and litter the pages of weekend colour* supplements. Sport utility vehicles or SUVs, otherwise known as 4X4s, four-wheel drives, and all-terrain wagons, have become badges of middle-class aspiration. They are also dangerous, fabulously polluting, and, as part of a general transport problem, set to become, according to the World Health Organisation, one of the world's most common causes of death and disability—ahead of TB, HIV, and war. . . .

2   With the Kyoto Protocol about to kick in and a major conference on global warming starting in Buenos Aires in two weeks, it is time for some fresh thinking on SUVs. . . . The gap between image and reality with SUVs is reminiscent of that in tobacco industry advertising. After all, the scientific consensus over the causes and conse-

---

*This article was published in England; therefore, you will see variations in spelling that are used and accepted in England.

quences of climate change closely mirrors that about smoking and cancer. And in the same way as the tobacco advertisers, car advertisers have tried to associate their product with masculinity, health, and the outdoor life. So shouldn't SUVs now be labelled in the same way as cigarette packets, with messages such as . . . "Climate change can seriously damage your health"? This might not entirely stop people driving SUVs, but it would force them to accept the consequences. The case for regulation of this sort is growing like a giant cloud of vehicle exhaust.

According to a 2004 World Health Organisation report, 1.2 million people across the world are killed in road crashes each year and 50 million injured. If nothing changes, the numbers are projected to rise by 65 per cent in 20 years. In Britain alone, there were 290,607 reported road casualties in 2003, including 3,508 deaths.

3

The WHO compares the global burden of diseases by looking at the years of potential life lost as a result of premature death and the years of productive life lost due to disability. In 1990, road traffic accidents ranked ninth on these criteria. By 2020, they will be third. And this does not include the contribution of vehicle emissions to respiratory disease and deaths or to the injuries caused by climate change.

4

SUVs, by almost any measurements, are more dangerous than other passenger cars. The Ford Explorer, America's biggest-selling SUV, is 16 times more likely than the typical family car to kill the occupants of another car in a crash. Pedestrians, too, are more at risk. You're twice as likely to be killed if you get hit by a 4X4. Even the widespread belief that, come the crunch, so to speak, the SUV owner is better off is a myth. New US federal traffic data reported in the *New York Times* shows that "people driving or riding in a sport utility vehicle in 2003 were nearly 11 per cent more likely to die in an accident than people in cars." One of the SUV's key selling points, its height, which is meant to make you feel safer, makes these cars twice as likely to be caught in fatal "rollover" accidents as ordinary cars. The US Consumers Union also reports that SUVs suffer from greater rearview blind spots — which may account for the rise of more than 50 per cent (to 91) last year in the number of US parents who killed their children by reversing over them.

5

As the [British] Health Secretary, John Reid, put it the other day: "In a free society, men and women ultimately have the right within the law to choose their own lifestyle, even when it may damage their own health." But, he added, "people do not have the right to damage the health of others, or to impose an intolerable degree of nuisance on others." And when it comes to choosing cars, it seems that neither industry nor the self-absorbed consumer can be trusted to do the right thing.

6

7   In the US, by the end of the 20th century, overall vehicle economy had dropped to its lowest level in 20 years. According to the Union of Concerned Scientists, "two decades of fuel-saving technologies, that could have helped curb carbon dioxide emissions, have instead gone into increasing vehicle weight and performance." The figures bear them out. In 1985, SUVs accounted for only one in 50 vehicles sold in the US. Now they make up one in four. . . .

8   In the US, people don't drive them just because they like them. Amazingly, the US government waves them on with tax breaks. Even the most costly SUVs—owned by lawyers, real estate agents, plastic surgeons, film stars, and so on—get breaks that can be worth up to $35,000. This is because SUVs are modelled on the frames of commercial vehicles. In other words, as far as the US taxman is concerned, they're really trucks. A sales tax credit designed for light trucks of more than 6,000 lb ended up being applied to the full range of big cars. This encourages manufacturers to build larger, weightier, and more polluting vehicles. Adding transport insult to climate injury, such vehicles are also exempted from emissions limits imposed on US manufacturers.

9   None of this is a problem if you listen to the industry. "CO_2 is not a pollutant. Repeat, not a pollutant," says the SUV Owners of America, an industry front group run by a PR firm that has worked for General Motors, DaimlerChrysler, and Ford. "It is a naturally occurring part of the air we breathe." Carbon dioxide is "not" a pollutant only in the way that arsenic is "not" a poison. It's all a question of dosage. And that's the problem with SUVs.

10   So would fuel taxes change behaviour? Yes, in part. But fuel duties have been politically out of favour since the country was held to ransom during the fuel blockades. And to change behaviour significantly, the taxes have to be very high. The Society of Motor Manufacturers says that "environmental factors are very low on people's list of priorities when it comes to buying a car." So the New Economics Foundation is looking at the model of tobacco labelling as a way to help people kick the SUV habit. Canadian government research, backed by World Bank findings, shows that there is a direct relationship between the size of warnings and the effect on personal behaviour. "The larger the health warning message," reports Health Canada, "the more effective it is at encouraging smokers to stop smoking."

11   Where cigarette smoke contains benzene, nitrosamines, formaldehyde, and hydrogen cyanide, as the warnings tell us, car exhaust has benzene, particulates, nitrogen oxides, and carbon monoxide. Smoking kills, but so do SUVs, their exhaust, and the global warming to which they disproportionately contribute.

Opinion is already turning against the vehicles. It is not only   12
London's [mayor] Ken Livingstone who wants to restrict them. Paris
city council has declared that SUVs are "totally unacceptable." In
Rome, the city government has proposed to treble the permit rate for
SUV owners to enter the city centre. So labelling is the logical next
step. The only issue would be classifying the guilty parties. The urban
off-roader, crossover SUV, Chelsea tractor, four-wheel drive, or 4X4 is
instantly recognisable with or without the bullbars. The group
encompasses vehicles with similar size and style that are marketed as
sport utility vehicles but which may not incorporate substantial off-
road features. Styling aside, a threshold could be set to trigger the
labelling, such as having a certain number of typical features, on the
basis that "if it walks like a duck and talks like a duck. . . ."

Fuel efficiency, already used as a basis for assessing vehicle excise   13
duty, could also be key, with the labelling kicking in when efficiency
drops below a certain threshold. Like those for cigarettes, the warnings could cover 30–50 per cent of the vehicles' surface area. People
could still drive them, but when they did, they would publicly accept
the consequences of their actions and help the education drive on
traffic safety and global warming.

At the least, cigarette-style car labelling would help the industry   14
move out of denial. A recent advert for the Chrysler Crossfire invited
the reader to "kiss the sky" with the car. But in an age of global warming, a more honest slogan for a 23 mpg vehicle would have been "rip
it apart." Label up, and let's go.   ■

Examining the Reading

1. Why does Simms believe that SUVs should have warning labels?

2. What emotional appeals does Simms make?

3. According to the author, why do people drive SUVs?

4. In what ways does Simms believe our lives would be better without SUVs?

5. Explain the meaning of each of the following words as used in the reading:
   aspiration (para. 1), *reminiscent* (2), *consensus* (2), *disproportionately* (12), and *treble*
   (13). Refer to your dictionary as needed.

Analyzing the Reading

1. Highlight Simms's claim and evaluate its placement in the essay.

2. What types of evidence does Simms use to support his argument? Which of these do you find most compelling? Explain your answer.

3. What arrangement of details does the author use to present the argument? What other arrangement could have been used?

4. Identify the opposing viewpoints that Simms refutes. How does he refute them? How effective are his refutations?

5. Explain the author's conclusion.

Reacting to the Reading: Discussion and Journal Writing

1. What solutions, other than warning labels, might encourage people not to buy SUVs?

2. Discuss citizens' right to choose habits and behaviors that might harm or injure them. Is this an essential part of a free society?

3. Write a journal entry about the labeling of dangerous products. Is it appropriate for automobiles?

Why Consumers Have Been Choosing SUVs
John Merline

John Merline, formerly the Washington, D.C., bureau chief of Investors Business Daily *and editor of* Consumers' Research *magazine, is an editorial writer for* USA Today. *He has covered the air bag controversy extensively in his various positions. As you read, notice how Merline anticipates and refutes opposing evidence as he argues in favor of SUVs.*

1   In recent months, a variety of consumer groups and environmentalists have launched a ferocious campaign aimed at disarming American drivers of sport utility vehicles (SUVs). One group, the Detroit Project, went so far as to charge that SUV drivers were supporting terrorism every time they filled up their gas tanks. A Christian group complained that driving SUVs was not in keeping with the teachings of Jesus Christ. Consumer activist Joan Claybrook, head of Public Citizen, charged that SUVs are "a bad bargain for society and a nightmare for American roads." They are, she said, "the dangerous offspring of a heady mix of profit-driven special interest politics and corporate deception."

2   According to these critics, SUVs are:

- *Road hazards:* They are prone to deadly rollovers and crush cars unlucky enough to crash into them.

- *Gas hogs:* Their relatively low mileage increases the nation's dependence on foreign oil.

- *Pollution machines:* They emit more pollutants than smaller cars, thereby increasing global warming and smog.

The only problem with all these pointed barbs is that few of them   3
withstand close scrutiny. SUVs are not nearly as dangerous as critics allege, and they are getting safer both for their own occupants and those in other cars colliding with them in accidents. Forcing SUVs to be more fuel efficient, or pushing buyers to buy allegedly more sensible smaller cars would have little meaningful impact on the nation's dependence on foreign oil. SUVs aren't increasing air pollution in cities, and their effect on global warming, if any, is negligible.

Road Hazards? According to Public Citizen's Claybrook, SUVs   4
"are no safer for their drivers than midsize and large cars, and are extremely dangerous for others on the road." Claybrook claims that fatality rates for SUVs are actually higher than for regular cars, despite the fact that they are generally larger and heavier than such cars. Claybrook and others argue that one safety weakness of SUVs is their higher rollover risk. Because they are taller than ordinary cars, SUVs have a higher center of gravity, making them more likely to roll over in extreme driving conditions. And, she and others say, because SUVs' bumpers are higher than those on cars, they can impose severe crash penalties on car drivers. The higher bumpers can ride over car bumpers and safety bars in doors, imposing more deadly crash forces on car passengers.

A close look at the data reveals a different picture. According to   5
the Insurance Institute for Highway Safety, drivers are less likely to die in SUVs than in passenger cars. In 2001, there were 73 driver deaths per million 1- to-3-year-old SUVs, the study found, compared with 83 deaths per million cars of the same vintage. So, whatever the propensity to roll over, SUVs apparently make up for it by being safer in other areas.

The second concern is that SUVs have a tendency to overpower   6
smaller cars in crashes. They might protect their own occupants, but make the highways less safe for others. This compatibility problem is a reasonable concern, to some extent. In 1990, for example, the average weight difference between cars and light trucks — a category that includes minivans and pickups as well as SUVs — was 830 pounds. According to the National Highway Traffic Safety Administration, this difference had increased to 1,130 pounds by 2001. All other

things being equal, heavier cars have an advantage in a crash over lighter cars. And because the bumpers don't always match up, an SUV can ride over a car's crumple zone.

7   But those who argue that SUVs must change to fix this problem overlook the other possible solution: making smaller cars heavier and more crash resistant. That would arguably not only protect drivers and passengers in these cars when they collide with an SUV, but in the many other crashes that involve trucks, buses, or fixed objects.

8   Finally, the overall fatality rate on the highways has dropped 27.4% since 1990, a time that saw sales of SUVs explode. If SUVs were the incredible safety menace that Joan Claybrook alleges, one would expect to have seen the opposite trend in fatalities.

9   **Gas Hogs?** Because SUVs get less mileage than do cars, critics charge that they contribute to the nation's dependence on foreign oil. Indeed, in the past 10 years, the nation's dependence on imports has climbed from 42% to 54% of oil consumption. Syndicated columnist and book author Arianna Huffington mounted an ad campaign complaining that, because SUVs consume more gasoline than cars, drivers were guilty of supporting the oil-producing regimes in the Persian Gulf—some of which have been accused of providing financial support to terrorists. "What is your SUV doing to our national security?" asked one ad sponsored by Huffington's group, the Detroit Project. At the very least, SUV critics insist that these cars be mandated by the federal government to be more fuel-efficient.

10   The connection seems to make sense until the data are more closely examined. First, while SUVs generally consume more gasoline than do cars, they are not the rapacious gas hogs critics suggest. True, the largest SUVs get, on average, just 17 miles per gallon. But relatively few of these vehicles sell each year. Indeed, the most popular SUVs are midsize ones, which get an average 20.7 mpg, according to the Oak Ridge National Laboratory. That's just 5 mpg less than a large car, and just 3 mpg less than an average minivan.

11   What's more, despite the surge in sales of SUVs over the past ten years, overall fuel economy on the road has actually improved. Consider: In this decade, SUVs went from 5% of all registered cars on the road to 11%. Yet fuel economy of all cars on the road climbed nearly 7% between 1990 and 2000, according to the Oak Ridge National Laboratory. It appears then, that many new car buyers, even those buying SUVs, are trading in less fuel-efficient cars for more fuel-efficient ones.

12   **Pollution Machines?** Environmentalists argue that dirtier SUVs are creating an intense new air-pollution burden on cities, and contributing to global warming because they emit more carbon dioxide than do more fuel-efficient vehicles. As one environmentalist group

puts it: "Sport utility vehicles can spew 30% more carbon monoxide and hydrocarbons and 75% more nitrogen oxides than passenger cars." These are pollutants that combine with sun and heat to form smog. The critics note that several popular SUVs get among the lowest rankings for air pollution put out by the Environmental Protection Agency.

Yet even as SUVs have come to dominate new car sales, air quality has improved. According to the Environmental Protection Agency, the amount of nitrogen oxide in the air dropped 11% between 1992 and 2001. Ozone dropped 3%. Carbon monoxide was down 38%. Those gains came not only as the car market shifted over towards more SUVs, minivans, and light trucks, but as cars overall were driven more. Miles traveled over the past 10 years climbed 30%. The reason may be similar to the reason for the improvements seen over the past decade in overall fuel economy. A driver who trades in a dirty old car for a slightly less polluting new SUV has helped improve the environment, even if the SUV isn't the cleanest new car coming off the assembly line.

The claim that SUVs are contributing meaningfully to global warming is also a stretch. Gasoline consumption in the United States is but one source of so-called greenhouse gases in this country, which themselves are just one source of global greenhouse gas emissions. Assuming that greenhouse gases are warming the planet in a way that will be harmful to humans, a claim that is still subject to much dispute, even eliminating all SUVs would do nothing measurable to warming trends over the next 100 years. All cars on the road account for only about half of oil consumption in this country, and SUVs account for a fraction of that. According to the United Nations, even if all countries in the world cut their emissions of greenhouse gases back to 1990 levels—which would take a far more radical and widespread effort to reduce energy consumption than just making SUVs more efficient—the result would push back eventual temperature increases by roughly 10 years.

The Role of Consumers. Overlooked in such attacks on SUVs is the important role consumers play, not just in the shape of the car market, but in overall highway safety. Over the past decade, sales of SUVs climbed an eye-popping 312%. Sales of cars—a category that excludes SUVs, minivans, and light trucks—actually dropped 10%. Joan Claybrook and other SUV critics attribute this to clever marketing on the part of carmakers, who allegedly make fat profits on SUV sales. But no amount of slick advertising can convince families living on a budget to buy an expensive SUV if more modestly priced vehicles are available to meet their needs. More likely, SUVs, along with minivans, are popular because they do, in fact, serve so many families' needs. Those with children who want to travel or carry sporting equipment or tow things have few reasonable choices aside from these large vehicles.

16   Driver behavior is also completely overlooked by SUV critics. Almost all rollover fatalities could be prevented, for example, if drivers and passengers of SUVs simply buckled up. As Runge of the National Highway Traffic Safety Administration, puts it: "We can reduce the effects of the rollover problem overnight if all occupants would simply buckle their safety belts. They are 80% effective in preventing deaths in rollovers involving light trucks." Yet, Runge notes, "72% of the occupants of these vehicles who die in rollover crashes are not wearing safety belts."

17   In the end, SUVS may not be perfect. And they may not be the sort of car some consumers would choose to buy. But that's the beauty of the free market. Consumers get to decide what cars and what toasters and what homes and what computers best serve their needs. Despite what SUV critics might think, it appears that consumers are making reasonable choices with their hard-earned money.   ■

Examining the Reading

1. According to Merline, why do people buy SUVs?
2. Identify the three opposing viewpoints that the author refutes.
3. Merline refutes SUV critics. What direct reasons of his own does he give in support of SUVs?
4. According to the author, how can manufacturers improve the outcome of accidents between SUVs and smaller cars?
5. Explain the meaning of each of the following words as used in the reading: *barbs* (para. 3), *syndicated* (9), *mandated* (9), and *rapacious* (10). Refer to your dictionary as needed.

Analyzing the Reading

1. Evaluate the expert opinion that the author provides. Are these sources you know and respect?
2. What types of evidence does Merline offer to refute the opposing viewpoints?
3. What types of emotional appeal does Merline use? How do they contribute to the article?

4. Merline briefly identifies the opposing viewpoints and then addresses each in detail. Why does he do this, and is it effective?

5. What is the author's conclusion? Is it an appropriate ending? How does it establish common ground with his audience?

Reacting to the Reading: Discussion and Journal Writing

1. What factors, other than increased sale of SUVs, might account for the decrease in the overall highway fatality rate since 1990?

2. Discuss whether the rollover threat is sufficient to prevent you from purchasing or riding in an SUV.

3. Write a journal entry about environmental hazards. Choose one hazard and describe your personal experiences with it. Examine possible solutions to the problem.

Integrating the Readings

1. Which essay did you find more convincing? Why?

2. Compare the ways in which the authors present and support their arguments.

3. How do you think the two authors would respond to each other on issues of safety, pollution, and fuel economy?

4. What further information would you need to clarify the issues examined in these essays?

APPLYING YOUR SKILLS: ADDITIONAL ESSAY ASSIGNMENTS

To Persuade Your Reader

Write an argument essay on one of the following topics. Narrow the topic to focus on an issue that can be debated, such as a problem that could be solved by reforms or legislation. Depending on the topic you choose, you may need to do library or Internet research. Your audience is made up of your classmates and instructor.

For more on locating and documenting sources, see Part 5.

1. Professional sports

2. College policies

3. Traffic laws

4. Television or movie ratings

5. Term limits for members of Congress

Cases Using Argument

1. Write an essay for a sociology course, arguing your position on the following statement: The race of a child and that of the prospective parents should be taken into consideration in making adoption decisions.

2. You have a job as a copy editor at a city newspaper. Write a proposal that explains and justifies your request to work at home one day per week. Incorporate into your argument the fact that you could use your home computer, which is connected to the newspaper's computer network.

EVALUATING YOUR PROGRESS
Part A: Using Argument

Write a paragraph that evaluates your use of argument. Be sure to include

- Identify one everyday, one academic, and one workplace situation in which argument will be useful.
- How did you adapt your argument essay to suit your audience? How would your essay change if you were writing for an audience either more or less agreeing?
- Identify any problems or trouble spots you experienced in using argument and explain how you dealt with them.

Part B: Analyzing Argument Readings

Describe what you learned about building and presenting a strong and convincing argument from each reading you were assigned.

Part C: Proofreading and Editing

List the errors your instructor identified in your argumentative essay(s). For more help with these problems, refer to Exercise Central (www.bedfordstmartins.com/successfulwriting).

PART 5

Writing with
Sources

Planning a Paper with Sources

CHAPTER QUICK START

Suppose you are enrolled in a public speaking class. Your instructor gives the class a number of photographs of significant national monuments and directs each student to choose one photograph and prepare a speech on what the history of the monument is and what it is intended to represent. You've chosen the picture of the Vietnam Veterans' Memorial Wall in Washington, D.C., shown on the opposite page.

Writing Quick Start

Write a brief statement summarizing what you already know about the Vietnam Veterans' Memorial Wall and indicating what further information you would need to speak or write in detail about this monument.

Before planning a speech about the monument shown in the photograph, you would probably need to consult several sources to learn more about it. What further information would you need to support your ideas? How would you be sure the information contained in your sources is relevant and reliable? How would you detect a writer's bias? This chapter will answer these and other questions about choosing and evaluating useful sources. It will also lead you through the process of planning a paper with sources.

Sources of information come in many forms. They include all print materials (books, newspapers, magazines, brochures, scholarly journals), media sources (television, radio, videotapes), and electronic sources (Internet, CD-ROM, email). Interviews, personal observations, and surveys are also sources of information. The various kinds of sources are discussed in more detail in Chapter 19.

You can use sources in a variety of ways. For instance, you may plan a paper that is based primarily on your own experiences but discover aspects of the topic that need additional support from outside sources. At other times, you may start a paper by checking several sources to narrow your topic or become more familiar with it. Finally, you may be asked to write a research paper, which requires the most extensive use of sources. See the accompanying box for a few other examples of situations that would require using sources.

WHEN SHOULD YOU USE SOURCES?

You should use sources whenever your topic demands more factual information than you can provide from your own personal knowledge and experience. Sources are classified as *primary* or *secondary*. **Primary sources** include historical docu-

---

SCENES FROM COLLEGE AND THE WORKPLACE

- For an *astronomy* course, you are asked to write a two-page report on black holes. Your textbook contains basic information on the subject, but you need to consult other sources to complete the assignment.

- For a *contemporary American history* assignment, you need to write a five-page research paper on a current issue (such as national health insurance), explaining the issue and reporting on current developments.

- You are a *journalist* and will interview your state governor. You need background information on the governor's position on several issues of local concern.

ments (letters, diaries, speeches), literary works, autobiographies, original research reports, eyewitness accounts, and your own interviews, observations, or correspondence. For example, a report on a study of heart disease written by the researcher who conducted the study is a primary source, as is a novel by William Faulkner. In addition, what *you* say or write can be a primary source. Your own interview with a heart-attack survivor for a paper on heart disease is a primary source. **Secondary sources** report or comment on primary sources. A journal article that reviews several previously published research reports on heart disease is a secondary source. A book written about Faulkner by a literary critic or biographer is a secondary source.

Using Sources to Add Details to an Essay

The following suggestions will help you use sources to add details to a paper and thus provide stronger support for your thesis.

- **Make general comments more specific.** For example, instead of saying that "the crime rate in New York City has decreased over the past few years," use a source that offers statistics indicating the exact percentage of the decrease.

- **Give specific examples that illustrate your main points.** If you are writing about why some companies refuse to accept orders over the Internet, for instance, locate a business that has such a policy and give details about its rationale.

- **Supply technical information.** If you are writing about a drug that lowers high blood pressure, gather information from sources about its manufacture, ingredients, effectiveness, cost, and side effects so that you can make informed, accurate comments.

- **Support opinions with evidence.** If you state that more federal assistance is needed for public education, you might provide statistics, facts, expert opinion, or other evidence to back up your statement.

- **Provide historical information.** If you are writing about space stations, for example, find out when the first one was established, what country launched it, and so forth to add background information to your paper.

- **Locate information about similar events or ideas.** For example, if you are writing about a president's intervention in a labor strike, find out if other presidents have intervened in similar strikes. You can then point out similarities and differences. You can also compare different writers' ideas on an issue. For example, in a paper about the consequences of divorce, you could use a source that deals with negative consequences and one that deals with benefits.

Using Sources to Write a Research Paper

A research paper requires you to collect and analyze information on a topic from a variety of sources. Depending on your topic, you may use primary sources, secondary sources, or both. For a research paper comparing the speeches of Abraham Lincoln to those of Franklin D. Roosevelt, you would probably read and analyze the speeches (primary sources). You might also create your own primary source by interviewing a local historian. But for a research paper comparing Lincoln's and Roosevelt's domestic policies, you would probably rely on several histories or biographies (secondary sources). Many research papers incorporate both primary and secondary sources. While researching Lincoln's and Roosevelt's domestic policies, for instance, you might consult some original documents (primary sources).

Regardless of the sources you use, your task is to organize and present your findings in a meaningful way. When you write a research paper, you don't simply "glue together" the facts, statistics, information, and quotations you find in sources. Like any other essay-length writing, a research paper has a thesis, and the thesis is supported throughout the paper. Although the information from outside sources is not your own, the interpretation you give it should be your own.

For more on systems for documenting sources, see Chapter 20, pp. 716 (MLA) and 734 (APA).

In a research paper or in any paper with sources, it is essential to acknowledge your sources fairly and correctly. To do so, you include parenthetical, or in-text, citations in the body of the paper and a corresponding list of works cited or references at the end of the paper.

Whether you use sources to add details to an essay or to write a research paper, it is helpful to approach the process of locating, evaluating, and using sources in a systematic way. Figure 18.1 presents an overview of this process. The following sections of this chapter will help you plan a paper with sources and learn how to evaluate source material.

PLANNING YOUR PAPER

Although starting your research in the library or on the Internet may seem like a good idea, usually the best place to begin is at your desk. There you can think about the assignment and devise a plan for completing it. This section describes several tasks that you should accomplish before you begin your research, as shown in Figure 18.2.

Defining the Assignment

Not all assignments have the same purpose. Many are informative, asking you to explain (for example, "Explain the treatment options for breast cancer") or to explore an issue (for example, "Examine the pros and cons of legalizing casino

FIGURE 18.1
LOCATING AND USING SOURCES: AN OVERVIEW

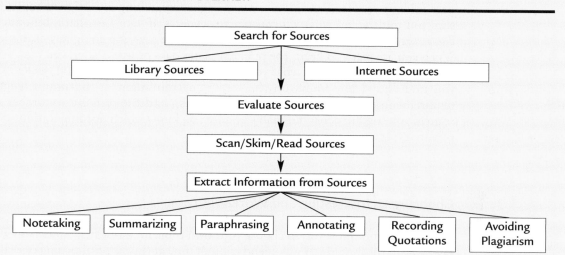

FIGURE 18.2
WRITING A PAPER USING SOURCES

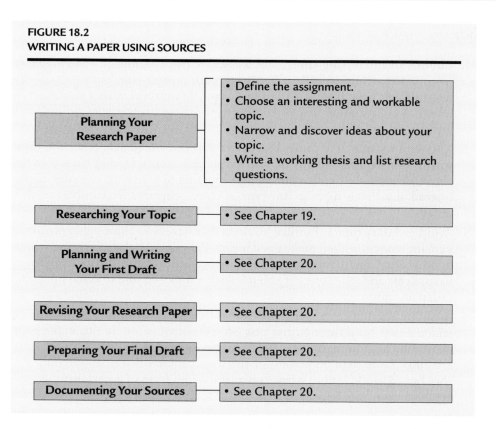

gambling"). Still others are persuasive, asking you to take and support a particular position (for example, "Defend or argue against your college's proposal to eliminate athletic scholarships"). Before you begin researching an assigned topic, be sure you understand what your instructor expects. If your instructor announces the assignment in class, write down what he or she says, including any examples. When you are ready to begin the research paper days or weeks later, you may find it helpful to review exactly what your instructor told you. In addition, make sure you understand any limits on the topic, any minimum or maximum length requirements, the due date (and late penalties), and the minimum number of sources you need to consult. Finally, be sure you know which documentation style you are expected to use.

Choosing an Interesting and Workable Topic

Most instructors allow you to choose your own topic for a research paper. You will save time in the long run if you spend enough time at the outset choosing one that is interesting and workable. Too many students waste hours researching a topic that they finally realize is too difficult, broad, or ordinary. The following tips will help you avoid such pitfalls.

1. **Choose an interesting topic.** You will enjoy the assignment and be able to write more enthusiastically if you work with a topic that captures your interest. If you have trouble choosing a topic, brainstorm with a classmate or friend. A conversation will often help you discover new angles on ordinary topics.

2. **Choose a manageable topic.** Make sure you can adequately cover the topic within the required length of your paper. For example, don't try to write about all kinds of family counseling programs in a five- to ten-page paper. Instead, limit your topic to one type, such as programs for troubled adolescents.

3. **Avoid ordinary topics.** Familiar subjects that have been thoroughly explained in many sources seldom make good topics. For example, the subjects of "childhood obesity" or "the dieting craze" have been thoroughly discussed in many newspapers and magazines. If you use such a topic, be sure to come up with a different slant on it.

4. **Avoid topics that are too current.** Topics that are currently in the news or for which a new breakthrough has just been reported often do not make good choices because in many cases little reliable information is available. In January 2005, more than 50 percent of the Iraqi people voted in an election that they hoped would lead to a new constitution and form of government. February 2005 would not have been a good time to do a research paper on the effects

of the election because too little was known about how successful the elected parties and their representatives would be.

5. **Choose a practical topic.** Choose a topic for which sources are readily available—on the Internet, at your college library, or through interlibrary loan. Avoid topics that require extensive technical knowledge that you lack. Most of us, for example, should not do a paper comparing the mechanical performance of two hybrid engines or the chemical makeup of two drugs.

Narrowing and Discovering Ideas about Your Topic

The following techniques will help you narrow your topic and discover ideas about it.

Do Some Preliminary Reading

It is often a good idea to do some preliminary reading to discover the scope, depth, and breadth of your topic. Either at your library or online, you might glance through part of a general encyclopedia, such as *Encyclopaedia Britannica,* to gain a brief overview of your topic. For example, one student researching eating disorders quickly discovered through preliminary reading that the major types are obesity, anorexia nervosa, and bulimia. She then used this information to come up with a narrowed topic.

For more on library and Internet sources, see Chapter 19.

Be sure to consider other kinds of sources as well. A specialized encyclopedia, such as *The McGraw-Hill Encyclopedia of Science and Technology,* and your library's electronic catalog can help you identify the subtopics into which a topic can be broken. The weekly *CQ Researcher,* whose database contains thousands of articles on current topics, is another useful reference to consult for background information and to get ideas for topics. Or consider scanning a current magazine index for coverage of controversial issues. You can also ask a reference librarian for assistance.

Try Prewriting

To uncover interesting topics or to narrow a broad topic, use one or more prewriting techniques. Prewriting may also reveal an interesting idea that may eventually become your thesis. A branching diagram may be particularly helpful in narrowing a topic.

For more on prewriting, see Chapter 3.

View Your Topic from Different Perspectives

Another technique, questioning, can help you view your topic in different ways. Try asking questions about your topic from a variety of perspectives—psychological, sociological, scientific or technical, historical, political, and economic. Add other perspectives that apply to your topic. Here is how one student used questioning to analyze different perspectives on television advertising.

TOPIC: TELEVISION ADVERTISING

Perspective	*Questions*
Psychological	• How does advertising affect people? • Does it affect everyone the same way? • What emotional appeals are used? • How do emotional appeals work?
Sociological	• How do different groups of people respond differently to ads? • Is advertising targeted toward specific racial and ethnic groups?
Scientific or technical	• How are ads produced? • Who writes them? • Are the ads tested before they are broadcast?
Historical	• What is the history of advertising? • When and where did it begin?
Political	• What is the history of political advertising? • Why are negative political advertisements effective?
Economic	• How much does a television ad cost? • Is the cost of advertising added on to the price of the product?

This list of questions yielded a wide range of interesting subtopics about advertising, including emotional appeals, targeting ads to particular racial or ethnic groups, and negative political advertising. You might try this technique with a friend or classmate, working together to devise questions.

EXERCISE 18.1

Working with one or two classmates, narrow each of the following topics until you reach a topic that would be manageable for a five- to ten-page research paper.

1. Job interviews
2. U.S. prison system
3. Mail-order companies
4. At-home schooling
5. Extinction of animal species

RESEARCH PAPER IN PROGRESS 1

Choose a broad topic for your research paper. In your paper you will state a thesis and provide evidence for your thesis. Your audience is your classmates. Begin by using one or more prewriting techniques to narrow and generate ideas about your topic. Then reread your work and highlight useful ideas. Choose one of the following broad topics or come up with one on your own. Refer to Table 3.2 on page 78 for other general topic suggestions.

1. Mandatory public works projects for the homeless
2. Cross-racial child adoptions
3. Sexual harassment: what it is and is not
4. How credit card use can lead to violations of privacy
5. Mandatory family planning

If you are uncertain about the topic you have chosen, be sure to check with your instructor. Most instructors don't mind if you clear your topic with them; in fact, some encourage or even require this step. Your instructor may also suggest a way to narrow your topic, recommend a useful source, or offer to review your outline at a later stage.

Writing a Working Thesis and Listing Research Questions

Once you choose and narrow a topic, try to determine, as specifically as possible, the kinds of information you need to know about it. Begin by writing a working thesis for your paper and listing the research questions you need to answer.

One student working on the general topic of child abuse, for example, used prewriting and preliminary reading to narrow his focus to physical abuse and its causes. Since he already had a few ideas about possible causes, he used those ideas to write a working thesis. He then used his thesis to generate a list of research questions. Notice how the student's questions follow from his working thesis.

WORKING THESIS	The physical abuse of children often stems from parents' emotional instability and a family history of child abuse.
RESEARCH QUESTIONS	If a person was physically abused as a child, how likely is that person to become an abusive parent?
	What kinds of emotional problems seem to trigger the physical abuse of children?
	Which cause is more significant—a family history of abuse or emotional problems?
	Is there more physical abuse of children now than there was in the past, or is more abuse being reported?

A working thesis and a list of research questions will enable you to approach your research in a focused way. Instead of running helter-skelter from one aspect of your topic to another, you will be able to zero in on the specific information you need from sources.

EXERCISE 18.2

For one of the following topics, write a working thesis and four or more research questions.

1. Methods of controlling pornography on the Internet
2. The possibility that some form of life has existed on other planets
3. Reasons for the extinction of dinosaurs

4. Benefits of tracing your family's genealogy (family tree)
5. How elderly family members affect family life

RESEARCH PAPER IN PROGRESS 2

Review the list of ideas you generated in Research Paper in Progress 1. Underline the ideas for which you need further details or supporting evidence and list the information you need. Then, using the preceding guidelines, write a working thesis and a list of research questions.

CHOOSING AND EVALUATING USEFUL SOURCES

Once you have a working thesis and a list of research questions, stop for a moment before you charge off to the library or your computer. Many students make the mistake of photocopying many articles, printing out dozens of Web pages, and lugging home numerous books only to find that the sources are not useful or that several contain identical information. Save yourself time by taking a few minutes to think about print and electronic sources and about which sources will be most relevant and reliable. Consider as well how to distinguish between facts and opinions, how to identify bias, and how to recognize generalizations or assumptions.

Choosing between Print and Electronic Sources

Although many people think that the Internet is the best way to find any kind of information, the truth is that sometimes a print source is preferable to an Internet source. This is often the case in the following situations:

- **To find specific facts.** It may be easier to find a single fact, such as the date of a president's inauguration, by looking in a reference book rather than doing research on the Web.
- **For historic or in-depth research of a topic.** Books may be essential to some types of research because they represent years of study by authorities on the subject. Some historical information and data are not available on the Internet.
- **To locate graphics.** Many of the best photographs, art reproductions, and illustrations are found in print sources.

Choosing Relevant Sources

A *relevant* source contains information that helps you to answer one or more of your research questions. Answering the following questions will help you determine whether a source is relevant.

1. **Is the source too general or too specialized for your intended audience?** Some sources may not contain the detailed information your audience requires; others may be too technical and require background knowledge that your audience does not have. For example, suppose you are researching the environmental effects of recycling cans and bottles. If your audience consists of science majors, an article in *Reader's Digest* might be too general. Conversely, an article in *Environmental Science and Technology* would be written for scientists and may be a bit too technical for your purposes. *For more on audience, see Chapter 3, p. 66.*

2. **Is the source recent enough for your purposes?** In rapidly changing fields of study, outdated sources are not useful, except when you need to give a historical perspective. For example, a five-year-old article on using air bags to improve car safety may not include information on recent discoveries about the dangers that air bags pose to children riding in the front passenger seat.

Choosing Reliable Sources

A *reliable* source is honest, accurate, and credible. Answering the following questions will help you determine whether a source is reliable. (To check the reliability of an Internet source, consult pp. 650–53 as well.)

1. **Is the source scholarly?** Although scholars often disagree with each other, they make a serious attempt to present accurate information. In addition, an article that appears in a scholarly journal or textbook has been reviewed by a panel of professionals in the field prior to publication. Therefore, scholarly sources tend to be trustworthy. For more on the differences between scholarly and popular sources, refer to Table 19.1 on page 671.

2. **Does the source have a solid reputation?** Some magazines, such as *Time* and *Newsweek*, are known for responsible reporting, whereas other periodicals have a reputation for sensationalism and should be avoided or approached skeptically. Web sites, too, may or may not be reputable.

3. **Is the author an expert in the field?** Check the author's credentials. Information about authors may be given in a headnote, at the end of an article, on a home page or title page, or in the preface of a book. You might also check a reference book such as *Contemporary Authors* to verify an author's credentials.

4. **Does the author approach the topic fairly and objectively?** A writer who states a strong opinion or assertion is not necessarily biased. However, a writer who ignores opposing views, distorts facts, or ignores information that does not fit his or her opinion may present a biased and incomplete view of a topic. Although you can use a biased source to understand a particular viewpoint, you must also seek out other sources that present the alternative views. For more on bias and viewpoint, see pp. 655–56.

EXERCISE 18.3

Working in a small group, discuss why the sources listed for each topic below would or would not be considered relevant and reliable. Assume that the classmates in your writing course are your audience.

1. Topic: Caring for family members with Alzheimer's disease
   a. Introductory health and nutrition textbook
   b. Article in *Women's Day* titled "Mother, Where Are You?"
   c. Article from a gerontology journal on caring for aging family members
2. Topic: Analyzing the effects of heroin use on teenagers
   a. Newspaper article written by a former heroin user
   b. Article from the *Journal of Neurology* on the biochemical effects of heroin on the brain
   c. Pamphlet on teenage drug use published by the National Institutes of Health
3. Topic: Implementing training programs to reduce sexual harassment in the workplace
   a. Article from the *Christian Science Monitor* titled "Removing Barriers for Working Women"
   b. A personal Web site relating an incident of harassment on the job
   c. Training manual for employees of General Motors

Evaluating Internet Sources

For more practice evaluating Web sites, visit www.bedfordstmartins .com/successfulwriting /tutorials.

The Internet offers many excellent and reputable sources. Not all sites are accurate and unbiased, however, and misinformation often appears on the Web. Use the following questions to evaluate the reliability of Internet sources. (Table 18.1 on p. 651 summarizes these questions.)

What Is the Site's Purpose?

For more about bias, see pp. 655–56.

Web sites have many different purposes. They may provide information or news, advocate a particular point of view, or try to sell a product. Many sites have more than one purpose. A pharmaceutical company's site, for instance, may offer health advice in addition to advertising its own drugs. Understanding the purposes of an Internet source will help you deal with its potential biases. Some of the different purposes of Web sites are summarized in Table 18.2.

For a more complete list of URL endings, see Chapter 19, p. 674.

To determine the purpose of any site, start by identifying the sponsor of the site—the organization or person who paid to place it on the Web. The copyright usually reveals the owner of a site, and the ending of a Web address (the uniform resource locator, or URL) shows the type of sponsorship. The ending *.com,* for instance, refers to a commercial site, *.gov* to a government site, *.edu* to education or a school, and *.org* to a nonprofit organization. Look, for example, at the health and science site National Institutes of Health (at www.nih.gov). This site is sponsored by the U.S. Department of Health and Human Services, a government agency that deals with public health and the health of individual citizens. Because the NIH site is government sponsored, its information should be reliable and fairly objective.

TABLE 18.1
EVALUATING INTERNET SOURCES

Purpose	• Who sponsors or publishes the site — an organization, corporation, government agency, or individual? • What are the sponsor's goals — to present information or news, opinions, products to sell, or fun?
Author	• Who wrote the information on the site? • Is the information clearly presented and well written?
Accuracy	• Are ideas supported by credible evidence? Is there a works cited list or bibliography? • Is the information presented verifiable? • Are opinions clearly identified as such?
Timeliness	• When was the site first created? What is the date of the last revision? • Does the specific document you are using have a date? • Are the links up-to-date?

TABLE 18.2
TYPES OF WEB SITES

Type	*Purpose*	*Example*
Informational	Provides reports, bibliographies, statistics, data, and other types of factual information; URL generally ends in *.edu* or *.gov*	www.pcwebopedia.com www.jhu.edu/~welfare thomas.loc.gov
Commercial	Sponsored by corporations or businesses to publicize and/or sell their services or products; URL usually ends in *.com*	www.chipsahoy.com www.mcdonalds.com www.amazon.com
News	Offers up-to-date local, national, or international news; often helpful in finding breaking news, photographs, or more information on a particular story; URL usually ends in *.com*	www.cnn.com www.abcnews.go.com www.nytimes.com
Advocacy	Promotes a particular point of view or cause, often involving a controversial topic; usually sponsored by a public service group or nonprofit organization; URL often ends in *.org*	www.sierraclub.org www.nra.org www.amnesty.org
Combined	Provides information or news but also sells or promotes products and services or encourages membership and fundraising; URL usually ends in *.com* or *.org*	www.acs.org www.icrc.org www.olympic-usa.org

Other sites may be reliable but also advocate definite opinions. For example, Amnesty International's advocacy Web site (at www.amnesty-usa.org) contains a great deal of information about the lack of human rights for political prisoners. Amnesty International is a well-known and reputable organization, so the information on its site is likely to be reliable, but it also presents a particular point of view. At this Web site, then, you will not learn the viewpoints of countries that have been charged with human rights violations. Understanding the purpose of Amnesty International's site helps you determine whether the material is fair and what information might be missing.

What Are the Author's Credentials?

It helps to know who wrote the specific Web page you are looking at. The sponsors of many Web sites have professionals write their content. When this is the case, the writer's name and credentials are usually listed, and his or her email address may be provided. This kind of information can help you determine whether the Web page is a reliable resource. If information about an author is not available on the site or is sketchy, you might conduct a search for the author's name on the Web.

Regardless of who the author of the site is, the information should be well written and organized. If it is carelessly put together, you should be wary of it. In short, if the sponsor did not spend time presenting information correctly and clearly, the information itself may not be very accurate.

Is the Site's Information Accurate?

In addition to paying attention to how a site's material is written and organized, ask yourself the following questions:

- **Is a bibliography or a list of works cited provided?** If sources are not included, you should question the accuracy of the site.
- **Can the accuracy of the information be checked elsewhere?** In most instances you should be able to verify Internet information by checking another source, preferably a print source.
- **Is it clear that opinions are opinions?** It is not a good idea to trust writers who treat their own opinions as facts. (For more on fact, opinion, and expert opinion, see p. 653.)
- **Is the document in complete form?** If you're looking at a summary, use the site to try to find the original source. If you can't locate the original, be skeptical of the source that contains the summary. Original information generally has fewer errors and is often preferred in academic papers.

If Internet information is available in print form, it is usually a good idea to try to obtain the print version. There are several reasons for doing so. First, when an article goes on the Web, errors may creep in. In addition, since Web sites often change addresses or information, a reader of your paper may not be able to find the Web site that you used. Finally, page numbers in print sources are easier to cite than those in electronic ones (which may not include standard page numbering).

Is the Site Up-to-Date?

Even though the Web has a reputation for providing current information, not all Web sites are up-to-date. You can check the timeliness of a site by asking yourself the following questions about dates:

- When was the site first established?
- If the site has been revised, what is the date of the last revision?
- When was the document you are looking at posted to the site? Has it been updated?

This kind of information generally appears at the bottom of a site's home page or at the end of a particular document. If no dates are given, check some of the links. If links are outdated and nonfunctioning, the information at the site is probably outdated as well.

ANALYZING AND THINKING CRITICALLY ABOUT SOURCES

Whether you search a library for sources, like relevant books or journal articles, or find them on the Internet, you should first make sure that your sources are relevant and reliable. In addition, when you use sources in your paper, you will need to analyze them and think critically. As a critical reader, you need to recognize that multiple viewpoints exist and to find the sources that express them. If you can sort through each writer's ideas and watch for opinions, bias, generalizations, and assumptions, you will be well on your way to locating useful research.

Separating Facts from Opinions

It is important to understand the difference between facts and opinions. **Facts** are statements that can be proven to be either true or false; evidence exists to verify facts. **Opinions,** on the other hand, are statements that reveal beliefs or feelings and are neither true nor false. For example, "The Boston Red Sox won the 2004 World Series" is a fact, whereas "The Boston Red Sox are the best team in baseball" is an opinion. For more examples of facts and opinions, see the box on page 654.

Facts are considered reliable if they are taken from a reputable source or can be verified. For example, the date of President John F. Kennedy's assassination—

DON'T CONFUSE FACTS AND OPINIONS

FACT	The planet Earth has six times the volume of Mars.
OPINION	Humans will probably destroy the planet Earth if they don't stop polluting it.
FACT	After inventing the telephone in 1876, Alexander Graham Bell worked on dozens of other inventions, many of which aided the deaf.
OPINION	Alexander Graham Bell's invention of the telephone is considered the most important technological innovation of the nineteenth century.
FACT	Many vitamin-fortified foods are now available in supermarkets.
OPINION	Supermarkets need to carry a wider variety of organic foods.

November 22, 1963 — is a fact that can be found in many reputable sources, including books, newspapers, and magazines. Opinions, however, are not always based on facts and should be evaluated carefully. Before accepting someone's opinion, try to find evidence that supports it. Several opinions exist, for instance, concerning why and how President Kennedy was shot. Some of these opinions may be more reliable than others.

When authors present an opinion, they often alert their readers by using certain words and phrases, such as the following:

as I see it	possibly
in my opinion	some experts believe
in my view	supposedly
it is probable	this seems to indicate

A special type of opinion is **expert opinion** — the attitudes or beliefs expressed by authorities on the topic. Like other writers, experts often use qualifying words and phrases when they offer an opinion. An expert on government finance may write, for example, "*It seems likely* that Social Security payments will decline for future generations of Americans."

When collecting information from a source, be sure not to confuse personal expressions of opinion with support. Personal expressions may be useful to read and consider as a means of shaping your own opinions, but they do not belong in a source-based paper. Expert opinion, however, is definitely usable. When you quote or paraphrase it, be sure to give appropriate credit to your source.

For more on documenting sources, see Chapter 20.

EXERCISE 18.4

Label each of the following statements as fact (F), opinion (O), or expert opinion (EO).

1. According to child psychologists Gerber and Gerber, children who watch prime-time television shows that depict crime consider the world more dangerous than those who do not watch crime shows.
2. The best symphonies are shorter than twenty minutes.
3. Most medical experts recommend that women age forty and older should have a mammogram once every one to two years.
4. About half the population of Uruguay lives in Montevideo.
5. More women earned doctoral degrees in engineering in 2004 than in 1984.
6. Private companies should not be allowed to sell concessions inside our national parks.
7. The mountains of Northern Idaho contain the most scenic landscapes in the country.
8. Many business leaders agree that it is important to hire people who love their work.

Identifying Bias or Viewpoint

Many relevant and reliable sources may provide only a portion of the information you need for your essay. For example, if you are writing about the pros and cons of the space shuttle program, you would expect the NASA Web site (at www.nasa.gov) to be a reliable source of information, but you would not expect it to critique the program's shortcomings. If you are writing an essay on problems in the nursing profession, the *American Journal of Nursing* might be a reliable source, but it, too, probably would not contain articles that are critical of nurses.

Many writers have a particular point of view and interpret information in their own way. For example, suppose you are writing an essay on home schooling for an introductory education class. You find a book that is titled *The Home Schooling Movement: What Children Are Missing* and was written by someone who taught high school for thirty years. While the book may offer valuable information, its title suggests that the book presents a biased, or one-sided, view of home schooling. The author would probably support classroom instruction and perhaps discuss the shortcomings of home schooling in detail but downplay its advantages. This one-sided view of home schooling, then, would be biased. **Bias** refers to a publisher's or writer's own views or particular interest in a topic. A biased source is not necessarily unreliable, but you need to notice the bias and find additional sources that present other opinions.

To find bias in someone's writing, first consider the author's background. For example, the viewpoint of a father who has written a book about home schooling his five children is likely to be very different from that of a long-term high school teacher. Then look carefully at the author's descriptive and connotative language. In the father's book, for instance, how does he describe his children and their educational achievements? Is he choosing specific words to create a particular response in the reader? Does he tend to use many words with negative connotations when

For more information on descriptive language, connotative language, and tone, see pp. 188, 189, and 242.

he is talking about traditional classroom education? Finally, consider the author's overall tone. Can you tell how the father feels about home schooling? Does he sound enthusiastic and positive?

EXERCISE 18.5

Examine each of the following sources and their annotations. Discuss whether the source is likely to be objective (O), somewhat biased (SB), or heavily biased (HB).

1. Cothran, Helen, ed. <u>Gun Control: Opposing Viewpoints</u>. Farmington Hills, MI: Greenhaven Press, 2003.

   > This book contains several articles that present the pros and cons of different issues relating to gun control. The articles are written by experts and give bibliographic references.

2. Malcolm X. <u>The Autobiography of Malcolm X</u>. New York: Ballantine, 1965.

   > Malcolm X tells his life story in this autobiography, which was published just before his death.

3. Markel, Susan. <u>Discipline</u>. From the Web site http://www.attachmentparentingdoctor.com/discipline.html.

   > This article describes ways for parents to discipline their children.

4. Guroianm, Vigen. "Dorm Brothel." <u>Christianity Today</u> 49 (2005): 44.

   > This article deals with the sexual behavior of college students.

5. Ponzetti, James J., Jr., ed. <u>International Encyclopedia of Marriage and Family</u>. New York: Macmillan Reference USA, 2003.

   > Four volumes of in-depth coverage related to family life.

Recognizing Generalizations

A **generalization** is a statement about a large group of items based on experience with or observation of only a limited part of that group. If, for example, you often saw high school students in your town hanging out on the streets and creating disturbances, you might make the following generalization: "The high school students in this town are not well behaved." You could not be sure about your generalization, however, unless you observed every high school student in town, and doing so might well cause you to change your generalization. Look at the following generalizations. You probably won't agree with all of them.

- U.S. colleges and universities give more funding to their athletic programs than to their libraries.
- Home-schooled children do not interact socially with other children their own age.
- Banks in this country no longer provide basic customer services.
- Big companies are laying off great portions of their workforces.
- Circus animals are abused.

A writer's generalization is his or her interpretation of a particular set of facts. If generalizations are backed up by experience or sufficient evidence, they are probably trustworthy. An expert on heart disease, for example, would probably make reliable generalizations about the risks of high cholesterol. If a writer is not an expert, however, and does not provide solid support for generalizations, you would be wise to consult different sources.

EXERCISE 18.6

Label each of the following statements either fact (F) or generalization (G). Indicate what support or documentation would be necessary for you to evaluate its accuracy.

1. Many women want to become pilots.
2. Elephants can vocalize at frequencies below the range of human hearing.
3. In certain parts of the Red Sea, the temperature of the water can reach 138 degrees Fahrenheit.
4. Most people who live in San Diego are associated with the U.S. Navy.
5. People all over the world donated money to help the survivors of the 2004 tsunamis.

Identifying Assumptions

As you may recall from Chapter 16, assumptions are ideas or generalizations that people accept as true without questioning their validity. Writers often use an assumption at the beginning of an essay and then base the rest of the essay on that assumption. If the assumption is false or cannot be proven, however, then the ideas that flow from it also may be incorrect. For instance, the following excerpt begins with an assumption (highlighted) that the writer makes no attempt to prove or justify.

> Childbirth is a painful experience, intolerable even with appropriate medications. In response to this pain, modern women should accept the painkillers offered to them by their doctors. Why be a martyr? You have to suffer sleepless nights because of your child for the rest of your life; bring them into this world on your terms—pain free. Women should not be embarrassed or reluctant to request anesthesia during labor.

The author assumes that all women find childbirth intolerably painful and then argues that women should request anesthesia during labor. But if the writer's initial assumption is false, much of the argument that follows should be questioned.

As you read, be aware of assumptions, especially those at the start of an essay. Ask yourself how the essay would be affected if the initial assumption were untrue. If you disagree with some of the assumptions in a source, check other sources to obtain different viewpoints.

EXERCISE 18.7

Each of the following statements contains one or more assumptions. Identify the assumption(s) made in each statement.

1. Computer users expect Web sites to entertain them with graphics, sound, and video.
2. In response to the problem of ozone depletion, the U.S. Environmental Protection Agency has designed various programs to reduce harmful emissions. The EPA wants to stop the production of certain substances so that the ozone can repair itself over the next fifty years.
3. Only the routine vaccination of all children can eliminate the threat of serious disease and ensure optimum public health. These shots should be administered without hesitation. Parents must have full confidence in their doctors on this matter.
4. Since so many athletes and coaches approve of the use of performance-enhancing drugs, these substances should be allowed without regulation.
5. Because they recognize that meat consumption is environmentally damaging, environmentalists are often vegetarians.

WORKING WITH TEXT: READING SOURCES

Reading sources involves some special skills. Unlike textbook reading, where your purpose is to learn and recall the material, you usually read sources to extract the information you need about a topic. Therefore, you can often read sources selectively, reading only the relevant parts and skipping over the rest. Use the following strategies for reading sources: scan, skim, and read.

Scanning a Source

Scanning means "looking for" the information you seek without actually reading a source from beginning to end. Just as you scan a phone directory to locate a phone number, you scan a source to extract needed information.

Use the following guidelines to scan sources effectively.

1. **Determine how the source is organized.** Is it organized chronologically or by topic? It could also be organized by chapter, subject, or author.

2. **Check the abstract or summary for journal articles; scan the index and table of contents for books.** You can quickly determine whether the source contains the information you need and approximately where to find it.

3. **Keep key words or phrases in mind as you scan.** For example, if you are searching for information on welfare reform, key phrases might include *welfare system, entitlement programs, benefits,* and *welfare spending.*

4. **Scan systematically.** Don't scan a source randomly, hoping to see what you need. Instead, follow a pattern as you sweep your eyes across the material. For charts, tables, and indexes, use a downward sweep. For prose material, use a zigzag or Z-pattern, sweeping across several lines of print at a time.

Skimming a Source

Skimming (also called *previewing*) is a quick way to find out whether a source suits your purposes without taking the time to read it completely. Skimming also allows you to determine whether any sections deserve close reading. As you skim a source, mark or jot down sections that might be worth returning to later.

For more on previewing, see Chapter 2, p. 24.

Use the following guidelines to skim a source effectively; adapt them to fit a particular source.

1. **Read the title.** It announces the subject and may provide clues about the author's approach to or attitude toward the subject.

2. **Read the introductory paragraph.** It may provide important background information, introduce the subject, and provide a brief overview.

3. **Read the headings.** A heading announces the topic to be discussed. When read successively, the headings may form a brief outline of the material.

4. **Read the first sentence of each paragraph.** Often it is the topic sentence of the paragraph and announces the main point. If it is transitional, then read the next sentence as well.

5. **Read key words and phrases.** Glance quickly through the remainder of each paragraph. Notice numbered lists, capitalized or italicized words, boldfaced terms, names, numbers, dates, and the like.

6. **Notice any graphics.** Read the legend or title given for any maps, charts, photographs, or diagrams.

7. **Read the last paragraph or summary.** It may review the key points in the article or essay.

Reading a Source Closely

Once you identify the sections within a source that contain the information you need — by scanning, skimming, or both — *read* those sections closely and carefully.

For more on strategies for close reading, see Chapter 2, pp. 28–39.

To be sure you do not take information out of context, also read the paragraphs before and after the material you have chosen.

Improving Your Reading of Electronic Sources

When you read material on the Internet, you often need some different reading strategies. The following information and advice should help you read Web sites more productively.

For more practice reading Web sites, visit www .bedfordstmartins.com /successfulwriting /tutorials.

- **Readers of Web sites should understand a site's design and features.** When you reach a new site, scroll through it quickly to discover how it is organized and what information is available. Remember that the first screen may grab your attention but rarely contains substantive information. Find out if there is a search option or a guide to the site (a site map). Doing an initial exploration is especially important on large and complex sites, where you may have a number of different choices for locating information.

- **Text on Web sites often does not follow the traditional text pattern.** Instead of containing typical paragraphs, a Web page may show a list of topic sentences without details. In addition, electronic pages are often designed to stand alone: They are brief and do not depend on other pages for meaning. In many instances, background information is not supplied.

- **Web sites involve graphics, movement, and sound as well as words.** Several of your senses may be engaged simultaneously when you visit a Web site. If you are distracted by the sound and graphics, check to see if a text-only version of the site is available.

Learning Style Options

- **Readers of Web sites can follow their own learning styles and make their own decisions about what paths to follow.** Because screens have menus and links, readers create their own texts by following or ignoring different paths. This is quite different from print text, which offers readers far fewer choices. Some readers may prefer to begin with "the big picture" and then move to the details; others may prefer to do the opposite. A pragmatic learner may move through a site systematically, either clicking on or ignoring links as they appear on the screen. A spatial learner, in contrast, would probably look at the graphics first. All readers should make sure that they don't skip over important content.

- **Readers of Web sites need to focus on their purpose.** Regardless of your learning style, keep in mind the information you are looking for. If you don't focus on your purpose, you may wander aimlessly through the site and waste valuable research time.

Finding Sources
and
Taking Notes

CHAPTER QUICK START

Suppose you are enrolled in a seminar on the environment. Your instructor gives the class a number of photographs and directs each student to choose one and write a paper about the environmental issues it reflects. You've chosen the photograph shown on the opposite page.

Writing Quick Start

Write a brief statement describing the environmental issue the photograph represents. Consider where you might go to learn more about this issue and make a list of the sources you would consult.

What issue did you write about? What sources of information did you list? Did you include both print and Internet sources? Do you need to conduct a personal interview or do a survey? Once you find information that is useful for your paper, what procedures should you use to record information for later use? This chapter will answer these and other questions about how to locate sources and take accurate notes.

Regardless of the kind of research you are doing, it is helpful to approach the process of locating and using sources in a systematic way, as shown in Figure 19.1. If you already have a narrowed topic for a research paper, be sure to write a working thesis and research questions before you start looking for specific sources. If you have a general topic and need help narrowing it, several kinds of library or online sources—such as encyclopedias and subject directories—may be helpful. In either case, it is a good idea to consult the advice in Chapter 18 about planning a paper and evaluating sources.

You will have many opportunities to use sources in the writing you do in college and at work (see the accompanying box for a few examples).

AN OVERVIEW OF LIBRARY SOURCES

Your college library is an immense collection of print, media, and computerized sources on a wide variety of topics. Learning to use this library will help you locate sources effectively.

Learning Your Way around the Library

It is a good idea to become familiar with your college library *before* you need to use it. Following are a few ways to do so.

1. **Take a formal tour of the library.** Many colleges offer library tours during the first few weeks of the term. On a tour, you'll learn where everything is located

> **SCENES FROM COLLEGE AND THE WORKPLACE**
>
> - For an *anthropology* course, you are asked to analyze the differences between the religious practices of two cultures.
> - For an *art history* course, you are asked to write a biography of a famous Renaissance artist.
> - As *supervisor* of a health-care facility, you decide to conduct a survey of the staff to determine employees' interest in flexible working hours.

FIGURE 19.1
WRITING A PAPER USING SOURCES

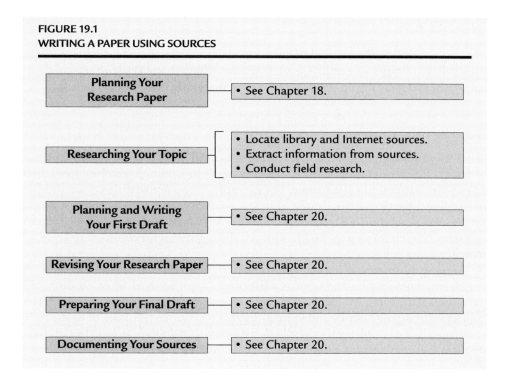

Planning Your Research Paper	• See Chapter 18.
Researching Your Topic	• Locate library and Internet sources. • Extract information from sources. • Conduct field research.
Planning and Writing Your First Draft	• See Chapter 20.
Revising Your Research Paper	• See Chapter 20.
Preparing Your Final Draft	• See Chapter 20.
Documenting Your Sources	• See Chapter 20.

and discover how to use important services, such as interlibrary loans and computerized database searches.

2. **Take your own tour.** Obtain a map or floor plan from the circulation desk and use it to tour the library. Inspect the popular magazine collection; see what electronic resources are available. Try to become comfortable with the library so that the first time you need to use it, you can get to work easily. Keep the floor plan in your bag or notebook for future reference.

3. **Consult reference librarians.** Librarians are usually available at the reference desk to advise you about what sources to use and where to locate them. Reference librarians often can save you time, so don't hesitate to ask them for help.

4. **Check the library's Web site.** Most libraries have a Web site created by librarians to present all the resources that are available to you. Look for a link to the library's catalog, including a way to check your library account. If your library subscribes to any online databases for journal articles, these will be listed on the Web site along with access instructions. Your librarians may also have posted lists of helpful Web sites that they have used with students over many semesters. Finally, library hours, services, policies, maps, and ways to contact the library staff should also appear on the site.

For guided practice touring the library, visit www.bedfordstmartins .com/successfulwriting /tutorials.

Locating Useful Library Sources

The sources you need often will be stored in electronic databases available through your college library or an online service. Learning how to use keyword searches and subject headings will help you locate relevant materials.

Searching Using Keywords

Whether you use an online catalog, a database on CD-ROM, or an online database to search for information, you will need to perform keyword searches. **Keywords** are words that describe your topic. For example, if you are writing about alternative political parties in the United States, keywords would include *politics, political parties, third parties,* or *U.S. politics.* Notice that keywords often include more than one term. The chart on page 667 has practical suggestions for conducting keyword searches.

Once you enter a keyword, a system (either an online catalog or a search engine) searches its files and returns a list of pertinent sources. Most catalogs and databases also search by using standard **subject headings.** Keep in mind that a subject heading may not be the same as the words you are thinking of to describe your topic. For example, you might look for articles on *drug abuse,* but the database might use the subject heading *substance abuse.* In this case, searching for *substance abuse* could give you more relevant search results.

Most databases publish a list of the subject headings (sometimes they call it a *thesaurus*). In general, it is best to start with a keyword search until you discover the controlled vocabulary terms for your topic, especially since all databases have a different controlled vocabulary. For example, if you are searching for information on *welfare reform,* keywords might include *welfare system, entitlement programs, benefits,* and *welfare spending.* The following sections describe how to locate books and articles in the library and in electronic databases using keywords and subject headings.

Library of Congress Subject Headings (LCSH)

The *Library of Congress Subject Headings (LCSH)* is a major reference work that lists standard subject headings used by the Library of Congress. These headings can give you ideas for a topic or help you narrow a broad topic. For example, if your broad subject is *animal communication* and you're interested in finding a narrowed topic for a ten-page research paper, the accompanying excerpt from the *LCSH* would give you several options to explore further, including *language learning by animals* and *human-animal communication.* Because the *LCSH* subject headings are so comprehensive, they are also an excellent source of keywords for database and online searches.

SUGGESTIONS FOR CONDUCTING KEYWORD SEARCHES

- Place quotation marks around a phrase to limit your search. For example, **"single motherhood"** will give you topics related to *single motherhood*. Without quotation marks, a keyword search would provide all sources that use the word *single* as well as all the sources that use the word *motherhood*.

- Use *AND* to join words that must appear in a document. For example, **psychology AND history** would provide sources that mention both *psychology* and *history*. For some searches, you may need to use a plus (+) sign instead of *AND*.

- Use *OR* to indicate synonyms when only one needs to appear in the document. For example, **job OR career** would provide more options than just *job* or just *career*.

- Place *NOT* before words that should not appear in the document. For example, **camels NOT cigarettes** would provide sources on the animal. In some searches, you may need to use a minus (-) sign instead of *NOT*.

- Use parentheses to group together keywords and combine the group with another set of keywords. For example, **(timepiece OR watch OR clock) AND production** would provide sources on the production of any of these three items.

- Use an asterisk (*) to indicate letters that may vary in spelling or words that may have variant endings. For example, a search for **"social psycholog*"** will find sources with the words *psychology, psychologist, psychologists,* and so forth.

SAMPLE ENTRY FROM THE *LCSH*

Animal communication

[QL776] ◄———— Library of Congress call number

Used for ———► UF Animal language
Communication among animals
Language learning by animals

Broader term ———► BT Animal behavior

Narrower term ———► NT Animal sounds
Human-animal communication
Sound production by animals
Animal communication with humans

See or refer to ———► USE Human-animal communication

Locating Books in the Library Catalog

A library's catalog lists books owned by the library. It may also list available magazines, newspapers, government documents, and electronic sources. However, it does not list individual articles included in magazines and newspapers. Before the widespread use of computers, a library's catalog was made up of three- by five-inch index cards. Now, though, almost all libraries have a computerized catalog, which allows you to search for sources electronically — by title, author, or subject — from terminals in the library. Directions usually appear on or near the screen, and most libraries also allow access to their catalogs from outside computers, at home, or in a computer lab on campus. Figure 19.2 shows a typical search page of an online library catalog.

When searching the library catalog for books on a specific topic, you may have to view two or three screens until you find information about a specific book because you first get a list of relevant titles. Then you need to select the title that interests you. On the next screen you will get more about that item. The call num-

FIGURE 19.2
LIBRARY CATALOG SEARCH PAGE

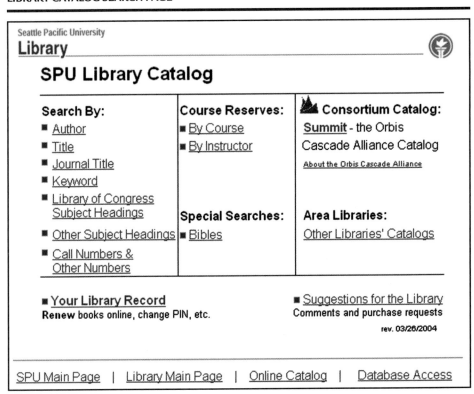

FIGURE 19.3
LIBRARY CATALOG SEARCH RESULTS

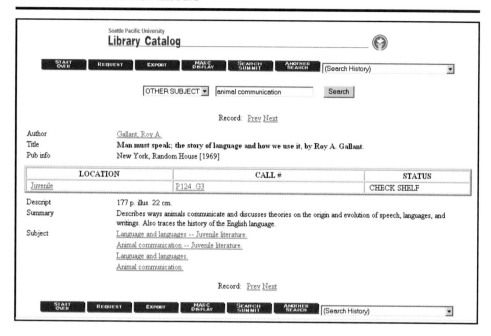

ber, location, and availability may be on this screen, or you might have to click once more to find specific information on obtaining that item. Figure 19.3 shows the results of a computerized search by subject for the topic *animal communication*. Computerized catalogs offer many conveniences. The screen often indicates whether the book is on the shelves, whether it has been checked out, and when it is due back. Some systems allow you to reserve the book by entering your request on the computer. Terminals often are connected to printers that enable you to print the screen, providing you with an accurate record of each source and saving you the time it would take to write down source information. Computerized catalogs allow you to enter more than one keyword at a time. Use the previous tips on keyword searches to help you use computerized catalogs.

For more practice using your library's catalog, visit www .bedfordstmartins.com /successfulwriting /tutorials.

For older or special collections, some libraries still maintain card catalogs that index all the items in that particular collection. A traditional card catalog includes three types of cards: title, author, and subject. Arranged alphabetically, the three types of cards may be filed together, or there may be a separate catalog for the subject cards.

The catalog provides call numbers that tell you where to locate books on the library's shelves. Once you have a specific call number, use your library floor plan and the call-number guides posted on shelves to locate the appropriate section of the library. Then scan the letters or numbers on the spines of books until you find the book you need. Be sure to scan the surrounding books, which are usually on related topics. You may discover other useful sources that you overlooked in the catalog.

Bibliographies

A **bibliography** lists sources on a particular subject, including books, articles, government publications, and other sources. Some bibliographies also provide brief summaries or descriptions of the sources they list.

To locate a bibliography on your subject, combine the word *bibliography* with a relevant keyword for your topic. For example, you could search your library's online catalog for *animal communication* and *bibliography*. Also, some libraries publish their own bibliographies or pathfinders to guide students to important sources on certain topics. Look for these on the library's Web site or ask the librarians if they have any such guides available as handouts.

Locating Articles Using Periodical Indexes

Periodicals include newspapers, popular magazines, and scholarly journals. Periodicals differ by content and frequency of publication. Table 19.1 summarizes the differences between popular magazines (such as *People*) and scholarly journals (such as the *American Journal of Psychology*). For academic essays, it is best not to rely solely on information from popular magazines.

Because periodicals are published daily, weekly, or monthly, they often contain up-to-date information about a subject. A library's catalog does not list specific articles from a magazine or journal. However, it does list the periodicals the library subscribes to and the indexes and abstracts it holds. **Indexes** list articles by title, author, and subject. **Abstracts** list articles and also provide a brief summary of each one.

Most indexes and abstracts are available as computer databases as well as in print form. These online indexes and abstracts may be accessed through the Internet, or they may be available on a campus network. Keep in mind that the name of the electronic version of an index or abstract may be different from that of the print version. Check with your librarian to see what databases are available and whether the library charges a fee for online services. Because online indexes are updated frequently, sometimes every week, you can use them to locate current information. Most computerized indexes and abstracts cover only recent years, so you may need to consult print indexes if you need older material. There are two types of periodical indexes—general and specialized.

More and more of the periodical databases provided by libraries give users access to full-text articles as Web documents (in hypertext markup language, or HTML) or as scanned images (in portable document format, or PDF). Since most libraries subscribe to more than one database provider, it may be necessary to check for the full text in a database other than the one in which you found the cita-

TABLE 19.1

A COMPARISON OF SCHOLARLY JOURNALS AND POPULAR MAGAZINES

	Scholarly Journal	Popular Magazine
Who reads it?	Researchers, professionals, students	General public
Who writes it?	Researchers, professionals	Reporters, journalists, freelance writers
Who decides what to publish in it?	Other researchers (peer review)	Editors, publishers
What does it look like?	Mostly text, some charts and graphs, little or no advertising	Many photos, many advertisements, eye-catching layout
What kind of information does it contain?	Results of research studies and experiments, statistics and analysis, in-depth evaluations of specialized topics, overviews of all the research on a subject (literature review), bibliographies and references	Articles of general interest, easy-to-understand language, news items, interviews, opinion pieces, no bibliographies (sources cited informally within the article)
Where is it available?	Sometimes by subscription only, large bookstores, large public library branches, college/-university libraries, online	Newsstands, most bookstores, most public library branches, online
How often is it published?	Monthly to quarterly	Weekly to monthly
What are some examples?	*Journal of Bioethics, American Journal of Family Law, Film Quarterly*	*Newsweek, Popular Science, Psychology Today*

tion or abstract. Look for an article linker that checks your library's other databases for you with one click.

Finally, when you are searching, look for options that allow you to refine your search. Many databases allow users to limit by date and publication type. Look for a place to choose "peer reviewed" or "newspapers and magazines" if you need to locate an article from a particular kind of source. Once you locate a relevant article, find out what your options are for emailing, printing, and saving it to a disk. Also, check with the librarian for interlibrary loan options if you cannot locate the full text or hard copy of an article that you want.

General periodical indexes. General indexes list articles on a wide range of subjects that have been published in popular magazines. The following common general indexes are available in most college libraries.

- *Readers' Guide to Periodical Literature (print, online, and CD-ROM)* The print version of the *Readers' Guide to Periodical Literature* indexes articles published in roughly two hundred popular periodicals beginning with the year 1900. It is of limited use for academic topics because it does not index scholarly journals. However, it can help you find articles of general interest and on current topics. The older paper editions are particularly useful for assignments that require historical research. For example, you may need to find a review of a play's first performance in New York. Or you may need an interview with a soldier's wife dating from World War II.

- *InfoTrac databases (online and CD-ROM)* InfoTrac's extensive computer databases list articles published in thousands of magazines, journals, and newspapers. Some entries include only abstracts, but depending on the type of agreement your library has, you may have access to full-text articles as well.

  Since InfoTrac is organized by subject headings, it may list subdivisions of the topic being searched. A partial list of subdivisions for the topic *animal communication* is shown in the following example.

SAMPLE INFOTRAC ENTRY

Subdivisions of: Animal Communication

analysis
  41 articles
behavior
  1 article
beliefs, opinions and attitudes
  3 articles
bibliography
  1 article
case studies
  2 articles
comparative analysis
  1 article
directories
  1 article
discovery and exploration
  1 article
environmental aspects
  7 articles
ethical aspects
  1 article

Specialized periodical indexes and abstracts. Specialized indexes and abstracts reference scholarly or technical articles within a specific academic field of study. The

Essay and General Literature Index (1900–, online, CD-ROM) is useful for locating articles and essays published in books. Many academic disciplines have one or more specialized indexes or abstracts. Some are specialized by subject; others by the type of material they index. Here is a list of common specialized indexes. Each is available in a print version as well as on CD-ROM and on the Internet. CD-ROM and online versions, however, may contain only recent files, although many databases continue to add back files.

Applied Science and Technology Index (1958–)
Art Index (1929–)
Biological and Agricultural Index (1983–)
Book Review Digest (1905–)
Business Index (1958–)
Dissertation Abstracts (1933–)
Education Index (1929–)
Engineering Index (1920–)
Historical Abstracts (1955–)
Humanities Index (1974–)
MLA International Bibliography of Books and Articles in the Modern Languages and Literature (1921–)
Monthly Catalog of U.S. Government Publications (1895–)
Music Index (1949–)
Physics Abstracts (1898–)
Psychological Abstracts (1927–)
Science Index (1984–)
Sociological Abstracts (1952–)

Here is a sample entry on the topic of *mammals* from the *Art Index*.

SAMPLE ENTRY FROM THE *ART INDEX*

Mammals

1. Haynes, G. The catastrophic extinction of North American mammoths and mastodonts. *World Archaeology* v. 33 no. 3 (February 2002) p. 391–416

2. Powell, E. A. Curtains for overkill? [extinction of mammoths]. *Archaeology* v. 55 no. 1 (January/February 2002) p. 16–17

RESEARCH AND THE INTERNET

The Internet is a huge network of computers located all over the world that allows those computers to share information. It has become another major resource for all types of research. Most colleges offer Internet access in dormitories, through campus computer centers, and in the library.

The Internet offers a wide variety of sources, including the World Wide Web (WWW or the Web), listservs, newsgroups, and email. You will most likely find the Web to be the most helpful of these sources in both academic and workplace research because it offers you access to millions of diverse sources.

The World Wide Web

The World Wide Web is made up of a vast collection of Web sites — linked electronic documents that can include video and audio excerpts as well as text and graphics. Web sites have been created for thousands of topics, from the most serious to the entirely silly. Corporations, government agencies, nonprofit organizations, schools, and individuals create and publish Web sites for various purposes.

Each Web site has a home page, which usually includes information about the site and a directory of links to other pages on the site. To access a Web site, you use a Web address, called a *uniform resource locator* (URL), and a Web browser, such as Netscape Navigator or Microsoft Internet Explorer. Most Web pages also include underlined topics called *links,* which you click on to access related pages or sites.

Every Web site has a unique URL, which consists of three basic parts.

$$\overbrace{}^{1}\quad\overbrace{}^{2}\quad\overbrace{}^{3}$$

http://www.spu.edu/info/facts/index.html

1. **Retrieval method or protocol** These are the rules computers use to communicate with each other and indicate where the user wants to go on the Internet. Common protocols include the following:

   - *http (hypertext transfer protocol):* This protocol is used to view Web pages and to allow users to follow links. It is the most common protocol.

   - *gopher:* This format presents information in a text-based, menu style.

   - *ftp (file transfer protocol):* This protocol moves files from one Internet site to another.

   - *telnet:* This method allows the user to log in to one network from another. This is commonly used for online catalogs.

2. **Computer where the information resides (also called "the server")** This information commonly consists of *www* (World Wide Web) and the domain name. Every domain name has an extension that can give a clue about the site's publisher. You should know the following common extensions:

   .com = commercial, a business-owned or profit-driven site
   .edu = education, usually associated with a school
   .gov = government
   .mil = military
   .net = network
   .org = nonprofit organization

.info = unrestricted use
.biz = business
.name = individual

3. Path This information communicates the location of the desired Web page. It takes the computer through one or several directories to the appropriate file.

The following section discusses how to optimize the World Wide Web for research.

Doing Research on the World Wide Web

The Web contains millions of Web sites, most of which are not grouped together in any organized way. Therefore, you will need to use a subject directory or search engine to locate the information you need.

Subject directory. A **subject directory** uses various categories and subcategories to classify Web resources. Some subject directories also include reviews or evaluations of sites. A subject directory can be especially helpful when you have decided on a general topic for an essay but need to narrow it further. Some subject directories are part of a search engine, whereas others are stand-alone sites.

Search engine. A **search engine** is an application that can help you find information on a particular topic. When you use a search engine, you begin by typing a keyword, phrase, or question into a search box. The search engine then looks for documents that contain the keyword or phrase you told it to search for. Seven commonly used search engines and their URLs follow.

USEFUL SEARCH ENGINES

Search Engine	URL
AltaVista	www.altavista.com
Go.com	www.go.com
Google	www.google.com
Hot Bot	www.hotbot.com
Kartoo	www.kartoo.com
Lycos	www.lycos.com
Yahoo!	www.yahoo.com

If a keyword or phrase is too general, a search could turn up hundreds or perhaps thousands of sites, most of which will not be helpful to you. Your searches will be more productive if you use the guidelines for keyword searches on page 667.

Since different search engines usually generate different results, it is a good idea to use more than one search engine when you are researching a given topic. For a general search, you might start with a search engine such as Google. Once you've narrowed your topic, however, you might want to use a more specialized search

For more practice selecting and evaluating a search engine, visit www.bedfordstmartins .com/successfulwriting /tutorials.

engine, such as one that is geared to a particular discipline or specialty. For example, if your topic involves the Democratic Party, Google might point you to a site entitled Political Science Resources on the Web, which has its own search engine.

Locating Useful Internet Sources

For more on evaluating Internet sources, see Chapter 18, pp. 650–53.

Although the Internet offers vast amounts of information, it does have one major drawback: Its information is often less reliable than information in print sources because anyone can post information and documents on the Internet. To be certain that your information is reliable, you will want to evaluate it, and you might want to maintain a list of reliable Web sites that provide accurate and thorough information.

Once you identify usable sources, be sure to keep track of their URLs so you can find the sites again easily and cite them in your paper. You can save Web addresses on your own computer as bookmarks or favorites (depending on the Web browser you use) that allow you to return to a site by clicking on its name. You can also organize your bookmarks or favorites into folders such as *career, library information,* or *new sites,* so that you can easily find your sources.

Following are some generally useful and reliable Web sites that you should know.

News Web sites.   Newspapers, television networks, and popular magazines often have companion Web sites that provide current information and late-breaking news stories. Useful sites include

- *The New York Times*   http://www.nytimes.com
- CNN Interactive   http://www.cnn.com
- *The Washington Post*   http://www.washingtonpost.com
- MSNBC   http://www.msnbc.com

Academic research sites.   Both general reference information and discipline-specific information can be found on the Internet. The following sites offer general reliable reference information:

- Altapedia Online   http://www.altapedia.com
- Britannica Online   http://www.eb.com
- Encyclopedia Smithsonian   http://www.si.edu/resource/faq

Table 19.2 lists some good places to begin research in academic disciplines.

Listservs and Newsgroups

The Internet's listservs and newsgroups are discussion forums where people interested in a particular topic or field of research can communicate and share information about it. A listserv is an email discussion group; messages are sent

TABLE 19.2
WEB SOURCES FOR ACADEMIC RESEARCH

Academic Discipline	Site Title and Affiliation	Site URL
Humanities	Voice of the Shuttle (University of California, Santa Barbara)	http://vos.ucsb.edu
	Edsitement (National Endowment for the Humanities)	http://edsitement.neh.gov /websites_all.asp
	Humbul Humanities Hub (Resource Discovery Network)	http://www.humbul.ac.uk /help/subjects.html
Literature	LitLinks (Bedford/St. Martin's)	http://www.bedfordstmartins .com/litlinks/
	Representative Poetry Online (University of Toronto)	http://eir.library.utoronto.ca /rpo/display/index.cfm
	Literary Resources on the Net (Jack Lynch, Rutgers University)	http://andromeda.rutgers .edu/~jlynch/Lit/
History	History@Bedford/St. Martin's	http://www.bedfordstmartins .com/history/
	Librarians' Index to the Internet history links	http://lii.org/search/file /history
	History Internet Resources (James Madison University Libraries)	http://www.lib.jmu.edu /history/internet.html
Social Sciences	Social Sciences Information Gateway (Resource Discovery Network)	http://sosig.esrc.bris.ac.uk
	Research Methods in the Social Sciences (University of Miami Libraries)	http://www.library.miami .edu/netguides/psymeth.html
	Social Science Libraries and Information Services (Yale University Library)	http://www.library.yale.edu /socsci/subjguides/
Science	Eurekalert (American Association for the Advancement of Science)	http://www.eurekalert.org/
	Nature.com (Nature Publishing Group)	http://www.nature.com /index.html
	SciCentral	http://www.scicentral.com/
Medicine	Health Information (National Institutes of Health)	http://health.nih.gov/

(Continued on next page)

TABLE 19.2 *(Continued)*

Academic Discipline	Site Title and Affiliation	Site URL
Medicine (cont'd)	WebMD	http://www.webmd.com/
	PubMed Central (National Institutes of Health)	http://www.pubmedcentral.org/
Business	Hoover's Online	http://www.hoovers.com/free/
	Bureau of Labor Statistics	http://stats.bls.gov/
	EdgarScan (PricewaterhouseCoopers)	http://edgarscan.pwcglobal.com/servlets/edgarscan

automatically to subscribers' email accounts. Some listservs allow anyone to subscribe, whereas others require a moderator's permission. A newsgroup, in contrast, does not require membership, and messages are posted to a news server for anyone to read and respond to. A central network called *Usenet* provides access to thousands of newsgroups.

Consult the frequently asked questions (FAQs) for a listserv or newsgroup to determine if it suits your needs and, for a listserv, to see how to subscribe. Keep in mind that messages posted to listservs and newsgroups are not usually checked for accuracy and are not always reliable sources of information (though in general listserv discussions tend to be more serious and focused than newsgroup discussions). You can use electronic discussion forums to become familiar with a topic; obtain background information; discover new issues, facets, or approaches; identify print sources of information; and build your interest in a topic. To locate discussion groups, use a World Wide Web search engine to search the term *discussion groups* or *Usenet.*

Email Addresses

Many authors, researchers, and corporations have email addresses that allow you to send correspondence directly to their computers. Many authorities are willing to respond to requests for specific information, but you should first make sure the information you need is not already available through more traditional sources. To locate email addresses, consult an online directory such as Bigfoot (at bigfoot.com) or Internet Address Finder (at www.iaf.net). (Any directory may include obsolete entries.) Email search directories are also available through Yahoo! and elsewhere. While not complete, they do contain a great deal of information.

When you send an email message to someone you don't know, be sure to introduce yourself and briefly describe the purpose of your inquiry. Provide complete information about yourself, including the name of your school and how to contact you, and politely request the information you need.

EXTRACTING INFORMATION FROM SOURCES

As you read sources, you will need to take notes to use later. The following section discusses systems for note-taking and explains how to write various types of notes—for summaries, paraphrases, and quotations. It also offers advice for avoiding plagiarism.

Gathering Necessary Citation Information

As you work with sources, be sure to record complete information for each source, using a form like the one shown in Figure 19.4. Filling out an information work-

For more on Works Cited lists, see Chapter 20, pp. 716 (MLA) and 734 (APA).

FIGURE 19.4
BIBLIOGRAPHIC INFORMATION WORKSHEET

Author(s) _____

Title _____

Beginning Page _____   Ending Page _____

Title of Journal _____

Volume Number _____   Issue Number _____

Date of Issue _____

Call Number _____

Publisher _____

Place of Publication _____

Copyright Date _____

sheet will help you locate the source again—in case you need to verify something or find additional information. Later on, when you have completed worksheets for all the sources you are using, you can easily alphabetize them and prepare your Works Cited list.

Constructing an Annotated Bibliography

Another approach, which some instructors require, is to prepare an **annotated bibliography**—a list of all the sources you *consulted* in researching your topic and a brief summary of each source's content and focus. You will find that it is easier to write the annotations as you do your research—while each source is fresh in your mind. Although preparing an annotated bibliography may be a bit more time-consuming, it can be very helpful during the drafting or revising stage. If you realize, for instance, that you need more information on a particular subtopic, your annotations can often direct you to the most useful source.

If you are putting together an annotated bibliography intended only for your own use, you might simply write your annotations at the bottom of each information worksheet. For an annotated bibliography that will be submitted to your instructor, you would need to alphabetize it and use correct bibliographic format. Here is a sample annotated bibliography for researching the benefits of cooperative learning in the classroom.

SAMPLE ANNOTATED BIBLIOGRAPHY

Ataiyero, Kayce T. "Spellman Spelling Success." The Washington
    Post 3 Apr. 2000: M12.
        Article in a leading newspaper about one school's
        experience with cooperative learning. Students,
        parents, teachers, researchers, and administrators
        are quoted.
Johnson, Roger T., and David W. Johnson. The Cooperative
    Learning Center of the University of Minnesota. 17 Apr.
    2002. 23 Apr. 2005. <http://www.co-operation.org/>.
        Huge Web site maintained by top authorities on the
        subject; provides dozens of research articles on
        many issues.
Littleton, Karen, Dorothy Miell, and Dorothy Faulkner, eds.
    Learning to Collaborate, Collaborating to Learn. New
    York: Nova Science, 2004.
        Collection of essays written by experts in the field
        of group learning. Applies the concept of collabora-

tive learning to a variety of subject areas and student populations.

Marzano, Robert J., Debra J. Pickering, and Jane E. Pollack.
Classroom Instruction That Works: Research-Based
Strategies for Increasing Student Achievement. Alexan-
dria, VA: ASCD, 2001.

> Contains one chapter on cooperative learning with
> a simplified overview of all the major research on
> this topic.

Vermette, Paul, Laurie Harper, and Shelley DiMillo. "Coopera-
tive and Collaborative Learning with Four- to Eight-Year-
Olds: How Does Research Support Teachers' Practice?"
Journal of Instructional Psychology June (2004): 130.

> Scholarly article reporting on several studies
> that deal with cooperative learning. Relates these
> studies to actual classroom practices. Includes
> references.

For more on bibliographic format, see Chapter 20, pp. 716 (MLA) and 734 (APA).

Systems of Note-Taking

When you take research notes, you'll probably need to copy quotes, write paraphrases, and make summary notes. There are three ways to record your research:
on note cards, on your computer, or on copies of source material.

Regardless of the system you use, be sure to designate a place to record your
own ideas, such as different-colored index cards, a notepad, or a computer folder.
Be careful as well not to simply record (or highlight) quotations. Writing summary
notes or paraphrases helps you think about the ideas in your source, how they fit
with other ideas, and how they might work in your research paper.

Note Cards

Some researchers use four- by six-inch or five- by eight-inch index cards for note-
taking. If you use this system, put information from only one source or about only
one subtopic on each card. At the top of the card, indicate the author of the source
and the subtopic that the note covers. Be sure to include page numbers in case you
need to go back and reread the article or passage. If you copy an author's exact
words, place the information in quotation marks and include the term *direct quotation* and the page number in parentheses. If you write a summary note (see
p. 683) or paraphrase (see p. 684), write *paraphrase* or *summary* on the card and the
page number of the source. When you use this system, you can rearrange your

FIGURE 19.5
SAMPLE NOTE CARD

Schmoke & Roques, 17-25

Medicalization

    Medicalization is a system in which the government would control the release of narcotics to drug addicts.
    — would work like a prescription does now — only gov't official would write prescription
        — addicts would be required to get counseling and health services
        — would take drug control out of hands of drug traffickers   (paraphrase, 18)

---

cards and experiment with different ways of organizing as you plan your paper. Figure 19.5 shows a sample note card.

Computerized Note-Taking

Another option is to type your notes into computer files and organize your files by subtopic. To do so, use a computer notebook to create small "note cards," or use a hypertext card program. As with note cards, keep track of sources by including the author's name and the page numbers for each source and make a back-up copy of your notes. If you have access to a computer in the library, you can type in summaries, paraphrases, and direct quotations while you are doing the research, eliminating the need to type or recopy them later.

Annotated Copies of Sources

For more on highlighting and annotating, see Chapter 2, p. 32.

This approach· is most appropriate for very short papers that do not involve numerous sources or extensive research. To use this system, photocopy or print the source material, underline or highlight useful information, and write your reactions, paraphrases, and summary notes in the margins or on attachments to the appropriate page. Annotating source material often saves time because you don't need to copy quotations or write lengthy notes. The disadvantage is that in addition to the expense of photocopying, this system does not allow you to sort and rearrange notes by subtopic.

When you highlight and annotate a source, be selective about what you mark or comment on, keeping the purpose of your research in mind. One student who was researching anthropomorphism annotated the following excerpt from *When Elephants Weep: The Emotional Lives of Animals* by Jeffrey Masson and Susan McCarthy. Note how this student underlined key points related to his research. Notice also how his annotations comment on, summarize key points of, and question the text.

SAMPLE ANNOTATIONS AND UNDERLINING

The greatest obstacle in science to investigating the emotions of other animals has been an inordinate desire to avoid anthropomorphism. <u>Anthropomorphism* means the ascription of human characteristics—thought, feelings, consciousness, and motivation—to the nonhuman.</u> When people claim that the elements are conspiring to ruin their picnic or that a tree is their friend, they are anthropomorphizing. Few believe that the weather is plotting against them, but anthropomorphic ideas about animals are held more widely. Outside scientific circles, it is common to speak of the thoughts and feelings of pets and wild and captive animals. Yet many scientists regard the notion that animals feel pain as the grossest sort of anthropomorphic error.

*def

!
Wrong! If so, then why do vets use anesthesia?

<u>Cats and dogs are prime targets of anthropomorphism, both wrongly and rightly.</u> Ascribing unlikely thoughts and feelings to pets is common: "She understands every word you say." "He sings his little heart out to show how grateful he is." Some people deck reluctant pets in clothing, give them presents in which they have no interest, or assign their own opinions to the animals. Some dogs are even taught to attack people of races different from their owners'. Many dog lovers seem to enjoy believing that cats are selfish, unfeeling creatures who heartlessly use their deluded owners, compared with loving, loyal, and naive dogs. More often, however, <u>people have quite realistic views about their pets' abilities and attributes. The experience of living with an animal often provides a strong sense of its abilities and limitations</u>—although even here, as for people living intimately with people, <u>preconceptions</u> can be <u>more persuasive than lived experience</u>, and can create their own reality.

dog lovers vs. cat lovers
why?

People have preconceived notions of certain breeds of dogs as vicious.

> JEFFREY MASSON and SUSAN MCCARTHY,
> *When Elephants Weep: The Emotional Lives of Animals*

Writing Summary Notes

Much of your note-taking will be in the form of summary notes, which condense information from sources. Take summary notes when you want to record the gist of an author's ideas but do not need the exact wording or a paraphrase. Use the following guidelines to write effective summary notes. Remember that everything you put in summary notes must be in your own words.

For more on writing summaries, see Chapter 2, p. 42.

1. **Record only information that relates to your topic and purpose.** Do not include irrelevant information.

2. **Write notes that condense the author's ideas in your own words.** Include key terms and concepts, procedures, or principles. Do not include specific examples, quotations, or anything that is not essential to the main point. Do not include your opinion, even a positive one. (You can include any comments in a separate note, as suggested earlier.)

3. **Record the ideas in the order in which they appear in the original source.** Reordering ideas might affect the meaning.

4. **Reread your summary to determine whether it contains sufficient information.** Would it be understandable to someone who has not read the original source? If not, revise the summary to include additional information.

5. **Jot down the publication information for the sources you summarize.** Unless you summarize an entire book or poem, you will need page references when you write your paper and prepare a works cited list.

A sample summary is shown below. It summarizes the first four paragraphs of the essay "Too Immature for the Death Penalty?" by Paul Raeburn, which appears in Chapter 15 (pp. 516–20). Read the essay and then study the summary.

SAMPLE SUMMARY

Two teenagers committed, confessed to, and were convicted of an abduction and murder. Their sentences have been overturned and are now being considered by the U.S. Supreme Court. The case is of interest to several professional groups because the case argues that teenagers should not be executed because their brains are not fully developed.

Writing Paraphrases

When you paraphrase, you restate the author's ideas in your own words. You do not condense ideas or eliminate details as you do in a summary. Instead, you use different sentence patterns and vocabulary but keep the author's intended meaning. In most cases, a paraphrase is approximately the same length as the original material. Compose a paraphrase when you want to record the author's ideas and details but do not want to use a direct quotation. Remember to paraphrase only the ideas or details you intend to use—not an entire article.

When paraphrasing, be especially careful not to *plagiarize*—to use an author's words or sentence structure as if they were your own (see p. 687). Read this excerpt from a source; then compare it to the acceptable paraphrase that follows and to the example that includes plagiarism.

EXCERPT FROM ORIGINAL

Learning some items may interfere with retrieving others, especially when the items are similar. If someone gives you a phone number to remember, you may be able to recall it later. But if two more people give you their numbers, each successive number will be more difficult to recall. Such proactive interference occurs when something you learned earlier disrupts recall of something you experienced later. As you collect more and more information, your mental attic never fills, but it certainly gets cluttered. DAVID G. MYERS, *Psychology*

ACCEPTABLE PARAPHRASE

When proactive interference happens, things you have already learned prevent you from remembering things you learn later. In other words, details you learn first may make it harder to recall closely related details you learn subsequently. You can think of your memory as an attic. You can always add more junk to it. However, it will become messy and disorganized. For example, you can remember one new phone number, but if you have two or more new numbers to remember, the task becomes harder.

UNACCEPTABLE PARAPHRASE — INCLUDES PLAGIARISM

When you learn some things, it may interfere with your ability to remember others. This happens when the things are similar. Suppose a person gives you a phone number to remember. You probably will be able to remember it later. Now, suppose two persons give you numbers. Each successive number will be harder to remember. Proactive interference happens when something you already learned prevents you from recalling something you experience later. As you learn more and more information, your mental attic never gets full, but it will get cluttered.

Although the preceding paraphrase does substitute some synonyms — *remember* for *retrieving,* for example — it is still an example of plagiarism. The underlined words are copied directly from the original. The shaded words show substitution of synonyms. Notice, too, that the style and sentence order of the unacceptable paraphrase are nearly identical to those of the original.

Writing paraphrases can be tricky because simply rewording an author's ideas is not acceptable and letting an author's language "creep in" is easy. There are also many ways to write an acceptable paraphrase of a particular passage. The following guidelines should help you write effective paraphrases.

1. **Read first; then write.** You may find it helpful to read material more than once before you try paraphrasing.

2. **If you must use any of the author's wording, enclose it in quotation marks.** If you do not use quotation marks, you may inadvertently use the same wording in your paper, which would result in plagiarism.

3. **Work sentence by sentence, restating each in your own words.** To avoid copying an author's words, read a sentence, cover it up, and then write. Be sure your version is accurate but not too similar to the original. As a rule of thumb, no more than two or three consecutive words should be the same as in the original.

4. **Choose synonyms that do not change the author's meaning or intent.** Consult a dictionary, if necessary.

5. **Use your own sentence structure and sentence order.** Using an author's sentence structure can be considered plagiarism. Also rearrange the order of ideas within a sentence.

6. **Use short sentences instead of a long one.** If the original has a lengthy sentence, write your paraphrase of it in shorter sentences.

Be sure to record the publication information (including page numbers) for the sources you paraphrase. You will need this information to document the sources in your paper.

EXERCISE 19.1

Write a paraphrase of the following excerpt from a source on animal communication.

> Another vigorously debated issue is whether language is uniquely human. Animals obviously communicate. Bees, for example, communicate the location of food through an intricate dance. And several teams of psychologists have taught various species of apes, including a number of chimpanzees, to communicate with humans by signing or by pushing buttons wired to a computer. Apes have developed considerable vocabularies. They string words together to express meaning and to make and follow requests. Skeptics point out important differences between apes' and humans' facilities with language, especially in their respective abilities to order words using proper syntax. Nevertheless, these studies reveal that apes have considerable cognitive ability.
>
> DAVID G. MYERS, *Psychology*

Recording Quotations

Sometimes it is advisable, and even necessary, to use a direct quotation—a writer's words exactly as they appear in the original source. Use quotations to record wording that is unusual or striking or when you want to report the exact words of an expert on your topic. Such quotations, when used sparingly, can be effective in a paper. When using a direct quotation, be sure to record it precisely as it appears in the source. The author's spelling, punctuation, and capitalization must be recorded exactly. Also write down the page number on which the material being quoted appears in the original source. Be sure to indicate that you are copying a direct quotation by including the term *direct quotation* and the page number in parentheses.

You may delete a phrase or sentence from a quotation as long as you do not change the meaning of the quotation. When you delete a phrase or sentence, use an ellipsis mark (three spaced periods)—...—to indicate that you have made a deletion.

AVOIDING PLAGIARISM

Plagiarism is the use of someone else's ideas, wording, or organization without any acknowledgment of the source. If you take information on uses of eye contact in communication and do not indicate where you got the information, you have plagiarized. If you copy the six-word phrase "Eye contact, particularly essential in negotiations" from a reference source without enclosing it in quotation marks, you have plagiarized.

Plagiarism is intellectually dishonest and is considered a form of cheating because you are submitting someone else's work as your own. Harsh academic penalties are applied to students found guilty of plagiarism; these often include, at minimum, receiving a failing grade on the paper, failing the entire course, or even being dismissed from the institution.

What Counts as Plagiarism

There are two types of plagiarism — intentional (deliberate) and unintentional (done by accident). Both are equally serious and both carry the same academic penalties. Below is a quick reference guide to determining if you have plagiarized.

To avoid plagiarism, be especially careful when taking notes from a source. Place anything you copy directly in quotation marks and record the source. Record the source for any information you paraphrase or summarize. Be sure to separate your own ideas from ideas expressed in the sources you are using. One way to do this is to use two different colors of ink or two different print sizes (if using a

For more on documentation, see Chapter 20.

YOU HAVE PLAGIARIZED IF YOU HAVE . . .

- Directly copied information word for word from a source without using quotation marks.
- Directly copied information word for word without using quotation marks, even though you acknowledged the source.
- Reworded and reorganized (paraphrased) information from a source without acknowledging the source.
- Borrowed someone else's organization or sequence of ideas.
- Reused someone else's visual material (graphs, tables, charts, maps, diagrams).
- Submitted another student's work as your own.

computer). Another way is to use different sections of a notebook or different computer files to distinguish your own ideas from those of others.

Cyberplagiarism

For more on citing Internet sources, see Chapter 20.

The term *cyberplagiarism* refers to borrowing information from the Internet without giving credit to the source posting the information. It also refers to "cut-and-paste plagiarism"—the practice of cutting information from an Internet source and pasting it into your own essay. Purchase of a student paper for sale on the Internet and submitting it as your own work is a third form of cyberplagiarism. Use the following suggestions to avoid unintentional plagiarism:

- Never copy and paste directly from an Internet source into your paper. Instead, cut and paste information you want to save into a separate file. Enclose the material you pasted in quotation marks to remind yourself that it is someone else's wording.

- Be sure to record all the source's information, including the name of the site, URL, date of access, and so on.

- When you make notes on ideas, opinions, or theories you encounter on the Internet, be sure to include complete source information for each item.

EXERCISE 19.2

The following piece of student writing is a paraphrase of a source on the history of advertising. Working with another student, evaluate the paraphrase and discuss whether it would be considered an example of plagiarism. If you decide the paraphrase is plagiarized, rewrite it so it is not.

ORIGINAL SOURCE

Everyone knows that advertising lies. That has been an article of faith since the Middle Ages—and a legal doctrine, too. Sixteenth-century English courts began the Age of Caveat Emptor by ruling that commercial claims—fraudulent or not—should be sorted out by the buyer, not the legal system. ("If he be tame and have ben rydden upon, then caveat emptor.") In a 1615 case, a certain Baily agreed to transport Merrell's load of wood, which Merrell claimed weighed 800 pounds. When Baily's two horses collapsed and died, he discovered that Merrell's wood actually weighed 2,000 pounds. The court ruled the problem was Baily's for not checking the weight himself; Merrell bore no blame.

CYNTHIA CROSSEN, *Tainted Truth*

PARAPHRASE

It is a well-known fact that advertising lies. This has been known ever since the Middle Ages. It is an article of faith as well as a legal doctrine. English courts in the sixteenth century started the Age of Caveat Emptor by finding that claims by businesses, whether legitimate or not, were the responsibility of the consumer, not the courts. For example, there was a case in which one person (Baily) used his horses to haul wood for a person named Merrell. Merrell told Baily that the wood weighed 800 pounds, but it actually weighed 2,000 pounds. Baily discovered this after his horses died. The court did not hold Merrell responsible; it stated that Baily should have weighed the wood himself instead of accepting Merrell's word.

CONDUCTING FIELD RESEARCH

Depending on your research topic, you may need — or want — to do field research to collect original information. Check with your instructor before doing so. This section discusses three common types of field research — interviews, surveys, and observation — all of which generate primary source material.

Interviewing

An interview lets you obtain firsthand information from a person who is knowledgeable about your topic. For example, if the topic of your research paper is *treatment of teenage alcoholism,* it might be a good idea to interview an experienced substance abuse counselor who works with teenagers. Use the following suggestions to conduct effective interviews.

1. **Choose interview subjects carefully.** Be sure your subjects work in the field you are researching or are experts on your topic. Also try to choose subjects that may provide you with different points of view. If you are researching a corporation, for example, try to interview someone from upper management as well as white- and blue-collar workers.

2. **Arrange your interview by letter, phone, or email well in advance.** Describe your project and purpose, explaining that you are a student working on an assignment. Indicate the amount of time you think you'll need, but don't be disappointed if the person shortens the time allotted for the interview or denies your request altogether. You should also be somewhat flexible about whom you interview. For example, a busy vice president may refer you to an assistant or to another manager.

3. **Plan the interview.** Come to the interview with a list of questions you want to ask; your subject will appreciate the fact that you are prepared and not wasting his or her time. Try to ask open rather than closed questions, which can be answered in a word or two. "Do you think your company has a promising future?" could be answered yes or no, whereas "How do you account for your company's turnaround last year?" might spark a detailed response. Open questions usually encourage people to "open up" and reveal attitudes as well as facts.

4. **Take notes during the interview.** Take a notebook to write in, since you probably will not be seated at a table or desk. Write the subject's responses in note form and find out whether you may quote him or her directly. If you want to tape-record the interview, be sure to ask the subject's permission.

5. **Evaluate the interview.** As soon as possible after the interview, reread your notes and fill in information you did not have time to record. Also write down your reactions while they are still fresh in your mind. Record these in the margin or in a different color ink so they are distinguishable from the interview notes. Try to write down your overall impression and an answer to this question: "What did I learn from this interview?"

Using a Survey

A survey is a set of questions designed to get information quickly from a large number of people. Surveys can be conducted face-to-face, by phone, by email, or by regular mail. Surveys are often used to assess people's attitudes or intended actions. For example, we frequently read the results of surveys that measure the popularity of political figures.

Use the following suggestions to prepare effective surveys.

1. **Clarify the purpose of the survey.** Write a detailed list of what you want to learn from the survey.

2. **Design your questions.** A survey can include closed or open questions or both, but most use closed questions in either a multiple-choice or ranking-scale format (see box). Closed questions usually work better in surveys because their

---

EXAMPLES OF CLOSED QUESTIONS

MULTIPLE CHOICE

How often do you purchase lunch in the campus cafeteria?

a. 1–2 days per week
b. 3–4 days per week
c. 5–6 days per week
d. Every day of the week

RANKING

On a scale of 5 to 1 (1 = poor and 5 = excellent), rate the quality of food in the campus cafeteria.

Poor			*Excellent*	
1	2	3	4	5

short, direct answers are easy to tally and interpret. An open question such as "What do you think of the food served in the cafeteria?" would elicit a variety of responses that would be difficult to summarize in your paper.

3. **Test your survey questions.** Try out your questions on a few classmates, family members, or friends to be sure they are clear and that they will provide the information you need.

4. **Select your respondents.** Your respondents, the people who provide answers to your survey, must be *representative* of the group you are studying and must be *chosen at random*. For example, if you are planning a survey to learn what students on your campus think about mandatory drug testing for athletes, you should choose a group of respondents — or a sample — that is similar to your school's student population. For most campuses, then, your group of respondents would contain both men and women, be racially and ethnically diverse, and represent the various ages and socioeconomic groups of students. Your sample should also be random; respondents should be unknown to you and not chosen for a specific reason. One way to draw a random sample is to give the survey to every fifth or tenth name on a list or every fifteenth person who walks by.

5. **Summarize and report your results.** Tally the results and look for patterns in the data. If the sample is fairly large, use a computer spreadsheet to tabulate results. In your paper, discuss your overall findings, not individual respondents' answers. Explain the purpose of the survey as well as how you designed it, selected a sample, and administered the survey to respondents. You may also want to include a copy of the survey and tabulations in an appendix.

Conducting Observations

The results obtained from observation — the inspection of an event, scene, or activity — can be an important primary source in a research paper. For instance, you might observe and report on a demonstration at a government agency or a field trial at a dog show. Firsthand observation can give you valuable insights on the job as well. You might, for example, need to observe and report on the condition of hospital patients or on the job performance of your employees.

Use the following tips to conduct observations effectively.

1. **Arrange your visit in advance.** Unless you are doing an observation in a public place, obtain permission of the company or organization in advance, and make the purpose of your visit clear when arranging your appointment.

2. **Take detailed notes on what you observe.** Write down the details you will need to describe the scene vividly in your paper. For instance, if you visit a mental health clinic, note details about patient care, security, hygiene, and the like. You might sketch the scene, especially if you are a spatial learner, or use a tape recorder or video camera if you have permission to do so. Try to gather

enough information to reconstruct your visit when you draft your research paper.

3. **Approach the visit with an open mind.** A closed-minded approach can defeat the purpose of observation. For example, if you observe a dog show with the preconceived notion that the dogs' owners are only interested in winning, your closed-minded view might keep you from discovering that dog shows serve many useful purposes (such as promoting the responsible breeding of pure-bred dogs).

4. **Create a dominant impression.** As soon as possible after your visit, evaluate your observations. Ask yourself about what you saw and heard. Then describe your dominant impression of what you observed and the details that support it. Details from the dog show, for example, might include the attitude and attire of owners and judges and the way the dogs were groomed.

FINDING SOURCES FOR YOUR OWN TOPIC

Before you begin to locate sources for your topic, you should review the information in Chapter 18, which describes how to plan a paper with sources and how to choose and evaluate useful sources, whether in the library or online. Here are a few pointers that will help you conduct your own research.

1. Begin with a narrowed topic, a working thesis, and some research questions (see pp. 642–48).

2. Decide what kinds of sources will best answer your research questions — recent journal articles, historical works, personal interviews, and so forth (see pp. 648–53).

3. Remember to consider whether each source will be truly useful. Is it relevant and reliable (see pp. 648–50)? Is it biased in some way (see pp. 653–58)?

4. Keep track of citation information for each source while you do your research (see pp. 679–81).

5. Decide what system of note-taking you will use — note cards, computer files, or annotated copies (see pp. 681–83).

6. As you take notes, paraphrase or summarize information appropriately and copy quotations word for word (see pp. 683–86).

RESEARCH PAPER IN PROGRESS 3

For the topic you worked on in Research Papers in Progress 1 and 2, locate a minimum of six sources that answer one or more of your research questions. Your sources should include at least one book, one magazine article, one scholarly journal article, one Internet source, and two other sources of any type. On a scale from 1 to 5 (where 1 is low, 5 is high), rank the relevancy and reliability of each source you located using the guidelines provided in Chapter 18, pages 648 to 650. Use the following chart to structure your responses.

Source	Relevancy Rating	Reliability Rating
1.		
2.		
3.		
4.		
5.		
6.		

RESEARCH PAPER IN PROGRESS 4

For the three most relevant and reliable sources you identified in Research Paper in Progress 3, use the suggestions on pages 681 to 686 to take notes on your sources. Your goal is to provide information and support for the ideas you developed earlier. Choose a system of note-taking, writing summary notes and paraphrases and recording quotations as needed. As you work, try to answer your research questions and keep your working thesis in mind.

Writing a Paper Using Sources

CHAPTER QUICK START

Suppose you have been assigned to write a research paper for a mass communication course on a topic related to human communication involving more than two people. You struggle with choosing a topic for nearly a week, when suddenly, as you walk down a busy street, you notice several bumper stickers on a parked car. You decide to write about bumper stickers and begin to think about how to categorize them into types.

Writing Quick Start

Write a list of the bumper stickers in the photograph on the opposite page plus five or more bumper stickers you have seen. Then try to group the bumper stickers into categories.

By creating categories of bumper stickers, you took the first steps in writing a research paper—synthesizing and condensing information from sources, in this case, a primary source. In Chapter 18 you learned how to plan a paper with sources and how to choose and evaluate useful information. Chapter 19 gave you advice on finding sources and taking notes. This chapter continues the research process by showing you how to organize, draft, revise, and document a paper using sources.

You will have numerous opportunities to write research papers in your college courses. Many jobs require research skills as well. You might, for instance, need to justify a proposed change in your company's vacation policy by citing the vacation policies of other companies, or you might need to research information about a company before going on a job interview. See the box below for a few other examples of situations that would require research skills.

Think of a research paper as an opportunity to explore information about a topic, pull ideas from sources together, and present what you discover. This chapter will guide you through the process of writing a paper using sources. Figure 20.1 presents an overview of the process.

ORGANIZING AND WRITING YOUR FIRST DRAFT

After you conduct library and Internet research on your topic and take notes on your sources (as detailed in Chapter 19), you are ready to evaluate your work in preparation for writing a first draft. This stage of the research process involves evaluating your research and working thesis, developing an organizational plan, and drafting the research paper.

SCENES FROM COLLEGE AND THE WORKPLACE

- For a *business* course, you are required to research a Fortune 500 company and write a report on its history and current profitability. At least two of your sources must be from the Internet.

- For a *social problems* course, you are asked to conduct your own field research (interviews or surveys) on a local or campus issue and to report your findings in a research paper.

- As *personnel director* of a publishing company, you are asked to research editorial salaries in the publishing industry and submit a report that your company will use to decide whether to change salary levels for editors.

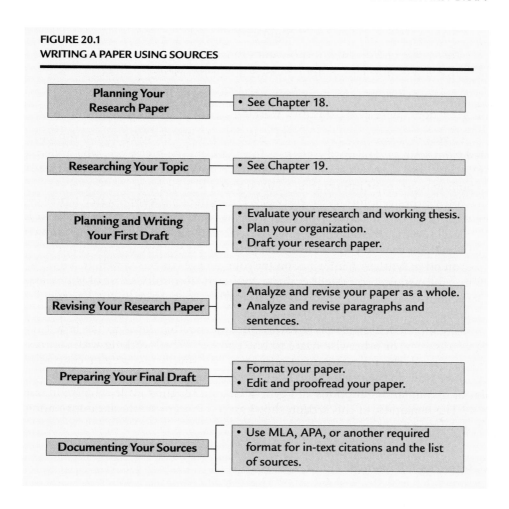

FIGURE 20.1
WRITING A PAPER USING SOURCES

Planning Your Research Paper	• See Chapter 18.
Researching Your Topic	• See Chapter 19.
Planning and Writing Your First Draft	• Evaluate your research and working thesis. • Plan your organization. • Draft your research paper.
Revising Your Research Paper	• Analyze and revise your paper as a whole. • Analyze and revise paragraphs and sentences.
Preparing Your Final Draft	• Format your paper. • Edit and proofread your paper.
Documenting Your Sources	• Use MLA, APA, or another required format for in-text citations and the list of sources.

Evaluating Your Research and Synthesizing Information

Before you began researching your topic, you probably wrote a *working thesis*—a preliminary statement of your main point about the topic—and a list of research questions you hoped to answer. Then, as you researched your topic, you may have discovered new facts about your topic, statistics you were unaware of, or expert testimony that surprised you. In most cases, the discoveries you make during the research process influence your thinking on the topic, requiring you to modify your working thesis. In some cases, you may even need to rethink the direction of your paper.

For more on writing a working thesis and research questions, see Chapter 18.

As you evaluate your research notes and modify your thesis, keep the following questions in mind.

1. What research questions did I begin with?
2. What answers did I find to those questions?
3. What other information did I discover about my topic?
4. What conclusions can I draw from what I've learned?
5. How does my research affect my working thesis?

To answer these questions, you'll need to **synthesize** the information you gathered from sources. The word *synthesis* is formed from the prefix *syn-,* which means "together," and *thesis,* which means "main or central point." *Synthesis,* then, means "a pulling together of information to form a new idea or point."

You synthesize information every day. For example, after you watch a preview of a movie, talk with friends who have seen the film, and read a critique of it, you then pull together the information you have acquired and come up with your own idea—perhaps that you do not want to see the movie because it is too juvenile.

You often synthesize information for your college courses as well. In a biology course, for instance, you might evaluate your own lab results, those of your classmates, and the data in your textbook to reach a conclusion about a particular experiment.

As you can see, synthesis involves putting together ideas to see how they agree, disagree, or otherwise relate to one another. When working with sources, you could ask the following questions: Does one source reinforce or contradict another? How do their claims and lines of reasoning compare? Do they make similar or dissimilar assumptions and generalizations? Is their evidence alike in any way? The remainder of this section shows several ways to synthesize information from sources.

Categorizing Information

One way to arrive at a synthesis is to condense the information into categories. For example, one student found numerous sources on and answers to this research question: "What causes some parents to physically abuse their children?" After rereading his research notes, the student realized he could synthesize the information by putting it into three categories—lack of parenting skills, emotional instability, and family history of child abuse. He then made this two-column list of the categories and his sources.

Category	Sources
Lack of parenting skills	Lopez, Wexler, Thomas
Emotional instability	Wexler, Harris, Thompson, Wong
Family history of child abuse	Thompson, Harris, Lopez, Strickler, Thomas

While evaluating his research in this way, the student also realized he needed to revise both his working thesis and the scope of his paper to include lack of parenting skills as a major cause of child abuse. Notice how he modified his working thesis accordingly.

WORKING THESIS

Some children are physically abused because of their parents' emotional instability and family history of child abuse.

REVISED THESIS

Some children are physically abused because of their parents' emotional instability, family history of child abuse, and lack of parenting skills.

As you work on synthesizing information from sources, keep in mind that you can categorize many kinds of events or phenomena, such as types of life insurance, effects of education level on salary, views on environmental problems, and so forth.

EXERCISE 20.1

Imagine that you have done research on one of the following topics; write a list of some of the information you have found. Then, working with one or two classmates, discuss how you might categorize the information. Write a thesis statement that reflects your research.

1. The health hazards of children's toys
2. The fairness of college entrance exams
3. The advantages of college athletic programs

Drawing an Organizer for Multiple Sources

Using a graphic organizer is another way to synthesize information from sources. Your organizer may reveal patterns and show similarities and differences. It will also show you how main ideas and supporting details connect with each other.

Suppose you are writing an essay on voluntary simplicity—the idea that minimizing personal possessions and commitments leads to a happier, more manageable lifestyle. You have located three reliable and relevant sources that define voluntary simplicity, but each develops the idea somewhat differently. Source 1 (Walker) is a practical how-to article that includes some personal examples. Source 2 (Parachin) is a theoretical look at statistics about workloads and complicated lifestyles and the reasons that voluntary simplicity is appealing. Source 3 (Remy) also presents strategies for simplifying but emphasizes the values of a simplified lifestyle. Figure 20.2 presents a sample organizer for information from these three sources.

Depending on your sources and the type of information they contain, you can use a variety of organizer formats. If all your sources compare and contrast the same things, such as the functioning and effectiveness of two presidents, you could adapt one of the graphic organizers for comparison and contrast shown in Chapter 12, pages 382 to 383. If most of your sources focus on effects, such as the economic effects of a recession on jobs and employment, you could adapt one of the cause-and-effect graphic organizers shown in Chapter 15, pages 514 to 516. Whatever style of organizer you use, be sure to keep track of the sources for each idea and to use them in your organizer (as shown in Figure 20.2).

FIGURE 20.2
GRAPHIC ORGANIZER FOR THREE SOURCES ON VOLUNTARY SIMPLICITY

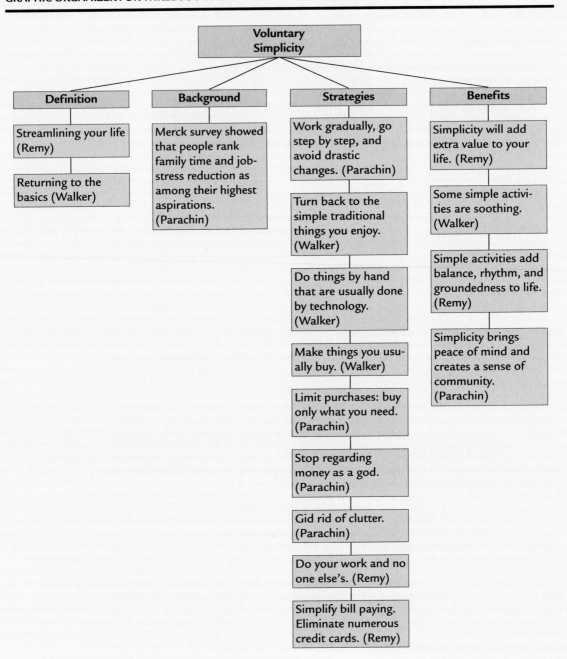

Using a Pro-and-Con List to Synthesize Confirming and Conflicting Sources

As you research a topic, especially if it is controversial, you are likely to find sources from many sides of the issue. For example, some sources may favor gun control legislation, others may oppose it, and still others may present both viewpoints. Even sources that agree or disagree, however, often do so for different reasons. On the issue of gun control legislation, one source may favor it for moral reasons: Gun control prevents a major crime — killing. Another source may favor legislation for a statistical reason: Statistics prove that owning a gun does not prevent crime.

As you encounter varying opinions in sources, a pro-and-con list may help you organize and synthesize your information. For the issue of gun control, you might create a two-column list such as the one shown in the box on page 702. Be sure to include the source of each entry.

Planning Your Organization

Your next step involves developing an organizational plan for your paper — deciding both what you'll say and the order in which you will say it. Think about whether you want to use chronological order, spatial order, or most-to-least or least-to-most important order or one of the patterns of development discussed in Parts 3 and 4 of this text.

Following are some guidelines for organizing your research paper.

Arranging Your Information

If you used note cards, begin by sorting them into piles by subtopics or categories. (You may already have developed categories when you evaluated your research and thesis and worked on synthesizing source information.) For example, note cards for the thesis "Prekindergarten programs provide children with long-lasting educational advantages" might be sorted by type of educational advantage, such as reading readiness, social skills, and positive self-image.

If you took notes on a computer, you may have arranged your research information by category as you went along. If not, this is the time to do so. As you move information within or among computer files, be careful to keep track of which material belongs to which source.

If you used photocopies of sources, attach self-stick notes to indicate the various subtopics each source covers.

Once your note cards, computer files, or photocopies are organized, you are ready to develop your outline or graphic organizer.

Developing an Outline or Graphic Organizer

Use an outline or a graphic organizer to show the divisions and subdivisions you intend for your paper. Preparing such a plan is especially important for a research

For more on outlines and graphic organizers, see Chapter 5, pp. 114–18.

PRO-AND-CON VIEWS ON GUN CONTROL LEGISLATION

Pro	Con
Stronger federal regulations are necessary to increase homeland security following the September 11, 2001, terrorist attacks on the United States. (Melissa Robinson)	Stricter gun control creates vulnerable targets for enemies of a free society. (Phyllis Schafly)
The crackdown on terrorism must close the loophole that allows many people to buy weapons at gun shows without background checks. (Fox Butterfield)	Gun control laws do not remove guns from the hands of criminals; they disarm victims. (Jack Duggan)
By 2000 violent crime had fallen for six consecutive years, due, in part, to mandating background checks, banning types of assault weapons, and limiting access for kids and criminals. (Brady Campaign)	We should enforce the laws we have before creating new ones that may or may not provide any benefits. (Warren Ockrassa)
A study by the Justice Department shows that background checks by the FBI and by state and local agencies have barred criminals from acquiring weapons hundreds of thousands of times. (*New York Times* editorial)	It is unrealistic to pass gun laws that prevent Americans from protecting themselves and their families. (Libertarian Party)
In the five years after the Brady Bill was passed (1994), background checks blocked 536,000 convicted felons and other illegal buyers from getting a gun. (Americans for Gun Safety)	Existing laws preventing illegal purchase have proven to be effective in catching suspected terrorists, so new laws that target gun shows are not needed. (National Rifle Association)

paper because you are working with a substantial amount of information. Without something to follow, it is easy to get lost and write an unfocused paper.

Pragmatic learners tend to prefer organizing in detail before beginning to write. If this is your tendency, make sure that you are open to change and new ideas as you write your draft. Creative learners, on the other hand, may prefer to start writing and try to structure the paper as they work. Most students should not take this approach, however; those who do should allow extra time for reorganizing and making extensive revisions.

Whatever your learning style, consider writing your outline or graphic organizer on a computer so that you can reorganize material easily and test several different organizations. Be sure to save your original outline or graphic organizer and any revised versions as separate files in case you need to return to earlier versions.

> **RESEARCH PAPER IN PROGRESS 5**
>
> Using the research notes you developed for Research Paper in Progress 4 (p. 693), sort your source notes and information into several categories and evaluate your working thesis. Then prepare an outline or a graphic organizer for your paper.

Drafting Your Research Paper

The following guidelines will help you write the first draft of a research paper.

1. **Follow the introduction, body, and conclusion format.** A straightforward organization is usually the best choice for a research paper.

2. **Take a serious, academic tone and avoid using the first or second person.** Your credibility will be enhanced if you use the third person, which is more objective and gives you some distance from your topic.

   For more on organization, see Chapter 5, pp. 110–18.

3. **For most research papers, place your thesis in the introduction.** However, for papers analyzing a problem or proposing a solution, try placing your thesis near the end. For example, if you were writing an essay proposing stricter traffic laws on campus, you might begin by documenting the problem — describing accidents that have occurred and detailing their frequency. You might conclude your essay by suggesting that your college lower the speed limit on campus and install two new stop signs.

4. **Keep your audience in mind.** Although you now know a great deal about your topic, your readers may not. When appropriate, be sure to provide background information, explain concepts and processes, and define terms for your readers. For example, if you were writing a paper on recycling plastics for a chemistry class, your audience might already understand some of the technical terms and concepts in your paper. You wouldn't need to explain everything. But if you were writing on the same topic for a composition class, you would need to provide thorough explanations and use more nontechnical terms.

5. **Follow your outline or graphic organizer but feel free to make changes as you work.** You may discover a better organization, think of new ideas about your topic, or realize that a subtopic belongs in a different section. Don't feel compelled to follow your outline to the letter but be sure to address the topics you list.

6. **Determine the purpose and main point of each paragraph.** State the main point of each body paragraph in a topic sentence. Then use your sources to substantiate, explain, or provide detail in support of that main point.

For more on using transitions, see Chapter 5, pp. 128–31.

7. **Use strong transitions.** Because a research paper may be lengthy or complex, strong transitions are needed to hold the paper together as a whole. In addition, transitions help your readers understand how you have divided the topic and how one point relates to another.

8. **Support your key points with evidence.** Be sure to identify your major points first, and support each major point with evidence from several sources. Keep in mind that relying on only one or two sources weakens your thesis, suggesting to readers that you did insufficient research. Bring together facts, statistics, details, expert testimony, and other types of evidence from a variety of sources to strengthen your thesis.

9. **Include source material only for a specific purpose.** Just because you discovered an interesting statistic or a fascinating quote, don't feel that you must use it. Information that doesn't support your thesis will distract your reader and weaken your paper.

10. **Refer to your source notes frequently as you write.** If you do so, you will be less likely to overlook an important piece of evidence. If you suspect that a note is inaccurate in some way, check the original source.

11. **Do not overuse sources.** Make sure your paper is not just a series of facts, quotations, and so forth taken from sources. Your research paper should not merely summarize what others have written about the topic: The basis of the paper should be your ideas and thesis.

12. **Use source information in a way that does not mislead your readers.** Even though you are presenting only a portion of someone's ideas, make sure you are not using them in a way that is contrary to the writer's original intentions.

13. **Incorporate in-text citations for your sources.** Whenever you paraphrase, summarize, or quote a source, be sure to include an in-text citation. (See pp. 706–08.)

INTEGRATING INFORMATION FROM SOURCES

After you have decided what source information to use, you will need to build that information into your essay. The three methods for extracting information—paraphrasing, summarizing, or quoting—have been discussed in Chapter 19 (pp. 683–86). In general, try to paraphrase or summarize information rather than quote it directly. Use a quotation only if the wording is unusual or unique or if you want to provide the actual statement of an expert on the topic. Regardless of how you integrate sources, be sure to acknowledge and document all direct quotations as well as the paraphrased or summarized ideas of others. You must make it clear to your readers that you have borrowed ideas or information by citing the source, whether it is a book, a Web page, a journal article, a drawing, a CD, or another type of source. The following section provides advice on what does and does not need to be documented as well as guidelines for writing in-text citations and using quotations appropriately.

Deciding What to Document

You can use another person's material in your paper as long as you give that person credit. **Plagiarism** occurs when you present the ideas of others as your own. Whether intentional or not, plagiarism is a serious error that must be avoided. The accompanying box identifies the types of material that *do* and *do not* require documentation. If you are unsure about whether to document something, ask your instructor or a reference librarian.

For more on what constitutes plagiarism, see Chapter 19, pp. 687–89.

In the last few years, deliberate plagiarism has become widespread, and unethical students have begun to exchange or sell papers over the Internet. To combat

---

WHAT DOES AND DOES NOT REQUIRE DOCUMENTATION

Documentation Required

Summaries, paraphrases, and quotations

Obscure or recently discovered facts (such as a little-known fact about Mark Twain or a recent discovery about Mars)

Others' opinions

Others' field research (results of opinion polls, case studies, statistics)

Quotations or paraphrases from interviews you conduct

Others' visuals (photographs, charts, maps, Web images, and so forth)

Information from others that you use to create visuals (statistics or other data that you use to construct a table, graph, or other visual)

Documentation Not Required

Common knowledge (George Washington was the first U.S. president, the Earth revolves around the sun, and so forth)

Facts that can be found in numerous sources (winners of Olympic competitions, names of Supreme Court justices, and so forth)

Standard definitions of academic terms

Your own ideas or conclusions

Your own field research (surveys or observations)

Your own visuals (such as photographs you take)

this problem, many instructors commonly use Internet tracking resources to check for plagiarized material. Be sure all your sources are clearly documented. You do not want to plagiarize anyone's ideas, even inadvertantly.

Writing In-Text Citations

Many academic disciplines have their own preferred format or style for documenting sources within the text of a paper. For example, in English and the humanities, the preferred documentation format is that of the Modern Language Association and is known as *MLA style.* In the social sciences, the guidelines of the American Psychological Association, commonly called *APA style,* are often used. Many scientists follow a format used by the Council of Science Editors (CSE) (formerly the Council of Biology Editors, CBE). This format is now known as either *CSE style* or *CBE style.* The two most widely used formats—MLA and APA—are discussed in detail later in this chapter. (See pp. 716–34 for MLA style; see pp. 734–46 for APA style.)

When you paraphrase, summarize, or quote from a source in the text of your paper, you must give credit to the source of the borrowed material. You give credit by providing an in-text citation, a brief reference that lets readers know that a complete description of the source can be found in a list of sources at the end of your paper. The list is headed *Works Cited* in MLA style and *References* in APA style. Because this list includes only those sources you cite in your paper, it is different from a bibliography, which includes all the sources you consulted, whether or not you used them.

What Should I Include in an In-Text Citation?

An in-text citation usually includes the author's name and the page number(s) of the source information. Many writers put the author's name in an introductory phrase, called an **attribution,** and the page number(s) in parentheses at the end of the sentence. Sometimes, however, both the author and the page number(s) may appear in parentheses at the end of the sentence. The following examples, which are in MLA style, show several ways to write an in-text citation of a paraphrase.

As Jo-Ellan Dimitrius observes, big spenders often suffer from low self-esteem (143).

Some behavioral experts claim that big spenders often suffer from low self-esteem (Dimitrius 143).

Jo-Ellan Dimitrius, a jury-selection consultant whose book Reading People discusses methods of predicting behavior,

```
observes that big spenders often suffer from low self-esteem
(143).
```

As the last example shows, it is often a good idea to provide some background information about sources the first time you mention them, especially if the source is not commonly known. Such information helps readers understand that the source is relevant or important.

How Can I Integrate Sources Most Effectively?

To integrate most paraphrases and summaries and *all* quotations, use an introductory phrase or clause, such as "As Markham points out" or "Bernstein observes that," that allows information to flow smoothly to your readers. When you integrate a number of sources in a paper, try to vary both the structure of the phrase and the verb used. The following verbs are useful for introducing many kinds of source material.

advocates	contends	insists	proposes
argues	demonstrates	maintains	shows
asserts	denies	mentions	speculates
believes	emphasizes	notes	states
claims	explains	points out	suggests

When integrating paraphrases or summaries, you may sometimes decide not to use an introductory phrase. In these instances, be sure that the source material is clear to the reader. If an in-text citation is in the wrong spot, readers may not be able to tell whether an idea is yours or the source's.

When integrating quotations, you should *always* include a lead-in or introduction. Quotations should blend into your sentences and paragraphs; they should not simply be "dropped in" to your paper.

QUOTATION NOT INTEGRATED

```
Anecdotes indicate that animals experience emotions, but they
are not considered scientifically valid. "Experimental evi-
dence is given almost exclusive credibility over personal
experience to a degree that seems almost religious" (Masson
and McCarthy 3).
```

QUOTATION INTEGRATED

```
Anecdotes indicate that animals experience emotions, but they are
not considered scientifically valid. Masson and McCarthy, who
```

have done extensive field observation, comment, "Experimental
evidence is given almost exclusive credibility over personal
experience to a degree that seems almost religious" (3).

Using Quotations Appropriately

Although quotations can lend interest to your paper and support for your ideas, they need to be used appropriately. The following section answers some common questions about the use of quotations. The in-text citations in this section follow the MLA style, as do the rules about changing quotations.

When Should I Use Quotations?

For more practice integrating quotations into your writing, visit www.bedfordstmartins .com/successfulwriting /tutorials.

1. **Use quotations sparingly.** Do not use quotations to reveal ordinary facts and opinions. Look carefully at what you intend to quote: If a quotation does not achieve one of the following purposes, use a paraphrase instead.

   • Quote when the author's wording is unusual, noteworthy, or striking. The quotation "Injustice anywhere is a threat to justice everywhere" from Martin Luther King Jr.'s "Letter from Birmingham Jail" probably is more effective than any paraphrase, for instance.

   • Quote when a paraphrase might alter or distort the statement's meaning.

   • Quote when the original words express the exact point you want to make.

   • Quote when the statement is a strong, opinionated, exaggerated, or disputed idea that you want to make clear is not your own.

2. **Use quotations to support your ideas.** Never use a quotation as the topic sentence of a paragraph. The topic sentence should state in your own words the idea you are about to explain or prove.

3. **Use quotations that are self-explanatory.** If a quotation needs to be restated or explained, paraphrase it instead.

What Format Do I Follow for Long Quotations?

In MLA style, lengthy quotations (more than three lines of poetry or more than four typed lines of prose) are indented in *block form,* ten spaces from the left margin. In APA style, the block format is used for quotations of more than forty words, and the block quotation is indented five spaces from the left margin. Both styles omit quotation marks and use a double-spaced format. Introduce a block quotation in the sentence that precedes it; a colon is used at the end of the introduction if it is a sentence. Note that for a block quotation, the parenthetical citation appears *after* the final sentence period. This is different from the style for short quotations within the text, in which the parenthetical citation precedes the period.

BLOCK QUOTATION, MLA STYLE

```
Although a business is a profit-making organization, it is
also a social organization. As Hicks and Gwynne note,
          In Western society, businesses are essentially
          economic organizations, with both the organizations
          themselves and the individuals in them dedicated to
          making as much money as possible in the most effi-
          cient way. But businesses are also social organiza-
          tions, each of which has its unique culture. Like
          all social groups, businesses are made up of people
          of both sexes and a wide range of ages, who play
          different roles, occupy different positions in the
          group, and behave in different ways while at work.
          (174)
```

How Do I Punctuate Quotations?

There are specific rules and conventions for punctuating quotations. The most important rules follow.

1. **Use single quotation marks to enclose a quotation within a quotation.**

```
Coleman and Cressey argue that "concern for the 'decaying fam-
ily' is nothing new" (147).
```

2. **Use a comma after a verb that introduces a quotation.**

```
As Thompson and Hickey report, "There are three major kinds
of 'taste cultures' in complex industrial societies: high
culture, folk culture, and popular culture" (76).
```

3. **Use a colon to introduce a quotation preceded by a complete sentence.** Begin the first word of the quotation with a capital letter (enclosed in brackets if it is not capitalized in the source).

```
The definition is clear: "Countercultures reject the con-
ventional wisdom and standards of the dominant culture and
provide alternatives to mainstream culture" (Thompson and
Hickey 76).
```

Note that in MLA style, the period *follows* a parenthetical citation for a short quotation that is integrated within the text.

4. When a quotation is built into your own sentence, it is not necessary to use a comma or capitalize the first word.

   ```
   Buck reports that "pets play a significant part in both physi-
   cal and psychological therapy" (4).
   ```

5. Place periods and commas inside quotation marks.

   ```
   "The most valuable old cars," notes antique car collector
   Michael Patterson, "are the rarest ones."
   ```

6. Place colons and semicolons outside quotation marks.

   ```
   "Petting a dog increases mobility of a limb or hand"; petting
   a dog, then, can be a form of physical therapy (Buck 4).
   ```

7. Place question marks and exclamation points inside quotation marks when they are part of the original quotation. No additional period is needed.

   ```
   "Does the text's description of alternate lifestyles agree
   with your experience?" the instructor asked.
   ```

8. Place question marks and exclamation points that belong to your own sentence outside quotation marks.

   ```
   Is the following definition accurate: "Sociolinguistics is the
   study of the relationship between language and society"?
   ```

How Can I Change Quotations?

1. When you use a quotation, the spelling, punctuation, and capitalization must be copied exactly as they appear in the original source, even if they are in error. If a source contains an error, copy it with the error and add the word *sic* (Latin for "thus") in brackets immediately following the error.

   ```
   According to Bernstein, "The family has undergone rapid de-
   centralization since Word [sic] War II" (39).
   ```

2. You can emphasize words by underlining or italicizing them, but you must add the notation *emphasis added* in parentheses at the end of the sentence to indicate the change.

   ```
   "In unprecedented and increasing numbers, patients are con-
   sulting practitioners of every type of complementary medicine"
   (emphasis added) (Buckman and Sabbagh 73).
   ```

3. You can omit part of a quotation, but you must add ellipsis points — three spaced periods (. . .) — to indicate that material has been deleted. You may delete words, sentences, paragraphs, or entire pages, as long as you do not distort the author's meaning by doing so.

```
According to Buckman and Sabbagh, "Acupuncture . . . has been
rigorously tested and proven to be effective and valid" (188).
```

When an omission falls at the end of a quoted sentence, use the three spaced periods in addition to the sentence period.

```
Thompson maintains that "marketers need to establish ethical
standards for personal selling. . . . They must stress fair-
ness and honesty in dealing with customers" (298).
```

4. You can add words or phrases in brackets to make a quotation clearer or to make it fit grammatically into your sentence; be sure that in doing so, you do not change the original sense.

```
Masson and McCarthy note that the well-known animal researcher
Jane Goodall finds that "the scientific reluctance to accept
anecdotal evidence [of emotional experience is] a serious
problem, one that colors all of science" (3).
```

5. You can change the first word of a quotation to a capital or lowercase letter to fit into your sentence. If you change it, enclose it in brackets.

```
As Aaron Smith said, "The . . ." (32).
Aaron Smith said that "[t]he . . ." (32).
```

RESEARCH PAPER IN PROGRESS 6

Using your research notes, revised thesis, and the organizational plan you developed for your research paper, write a first draft. Be sure to integrate sources carefully and to include in-text citations. (See pp. 716–20 for MLA style guidelines for in-text citations; see pp. 734–38 for APA style.)

REVISING YOUR RESEARCH PAPER

Revise a research paper in two stages. First focus on the paper as a whole; then consider individual paragraphs and sentences for effectiveness and correctness. If time allows, wait at least a day before rereading your research paper.

For more on revision, see Chapter 6.

Analyzing and Revising Your Paper as a Whole

Begin by evaluating your paper as a unified piece of writing. Focus on general issues, overall organization, and the key points that support your thesis. Use Figure 20.3 to help you discover the strengths and weaknesses of your research paper as a whole. You might also ask a classmate to review your draft paper by using the questions in the flowchart.

Analyzing and Revising Paragraphs and Sentences

After evaluating your paper as a whole, check each paragraph to be sure that it supports your thesis and integrates sources appropriately. Then check your sentences for correct structure, transitions, and in-text citation format. Use your earlier work with Figure 20.3 to guide your analysis.

> **RESEARCH PAPER IN PROGRESS 7**
>
> Using the questions in Figure 20.3, revise the first draft of your research paper.

PREPARING YOUR FINAL DRAFT

After you have revised your paper and compiled a list of references or works cited, you are ready to prepare the final draft. Following are some guidelines to help you format, edit, and proofread your final paper. For an example, see the essay "Do Animals Have Emotions?" by Nicholas Destino on pages 748 to 756.

Formatting Your Paper

Academic papers should follow a standard manuscript format whether or not they use sources. The following guidelines are recommended by the Modern Language Association (MLA). If your instructor suggests or requires a different format, be sure to follow it. If your instructor does not recommend a format, these guidelines would probably be acceptable.

1. **Paper.** Use 8½- by 11-inch white paper. Separate the sheets if you use continuous-feed printer paper. Use a paper clip; do not staple or use a binder.

2. **Your name and course information.** Do not use a title page unless your instructor requests one. Position your name at the left margin about one inch from the top of the page. Underneath it, list your instructor's name, your course name and number, and the date. Use separate lines for each and double-space between the lines.

FIGURE 20.3
FLOWCHART FOR REVISING A RESEARCH PAPER

Questions		Revision Strategies

1. Highlight your thesis statement. Is it stated clearly and specifically? Is the assertion based on your own (and not the sources') ideas about the subject?

No

- Delete your thesis statement. Then have a peer read the paper and tell you what he or she believes the thesis to be.
- Brainstorm about the main point you wish to make.
- Review the guidelines for writing a thesis in Chapter 4, pp. 89–95.

Yes

2. Underline the topic sentence of each paragraph. Does each topic sentence support your thesis?

No

- Ask yourself, "Would my paper be stronger if this point were eliminated?" If so, eliminate the point.
- Reread your research notes to see if you overlooked any major points.

Yes

3. [Bracket] the ideas that support each topic sentence. Are these your own ideas? Do you avoid a string of quotations, paraphrases, and summaries from sources?

No

- Rewrite to focus on your ideas, using source material to support them.
- Delete facts, statistics, and other evidence that do not support each topic sentence.

Yes

4. Draw a (circle) around terms that are essential to your thesis or that your audience might not know. Is each defined?

No

- Add definitions where necessary.
- Read the circled terms and definitions to a classmate and ask if he or she understands them.
- Ask the classmate to read your paper and circle any terms he or she doesn't understand.

Yes

(Continued on next page)

FIGURE 20.3 *(Continued)*

Questions		Revision Strategies
5. Place a checkmark ✔ next to each idea that came from an outside source. Do you give credit to each source you cite in an in-text citation?	**No** →	• Add in-text citations wherever you paraphrase, summarize, or quote from sources.

Yes ↓

| 6. Is it clear where information from each source (✔) begins and ends? | **No** → | • Add introductory phrases and clauses (p. 707).
• Change some of your introductory phrases so that you don't use the same phrase repeatedly (p. 707). |

Yes ↓

| 7. Draw a box around your introduction and conclusion. Does the introduction provide a context for your research? Is the conclusion satisfying and relevant to the research? | **No** → | • Revise your introduction to meet the guidelines in Chapter 5, p. 131.
• Review what the research suggests and then revise your conclusion.
• Propose an action or way of thinking that is appropriate in light of the research.
• Revise your conclusion to meet the guidelines in Chapter 5, p. 135. |

Yes ↓

8. Print out another draft to edit and proofread. Add a Works Cited page to your research paper before turning it in.

3. **Title.** Place the title two lines below the date. Center the title on the page. Capitalize the first word and all other words except articles, coordinating conjunctions, and prepositions. Double-space after the title and type your first paragraph. Do not underline your title or put quotation marks around it.

4. **Margins, spacing, and indentation.** Use one-inch margins. Double-space between all lines of your paper. Indent each paragraph five spaces.

5. **Numbering of pages.** Number all pages in the upper right corner. Place the numbers one-half inch below the top of the paper. (If your instructor requests a title page, do not number it and do not count it in your numbering.) Use arabic numerals (1, 2, 3), and include your last name, with a space between your name and the number.

6. **Headings.** The MLA does not provide any guidelines for using headings. However, the system recommended by the American Psychological Association (APA) should work for most papers. Main headings should be centered, and the first letter of key words capitalized. Subheadings, underlined, should begin at the left margin, with important words in the subheadings capitalized.

7. **Visuals.** You may include tables and figures (graphs, charts, maps, photographs, and drawings) in your paper. Label each table or figure with an arabic numeral (*Table 1, Table 2; Fig. 1, Fig. 2*) and give it a title. Place the title on a separate line above the table. Give each figure a number and title and place the figure number and title on a separate line below the figure.

Editing and Proofreading Your Paper

As a final step, edit and proofread your revised paper for errors in grammar, spelling, punctuation, mechanics, and documentation style. In addition, be sure to check your error log for the types of errors you commonly make.

For more on editing and proofreading, see Chapter 7.

As you edit and proofread, watch out for the following common problems.

1. Does your paper contain any long, cumbersome sentences? If so, try splitting them into two separate sentences.

2. Do you use a consistent verb tense throughout your paper? Don't shift from present to past to future tense unless there is a good reason to do so.

3. Do you punctuate and style in-text citations correctly? Make sure that they conform to MLA style or that of another system of documentation.

4. Do you reproduce direct quotations exactly as they appear in the original source? In addition to checking the accuracy of individual words, be sure to check your use of quotation marks, capital letters, commas, and ellipses within quotations.

5. Do you avoid plagiarism by carefully quoting, paraphrasing, and summarizing the ideas of others?

6. Is your paper typed and spaced according to the format you need to follow? Be sure that block quotations are also typed appropriately.

7. Is your list of works cited or references complete? Make sure all sources cited in your paper are included in the list and are formatted correctly.

RESEARCH PAPER IN PROGRESS 8

Edit and proofread your paper, paying particular attention to the questions in the preceding list.

DOCUMENTING YOUR SOURCES: MLA STYLE

The system described in this section is recommended by the Modern Language Association (MLA). If you are unsure whether to use the MLA system, check with your instructor.

The MLA style uses in-text citations to identify sources within the text of a research paper. A corresponding list of works cited appears at the end of the paper.

MLA Style for In-Text Citations

The MLA style for citing sources is commonly used in English and the humanities. Both in-text citations and a list of works cited are used to document sources, as the models in this chapter show. For more information, consult the following source.

> Gibaldi, Joseph. *MLA Handbook for Writers of Research Papers,* 6th ed. New York: MLA, 2003.

The student paper that appears later in this chapter uses MLA style (see pp. 748–56), as do all student papers in Chapters 5 to 13.

Your paper must include in-text citations for all material you borrow or quote from sources. There are two basic ways to write an in-text citation.

For more on attributions, see p. 706.

1. **Use an attribution.** Mention the author's name early in the sentence or paragraph and include only the page number(s) in parentheses. Use the author's full name the first time you mention the author. After the first mention, give only the author's last name in subsequent citations to the same source.

2. **Use only a parenthetical citation.** Include both the author's last name and the page number(s) in parentheses at the end of the sentence. Do not separate the name and page number with a comma.

Many instructors prefer that you use attributions rather than parenthetical citations. For either type of citation, use the following rules.

- Do not use the word *page* or the abbreviation *p.* or *pp.*
- Place the sentence period after the closing parenthesis, unless the citation follows a block quotation. (See p. 708.)
- If a quotation ends the sentence, insert the closing quotation marks before the parentheses.

The following section provides guidelines for formatting in-text citations in the MLA style.

A single author

```
According to Vance Packard . . . (58).
. . . (Packard 58).
```

Two or three authors.   Include all authors' names, in either an attribution or a parenthetical citation.

```
Marquez and Allison assert . . . (74).
. . . (Marquez and Allison 74).
```

Four or more authors.   You may use either the first author's last name followed by *et al.* (Latin for "and others") or all of the authors' last names. Whichever option you choose, apply it consistently within your paper.

```
Hong and colleagues maintain . . . (198).
. . . (Hong et al. 198).
```

Two or more works by the same author.   When citing two or more sources by the same author or group of authors in your paper, include the full or abbreviated title in the citation to indicate the proper work.

FIRST WORK

```
In For God, Country, and Coca-Cola, Pendergrast describes . . .
(96).
Pendergrast describes . . . (Coca-Cola 96).
. . . (Pendergrast, Coca-Cola 96).
```

SECOND WORK

```
In Uncommon Grounds, Pendergrast maintains . . . (42).
Pendergrast maintains . . . (Grounds 42).
. . . (Pendergrast, Grounds 42).
```

Corporate or organizational author.   When the author of the source is given as a corporation, an organization, or a government office, reference the organization's name as the author name. Use abbreviations such as *Natl.* and *Cong.* in parenthetical references of government authors.

```
According to the National Institute of Mental Health . . . (2).
. . . (Natl. Institute of Mental Health 2).
```

Unknown author.   If the author is unknown, use the full title in an attribution or a shortened form in parentheses.

```
According to the article "Medical Mysteries and Surprises,"
. . . (79).
. . . ("Medical Mysteries" 79).
```

Authors with the same last name.   Include the first initial of these authors in all parenthetical citations. Use the complete first name in an attribution or if both authors have the same first initial.

```
John Dillon proposes . . . (974).
. . . (J. Dillon 974).
```

Two or more sources in the same citation.   When citing two or more sources of one idea in parentheses, separate the citations with a semicolon.

```
. . . (Breakwater 33; Holden 198).
```

Entire work.   To refer to an entire work, use only the author's name, preferably within the text rather than in a parenthetical reference. The title is optional; do not include page numbers.

```
Pendergrast in For God, Country, and Coca-Cola presents an
unauthorized history of Coca-Cola, the soft drink, and of the
company that produces it.
```

Work within an anthology or textbook.   An *anthology* is a collection of writings (articles, stories, poems) by different authors. In the in-text citation, name the author who wrote the work (not the editor of the anthology) and include the page number(s) from the anthology. The corresponding entry in the list of works cited begins with the author's last name; it also names the editor of the anthology.

IN-TEXT CITATION

```
According to Nora Crow . . . (226).
. . . (Crow 226).
```

WORKS CITED ENTRY

```
Crow, Nora F. "Swift and the Woman Scholar." Pope, Swift, and
     Women Writers. Ed. Donald C. Mell. Newark: U of Delaware
     P, 1996. 222-38.
```

Multivolume work. When citing two or more volumes of a multivolume work, indicate the volume number, followed by a colon and the page number.

```
Terman indicates . . . (2: 261).
. . . (Terman 2: 261).
```

Indirect sources. When quoting an indirect source (someone whose ideas came to you through another source, such as a magazine article or book), make this clear by adding, in parentheses, the last name and page number of the source in which the quote or information appeared, preceded by the abbreviation *qtd. in.*

```
According to Ephron (qtd. in Thomas 33), . . .
```

Personal interviews, letters, email, conversations. Give the name of the person in your text.

```
In an interview with Professor Lopez, . . .
```

Literature and poetry. Include information that will help readers locate the material in any edition of the literary work. Include page numbers from the edition you use.

- *For novels:* Cite page and chapter numbers.

  ```
  (109; ch. 5)
  ```

- *For poems:* Cite line numbers instead of page numbers; use the word *line* or *lines* in the first reference only.

  FIRST REFERENCE   `(lines 12-15)`

  LATER REFERENCES   `(16-18)`

- *For plays:* Give the act, scene, and line numbers in arabic numerals, separated by periods.

  ```
  (Macbeth 2.1.32-37)
  ```

Include complete publication information for the edition you use in the list of works cited.

Internet and nonprint sources.   In general, Internet sources are cited like their printed counterparts. Give enough information in the citation so that readers can locate the source in your list of works cited. If the electronic source provides page numbers, you should provide them too. If the source uses another ordering system, such as paragraphs (*par.* or *pars.*), sections (*sec.*), or screens (*screen*), provide the abbreviation with the appropriate number.

```
Brian Beckman argues that "centrifugal force is a fiction"
(par. 6).
. . . (Beckman, par. 6).
```

If the source does not have paragraphs or page numbers, which is often the case, then cite the work by title or author.

TITLE

```
According to a Web page posted by the Council for Indigenous
Arts and Culture, . . .
```

AUTHOR

```
Teresa Schmidt discusses . . .
. . . (Schmidt).
```

MLA Style for the List of Works Cited

For more practice using the MLA style of documentation, visit www .bedfordstmartins.com /successfulwriting /tutorials.

On a separate page at the end of your paper, you must include an alphabetical list of all the sources you cite. The list is headed *Works Cited.* Follow these general guidelines for preparing the list.

1. **List only the sources you cite in your paper.** If you consulted a source but did not cite it in your paper, do not include it in the list of works cited.

2. **Put the list on a separate page at the end of your paper.** The heading *Works Cited* should be centered an inch below the top margin of the page. Do not use quotation marks, underlining, or bold type for the heading.

3. **Alphabetize the list by authors' last names.** For works with multiple authors, invert only the first author's name.

```
Kaplan, Justine, and Anne Bernays. The Language of Names. New
     York: Simon, 1997.
```

4. **Capitalize the first word and all other words in a title except** *a, an, the, to,* coordinating conjunctions, and prepositions.

5. Italicize or underline titles of books and names of periodicals.

6. **Give inclusive page numbers of articles in periodicals.** Do not use the word page or the abbreviation *p.* or *pp.*

7. **Indent the second and all subsequent lines five spaces.** This is known as the *hanging indent* style.

8. **Double-space the entire list.**

The following sections describe how to format Works Cited entries for books, periodicals, Internet sources, and other sources.

Books

General guidelines and sample entries for books follow. Include the following elements, which you will find on the book's title page and copyright page. See Figure 20.4 on page 722 for an example.

1 *Author.* Begin with the author's last name, followed by the first name.

2 *Title.* Provide the full title of the book, including the subtitle. It should be capitalized and italicized or underlined.

3 *Place of publication.* Do not abbreviate city names (use *Los Angeles,* not *LA*). Unless the city is not easily recognizable, it is not necessary to include an abbreviation for the state. When you do need to include the state, use the two-letter postal style (e.g., AK, MT).

4 *Publisher.* Use a shortened form of the publisher's name; usually one word is sufficient (*Houghton Mifflin* is listed as *Houghton*). For university presses, use the abbreviations *U* for *University* and *P* for *Press* with no periods.

5 *Date.* Use the most recent publication date listed on the book's copyright page.

MLA FORMAT FOR CITING A BOOK

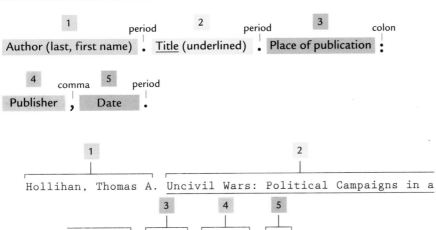

FIGURE 20.4
WHERE TO FIND DOCUMENTATION INFORMATION FOR A BOOK

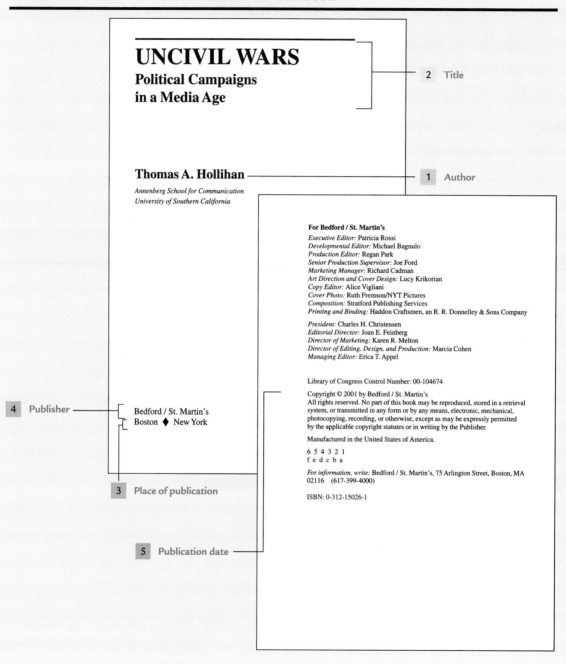

UNCIVIL WARS
Political Campaigns
in a Media Age

2   Title

Thomas A. Hollihan ——————————————— **1**   Author

Annenberg School for Communication
University of Southern California

For Bedford / St. Martin's
Executive Editor: Patricia Rossi
Developmental Editor: Michael Bagnulo
Production Editor: Regan Park
Senior Production Supervisor: Joe Ford
Marketing Manager: Richard Cadman
Art Direction and Cover Design: Lucy Krikorian
Copy Editor: Alice Vigliani
Cover Photo: Ruth Fremson/NYT Pictures
Composition: Stratford Publishing Services
Printing and Binding: Haddon Craftsmen, an R. R. Donnelley & Sons Company

President: Charles H. Christensen
Editorial Director: Joan E. Feinberg
Director of Marketing: Karen R. Melton
Director of Editing, Design, and Production: Marcia Cohen
Managing Editor: Erica T. Appel

Library of Congress Control Number: 00-104674

Copyright © 2001 by Bedford / St. Martin's
All rights reserved. No part of this book may be reproduced, stored in a retrieval system, or transmitted in any form or by any means, electronic, mechanical, photocopying, recording, or otherwise, except as may be expressly permitted by the applicable copyright statutes or in writing by the Publisher.

Manufactured in the United States of America.

6 5 4 3 2 1
f e d c b a

For information, write: Bedford / St. Martin's, 75 Arlington Street, Boston, MA 02116   (617-399-4000)

ISBN: 0-312-15026-1

4   Publisher ——— Bedford / St. Martin's
                      Boston ◆ New York

3   Place of publication

5   Publication date

If applicable, also include the original publication date, editor, translator, edition, and volumes used; these should be placed immediately after the title of the work.

Book with one author

```
Rybczynski, Witold. The Look of Architecture. New York: Oxford
     UP, 2001.
```

Book with two or more authors.   List the names in the order they appear on the title page of the book, and separate the names with commas. The second and subsequent authors' names are *not* reversed. For books with four or more authors, you can either list all names or list only the first author's name followed by *et al.*

TWO AUTHORS

```
Postel, Sandra, and Brian Richter. Rivers for Life: Managing
     Water for People and Nature. Washington: Island, 2003.
```

FOUR OR MORE AUTHORS

```
Kelly, Rita Mae, et al. Gender, Globalization, and
     Democratization. Lanham: Rowman, 2001.
```

Book with no named author.   Put the title first and alphabetize the entry by title. (Do not consider the words *A, An,* and *The* when alphabetizing.)

```
The Ticker Symbol Book. New York: McGraw, 1997.
```

Book by a corporation or organization.   List the organization or corporation as the author, omitting any initial article (*A, An, The*).

```
American Medical Association. American Medical Association
     Family Medical Guide. Hoboken: Wiley, 2004.
```

Government publication.   If there is no author, list the government followed by the department and agency of the government. Use abbreviations such as *Dept.* and *Natl.* if the meaning is clear.

```
United States Dept. of Health and Human Services. Natl. Insti-
     tute of Mental Health. Helping Children and Adolescents
     Cope with Violence and Disasters. Bethesda: NIMH, 2001.
```

Edited book or anthology.   List the editor's name followed by a comma and the abbreviation *ed.* or *eds.*

> Frazier, Ian, and Jason Wilson, eds. The Best American Travel
>   Writing 2003. Boston: Houghton, 2003.

Work within an anthology.   List the author and title of the work, followed by the title and editor of the anthology (*Ed.* is the abbreviation for "Edited by"); city, publisher, and date; and the pages where the work appears.

> Tan, Amy. "Two Kinds." The Story and Its Writer: An Introduc-
>   tion to Short Fiction. Ed. Ann Charters. Boston: Bedford,
>   2003. 1278-86.

Introduction, preface, foreword, or afterword

> Sacks, Oliver. Foreword. Thinking in Pictures: And Other
>   Reports from My Life with Autism. By Temple Grandin. New
>   York: Vintage, 1996.

Translated book.   After the title include the abbreviation *Trans.* followed by the first and last names of the translator.

> Houellebecq, Michel. The Elementary Particles. Trans. Frank
>   Wynne. New York: Knopf, 2000.

Two or more works by the same author(s).   Use the author's name for only the first entry. For subsequent entries, use three hyphens followed by a period. List the entries in alphabetical order by title.

> Covey, Stephen R. Principle-Centered Leadership. New York:
>   Simon, 1991.
> ---. The Seven Habits of Highly Effective People: Restoring
>   the Character Ethic. New York: Simon, 1989.
> Ehrenreich, Barbara. Nickel and Dimed: On (Not) Getting By in
>   America. New York: Metropolitan, 2001.
> Ehrenreich, Barbara, and Deirdre English. Witches, Midwives,
>   and Nurses: A History of Women Healers. London: Com-
>   pendium, 1974.

Edition other than the first.   Indicate the number of the edition following the title.

> Myers, David G. Exploring Psychology. 5th ed. New York: Worth,
>   2002.

Multivolume work.   Give the number of volumes after the title.

> Kazdin, Alan E., ed. <u>Encyclopedia of Psychology</u>. 8 vols.
>
>   Washington: American Psychological Association,
>
>   2000.

Encyclopedia or dictionary entry.   Note that when citing well-known reference books, you do not need to give the full publication information, just the edition and year.

> "Triduum." <u>Merriam-Webster's Collegiate Dictionary</u>. 11th ed.
>
>   2003.
>
> Levi, Anthony. "Maxim." <u>Encyclopedia of the Essay</u>. Ed. Tracy
>
>   Chevalier. London: Fitzroy, 1997.

One volume of a multivolume work.   Give the volume number after the title, and list the number of volumes in the complete work after the date, using the abbreviations *Vol.* and *vols.*

> Kazdin, Alan E., ed. <u>Encyclopedia of Psychology</u>. Vol. 3. Wash-
>
>   ington: American Psychological Association, 2000. 8 vols.

Article or chapter in a compilation.   List the author and title of the article first and then the title of the anthology, the editor's name (introduced by the abbreviation *Ed.*, for "Edited by"), and the publication information.

> McGowan, Moray. "Multiple Masculinities in Turkish-German
>
>   Men's Writing." <u>Conceptions of Postwar German Masculinity</u>.
>
>   Ed. M. Kimmel. Albany: State U of New York P, 2001.
>
>   310-20.

If more than one of these rules applies to a source, cite the necessary information in the order given in the preceding examples. For instance, to cite a reading from this textbook, treat it as a **work within an anthology (p. 724) in an edition other than the first (p. 724).** To do this, list the author and title of the reading, followed by the title of this book, the editor, the edition number, and all other publication information.

> Bernstein, Nell. "Goin' Gangsta, Choosin' Cholita: Claiming
>
>   Identity." <u>Successful College Writing: Skills, Strategies,</u>
>
>   <u>Learning Styles</u>. Ed. Kathleen T. McWhorter. 3rd ed.
>
>   Boston: Bedford, 2006. 311-15.

Articles in Periodicals

General guidelines and sample entries for various types of periodical articles follow. Include the following elements, most of which you should find on the first page of the article. See Figure 20.5 for an example.

1. *Author.* Use the same format for listing authors' names as for books (see p. 721). If no author is listed, begin the entry with the article title and alphabetize the entry by its title.

2. *Article title.* The title should appear in double quotation marks; a period falls inside the ending quotation mark.

3. *Periodical title.* Italicize or underline the title of the periodical. Do *not* include the word *A, An,* or *The* at the beginning: *Journal of the American Medical Association, New York Times.*

4. *Volume/issue and date.* For magazines and newspapers, list just the date in the following order: day, month, year; abbreviate the names of months except for *May, June,* and *July.* For scholarly journals, give the volume and issue numbers and then just the year in parentheses.

5. *Page(s).* If an article begins in one place, such as pages 19 to 21, and is continued elsewhere, such as on pages 79 to 80, just write *19+* for the page numbers (do *not* write 19–80).

The basic format for citing a periodical article is as follows.

MLA FORMAT FOR CITING A PERIODICAL ARTICLE

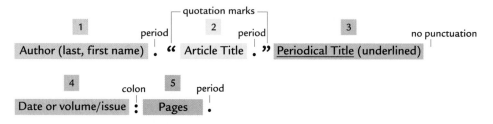

Magazine or newspaper article

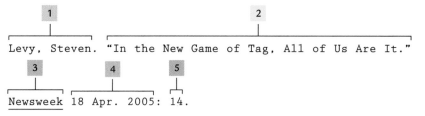

FIGURE 20.5

WHERE TO FIND DOCUMENTATION INFORMATION FOR AN ARTICLE

TheTechnologist

1 Author

2 Article title

BY STEVEN LEVY

In the New Game of Tag, All of Us Are It

MELVIL DEWEY HAD it easy. In 1876, when he created his famous system of ordering information, the Dewey Decimal Classification System, there weren't Web sites, video clips or blogs. Today's digital world—where millions of items are generated on an hourly basis, and even fantastic search engines can't find all the good stuff—is tougher to organize than a herd of Democrats. But Internet pundits now claim a solution: let the people do the categorizing. Using a practice called tagging, we can collectively label everything from great literature to pictures of your puppy. Bye-bye, Dewey. Hello, do-it-yourself.

As the name implies, tagging something means putting a virtual label on it. (Software lets you do this by simply typing a word; from then on, it's linked to the content.) What the tag says is totally up to you. The important thing is that later you—and others—can find things simply by the tag name. Think of tagging as the opposite of search. By leaving linguistic bread crumbs behind on your wanderings through cyberspace, you can easily relocate the sights (and sites) you saw along the way.

But "keeping found things found"—as Clay Shirky, a teacher at NYU's Interactive Telecommunications Program, explains—is only the first benefit of a grass-roots tagging system. Whereas the old, Dewey-style taxonomies involved graybeards figuring out in advance how things should be categorized, tagging is done on the fly, adapting to the content itself. What's more, because all this is digital, there's no limit to the number of tags people can slap on an item. In a library you can put "Frederick the Great" in the history or the biography section, but you'd need a second copy to put it in both. With digital tags you could use both, and more: *military, Prussia, really great reads.*

The big question about tagging is whether the lack of rules will lead to anarchy. Early results from the Web sites that exploit tagging show quite the opposite: order seems to emerge from the chaos of freestyle labeling. On a site called del.icio.us, participants put tags on their favorite Web sites, making it not only easy to find information on specific topics, but allowing visitors to view the most popular sites of the whole community. The photo-sharing site Flickr, which classifies images by user-selected labels, has generated a sometimes quirky but totally coherent form of organization, simply because people can

Will free-style information tagging lead to anarchy? Early results are showing quite the opposite.

check out which tag words get the best responses from the community, and do their own tagging accordingly. "Think of the process as similar to that of language, which is also a self-organized process," says author and tagging proponent David Weinberger. That process is also at work on a Web site called 43 Things, where people express their goals, tag them and comment and commiserate on the goals of others. It turns out that a lot of people on the site read a book called "Getting Things Done." When someone came up with the idea of making a tag called "GTD," others recognized that the abbreviation was an ideal label, and thereafter anyone who posted a goal inspired by that book stuck a GTD tag on it. That's a classic example of how the group effort of tagging can discover its own kind of compelling logic. Tagging enthusiasts call such systems "folksonomies."

Incidentally, 43 Things is funded by Amazon.com. The company won't comment on whether it's considering a customer-generated tagging system to organize its millions of items. But some think it inevitable that not only Amazon but other Net giants—eBay, iTunes and even Google and Yahoo—will let users do the organizing. "Traditionalists may go crazy," says Weinberger, "but the Internet makes them crazy anyway." Let's tag this scheme "promising." ∎

THE DIGIT

2 Rank of videogames among entertainment purchases made by active gamers, behind DVDs and ahead of CDs and MP3s.

NIELSEN ENTERTAINMENT

Blog Watch

A WEEKLY MAINSTREAM MEDIA SNAPSHOT OF WHAT'S HOT (AND WHAT'S NOT) IN THE WORLD OF WEB LOGS. FOR FULL LINKS GO TO NEWSWEEK.COM

$ Gawker Media tries to poach on Matt Drudge's territory with **sploid.com**, which puts a tabloid spin on news updates.

DELETE Right-wing blogs **intheagora.com** and **powerlineblog.com** falsely accused Dems of faking GOP talking points on Terri Schiavo; **theagitator.com** would like to see them eat a bit of crow.

! Football season doesn't start for several months, but **nflcheerleader.blogspot.com** might tide you over.

14 NEWSWEEK APRIL 18, 2005

ILLUSTRATION BY GREG MABLY FOR NEWSWEEK

© 2005 Newsweek, Inc.

5 **3** Periodical title   **4** Date

Page

Scholarly journal article

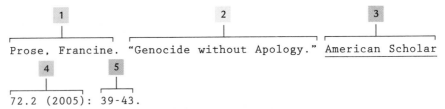

```
Prose, Francine.  "Genocide without Apology."  American Scholar
72.2 (2005):  39-43.
```

Article in a scholarly journal when each issue begins with page 1.   After the journal title, include the volume number, a period, and the issue number, followed by the year in parentheses, a colon, and the inclusive page numbers.

```
Schug, Mark C., and J. R. Clark.  "Economics for the Heart and
    the Head."  International Journal of Social Education 16.1
    (2001):  45-54.
```

Article in a scholarly journal with issues paged continuously through each volume.   Only the volume number precedes the year.

```
Lawson, David M.  "The Development of Abusive Personality: A
    Trauma Response."  Journal of Counseling and Development
    79 (2001):  505-09.
```

Article in a newspaper

```
Gay, Joel.  "Glorious Wreck Rears Its Head."  Anchorage Daily
    News 8 Sept. 2004, final ed.: A1+.
```

Article in a monthly magazine

```
Bethell, Tom.  "Democracy: A Little Goes a Long Way."  American
    Spectator Nov. 2003:  42-43.
```

Article in a weekly magazine

```
Henneberger, Melinda.  "Tending to the Flock."  Newsweek 13
    Sept. 2004:  34-36.
```

Editorial or letter to the editor.   Cite the article or letter beginning with the author's name, and add the word *Editorial* or *Letter* followed by a period after the title. An author's name or a title may be missing.

```
"The Search for Livable Worlds."  Editorial.  New York Times
    8 Sept. 2004:  A22.
```

Wolansky, Taras. Letter. <u>Wired</u> May 2004: 25.

Book or film review.   List the reviewer's name and title of the review. After the title add the words *Rev. of* and give the title and author or director of the book or film reviewed. Include publication information for the review itself, not for the material reviewed.

Gabler, Neal. "The Rise and Rise of Celebrity Journalism."
       Rev. of <u>The Untold Story: My Twenty Years Running the</u>
       <u>National Enquirer</u>, by Iain Calder, and <u>The Importance</u>
       <u>of Being Famous: Behind the Scenes of the Celebrity</u>
       <u>Industrial Complex</u>, by Maureen Orth. <u>Columbia Journalism</u>
       <u>Review</u> July/Aug. 2004: 48-51.

Internet Sources

Citations for Internet sources should include enough information to enable readers to locate the sources. Because electronic sources change frequently, it is often necessary to provide more information than you do for print sources. To help readers locate an online source easily, give its network address, or URL (uniform resource locator), at the end of your citation, enclosed in angle brackets (< >). If a URL is too long to fit on one line, divide it only following a slash.

Citing Internet sources may not be as straightforward as citing print sources because Web sites differ in how much information they provide and where and how they provide it. As a general rule, give as many of the following elements as possible, and list them in the order shown.

1   *Author.* Include the name of the person or organization if it is available.

2   *Title of the work.* Enclose titles of articles in quotation marks; italicize or underline the titles of longer works.

3   *Print publication information.* If the material was originally published in print, tell where and when it was originally published. Include volume and issue numbers, names of periodicals, names of publishers, dates, and so forth.

4   *Electronic publication information.* The information here will differ depending on the type of Web site.

   a. To cite an entire Web site or a document on a general Web site, provide as many of the following as are available: title of site (underlined or italicized); names of editors, compilers, or translators; date of publication or last update; and the sponsoring organization.

   b. To cite an article in an online periodical, give all the information you would give for a print source: periodical title, volume/issue, and date.

5   *Access date.* Include the date you accessed the document (day, month, year).

6 *URL.* Provide the full URL for the work or the URL for the site and the path you followed to find the work. Include any page, section, or paragraph numbers, if they are provided.

Some sample citations for different kinds of Internet sources are given below.

MLA FORMAT FOR CITING INTERNET SOURCES

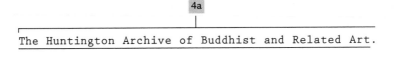

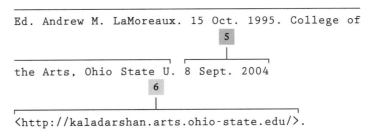

Entire Web site

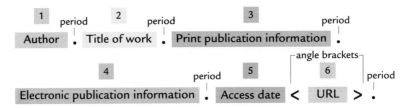

The Huntington Archive of Buddhist and Related Art.

Ed. Andrew M. LaMoreaux. 15 Oct. 1995. College of

the Arts, Ohio State U. 8 Sept. 2004

<http://kaladarshan.arts.ohio-state.edu/>.

Document on a Web site

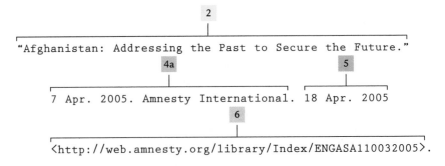

"Afghanistan: Addressing the Past to Secure the Future."

7 Apr. 2005. Amnesty International. 18 Apr. 2005

<http://web.amnesty.org/library/Index/ENGASA110032005>.

Work originally published in print

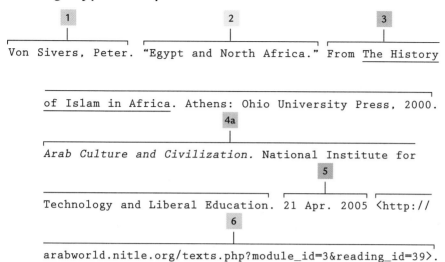

Von Sivers, Peter. "Egypt and North Africa." From The History

of Islam in Africa. Athens: Ohio University Press, 2000.

Arab Culture and Civilization. National Institute for

Technology and Liberal Education. 21 Apr. 2005 <http://

arabworld.nitle.org/texts.php?module_id=3&reading_id=39>.

Article in an online periodical

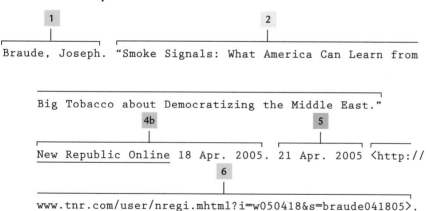

Braude, Joseph. "Smoke Signals: What America Can Learn from

Big Tobacco about Democratizing the Middle East."

New Republic Online 18 Apr. 2005. 21 Apr. 2005 <http://

www.tnr.com/user/nregi.mhtml?i=w050418&s=braude041805>.

Internet. Include the author's name (if it is not known, begin the entry with the title), title or site description (such as *Home page* if the site is untitled), date of publication, name of any sponsoring organization, date of access, and URL.

The Bulwer-Lytton Fiction Contest. Ed. Scott Rice. 7 Sept.
    1997. English Dept., San Jose State U. 8 Sept. 2004
    <http://www.bulwer-lytton.com>.

Email.   Provide the writer's name, the subject line (if available) in quotation marks, the words *Email to,* and the recipient's name. End with the date of the message.

> Morales, Anita. "Antique China." Email to Ruth E. Thompson. 11
>   Jan. 2002.

Article from an online journal

> Kimball, Bobbi. "Health Care's Human Crisis: Rx for an
>   Evolving Profession." Online Journal of Issues in Nursing
>   9.2 (2004). 8 Sept. 2004 <http://www.nursingworld.org/
>   ojin/tpc24_1.htm>.

Article from an online subscription service

> Wood, Robert A. "School as a Risk Environment for Children
>   Allergic to Cats and a Site of Transfer of Cat Allergen
>   to Homes." Pediatrics 106.2 (Aug. 2000): 431. Expanded
>   Academic ASAP. InfoTrac. Shoreline Lib., King County Lib.
>   System, Shoreline, WA. 4 Oct. 2001 <http://
>   infotrac.galegroup.com/itweb/kcls_remote>.

Posting to a listserv or newsgroup.   Include the author's name, the title or subject line enclosed in quotation marks, the phrase *Online posting,* the date of posting, the name of the list, the date of access, and the list's URL or the moderator's or supervisor's email address. If possible, cite an archival version.

> McCarty, Willard. "Smart Medicines?" Online posting. 10 May
>   2004. Humanist Discussion Group. 8 Sept. 2004 <http://
>   lists.village.virginia.edu/lists_archive/Humanist/v18/
>   0002.html>.

Online book.   Include the author's name; title (underlined); the name of any editor, translator, or compiler; original publication information (if available); electronic publication information; date of access; and URL.

> Twain, Mark. A Connecticut Yankee in King Arthur's Court.
>   New York: Harper, 1889. Electronic Text Center. U of
>   Virginia. 8 Sept. 2004 <http://etext.lib.virginia.edu/
>   modeng/modengT.browse.html>.

Other Sources

Publication on diskette, CD-ROM, or another electronic medium.   These sources are cited much like a book. Include the author's name and title. If the work is available in print, include publication information.

> The Time-Life Works of Shakespeare. Videodisc. Chicago:
>   Clearvue, 1995.

Material from a CD-ROM database.   Give the title of the material (in quotation marks), the title of the database (underlined), and all other publication details. Place the date of electronic publication at the end of the reference.

> Hurley, Patrick J. "Writing Basic Arguments." A Concise Intro-
>   duction to Logic. CD-ROM. Australia: Wadsworth, 2000.

Personal interviews or personal communication.   Indicate the name of the person, followed by the type of communication. For interviews you conducted, indicate the type of interview (telephone, personal, email, and so forth).

> Thompson, Alan. Telephone interview. 19 Jan. 2002.
>
> Chevez, Maria. Letter to the author. 14 July 2001.

See page 732 for help with citing an email message.

Published interviews.   List the person interviewed, and then list the title of the interview (if available) in quotation marks (underline the title if it is a complete work). If the interview has no title, label it *Interview* and give the source. Include the date of the interview.

> Everett, Percival. Interview. Bomb Summer 2004: 46-51.

Published letters.   If the letter was published, cite it as you would a selection in a book.

> Lewis, C. S. "To His Father (LPIII: 82)." 4 Sept. 1907. The
>   Collected Letters of C. S. Lewis, Vol. 1: Family Letters,
>   1905-1931. Ed. Walter Hooper. San Francisco: Harper,
>   2004. 5.

Film, video, or DVD.   List the title, director, and key performer(s). Include the original release date and the medium, if relevant, before the name of the distributor and the year of distribution.

> The Big Sleep. Dir. Howard Hawks. Perf. Humphrey Bogart and
>   Lauren Bacall. 1946. DVD. Warner Home Video, 2000.

Television or radio program.   List the title of the program (underlined), then give key names (narrator, producer, director, actors) as necessary and the title of the series (neither underlined nor in quotation marks). Identify the network, local station and city, and broadcast date. When citing a particular episode or segment, include its title in quotation marks before the title of the program.

> "Beyond Vietnam." Narr. David Barsamian. Alternative Radio.
>   Natl. Public Radio. KUOW, Seattle. 25 Aug. 2004.

Music recording.   List the composer or performer, the title of the recording or composition, the names of the artists, the medium if not a CD (audiocassette, LP, audiotape), the production company, and the date. Titles of recordings should be underlined, but titles of compositions identified by form (for example, Symphony No. 5) should not.

> Lloyd-Webber, Andrew. Phantom of the Opera. Perf. Michael
>   Crawford, Sarah Brightman, and Steve Barton. Polydor,
>   1987.

DOCUMENTING YOUR SOURCES: APA STYLE

APA style, recommended by the American Psychological Association, is commonly used in the social sciences. Both in-text citations and a list of references are used to document sources, as the following models show. For more information, consult the following reference work.

> American Psychological Association. *Publication Manual of the American Psychological Association.* 5th ed. Washington, DC: APA, 2001.

APA Style for In-Text Citations

Your paper must include in-text citations for all material you borrow or quote from sources. There are two basic ways to write an in-text citation.

1. **Use an attribution.** Mention the author's name in a phrase or sentence introducing the material, and include the date in parentheses immediately following the author's name. For quotations, include a page number at the end of the cited material.

2. **Use only a parenthetical citation.** Include both the author's last name and the date of publication in parentheses at the end of the sentence. Separate the name, date, and page number with commas.

Many instructors prefer that you use attributions rather than parenthetical citations. For either type of citation, use the following rules.

- Place the sentence period after the closing parenthesis. When a quotation ends the sentence, insert the closing quotation mark before the opening parenthesis. Block quotations are an exception to these rules; see page 708.

- For direct quotations and paraphrases, include the page number after the date, separating it from the date with a comma. Use the abbreviation *p.* or *pp.* followed by a space and the page number.

ATTRIBUTION

```
Masson and McCarthy (1995) maintain that emotions of "captive
wild animals are as real as those of wild animals" (7).
```

PARENTHETICAL CITATION

```
The emotions of "captive wild animals are as real as those of
wild animals" (Masson & McCarthy, 1995, p. 7).
```

The following section provides guidelines for formatting in-text citations in the APA style.

A single author.

```
According to Packard (1957), . . .
. . . (Packard, 1957).
```

Two authors.   Include both authors' last names and the date in an attribution or a parenthetical citation. In the latter case, use an ampersand (*&*) in place of the word *and*.

```
Masson and McCarthy (1995) assert . . .
. . . (Masson & McCarthy, 1995).
```

Three to five authors.   Include all authors' last names the first time the source is mentioned. In subsequent references to the same source, use the first author's last name followed by *et al.* (Latin for "and others").

FIRST REFERENCE

```
Hong, Kingston, DeWitt, and Bell (1996) have found . . .
. . . (Hong, Kingston, DeWitt, & Bell, 1996).
```

LATER REFERENCES

```
Hong et al. (1996) discovered . . .
. . . (Hong et al., 1996).
```

Six or more authors.   Use the first author's last name followed by *et al.* in all in-text citations.

Two or more works by the same author in the same year.   Add the lowercase letter *a* after the publication date for the first source as it appears alphabetically by title in your reference list. Add the letter *b* to the publication date for the source that appears next, and so forth. Include the dates with the corresponding lowercase letters in your in-text citations. (See p. 741 for the corresponding reference entries.)

```
Gardner (1995a) believes that . . .
. . . (Gardner, 1995a).
```

Two or more works by the same author(s).   Cite the works chronologically, in order of publication.

```
Gilbert (1988, 1993) believes that . . .
. . . (Gilbert, 1988, 1993).
```

Authors with the same last name.   Use the authors' initials with their last names.

```
Research by F. P. Lopez (1997) demonstrated . . .
According to C. Lopez (1993), . . .
```

Unknown author.   Use the title and date in the attribution or parenthetical citation. Give only the first two or three important words of a long title. Underline a book title; put the title of a journal article in quotation marks. Unlike the entry in the list of references, use standard capitalization in the in-text citation. (See p. 738.)

```
As noted in "Medical Mysteries" (1993), . . .
. . . ("Medical Mysteries," 1993).
```

Two or more sources in the same citation.   When citing two or more sources in parentheses, put a semicolon between them and list them in alphabetical order.

```
(Breakwater, 1986; Holden, 1996)
```

Entire work.   To refer to an entire work, give the author's name and the date. The title is optional; do not include page numbers.

```
Pendergrast (1997) presents an unauthorized history of Coca-
Cola, the soft drink, and of the company that produces it.
```

Work within an anthology.   An *anthology* is a collection of writings by different authors. In the in-text citation, name the author who wrote the work (*not* the editor of the anthology) and give the date. The corresponding entry in the list of references begins with the author's last name; it also names the editor of the anthology.

IN-TEXT CITATION

```
As Kaul (1995) notes, . . .
. . . (Kaul, 1995).
```

REFERENCES ENTRY

```
Kaul, P. (1995). The unraveling of America. In L. Chiasson,
Jr. (Ed.), The press in times of crisis (pp. 169-187).
Westport, CT: Greenwood.
```

Multivolume work.   When you cite one volume of a multivolume work, include the year of publication for that volume.

```
Terman (1990) indicates . . .
. . . (Terman, 1990).
```

When you cite two or more volumes of a multivolume work, give inclusive dates for the volumes.

```
Terman (1990-1991) indicates . . .
```

Indirect sources.   When you quote a source indirectly (rather than from the original source), include the abbreviation *qtd. in* along with the information for the source in which you found the quote.

```
According to Ephron, . . . (qtd. in Thomas, 1994, p. 33).
```

Personal interviews, letters, email, and conversations.   Give the last name and initial of the person, the source of the communication, and an exact date. Do not include these sources in the list of references.

```
Professor B. Lopez (personal communication, October 30, 2001)
asserts that . . .
```

Internet sources.   For direct quotations, give the author, year, and page (if available) in the attribution or parenthetical citation. If paragraph numbers are available, cite them with the paragraph symbol (¶) or the abbreviation *para.* If the author is unknown, use the document title in place of the author. If the date is unknown, use the abbreviation *n.d.*

```
Stevens (1997) maintains . . .
. . . (Stevens, 1997).
```

APA Style for the List of References

For more practice using the APA style of documentation, visit www.bedfordstmartins.com /successfulwriting /tutorials.

On a separate page at the end of your paper, you must include an alphabetical list of all the sources you cite. The list is headed *References.* Follow these general guidelines for preparing the list.

1. **List only the sources you cite in your paper.** If you consulted a source but did not cite it in your paper, do not include it in the list of references.

2. **Put the list on a separate page at the end of your paper.** The heading *References* should be centered about an inch below the top margin of the page. Do not use quotation marks, underlining, or bold type for the heading.

3. **Alphabetize the list by authors' last names.** Give the last name first followed by a comma and an initial or initials. Do not spell out authors' first names; use a space between initials: *Myers, D. G.* For works with multiple authors, list all authors' names in inverted order.

```
Kaplan, J., & Bernays, A. (1997). The language of names. New
     York: Simon.
```

4. **Put the publication date in parentheses after the author's name.**

5. **Capitalize the first word of the titles of books and articles, the first word following a colon, and any proper nouns.** All other words are lowercase.

6. **Include the word *A, An,* or *The* at the beginning of titles.** The word *The* is dropped from the titles of journals, however.

7. **Italicize titles of books and names of journals.** If your instructors prefer, use underlining instead of italics. Do not italicize, underline, or use quotation marks with article titles.

8. **For magazine and journal articles, italicize the name of the publication and the volume number.** The punctuation and spaces between these elements are also italicized. Italicize the names of newspapers. Capitalize all important words in the names of periodicals.

9. **Indent the second and all subsequent lines five spaces.** This is the hanging indent style, which the APA recommends for student papers.

10. **Double-space the entire list.**

The following sections describe how to format reference list entries for books, articles in periodicals, Internet sources, and other sources.

Books

The basic format for a book is as follows.

1 *Author.* Give the author's last name and initial(s). Do not spell out authors' first names; include a space between initials: *Myers, D. G.*

2 *Date.* Include the date in parentheses following the author's name. Use the most recent copyright date if more than one is given.

3 *Title.* Italicize the title of the book. If you underline instead of italicize, be sure to underline the period that follows the title.

4 *Place of publication.* Give the city of publication followed by a colon. If the city is not well known, add the postal abbreviation for the state (*Hillsdale, NJ:*).

5 *Publisher.* Include the name of the publisher followed by a period. Use a shortened form of the publisher's name: *Houghton Mifflin* would be listed as *Houghton,* for example. Do not omit the word *Books* or *Press* if it is part of the publisher's name: *Academic Press, Basic Books.*

APA FORMAT FOR CITING A BOOK

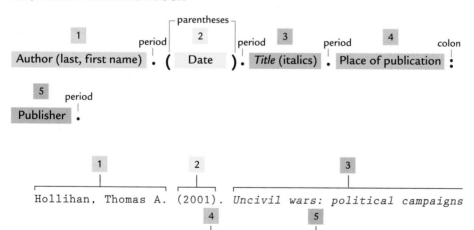

Book with one author

> Rybczynski, W. (2001). *The look of architecture.* New York:
> Oxford University Press.

Book with two or more authors.   List all authors' names in the order they appear on the book's title page. Use inverted order (*last name, initial*) for all authors' names. Separate the names with commas and use an ampersand (*&*) in place of the word *and.* Do not use *et al.* in the reference list unless the book has six or more authors.

> Douglas, S., & Michaels, M. (2004). *The mommy myth: The ideal-*
> *ization of motherhood and how it has undermined women.*
> New York: Free Press.
> Postel, S., & Richter, B. (2003). *Rivers for life: Managing*
> *water for people and nature.* Washington, DC: Island
> Press.

Book with no named author.   Give the full title first, and alphabetize the entry by title. (Do not consider the word *A, An,* or *The* when alphabetizing.)

> *The ticker symbol book.* (1997). New York: McGraw.

Book by an agency or corporation.   List the agency as the author. If the publisher is the same as the author, write *Author* for the name of the publisher.

> Ford Foundation. (2003). *Celebrating Indonesia: Fifty years*
> *with the Ford Foundation, 1953-2003.* Jakarta: Author,
> 2003.

Government publication.   List the agency as the author followed by the date. Include the document or publication number if available.

> Environmental Protection Agency. (2001). *Providing*
> *solutions for a better tomorrow: Reducing the risks*
> *associated with lead in soil.* EPA Publication No.
> EPA/600/F-01/014). Washington, DC: U.S. Government
> Printing Office.

Edited book or anthology.   List the editor's or editors' names followed by the abbreviation *Ed.* or *Eds.* in parentheses followed by a period.

```
Penzler, O., & Cook, T. H. (Eds.). (2004). The best American
    crime writing. New York: Vintage.
```

Work within an anthology.   List the author of the work first and then the date the work was published in the anthology. The title of the work follows. Then name the editor of the anthology (not in inverted order), give the title of the anthology (italicized), and include the inclusive page numbers in parentheses for the work (preceded by *pp.*). The publication information follows in normal order.

```
Kaul, P. (1995). The unraveling of America. In L. Chiasson,
    Jr. (Ed.), The press in times of crisis (pp. 169-187).
    Westport, CT: Greenwood.
```

Translated book.   After the title, include the initial(s) and last name of the translator followed by a comma and *Trans.*

```
Tolstoy, L. (1972). War and peace. (C. Garnett, Trans.).
    London: Pan. (Original work published 1869)
```

Two or more works by the same author(s).   Begin each entry with the author's name. Arrange the entries in chronological order of publication.

```
Gilbert, L. A. (1988). Sharing it all: The rewards and strug-
    gles of two-career families. New York: Plenum.
Gilbert, L. A. (1993). Two careers, one family: The promise of
    gender equity. Newbury Park, CA: Sage.
```

Two or more works by the same author in the same year.   Arrange the works alphabetically by title; then assign a lowercase letter (*a, b, c*) to the year of publication for each source. (See p. 736 for the corresponding in-text citation.)

```
Orman, S. (2003a). The laws of money, the lessons of life:
    Keep what you have and create what you deserve. New York:
    Free Press.
Orman, S. (2003b). The road to wealth: A comprehensive guide
    to your money. New York: Riverhead.
```

Edition other than the first

```
Myers, D. G. (2002). Exploring psychology (5th ed.). New York:
    Worth.
```

Multivolume work.   Give the inclusive volume numbers in parentheses after the title. If all volumes were not published in the same year, the publication date should include the range of years.

> Hawkins-Dady, M. (Ed.). (1992-1995). *International dictionary*
>   *of theatre* (Vols. 1-3). New York: St. James Press.

Article in a multivolume work.   Include the author and title of the article, as well as the title, volume number, and publication information for the work.

> Norton, M. J. (1995). Sleep disorders. In *Encyclopedia of*
>   *human behavior* (Vol. 4, pp. 738-741). San Diego: Academic
>   Press.

If more than one of these rules applies to a source, cite the necessary information in the order given in the preceding examples. For instance, to cite a reading from this textbook, treat it as a **work within an anthology (p. 741) in an edition other than the first (p. 741).** To do this, list the author of the reading, the date the reading was published in the anthology, the title of the reading, the editor and the title of this book, the edition number, the pages where the reading appears, and all other publication information.

> Bernstein, N. (2006). Goin' gangsta, choosin' cholita:
>   Claiming identity. In K. T. McWhorter (Ed.), *Successful*
>   *college writing: Skills, strategies, learning styles* (3rd
>   ed., pp. 311-15). Boston: Bedford.

Articles in Periodicals

General guidelines and sample entries for various types of periodical articles follow.

1 *Author.* Follow the basic format for listing authors' names (see p. 738). If no author is listed, begin with the article title and alphabetize the entry by its title.

2 *Date.* The year of publication appears in parentheses following the author's name. For articles in newspapers and magazines, the issue month and day follow the year.

3 *Article title.* Do not enclose article titles in quotation marks and do not use standard capitalization. Only the first word of an article title is capitalized, along with any proper nouns and the first word following a colon.

4 *Periodical title.* Italicize the name of the periodical. Use standard capitalization for the titles of periodicals.

5 *Volume/issue.* For scholarly journals only, give the volume number in italics; if needed, give the issue number in parentheses and roman type.

6 *Pages.* The abbreviation *p.* or *pp.* is used only in entries for newspaper articles.

APA FORMAT FOR CITING A PERIODICAL ARTICLE

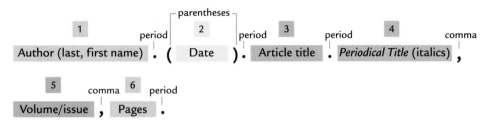

Magazine or newspaper article

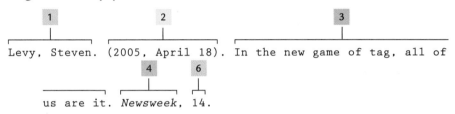

Scholarly journal article

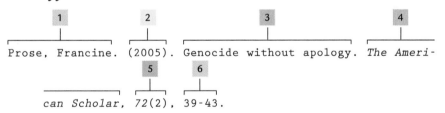

Article in a scholarly journal when each issue begins with page 1

Schug, M. C., & Clark, J. R. (2001). Economics for the heart and the head. *International Journal of Social Education,* *16*(1), 45-54.

Article in a scholarly journal with issues paged continuously through each volume

Lawson, D. M. (2001). The development of abusive personality: A trauma response. *Journal of Counseling and Development,* *79*, 505-509.

Article in a newspaper.   Include the year, month, and day in parentheses following the author's name. Page numbers for newspaper articles should be preceded by a *p.* or *pp.*

> Norris, F. (2001, September 13). A symbol was destroyed, not
>   America's financial system. *The New York Times,* p. C1.

Article in a monthly magazine.   Include the month of publication after the year.

> Bethell, T. (2003, November). Democracy: A little goes a long
>   way. *American Spectator,* 42-43.

Article in a weekly magazine.   Give year, month, and day of publication.

> Henneberger, M. (2004, September 13) Tending to the flock.
>   *Newsweek,* 34-36.

Editorial or letter to the editor.   Cite the editorial or letter beginning with the author's name (if available) and *Editorial* or *Letter to the editor* in brackets. If the author's name is not available, begin with the title.

> The search for livable worlds [Editorial]. (2004, September
>   8). *The New York Times,* p. A22.
> Wolansky, T. (2004, May) [Letter to the editor]. *Wired,* 25.

Book or film review.   List the reviewer's name, the date, and the title of the review. In brackets, give a description of the work reviewed, including the medium (*book* or *motion picture*) and the title.

> Gabler, N. (2004, July-August). Ephemera: The rise and fall
>   of celebrity journalism. [Review of the books *The untold*
>   *story: My twenty years running the* National Enquirer and
>   *The importance of being famous: Behind the scenes of the*
>   *celebrity industrial complex]. CJR,* 48-51.

Article with no author.   Use the full title as the author.

> The economy's bonus setback. (2002, January 14). *Business*
>   *Week,* 24.

Internet Sources

For Internet sources, include enough information to allow readers to locate the sources online. Guidelines for documenting Internet sources follow. For more help with formatting entries for Internet and other electronic sources in the APA style, consult *General Forms for Electronic References* from the American Psychological Association, available at http://www.apastyle.org/elecref.html .

1. Give the author's name, if available.

2. Include in parentheses the year of Internet publication or the year of the most recent update, if available. If there is no date, use the abbreviation *n.d.*

3. Capitalize the first word of the title of the document or subject line of the message, the first word following a colon, and any proper nouns. The other words are lowercase.

4. Give the date you retrieved the document, preceded by *Retrieved* and followed by a comma, the word *from,* and the URL (the Internet address at which you accessed the source). The URL is not followed by a period.

The basic APA format for an Internet source is as follows.

APA FORMAT FOR CITING INTERNET SOURCES

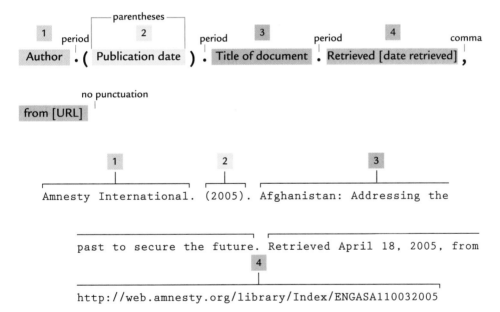

A document posted on a World Wide Web site

```
American Civil Liberties Union. (2004). Death penalty: A
    question of innocence. Retrieved September 8, 2004,
    from http://www.aclu.org/DeathPenalty/
    DeathPenalty.cfm?ID=9316&c=65
```

Article from an online journal.   Provide page numbers if available.

> Treharne, G. J., Lyons, A. C., & Tupling, R. E. (2001, December 17). The effects of optimism, pessimism, social support, and mood on the lagged relationship between daily stress and symptoms. *Current Research in Social Psychology, 7*(5). Retrieved September 8, 2004, from http://www.uiowa.edu/~grpproc/crisp/crisp.7.5.htm

A document from a university or college department Web site.   After the author, date, title, and retrieval date, be sure to include the name of the host institution followed by the program or department. Then put a colon and the URL.

> Abramson, C. (2000). *Laboratory of comparative psychology and behavioral biology.* Retrieved September 8, 2004, from Oklahoma State University, Department of Psychology Web site: http://psychology.okstate.edu/faculty/abramson/index.html

An online version of a print journal article.   Use the basic format for a journal reference, but add *Electronic version* in brackets following the title of the article. Add on the retrieval date and the URL at the end of the reference if you believe the material has changed from the print version (if it has graphics, for example).

> Wolfe, Henry B. (2001) An introduction to computer forensics. [Electronic version]. *Informing Science 4*, 47-52. Retrieved September 8, 2004, from http://inform.nu/Articles/Vol4/v4n2p047-052.pdf

Posting to a listserv or newsgroup.   Reference a listserv or newsgroup only if it provides a searchable archive. If not, cite it as personal or email communication.

> Maenpaa, S. (2004, September 8). Women and informal port economies. H-Labor Discussion Group. Retrieved September 8, 2004, from http://www.h-net.msu.edu/~labor

Other Sources

Material from an information service or a database

> Sherer, J. (2002, February). Downplaying the scale. *Shape, 21*(6). 60. Retrieved January 16, 2002, from InfoTrac online database (Health Reference Center A81825798)

Film, video, or DVD

> Jhally, S. (Producer and Director). (1995). *Slim hopes: Adver-*
>   *tising and the obsession with thinness* [Motion Picture].
>   Northampton, MA: Media Education Foundation.

Television program.   Use the producer's name as the author unless you are citing a dramatic or fictional series. In that case, use the script writer's name as the author, followed by the director. Give titles for individuals in parentheses after their names.

> Dochtery, N. (Producer). (2001, February 13). Hackers. [Tele-
>   vision series episode]. *Frontline*. Boston: WGBH.

Computer software.   If a person has proprietary rights to the software, list that person's name. If not, use the format for a work with an unknown author.

> Mitterer, J. (1993). Dynamic concepts in psychology [Computer
>   software]. Orlando, FL: Harcourt.

RESEARCH PAPER IN PROGRESS 9

For the final paper you prepared in Research Paper in Progress 8, prepare a Works Cited or References list, following your instructor's preference.

STUDENTS WRITE

The following research paper was written by Nicholas Destino for his first-year writing course while he was a student at Niagara County Community College. Destino used the MLA style for formatting his paper and documenting sources. Notice his use of in-text citations and quotations to provide evidence in support of his thesis.

Destino 1

Nicholas Destino
Professor Thomas
English 101
10 November 2005

Double-spaced

Centered title

Do Animals Have Emotions?

Somewhere in the savannas of Africa a mother elephant is dying in the company of many other pachyderms.
Some of them are part of her family; some are fellow
members of her herd. The dying elephant tips from side
to side and seems to be balancing on a thin thread in
order to sustain her life. Many of the other elephants
surround her as she struggles to regain her balance.
They also try to help by feeding and caressing her.
After many attempts by the herd to save her life, they
seem to realize that there is simply nothing more that
can be done. She finally collapses to the ground in the
presence of her companions. Most of the other elephants
move away from the scene. There are, however, two
elephants who remain behind with the dead elephant--
another mother and her calf. The mother turns her back
to the body and taps it with one foot. Soon the other
elephants call for them to follow and eventually they
do (Masson and McCarthy, Elephants 95). These movements, which are slow and ritualistic, suggest that
elephants may be capable of interpreting and responding
to the notion of death.

The topic of animal emotions is one that, until
recently, has rarely been discussed or studied by scientists. However, since the now famous comprehensive
field studies of chimpanzees by the internationally
renowned primatologist Jane Goodall, those who study
animal behavior have begun to look more closely at the
notion that animals feel emotions. As a result of their

Destino 2

observations of various species of animals, a number of
these researchers have come to the conclusion that animals do exhibit a wide range of emotions, such as
grief, sympathy, and joy.

    One of the major reasons that research into animal
emotions traditionally was avoided is that scientists
fear being accused of anthropomorphism--the act of
attributing human qualities to animals. To do so is
perceived as unscientific (Masson and McCarthy, "Hope
and Joy" xviii). Frans de Waal, of the Yerkes Regional
Primate Research Center in Atlanta, believes that if
people are not open to the possibility of animals
having emotions, they may be overlooking important
information about both animals and humans. He explains
his position in his article "Are We in Anthropodenial?"
The term anthropodenial, which he coined, refers to "a
blindness to the humanlike characteristics of other
animals, or the animal-like characteristics of ourselves" (52). He proposes that because humans and animals are so closely related, it would be impossible for
one not to have some characteristics of the other. He
contends, "If two closely related species act in the
same manner, their underlying mental processes are
probably the same, too" (53). If de Waal is correct,
then humans can presume that animals do have emotions
because of the many similarities between human and animal behavior.

    Grief has been observed in many different species.
In many instances, their behaviors (and presumably,
therefore, their emotions) are uncannily similar to the
behaviors of humans. Birds, which mate for life, have
been observed showing obvious signs of grief when their
mates die. In The Human Nature of Birds, Theodore

Thesis statement

Attribution of quotation within text

Page number follows quotation

First main point

Destino 3

Barber includes a report from one Dr. Franklin, who witnessed a male parrot caring for his mate by feeding her and trying to help her raise herself when she was dying. Franklin observed the following scene:

> Her unhappy spouse moved around her inces-
> santly, his attention and tender cares redou-
> bled. He even tried to open her beak to give
> her some nourishment. . . . At intervals, he
> uttered the most plaintive cries, then with
> his eyes fixed on her, kept a mournful
> silence. At length his companion breathed her
> last; from that moment he pined away, and
> died in the course of a few weeks. (qtd. in
> Barber 116)

Veterinarian Susan Wynn, discussing the physio-logical symptoms brought on by emotional trauma in animals, notes that "[a]nimals definitely exhibit grief when they lose an owner or another companion ani-mal. . . . Signs of grief vary widely, including lethargy, loss of appetite, hiding . . ." (5). This observation reinforces de Waal's position that animals experience some of the same emotions as humans.

Perhaps the most extreme case of grief experienced by an animal is exemplified by the true story of Flint, a chimp, when Flo, his mother, died. In her book, Through a Window, which elaborates on her thirty years of experience studying and living among the chimps in Gombe, Tanzania, Jane Goodall gives the following account of Flint's experience with grief.

> Flint became increasingly lethargic, refused
> most food and, with his immune system thus
> weakened, fell sick. The last time I saw him
> alive, he was hollow-eyed, gaunt and utterly

Quotation longer than four lines indented ten spaces and not enclosed in quotation marks; period precedes citation

Citation for an indirect source

First letter of a quotation changed to lowercase to fit into sentence; ellipsis mark used to indicate omitted material

Source's credentials included within the text

Destino 4

depressed, huddled in the vegetation close to
where Flo had died. . . . The last short
journey he made, pausing to rest every few
feet, was to the very place where Flo's body
had lain. There he stayed for several hours,
sometimes staring and staring into the water.
He struggled on a little further, then curled
up--and never moved again. (196-97)

Of course, animal emotions are not limited to
despair, sadness, and grief. Indeed, substantial evidence indicates that animals experience other, more
uplifting emotions, such as sympathy, altruism, and
joy.

Many scientists who study animal behavior have
found that several species demonstrate sympathy to one
another. In other words, they act as if they care about
one another in much the same way as humans do. It is
probably safe to assume that no animal is more sympathetic, or at least displays more behaviors associated
with the emotion of sympathy, than chimpanzees. Those
who have studied apes in the wild, including de Waal,
have observed that animals who had been fighting make
up with one another by kissing and hugging. Although
other primates also engage in similar behaviors, chimps
even go so far as to embrace and attempt to console
the defeated animal ("Going Ape"). Another striking
example of one animal showing sympathy for another is
the account cited by Barber of a parrot comforting its
sick mate. It is not, however, the only example of this
type of behavior, especially among birds. Barber cites
several other instances as well. According to Barber,
documented records show that responsible observers have
seen robins trying to keep each other alive. Also,

Transition to the second main point

Clear topic sentence

Information from a source paraphrased

Title used in citation since there is no author indicated

Page number not given since the article occupies only one page in the journal

Information from a source summarized

Destino 5

terns have been known to lift another handicapped tern
by its wing and transport it to safety. Likewise, a jay
has been known to successfully seek human help when a
newborn bird of a different species falls out of its
nest. What makes this latter example particularly noteworthy is that the newborn wasn't a jay but an altogether different type of bird.

Had the jay been helping another jay, it would be
easy to assume that the act of caring was the result of
what scientists call genetic altruism--the sociobiolog-
ical theory that animals help each other to keep their
own genes alive so they can reproduce and not become
extinct. Simply put, scientists who believe in genetic
altruism assume that when animals of the same species
help each other out, they do so because there is something in it for them--namely, the assurance that their
species will continue. This theory certainly provides
an adequate, unbiased scientific explanation for why
animals such as birds might behave in a caring manner.
However, if animals really help each other out only
when doing so will perpetuate their species, then the
jay would have had no genetic reason to help the newborn bird.

There is another popular explanation for why a
bird of one species might help a bird of another
species, however. Scientists who favor a related scientific theory called mutual altruism believe that animals will help each other because some day they
themselves may need help, and then they will be able to
count on reciprocal help (Hemelrijk 479-81). This theory is a plausible, nonanthropomorphic explanation for
why animals show sympathy, regardless of whether they

Transitional sentence
refers to incident
reported in preceding
paragraph.

Information that can
be found in many
sources; does not
need to be docu-
mented

Destino 6

actually feel sympathy. This point is crucial because after all, humans can't actually observe how an animal feels; we can only observe how it behaves. It is then up to the observer to draw some logical conclusion about why animals behave in the ways they do. The mutual altruism theory, however, also can be disputed. In many cases, animals have helped others even when the receiver of the help would probably never be in a position to return the favor. For example, there are many accounts of dolphins helping drowning or otherwise endangered swimmers. Phil Mercer, on the BBC Web site, reported that dolphins stopped a shark from attacking swimmers off the coast of New Zealand. The animals surrounded the swimmers for about forty minutes while the great white shark circled. When the swimmers reached the shore, they remarked that they were sure that the dolphins acted deliberately to save them.

Not only do animals show sympathy, but they are also clearly able to express joy. For example, on many occasions primate experts have heard apes laugh while in the presence of other apes. These experts are sure that the noise they heard was laughter because of the clarity and tone of the sound. In their book, <u>Visions of Caliban</u>, Dale Peterson and Jane Goodall describe this laughter in detail.

> I'm not referring to a sort of pinched vocalization that might be roughly compared with human laughter, as in the "laughter" of a hyena. I'm referring to real laughter, fully recognizable laughter, the kind where you lie down on the ground and shake in a paroxysm of clear amusement and simple pleasure. (181)

Transition to the final main point

Destino 7

According to Peterson and Goodall, only four species, in addition to humans, have the capacity to be amused and to show their amusement by laughing: chimpanzees, gorillas, bonobos, and orangutans.

Even the actions of animals who are not able to laugh uproariously indicate that they feel joy. Many animals engage in playful behavior that can emanate only from a sense of joy. In "Hope and Joy among the Animals," Masson and McCarthy tell an amusing, yet true, story about an elephant named Norma.

> A traveling circus once pitched its tents next to a schoolyard with a set of swings. The older elephants were chained, but Norma, a young elephant, was left loose. When Norma saw children swinging, she was greatly intrigued. Before long, she went over, waved the children away with her trunk, backed up to a swing, and attempted to sit on it. She was notably unsuccessful, even using her tail to hold the swing in place. (45)

Geese, according to experts, have an "emotional body language which can be read: goose posture, gestures, and sounds can indicate feelings such as uncertain, tense, glad, victorious, sad, alert, relaxed or threatening." Additionally, birds sometimes can be seen moving their wings back and forth while listening to sounds they find pleasant (McHugh).

In short, animals exhibit a large number of behaviors that indicate that they possess not only the capacity to feel but the capacity to express those feelings in some overt way, often through body language. If these are not proof enough that animals have emotions, people need look no further than their own

Entire title of article included in attribution because two works by Masson and McCarthy are cited

Citation of Internet source consists of author's name only; no page numbers available

Transition to the conclusion of the essay

Destino presents his own conclusion about animal emotions.

beloved cat or dog. Pets are so frequently the cause of joy, humor, love, sympathy, empathy, and even grief that it is difficult to imagine animals could elicit such emotions in humans without actually having these emotions themselves. The question, then, is not "Do animals have emotions?" but rather, "Which emotions do animals have, and to what degree do they feel them?"

Destino 9

Works Cited

Barber, Theodore Xenophone. The Human Nature of Birds:
    A Scientific Discovery with Startling Implica-
    tions. New York: St. Martin's, 1993.

de Waal, Frans. "Are We in Anthropodenial?" Discover
    July 1997: 50-53.

"Going Ape." Economist 17 Feb. 1997: 78.

Goodall, Jane. The Chimpanzees of Gombe: Patterns of
    Behavior. Cambridge: Belknap Press, 1986.

---. Through a Window. Boston: Houghton, 1990.

Hemelrijk, Charlotte K. "Support for Being Groomed in
    Long-Tailed Macaques, Macaca Fascicularis." Animal
    Behaviour 48 (1994): 479-81.

Masson, Jeffrey Moussaleff, and Susan McCarthy. "Hope
    and Joy among the Animals." Utne Reader July-Aug.
    1995: 44-46.

---. When Elephants Weep: The Emotional Lives of
    Animals. New York: Delacorte, 1995.

McHugh, Mary. "The Emotional Lives of Animals." The
    Global Ideas Bank. Ed. Nicholas Albery and
    Stephanie Wienrich. 1998. Institute for Social
    Inventions, London. 19 Dec. 2004 <http://
    www.globalideasbank.org/BI/BI-170.html>.

Mercer, Phil. "Dolphins Prevent NZ Shark Attack."
    BBC News. 23 Nov. 2004. BBC. 21 Jan. 2005.
    <http://news.bbc.co.uk/1/hi/world/asia-pacific/
    4034383.stm>.

Peterson, Dale, and Jane Goodall. Visions of Caliban: On
    Chimpanzees and People. New York: Houghton, 1993.

Wynn, Susan G. "The Treatment of Trauma in Pet Animals:
    What Constitutes Trauma?" Homeopathy Online 5 (1998):
    7 pp. 15 Dec. 2004 <http://www.lyghtforce.com/
    HomeopathyOnline/issue5/articles/wynn.html>.

Heading centered

Double-space between heading and first line, and between all subsequent lines.

Entries are alphabetized by authors' last names.

First line of each entry is flush with the left margin; subsequent lines indent five spaces.

PART 6

Academic Applications

The Bean Eaters

Gwendolyn Brooks

They eat beans mostly, this old yellow pair.
Dinner is a casual affair.
Plain chipware on a plain and creaking wood,
Tin flatware.

Two who are Mostly Good.   5
Two who have lived their day,
But keep on putting on their clothes
And putting things away.

And remembering . . .
Remembering, with twinklings and twinges,   10
As they lean over the beans in their rented back room that
    is full of beads and receipts and dolls and cloths,
    tobacco crumbs, vases and fringes.

Reading and Writing about Literature

Suppose your American literature instructor asks you to read carefully the poem by Gwendolyn Brooks (1917–2000), a major American writer of poetry as well as fiction and nonfiction prose. Brooks was the first African American woman to win a Pulitzer Prize for poetry (for *Annie Allen,* 1949). "The Bean Eaters" was originally published in a collection of poems, *The Bean Eaters,* in 1960.

Writing Quick Start

After reading Brooks's "The Bean Eaters," how can you describe the life of the elderly couple shown in the photo? Note that the elderly couple in the photo is not the couple described in the poem. Using information about the elderly lifestyle presented in "The Bean Eaters," as well as your own experience with elderly people, write a paragraph describing in your own words what you think the couple's relationship might be like.

Brooks's poem and the paragraph you just wrote both paint a picture of an elderly couple. Through carefully selected details, the poem tells about the couple's daily activities, memories of the past, and current economic situation (for example, "They eat beans mostly," "Plain chipware," and "rented back room" reveal that the couple is poor). Brooks also suggests that routine is important to the couple ("But keep on putting on their clothes / And putting things away") and that their memories of the past are both good ("twinklings") and bad ("twinges").

Now think of an elderly couple you know, such as your grandparents or neighbors. Do some of the characteristics of Brooks's couple apply to the couple you know? How does Brooks's picture of one elderly couple help you understand other elderly people like the ones in the photo?

"The Bean Eaters" suggests an answer to the question many students ask: "Why should I read or write about literature?" This poem, like all literature, is about the experiences people share. Literature often deals with large issues: "What is worthwhile in life?" "What is moral?" "What is beautiful?" When you read and write about literature, you gain new insights into many aspects of human experience and thereby enrich your own life.

Understanding literature has practical purposes as well (see the accompanying box for a few examples). You may be asked to write about literature in many college courses — not only in English classes. Even in work situations, a knowledge of literature will make some tasks easier or more meaningful.

This chapter will help you read and respond to works of literature. The first half of the chapter offers a general approach to reading and understanding literature, including discussions of the language and other elements of short stories and poetry. The second half of the chapter focuses on the characteristics of literary analysis and helps you through the process of writing one in a Guided Writing

---

SCENES FROM COLLEGE AND THE WORKPLACE

- Your *art history* professor asks you to read Ernest Hemingway's *For Whom the Bell Tolls* (a novel set in the time of the Spanish Civil War) and to write a paper discussing its meaning in conjunction with Picasso's *Guernica,* a painting that vividly portrays a scene from that war.

- In a *film* class, you watch the film *Romeo and Juliet,* directed by Franco Zeffirelli. Your instructor then asks you to read excerpts from Shakespeare's *Romeo and Juliet* and write a paper evaluating how successfully Juliet is portrayed in the film.

- You work for a *children's book store.* Your supervisor has asked you to read several children's books that she is considering featuring during story hour and write an evaluation of each.

Assignment. Although literature can take many forms, including poetry, short stories, biography, autobiography, drama, essays, and novels, this chapter concentrates on two literary genres: short stories and poetry.

A GENERAL APPROACH TO READING LITERATURE

Textbooks focus primarily on presenting factual information, but literature does not. Instead, *works of literature* are concerned with interpreting ideas, experiences, and events. They employ facts, description, and detail to convey larger meanings.

Use the following general guidelines to read a literary work effectively.

1. **Read with an open mind.** Be ready to respond to the work; don't make up your mind about it before you start reading.

2. **Preview the work before reading it.** Read background information about the author and the work and study the title. For a short story, read the first few and last few paragraphs and quickly skim through the pages in between, noticing the setting, the names of the characters, the amount of dialogue, and so forth. For a poem, read it through once to get an initial impression. *For more on previewing, see Chapter 2, p. 24.*

3. **Read slowly and carefully.** Works of literature use language in unique and creative ways, requiring you to read them slowly and carefully with a pen in hand. Mark interesting uses of language, such as striking phrases or descriptions, as well as sections that hint at the theme of the work.

4. **Note that literature often "bends the rules" of grammar and usage.** Writers of literature may use sentence fragments, ungrammatical dialogue, or unusual punctuation to create a particular *effect* in a short story or poem. When you see such instances in literature, remember that the writers bend the rules for a purpose.

5. **Establish the literal meaning first.** During the first reading of a work, try to establish its literal meaning. Who is doing what, when, and where? Identify the general subject, specific topic, and main character. What is happening? Describe the basic plot, action, or sequence of events. Establish where and during what time period the action occurs.

6. **Reread the work to focus on your interpretation.** To analyze a literary work, you will need to reread parts of the work or the entire work several times.

7. **Anticipate a gradual understanding.** Literary works are complex; you should not expect to understand a poem or short story immediately after reading it. As you reread and think about the work, its meanings will often come to mind gradually. Consider why the writer wrote the work and what message the writer is trying to communicate. Then ask "So what?" to discover deeper meanings. Try to determine the work's view of, comment on, or lesson about the human experience.

8. **Interact with the work.** Jot down your reactions to it in the margins as you read. Include hunches, insights, and feelings as well as questions about the work. Highlight or underline key words, phrases, or actions that seem important or that you want to reconsider later.

9. **Identify themes and patterns.** Study your annotations to discover how the ideas in the work link together to suggest a theme. **Themes** are large or universal topics that are important to nearly everyone. For example, the theme of a poem or short story might be that death is inescapable or that aging involves a loss of the innocence of youth. Think of the theme as the main point a poem or short story makes. (Themes are discussed in greater detail later in the chapter.)

THE LANGUAGE OF LITERATURE

Many writers, especially writers of literary works, use figures of speech to describe people, places, or objects and to communicate ideas. In general, **figures of speech** are comparisons that make sense imaginatively or creatively but not literally. Three common types of figurative language are *similes, metaphors,* and *personification.* Writers often use another literary device, *symbols,* to suggest larger themes. Finally, writers use *irony* to convey the incongruities of life.

Similes, Metaphors, and Personification

For more on figures of speech, see Chapter 7, p. 190, and Chapter 9, p. 246.

Similes and metaphors are comparisons between two unlike things that have one common trait. A **simile** uses the word *like* or *as* to make a comparison, whereas a metaphor states or implies that one thing is another thing. If you say, "My father's mustache is a housepainter's brush," your metaphor compares two dissimilar things — a mustache and paintbrush — that share one common trait — straight bristles. Such comparisons appeal to the reader's imagination. If you say, "Martha's hair looks like she just walked through a wind tunnel," your simile creates a more vivid image of Martha's hair than if you simply stated, "Martha's hair is messy." Here are examples from literary works.

SIMILE

My soul has grown deep like the rivers.

LANGSTON HUGHES, "The Negro Speaks of Rivers"

METAPHOR

Time is but the stream I go a-fishing in.

HENRY DAVID THOREAU, *Walden*

When writers use **personification,** they attribute human characteristics to objects or ideas. A well-known example of personification is found in Carl Sandburg's poem "Fog." Sandburg likens fog to a cat and says the fog "comes on little cat feet" and sits "on silent haunches" as it looks over the city. Like similes and metaphors, personification often creates a strong visual image.

Symbols

A **symbol** suggests more than its literal meaning. A flag, for instance, suggests patriotism; the color white often suggests innocence and purity. Because the abstract idea that a symbol represents is not stated but is left for the reader to infer, a symbol may suggest more than one meaning. A white handkerchief, for example, might symbolize retreat in one context but good manners in another. Some literary critics believe the white whale in Herman Melville's novel *Moby Dick* symbolizes evil, whereas others see the whale as representing the forces of nature.

To recognize symbols in a literary work, look for objects that are given a particular or unusual emphasis. The object may be mentioned often, suggested in the title, or appear at the beginning or end of the work. Also be on the lookout for familiar symbols, such as flowers, doves, and colors.

Irony

Irony is literary language or a literary style in which actions, events, or words are the opposite of what readers expect. For example, a prize fighter cowering at the sight of a spider is an ironic action, a fire station burning down is an ironic event, and a student saying that she is glad she failed an important exam is making an ironic statement.

EXERCISE 21.1

Working with another student, make a list of common metaphors and similes, examples of personification, and symbols you have heard or seen in everyday life, in films or television programs, or in works of literature.

ANALYZING SHORT STORIES

A **short story** is a brief fictional narrative. It contains five key elements: setting, characters, point of view, plot, and theme. Short stories are shorter than novels, and their scope is much more limited. A short story, for example, may focus on one event in a person's life, whereas a novel may chronicle the events in the lives of an entire family. Like a novel, however, a short story makes a point about some aspect of the human experience.

Read the following short story, "The Secret Lion," before continuing with this section of the chapter. Then, as you continue with the chapter, you will discover how each of the key short-story elements works in "The Secret Lion."

The Secret Lion
Alberto Ríos

Alberto Ríos (b. 1952), the son of a Guatemalan father and an English mother, was raised in Nogales, Arizona, near the Mexican border. His work has appeared in numerous national and international literature anthologies. In addition to fellowships from the Guggenheim Foundation and the National Endowment for the Arts, Ríos has won several awards: the Walt Whitman Award from the Academy of American Poets, the Arizona Governor's Arts Award, and the Western States Book Award for The Iguana Killer: Twelve Stories of the Heart *(1984), a collection of stories that includes the one reprinted here. Ríos is currently a Regents Professor of English at Arizona State University.*

1   I was twelve and in junior high school and something happened that we didn't have a name for, but it was there nonetheless like a lion, and roaring, roaring that way the biggest things do. Everything changed. Just that. Like the rug, the one that gets pulled — or better, like the tablecloth those magicians pull where the stuff on the table stays the same but the gasp! from the audience makes the staying-the-same part not matter. Like that.

2   What happened was there were teachers now, not just one teacher, teach-erz, and we felt personally abandoned somehow. When a person had all these teachers now, he didn't get taken care of the same way, even though six was more than one. Arithmetic went out the door when we walked in. And we saw girls now, but they weren't the same girls we used to know because we couldn't talk to them anymore, not the same way we used to, certainly not to Sandy, even though she was my neighbor, too. Not even to her. She just played the piano all the time. And there were words, oh there were words in junior high school, and we wanted to know what they were, and how a person did them — that's what school was supposed to be for. Only, in junior high school, school wasn't school, everything was backward-like. If you went up to a teacher and said the word to try and find out what it meant you got in trouble for saying it. So we

didn't. And we figured it must have been that way about other stuff, too, so we never said anything about anything—we weren't stupid.

But my friend Sergio and I, we solved junior high school. We would come home from school on the bus, put our books away, change shoes, and go across the highway to the arroyo.[1] It was the one place we were not supposed to go. So we did. This was, after all, what junior high had at least shown us. It was our river, though, our personal Mississippi, our friend from long back, and it was full of stories and all the branch forts we had built in it when we were still the Vikings of America, with our own symbol, which we had carved everywhere, even in the sand, which let the water take it. That was good, we had decided; whoever was at the end of this river would know about us.

At the very very top of our growing lungs, what we would do down there was shout every dirty word we could think of, in every combination we could come up with, and we would yell about girls, and all the things we wanted to do with them, as loud as we could—we didn't know what we wanted to do with them, just things—and we would yell about teachers, and how we loved some of them, like Miss Crevelone, and how we wanted to dissect some of them, making signs of the cross, like priests, and we would yell this stuff over and over because it felt good, we couldn't explain why, it just felt good and for the first time in our lives there was nobody to tell us we couldn't. So we did.

One Thursday we were walking along shouting this way, and the railroad, the Southern Pacific, which ran above and along the far side of the arroyo, had dropped a grinding ball down there, which was, we found out later, a cannonball thing used in mining. A bunch of them were put in a big vat which turned around and crushed the ore. One had been dropped, or thrown—what do caboose men do when they get bored—but it got down there regardless and as we were walking along yelling about one girl or another, a particular Claudia, we found it, one of these things, looked at it, picked it up, and got very very excited, and held it and passed it back and forth, and we were saying "Guythisis, this is, geeGuythis . . .": we had this perception about nature then, that nature is imperfect and that round things are perfect: we said "GuyGodthis is perfect, thisisthis is perfect, it's round, round and heavy, it'sit's the best thing we'veeverseen. Whatisit?" We didn't know. We just knew it was great. We just, whatever, we played with it, held it some more.

---

[1]*arroyo:* A creek or stream in a dry part of the country.

3
4
5

6   And then we had to decide what to do with it. We knew, because of a lot of things, that if we were going to take this and show it to anybody, this discovery, this best thing, was going to be taken away from us. That's the way it works with little kids, like all the polished quartz, the tons of it we had collected piece by piece over the years. Junior high kids too. If we took it home, my mother, we knew, was going to look at it and say "throw that dirty thing in the, get rid of it." Simple like, like that. "But ma it's the best thing I" "Getridofit." Simple.

7   So we didn't. Take it home. Instead, we came up with the answer. We dug a hole and buried it. And we marked it secretly. Lots of secret signs. And came back the next week to dig it up and, we didn't know, pass it around some more or something, but we didn't find it. We dug up that whole bank, and we never found it again. We tried.

8   Sergio and I talked about that ball or whatever it was when we couldn't find it. All we used were small words, neat, good. Kid words. What we were really saying, but didn't know the words, was how much that ball was like that place, that whole arroyo: couldn't tell anybody about it, didn't understand what it was, didn't have a name for it. It just felt good. It was just perfect in the way it was that place, that whole going to that place, that whole junior high school lion. It was just iron-heavy, it had no name, it felt good or not, we couldn't take it home to show our mothers, and once we buried it, it was gone forever.

9   The ball was gone, like the first reasons we had come to that arroyo years earlier, like the first time we had seen the arroyo, it was gone like everything else that had been taken away. This was not our first lesson. We stopped going to the arroyo after not finding the thing, the same way we had stopped going there years earlier and headed for the mountains. Nature seemed to keep pushing us around one way or another, teaching us the same thing every place we ended up. Nature's gang was tough that way, teaching us stuff.

10   When we were young we moved away from town, me and my family. Sergio's was already out there. Out in the wilds. Or at least the new place seemed like the wilds since everything looks bigger the smaller a man is. I was five, I guess, and we had moved three miles north of Nogales where we had lived, three miles north of the Mexican border. We looked across the highway in one direction and there was the arroyo; hills stood up in the other direction. Mountains, for a small man.

11   When the first summer came the very first place we went to was of course the one place we weren't supposed to go, the arroyo. We went down in there and found water running, summer rain water mostly, and we went swimming. But every third or fourth or fifth day,

the sewage treatment plant that was, we found out, upstream, would release whatever it was that it released, and we would never know exactly what day that was, and a person really couldn't tell right off by looking at the water, not every time, not so a person could get out in time. So, we went swimming that summer and some days we had a lot of fun. Some days we didn't. We found a thousand ways to explain what happened on those other days, constructing elaborate stories about the neighborhood dogs, and hadn't she, my mother, miscalculated her step before, too? But she knew something was up because we'd come running into the house those days, wanting to take a shower, even — if this can be imagined — in the middle of the day.

That was the first time we stopped going to the arroyo. It taught 12 us to look the other way. We decided, as the second side of summer came, we wanted to go into the mountains. They were still mountains then. We went running in one summer Thursday morning, my friend Sergio and I, into my mother's kitchen, and said, well, what'zin, what'zin those hills over there — we used her word so she'd understand us — and she said nothingdon'tworryaboutit. So we went out, and we weren't dumb, we thought with our eyes to each other, ohhoshe'stryingtokeepsomethingfromus. We knew adults.

We had read the books, after all; we knew about bridges and 13 castles and wildtreacherousraging alligatormouth rivers. We wanted them. So we were going to go out and get them. We went back that morning into that kitchen and we said, "We're going out there, we're going into the hills, we're going away for three days, don't worry." She said, "All right."

"You know," I said to Sergio, "if we're going to go away for three 14 days, well, we ought to at least pack a lunch."

But we were two young boys with no patience for what we 15 thought at the time was mom-stuff: making sa-and-wiches. My mother didn't offer. So we got out little kid knapsacks that my mother had sewn for us, and into them we put the jar of mustard. A loaf of bread. Knivesforksplates, bottles of Coke, a can opener. This was lunch for the two of us. And we were weighed down, humped over to be strong enough to carry this stuff. But we started walking anyway, into the hills. We were going to eat berries and stuff otherwise. "Goodbye." My mom said that.

After the first hill we were dead. But we walked. My mother could 16 still see us. And we kept walking. We walked until we got to where the sun is straight overhead, noon. That place. Where that is doesn't matter; it's time to eat. The truth is we weren't anywhere close to that place. We just agreed that the sun was overhead and that it was time to eat, and by tilting our heads a little we could make that the truth.

"We really ought to start looking for a place to eat." 17

18   "Yeah. Let's look for a good place to eat." We went back and forth saying that for fifteen minutes, making it lunchtime because that's what we always said back and forth before lunchtimes at home. "Yeah, I'm hungry all right." I nodded my head. "Yeah, I'm hungry all right too. I'm hungry." He nodded his head. I nodded my head back. After a good deal more nodding, we were ready, just as we came over a little hill. We hadn't found the mountains yet. This was a little hill.

19   And on the other side of this hill we found heaven.

20   It was just what we thought it would be.

21   Perfect. Heaven was green, like nothing else in Arizona. And it wasn't a cemetery or like that because we had seen cemeteries and they had gravestones and stuff and this didn't. This was perfect, had trees, lots of trees, had birds, like we had never seen before. It was like The Wizard of Oz, like when they got to Oz and everything was so green, so emerald, they had to wear those glasses, and we ran just like them, laughing, laughing that way we did that moment, and we went running down to this clearing in it all, hitting each other that good way we did.

22   We got down there, we kept laughing, we kept hitting each other, we unpacked our stuff, and we started acting "rich." We knew all about how to do that, like blowing on our nails, then rubbing them on our chests for the shine. We made our sandwiches, opened our Cokes, got out the rest of the stuff, the salt and pepper shakers. I found this particular hole and I put my Coke right into it, a perfect fit, and I called it my Coke-holder. I got down next to it on my back, because everyone knows that rich people eat lying down, and I got my sandwich in one hand and put my other arm around the Coke in its holder. When I wanted a drink, I lifted my neck a little, put out my lips, and tipped my Coke a little with the crook of my elbow. Ah.

23   We were there, lying down, eating our sandwiches, laughing, throwing bread at each other and out for the birds. This was heaven. We were laughing and we couldn't believe it. My mother was keeping something from us, ah ha, but we had found her out. We even found water over at the side of the clearing to wash our plates with — we had brought plates. Sergio started washing his plates when he was done, and I was being rich with my Coke, and this day in summer was right.

24   When suddenly these two men came, from around a corner of trees and the tallest grass we had ever seen. They had bags on their backs, leather bags, bags and sticks.

25   We didn't know what clubs were, but I learned later, like I learned about the grinding balls. The two men yelled at us. Most specifically, one wanted me to take my Coke out of my Coke-holder so he could sink his golf ball into it.

26   Something got taken away from us that moment. Heaven. We grew up a little bit, and couldn't go backward. We learned. No one

had ever told us about golf. They had told us about heaven. And it went away. We got golf in exchange.

We went back to the arroyo for the rest of that summer, and tried 27 to have fun the best we could. We learned to be ready for finding the grinding ball. We loved it, and when we buried it we knew what would happen. The truth is, we didn't look so hard for it. We were two boys and twelve summers then, and not stupid. Things get taken away.

We buried it because it was perfect. We didn't tell my mother, but 28 together it was all we talked about, till we forgot. It was the lion. ■

Setting

The **setting** of a short story is the time, place, and circumstance in which the story occurs. The setting provides the framework and atmosphere in which the plot develops and characters interact. For example, Charles Dickens's "A Christmas Carol" is set in nineteenth-century London. The setting of "The Secret Lion" is between the arroyo and the mountains just outside of Nogales, Arizona. The action occurs near the arroyo and on the golf course.

Characters

The **characters** are the actors in the story. They are revealed through their dialogue, actions, appearance, thoughts, and feelings. The **narrator,** the person who tells the story, may also comment on or reveal information about the characters. The narrator is not necessarily the author of the story. The narrator can be one of the characters in the story or an onlooker who observes but does not participate in the action. Therefore, you need to think critically about what the narrator reveals about the personalities, needs, and motives of the characters and whether the narrator's opinions may be colored by his or her perceptions and biases. "The Secret Lion" involves two principal characters: the narrator and his childhood friend, Sergio. Both twelve-year-old boys are playful, spirited, and inquisitive. They explore, disobey, and test ideas. The narrator's mother is a secondary character in the story.

Point of View

The **point of view** is the perspective from which a story is told. There are two common points of view: first person and third person. In the first-person (*I*) point of view, the narrator tells the story as he or she sees or experiences it ("*I* saw the crowd gather at the cemetery"). A first-person narrator may be one of the characters or someone observing but not participating in the story. In the third-person (*they*) point of view, the narrator tells the story as if someone else is experiencing it ("*Laura* saw the crowd gather at the cemetery"). A third-person narrator may be able to report only the actions that can be observed from the outside or may be able to enter the minds of one or more characters and tell about their thoughts and motives. An *omniscient* or all-knowing third-person narrator is aware of the thoughts and actions of all characters in the story.

To identify the point of view of a story, then, consider who is narrating and what the narrator knows about the characters' actions, thoughts, and motives. "The Secret Lion" is told by a first-person narrator who both participates in the action and looks back on the events to interpret them. For example, he says of their preparations for their trip to the mountains, "But we were two young boys with no patience for what we thought at the time was mom-stuff" (para. 15). He also uses a fast-talking narrative style characteristic of twelve-year-old boys, intentionally bending rules of spelling and grammar to achieve this effect. For example, he uses sentence fragments — "Lots of secret signs" (7), "Out in the wilds" (10) — and runs words together or emphasizes syllables to show how they are pronounced — "wildtreacherousraging alligatormouth rivers" (13), "sa-and-wiches" (15). He also uses slang words — "neat" (8) — and contractions to create an informal tone.

Plot

The **plot** is the basic story line — that is, the sequence of events and actions through which the story's meaning is expressed. The plot is often centered on a **conflict,** a problem or clash between opposing forces, and the resolution of the conflict. Once the scene is set and the characters are introduced, a problem or conflict arises. Suspense builds as the conflict unfolds and the characters wrestle with the problem. Near the end of the story, the events come to a **climax** — the point at which the conflict is resolved. The story ends with a conclusion.

In "The Secret Lion" two childhood friends, while playing near an arroyo, discover a grinding ball. They bury the ball but are unable to find it when they return. The narrator recollects an earlier time, when they had planned a trip to the mountains and stopped to have lunch on what they soon discovered was a golf course. The conflict, illustrated by several events, is between the boys' imaginations and adult realities.

Theme

The **theme** of a story is its central or dominant idea, the main point the author makes about the human experience. Readers do not always agree about a story's theme. Therefore, in a literary analysis of a short story, you must give evidence to support your interpretation of the theme. The following suggestions will help you uncover clues.

1. **Study the title.** What meanings does it suggest?

2. **Analyze the main characters.** Do the characters change? If so, how, and in response to what?

3. **Look for broad statements about the conflict.** What do the characters and narrator say about the conflict or their lives?

4. **Analyze important elements.** Look for symbols, figures of speech, and meaningful names (Young Goodman Brown, for example).

Once you uncover a theme, try expressing it in sentence form rather than as a single word or brief phrase. For example, to say the theme is "dishonesty" or "parent-child relationships" does not reveal the meaning of a story. When expressed as a sentence, however, a story's theme becomes clear: "Dishonesty sometimes pays" or "Parent-child relationships are often struggles for power and control."

One possible theme of "The Secret Lion" is that change is inevitable, that nothing remains the same. After the boys discover that they can't find the buried grinding ball, the narrator hints at this theme: "The ball was gone . . . like everything else that had been taken away" (9). When the boys encounter the two men on the golf course, the narrator again comments on the theme of change: "Something got taken away from us that moment. Heaven. We grew up a little bit, and couldn't go backward" (26).

Another possible theme of Ríos's story is that perfection is unattainable. The boys are attracted to the ball because it is perfect: "GuyGodthis is perfect, thisisthis is perfect . . . it'sit's the best thing we'veeverseen" (5). But once the "perfect" ball is buried, it can never be found again. In much the same way, the boys cannot return to the "heaven" they once knew at the golf course.

EXERCISE 21.2

Working in groups of two or three, choose a television situation comedy and watch one episode, either together, if possible, or separately. After viewing the program, identify each of the following elements: setting, character, point of view, and plot. Then consider whether you think the episode has a theme.

Use the questions in the box on page 772 to guide your analysis of short stories. As you read the story that follows, "The Story of an Hour" by Kate Chopin (p. 773), keep these questions in mind. You may choose to write an analysis of this story in response to the Guided Writing Assignment on page 782.

QUESTIONS FOR ANALYZING SHORT STORIES

Setting: Time

1. In what general time period (century or decade) does the story take place?

2. What major events (wars, revolutions, famines, political or cultural movements) occurred during that time, and what bearing might they have on the story?

Setting: Place

1. In what geographic area does the story take place? (Try to identify the country and the city or town, as well as whether the area is an urban or rural one.)

2. Where does the action occur? (For example, does it occur on a battle-field, in a living room, or on a city street?)

3. Why is the place important? (Why couldn't the story occur elsewhere?)

Characters

1. Who are the main characters in the story?

2. What are the distinguishing qualities and characteristics of each character?

3. Why do you like or dislike each character?

4. How and why do characters change (or not change) as the story progresses?

Point of View

1. Is the narrator a character in the story or strictly an observer?

2. Is the narrator knowledgeable about the motives, feelings, and behavior of any or all of the characters?

3. Does the narrator affect what happens in the story? If so, how? What role does the narrator play?

Plot

1. What series of events occurs? Summarize the action.

2. What is the conflict? Why does it occur? How does it build to a climax?

3. How is the conflict resolved?

4. Is the outcome satisfying? Why or why not?

Theme

1. What is the theme? What broad statement about life or the human experience does the story suggest?

2. What evidence from the story supports your interpretation of the theme?

The Story of an Hour
Kate Chopin

Kate Chopin (1851–1904), a nineteenth-century American writer, is best known for her novel The Awakening *(1899), which outraged early literary critics with its portrayal of a woman in search of sexual and professional independence. As you read the following short story, originally published in* Vogue *magazine in 1894, look for, highlight, and annotate the five primary elements of short stories discussed in this chapter.*

1   Knowing that Mrs. Mallard was afflicted with a heart trouble, great care was taken to break to her as gently as possible the news of her husband's death.

2   It was her sister Josephine who told her, in broken sentences, veiled hints that revealed in half concealing. Her husband's friend Richards was there, too, near her. It was he who had been in the newspaper office when intelligence of the railroad disaster was received, with Brently Mallard's name leading the list of "killed." He had only taken the time to assure himself of its truth by a second telegram, and had hastened to forestall any less careful, less tender friend in bearing the sad message.

3   She did not hear the story as many women have heard the same, with a paralyzed inability to accept its significance. She wept at once, with sudden, wild abandonment, in her sister's arms. When the storm of grief had spent itself she went away to her room alone. She would have no one follow her.

4   There stood, facing the open window, a comfortable, roomy armchair. Into this she sank, pressed down by a physical exhaustion that haunted her body and seemed to reach into her soul.

5   She could see in the open square before her house the tops of trees that were all aquiver with the new spring life. The delicious breath of rain was in the air. In the street below a peddler was crying his wares. The notes of a distant song which someone was singing reached her faintly, and countless sparrows were twittering in the eaves.

6   There were patches of blue sky showing here and there through the clouds that had met and piled one above the other in the west facing her window.

7   She sat with her head thrown back upon the cushion of the chair, quite motionless, except when a sob came up into her throat and shook her, as a child who has cried itself to sleep continues to sob in its dreams.

8   She was young, with a fair, calm face, whose lines bespoke repression and even a certain strength. But now there was a dull stare in her eyes, whose gaze was fixed away off yonder on one of those patches of blue sky. It was not a glance of reflection, but rather indicated a suspension of intelligent thought.

9   There was something coming to her and she was waiting for it, fearfully. What was it? She did not know, it was too subtle and elusive to name. But she felt it, creeping out of the sky, reaching toward her through the sounds, the scents, the color that filled the air.

10   Now her bosom rose and fell tumultuously. She was beginning to recognize this thing that was approaching to possess her, and she was striving to beat it back with her will—as powerless as her two white slender hands would have been.

11   When she abandoned herself a little whispered word escaped her slightly parted lips. She said it over and over under her breath: "Free, free, free!" The vacant stare and the look of terror that had followed it went from her eyes. They stayed keen and bright. Her pulses beat fast, and the coursing blood warmed and relaxed every inch of her body.

12   She did not stop to ask if it were not a monstrous joy that held her. A clear and exalted perception enabled her to dismiss the suggestion as trivial.

13   She knew that she would weep again when she saw the kind, tender hands folded in death; the face that had never looked save with love upon her, fixed and gray and dead. But she saw beyond that bitter moment a long procession of years to come that would belong to her absolutely. And she opened and spread her arms out to them in welcome.

14   There would be no one to live for during those coming years; she would live for herself. There would be no powerful will bending her in that blind persistence with which men and women believe they have a right to impose a private will upon a fellow creature. A kind intention or a cruel intention made the act seem no less a crime as she looked upon it in that brief moment of illumination.

15   And yet she had loved him—sometimes. Often she had not. What did it matter! What could love, the unsolved mystery, count for in face of this possession of self-assertion which she suddenly recognized as the strongest impulse of her being.

16   "Free! Body and soul free!" she kept whispering.

17   Josephine was kneeling before the closed door with her lips to the keyhole, imploring for admission. "Louise, open the door! I beg; open the door—you will make yourself ill. What are you doing, Louise? For heaven's sake open the door."

"Go away. I am not making myself ill." No; she was drinking in a 18
very elixir of life through that open window.

Her fancy was running riot along those days ahead of her. Spring 19
days, and summer days, and all sorts of days that would be her own.
She breathed a quick prayer that life might be long. It was only yesterday she had thought with a shudder that life might be long.

She arose at length and opened the door to her sister's importu- 20
nities. There was a feverish triumph in her eyes, and she carried herself unwittingly like a goddess of Victory. She clasped her sister's
waist, and together they descended the stairs. Richards stood waiting
for them at the bottom.

Some one was opening the front door with a latchkey. It was 21
Brently Mallard who entered, a little travel-stained, composedly carrying his gripsack and umbrella. He had been far from the scene of
accident, and did not even know there had been one. He stood
amazed at Josephine's piercing cry; at Richards' quick motion to
screen him from the view of his wife.

But Richards was too late. 22

When the doctors came they said she had died of heart disease — 23
of joy that kills. ∎

ANALYZING POETRY

Poetry is written in lines and stanzas, instead of in paragraphs. Because of poetry's
unique format, ideas in poems are often expressed in compact and concise language, and reading and analyzing a poem may take as much time and effort as
analyzing an essay or a short story. To grasp the meaning of a poem, it is important to pay attention to the sound and meaning of individual words and to consider how the words in the poem work together to convey meaning.

Use the following general guidelines to read and analyze poetry effectively.

1. **Read the poem through once,** without any defined purpose. Read with an
   open mind; try to get a general sense of what the poem is about. If you come
   across an unfamiliar word or a confusing reference, keep reading.

2. **Use punctuation to guide your comprehension.** Although poetry is written
   in lines, each line may not make sense by itself. Meaning often flows from line
   to line, and a single sentence can be composed of several lines. Use the poem's
   punctuation to guide you. If there is no punctuation at the end of a line, read
   it with a slight pause at the end and with an emphasis on the last word. Think
   about how the poet breaks lines to achieve a certain effect.

3. **Visualize as you read.** Especially if you tend to be a spatial or an abstract learner, try to visualize or see what the poem is about.

4. **Read the poem several more times.** The meaning of the poem will become clearer with each successive reading. At first, you may understand some parts but not others. If you tend to be a pragmatic or rational learner, you will probably want to work through the poem line by line, from beginning to end. With poetry, however, that approach does not always work. Instead, you may need to use later stanzas to help you understand earlier ones. If you find certain sections difficult or confusing, read these sections aloud several times. You might try copying them, word for word, on a piece of paper. Look up the meanings of any unfamiliar words in a dictionary.

5. **Check unfamiliar references.** A poet may make **allusions**—references to people, objects, or events outside of the poem. Understanding an allusion is often essential to understanding the overall meaning of a poem. If you see Oedipus mentioned in a poem, for example, you may need to use a dictionary or encyclopedia to learn that he was a figure in Greek mythology who unwittingly killed his father and unknowingly married his mother. Your knowledge of Oedipus would then help you interpret the poem.

6. **Identify the speaker and tone.** Poems often refer to an unidentified *I* or *we.* Try to describe the speaker's viewpoint or feelings to figure out who he or she is. Also consider the speaker's tone: Is it serious, challenging, sad, frustrated, or joyful? To help determine the tone, read the poem aloud. Your emphasis of certain words or the rise and fall of your voice may provide clues to the tone; that is, you may "hear" the poet's anger, despondency, or elation.

7. **Identify to whom the poem is addressed.** Is it written to a person, to the reader, to an object? Consider the possibility that the poet may be writing to work out a personal problem or to express strong emotions.

For more on connotations, see Chapter 7, p. 88; for more on descriptive language, see Chapter 9, p. 242.

8. **Analyze the language of the poem.** Consider the *connotations,* or shades of meaning of words in the poem. Study the poem's use of descriptive language, similes, metaphors, personification, and symbols (see pp. 762–63).

9. **Analyze the poem's theme.** Does its overall meaning involve a feeling, a person, a memory, or an argument? Paraphrase the poem; express it in your own words and connect it to your own experience. Then link your ideas together to discover the poem's overall meaning. Ask yourself: "What is the poet trying to tell me?" and "What is the theme?"

Use questions in the accompanying box to guide your analysis of poetry. As you read the following poem by Robert Frost, "Two Look at Two," keep these questions in mind.

> ### QUESTIONS FOR ANALYZING POETRY
>
> 1. How does the poem make you feel—shocked, saddened, angered, annoyed, happy? Write a sentence or two describing your reaction.
>
> 2. Who is the speaker? What do you know about him or her? What tone does the speaker use? To whom is he or she speaking?
>
> 3. What is the poem's setting? If it is unclear, why does the poet not provide a setting?
>
> 4. What emotional atmosphere or mood does the poet create? Do you sense, for example, a mood of foreboding, excitement, or contentment?
>
> 5. How does the poet use language to create an effect? Does the poet use similes, metaphors, personification, or symbols?
>
> 6. Does the poem tell a story? If so, what is its point?
>
> 7. Does the poem express emotion? If so, for what purpose?
>
> 8. Does the poem rhyme? If so, does the rhyme affect the meaning? (For example, does the poet use rhyme to emphasize key words or phrases?)
>
> 9. What is the meaning of the poem's title?
>
> 10. What is the theme of the poem?

Two Look at Two

Robert Frost

Robert Frost (1874–1963) is a major American poet whose work often focuses on familiar objects, natural scenes, and the character of New England. In his early life, Frost was a farmer and teacher; later, he became a poet in residence at Amherst College and taught at Dartmouth, Yale, and Harvard. Frost was awarded Pulitzer Prizes for four collections of poems: New Hampshire *(1923), from which "Two Look at Two" is taken;* Collected Poems *(1930);* A Further Range *(1936); and* A Witness Tree *(1942). As you read the selection, use the questions in the accompanying box to think critically about the poem.*

Love and forgetting might have carried them
A little further up the mountain side
With night so near, but not much further up.
They must have halted soon in any case
With thoughts of the path back, how rough it was   5
With rock and washout, and unsafe in darkness;

When they were halted by a tumbled wall
With barbed-wire binding. They stood facing this,
Spending what onward impulse they still had
In one last look the way they must not go,   10
On up the failing path, where, if a stone
Or earthslide moved at night, it moved itself;
No footstep moved it. "This is all," they sighed,
"Good-night to woods." But not so; there was more.
A doe from round a spruce stood looking at them   15
Across the wall, as near the wall as they.
She saw them in their field, they her in hers.
The difficulty of seeing what stood still,
Like some up-ended boulder split in two,
Was in her clouded eyes: they saw no fear there.   20
She seemed to think that two thus they were safe.
Then, as if they were something that, though strange,
She could not trouble her mind with too long,
She sighed and passed unscared along the wall.
"*This*, then, is all. What more is there to ask?"   25
But no, not yet. A snort to bid them wait.
A buck from round the spruce stood looking at them
Across the wall, as near the wall as they.
This was an antlered buck of lusty nostril,
Not the same doe come back into her place.   30
He viewed them quizzically with jerks of head,
As if to ask, "Why don't you make some motion?
Or give some sign of life? Because you can't.
I doubt if you're as living as you look."
Thus till he had them almost feeling dared   35
To stretch a proffering hand—and a spell-breaking.
Then he too passed unscared along the wall.
Two had seen two, whichever side you spoke from.
"This *must* be all." It was all. Still they stood,
A great wave from it going over them,   40
As if the earth in one unlooked-for favor
Had made them certain earth returned their love.

The poem takes place on a mountainside path, near dusk. A couple walking the path finds a tumbled wall. Looking beyond the wall, the couple first encounters a doe and then a buck. The doe and buck stare at the human couple and vice versa; hence the title "Two Look at Two." Neither the animals nor the humans are frightened; both couples observe each other and continue with their lives. The action is described by a third-person narrator who can read the thoughts of the humans. The speaker creates an objective tone by reporting events as they occur.

In "Two Look at Two," Frost considers the important relationship between humans and nature. The wall is symbolic of the separation between them. Beyond the wall the couple looks at "the way they must not go" (line 10). Although humans and nature are separate, they are also equal and in balance. These qualities are suggested by the title as well as by the actions of both couples as they observe each other in a nonthreatening way. The third-person point of view contributes to this balance in that the story is narrated by an outside observer rather than a participant. One possible theme of the poem, therefore, is the balance and equality between humans and nature.

As you read the following poem, "Filling Station," by Elizabeth Bishop, use the guidelines on pages 775 to 776 and the questions in the box on page 777 to help you analyze its elements and discover its meaning. You may choose to write an analysis of this poem in response to the Guided Writing Assignment on page 782.

Filling Station
Elizabeth Bishop

Elizabeth Bishop (1911–1979) is an American poet who traveled most of her life. Much of her poetry recounts the places she visits and the intimate details of everyday things. She published several collections of poems, including North and South *(1946);* Poems: North and South—A Cold Spring *(1956), for which she was awarded a Pulitzer Prize;* Questions of Travel *(1965);* The Complete Poems *(1969), for which she received the National Book Award; and* Geography III *(1976). The following poem was originally published in* Questions of Travel. *As you read, respond to the poem by making notes in the margin.*

Oh, but it is dirty!
—this little filling station,
oil-soaked, oil-permeated
to a disturbing, over-all
black translucency,   5
Be careful with that match!

Father wears a dirty,
oil-soaked monkey suit
that cuts him under the arms,
and several quick and saucy   10
and greasy sons assist him

(it's a family filling station),
all quite thoroughly dirty.

Do they live in the station?
It has a cement porch   15
behind the pumps, and on it
a set of crushed and grease-
impregnated wickerwork;
on the wicker sofa
a dirty dog, quite comfy.   20

Some comic books provide
the only note of color—
of certain color. They lie
upon a big dim doily
draping a taboret*   25
(part of the set), beside
a big hirsute begonia.

Why the extraneous plant?
Why the taboret?
Why, oh why, the doily?   30
(Embroidered in daisy stitch
with marguerites, I think,
and heavy with gray crochet.)

Somebody embroidered the doily.
Somebody waters the plant,   35
or oils it, maybe. Somebody
arranges the rows of cans
so that they softly say:
ESSO**—SO—SO—SO

to high-strung automobiles.   40
Somebody loves us all.

---

taboret: low cylindrical stool
**ESSO:* The mid-twentieth-century name for a petroleum products company that began in the late nineteenth century as Standard Oil Trust and continues today as ExxonMobil.

Now that you have a better understanding of the elements of poetry and short stories, you are ready to write about a literary work. In English and humanities courses, you will often be asked to read and analyze works of literature and then write literary analyses. The following sections will discuss this type of essay and take you step by step through a Guided Writing Assignment.

WHAT IS LITERARY ANALYSIS?

A **literary analysis** essay, sometimes called *literary criticism* or a *critique,* analyzes and interprets one or more aspects of a literary work. As with other types of essays, writing a literary analysis involves generating ideas through prewriting, developing a thesis, collecting supporting evidence, organizing and drafting, analyzing and revising, and editing and proofreading.

Keep in mind that a literary analysis does *not* merely summarize the work; rather, it focuses on *analysis* and *interpretation* of the work. Therefore, in a literary analysis, you take a position on some aspect of the work and support your position with evidence. In other words, you assume the role of a critic, in much the same way that a film critic argues for his or her judgment of a film rather than simply reporting its plot. For this chapter's assignment, your literary analysis should focus on *one* element of the work, even though some literary analyses cover multiple elements or more than one work.

Characteristics of Literary Analysis

A literary analysis has the following characteristics.

- It makes a point about one or more elements of a literary work.
- It includes and accurately documents evidence from the work. (It may also include evidence from outside sources.)
- It assumes that the audience is somewhat familiar with the work but not as familiar as the writer of the analysis.
- It has a serious tone and is written in the present tense.

A GUIDED WRITING ASSIGNMENT

The following guide will help you write a literary analysis of a poem or short story. Depending on your learning style, you may find some of the suggested strategies more suitable than others. Social or verbal learners, for instance, may prefer to generate ideas about the poem or short story through discussion with classmates. Spatial or creative learners may decide to draw a character map. Independent or concrete learners may choose to draw a time line or write a summary. This Guided Writing Assignment will provide you with alternatives.

The Assignment

Write a literary analysis of a poem or short story. Choose one of the following works reprinted in this chapter, a work you select on your own, or a work assigned by your instructor. Your classmates are your audience.

1. Gwendolyn Brooks, "The Bean Eaters" (p. 758)
2. Alberto Ríos, "The Secret Lion" (p. 764)
3. Kate Chopin, "The Story of an Hour" (p. 773)
4. Robert Frost, "Two Look at Two" (p. 777)
5. Elizabeth Bishop, "Filling Station" (p. 779)

For more on illustration, comparison and contrast, and cause and effect, see Chapters 10, 12, and 15.

As you develop your literary analysis essay, you will probably use one or more patterns of development. You will use illustration, for instance, to cite examples from the poem or short story that support your analysis of it. In addition, you might compare or contrast two main characters or analyze a plot by discussing causes and effects.

Generating Ideas

The following guidelines will help you explore the short story or poem you have selected and generate ideas for writing about it.

Learning Style Options

For more on annotating, see Chapter 2, p. 32.

1. **Highlight and annotate as you read.** Record your initial impressions and responses to the work in marginal annotations as you read. For recording lengthy comments, use a separate sheet of paper. Look for and highlight figures of speech, symbols, revealing character descriptions, striking dialogue, and the like. Here is a sample annotated portion of Frost's "Two Look at Two."

SAMPLE ANNOTATED PASSAGE

Love and forgetting might have carried them
A little further up the mountain side
With night so near, but not much further up.   ← limitations of humans
They must have halted soon in any case
With thoughts of the path back, how rough it was   ← road of life? difficulty of life
With rock and washout, and unsafe in darkness;
When they were halted by a tumbled wall   ← separates man and nature — Why is it tumbled?
With barbed-wire binding. They stood facing this,   ← sharp, penetrating
Spending what onward impulse they still had
In one last look the way they must not go,   ← prohibited from crossing

ROBERT FROST, "Two Look at Two"

2. **Discuss the literary work with classmates.** Discussing the short story or poem with others will help you generate ideas about it. Plan your discussion, moving from the general meaning of the work to a more specific paragraph-by-paragraph or line-by-line examination. Then consider your interpretation of the work's theme.

3. **Write a summary.** Especially when you draw a blank about a work, try writing a summary of it in your own words. You may find yourself raising and answering questions about the work as you summarize it. Jot down ideas as they occur to you, either on your summary page or a separate sheet of paper.

For more on writing a summary, see Chapter 2, p. 42.

4. **Draw a time line.** For a short story, especially one with a complex plot that flashes back or forward in time, draw a time line of the action in chronological sequence on paper or a computer. Here is a sample time line for Ríos's "The Secret Lion."

Sample Time Line: "The Secret Lion"

Age 5 ——————→ Main character moves three miles north of Nogales.

First half of summer ——→ He visits the arroyo with Sergio; goes swimming, mother suspects.

Second half of summer ——→ Boys visit mountains; think they have found heaven but learn it is a golf course.

They return to the arroyo; try to have fun.

Age 12 (junior high school) ——→ They visit the arroyo.

They shout dirty words and yell about girls.

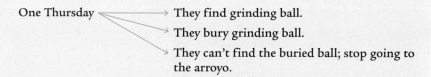

One Thursday → They find grinding ball.
→ They bury grinding ball.
→ They can't find the buried ball; stop going to the arroyo.

5. **Draw a character map.** To explore the connections and interactions among the characters in a story, draw a character map. In the center of a blank piece of paper, put a main character's name inside a circle. Then add other characters' names, connecting them with lines to the main character. On the connecting lines, briefly describe the relationships between characters and the events or other factors (such as emotions) that affect their relationship. You might use a drawing or symbol to represent some aspect of a character or relationship (for instance, *$* for "wealthy" or a smiley face for "happy"). Here is a sample character map for Ríos's "The Secret Lion."

Sample Character Map: "The Secret Lion"

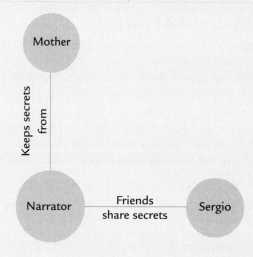

For more on finding sources, see Chapter 19.

6. **Investigate the background of the work and author.** Research the historical context of the work and biographical information about the author. Look for connections among the work, the author's life, and the social, economic, and political events of the time. Investigating the background of a work and its author can give you valuable insights into the writer's meaning (or theme) and purpose. For example, an interpretation of Charles Dickens's "A Christmas Carol" might be

more meaningful if you understood how the author's difficult childhood and the conditions of the poor in nineteenth-century England contributed to his portrayal of the Cratchit family.

7. **Use a two-column response journal.** Divide several pages of your journal into two vertical columns. Label the left column *Text* and the right column *Response.* In the left column, record five to ten quotations from the poem or short story. Choose only quotations that convey a main point or opinion, reveal a character's motives, or say something important about the plot or theme. In the right column, describe your reaction to each quotation. You might interpret, disagree with, or question the quotation. Try to comment on the language of the quotation and to relate it to other quotations or elements in the work. Here is a sample two-column journal response to Frost's "Two Look at Two."

For more on journal writing, see Chapter 1, p. 7, and Chapter 2, p. 48.

Sample Two-Column Response to "Two Look at Two"

Text	Response
"With thoughts of the path back, how rough it was" (line 5)	The couple's past has been difficult; returning to daily life may be difficult, too. Nature is rough and challenging.
"'This is all,' they sighed, / 'Good-night to woods.'" (lines 13–14)	The couple will soon come to the end—of their relationship or their lives.

8. **Discover parallel works or situations.** You can often evoke a response to a work by comparing it to other literary works, another narrative form (such as a film or television show), or a familiar situation. For example, after reading the poem "On His Blindness" by John Milton, one student connected it to the movie *Scent of a Woman,* in which one central character is blind. By comparing the literary work to the more familiar film, the student was better able to analyze the meaning of the poem.

9. **Use prewriting.** Prewriting helps you generate ideas for all types of essays, including a literary analysis. Try freewriting, brainstorming, sketching, questioning, or any of the other prewriting strategies discussed in Chapter 3.

ESSAY IN PROGRESS 1

Use one or more of the preceding techniques to generate ideas about the short story or poem you've chosen for your analysis.

Evaluating Your Ideas

Once you generate sufficient ideas about the work, begin your evaluation by reviewing your notes and prewriting. Look for a perspective or position that reflects your understanding of some aspect of the work. Here are several possible approaches you might take in a literary analysis.

1. **Evaluate symbolism.** Discuss how the author's use of images and symbols creates a particular mood and contributes to the overall meaning of the work.

2. **Analyze conflicts.** Focus on their causes, effects, or both.

3. **Evaluate characterization.** Discuss how characters are presented, whether a particular character's actions are realistic or predictable, or what the author reveals or hides about a character.

4. **Interpret characters or relationships among them.** Analyze how the true nature of a character is revealed or how a character changes in response to circumstances.

5. **Explore themes.** Discover the important point or theme the work conveys and back up your ideas with examples from the work.

Developing Your Thesis

After evaluating your ideas and choosing an aspect of the work to focus on, it is time to write a thesis statement. Your thesis should indicate the element of the work you will analyze (its theme, characters, or use of symbols, for example) and state the main point you will make about that element, as in the following sample thesis statements.

- Flannery O'Connor's short story "A Good Man Is Hard to Find" uses color to depict various moods throughout the story.

- In Susan Glaspell's play *Trifles,* the female characters are treated condescendingly by the males, and yet the women's interest in so-called trivial matters leads them to interpret the "trivial" pieces of evidence that solve the murder mystery.

Be sure your thesis statement focuses on your interpretation of one specific aspect of the work. As in other types of essays, the thesis for a literary analysis should identify your narrowed topic.

For more on thesis statements, see Chapter 4, p. 89.

ESSAY IN PROGRESS 2

Using the preceding guidelines, write a working thesis for your literary analysis essay. Then review the poem or short story and your notes to make sure you have enough evidence to support your thesis. In the body paragraphs of your essay, you will need to cite examples from the work that show why your thesis is valid. You might, for example, include relevant descriptions of characters or events, snippets of dialogue, examples of imagery and figures of speech, or any other details from the work that confirm or explain your thesis.

As you review the work and your notes about it, try to meet with one or two classmates who are working on the same poem or short story. They may have noticed evidence that you have overlooked or offer insights into the work that enrich your own reading of it. No two readers will have the same interpretation of a literary work, however, so don't be alarmed if their ideas differ from yours.

TRYING OUT YOUR IDEAS ON OTHERS

Working in a group of two or three students, discuss each other's thesis and supporting evidence for this chapter's assignment. Encourage your peers to ask questions about your work and suggest improvements.

ESSAY IN PROGRESS 3

Use your own analysis and the feedback you received from peer reviewers to evaluate your thesis and supporting evidence. Gather additional examples from the work if necessary and delete any examples that do not support your thesis.

Organizing and Drafting

Use the following guidelines to organize and draft your literary analysis.

1. **Choose a method of organization.** See Chapter 5 for more detailed suggestions about organizing an essay.

2. **Focus your essay on ideas and not on events.** Remember that your literary analysis should not merely summarize the work or the plot. Instead, focus on your ideas and interpretations.

3. **Write in the present tense.** Treat the events in the work as if they are happening now rather than in the past. For example, write "Brooks describes an elderly couple . . . ," *not* "Brooks described. . . ."

For help with citing examples from a literary work, see Chapter 20, p. 719.

4. **Include sufficient examples from the work and cite them correctly.** Use enough examples to support your thesis but not so many that your essay becomes one long string of examples with no clear main point. In addition, provide in-text citations (including paragraph or page numbers for a short story or line numbers for a poem) in parentheses immediately after any quotations from the work. Include a works-cited entry at the end of your paper indicating the edition of the work you used.

5. **Write an effective introduction.** The introduction for a literary analysis should engage readers, name the author and title of the work, present your thesis, and suggest why your analysis of the work is useful or important. For example, to engage your readers' interest, you might include a meaningful quotation from the work, comment on the universality of a character or theme, or briefly state your response to the work.

For more on writing effective introductions and conclusions, see Chapter 5, p. 131.

6. **Write a satisfying conclusion.** To conclude your essay, you can use techniques similar to those just described for introductions. Your purposes are to give the essay a sense of closure as well as to reaffirm your thesis. You may want to tie your conclusion directly to your introduction, offering a final word or comment on your main point.

ESSAY IN PROGRESS 4

Using the preceding guidelines for organizing and drafting and the thesis you developed in Essay in Progress 2 (p. 787), draft your literary analysis essay.

Analyzing and Revising

If possible, set aside your draft for a day or two before rereading and revising it. Then, as you reread your draft, concentrate on your ideas and organization, not on grammar or mechanics. Use Figure 21.1 to guide your evaluation. You might also ask a classmate to review your draft by using the questions in the flowchart.

For more on the benefits of peer review, see Chapter 6, p. 155.

FIGURE 21.1
FLOWCHART FOR REVISING A LITERARY ANALYSIS ESSAY

Questions		Revision Strategies
1. Highlight your thesis statement. Does it identify the work, the one aspect of it you are analyzing, and the main point of your analysis?	**No**	• Revise your thesis so that all of these items are included. • Ask a classmate to read your thesis and convey his or her understanding of your main point.
Yes		
2. Place a checkmark (✔) by the evidence from the literary work that supports your thesis. Is your evidence relevant to the one aspect of the work you identify in your thesis?	**No**	• Delete examples that do not support your thesis or that might be confusing to readers. • Include relevant quotations.
Yes		
3. Place [brackets] around each quotation from the work. Do you include in-text citations or line numbers for each?	**No**	• Add in-text citations where they are required. • Give a works-cited entry for the edition of the work used at the end of the essay.
Yes		

(Continued on next page)

FIGURE 21.1 *(Continued)*

Questions		Revision Strategies

4. *Write* a sentence describing your audience. Do you assume that the audience is less familiar with the work than you are?

No →

- Assume your readers have only limited knowledge of the work and have read it only once or twice.
- Provide information (about the author, plot, characters, and so on) that your readers will need to understand your analysis of the work.

Yes

5. (Circle) each verb. Have you used the present tense consistently throughout?

No →

- When writing about events in the work, maintain the present tense unless you are writing about an event that preceded another event in the story.

Yes

6. Place an *X* next to words that reveal your feelings or judgments about the work. Does your tone suggest a serious, objective view of the work?

No →

- Eliminate any overly critical or enthusiastic statements.

Yes

7. Underline the topic sentence of each paragraph. Does each paragraph focus on one main point or idea? Does each topic sentence relate to your thesis?

No →

- Be sure each body paragraph has a topic sentence (see Chapter 5) and supporting evidence from the work.
- Consider combining closely related paragraphs.
- Split paragraphs that cover two or more main points or ideas.

Yes

(Continued on next page)

FIGURE 21.1 *(Continued)*

Questions	Revision Strategies
8. Draw a box around your introduction and conclusion. Does the introduction suggest the importance of your thesis and engage your readers' interest? Is your conclusion satisfying? **No**	• Begin and end your essay with a meaningful quotation or brief statement about a character, a theme, or your response to the work. • Ask yourself, "Why would my audience be interested in my thesis?" Incorporate the answer into your introduction. • Revise your introduction and conclusion so that they meet the guidelines covered in Chapter 5 (pp. 131–36).

ESSAY IN PROGRESS 5

Revise your draft essay using Figure 21.1 and the comments you received from peer reviewers.

Editing and Proofreading

The last step is to check your revised essay for errors in grammar, spelling, punctuation, and mechanics. In addition, be sure to check your error log for the types of errors you tend to make.

For more on keeping an error log, see Chapter 7, p. 193.

As you edit and proofread your literary analysis, watch out for the following errors that are often found in this type of writing.

1. **Use the literary present tense.** Even though the poem or short story was written in the past, as a general rule you should write about the events in it and the author's writing of it as if they were happening in the present. This is called the *literary present tense.* An exception to this rule occurs when you are referring to a time earlier than that in which the narrator speaks, in which case a switch to the past tense is appropriate.

> *refers*
> ▶ Keats in "Ode on a Grecian Urn" ~~referred~~ to the urn as a "silent form"
> (line 44).

> ▶ In "Two Look at Two," it is not clear why the couple *decided* to walk up
> the mountainside path.

The couple made the decision before the action in the poem began.

2. **Punctuate quotations correctly.** Direct quotations from a literary work, whether spoken or written, must be placed in quotation marks. Omitted material is marked by an ellipsis mark. The lines of a poem are separated by a slash (/).

> ▶ In "Two Look at Two," Frost concludes that the earth in one unlooked-for
>   "
> favor / Had made them certain earth returned their love (lines 41–42).
>   "

Periods and commas appear within quotation marks. Question marks and exclamation points go within or outside of quotation marks, depending on the meaning of the sentence. Here the question mark goes inside the closing quotation marks because it is part of Frost's poem (line 32). Notice, too, that double and single quote marks are required for a quotation within a quotation.

> ▶ The buck seems "to ask, 'Why don't you make some motion'"? (line 32).
>   ?

! **ESSAY IN PROGRESS 6**
!
! Edit and proofread your literary analysis essay, paying particular attention to
! verb tense and punctuation of quotations.

STUDENTS WRITE

Andrew Decker was a student at Niagara County Community College when he wrote the following literary analysis of Ríos's "The Secret Lion" in response to an assignment in his first-year writing class. As you read the essay, identify the one aspect of the literary work that Decker focuses on. Also underline or highlight his thesis and the evidence he uses to support it.

The Keeping of "The Secret Lion"
Andrew Decker

Alberto Ríos's "The Secret Lion" charts the initiation of a young boy into adolescence. During this climactic period of growth, the narrator experiences several shifts in perception that change him from a child to an adolescent by teaching him the value of secrets.

Within the first paragraph, the author introduces the reader to the new and perplexing feelings of the main character during his junior high years. His impression of what happened during those years remains nameless, "but it was there nonetheless like a lion, and roaring, roaring that way the biggest things do. Everything changed. Just that" (paragraph 1). It is as if the boy is being swept away by a great swell, the wave of anticipation traditionally associated with the child's entry into adolescence.

He finds that these changes are confusing and yet enticing. Evident within the context of the first page is the boy's newfound curiosity about and fascination with the opposite sex. He is also bewildered by the use of profanity and delights in the opportunity to verbally (and very loudly) explore his own feelings with respect to the use of such words.

Although adults scold him when he questions them about the meaning of these words, their dismay does not discourage him from saying the words privately. He and his friend Sergio like to hide away from such authoritarian voices, and so they cross the highway to the arroyo where they are not supposed to play. In the arroyo, they "shout every dirty word we could think of, in every combination we could come up with, and we would yell about girls, and all the things we wanted to do with them, as loud as we could" (4). Of course, they take great pleasure in this youthful audacity for "it just felt good and for the first time in our lives there was nobody to tell us we couldn't" (4). All is new. All is fresh. Opportunity abounds, and possibilities remain infinite, for time has not yet become an enemy.

5   One day when the two boys are playing and cussing in the arroyo, they find a perfectly round iron ball. It is heavy and smooth and to them it is the perfect object. In the eyes of the two children, the world is formless and pure, as is the ball. Similarly, they consider the arroyo to be the perfect place--their perfect place. When faced with deciding what to do with the ball, they choose to bury it so that nobody can take it away--if only in a less literal sense.

6   Their minds are still free of the narrow vision of an adult. They are free to roam and roar and echo the spirit of the lion, which is for Sergio and the narrator the spirit of that time. In their own words, when they talk of that ball, they speak of "how much that ball was like that place, that whole arroyo: couldn't tell anybody about it, didn't understand what it was, didn't have a name for it. It just felt good. It was just perfect in the way it was that place, that whole going to that place, that whole junior high school lion" (8). They know that once they bury the grinding ball (they only learn later what it is), it will be gone forever and yet thereby preserved.

7   The two boys are applying a lesson they have already learned. They understand that an experience can be stolen or changed by a shift in perception so that the original feeling, the original reality, ceases to exist in its more pure and innocent form. The boys had experienced disillusion before; when they were very young, they had also played in the arroyo and gone swimming in the stream. It was a time of naiveté, but their naiveté had been challenged when they learned that the water was at times filled with the waste flushed downstream by a local sewage plant.

8   Another shift in perception happened later that same summer, when the boys think they have found a new haven beyond some small hills near their houses. On the other side of a hill they find a green clearing, and they declare its lush beauty their "heaven." They learn, however, that this heaven is merely a product of their

unworldly imagination; the boys have youthfully glorified
a simple golf course, in which they were unwelcome visitors.

These events and others teach the boys to protect   9
a new experience, to keep new feelings safe and virginal
so as not to lose them to the ravages of time and change.
When they return to the arroyo several years later, when
they are twelve and experiencing the exuberance and
excitement of adolescence, they know enough not to share
or expose their experiences. The grinding ball is a symbol of that age, that sense of newness, and as they
say, "when we buried it we knew what would happen" (27).
Burying the ball is an attempt on their part to crystal-
lize a certain time, a certain perception, "because it
was perfect" (28). "It was the lion," and the lion was
the "roaring" of both that time and that place, and they
bury it so that it might never truly be lost.

Work Cited

Ríos, Alberto. "The Secret Lion." The Iguana Killer:
     Twelve Stories of the Heart. Lewiston: Blue Moon,
     1984.

Analyzing the Essay

1. What one element of "The Secret Lion" does Decker address?
2. Evaluate Decker's thesis statement. Does it indicate the element he analyzes and make a point about that element?
3. Does Decker provide sufficient evidence to support his thesis? Choose one example Decker offers and evaluate its effectiveness.
4. Evaluate Decker's introduction and conclusion. In what ways could they be improved?
5. Which paragraphs are particularly well developed? Which, if any, need further development?

Reacting to the Essay: Discussion and Journal Writing

1. How does Decker's interpretation of "The Secret Lion" compare with yours?
2. Evaluate Decker's perception of childhood and adolescence. Write a journal entry comparing his perception to your own.

"ALTHOUGH HUMANS MAKE SOUNDS WITH THEIR MOUTHS AND OCCASIONALLY LOOK AT EACH OTHER, THERE IS NO SOLID EVIDENCE THAT THEY ACTUALLY COMMUNICATE WITH EACH OTHER."

Essay Examinations, Timed Writings, and Portfolios

CHAPTER QUICK START

Suppose you have to take a short timed writing test. You have to write about one of the images on the opposite page. Assume that your grade on the test will influence your grade in the writing course.

Writing Quick Start

Choose one of the images and write a paragraph that either explains your reaction to the photograph or interprets the meaning of the cartoon. You have fifteen minutes to complete the writing test.

In completing the timed writing test, did you feel pressured by the fifteen-minute limit? How did you decide which assignment to complete? Did you have as much time as you would have liked to organize, plan, develop, and revise your ideas? Probably not.

Many college instructors use timed writings, essay exams, or portfolios to assess students' knowledge and writing ability. As you progress through college, you will be required to take many essay exams, especially in advanced courses. In other courses you may be asked to collect and present samples of your work in a portfolio. In the workplace, too, you may be asked to produce a memo, report, or proposal and have it on your supervisor's desk "by five o'clock." See the accompanying box for a few examples of writing assessment.

You may ask, "Why do instructors give essay exams and other kinds of timed writing assignments?" In many college courses, essay exams allow instructors to determine how well students have grasped important concepts and whether they can organize and integrate key concepts with other material. In addition, instructors realize that an essay exam requires students to use different and more advanced thinking skills than they use when taking a more objective type of exam, such as a multiple-choice test. For instance, an essay exam for a history course would require you to pull ideas together and focus on larger issues, perhaps analyzing historical trends or making comparisons between two political figures. Timed writing assignments serve a similar purpose in a composition course. When you are given forty-five minutes to write a brief process analysis of something you know how to do, a short comparison of two television shows, or a description of someone you admire, your instructor wants to make sure you are learning how to write various types of essays and can do so quickly and efficiently. Finally, some colleges require students to demonstrate their writing expertise in a competency test given shortly after admission to the college, at the end of a writing course, or at the completion of a program of study.

This section will help you prepare for the timed essay writings you will encounter in college and in your career. Developing good study skills is a key to success on such exams. You will learn how to anticipate the types of questions

---

SCENES FROM COLLEGE AND THE WORKPLACE

- For a *business communication* class, you are asked to assemble a portfolio that illustrates your mastery of the six course objectives.

- For the midterm exam in your *philosophy of religion* course, you have one hour to complete the following essay: "Contrast the beliefs of Islam with those of either Judaism or Christianity."

- As the *sales manager* of an auto parts store, you are required to write an evaluation of two sales trainees and to fax your report to national headquarters by noon that day.

instructors ask, how to organize your ideas quickly and efficiently, and how to work within the time constraints of essay exams. Although the chapter focuses on essay exams, the skills you learn here also apply to other kinds of timed writing assignments. You will also learn how to create a writing portfolio and write a reflective essay that introduces it.

ESSAY EXAMINATIONS

PREPARING FOR ESSAY EXAMS

Because essay exams require you to produce a written response, the best way to prepare for them is by organizing and writing. The following guidelines will help you prepare for such exams.

Write Study Sheets That Synthesize Information

Most essay exams require you to *synthesize* or pull together information. To prepare for this task, try to identify the key topics in a course and write a study sheet for each main topic. Study sheets help you organize and consolidate complex or detailed information and give you brief topic outlines to study. To prepare a study sheet, draw on information from your textbook as well as from your class notes, in-class handouts, papers (note key topics), previous exams (look for emphasized topics), and assigned readings.

For more on synthesizing information, see Chapter 20, p. 697.

You can organize a study sheet in a variety of ways. For example, you might draw a graphic organizer to create a visual study sheet, create a time line to connect historical events, write an outline to organize information, or construct a comparison and contrast chart to see relationships between different topics. Whatever method of organization you use for your study sheet, be sure to include key information about topics: definitions, facts, principles, theories, events, research studies, and the like.

Here is part of one student's study sheet for a speech communication course on the topic *audience analysis*.

SAMPLE STUDY SHEET

Topic: Audience Analysis

1. Demographic characteristics
   — Age and gender
   — Educational background (type and level of education)
   — Group membership (people who share similar interests or goals)

——Social activities
——Religious activities
——Hobbies and sports

2. Psychological characteristics
   ——Beliefs (about what is true or false, right or wrong)
   ——Attitudes (positive or negative)
   ——Values (standards for judging worth of thoughts and actions)

EXERCISE 22.1

Use the preceding guidelines to prepare a study sheet on a general topic that you expect will be covered on an upcoming exam in one of your courses.

Predict Essay Exam Questions

Once you prepare study sheets for a particular course, the next step is to predict questions that might be asked on an essay exam. Although essay exam questions usually focus on general topics, themes, or patterns, you will probably need to supply details in your response. For example, an essay question on an economics exam might ask you to compare and contrast the James-Lange and Cannon-Bard theories of motivation. Your answer would focus on the similarities and differences between these key theories, incorporating relevant details where necessary.

Use the following strategies to help you predict the types of questions you might be asked on an essay exam.

1. **Group topics into categories.** Review your textbook, class notes, and study sheets. Look to see how you can group topics into general subject areas or categories. For example, if you find several chapters that deal with kinship in your anthropology textbook, a question on kinship is likely to appear on one or more essay exams for the course.

2. **Study your course syllabus and objectives.** These documents contain important clues about what your instructor expects you to know at various points during the course.

3. **Study previous exams.** Notice which key ideas are emphasized in previous exams. If you had to explain the historical significance of the Boston Tea Party on your first American history exam, you can predict that you will be asked to explain the historical significance of other events on subsequent exams.

4. **Listen to your instructor's comments.** When your instructor announces or reviews material for an upcoming essay exam, pay close attention to what is said. He or she may reveal key topics or suggest areas that will be emphasized on the test.

5. **Draft some possible essay questions.** Use Table 22.1 (on p. 805) to help you draft possible essay questions using key verbs. The verb in a question affects the way

you answer it. It takes time to learn how to predict exam questions, so don't get discouraged if at first you predict only one question correctly. Even if you predict none of the questions, the attempt to do so will help you to learn the material.

EXERCISE 22.2

Suppose your business marketing textbook includes a chapter with the following headings. Using the preceding guidelines for predicting essay exam questions and the key verbs in Table 22.1 (p. 805), write three possible questions that the course instructor might ask about the chapter material.

Textbook: *Marketing*, by William G. Nickels and Marian Burk Wood
Chapter: "Consumer Buying Behavior"
Headings:
    Marketing, Relationships, and Consumer Behavior
        Real People, Real Individuals
        Consumers as Moving Targets
    How Consumers Buy
        The Need-Recognition Stage
        The Information-Seeking Stage
        The Evaluation Stage
        The Purchase Stage
        The Postpurchase Evaluation Stage
        Involvement and the Purchase-Decision Process
    External Influences on Consumer Behavior
        Family and Household Influences
        Opinion Leaders and Word of Mouth
        Reference Groups
        Social Class
        Culture, Subculture, and Core Values
        Situational Influences
    Internal Influences on Consumer Behavior
        Perception
        Motivation
        Attitudes

ESSAY IN PROGRESS 1

For an upcoming essay exam in one of your courses, predict and write at least three possible questions your instructor might ask about the course material.

Draft Answers in Outline Form

Once you predict several possible essay exam questions, the next step is to write a brief, rough outline of the information that answers each question. Be sure each outline responds to the *wording* of the question; that is, it should *explain, compare, describe,* or do whatever else the question asks (see Table 22.1 on p. 805). Writing a rough outline will strengthen your recall of the material. It will also save you time during the actual exam because you will have already spent some time thinking about, organizing, and writing about the material.

Here is a sample essay question and an informal outline written in response to it.

ESSAY QUESTION

Explain the ways in which material passes in and out of cells by crossing plasma membranes.

INFORMAL OUTLINE

Types of Transport

1. Passive — no use of cellular energy; random movement of molecules
   a. Diffusion — movement of molecules from areas of high concentration to areas of low concentration (example: open bottle of perfume, aroma spreads)
   b. Facilitated diffusion — similar to simple diffusion; differs in that some kinds of molecules are moved more easily than others (helped by carrier proteins in cell membrane)
   c. Osmosis — diffusion of water across membranes from area of lower to area of higher solute concentration

2. Active — requires cellular energy; usually movement against the concentration gradient
   a. Facilitated active transport — carrier molecules move ions across a membrane
   b. Endocytosis — material is surrounded by a plasma membrane and pinched off into a vacuole
   c. Exocytosis — cells expel materials

ESSAY IN PROGRESS 2

For one of the questions you predicted in Essay in Progress 1, prepare a brief informal outline in response to the question.

Reduce Informal Outlines to Key-Word Outlines

To help you recall your outline answer at the time of the exam, reduce it to a brief key-word outline or list of key topics. Here is a sample key-word outline for the essay question about cells.

KEY-WORD OUTLINE

Types of Transport

1. Passive
    —Diffusion
    —Facilitated diffusion
    —Osmosis

2. Active
    —Facilitated active transport
    —Endocytosis
    —Exocytosis

ESSAY IN PROGRESS 3

Reduce the outline answer you wrote in Essay in Progress 2 to a key-word outline.

TAKING ESSAY EXAMS

Once you have done some preparation, you should be more confident about taking an essay exam. Although the time limit for an essay exam may make you feel somewhat pressured, remember that your classmates are working under the same conditions.

Some General Guidelines

Keep the following general guidelines in mind when you take essay exams.

1. **Arrive at the room where the exam is to be given a few minutes early.** You can use this time to collect your thoughts and get organized.

2. **Sit in the front of the room.** You will be less distracted and better able to see and hear the instructor as last-minute directions or corrections are announced.

3. **Read the directions carefully.** For example, some exams may direct you to answer only one of three questions, whereas other exams may ask you to answer all questions.

4. **Preview the exam and plan your time carefully.** Get a complete picture of the task at hand and then plan how you will complete the exam within the allotted time. For example, if you are given fifty minutes to complete an essay exam, spend roughly ten minutes planning, thirty minutes writing, and ten minutes editing, proofreading, and making last-minute changes. If an exam contains

both objective and essay questions, do the objective questions first so you have the remaining time to concentrate on the essay questions.

5. **Notice the point value of each question.** If your instructor assigns points to each question, use the point values to plan your time. For example, you would spend more time answering a thirty-point question than one worth ten points.

6. **Choose topics or questions carefully.** Often you will be given little or no choice of topic or question. If you do have a choice, choose the topics or answer the questions that you know the most about. If you are given a broad topic, such as a current social issue, narrow the topic to one you can write about in the specified amount of time.

7. **Answer the easiest question first.** Answering the easiest question first will boost your confidence and allow you to spend the remaining time working on the more difficult questions.

8. **Consider your audience and purpose.** For most essay exams, your instructor is your audience. Since your instructor is already knowledgeable about the topic, your purpose is to demonstrate what *you know* about the topic. Therefore, you should write thorough and complete answers, pretending that your instructor knows only what you tell him or her.

9. **Remember that your first draft is your final draft.** Plan on writing your first draft carefully and correctly so that it can serve as your final copy. You can always make minor changes and additions as you write or while you edit and proofread.

10. **Plan and organize your answer.** Because time is limited, your first response may be to start writing immediately. However, planning and organizing are especially important first steps because you will not have the opportunity to revise your essay. (If you usually write whatever comes to mind and then spend a great deal of time revising, you will need to modify your approach for essay exams.) Begin by writing a brief thesis statement. Then jot down the key supporting points and number them in the order you will present them. Leave space under each supporting point for your details. If the question is one you predicted earlier, write down your key-word outline. If an idea for an interesting introduction or an effective conclusion comes to mind, jot it down as well. As you write your answers, be sure to reserve enough time to reread your essay and correct surface errors.

Analyzing Essay Exam Questions

Essay exam questions are often concise, but if you read them closely, you will find that they *do* tell you specifically what to write about. Consider the following sample essay question from a sociology exam.

Choose a particular institution, define it, and identify its primary characteristics.

The question tells you exactly what to write about—*a particular institution*. In addition, the key verbs *define* and *identify* tell you how to approach the subject. For this essay question, then, you would give an accurate definition of an institution and discuss its primary characteristics.

Table 22.1 lists key verbs commonly used in essay exam questions along with sample questions and tips for answering them. As you study the list, notice that

TABLE 22.1
RESPONDING TO KEY VERBS IN ESSAY EXAM QUESTIONS

Key Verb	Sample Essay Question	Tips for Answering Questions
Compare	Compare the poetry of Judith Ortiz Cofer to that of Julia Alvarez.	Show how poems are similar as well as different; use details and examples.
Contrast	Contrast classical and operant conditioning.	Show how they are different; use details and examples.
Define	Define *biofeedback* and describe its uses.	Give an accurate explanation of the term with enough detail to demonstrate that you understand it.
Discuss	Discuss the halo effect and give examples of its use.	Consider important characteristics and main points; include examples.
Evaluate	Evaluate the accomplishments of the feminist movement over the past fifty years.	Assess its merits, strengths, weaknesses, advantages, or limitations.
Explain	Explain the functions of amino acids.	Use facts and details to make the topic or concept clear and understandable.
Illustrate	Illustrate with examples from your experience how culture shapes human behavior.	Use examples that demonstrate a point or clarify an idea.
Justify	Justify laws outlawing smoking in federal buildings.	Give reasons and evidence that support an action, decision, or policy.
List	List the advantages and disadvantages of sales promotions.	List or discuss one by one; use most-to-least or least-to-most organization.
Summarize	Summarize Maslow's hierarchy of needs.	Briefly review all the major points.
Trace	Trace the life cycle of a typical household product.	Describe its development or progress in chronological order.

many of the verbs suggest a particular pattern of development. For example, *trace* suggests using a narrative sequence, and *justify* suggests using argumentation. For a more vague key verb such as *explain* or *discuss,* you might use a combination of patterns.

Writing Essay Answers

Since your first-draft essay exam is also your final draft, be sure to write in complete and grammatically correct sentences, to supply sufficient detail, and to follow a logical organization. For essay exams, instructors do not expect your writing to be as polished as it might be for an essay or research paper assignment. It is acceptable to cross out words or sentences neatly and to indicate corrections in spelling or grammar. If you think of an idea to add, write the sentence at the top of your paper and draw an arrow to indicate where it should be inserted.

Essay exam answers tend to have brief introductions and conclusions. The introduction, for instance, may include only a thesis statement. If possible, include any necessary background information on the topic and write a conclusion only if the question seems to require a final evaluative statement.

If you run out of time on an essay exam, jot the unfinished portion of your outline at the end of the essay. Your instructor may give you partial credit for your ideas.

Writing Your Thesis Statement

For more on thesis statements, see Chapter 4.

Your thesis statement should be clear and direct, identify your subject, and suggest your approach to the topic. Often the thesis rephrases or answers the essay exam question. Consider the following examples.

Essay Exam Question	*Thesis Statement*
Explain how tides are produced in the earth's oceans. Account for seasonal variations.	The earth's gravitational forces are responsible for producing tides in the earth's oceans.
Distinguish between bureaucratic agencies and other government decision-making bodies.	Bureaucratic agencies are distinct from other government decision-making bodies because of their hierarchical organization, character and culture, and professionalism.

For some essay exam questions, your thesis should also suggest the organization of your essay. For example, if you are asked to explain the differences between primary and secondary groups, your thesis might be stated as follows: "Primary groups differ from secondary groups in their membership, purpose, level of interaction, and level of intimacy." Your essay, then, would be organized accordingly, discussing membership first, then purpose, and so forth.

EXERCISE 22.3

Write thesis statements for two of the following essay exam questions.

1. Define and illustrate the meaning of the term *freedom of the press.*
2. Distinguish between the medical care provided by private physicians and that provided by medical clinics.
3. Choose a recent television advertisement and describe its rational and emotional appeals.
4. Evaluate a current news program in terms of its breadth and depth of coverage, objectivity, and political and social viewpoints.

Developing Supporting Details

Write a separate paragraph for each of your key points. In an essay answer distinguishing primary from secondary groups, for example, you would devote one paragraph to each distinguishing feature: membership, purpose, level of interaction, and level of intimacy. The topic sentence for each paragraph should identify and briefly explain a key point. For example, a topic sentence for the first main point about groups might read like this: "Membership, or who belongs, is one factor that distinguishes primary from secondary groups." The rest of the paragraph would explain membership: what constitutes membership, what criteria are used to decide who belongs, and who decides. Whenever possible, supply examples to make it clear that you can apply the information you have learned. Keep in mind that on an essay exam your goal is to demonstrate your knowledge and understanding of the material.

For more on topic sentences, see Chapter 5, p. 118.

Rereading and Proofreading Your Answer

Be sure to leave enough time to reread and proofread your essay answer. Begin by rereading the question to make sure you have answered all parts of it. Then reread your answer, checking it first for content. Add missing information, correct vague or unclear sentences, and add facts or details. Next, proofread for errors in spelling, punctuation, and grammar. Before taking an essay exam, check your error log and then evaluate your answer with those errors in mind. A neat, nearly error-free essay makes a positive impression on your instructor and identifies you as a serious, conscientious student. An error-free essay may also improve your grade.

For more on proofreading and on keeping an error log, see Chapter 7, p. 193.

ESSAY IN PROGRESS 4

For the essay question you worked on in Essay in Progress 3, use the preceding guidelines to write a complete essay answer.

STUDENTS WRITE

The following model essay exam response was written by Ronald Robinson for his sociology course. As you read the student's essay, note that it has been annotated to identify key elements of its organization and content.

Essay Exam Response

ESSAY EXAM QUESTION

Distinguish between fads and fashions, explaining the characteristics of each type of group behavior and describing the phases each usually goes through.

Thesis statement

> Fashions and fads, types of collective group behavior, are distinct from one another in terms of their duration, their predictability, and the number of people involved. Each type follows a five-stage process of development.

Definition and characteristics of *fashion*

> A fashion is a temporary trend in behavior or appearance that is followed by a relatively large number of people. Although the word *fashion* often refers to a style of dress, there are fashions in music, art, and literature as well. Trends in clothing fashions are often engineered by clothing designers, advertisers, and the media to create a particular "look." The hip-hop look is an example of a heavily promoted fashion. Fashions are more universally subscribed to than fads. Wearing athletic shoes as casual attire is a good example of a universal fashion.

Definition and characteristics of *fad*

> A fad is a more temporary adoption of a particular behavior or look. Fads are in-group behaviors that often serve as identity markers for a group. Fads also tend to be adopted by smaller groups, often made up of people who want to appear different or unconventional. Unlike fashions, fads tend to be shorter-lived, less predictable, and less influenced by people outside the group. Examples of recent fads are bald heads, tattoos,

and tongue piercings. Fads are usually harmless and have
no long-range effects.

    Fashions and fads each follow a five-phase process
of development. In the first phase, latency, the trend
exists in the minds of a few people but shows little
evidence of spreading. In the second phase, the trend
spreads rapidly and reaches its peak. After that, the
trend begins a slow decline (phase three). In the fourth
phase, its newness is over and many users drop or abandon the trend. In its final phase, quiescence, nearly
everyone has dropped the trend, and it is followed by
only a few people.

Description of 5-phase process

THINKING CRITICALLY ABOUT ESSAY EXAMS

Read essay exam questions critically, approaching them from the viewpoint of the
instructor. Try to discover the knowledge or skill that your instructor is attempting to assess by asking the question. Then, as you write your answer, make sure
your response clearly demonstrates your knowledge or skill. For example, in posing the question "Discuss the issue of sexual behavior from the three major sociological perspectives," the instructor is assessing two things—how well you
understand the three sociological perspectives and *apply* them to a particular issue
(sexual behavior). You first would need to give a clear, complete, but brief definition of each perspective. Then you would explain how each of the three sociological perspectives approaches the issue of sexual behavior.

PORTFOLIOS

CREATING A WRITING PORTFOLIO

A portfolio is a collection of materials that is representative of a person's work. It
often demonstrates or exemplifies skill, talent, or proficiency. Architects create
portfolios that contain drawings and photographs of buildings they have
designed. Sculpturers' portfolios may include photographs of their work, as well as
copies of reviews, awards, or articles about the work. Similarly, your writing

instructor may ask you to create a portfolio that represents your skill and proficiency as a writer. Think of your portfolio as a picture of your development as a writer over time.

Purposes of a Writing Portfolio

Usually, a writing portfolio is assigned by your writing instructor to achieve one or more purposes. One purpose is assessment. Your instructor may use your collection of writing to evaluate your mastery of the objectives outlined in the course syllabus. That evaluation will become a part of your final grade in the course.

The second purpose is learning and self-assessment. Building a portfolio makes you think about yourself as a learner and as a writer. By building a writing portfolio, you can learn a great deal about the writing process, assess your strengths and weaknesses as a writer, and observe your own progress as you build writing proficiency. Think of building your writing portfolio as an opportunity to present yourself in the best possible way—highlighting the work you are proud of and demonstrating the skills you have mastered. It is also an opportunity, as you track your progress, to realize that your hard work in the course has paid off.

Deciding What to Include

Instructors often specify what their students' portfolios should include. If you are uncertain about what to include, be sure to ask your instructor for clarification. You might ask to see a sample of a portfolio that meets your instructor's expectations. Be sure you can answer each of the following questions.

- How many pieces of writing should I include? Are there limits?
- Should all writing done in the course be included, or am I allowed to choose what to include?
- What version should be included—drafts, outlines, and revisions or just the final essay?
- What types of writing should be included? Should essays be based on personal experience, library or Internet research, or field research?
- Is the portfolio limited to essays, or can research notes, downloaded Web pages, or completed class exercises be included?
- Can writing from other courses or pieces of writing for nonacademic audiences (email, work-related correspondence, or service learning projects, for example) be included?
- How should the portfolio be organized?
- What type of introductory letter or essay is required? What length and format are appropriate?

- How much does the portfolio count in my grade?
- What is the due date, or is the portfolio to be submitted at various intervals throughout the term?
- How will it be graded? That is, is the grade based on improvement or only on the quality of the work included?

Using Your Course Syllabus as a Guide

Your course syllabus is an important guide that can help you decide what to include in your portfolio, especially if your instructor has given you choices in structuring and organizing it. Your course syllabus contains objectives. These are statements of what your instructor expects you to learn from the course. You can use several or all of these to structure your portfolio. Suppose one objective states, "Students will develop prewriting strategies that accommodate their learning style." In your portfolio, then, you might include a copy of the results of the Learning Style Inventory (p. 10) and then show examples of your use of two or more prewriting strategies. If another objective states, "Students will demonstrate control over errors in sentence structure, spelling, and punctuation," you would want to include examples of essays in which you identified and corrected these types of errors. You might also include a copy of your error log and a list of exercises you completed using Exercise Central or other online resources.

For a sample syllabus, see Keys to Academic Success, p. l.

Organizing Your Portfolio

Begin collecting materials for your portfolio as soon as you know it is required. If you wait until the due date to assemble what you need, you may have discarded or misplaced important prewriting, revision materials, or drafts of essays.

Begin by deciding whether you will keep track of materials for your portfolio using printed copies or electronic copies. If you are using printed copies, use a file folder or accordion folder divided into sections to separate your work. Keep everything associated with each writing assignment you complete. This includes the original assignment, prewriting, outlines, graphic organizers, and all drafts. If you are using sources, keep your notes, photocopies, or printouts of sources. Be sure to keep peer-review comments, as well as papers with your instructor's comments.

If you are using an electronic system to collect materials for your portfolio, create a file system that will make it easy for you to locate all of your work. Be sure to make backup copies of your files on a disk or CD. Keep a paper file for hard copies of materials such as research notes or peer-review comments that are not on your computer.

Your portfolio represents you. Be sure it is neat, complete, and carefully assembled. Use the following suggestions to present a well-organized portfolio that demonstrates that you have taken care in its preparation.

- Include a cover or title page that gives your name, course number, instructor's name, and date.

- Include a table of contents that identifies the elements in the portfolio and the page number on which each piece begins. Number the portfolio consecutively from beginning to end. Since your essays may already have page numbers, put the new page numbers in a different position or use a different color of ink.

- Attach earlier drafts of papers behind the final draft, clearly labeling each draft.

- Be sure each piece is dated so your instructor can identify its place within your growth process.

- Label each piece, indicating what it is intended to demonstrate. For example, if an essay demonstrates your ability to use narration, be sure to label it as such.

- Plan the sequence of your portfolio. If your instructor has not expressed a preference, choose a method of organization that presents your work and skill development in the best possible way. If you are including two essays to demonstrate your effective use of narration, for example, you might present the better one first, thereby making the strongest possible first impression. If, on the other hand, you are trying to show the growth in your ability to use narration, you might present the weaker one first.

Choosing Pieces to Include

One key to creating a successful portfolio is choosing the *right* pieces to include, assuming that you have a choice. The right pieces depend on what your portfolio is intended to demonstrate. If you are supposed to demonstrate growth, it is a mistake to include only your best papers. If you are supposed to demonstrate your ability to write for a variety of purposes and audiences, it would be a mistake to include only argumentative essays. If the length is unlimited, do not include everything; be selective and choose pieces that illustrate what your instructor wants you to evaluate. Use Table 22.2 to guide your selection.

Writing the Introductory Letter or Essay

Most instructors expect you to include an essay or a letter that introduces your portfolio. It is often called a *reflective essay* or *letter* because in it you reflect on your development as a writer. This letter or essay is crucial to an effective portfolio, and

TABLE 22.2
GUIDELINES FOR BUILDING A WRITING PORTFOLIO

If You Are Asked To . . .	What to Include
Demonstrate your growth as a writer	• Include weak papers from early in the semester and conclude with your best papers written toward the end of the semester. • You might also include an essay that demonstrates major changes from first to final draft.
Demonstrate your ability to approach writing as a process	• For several essays, include work you did for topic selection, generating ideas, drafting, revising, and proof-reading. • Choose pieces that show your essay gradually developing and evolving as you worked; they should also show major changes in revised drafts. • Avoid pieces that were well developed in your early stages of writing and that required only final polishing.
Feature your best work of the semester	• Choose essays that solidly exemplify the method of organization you are using. • Use the revision flowcharts and the Evaluating Your Progress boxes in Chapters 8–15 and 17 to guide your selection.
Demonstrate your ability to write for a variety of audiences and purposes	• Review the section on audience and purpose in Chapter 3, p. 65. • Select pieces that are widely different. • Include non-course-related and nonacademic pieces, if allowed.
Demonstrate your ability to use library and Internet sources	• Review the appropriate sections of Chapters 18–20. • Choose an essay that uses both library and Internet sources, rather than only one.

you should spend a good amount of time composing it. In fact, you might begin thinking and making notes about it long before the portfolio is due, observing trends, problems, and patterns in your writing.

This essay is the key to the portfolio, since it reflects on and explains its contents. It should explain how your portfolio is organized and give an overview of what it includes. It also should explain *how* various items that you have placed in the portfolio demonstrate what you intend them to demonstrate. For example, if you have included two essays to illustrate your ability to write for a variety of audiences and purposes, then explain for whom and for what purpose each essay was written.

Your reflective letter may also include some or all of the following:

- An appraisal of what you have learned in the course, referring to specific materials included in the portfolio as evidence.

- A discussion of your strengths and weaknesses as a writer, again referring to portfolio materials that illustrate and explain your points.

- A discussion of your progress or development as a writer. Explain how you have changed, giving examples of new strategies you have learned. Point out examples of them in the portfolio.

The Evaluating Your Progress boxes at the end of Chapters 8 to 15 and 17 may be helpful as you assess and track your progress. Refer to them frequently as you draft this introductory essay.

Here are a few things to avoid when building your portfolio. Make sure you write about what you learned about *your* writing, not about writing in general. That is, do not repeat points from the book about the writing process. Instead, explain how you have used that information to become a better writer. Also, do not exaggerate your progress or try to say what you think the instructor wants to hear. Instead, be honest and forthright in assessing your progress. Finally, avoid flattery or praise of the instructor or the course. Most instructors will give you a separate opportunity to evaluate them and the courses they teach.

Here is a sample reflective essay written by Bryan Scott, a nursing student and former Marine, for his first-year writing course.

STUDENTS WRITE

The Portfolio Assignment

For your final assignment you will submit a portfolio containing:

- A table of contents listing the titles and page numbers of all included writing pieces,

- A reflective essay that introduces your portfolio,

- One series of writing pieces (prewriting, outlines, drafts) that demonstrates your ability to move successfully through the steps in the writing process,

- At least two pieces of writing that demonstrate your growth as a writer,
- One piece of writing done this term for another class,
- Essays that demonstrate your ability to use various methods of organization, and
- A limited number of materials of your own choice.

In your reflective essay, you are expected to include answers to the following questions.

1. What are your current strengths and weaknesses as a writer?
2. What specific writing skills have you developed?
3. How have you changed as a writer?
4. In what ways has your awareness of learning style improved your ability to write?
5. What critical reading and thinking skills have your learned, *or* in what ways have you strengthened your critical reading and thinking skills?

Sample Reflective Essay

TABLE OF CONTENTS

Bryan Scott
May 5, 2005
Final Portfolio
English 109

      From the Marines to the Writing Classroom

    I enrolled in this course because it was a required   1
course in my nursing curriculum, but I can now say that
I am glad that it was required. As a former Marine, I
had little experience with writing, other than writing
letters home to my wife and parents. Now, as I prepare

for a career as a nurse, I realize that writing is an important communication skill. Writing reports about patients, such as "Nursing Care Plan: Patient 4," requires me to present clear, precise, and accurate information about patients and their care. Through this course I have learned to do so. Although I improved in almost every area of writing, my greatest improvements were in approaching writing as a process, moving from personal to informative writing, and developing an awareness of audience.

2   Through this course I have learned to view writing as a process rather than a "write-it-once-and-I-am-done" activity. As shown in the packet of writing for "The Wall at Sunset," I have discovered the value of prewriting as a way of coming up with ideas. Before I started writing this essay, I knew that visiting the Vietnam Veterans Memorial had been an emotional experience for me, but I found that mapping helped me define and organize my feelings. Since I am a spatial learner, I could visualize the wall and map my responses to seeing the names of other soldiers. My first draft in the packet demonstrates my ability to begin with a thesis statement and build ideas around it. My second draft shows how I added detail and arranged my impressions into an organized essay. My final draft shows my ability to catch most errors in spelling, grammar, and punctuation.

3   Moving from personal writing to informative writing was a valuable learning experience that is essential for my career. My first essay, "The Wall at Sunset," was a very personal account of my visit to the Vietnam Veterans Memorial, as was the essay "How the Marines Changed My Life," a personal account of life in the U.S. Marine Corps. While I had a lot to say about my own experiences, I found it difficult to write about topics that did not directly involve me. I found that learning to use sources, especially Internet sources, helped me get started with informative writing. By visiting news Web

sites, doing Internet research, and reading blogs, I
learned to move outside of myself and begin to think
about and become interested in what other people were
saying and thinking. My essay "Miracle in the Operating
Room" demonstrates my ability to use sources, both print
and Internet, to learn how kidney transplants are done.

As I moved from personal to informative writing, I　　4
found that the patterns of development provided a framework for developing and organizing informative writing.
Process seemed to be an effective way to present information for the essay "Miracle in the Operating Room." My
essay "Emotional Styles of Athletes" initially contained
a lot of my own personal impressions (see the first
draft that I have included), but by using classification,
I was able to focus on characteristics of athletes
rather than on my opinions of them.

Before I took this course, I had no idea that I　　5
should write differently for different audiences. My
essay "How the Marines Changed My Life" was written for
my classmates, many of whom had no military experience.
I found I had to explain things about chain of command,
regimentation, and living conditions--all things that I
and other Marines are familiar with. In my case report
for my nursing class, "Nursing Care Plan: Patient 4,"
my audience was other nurses and medical staff, even
doctors. Because I was writing for a specialized audience, I could mention medical terms, procedures, and medications freely without defining them. However, in
"Miracle in the Operating Room," I was writing for a
general, nonspecialized audience, so I realized it was
necessary to explain terms such as *dialysis, laparoscopy,*
and *nephrectomy.* This essay and my nursing case report
demonstrate my ability to write in a clear, direct,
and concise manner in my chosen field for different
audiences.

While I developed many strengths as a writer, I am　　6
still aware of many weaknesses. I have difficulty with

descriptive writing; I just cannot come up with words to paint a visual picture as effectively as I would like. Fortunately, nursing will not require much creative description. I also have difficulty choosing a topic. Although I found the suggestions in our textbook helpful, I still feel as if I am overlooking important or useful topics. Finally, I have not benefited from peer review as much as others have. I still find myself uncomfortable when accepting criticism and revision ideas from other students. Perhaps my military training to look to authority for direction is still getting in the way.

7   As I developed strengths as a writer, I also became a more critical reader and thinker. I am enclosing my annotations for the professional essay "Bad Conduct, by the Numbers." These annotations demonstrate my ability to ask questions and challenge the author. I also found enlightening discussions in the text on connotative language, bias, and fact and opinion. These are things I had never thought much about, and now I find myself being aware of these things as I read.

8   Overall, by taking this course, I have become a more serious and aware writer and have come to regard writing as a rewarding challenge.

Note that Bryan organized his reflective essay using the principles of good writing he learned in the course. Within this organization, he was able to identify his strengths and weaknesses as a writer, discuss learning styles, and analyze his essays. Notice that Bryan identifies his strengths and weaknesses as a writer throughout the essay.

Classroom Communication Skills

CHAPTER QUICK START

Your friend at another college mentions in an email that he has to give an oral presentation in his history class in two weeks. He is unaccustomed to speaking in front of groups and says he is nervous about the assignment.

Writing Quick Start

Write a paragraph in which you offer advice to your friend. Include what you already know about making interesting and effective oral presentations.

In completing the assignment on the previous page, you began to think about oral presentations, one of the many ways in which you will be required to communicate in your college classes. So far this book has concentrated on two forms of communication, reading and writing, but you will also need to build your speaking and listening skills to be a productive and successful student. This chapter will give you advice on listening carefully, asking and answering questions, working on group projects, and making oral presentations.

LISTENING CAREFULLY AND CRITICALLY

Of the most common ways people communicate — reading, writing, speaking, and listening — listening is the skill that you perform most frequently. College students spend a large portion of their time in a classroom listening. Think about the classes you attended this week; you probably spent far more time listening than reading, writing, or speaking. Because you spend so much time doing it, you need to listen carefully and critically — grasping what is said and questioning and reacting to what you hear.

Becoming a Careful Listener

Did you know that you can process information faster than speakers can speak? As a result, your mind has time to wander while listening. Try using the following suggestions to maintain your attention in the classroom.

- Sit in the front of the room so you can see and hear a limited number of distractions and can focus more easily on the instructor.
- Take notes. Writing will help focus and maintain your attention.
- Try to anticipate the ideas the speaker will address next. This activity keeps your mind active.
- Sit comfortably but do not sprawl. A serious posture puts your mind in gear for serious work.
- Maintain eye contact with the speaker. You will feel more personally involved and will be less likely to drift off mentally.
- Avoid sitting among groups of friends. You will be tempted to talk to or think about them, and you risk missing information that the speaker is presenting.

Listening Critically

In many classes, you are expected to both understand what the speaker — either your instructor or another student — is saying and respond to it. Here are a few suggestions for developing your critical listening skills.

Maintain an Open Mind

It is easy to shut out ideas and opinions that do not conform to your values and beliefs. Try to avoid evaluating a message either positively or negatively until it is complete and understandable.

Avoid Selective Listening

Some listeners hear what they want to hear, especially when listening to ideas they disagree with. Other listeners do not remember ideas with which they disagree. This is dangerous, since you may miss important points in a discussion. Make a deliberate attempt to understand the speaker's viewpoint, and distract yourself from disagreeing by taking notes or creating an informal outline of the speaker's main points.

Avoid Oversimplification

When listening to difficult, unpleasant, emotional, or complex messages, it is tempting to simplify them by eliminating their details, reasons, and supporting evidence. For example, if you are listening to a speaker describe his wartime experiences in Iraq, the speaker's details may be unpleasant but are important to understanding his experience.

Focus on the Message, Not the Speaker

Try not to be distracted by the speaker's dress, mannerisms, speech patterns, or annoying quirks.

EXERCISE 23.1

Working with a classmate, identify at least five topics that you would need to listen to critically to avoid the pitfalls listed above.

ASKING AND ANSWERING QUESTIONS

You can learn more from your classes if you develop or polish your questioning skills. This means asking questions when you need information and clarification and answering questions posed by the instructor to demonstrate and evaluate your knowledge and express interest in the class. Use the following tips to strengthen your questioning and answering skills.

- Conquer your fear of speaking in class. Stop worrying what your friends and classmates will think: Speak out.

- As you read an assignment, jot down questions as they occur to you. Bring your list to class, and use it when your instructor invites questions.

- Form your questions concisely. Don't apologize for asking, and don't ramble.

- Don't worry if your questions seem unimportant or silly. Other students probably have the same questions but are reluctant to ask them.

- Focus on critical questions. Instead of asking factual questions, think about questions that focus on how the information can be used, how ideas fit together, how things work, what might be relevant problems and solutions, or what the long-term value and significance of the information are.

- When answering questions, try to think through your response before volunteering to answer.

EXERCISE 23.2

Working with a classmate, brainstorm a list of questions you could ask about the content presented in this chapter.

GROUP PROJECTS: WORKING WITH CLASSMATES

Many college assignments and class activities involve working with other students. For example, in this book, many chapters contain a box titled "Trying Out Your Ideas on Others" that asks you to work with other students. Group projects vary, and therefore your approach may vary depending on the discipline, the course, and the instructor. Some groups may be assembled to discuss problems; others may carry out an activity, such as examining a piece of writing; others may research a topic and present their findings.

Understanding the Purpose

Many students expect to learn from their instructors but do not realize they can learn from one another as well. Group projects enable students to share experiences, understand classmates' thinking, and evaluate new ideas and approaches to completing a task. For example, if you are working with several classmates to prepare a panel discussion, you may observe that different classmates approach the task differently. Some may begin by brainstorming about the topic; others may begin by asking questions; still others may start by reading about or researching the topic. To benefit most from group projects, be sure you understand the task and then analyze it. Ask yourself, "What can I learn from this?" You will get more out of an assignment if you are focused on outcomes.

Keeping Groups Functioning Effectively

Some students complain that group projects are time-consuming and often unproductive. If you feel that way about a project, take a leadership role and make it work. Here are some suggestions for making groups work more effectively.

Do . . .	Don't . . .
Set a good example as a committed and productive group member.	Take a passive role by allowing others in the group to do the bulk of the planning and work.
Work with serious, energetic, and creative classmates, if you have a choice.	Work with people who will be easily distracted and less likely to get their work done.
As a group, decide on an action plan, distribute responsibilities, and establish a firm schedule.	Work haphazardly, so that some tasks do not get done and others are duplicated.
Stay focused on the project during group meetings.	Waste time by allowing group discussions to wander off topic or turn into a social situation.
Do the best work you can, and get it done on time, since each member's work affects the grade for the project.	Complain about your workload or hold up the group by completing your part late or insufficiently.
Assign tasks wisely and equitably in a way that best uses members' strengths.	Assign important preliminary tasks to a member who works slowly or is disorganized.
Address potential problems quickly.	Allow interpersonal problems or other conflicts to get in the way of productivity.

Managing Conflicts

Despite your best efforts and those of other group members, not all groups function effectively. Conflicts may arise; members may complain; a group member may not do his or her share. Since your grade on the project may depend on every other member's work, your best interests require you to address these problems quickly and effectively if they occur. Use the following suggestions to do so.

- If members miss meetings, offer to call everyone to remind them of the time and place.

- Establish a more detailed timetable if the work is not getting done.
- Offer to take on a greater share of the work if it will help get the assignment done.
- Ask questions that may stimulate unproductive members' ideas and interest.
- Suggest that uncommunicative members share their ideas in written form.
- Encourage the students who are causing the problem to propose solutions.

If you are unable to resolve problems or conflicts, discuss them with your instructor.

GIVING ORAL PRESENTATIONS

Oral presentations are an important part of many college classes. In an ecology class, you may be asked to report on a local environmental problem. In a sociology class, you may have to summarize your findings from a survey about a campus issue. Presentations vary in type: You may express your own ideas, inform, or persuade. These purposes are similar to those you have learned for writing essays.

Effective presentations are important in academic situations and also in many jobs and careers. By learning to speak before groups, you will gain self-confidence and become a more effective communicator. As you work through this section, you will see that the steps you take in giving an oral presentation parallel the steps required in writing an essay: planning, organizing and drafting, rehearsing (similar to revising), and delivering (similar to the final submission of your essay).

Planning Your Presentation

The more carefully you plan your presentation, the more comfortable you will be in delivering it. Use the following steps.

Select Your Topic

Choosing a topic is as important for making a presentation as it is for writing an essay. The topic you choose should depend on the assignment. Make sure you understand the assignment and the type of speech you are to give. Is it to be informative or persuasive? Are visual aids permitted, encouraged, or required? Are you allowed to speak from an outline or note cards? What is the time limit? Also consider your audience, as you do when writing essays. What topics are important to your listeners and will sustain their interest? Here a few suggestions for choosing a topic.

- Choose a topic that is appropriate for your audience. You might be interested in choosing a day-care center, but if your audience is mostly young college students, you may have difficulty sustaining their interest with a speech titled "How to Choose the Best Day-Care Center."

- Choose a topic of value. Your topic should be worthwhile or meaningful to your audience. Trivial topics such as how to create a particular hairstyle or a report about characters on a soap opera may not have sufficient merit for college classrooms.

- Choose a narrow topic. As in writing, if you choose a topic that is too broad, you will have too much to say in the allotted time or may resort to generalities that lack supporting evidence.

- Choose a topic that you find interesting or know something about. You will find it easier to exude and generate enthusiasm if you are speaking about a topic that is familiar and that you enjoy.

Identify Your Purpose

As when you are writing, first determine if your purpose is to inform or persuade. Then more carefully define your purpose. For an informative speech, what information do you want to convey? If your topic is wrestling, do you want to explain its popularity, demonstrate several wrestling holds, or discuss it as a collegiate sport? If your purpose is to persuade, do you want to argue values, encourage action, or change your audience members' thinking or beliefs?

Research Your Topic

As you would for an essay, unless your presentation is to be based on your personal knowledge or experience, you will need to research your topic. As you give your speech, be sure to mention your sources. You might mention the author, the work, or both—whatever is meaningful and adds credibility to your presentation. If you use quotations, avoid tedious expressions such as "I quote here" or "I want to quote an example." Instead, integrate your quotations into your speech as you would quotations into an essay.

For more information on researching, see Chapters 18 and 19.

For more information on integrating quotations, see Chapter 20, p. 704.

Organizing and Drafting Your Presentation

Develop a Thesis and Identify Supporting Ideas

Once you have read about your topic, you are ready to draft a thesis statement and collect information that supports it. Again, these processes parallel those you have been using to write an essay. Be sure to include a variety of evidence, considering the types that would appeal to your audience. When you write an essay, your readers can reread if they miss a point. When you give an oral presentation, your listeners do not have that option, so reiterate your thesis frequently to make your presentation easier to follow.

Organize Your Speech

Using a method of organization will make your speech easier to follow and easier for you to present. By grouping your ideas together, you will be able to remember them better. If you are using classification to organize a speech titled "Types of Procrastinators," you can remember that you have four main categories, with descriptive details to explain each. Be sure to use plenty of transitions that signal your organization to ensure that your listeners don't get lost.

Use Appropriate Visuals

Visuals add interest to your presentation and can be used to reinforce your message and make your ideas clear and concrete. You may also find that using a visual aid builds your confidence and lessens apprehension. Presentation aids seem to relax speakers and distract them from thinking about themselves and how they look. A wide range of presentation aids are available, including related objects (if you are giving a speech about in-line skating, bring your skates), charts, maps, photographs, tapes, CDs, videotapes, flip charts, and Microsoft PowerPoint presentations. Ask your instructor what is permissible and what media are available for classroom use.

Plan Your Introduction and Conclusion

For more information on introductions, see Chapter 5, p. 131.

Your introduction should grab your audience's attention, introduce your topic, and establish a relationship between you and your audience. You can capture your reader's interest and introduce your topic in many of the same ways you do when you write essays. To build a relationship with your audience, try to make connections with them. You might mention others who are present, refer to a shared situation (a previous class or another student's speech), or establish common ground by referring to a well-known event, personality, or campus issue.

Your conclusion is a crucial part of your presentation because it is often the most memorable. It is the final impression with which you leave your audience. Your conclusion should summarize your speech, but it should also let your audience know your presentation is ending. You might also end your presentation with a statement that leaves a lasting final impression.

Rehearsing Your Presentation

Practicing your speech is the key to comfortable and effective delivery. Once you have drafted and organized your ideas, you need to prepare an outline or note cards that you can use to guide your presentation. Use the following rehearsal tips.

- Practice giving the entire speech, not just parts. Rehearse at least three or four times. Try to improve your speech during each rehearsal.
- Time yourself. If you are over or seriously under the time limit, make necessary cuts or additions.
- If possible, rehearse the speech in the room in which you will give it.
- Rehearse in front of an audience of a few friends or classmates. Ask them for constructive criticism. Some students videotape their presentations to build their confidence and look for areas that need improvement.

Overcoming Apprehension

Many students are nervous or afraid to make oral presentations to their class-mates. Often called "stage fright," this apprehension is normal and natural but also easily overcome. The first step to overcoming apprehension is to understand its causes.

Some speakers are apprehensive because they feel conspicuous — at the center of attention. Others feel they are competing with other, better speakers in the class. Still others are apprehensive because the task is new and they have never done it before. You can often overcome these feelings using the following sugges-tions.

- If you feel conspicuous, try to imagine that you are talking to one friend or one friendly and supportive classmate.
- To reduce the newness of the task, be sure to practice your speech. (See the sec-tion on rehearsal above.)
- Preparation — knowing you have put together a solid, interesting presenta-tion — can build your self-confidence and lessen your sense of competition.

Use Visualization to Enhance Your Performance

Many athletes, actors, and musicians use the technique of visualization to enhance their performances. Performance visualization involves imagining yourself suc-cessfully completing a task. For an oral presentation, visualize yourself successfully making the presentation. Create a mental videotape. It should begin with your arrival at the classroom and take you through each step: confidently walking to the front of the room, beginning your speech, engaging your audience, handling your notes, and so on. Be sure to visualize the presentation positively; avoid negative thoughts. Now you have the image of yourself as a successful speaker. You know what it looks and feels like to give an effective presentation. Review your "videotape" often, especially on the day of your presentation. As you give your presentation, try to model the look and feel of your videotape.

Use Desensitization

Desensitization is a method of overcoming fears by gradually building up your tolerance of the feared situation or object. If someone is afraid of snakes, for example, a desensitization therapist might begin by showing the person a photograph, then a videotape, then a small snake at a distance, and so forth, gradually building up the person's exposure time and tolerance. You can do the same thing to overcome your apprehension of oral presentations by gradually building up to making presentations. Begin by asking a question in class. When you are comfortable with that, move to answering questions in class. Then you might move toward speaking in front of small groups (practicing your speech on a group of friends, for example). Each step you take makes the next one easier. Eventually you will become more comfortable with public speaking and ready to make a presentation to the class.

Delivering an Effective Presentation

The delivery of your presentation ultimately determines its effectiveness. Use the following suggestions, as well as Table 23.1, to improve the delivery of your presentation.

- Avoid using too many notes or a detailed outline. Instead, construct a keyword outline that will remind you of major points in the order you wish to present them.
- Make eye contact with your audience. Make them part of your presentation.
- Move around a little, rather than standing stiffly. Use gestures to add an expressive quality to your presentation.
- Speak slowly. It is a common mistake to speak too fast. Your audience may miss your main points and lose interest in your presentation.

TABLE 23.1
FREQUENTLY ASKED QUESTIONS FOR MAKING PRESENTATIONS

Question	*Suggested Solutions*
What should I do if I go blank?	• Refer to your notes or index cards. • Ask if there are any questions. Even if no one asks any, the pause will give you time to regroup your ideas.
What should I do if classmates are restless, uninterested, or even rude?	• Make eye contact with as many members of the class as possible as you speak. • For a particularly troublesome person, you might lengthen your eye contact. • Change the tone or pitch of your voice. • Try to make your speech more engaging by asking questions or using personal examples.
What should I do if I skip over or forget to include an important part of the presentation?	• Go back and add it in. Say something like, "I neglected to mention . . . " and present the portion you skipped.
What if I realize that my speech will be too short or too long?	• If you realize it will be too short, try to add examples, anecdotes, or more detailed information. • If you realize it will be too long, cut out examples or summarize instead of fully explaining sections that are less important.

PART 7

Handbook
Writing Problems and How to Correct Them

HANDBOOK CONTENTS

REVIEW OF BASIC GRAMMAR

1 PARTS OF SPEECH

Each word in a sentence acts as one of eight parts of speech: *nouns, pronouns, verbs, adjectives, adverbs, conjunctions, prepositions,* and *interjections.* These are the building blocks of our language. Often, to revise your writing or to correct sentence errors, you need to understand how a word or phrase functions in a particular sentence.

1a Nouns

A **noun** names a person (*waiter, girlfriend*), a place (*classroom, beach*), a thing (*textbook, computer*), or an idea (*excitement, beauty*). **Proper nouns** name specific people (*Professor Wainwright*), places (*Texas*), things (*Game Boy*), or ideas (*Marxism*) and are always capitalized.

▶ *James* drove to *Williamsville* in a *Toyota* in *March.*

Common nouns name one or more of a general class or type of person, place, thing, or idea and are not capitalized.

▶ A *holiday* is a *celebration* of an *event.*

Collective nouns name groups: *class, jury, team.* **Concrete nouns** name tangible things that can be tasted, seen, touched, smelled, or heard: *instructor, exam, desk.* **Abstract nouns** name ideas, qualities, beliefs, and conditions: *love, faith, trust.*

Most nouns express **number** and can be singular or plural: *one test, two tests; one pen, five pens.* **Count nouns** name items that can be counted. Count nouns can be made plural, usually by adding *-s* or *-es: one telephone, three telephones; one speech, ten speeches.* Some count nouns form their plurals in an irregular way: *mouse, mice; goose, geese.* **Noncount nouns** such as *water, anger, courage,* and *knowledge* name ideas or entities that cannot be counted. Most noncount nouns do not have a plural form. (See Section 26 of this Handbook for more on count and noncount nouns.)

EXERCISE 1.1

Underline the nouns in the following sentences and identify each one as common or proper by writing *C* for common or *P* for proper above each.

            P
▶ Where did English come from?

    C   P   C   P   P
1. The language we call Old English was spoken by tribes known as Angles and Saxons.
           P   P
2. They invaded England from northern Europe.

For more exercises on nouns, refer to the Parts of Speech section of Exercise Central at www .bedfordstmartins.com /successfulwriting.

3. Old English was closely related to Germanic languages of that time.
4. The Normans, who came from France, later conquered England.
5. Our language then acquired many French words and characteristics.

1b Pronouns

Pronouns are words that take the place of nouns. The noun or pronoun to which a pronoun refers is called the pronoun's **antecedent.**

► Because the *researcher* developed a new drug, *she* became famous.

The noun *researcher* is the antecedent of the pronoun *she.*

Personal pronouns name specific people, places, or things. Personal pronouns come in three cases that describe a pronoun's function in a sentence. The **subjective case** indicates that a pronoun is a subject, a doer of an action (*I, you, he, she, it, we, they*).

► *She* asked questions about the job.

The **objective case** indicates that a pronoun is an object, a receiver of an action (*me, you, him, her, it, us, them*).

► The career counselor has been advising *her.*

The **possessive case** indicates ownership or belonging (*my, mine, your, yours, his, her, hers, its, our, ours, your, yours, their, theirs*).

► *His* enthusiasm for the company does not match *theirs.*

Personal pronouns also indicate **person,** to distinguish among the speaker (first person: *I, we*), the person spoken to (second person: *you*), and the person or thing spoken about (third person: *he, she, it, they*). The **gender** of personal pronouns identifies them as masculine (*he, him*), feminine (*she, her*), or neuter (*it*). Personal pronouns also show **number:** singular (one person or thing: *I, you, he, she, it*) or plural (more than one person or thing: *we, you, they*).

Demonstrative pronouns point out a particular person or thing: *this, that, these,* and *those.* A demonstrative pronoun can be used as an adjective to describe a noun.

► *These* research procedures are questionable.

Reflexive pronouns indicate that a subject performs actions to, for, or on itself. Reflexive pronouns end in *-self* or *-selves.*

	Singular	*Plural*
First person	myself	ourselves
Second person	yourself	yourselves
Third person	himself	themselves
	herself	
	itself	

▶ We allowed *ourselves* two hours to complete the experiment.

Intensive pronouns have the same forms as reflexive pronouns and are used to emphasize their antecedents.

▶ Not even the computer programmer *herself* could correct the error.

Reflexive and intensive pronouns cannot be used as the subject of a sentence, and their antecedents must appear in the same sentence as the pronoun.

INCORRECT	*Myself* disagreed with the speaker's proposal, despite my sympathy with the movement.
CORRECT	*I myself* disagreed with the speaker's proposal, despite my sympathy with the movement.

Interrogative pronouns introduce or ask a question.

REFER TO PEOPLE	who, whoever, whom, whomever, whose
REFER TO THINGS	what, which

▶ *Who* will pay the bill?

Relative pronouns introduce **dependent clauses** that function as adjectives. Relative pronouns refer back to a noun or pronoun that the clause modifies.

A dependent clause contains a subject and a verb but does not express a complete thought.

REFER TO PEOPLE	who, whoever, whom, whomever, whose
REFER TO THINGS	that, what, whatever, which, whose

▶ The research *that* caused the literacy test controversy was outdated.

▶ Sylvia Plath was married to Ted Hughes, *who* later became poet laureate of England.

Indefinite pronouns do not refer to specific nouns; rather, they refer to people, places, or things in general (*everyone, anywhere, everything*). Commonly used indefinite pronouns include the following.

Singular

another	either	nobody	somebody
anybody	enough	none	someone
anyone	everybody	no one	something
anything	everyone	nothing	
anywhere	everything	one	
each	neither	other	

Plural

both	many	several
few	others	

▶ Hardly *anyone* had heard of the Sapir-Wharf hypothesis.

▶ Although a number of psychologists have researched brain dominance, *few* have related it to learning style.

Several indefinite pronouns, such as *all, any, more, most, some,* and *none,* can be either singular or plural, depending on their antecedent (see 5e).

The **reciprocal pronouns** *each other* and *one another* indicate an interchange of information or physical objects between two or more parties.

▶ The debate semifinalists congratulated *each other* on their scores.

See Section 7 of the Handbook for more on pronoun usage.

For more exercises on pronouns, refer to the Parts of Speech section of Exercise Central at www .bedfordstmartins.com /successfulwriting.

EXERCISE 1.2

Underline the pronouns in the following sentences and identify each one as personal, demonstrative, reflexive, intensive, interrogative, relative, indefinite, or reciprocal. Some sentences may not contain pronouns.

       relative personal   personal   indefinite   personal
▶ The fact that our eyes deceive us is difficult for many of us to accept.

1. Our brains influence our eyes in ways that we ourselves may not realize.
2. Events that surprise us are especially hard to remember accurately.
3. In a famous study, psychologist Elizabeth Loftus staged sudden protests in college classrooms to see how students reacted.
4. The students were later asked to fill out questionnaires in which untrue details of these incidents were suggested.
5. Most of them were wrong about significant details.

1c Verbs

Verbs show action (*read, study*), occurrence (*become, happen*), or a state of being (*be, feel*). There are three types of verbs: action verbs, linking verbs, and helping verbs (also called auxiliary verbs).

Action verbs express physical or mental activities.

▶ My hair *grew* longer and longer.

▶ Amelia *thought* her answer was correct.

Action verbs may be either transitive or intransitive. A **transitive verb** (TV) has a **direct object** (DO) that receives the action and completes the meaning of the sentence. (In the examples, S stands for *subject*.)

     S   TV   DO
▶ Juan *wrote* lyrics for songs.

An **intransitive verb** (IV) does not need a direct object to complete the meaning of the sentence.

     S   IV
▶ The lights *flickered.*

Some verbs can be either transitive or intransitive, depending on how they are used in a sentence.

    INTRANSITIVE   The student *wrote* quickly.

    TRANSITIVE   The student *wrote* a paper on hypnotism.

Linking verbs show existence, explaining what something is, was, or will become. A linking verb connects a word to words that describe it.

▶ Dr. Miller *is* the new college president.

▶ Their answers *were* evasive.

The forms of the verb *be* (*am, is, are, was, were, be, being, been*) are linking verbs. Some action verbs can also function as linking verbs. These include *appear, become, feel, grow, look, prove, remain, seem, smell, sound, stay,* and *taste.*

▶ The sky *grew* dark.

▶ Something in the kitchen *smells* delicious.

Helping verbs, also called **auxiliary verbs,** are used along with action or linking verbs to indicate tense, mood, or voice or to add further information. A **verb phrase** is a combination of one or more helping verbs and a main verb.

SIMPLE VERB	The newspaper *reports* the incident.
SIMPLE VERB + HELPING VERB	The newspaper *should report* the incident.

Helping verbs include the different forms of *do, be,* and *have* (which can also serve as main verbs in a sentence) along with *can, could, may, might, must, shall, should, will,* and *would.*

For more exercises on
verbs, refer to the Parts
of Speech section of Exercise Central at www
.bedfordstmartins.com
/successfulwriting.

EXERCISE 1.3

Underline the verbs in the following sentences and identify each one as action, linking, or helping; for action verbs, identify the verb as transitive or intransitive.

action-intransitive   *helping action-intransitive*
▶ The California gold rush began when gold was discovered at Sutter's Mill in 1848.

1. Gold fever swept across the United States.
2. A few months later, over four thousand miners had arrived.
3. Some traveled west in wagons and faced hardship and disease.
4. Most "forty-niners" soon grew disillusioned.
5. Those prospectors who left mining for agriculture and storekeeping were better off.

Verb Forms

All verbs except *be* have five forms: the base form, the past tense, the past participle, the present participle, and the *-s* form for the present tense when the subject is singular and in the third person.

The first three forms are called the verb's principal parts. The base form is the form of the verb as it appears in the dictionary: *review, study, prepare.* For regular verbs, the past tense and past participle are formed by adding *-d* or *-ed* to the base form. For regular verbs ending in *y,* the *y* is changed to *i: rely, relied.* For one-syllable regular verbs ending in a vowel plus a consonant, the consonant is doubled: *plan, planned* (see 25c).

	Regular	*Irregular*
Base form	walk	run
Past tense	walked	ran
Past participle	walked	run
Present participle	walking	running
-s form	walks	runs

Irregular verbs follow no set pattern to form their past tense and past participle.

FORMS OF COMMON IRREGULAR VERBS

Base Form	*Past Tense*	*Past Participle*
be	was/were	been
become	became	become

FORMS OF COMMON IRREGULAR VERBS *(continued)*

Base Form	Past Tense	Past Participle
begin	began	begun
bite	bit	bitten, bit
blow	blew	blown
build	built	built
burst	burst	burst
catch	caught	caught
choose	chose	chosen
come	came	come
dive	dived, dove	dived
do	did	done
draw	drew	drawn
drive	drove	driven
eat	ate	eaten
fall	fell	fallen
feel	felt	felt
fight	fought	fought
find	found	found
fling	flung	flung
fly	flew	flown
get	got	gotten, got
give	gave	given
go	went	gone
grow	grew	grown
have	had	had
know	knew	known
lay	laid	laid
lead	led	led
leave	left	left
lie	lay	lain
lose	lost	lost
make	made	made
prove	proved	proved, proven
ride	rode	ridden

(Continued on next page)

FORMS OF COMMON IRREGULAR VERBS *(continued)*

Base Form	Past Tense	Past Participle
ring	rang	rung
rise	rose	risen
run	ran	run
say	said	said
set	set	set
sit	sat	sat
speak	spoke	spoken
swear	swore	sworn
swim	swam	swum
take	took	taken
tear	tore	torn
tell	told	told
think	thought	thought
throw	threw	thrown
wear	wore	worn
win	won	won
write	wrote	written

If you are unsure of a verb's principal parts, check your dictionary. See Section 6 of the Handbook for more about verb forms.

EXERCISE 1.4

For more exercises on verb forms, refer to the Parts of Speech and Verb Forms sections of Exercise Central at www.bedfordstmartins .com/successfulwriting.

Correct any errors in verb form in the following sentences. Some sentences may be correct as written.

▶ Muhammad Ali, who ~~wonned~~ the world heavyweight boxing title three separate
　　　　　　　　　　　won

　　times, ~~remain~~ a popular hero.
　　　　 remains

1. Muhammad Ali begun his boxing career under the name Cassius Clay.
2. Cassius Clay was boxing as an amateur in 1960, when he earned the Golden Gloves title and an Olympic gold medal.
3. In 1964, he defeated Sonny Liston and become the world heavyweight champion.
4. Ali growed increasingly well known for his quick moves in the ring and his quick wit everywhere else.
5. In 1967, Clay joined the Nation of Islam and taked the Muslim name Muhammad Ali.
6. He refused to be drafted that year for religious reasons and was baned from boxing and stripped of his title.
7. Ali returned to boxing in 1971 but lost his title to Joe Frazier the following year.

8. He get the title back in 1974 by defeating George Foreman.
9. Ali lost the title to Leon Spinks in 1978 but fighted him again and won it back later that year.
10. Although Ali retired in 1979 and has been in declining health, many Americans still admire him greatly.

Verb Tense

The **tenses** of a verb express time. They convey whether an action, a state of being, or an occurrence takes place in the present, past, or future. There are six basic tenses: present, past, future, present perfect, past perfect, and future perfect. There are also three groups of tenses: simple, perfect, and progressive.

Simple tenses indicate whether an action occurs in the present, past, or future.

▶ He *loves* Kabuki theater.

▶ I *purchased* their new CD immediately.

▶ Hitchcock's reputation *will continue to grow.*

Perfect tenses indicate that the action was or will be finished by the time of some other action.

▶ By now, Rosa *has taken* the exam.

▶ Dave Matthews *had* already *performed* when they arrived.

▶ The centennial celebration *will have begun* before he completes the sculpture.

Progressive tenses indicate that the action does, did, or will continue.

▶ She *is going* to kindergarten.

▶ When the ambulance arrived, he *was sweating* profusely.

▶ During spring break, we *will be basking* on a sunny beach.

A SUMMARY OF VERB TENSES

Present Tense

Simple present: happening now or occurring regularly

▶ He *performs* his own stunts.

Present progressive: happening now; going on (in progress) now

▶ The governor *is considering* a Senate campaign.

Present perfect: began in the past and was completed in the past or is continuing now

▶ The children's benefactor *has followed* their progress closely.

(Continued on next page)

(Continued)

Present perfect progressive: began in the past and is continuing now

▶ She *has been singing* in nightclubs for thirty years.

Past Tense

Simple past: began and ended in the past

▶ The doctor *treated* him with experimental drugs.

Past progressive: began and continued in the past

▶ They *were* not *expecting* any visitors.

Past perfect: occurred before a certain time in the past or was completed before another action was begun

▶ The birds *had eaten* all the berries before we knew they were ripe.

Past perfect progressive: was taking place until a second action occurred

▶ He *had been seeing* a psychiatrist before his collapse.

Future Tense

Simple future: will take place in the future

▶ The play *will begin* on time.

Future progressive: will both begin and end in the future

▶ After we get on the plane, we *will be sitting* for hours.

Future perfect: will be completed by a certain time in the future or before another action will begin

▶ By next month, the new apprentice *will have become* an expert.

Future perfect progressive: will continue until a certain time in the future

▶ By the time she earns her Ph.D., she *will have been studying* history for twelve years.

Most of the time you will not need to think about verb tense; you will use the correct tense automatically. There are, however, a few situations in which you need to pay special attention to verb tense.

- Use the present tense to make a generalization or to state a principle or fact.

    ▶ Thanksgiving *falls* on the fourth Thursday of November each year.
    ▶ Walking *is* excellent exercise.

- Use the present tense to indicate an action that occurs regularly or habitually.

    ▶ My sister *takes* frequent trips to Dallas.

- Use the present tense when referring to literary works and artworks, even though the work was written or created in the past.

  ▶ *Hamlet is* set in Denmark.

- Use the present tense to refer to authors no longer living when you are discussing their works.

  ▶ Borges frequently *employs* magical realism in his fiction.

For more exercises on verb tenses, refer to the Parts of Speech section of Exercise Central at www .bedfordstmartins.com /successfulwriting.

EXERCISE 1.5

Underline the verbs in the following sentences and identify the tense of each one.

present perfect
▶ Although the U.S. Constitution <u>has already celebrated</u> its 200th anniversary, it

simple present
<u>remains</u> the core of American democracy.

1. For several years after the end of the Revolutionary War, the United States had been struggling to establish principles of government.
2. While its writers were developing the Constitution, they studied important documents from other societies.
3. By 1789 they had created a Constitution that all of the states ratified.
4. The Constitution is adaptable and has been amended—for example, to ensure that female and nonwhite citizens have the right to vote.
5. Most Americans expect that future generations will find that the Constitution will have proved to be an enduring foundation for justice.

Voice

A verb is in the **active voice** when the subject of the clause or sentence performs the action of the verb.

▶ The diplomats *have arrived.*

▶ He *plays* soccer professionally.

A verb is in the **passive voice** when the subject of a clause or sentence is the receiver of the action that the verb describes. Passive verbs are formed using a form of *be* and the past participle of a verb.

▶ The child *was* badly *bitten* by mosquitoes.

▶ Her car *was stolen.*

Since the passive voice may make it difficult for your readers to understand who is performing the action of a sentence, in most writing situations, use the active voice. If you do not know who performed an action, however, or if you want to emphasize the receiver of the action, consider using the passive voice.

PASSIVE VOICE   The evidence had been carefully removed by the defendant.

ACTIVE VOICE   The defendant had carefully removed the evidence.

Mood

The **mood** of a verb indicates whether it states a fact or asks a question (**indicative**), gives a command or direction (**imperative**), or expresses a condition, wish, or suggestion (**subjunctive**). The subjunctive mood is also used for hypothetical situations or impossible or unlikely events.

INDICATIVE   Redwood trees can pull moisture from the air.

IMPERATIVE   Read the play and write an analysis of it.

SUBJUNCTIVE   It would be nice to win the lottery.

The subjunctive mood, often used in clauses that begin with *if* or *that,* expresses a wish, suggestion, or condition contrary to fact. Use the base form of the verb for the present subjunctive. For the verb *be,* the past tense subjunctive is *were,* not *was.*

▶ I suggested that she *walk* to the station.

▶ The new student in class wished that he *were* more outgoing.

For more exercises on verb mood and voice, refer to the Parts of Speech section of Exercise Central at www .bedfordstmartins.com /successfulwriting.

EXERCISE 1.6

Underline the verbs in the following sentences and identify the mood (indicative, imperative, or subjunctive) and voice (active or passive) of each verb.

indicative, active

▶ Opiate use and abuse has a long history.

1. Opium was eaten as a folk medicine in India for centuries.
2. In the seventeenth century, the practice of smoking opium spread from Java to China.
3. Smoking opium leads to severe addiction, and Chinese authorities attempted to ban the drug.
4. Morphine was used as an effective painkiller during the Civil War.
5. Heroin was discovered in 1898, and doctors hoped it would cure the "soldier's disease" of morphine addiction.

1d Adjectives

Adjectives modify a noun or pronoun by describing it, limiting it, or giving more information about it. They answer the following questions.

WHICH ONE?   The *cutest* puppy belongs to the neighbors.

WHAT KIND?   Use only *academic* sources for the paper.

HOW MANY? *Several hundred* protesters gathered at City Hall.

There are three types of adjectives: descriptive, limiting, and proper. **Descriptive adjectives** name a quality of the person, place, thing, or idea that they describe.

yellow backpack   *pretty* face   *disturbing* event

Limiting adjectives narrow the scope of the person, place, or thing they describe.

my laptop   *second* building   *that* notebook

Proper adjectives are derived from proper nouns. They are always capitalized.

Japanese culture   *Elizabethan* England   *Scandinavian* mythology

The articles *a, an,* and *the* appear immediately before nouns and are considered adjectives. *The* refers to a specific item, while *a* and *an* do not. *A* is used before words that begin with consonant sounds. *An* is used before words that begin with vowel sounds.

▶ *The* person behind us laughed.

  The refers to a specific person.

▶ *An* answer will be forthcoming.

  Some answer will be provided.

The can also be used to refer to a group or class of items.

▶ *The* cat is *a* playful animal.

For more on the use of adjectives, see Section 9 of the Handbook. For more on articles, see Section 26 of the Handbook.

EXERCISE 1.7

Underline the adjectives in the following sentences and identify each one as a descriptive, limiting, or proper adjective or as an article.

For more exercises on adjectives, refer to the Parts of Speech and Adjectives and Adverbs sections of Exercise Central at www.bedfordstmartins .com/successfulwriting.

      art. descrip.   art.   descrip.   art.   descrip.   art.
▶ A disease cluster is a higher-than-usual incidence of an uncommon illness in a
  community.

1. Computer tracking of cancer cases around the country has revealed many apparent clusters of illness.
2. These clusters have led some people to believe that the cancers have environmental causes.
3. In recent years, discoveries of clusters have usually been followed by intensive testing to find the source.

4. The Love Canal site was one of the first clusters to alert the American public.

5. Few cases of clusters have been traced to an identifiable cause.

1e Adverbs

Adverbs modify verbs, adjectives, other adverbs, entire sentences, or clauses by describing, qualifying, or limiting the meaning of the words they modify. They answer the following questions.

HOW?	Andrea Bocelli performed *brilliantly*.
WHEN?	*Later,* they met to discuss the proposal.
WHERE?	The taxi driver headed *downtown*.
HOW OFTEN?	The bobcat is *rarely* seen in the wild.
TO WHAT EXTENT?	He agreed to cooperate *fully* with the investigation.

Most adverbs end in *-ly:*

particular*ly*   beautiful*ly*   secret*ly*

Note that not all words ending in *-ly* are adverbs; some are adjectives (*scholarly, unfriendly*). Common adverbs that do not end in *-ly* include *almost, never, quite, soon, then, there, too,* and *very.* Some words can function as either adjectives or adverbs depending on their use in the sentence.

ADJECTIVE	The flu victims were finally *well*.
ADVERB	His paper was *well* written.

Adverbs that modify adjectives or other adverbs appear next to the word they modify.

▶ Tired sloths move *especially* slowly.

▶ A pregnant woman may feel *extremely* tired.

Adverbs that modify verbs can appear in several different positions, however.

▶ He *carefully* put the toys together.

▶ He put the toys together *carefully*.

For more exercises on adverbs, refer to the Parts of Speech and Adjectives and Adverbs sections of Exercise Central at www .bedfordstmartins.com /successfulwriting.

For more on the use of adverbs, see Section 9 of the Handbook.

EXERCISE 1.8

Underline the adverbs in the following sentences. Some sentences may not contain adverbs.

► Historically, the Japanese art of flower arranging, or ikebana, was practiced in private homes.

1. Today, ikebana appears almost everywhere in Japan.
2. Ikebana practitioners follow ancient rules that govern the placement of the chosen elements. *No adverbs*
3. Empty spaces, carefully arranged structures, and a natural appearance are all fundamentally important in ikebana.
4. Ikebana arrangements are typically triangular.
5. Seasonal flowers and foliage are more highly prized than rare or expensive ones.

1f Conjunctions

Conjunctions connect words, phrases, or clauses. **Coordinating conjunctions** connect words or word groups of equal importance. There are seven coordinating conjunctions: *and, but, or, nor, for, yet,* and *so.* *write on computer*

► He attended the inauguration *but* looked unhappy.

Coordinating conjunctions must connect words, phrases, or clauses of the same kind. For example, *and* may connect two nouns, but it cannot connect a noun and a clause.

NOUNS	Novels by *Tom Clancy* and *Robert Parker* appeared on the best-seller list.
PHRASES	We searched *in the closets* and *under the beds.* *Phrases*
CLAUSES	*Custer graduated last in his West Point class,* but *he distinguished himself in the Civil War.*

Conjunctions that are used in pairs are called **correlative conjunctions:** *as . . . as, both . . . and, either . . . or, just as . . . so, neither . . . nor, not . . . but, not only . . . but also,* and *whether . . . or.*

► *Neither* the strikers *nor* the management was satisfied with the compromise.

Subordinating conjunctions connect **dependent clauses** to **independent clauses.** They connect ideas of unequal importance. Often used at the beginning of a dependent clause, subordinating conjunctions indicate how a less important idea (expressed in a dependent clause) relates to a more important idea (expressed in an independent clause). Here is a list of common subordinating conjunctions and the relationships they express.

A **dependent clause** contains a subject and a verb but does not express a complete thought.

An **independent clause** contains a subject and a verb and can stand alone as a sentence.

Subordinating Conjunctions

Time	before, after, while, until, when
	► *While* the sky was still dark, the army prepared for battle.
Cause or effect	because, since, so that
	► *Since* he doesn't like math, he should avoid calculus.

Condition	whether, if, unless, even if
	▶ We don't do volunteer work *unless* it is for a good cause.
Circumstance	as, as far as, as soon as, as if, as though, even though, even if, in order to
	▶ In-line skating is a popular sport, *even though* it is somewhat dangerous.

Conjunctive adverbs link sentence parts that are of equal importance; they also serve as modifiers. Conjunctive adverbs show the following relationships between the elements they connect.

Conjunctive Adverbs

Time	afterward, finally, later, meanwhile, next, subsequently, then
	▶ The candidates campaigned for months; *finally,* a primary election was held.
Example	for example, for instance, to illustrate
	▶ Some members of the party—*for example,* the governor—supported another candidate.
Continuation or addition	also, furthermore, in addition, in the first place, moreover
	▶ He is poorly organized; *in addition,* his arguments are not logical.
Cause or effect	accordingly, as a result, consequently, hence, therefore, thus, unfortunately
	▶ *As a result,* he may convince few voters.
Differences or contrast	however, nevertheless, on the contrary, on the other hand, otherwise
	▶ *Nevertheless,* he has support from some groups.
Emphasis	in fact, in other words, that is, undoubtedly
	▶ *In fact,* some politicians are tired of constantly needing to raise money for campaigns.
Similarities or comparison	likewise, similarly, in contrast, conversely
	▶ *In contrast,* their opponents have received many large donations.

EXERCISE 1.9

For more exercises on conjunctions, refer to the Parts of Speech section of Exercise Central at www .bedfordstmartins.com /successfulwriting.

Underline the conjunctions in the following sentences and identify each one as a coordinating conjunction, correlative conjunction, subordinating conjunction, or conjunctive adverb.

> *subordinating conjunction*
▶ Sometimes academics behave as though there were a gap between the humanities

coordinating conjunction
and the sciences.

1. Writer and scientist C. P. Snow warned of this gap between the arts and sciences decades ago when he wrote *The Two Cultures*.
2. Since Snow wrote his speech, relations between the two groups have changed.
3. Snow addressed both the scientists who were proud of avoiding literature and the humanities professionals who were blissfully ignorant of basic scientific principles.
4. Today, some academics in the humanities have adopted not only scientific terms but also scientific theories in their work.
5. The gap between the arts and sciences has changed in the last few decades; unfortunately, it does not seem to be any smaller.

1g Prepositions

A **preposition** is a word or phrase that links and relates a noun or a pronoun (the object of the preposition) to the rest of the sentence. A **prepositional phrase** includes the preposition along with its object and modifiers. Prepositions often show relationships of time, place, direction, or manner.

▶ Steve Prefontaine could run *despite* excruciating pain.

▶ The continental shelf lies *beneath* the ocean.

Common Prepositions

about	below	except	outside	under
against	beneath	for	over	underneath
along	beside	from	past	unlike
among	between	in	since	until
around	beyond	near	through	up
as	by	off	throughout	upon
at	despite	on	till	with
before	down	onto	to	within
behind	during	out	toward	without

Compound prepositions consist of more than one word.

▶ *According to* historical records, the town is three hundred years old.

▶ The department gained its reputation *by means of* its diversity.

Common Compound Prepositions

according to	because of	in place of	out of
along with	by means of	in regard to	up to
aside from	except for	in spite of	with regard to
as of	in addition to	instead of	with respect to
as well as	in front of	on account of	

For more exercises on prepositions, refer to the Parts of Speech section of Exercise Central at www .bedfordstmartins.com /successfulwriting.

EXERCISE 1.10

Underline the prepositions in the following sentences.

▶ Generations <u>of</u> filmgoers have admired the work <u>of</u> Indian director Satyajit Ray.

1. After Satyajit Ray earned a degree in economics, his mother persuaded him to go to art school.
2. Until then, he had been interested in Western thought, but he became fascinated with Indian art.
3. Ray was an early fan of movies and helped to found the Calcutta Film Society in 1947.
4. Ray's first film, *Pather Panchali,* won a prize at the Cannes Film Festival in 1955.
5. His film career lasted for four decades, and Ray may be remembered as India's greatest filmmaker.

1h Interjections

Interjections are words that express surprise or some other strong feeling. An exclamation point or a period often follows an interjection; a comma may precede and/or follow an interjection if it is a mild one.

▶ *Oh,* it wasn't important.

▶ *Ouch!*

▶ There were no fires reported last month, *by the way.*

EXERCISE 1.11

Underline the interjections in the following sentences. Some sentences may not contain interjections.

▶ <u>Cool!</u> Baseball season starts soon!

1. Our local team did <u>badly</u> last year, <u>but oh well,</u> there's always hope we'll do better this year.
2. Our coach is a good guy, <u>but hey,</u> the team has to win, too.
3. The three things that our team <u>lacks most</u> desperately are pitching, batting, and coaching.
4. <u>Oh,</u> and a few good runners wouldn't hurt either.
5. <u>Awesome!</u> It's time to get fired up for a brand new season!

2 SENTENCE STRUCTURE

2a Sentence parts

A **sentence** is a group of words that expresses a complete thought about something or someone. Every sentence must contain two basic parts: a subject and a predicate.

Subjects

The **subject** of a sentence names a person, place, or thing and tells whom or what the sentence is about. It identifies the performer or receiver of the action expressed in the predicate.

▶ *Carmen Miranda,* the flamboyant performer, made savvy decisions about her career.

▶ The *clock* on the mantel was given to her by her grandmother.

The noun or pronoun that names what the sentence is about is called the **simple subject.**

▶ *Mozart* began composing at the age of four.

▶ The postal *worker* was bitten by a dog.

The simple subject of an imperative sentence is understood as *you,* but *you* is not stated directly.

▶ Be quiet.

　 The sentence is understood as *[You] be quiet.*

The **complete subject** is the simple subject plus its modifiers—words that describe, identify, qualify, or limit the meaning of a noun or pronoun.

　　┌──── complete subject ────┐
▶ A series of very bad *decisions* doomed the project.

　　┌──── complete subject ────┐
▶ There are too many *books* to fit on the shelves.

A sentence with a **compound subject** contains two or more simple subjects joined by a coordinating conjunction (*and, but, or, nor, for, yet,* or *so*).

▶ *Joel* <u>and</u> *Ethan Coen* produce and direct their films.

▶ *A doctor* <u>or</u> *a physician's assistant* will explain the results.

Predicates

The **predicate** of a sentence indicates what the subject does, what happens to the subject, or what is said about the subject. The predicate, then, can indicate an action or a state of being.

ACTION	Plant respiration *produces* oxygen.
STATE OF BEING	Stonehenge *has existed* for many centuries.

A **helping verb** (also called an **auxiliary verb**) combines with a main verb to indicate tense, mood, or voice or to add further information.

A **complement** is a word or group of words that describes or renames a subject or an object.

The **simple predicate** is the main verb along with its helping verbs.

▶ Reporters *should call* the subjects of their stories for comment.

▶ A snow bicycle for Antarctic workers *has been developed.*

The **complete predicate** consists of the simple predicate plus its modifiers and any objects or **complements**. (See p. 855 for more about **complements**.)

┌─────────── complete predicate ───────────┐
▶ The growth of Los Angeles *depended* to a large extent on finding a way to get water to the desert.

┌──────────── complete predicate ────────────┐
▶ Watching fishing boats *is* a relaxing and pleasant way to spend an afternoon.

A **compound predicate** contains two or more predicates that have the same subject and that are joined by *and, but, or, nor,* or another conjunction (see 1f).

▶ AIDS drugs *can save many lives <u>but</u> are seldom available in poor countries that need them desperately.*

▶ President Johnson *<u>neither</u> wanted to run for a second term <u>nor</u> planned to serve if elected.*

For more exercises on subjects and predicates, refer to the Sentence Structure section of Exercise Central at www .bedfordstmartins.com /successfulwriting.

EXERCISE 2.1

In each of the following sentences, underline the simple subject and the simple predicate, put the complete subject in brackets, and enclose the complete predicate in parentheses. Then identify and label any compound subjects and compound predicates that appear.

compound subject
▶ [Wildlife parks and nature preserves] (should be off-limits to human inhabitants).

1. Wildlife and the Maasai tribe's herds of livestock share much of the land at Amboseli Nature Reserve in Kenya.
2. Would this kind of human and wildlife cooperation work in other areas?
3. The Maasai people customarily do not <u>kill</u> local wildlife except during severe drought emergencies.
4. This custom both ensures the workability of the Amboseli Reserve's unusual system and indicates the difficulty of trying the same system elsewhere.
5. The Maasai neither <u>need</u> nor wish to destroy the wild animals with whom they share the land.

Objects

A **direct object** is a noun or pronoun that receives the action of a verb. A direct object answers the question "What?" or "Whom?"

▶ The Scottish fiddler played a lively *reel.*

The noun *reel* answers the question, "What did he play?"

▶ The crowd in the stadium jeered the *quarterback*.

The noun *quarterback* answers the question, "Whom did they jeer?"

An **indirect object** is a noun or pronoun that names the person or thing to whom or for whom something is done.

▶ Habitat for Humanity gave *him* an award for his work.

▶ A woman on a bench tossed the *pigeons* some crumbs.

Complements

A **complement** is a word or group of words that describes a subject or object and completes the meaning of the sentence. There are two kinds of complements: subject complements and object complements.

A **linking verb** (such as *be, become, seem, feel,* or *taste*) connects the subject of a sentence to a **subject complement**, a noun, a noun phrase, or an adjective that renames or describes the subject.

▶ Bill T. Jones is *a well-known choreographer.*

▶ She was *too disorganized to finish her science project.*

An **object complement** is a noun, a noun phrase, or an adjective that modifies or renames the **direct object**. Object complements appear with transitive verbs (such as *name, find, make, think, elect, appoint, choose,* and *consider*), which express action directed toward something or someone.

> A direct object receives the action of the verb: *He drove me home.*

▶ The council appointed him *its new vice president.*

▶ The undercooked meat made several children *sick.*

EXERCISE 2.2

Underline the objects and complements in the following sentences and identify each one as a direct object, an indirect object, a subject complement, or an object complement.

> For more exercises on objects and complements, refer to the Sentence Structure section of Exercise Central at www.bedfordstmartins.com/successfulwriting.

         indirect object   *direct object*

▶ A group of pioneers gave their neighbors | most of their belongings and headed west in 1846.

1. They were an inexperienced but hopeful group.
2. The travelers made the head of the wealthy Donner family their official leader.
3. Their untested route was more dangerous than they realized.
4. Unfortunately, heavy snows trapped the few remaining wagons in the Sierra Nevada mountains in October.
5. When some members of the Donner party died, cannibalism gave the others a way to survive.

2b Phrases

A **phrase** is a group of related words that lacks either a subject, a predicate, or both. A phrase cannot stand alone as a sentence. Phrases can appear at the beginning, middle, or end of a sentence and can help make your writing more detailed and interesting.

WITHOUT PHRASES   The burglars escaped.

Bus travel is an inexpensive choice.

WITH PHRASES   Startled by the alarm, the burglars escaped without getting any money.

For adventurers on a budget, bus travel, while not luxurious, is an inexpensive choice.

There are four common types of phrases: prepositional phrases, verbal phrases, appositive phrases, and absolute phrases.

Prepositional Phrases

A **prepositional phrase** consists of a preposition (*in, above, with, at, behind*), the object of the preposition (a noun or pronoun), and any modifiers of the object. Prepositional phrases usually function as adjectives or adverbs to tell more about people, places, objects, or actions. They can also function as nouns. A prepositional phrase generally adds information about time, place, direction, or manner.

ADJECTIVE   The plants *on the edge of the field* are weeds.
PHRASE

On the edge and *of the field* tell *where.*

ADVERB PHRASE   New Orleans is very crowded *during Mardi Gras.*

During Mardi Gras tells *when.*

NOUN PHRASE   *Down the hill* is the shortest way to town.

Down the hill acts as the subject of the sentence.

Each of the following sentences has been edited to include a prepositional phrase or phrases that expand the meaning of the sentence by adding detail.

▶   He fell/   *on the icy sidewalk.*
          ^

▶   The ship suddenly appeared/   *through the mist near the shore.*
                                 ^

Verbal Phrases

A **verbal** is a verb form used as a noun (the *barking* of the dog), an adjective (a *barking* dog), or an adverb (continued *to bark*). It cannot be used alone as the verb of a sentence, however. The three kinds of verbals are participles, gerunds, and infinitives. A **verbal phrase** consists of a verbal and its modifiers.

Participles and participial phrases. All verbs have two participles: present and past. The **present participle** is the *-ing* form of a verb (*being, hoping, studying*). The **past participle** of most verbs ends in *-d* or *-ed* (*hoped, consisted*). The past participle of irregular verbs has no set pattern (*been, ridden*). Both the present participle and the past participle can function as adjectives modifying nouns and pronouns.

▶ The planes flew over the foggy airport in a *holding* pattern.

▶ The pot was made of *molded* clay.

A **participial phrase**, which consists of a participle and its modifiers, can also function as an adjective in a sentence.

▶ The suspect, *wanted for questioning* on robbery charges, had vanished.

Gerunds and gerund phrases. A **gerund** is the present participle, or *-ing* form, of a verb that functions as a noun in a sentence.

▶ *Driving* can be a frustrating activity.

▶ The government has not done enough to build *housing*.

A **gerund phrase** consists of a gerund and its modifiers. Like a gerund, a gerund phrase is used as a noun and can therefore function in a sentence as a subject, a direct object, an indirect object, an object of a preposition, or a subject complement.

SUBJECT	*Catching the flu* is unpleasant.
DIRECT OBJECT	All the new recruits practiced *marching*.
INDIRECT OBJECT	One director gave his *acting* a chance.
OBJECT OF A PREPOSITION	An ambitious employee may rise by *impressing* her boss.
SUBJECT COMPLEMENT	The biggest thrill was the *skydiving*.

Infinitives and infinitive phrases. An **infinitive** is the base form of a verb preceded by *to: to study, to sleep*. An **infinitive phrase** consists of the infinitive plus any modifiers or objects. An infinitive phrase can function as a noun, an adjective, or an adverb.

SUBJECT   *To become* an actor is my greatest ambition.

ADJECTIVE   She had a job *to do.*

ADVERB   The weary travelers were eager *to sleep.*

Sometimes the *to* in an infinitive phrase is understood but not written.

▶ Her demonstration helped me learn the software.

Note: Be sure to distinguish between infinitive phrases and prepositional phrases beginning with the preposition *to.* In an infinitive phrase, *to* is followed by a verb (*to paint*); in a prepositional phrase, *to* is followed by a noun or pronoun (*to a movie*).

Appositive Phrases

An **appositive** is a word that explains, restates, or adds new information about a noun. An **appositive phrase** consists of an appositive and its modifiers.

▶ Bono, *the lead singer of the band U2,* is active in many political causes.

The appositive phrase adds information about the noun *Bono.*

Absolute Phrases

An **absolute phrase** consists of a noun or pronoun and any modifiers, usually followed by a participle. An absolute phrase modifies an entire sentence, not any particular word or words within the sentence. It can appear anywhere in a sentence and is set off from the rest of the sentence with commas.

▶ *Their shift completed,* the night workers walked out at sunrise.

▶ *An unsuspecting insect clamped in its mandible,* the praying mantis, *its legs folded piously,* appears serenely uninvolved.

EXERCISE 2.3

For more exercises on phrases, refer to the Sentence Structure section of Exercise Central at www .bedfordstmartins.com /successfulwriting.

Underline the phrases in the following sentences and identify each one as a prepositional phrase, participial phrase, gerund phrase, infinitive phrase, appositive phrase, or absolute phrase. If a phrase occurs within a phrase, double underline the overlapping phrase.

  prepositional   participial   / prepositional
  phrase   phrase   phrase
▶ In Indian culture, marriages arranged by the couple's parents are still very
  common.

1. India, a modern nation in many ways, still has ancient customs.
2. Young Indians living in the United States often try to maintain ties with their homeland.
3. A custom practiced for centuries, arranged marriages are one way to find a compatible mate.

4. In some cases, parents may approach their adult children with a proposed match.
5. In other instances, parents arrange the marriage when their children are quite young.

2c Clauses

A **clause** is a group of words that contains a subject and a predicate. A clause is either independent (also called *main*) or dependent (also called *subordinate*). An **independent clause** can stand alone as a grammatically complete sentence.

▶ Einstein was a clerk at the Swiss Patent Office.

▶ Ethnic disputes followed the disintegration of Yugoslavia.

A **dependent clause** has a subject and a predicate, but it cannot stand alone as a grammatically complete sentence because it does not express a complete thought. A dependent clause usually begins with either a subordinating conjunction or a relative pronoun that connects it to an independent clause.

Common Subordinating Conjunctions

after	in as much as	that
although	in case that	though
as	in order that	unless
as if	in so far as	until
as far as	in that	when
as soon as	now that	whenever
as though	once	where
because	provided that	wherever
before	rather than	whether
even if	since	while
even though	so that	why
how	supposing that	
if	than	

Relative Pronouns

that	whatever	who (whose, whom)
what	which	whoever (whomever)

┌── dependent clause ──┐
▶ *When the puppies were born,* the breeder examined them carefully.

dependent
┌─ clause ─┐
▶ Van Gogh's paintings began to command high prices *after he died.*

▶ Isadora Duncan, *who personified modern dance,* died in a bizarre accident.

     — dependent clause —

When joined to independent clauses, dependent clauses can function as adjectives, adverbs, or nouns and are known as **adjective clauses** (also called **relative clauses**) **adverb clauses,** or **noun clauses.** A noun clause can function as a subject, an object, or a complement.

     — adjective clause —

▶ Comic art, *which was once considered "kid stuff,"* is now taken seriously.

     — adverb clause —

▶ The whistle blew *as the train approached the crossing.*

     — noun clause —

▶ The starving artist ate *whatever he could get.*

Relative pronouns are generally the subject or object in their clauses. *Who* and *whoever* change to *whom* and *whomever* when they function as objects. Sometimes the relative pronoun or subordinating conjunction is implied or understood rather than stated.

▶ **African rituals are among the subjects [that] the essay discusses.**

That is the understood relative pronoun in the subordinate clause.

A dependent clause may contain an implied predicate. When a dependent clause is missing an element that can be inferred from the context of the sentence, it is called an **elliptical clause.**

     — elliptical clause —

▶ **The Watergate cover-up disturbed Americans** *more than the Iran-Contra hearings.*

The predicate *disturbed them* is implied.

EXERCISE 2.4

For more exercises on clauses, refer to the Sentence Structure section of Exercise Central at www .bedfordstmartins.com /successfulwriting.

Underline the dependent clauses in the following sentences.

▶ **An illness <u>that is believed to affect a high percentage of children</u> is attention deficit disorder, or ADD.**

1. Children <u>who have ADD</u> are easily distracted and may be hyperactive.
2. If a child has difficulty concentrating on ordinary tasks such as homework, he or she may have ADD.
3. Although treatment of ADD has become more commonplace recently, some people have started to ask questions.
4. Some people wonder whether ADD might be a phenomenon connected to modern life.
5. Other researchers believe that ADD is the result of a chemical deficiency in the brain.

2d Types of sentences

A sentence can be classified as one of four basic types: simple, compound, complex, or compound-complex.

Simple Sentences

A **simple sentence** has one main or **independent clause** and no subordinate or **dependent clauses**. A simple sentence contains at least one subject and one predicate. It may have a compound subject, a compound predicate, and various phrases, but it has only one clause.

> ▶ She sprints.

> ▶ She and her teammates sprint.

> ▶ She and her teammates sprint and run laps.

> ▶ She and her teammates in the track and field events sprint and run laps to achieve their goal of winning medals.

An independent clause contains a subject and a verb and can stand alone as a sentence.

A dependent clause contains a subject and a verb but does not express a complete thought.

Compound Sentences

A **compound sentence** consists of two or more independent clauses and no dependent clauses. The two independent clauses are usually joined with a comma and a coordinating conjunction (*and, but, nor, or, for, so,* or *yet*).

> ▶ She runs laps, but her teammates practice throwing the javelin.

Sometimes the two clauses are joined with a semicolon and no coordinating conjunction.

> ▶ She runs laps; her teammates practice throwing the javelin.

Or they may be joined with a semicolon and a conjunctive adverb (such as *nonetheless* or *still*), followed by a comma.

> ▶ She runs laps; however, her teammates practice throwing the javelin.

Complex Sentences

A **complex sentence** has one independent clause and one or more dependent clauses. The dependent clauses usually begin with a subordinating conjunction or a relative pronoun (see 2c for a list).

> ▶ They are training *while he recovers from a sprained ankle.*

▶ Runners *who win their event at more than one local track meet* will be eligible for the district trials.

Compound-Complex Sentences

A **compound-complex sentence** contains two or more independent clauses and one or more dependent clauses.

▶ She and her teammates won the meet, and as they were celebrating, a reporter approached for an interview.

▶ A reporter approached while they were celebrating their victory, and after they doused him with champagne, they answered his questions.

For more exercises on sentence types, refer to the Sentence Structure section of Exercise Central at www.bedfordstmartins.com/successfulwriting.

EXERCISE 2.5

Identify each of the following sentences as simple, compound, complex, or compound-complex.

▶ Trumpeter Louis Armstrong was a major influence on jazz music. *Simple*

1. Armstrong, who was born in New Orleans, played the cornet at first.
2. While he was a member of Fletcher Henderson's band, he began to create innovative jazz forms, and later, in Chicago, he switched to the trumpet.
3. He made important recordings in Chicago from 1925 to 1928.
4. Many jazz historians contend that he was the most influential jazz musician in the twentieth century.
5. Armstrong was also a singer and a film actor, but his contributions as a musician are his most enduring legacy.

WRITING CORRECT SENTENCES

3 SENTENCE FRAGMENTS

A **sentence fragment** is a group of words that cannot stand alone as a complete sentence. A fragment is often missing a subject, a complete verb, or both.

> A **sentence** is a group of words that must include at least one independent clause (a subject and a verb that express a complete thought).

> FRAGMENT   Are hatched in sand.

This group of words does not tell *who* or *what* are hatched in sand. It lacks a subject.

> FRAGMENT   Jamal is a basketball player of many talents. *Especially his rebounding ability.*

The second group of words has a subject, Jamal's rebounding ability, but lacks a verb.

> FRAGMENT   To notice a friendly smile.

This group of words lacks both a subject and a verb. *To notice* is not a complete verb. It is an infinitive.

A group of words can have both a subject and a verb but still be a fragment because it does not express a complete thought.

>   subject   verb
> FRAGMENT   Because the *number* of voters *has* declined.

This group of words does not tell what happened as a result of the voter decline. Its meaning is incomplete.

Notice that the preceding fragment begins with the subordinating conjunction *because*. A clause that begins with a subordinating conjunction cannot stand alone as a complete sentence. (For a list of common subordinating conjunctions, see 2c.)

Word groups that begin with a relative pronoun (*that, which, who*) are also not complete sentences.

>   subject   verb
> FRAGMENT   Which *scientists studied* for many years.

The group of words does not tell *what* the scientists studied.

Finally, when a word group begins with a transitional word or phrase (*for example, also*), make sure that it includes both a subject and a verb.

>   subject
> FRAGMENT   For example, the Gulf *Coast* of Florida.

Use the accompanying flowchart to help you decide whether a particular word group is a complete sentence or a sentence fragment. Also try reading your essays backward from the end to the beginning, sentence by sentence, to check for fragments. This method allows you to evaluate each sentence in isolation, without being distracted by the flow of ideas throughout the essay. You might also try

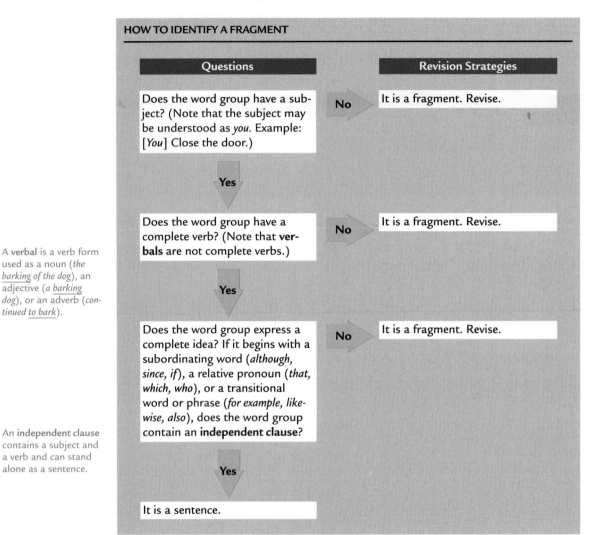

A **verbal** is a verb form used as a noun (*the barking of the dog*), an adjective (*a barking dog*), or an adverb (*continued to bark*).

An **independent clause** contains a subject and a verb and can stand alone as a sentence.

HOW TO IDENTIFY A FRAGMENT

Questions		Revision Strategies
Does the word group have a subject? (Note that the subject may be understood as *you*. Example: [*You*] Close the door.)	**No** →	It is a fragment. Revise.
↓ **Yes**		
Does the word group have a complete verb? (Note that **verbals** are not complete verbs.)	**No** →	It is a fragment. Revise.
↓ **Yes**		
Does the word group express a complete idea? If it begins with a subordinating word (*although, since, if*), a relative pronoun (*that, which, who*), or a transitional word or phrase (*for example, likewise, also*), does the word group contain an **independent clause**?	**No** →	It is a fragment. Revise.
↓ **Yes**		
It is a sentence.		

turning each sentence into a *yes* or *no* question by adding a helping verb, such as *do, does,* or *did.* A complete sentence can be turned into a *yes* or *no* question, but a fragment cannot.

SENTENCE   Sociology has wide applications.

YES/NO   Does sociology have wide applications?
QUESTION

FRAGMENT   While sociology has wide applications.

YES/NO   [Cannot be formed]
QUESTION

A sentence fragment can be revised in two general ways: (1) by attaching it to a nearby sentence or (2) by rewriting the fragment as a complete sentence. The method you choose depends on the element the fragment lacks as well as your intended meaning.

▶ *Certain turtle eggs are*
~~Are~~ hatched in sand.

▶ Jamal is a basketball player of many talents~~.~~, *E*specially his rebounding ability.

▶ *Sam was too busy to*
~~To~~ notice a friendly smile.

▶ *The*
~~Because the~~ number of voters has declined.

3a Join a fragment lacking a subject to another sentence or rewrite it as a complete sentence.

Attach a fragment lacking a subject to a neighboring sentence if the two are about the same person, place, or thing.

▶ *and*
Jenny speaks Italian fluently~~.~~ ~~And~~ reads French well.

As an alternative, you can add a subject to turn the fragment into a complete sentence.

▶ *She also*
Jenny speaks Italian fluently. ~~And~~ reads French well.

3b Add a helping verb to a fragment lacking a complete verb.

Make sure that every sentence you write contains a *complete* verb. For example, verb forms ending in *-ing* need helping verbs to make them complete. **Helping verbs** include forms of *do, be,* and *have* as well as such words as *will, can, could, shall, should, may, might,* and *must.* When you use an *-ing* verb form in a sentence without a helping verb, you create a fragment. To correct the fragment, add the helping verb.

▶ *is*
The college installing a furnace to heat the library.

3c Join a fragment that lacks both a subject and a verb to another sentence, or add the missing subject and verb.

Often, fragments lacking a subject and verb begin with an **infinitive** such as *to hope, to walk,* and *to play,* which are not complete verbs, or they begin with an *-ed* or *-ing* form of a verb. Revise a fragment that begins with an infinitive or an *-ed* or *-ing* verb form by combining it with a previous sentence.

An infinitive is a verb form made up of *to* plus the base form (*to run, to see*).

▶ I plan to transfer next semester,/~~To~~ live closer to home.
to

▶ Robert E. Lee and Ulysses S. Grant met on April 9, 1865,/ ~~Bringing~~ an end to the Civil War.
bringing

You can also revise a fragment beginning with an infinitive or an *-ed* or *-ing* verb form by adding both a subject and a verb to make it a complete sentence.

▶ Linda was reluctant to go out alone at night. ~~To~~ walk across campus from the library.
She was unwilling to

▶ Kyle was determined to do well on his math exam. ~~Studied~~ during every available hour.
He studied

Watch out for fragments that begin with a transitional word or phrase. They can usually be corrected by joining them to a previous sentence.

▶ Annie has always wanted to become an orthopedist,/ ~~That~~ is, a bone specialist.
—that

3d Join a fragment beginning with a subordinating word to another sentence, or drop the subordinating word.

You can correct a fragment beginning with a subordinating word by joining it to the sentence coming before or after.

▶ The students stared spellbound,/~~While~~ the professor lectured.
while

▶ Until Dr. Jonas Salk invented a vaccine,/ ~~Polio~~ was a serious threat to public health.
polio

As an alternative, you can revise this type of fragment by dropping the subordinating word.

▶ ~~Because~~ the 800 area code for toll-free dialing is overused. New codes — 888 and 877 — have been added.
The

3e Join a fragment beginning with a relative pronoun such as who or whom to another sentence, or rewrite it as a complete sentence.

Another common type of sentence fragment begins with a relative pronoun. **Relative pronouns** include *who, whom, whose, whoever, whomever, what, whatever, which,* and *that.*

> ▶ My contemporary fiction instructor assigned a novel by Stephen King, ~~Whose~~ *whose* work I admire.

> ▶ The dodo is an extinct bird. ~~That~~ *It* disappeared in the seventeenth century.

Professional writers sometimes use sentence fragments intentionally to achieve special effects, particularly in works of fiction or articles written for popular magazines. An *intentional* fragment may be used to emphasize a point, answer a question, re-create a conversation, or make an exclamation. However, you should avoid using intentional fragments in academic writing. Instructors and other readers may find the fragments distracting or too informal, or they may assume you used a fragment in error.

EXERCISE 3.1

Correct any fragments in the following sentences. Some groups of sentences may be correct as written.

For more exercises on sentence fragments, refer to the Sentence Fragments section of Exercise Central at www.bedfordstmartins .com/successfulwriting.

> ▶ The mail is delivered every afternoon. ~~While~~ *while* I am at school.

1. Nobody needs to tell you. That a person's mail is private.
2. In these days of computerized mailing lists. Your name and address are certainly not private.
3. The direct-mail business has exploded. Sixty-five billion pieces of unsolicited mail reach American homes and offices each year.
4. To put it another way. Four trees per person per year contribute to this tide of printed waste.
5. Now you can also get electronic junk mail, or "spam." Millions of advertisements sent over the Internet at the push of a button.
6. Email advertisers can target specific audiences. Such as small-business owners or college students.
7. If your Internet service provider charges by the hour or the minute. You will be paying to read unwanted spam.
8. Companies choosing from among more than 20,000 mailing lists. For just pennies per name, firms can target recipients with mass mailings, either paper or electronic. And make a profit from a relatively low response.
9. Even though you can delete the email. You can't remove your name from many computerized mailing lists.
10. Your name can be "sold" over and over. Until it's almost impossible to track it to the business that first listed it.

EXERCISE 3.2

Rewrite the following passage as needed to eliminate sentence fragments.

For more exercises on sentence fragments, refer to the Sentence Fragments section of Exercise Central at www.bedfordstmartins .com/successfulwriting.

▶ How much and what kind of intervention should be undertaken,/O̶n̶ ^{on} behalf of endangered species?

Gila trout are endangered in some stretches of water. That are managed as designated wilderness. A hands-off policy would be their doom. Because exotic trout species now swim in the same streams. Gila trout can survive the competition and the temptation to interbreed only if they swim in isolated tributaries. In which a waterfall blocks the upstream movement of other fish. Two decades ago, one such tributary was fortified. With a small concrete dam. In other words, a dam deliberately built in the wilderness. It is often difficult to choose the right way. To manage a wilderness area. A scientific grasp of the way the ecosystem works is essential. Yet not always available.

4   RUN-ON SENTENCES AND COMMA SPLICES

A **run-on sentence** occurs when two or more independent clauses are joined without a punctuation mark or a coordinating conjunction. Run-on sentences are also known as **fused sentences**.

RUN-ON SENTENCE ┌──── independent clause ────┐ ┌── independent clause ──
A television addict is dependent on television I have suffered this
└───────────────┐
addiction for years.

A **comma splice** occurs when two or more independent clauses are joined with a comma but without a coordinating conjunction (such as *and*, *or*, or *but*).

COMMA SPLICE ┌──── independent clause ────┐ ┌── independent
A typical magic act includes tricks and illusions, both depend
clause ──────┐
on deception.

Notice that only a comma separates the two independent clauses, causing the comma splice.

Another type of comma splice occurs when a word other than a coordinating conjunction is used with a comma to join two or more independent clauses.

COMMA SPLICE ┌──── independent clause ────┐
A typical magic act includes tricks and illusions, however,
┌── independent clause ──┐
both depend on deception.

In the preceding sentence, *however* is a conjunctive adverb, not a coordinating conjunction. There are only seven coordinating conjunctions: *and, or, nor, but, for, so,* and *yet.*

RECOGNIZING RUN-ON SENTENCES AND COMMA SPLICES

Many students have difficulty spotting run-on sentences and comma splices in their own writing. Use the accompanying flowchart to help you identify these types of errors in your sentences.

HOW TO IDENTIFY RUN-ON SENTENCES AND COMMA SPLICES

Questions		Revision Strategies
1. Does the sentence have two or more independent clauses?	No	It is not a run-on or a comma splice.
Yes		
2. Are the clauses joined by a comma and a coordinating conjunction (*and, or, nor, but, for, so,* or *yet*)?	Yes	The sentence is not a run-on or a comma splice.
No		
3. Are the clauses joined by a semicolon (;)?	Yes	The sentence is not a run-on or a comma splice.
No		
4. Are the clauses connected with only a comma?	Yes	The sentence is a comma splice. Revise.
No		
5. Does the sentence lack both a comma and a coordinating conjunction?	Yes	It is a run-on sentence. Revise.

CORRECTING RUN-ON SENTENCES AND COMMA SPLICES

There are four basic ways to correct a run-on sentence or comma splice. Choose the method that best fits your sentence or intended meaning.

4a Revise by creating two separate sentences.

Correct a run-on sentence or comma splice by creating two separate sentences. Make sure each independent clause has the appropriate end punctuation mark — a period, a question mark, or (on rare occasions) an exclamation mark.

period   period
↓   ↓

Independent clause . *Independent clause* .

RUN-ON SENTENCE   A resume should be directed to a specific audience. *It* it should emphasize the applicant's potential value to the company.

COMMA SPLICE   To evaluate a charity, you should start by examining its goals,/. *T* then you should investigate its management practices.

4b Revise by joining the clauses with a semicolon (;).

When the independent clauses are closely connected in meaning, consider joining them with a semicolon. Note that a coordinating conjunction (such as *and, or,* or *but*) is *not* included when you revise with a semicolon (see 4c).

semicolon
↓

Independent clause ; *independent clause* .

RUN-ON SENTENCE   Specialty products are unique items that consumers take time purchasing; these items include cars, parachutes, and skis.

COMMA SPLICE   Studies have shown that male and female managers have different leadership styles,/; as a result, workers may respond differently to each.

In the second example, the semicolon joins the two clauses connected by the conjunctive adverb *as a result.* When two independent clauses are joined by a conjunctive adverb, a semicolon is needed.

4c Revise by joining the clauses with a comma and a coordinating conjunction.

Two independent clauses can be joined by using *both* a comma and a coordinating conjunction (*and, or, nor, but, for, so,* or *yet*). The coordinating conjunction indicates how the two clauses are related.

comma + coordinating conjunction
↓

Independent clause , *and* *independent clause* .

RUN-ON SENTENCE	Closed-minded people often refuse to recognize opposing *and* views, they reject ideas without evaluating them.
COMMA SPLICE	*but* Some educators support home schooling, others oppose it vehemently.

4d Revise by making one clause dependent or by turning one clause into a phrase.

A **dependent clause** contains a subject and a verb but does not express a complete thought. It must always be linked to an independent clause. You can correct a run-on sentence or a comma splice by adding a **subordinating conjunction** (such as *because* or *although*) to one of the independent clauses, thereby making it a dependent clause. The subordinating conjunction makes the thought incomplete and dependent on the independent clause.

subordinating conjunction
↓

Because *dependent clause* , *independent clause* .

or   subordinating conjunction
↓

Independent clause *because* *dependent clause* .

RUN-ON SENTENCE	Facial expressions are very revealing they are an important communication tool.
INDEPENDENT CLAUSE	Facial expressions are very revealing.
DEPENDENT CLAUSE	*Because* facial expressions are very revealing
JOINED TO INDEPENDENT CLAUSE	Because facial expressions are very revealing, they are an important communication tool.

You can also correct a run-on sentence or a comma splice by changing one of the independent clauses to a phrase.

Phrase , *independent clause* .

or

Independent clause , *phrase* .

or

Beginning of independent clause , *phrase* , *end of independent clause* .

COMMA SPLICE	Medieval peasants in Europe ate a simple, hearty diet, they relied almost totally on agriculture.
INDEPENDENT CLAUSE	Medieval peasants in Europe ate a simple, hearty diet.
CLAUSE REDUCED TO PHRASE	having a simple, hearty diet
EMBEDDED IN INDEPENDENT CLAUSE	Medieval peasants in Europe, having a simple, hearty diet, relied almost totally on agriculture.

Note: A comma or commas may or may not be needed to separate a phrase from the rest of the sentence, depending on how the phrase affects the meaning of the sentence (see 12e). Here are two more examples that show how to revise run-on sentences and comma splices using subordination.

RUN-ON SENTENCE	Distributors open big-budget movies late in the week, ~~they hope~~ *hoping* moviegoers will flock to theaters over the weekend.
COMMA SPLICE	*Although the* ~~The~~ remote fishing lodge has no heat or electricity, ~~nevertheless~~ it is a popular vacation spot.

EXERCISE 4.1

For more exercises on run-on sentences and comma splices, refer to the Run-on Sentences and Comma Splices section of Exercise Central at www.bedfordstmartins.com/successfulwriting.

Correct any run-ons or comma splices in the following sentences.

▶ A deadly nerve poison is found on the skin of some Amazon tree frogs,/; native tribes use the poison on the tips of their arrows when they hunt.

1. Nearly every American child dreams of going to Disney World, it has become one of the most popular family vacation destinations.
2. Shopping through Internet bookstores is convenient, some people miss the atmosphere of a traditional bookstore.

3. Openness is one way to build trust in a relationship another is to demonstrate tolerance and patience.

4. In the 1960s many Americans treated Vietnam veterans disrespectfully this situation has changed dramatically since that time.

5. William Faulkner wrote classic novels about life in the U.S. South, Eudora Welty has also written vividly about southern life.

6. With large bodies and tiny wings, bumblebees have long been a puzzle, how do they fly?

7. The Taj Mahal is aptly called the "Pearl Mosque" it glows in the moonlight with unearthly beauty.

8. The Supreme Court often makes controversial decisions, the justices must decide how to interpret the Constitution.

9. Although the clouds were threatening, the storm had not yet struck, however, most boats turned toward shore.

10. Restoring a painting is, indeed, delicate work too much enthusiasm can be dangerous.

EXERCISE 4.2

Correct any run-on sentences and comma splices in the following paragraph. Some sentences may be correct as written.

For more exercises on run-on sentences and comma splices, refer to the Run-on Sentences and Comma Splices section of Exercise Central at www .bedfordstmartins.com /successfulwriting.

                                                                          but
▶ **Some people believe dreams are revealing, others think the brain is simply unloading excess information.**

    Throughout recorded history, people have been fascinated by dreams, they have wondered what meaning dreams hold Whether the dreams are ominous or beautiful, people have always wanted to understand them. There are many ancient stories about dream interpretation one of these is the biblical story of Daniel. Daniel is able to interpret a ruler's dream, this power to interpret convinces the ruler that Daniel is a prophet. Other early writers considered the topic of dream interpretation, to Latin writers, some dreams were meaningful and some were not. Meaningful dreams could reveal the future, these writers argued, but other dreams were simply the result of eating or drinking too much. Sigmund Freud, the founder of psychoanalysis, dramatically changed the field of dream interpretation he believed that dreams come from the subconscious. According to Freud, ideas too frightening for the waking mind often appear in dreams, patients in Freudian therapy often discuss dream images. Today, not everyone agrees with Freud, scientists trying to understand the brain still pay attention to dreams. They are certain that dreams reflect modern life more and more people today dream about computers.

5 SUBJECT-VERB AGREEMENT

Subjects and verbs must agree in person and number. **Person** refers to the forms *I* or *we* (first person), *you* (second person), and *he, she, it,* and *they* (third person). **Number** shows whether a word refers to one thing (singular) or more than one thing (plural). In a sentence, subjects and verbs need to be consistent in person and number: *I drive, you drive, she drives.*

Subject-verb agreement errors often occur in complicated sentences, in sentences with compound subjects, or in sentences where the subject and verb are separated by other words or phrases. The following sections will help you look for and revise common errors in subject-verb agreement.

5a Make sure the verb agrees with the subject, not with words that come between the subject and verb.

▶ The *number* of farm workers *has* remained constant over several decades.

The subject *number* is singular and requires a singular verb, even though the words *of farm workers* appear between the subject and verb.

5b Use a plural verb when two or more subjects are joined by *and*.

▶ A dot and a dash represents the letter *A* in Morse code.

▶ Supreme Court Justice Antonin Scalia, media magnate Rupert Murdoch, and news

                                were

   correspondent Sam Donaldson was born on March 11.

5c Revise to make the verb agree with the subject closest to it when two or more subjects are joined by *or, either . . . or,* or *neither . . . nor.*

When two or more singular subjects are joined by *or, either . . . or,* or *neither . . . nor,* use a singular verb.

▶ *Math* or *accounting appears* to be a suitable major for you.

▶ Either the *waiter* or the *customer has* misplaced the bill.

▶ Neither the *doctor* nor the *patient is* pessimistic about the prognosis.

When one singular and one plural subject are joined by *or, either . . . or,* or *neither . . . nor,* the verb should agree in number with the subject nearest to it.

▶ Neither the *sailors* nor the *boat was* harmed by the storm.

▶ Neither the *boat* nor the *sailors were* harmed by the storm.

                                     s

▶ Either my daughters or my wife water that plant daily.

5d Use a singular verb with most collective nouns, such as *family, couple,* and *class.*

When a **collective noun** refers to a group as one unit acting together, use a singular verb. When the members of the group are acting as individuals, use a plural verb.

To make their meaning clearer and avoid awkwardness, writers often add *members* or a similar noun.

▶ The school *committee has* voted to increase teachers' salaries.

  The committee is acting as a unit.

▶ The family ~~are~~ *is* living in a cramped apartment.

▶ The *team members are* traveling by train, bus, and bike.

  The team members are acting individually.

▶ The members of the jury ~~is~~ *are* divided and unable to reach consensus.

5e Use a singular verb with most indefinite pronouns, such as *anyone, everyone, each, every, no one,* and *something.*

Indefinite pronouns do not refer to a specific person, place, or object. They refer to people, places, or things in general. Singular indefinite pronouns include the following: *each, either, neither, anyone, anybody, anything, everyone, everybody, everything, one, no one, nobody, nothing, someone, somebody, something.*

▶ *Everyone* in this room *is* welcome to express an opinion.

▶ Neither of the candidates ~~have~~ *has* run for office before.

Other indefinite pronouns, such as *several, both, many,* and *few,* take a plural verb.

▶ Every year *many succeed* in starting new small businesses.

▶ Several of you jog~~s~~ at least three miles a day.

Some indefinite pronouns, such as *all, any, more, most, some,* and *none,* take either a singular or a plural verb depending on the noun they refer to. To decide which verb to use, follow this rule: Treat the indefinite pronoun as singular if it refers to something that cannot be counted and as plural if it refers to more than one of something that can be counted.

▶ Most of the water go*es* into this kettle.

  You cannot count water.

▶ Some of the children in the study choose~~s~~ immediate rather than delayed rewards.

  You can count children.

An **antecedent** is the noun or pronoun to which a pronoun refers.

A **relative pronoun** introduces a dependent clause that functions as an adjective: *the patient who injured her leg.*

5f Revise to make verbs agree with the antecedents of *who, which,* and *that.*

When a **relative pronoun** (*who, which, that*) refers to a singular noun, use a singular verb. When it refers to a plural noun, use a plural verb.

▶ *Toni Morrison, who enjoys* unique success as both a popular and a literary author, won the Nobel Prize in literature in 1993.

Who refers to Toni Morrison, and because *Toni Morrison* is singular, the verb *enjoys* is singular.

▶ Look for *stores that display* this sign.

That refers to *stores,* a plural noun.

Using *one of the* often leads to errors in subject-verb agreement. The phrase *one of the* plus a noun is plural.

▶ A pigeon is *one of the two birds that drink* by suction.

That refers to *birds,* and since *birds* is plural, the verb *drink* is plural.

However, *only one of the* plus a noun is singular: *The cheetah is the only one of the big cats that has nonretractable claws.*

5g Revise to make the verb agree with a subject that follows it.

A **prepositional phrase** is a group of words that begins with a preposition and includes the object or objects of the preposition and all their modifiers: *above the low wooden table.*

When a sentence begins with the word *here* or *there* (which cannot function as a subject) or with a **prepositional phrase**, the subject often follows the verb. Look for the subject after the verb and make sure the subject and verb agree.

▶ There *is* a false *panel* somewhere in this room.

▶ Under the stairs *lurks* a solitary *spider.*

5h Make sure a linking verb agrees with its subject, not a word or phrase that renames the subject.

Linking verbs, such as forms of *be* and *feel, look,* and *taste,* connect a subject with a word or phrase that renames or describes it. In sentences with linking verbs, the verb should agree with the subject.

▶ The *bluebell is* any of several plants in the lily family.

▶ The *issue* discussed at the meeting *was* the low wages earned by factory workers.

5i Use a singular verb when the subject is a title.

▶ *Gulliver's Travels* ~~are~~ ^is a satire by the eighteenth-century British writer Jonathan Swift.

5j Use singular verbs with singular nouns that end in *s*, such as *physics* and *news*.

▶ *Linguistics deals* with the study of human speech.

EXERCISE 5.1

Correct any subject-verb agreement errors in the following sentences. Some sentences may be correct as written.

▶ Most of the people in the world believes that learning a second language is important.

1. Many members of the international business community communicates by speaking English, the international language of business.
2. A student in most non-English-speaking industrialized nations expect to spend six or more years studying English.
3. The United States are different.
4. Working for laws that requires all Americans to speak English is a fairly common U.S. political tactic.
5. In American schools, often neither a teaching staff nor enough money have been available for good foreign language programs.
6. Some linguists joke that a person who speaks two languages are called "bilingual," while a person who speaks one language is called "American."
7. Some states around the country has begun to change this situation.
8. If a class is given lessons in a foreign language, the students feel that they will be better prepared for the new global economy.
9. In a Spanish or French class, children of immigrants for whom English was a second language learns a new language and perhaps gains a new appreciation of their parents' accomplishments.
10. Everyone who study a foreign language are likely to benefit.

For more exercises on subject-verb agreement, refer to the Subject-Verb Agreement section of Exercise Central at www.bedfordstmartins .com/successfulwriting.

EXERCISE 5.2

Correct any sentences with subject-verb agreement errors in the following paragraph. Some sentences may be correct as written.

Everyone in the colder climates want to know whether the next winter will be severe. The National Weather Service, however, usually predict the weather only a short time in advance. Another method of making weather predictions are popular with many Americans. According to folklore, there is a number of signs to alert people to a

For more exercises on subject-verb agreement, refer to the Subject-Verb Agreement section of Exercise Central at www.bedfordstmartins .com/successfulwriting.

hard winter ahead. Among these signs are the brown stripe on a woolly bear caterpillar. If the brown stripe between the caterpillar's two black stripes are wide, some people believe the winter will be a short one. Another of the signs that indicate a hard winter is a large apple harvest. And of course, almost everyone in the United States have seen news stories on February 2 about groundhogs predicting the end of winter. Folk beliefs, which are not based on science, seems silly to many people. Neither the National Weather Service nor folklore are always able to forecast the weather accurately, however.

6   VERB FORMS

Except for *be,* all English verbs have five forms.

Base Form	*Past Tense*	*Past Participle*	*Present Participle*	*-s Form*
move	moved	moved	moving	moves

▶ Many designers *visit* Milan for fashion shows each year.

▶ Sarah *visited* her best friend in Thailand.

▶ Students have *visited* the state capitol every spring for decades.

▶ His cousin from Iowa is *visiting* this week.

▶ Maria *visits* her grandmother in Puerto Rico as often as possible.

6a   Use *-s* or *-es* endings for present tense verbs that have third-person singular subjects.

The *-s* form is made up of the verb's base form plus *-s* or *-es.*

▶ Mr. King *teaches* English.

A third-person singular subject can consist of a singular noun, a singular pronoun (*he, she,* and *it*), or a singular indefinite pronoun (such as *everyone*).

SINGULAR NOUN	The flower opens.
SINGULAR PRONOUN	He opens the door.
SINGULAR INDEFINITE PRONOUN	Everybody knows the truth.

  wants
▶ She ~~want~~ to be a veterinarian.
        ^

                     understands
▶ None of the townspeople ~~understand~~ him.
                      ^

6b Do not omit *-ed* endings on verbs.

For regular verbs, both the past tense and the past participle are formed by adding *-ed* or *-d* to the base form of the verb. (For more on verb tense, see 1c and 27a.)

▶ She *claimed* to be the czar's daughter, Anastasia.

▶ The defendant *faced* his accusers.

Some speakers do not fully pronounce the *-ed* endings of verbs (*asked, fixed, supposed to, used to*). As a result, they may unintentionally omit these endings in their writing.

      talked
▶ He ~~talk~~ to the safety inspectors about plant security.

      used
▶ They ~~use~~ to dance to disco all night long.

6c Use the correct form of irregular verbs such as *lay* and *lie*.

The verb pairs *lay* and *lie* and *sit* and *set* have similar forms and are often confused. Each verb has its own meaning: *lie* means to recline or rest on a surface, while *lay* means to put or place something; *sit* means to be seated, as in a chair, while *set* means to place something on a surface.

      lie
▶ Our dog likes to ~~lay~~ on the couch all afternoon.

      sit
▶ Let me ~~set~~ in this chair for a while.

For more on irregular verbs, see 1c.

6d Use the active and passive voice appropriately.

When a verb is in the **active voice**, the subject performs the action.

    ACTIVE VOICE   The Mississippi River flows into the Gulf of Mexico.

When a verb is in the **passive voice**, the subject receives the action.

    PASSIVE VOICE   The computer file was deleted.

    Notice that the passive voice sentence does not tell *who* deleted the file.

    The active voice expresses ideas more vividly and emphatically than does the passive voice. Whenever possible, use the active voice in your sentences.

    The colonists threw tea
▶ ~~Tea was thrown~~ into Boston Harbor. ~~by the colonists.~~

> *No one is allowed to sell illegal*
> ~~Illegal~~ drugs. ~~are not allowed to be sold,~~
>   ^   ^

Passive voice sentences may seem indirect, as if the writer is purposely withholding information. In general, use the passive voice sparingly. There are two situations in which it is the best choice, however.

1. When you do not know or do not want to reveal who performed the action of the verb:

    PASSIVE   Several historic buildings had been torn down.

2. When you want to emphasize the object of the action rather than the person who causes the action:

    PASSIVE   The poem "My Last Duchess" by Robert Browning was discussed in class.

    In this sentence, the title of the poem is more important than the people who discussed it.

6e Use the present tense when writing about literary works, even though they were written in the past.

> *depicts*
> Chaucer's *Canterbury Tales* ~~depicted~~ a tremendously varied group of travelers.
>   ^

6f Be sure to distinguish between the immediate past and the less immediate past.

Use the past perfect form of the verb, formed by adding *had* to the past participle, to indicate an action that was completed before another action or a specified time.

    UNCLEAR   Roberto finished three research papers when the semester ended.

    Roberto did not finish all three right at the end of the semester.

    REVISED   Roberto had finished three research papers when the semester ended.

For more on verb tense, see 1c and 27a.

For more exercises on verb forms, refer to the Verb Forms section of Exercise Central at www .bedfordstmartins.com /successfulwriting.

EXERCISE 6.1

Correct the errors in verb form in the following sentences. Some sentences may be correct as written.

> *United States entered the*
> The Spanish-American War ~~was entered by the United States~~ in 1898.
>   ^

1. When the nineteenth century change into the twentieth, many people in the United States became eager to expel Spain from the Americas.

2. Cuba, an island that lays ninety miles off the Florida coast, provided them with an excuse to do so.

3. Cuban rebels were trying to free themselves from Spain, and many Americans wanted to help them.

4. In addition, many people in the United States wanted to take over Spain's territories for a long time.

5. The United States won the war very quickly and assume control of Cuba, the Philippines, Guam, and Puerto Rico.

6. Cuba was allow to take control of its own affairs right away.

7. Puerto Rico became a commonwealth in 1952, a position that place it between statehood and independence.

8. In a 1998 election, the people of Puerto Rico were offered the option of full statehood.

9. It was rejected by them.

10. Many Puerto Ricans are worried that statehood would destroy the native culture of their island, and none of them want that to happen.

EXERCISE 6.2

Correct the errors in verb form in the following paragraph. Some sentences may be correct as written.

For more exercises on verb forms, refer to the Verb Forms section of Exercise Central at www .bedfordstmartins.com /successfulwriting.

                        contains
▶ Walt Whitman's *Leaves of Grass* ~~contain~~ long, informally structured poems.
                             ^

      Walt Whitman was usually considered one of the greatest American poets. He spent almost his whole life in Brooklyn, New York, but he like to write about all of America. He was fired from several jobs for laziness and admitted that he liked to lay in bed until noon. But he had a vision: He wanted to create an entirely new kind of poetry. Rhyme was considered unimportant by him, and he did not think new American poetry needed formal structure. Unfortunately for Whitman, his great masterpiece, *Leaves of Grass,* was not an overnight success. Ralph Waldo Emerson admire it, but Whitman sold very few copies. He revise it continuously until his death. Today, people admires *Leaves of Grass* for its optimism, its beautiful language, its very modern appreciation of the diversity of America, and its astonishing openness about sexuality. Whitman's body of work still move and surprise readers.

7 PRONOUN PROBLEMS

Pronouns are words used in place of nouns. They provide a quick, convenient way to refer to a word that has already been named. Common problems in using pronouns include problems with pronoun reference, agreement, and case.

PRONOUN REFERENCE

    A pronoun should refer clearly to its **antecedent,** the noun or pronoun for which it substitutes.

If an antecedent is missing or unclear, the meaning of the sentence is also unclear. Use the following guidelines to make certain your pronoun references are clear and correct.

7a Make sure each pronoun refers clearly to one antecedent.

▶ The hip-hop radio station battled the alternative rock station for the highest ratings.

         the alternative station
Eventually, ~~it~~ won.

The revised sentence makes it clear which station won: the alternative rock station.

7b Be sure to check for vague uses of *they, it,* and *you.*

They, it, and *you* often refer vaguely to antecedents in preceding sentences or to no antecedent at all.

OMITTED ANTECEDENT	On the Internet, they claimed that an asteroid would collide with the earth.

On the Internet does not explain what *they* refers to.

CLEAR	On the Internet, a Web page claimed that an asteroid would collide with the earth.

Adding the noun *a Web page* clears up the mystery.

▶ When political scientists study early political cartoons, ~~it provides~~ *they gain* insight into historical events.

▶ In Florida, ~~you often hear~~ *people often talk* about hurricane threats of previous years.

7c Make sure pronouns do not refer to adjectives or possessives.

Pronouns must refer to nouns or other pronouns. Adjectives and possessives cannot serve as antecedents, although they may seem to suggest a noun the pronoun *could* refer to.

▶ He became so depressed that ~~it made him~~ *he was* unable to get out of bed.

The pronoun *it* seems to refer to the adjective *depressed,* which suggests the noun *depression.* This noun is not in the sentence, however.

▶ The stock market's rapid rise made ~~it~~ *stocks* appear to be an attractive investment.

The pronoun *it* seems to refer to *stock market's,* which is a possessive, not a noun.

7d Make sure the pronouns *who, whom, which,* and *that* refer to clear, specific nouns.

These storms make

▶ Lake-effect storms hit cities along the Great Lakes. ~~That makes~~ winter travel treacherous.

EXERCISE 7.1

Correct any errors in pronoun reference in the following sentences.

are

▶ Innovative codes are important because ~~it means that~~ they ~~will be~~ hard to break.

1. A country at war must be able to convey information to military personnel. That is always a challenge.
2. The information's importance often requires it to be transmitted secretly.
3. Military strategists use codes for these transmissions because they baffle the enemy.
4. They say that "invisible ink," which cannot be seen until the paper is heated, was once a popular way to communicate secretly.
5. Lemon juice and vinegar are good choices for invisible ink because you can't see them unless they are burned.
6. During World War II, U.S. government code specialists hired Navajo Indians because it is a difficult and little-studied language.
7. In early code writing, it involved substituting letters throughout the message.
8. These cryptograms are no longer used to transmit messages because they are too simple.
9. The Nazis' enigma code was extremely difficult to crack. This was an enormous problem for the Allied forces.
10. Alan Turing's mathematical genius saved the day. He was a British civil servant who finally solved the enigma code.

For more exercises on pronoun reference, refer to the Pronoun Problems section of Exercise Central at www.bedfordstmartins .com/successfulwriting.

PRONOUN-ANTECEDENT AGREEMENT

Pronouns and **antecedents** must agree in **person, number,** and **gender.** The most common agreement error occurs when pronouns and antecedents do not agree in number. If the antecedent is singular, use a singular pronoun. If the antecedent is plural, use a plural pronoun.

In most situations, you will instinctively choose the correct pronoun and antecedent. Here are a few guidelines to follow for those times when you are unsure of which pronoun or antecedent to use.

7e Use singular pronouns to refer to indefinite pronouns that are singular in meaning.

Singular indefinite pronouns include the following.

An **antecedent** is the noun or pronoun to which a pronoun refers.

Person indicates whether the subject is speaking (first person: *I, we*), is being spoken to (second person: *you*), or is being spoken about (third person: *he, she, it, they*).

Number is a term that classifies pronouns as singular (*I, you, he, she, it*) or plural (*we, you, they*).

another	anywhere	everyone	none	other
anybody	each	everything	no one	somebody
anyone	either	neither	nothing	someone
anything	everybody	nobody	one	something

▶ *Each* of the experiments produced *its* desired result.

▶ If *anyone* wants me, give *him or her* my email address.

▶ *Everyone* in America should exercise *his or her* right to vote so *his or her* voice can be heard.

If the pronoun and antecedent do not agree, change either the pronoun or the indefinite pronoun to which it refers. If you need to use a singular pronoun, use *he or she* or *him or her* to avoid sexism.

▶ ~~Everyone~~ *People* should check their credit card statements monthly.

▶ Everyone should check ~~their~~ *his or her* credit card statement monthly.

An alternative is to eliminate the pronoun or pronouns entirely.

▶ No one should lose ~~their~~ *a* job because of family responsibilities.

Note: Overuse of *him or her* and *his or her* can create awkward sentences. To avoid this problem, you can revise your sentences in one of two ways: by using a plural antecedent and a plural pronoun or by omitting the pronouns altogether.

The indefinite pronouns *all, any, more, most,* and *some* can be either singular or plural, depending on how they are used in sentences. When an indefinite pronoun refers to something that can be counted, use a plural pronoun to refer to it. When an indefinite pronoun refers to something that cannot be counted, use a singular pronoun to refer to it.

▶ Of the tropical plants studied, *some* have proven *their* usefulness in fighting disease.

Because the word *plants* is a plural, countable noun, the pronoun *some* is plural in this sentence.

▶ The water was warm, and *most* of it was murky.

The word *water* is not countable, so *most* is singular.

7f Use a plural pronoun to refer to a compound antecedent joined by *and*.

▶ *The walrus and the carpenter* ate *their* oysters greedily.

Exception: When the singular antecedents joined by *and* refer to the same person, place, or thing, use a singular pronoun.

▶ As *a father and a husband, he* is a success.

Exception: When *each* or *every* comes before the antecedent, use a singular pronoun.

▶ *Every nut and bolt* was in *its* place for the inspection.

When a compound antecedent is joined by *or* or *nor,* the pronoun should agree with the noun closer to the verb.

                                                              their
▶ Either the panda or the sea otters should have ~~its~~ new habitat soon.
                                                              ^

7g Use a singular or plural pronoun to refer to a collective noun, depending on the meaning.

A **collective noun** names a group of people or things acting together or individually (*herd, class, team*) and may be referred to by a singular or plural pronoun depending on your intended meaning. When you refer to a group acting together as a unit, use a singular pronoun.

▶ The *wolf pack* surrounds *its* quarry.

The pack is acting as a unit.

When you refer to the members of the group as acting individually, use a plural pronoun.

▶ After the false alarm, *members* of the bomb squad returned to *their* homes.

The members of the squad acted individually.

EXERCISE 7.2

Correct any errors in pronoun-antecedent agreement in the following sentences. Some sentences may be correct as written.

                         his or her
▶ Every scientist has ~~their~~ own idea about the state of the environment.
                         ^

For more exercises on pronoun-antecedent agreement, refer to the Pronoun Problems section of Exercise Central at www.bedfordstmartins .com/successfulwriting.

case

1. Neither the many species of dinosaurs nor the flightless dodo bird could prevent their own extinction.
2. A team of researchers might disagree on its conclusions about the disappearance of the dinosaur.
3. However, most believe that their findings indicate the dodo died out because of competition from other species.
4. In one way, animals resemble plants: Some are "weeds" because it has the ability to thrive under many conditions.
5. Any species that cannot withstand their competitors may be doomed to extinction.
6. When a "weed" and a delicate native species compete for its survival, the native species usually loses.
7. If the snail darter and the spotted owl lose their fight to survive, should humans care?
8. Everyone should be more concerned about the extinction of plants and animals than they seem to be.
9. Every extinction has their effect on other species.
10. The earth has experienced several mass extinctions in its history, but another would take their toll on the quality of human life.

PRONOUN CASE

Most of the time, you will know automatically which form or *case* of a pronoun to use: the **subjective, objective,** or **possessive** case. A pronoun's case indicates its function in a sentence. When a pronoun functions as a subject in a sentence, the subjective case (*I*) is used. When a pronoun functions as a **direct object,** an **indirect object,** or an **object of a preposition,** the objective case (*me*) is used. When a pronoun indicates ownership, the possessive case (*mine*) is used.

A **direct object** receives the action of the verb: *He drove me home.*

An **indirect object** indicates to or for whom an action is performed: *I gave her the keys.*

An **object of a preposition** is a word or phrase that follows a preposition: *with him, above the table.*

Subjective Case	Objective Case	Possessive Case
I	me	my, mine
we	us	our, ours
you	you	your, yours
he, she, it	him, her, it	his, her, hers, its
they	them	their, theirs
who	whom	whose

Use the following guidelines to correct errors in pronoun case.

7h **Read the sentence aloud without the noun and the word *and* to decide which pronoun to use in a compound construction (*Yolanda and I, Maria and me*).**

INCORRECT   Yolanda and me graduated from high school last year.

If you mentally delete *Yolanda and,* the sentence sounds wrong: *Me graduated from high school last year.*

REVISED   Yolanda and I graduated from high school last year.

If you mentally delete *Yolanda and,* the sentence sounds correct: *I graduated from high school last year.*

INCORRECT   The mayor presented the citizenship award to Mrs. King and I.

If you delete *Mrs. King and,* the sentence sounds wrong: *The mayor presented the citizenship award to I.*

REVISED   The mayor presented the citizenship award to Mrs. King and me.

If you delete *Mrs. King and,* the sentence sounds correct: *The mayor presented the citizenship award to me.*

7i   Read the sentence aloud with the pronoun as the subject when a pronoun follows a form of the verb *be* (*is, are, was, were*).

INCORRECT   The leader is him.

If you substitute *him* for *the leader,* the sentence sounds wrong: *Him is the leader.*

REVISED   The leader is he.

If you substitute *he* for *the leader,* the sentence sounds correct: *He is the leader.*

▶   The best singer in the group is ~~her.~~ *she*

7j   Read the sentence aloud without the noun to determine whether *we* or *us* should come before a noun.

▶   If we hikers frighten them, the bears may attack.

If you mentally delete *hikers,* the sentence sounds correct: *If we frighten them, the bears may attack.*

▶   The older children never paid attention to us kindergartners.

If you mentally delete *kindergartners,* the sentence sounds correct: *The older children never paid attention to us.*

7k   Choose the correct pronoun form for a comparison using *than* or *as* by mentally adding the verb that is implied.

▶   Alexandra is a better athlete than I [am].

▶   The coach likes her better than [he likes] me.

An **object** is the target or recipient of the action described by the verb: *I gave her the keys.*

An **object of a preposition** is a word or phrase that follows a preposition: *with him, above the table.*

7l Use *who* or *whoever* when the pronoun functions as the subject of a sentence. Use *whom* or *whomever* when the pronoun functions as the object of a verb or preposition.

To decide whether to use *who* or *whom* in a question, answer the question yourself by using the words *he* or *him* or *she* or *her*. If you use *he* or *she* in the answer, you should use *who* in the question. If you use *him* or *her* in the answer, use *whom* in the question.

QUESTION	(*Who, Whom*) photocopied the article?
ANSWER	*She* photocopied the article.
CORRECT PRONOUN	*Who* photocopied the article?
QUESTION	To (*who, whom*) is that question addressed?
ANSWER	It is addressed to *him.*
CORRECT PRONOUN	To *whom* is that question addressed?

A **dependent clause** contains a subject and a verb but does not express a complete thought.

Similarly, to decide whether to use *who* or *whom* in a **dependent clause**, turn the dependent clause into a question. The pronoun you use to answer that question will tell you whether *who* or *whom* should appear in the clause.

▶ Aphra Behn's *Oronooko* dramatizes the life of a slave ~~whom~~ *who* came from African royalty.

If you ask the question (*Who, whom*) *came from African royalty?* the answer, *He came from African royalty,* indicates that the correct pronoun is *who.*

A **gerund** is an *-ing* form of a verb that functions as a noun (*complaining, jogging*).

▶ The leader ~~who~~ *whom* we seek must unite the community.

If you ask the question (*Who, whom*) *do we seek?* the answer, *We seek him,* indicates that the correct pronoun is *whom.*

A **participle** is an *-ing* or *-ed* form of a verb that is used as an adjective (*the terrifying monster*) or with a helping verb to indicate tense (*he was running away*). Pronouns used with participles should be in the objective case; pronouns used with gerunds should be in the possessive case.

7m Use a possessive pronoun to modify a gerund.

▶ *His moralizing* has never been welcome.

The possessive pronoun *his* modifies the gerund *moralizing.*

Gerunds are often confused with **participles** because both end in *-ing.*

PARTICIPLE	Teenagers across the United States watched *them singing* on *Saturday Night Live.*

The teenagers watched them, not the singing.

GERUND   The professor discovered *their cheating* on the final exam.

The cheating was discovered, not the students doing the cheating.

EXERCISE 7.3

Correct any errors in pronoun case in the following sentences. Some sentences may be correct as written.

For more exercises on pronoun case, refer to the Pronoun Problems section of Exercise Central at www.bedfordstmartins .com/successfulwriting.

>   *who*
> ▶ Cave explorers, ~~whom~~ are called "spelunkers," sometimes find underground
>   rooms no one has seen before.

1. Whomever discovers a large cave is usually able to attract tourists.
2. Much of Kentucky's Mammoth Cave was explored in the 1830s by Stephen Bishop, a slave who worked as a cave guide.
3. Few spelunkers today are better known than he.
4. Following the success of Mammoth Cave, many Kentucky cavers hoped to make a fortune from them spelunking.
5. Floyd Collins was one Kentucky native whom searched his property for caves.
6. In January of 1925, a falling rock trapped Collins, whom was spelunking in a narrow passage in Sand Cave.
7. When his brothers found him, Collins and them worked unsuccessfully to free his trapped leg.
8. For several days, the most famous man in Kentucky was him.
9. The plea to rescue Floyd Collins was answered by whoever could travel to rural Kentucky.
10. Them failing to save Collins was a terrible tragedy for his family and the rescuers.

EXERCISE 7.4

Correct any errors in pronoun reference, agreement, and case in the following paragraph. Some sentences may be correct as written.

For more exercises on pronoun reference, agreement, and case, refer to the Pronoun Problems section of Exercise Central at www.bedfordstmartins .com/successfulwriting.

>   *She*
> ▶ ~~Her~~ and her husband married for love, which was unusual at the time.

    Lady Mary Wortley Montagu, whom was a wealthy aristocrat, was one of the eighteenth century's most interesting characters. Few women then were as well educated as her. Every parent wanted their daughter to be charming, not intellectual, so Lady Mary secretly taught herself Latin. When her husband was appointed ambassador to Turkey, she and he traveled there together. Her letters to friends in London, which were later published, were filled with detail. She described a Turkish bath's atmosphere so vividly that it became a popular setting for paintings and literature. She also learned that smallpox was rare in Turkey. Of the Turkish people she met, most had gotten his or her immunity to smallpox from a kind of inoculation. This had an effect on Lady Mary herself. Lady Mary's children were among the first British citizens who were inoculated against it.

8 SHIFTS AND MIXED CONSTRUCTIONS

A **shift** is a sudden, unexpected change in point of view, verb tense, voice, mood, or level of diction that may confuse your readers. Shifting from a direct to an indirect question or quotation can also confuse readers. A **mixed construction** is a sentence containing parts that do not sensibly fit together. This chapter will help you identify and correct shifts and mixed constructions in your sentences.

SHIFTS

8a Refer to yourself, your audience, and the people you are writing about in a consistent way.

Person shows the writer's point of view. Personal pronouns indicate whether the subject is the speaker (first person: *I, we*), the person spoken to (second person: *you*), or the person or thing spoken about (third person: *he, she, it, they, one*). (For more on person, see 1b and Chapter 3, p. 68.)

> INCONSISTENT   I discovered that *you* could touch some of the museum exhibits.

Notice that the writer shifts from first-person *I* to the second-person *you*.

> CONSISTENT   I discovered that *I* could touch some of the museum exhibits.

The writer uses the first-person *I* consistently within the sentence.

▶ When people study a foreign language, ~~you~~ *they* also learn about another culture.

8b Maintain consistency in verb tense throughout a paragraph or an essay, unless the meaning requires you to change tenses.

> INCONSISTENT   The virus *mutated* so quickly that it *develops* a resistance to most vaccines.

The sentence shifts from past to present.

> REVISED   The virus *mutates* so quickly that it *develops* a resistance to most vaccines.

Shifts between the present and past tense are among the most common shifts writers make.

▶ The city's crime rate continues to drop, but experts disagreed on the reasons.

8c Change verb tense when you want to indicate an actual time change.

Use the present tense for events that occur in the present; use the past tense for events that occurred in the past. When the time changes, be sure to change the tense. Notice the intentional shifts in the following passage (the verbs are in italics).

> Every spring migratory birds *return* to cooler climates to raise their young. This year a pair of bluejays *is occupying* a nest in my yard, and I *spy* on them. The hatchlings *are growing* larger and *developing* feathers. Last spring, robins *built* the nest that the jays now *call* home, and I *watched* them every morning until the young birds *left* home for the last time.

As the events switch from this year (present) to the previous year (past), the writer changes from the present tense (*is occupying*) to the past tense (*built*). (For more on verb tense, see 1c and 27a.)

8d Use a consistent voice.

Needless shifts between the **active voice** and **passive voice** can disorient readers and create wordy sentences.

In the **active voice,** the subject of the sentence performs the action.

► ~~One~~ group of volunteers ~~was given~~ a placebo, and ~~the researchers~~ treated another group with the new drug.
  The researchers gave one
  they

In the **passive voice,** the subject receives the action.

► Drought and windstorms made farming impossible, and many families ~~were forced~~ to leave Oklahoma. ~~by the specter of starvation.~~
  the specter of starvation forced

To change a sentence from the passive voice to the active voice, make the performer of the action the subject of the sentence. The original subject of the sentence becomes the direct object. Delete the form of the verb *be*.

PASSIVE	The restraining order was signed by the judge.
ACTIVE	The judge signed the restraining order.

For more on voice, see 1c and 6d.

8e Avoid sudden shifts from indirect to direct questions or quotations.

An indirect question tells what a question is or was.

INDIRECT QUESTION	The defense attorney asked where I was on the evening of May 10.
DIRECT QUESTION	"Where were you on the evening of May 10?"

Avoid shifting from direct to indirect questions.

he
▶ Sal asked what could ~~I~~ do to solve the problem.
 ^

8f   Use a consistent mood throughout a paragraph or an essay.

Mood indicates whether the sentence states a fact or asks a question (**indicative mood**), gives a command or direction (**imperative mood**), or expresses a condition contrary to fact, a wish, or a suggestion (**subjunctive mood**). The subjunctive mood is also used for hypothetical situations or impossible or unlikely events. (For more on mood, see 1c.)

INCONSISTENT

You shouldn't expect to learn ballroom dancing immediately, and remember that even Fred Astaire had to start somewhere. First, find a qualified instructor. Then, you should not be embarrassed even if everyone else seems more graceful than you are. Finally, keep your goal in mind, and you need to practice, practice, practice.

This paragraph contains shifts between the indicative and imperative moods.

CONSISTENT

Don't expect to learn ballroom dancing immediately, and remember that even Fred Astaire had to start somewhere. First, find a qualified instructor. Then, don't be embarrassed if everyone else seems more graceful than you are. Finally, keep your goal in mind, and practice, practice, practice.

This revised paragraph uses the imperative mood consistently.

8g   Use a consistent level of diction.

Your level of diction can range from formal to informal. The level you choose should be appropriate for your audience, your subject matter, and your purpose for writing. As you revise your essays, look for inappropriate shifts in diction, such as from a formal to an informal tone or vice versa.

William H. Whyte's studies of human behavior in public space yielded a number of surprises. Perhaps most unexpected was the revelation that people seem to be drawn toward, rather than driven from, crowded spaces. They tend to congregate near the entrances of stores or on street corners. Plazas and shopping districts crowded with pedestrians attract more pedestrians. For some reason, people seem

enjoy gathering together in public spaces.
to ~~get a charge out of hanging out where lots of other folks are hanging out, too.~~
      ^

For academic writing, including class assignments and research papers, use formal language. (For more on levels of diction, see Chapter 7, p. 187.)

EXERCISE 8.1

Correct the shifts in person, verb tense, voice, mood, and level of diction in the following sentences.

For more exercises on shifts in person, verb tense, voice, mood, and level of diction, refer to the Shifts and Mixed Constructions section of Exercise Central at www.bedfordstmartins .com/successfulwriting.

> *many parents have studied*
> ► Experts continue to break new ground in child psychology, and their research.
>   ^   ^
>   ~~has been studied by many parents.~~

1. A new idea about the development of children's personalities had surprised many American psychologists because it challenges widely accepted theories.
2. We wondered whether our professor knew of the new theory and did she agree with it.
3. Personality is believed by some experts to be the result of parental care, but other specialists feel that biology influences personality more strongly.
4. Most parents think you have a major influence on your child's behavior.
5. The new theory suggests that children's peers are a heck of a lot more influential than parents.
6. Peer acceptance is strongly desired by children, and they want to be different from adults.
7. If adults were to think about their childhood experiences, they realize that this idea has merit.
8. Most adults recall that, in childhood, your friends' opinions were extremely important to you.
9. The way people behave with family members is often different from the way we act with our friends.
10. Jittery moms and dads would be really, really relieved if this hypothesis were proven.

EXERCISE 8.2

Correct the shifts in person, verb tense, voice, mood, and level of diction in the following paragraph.

For more exercises on shifts in person, verb tense, voice, mood, and level of diction, refer to the Shifts and Mixed Constructions section of Exercise Central at www.bedfordstmartins .com/successfulwriting.

> *surprise*
> ► Some artists long ago used techniques that still ~~surprised~~ modern students of
>   ^
>   their work.

   Museum visitors can see paintings by the seventeenth-century Dutch artist Jan Vermeer, but you cannot see how he achieved his remarkable effects. Most of his paintings showed simply furnished household rooms. The people and objects in these rooms seem so real that the paintings resembled photographs. Vermeer's use of perspective and light would also contribute to the paintings' realism. Some art historians believe he used a gizmo called a *camera obscura*. This machine projected an image onto a flat surface so you could draw it. For most experts, Vermeer's possible use of technological aids does not make his totally fabulous results less impressive. It is agreed by art historians that the paintings are masterpieces. Vermeer's paintings are admired even more now than they are in his own lifetime.

MIXED CONSTRUCTIONS

8h Make sure clauses and phrases fit together logically.

A **mixed construction** contains phrases or clauses that do not work together logically and that cause confusion in meaning.

> MIXED The fact that the marathon is twenty-six miles, a length that explains why I never have finished it.

The sentence starts with a subject (*The fact*) followed by a dependent clause (*that the marathon is twenty-six miles*). The sentence needs a predicate to complete the independent clause; instead it includes a noun (*a length*) and another dependent clause (*that explains why I never have finished it*). The independent clause that begins with *The fact* is never completed.

> REVISED The marathon is twenty-six miles long, which is why I never have finished it.

In the revision, the parts of the sentence work together.

To avoid mixed constructions in your writing, it often helps to check the words that connect clauses and phrases, especially prepositions and conjunctions.

8i Make subjects and predicates consistent.

Faulty predication occurs when a subject does not work grammatically with its predicate.

> FAULTY The most valued trait in an employee is a person who is loyal.

A person is not a trait.

> REVISED The most valued trait in an employee is loyalty.

► Rising health-care costs decrease health insurance. *the number of people who can afford* ~~for many people.~~

Costs do not decrease health insurance.

8j Avoid the constructions *is when* or *is where* or *reason . . . is because.*

> FAULTY Indigestion is when you cannot digest food.
>
> REVISED Indigestion is the inability to digest food.

> the attraction of
> Gravitation is ~~where~~ one body ~~is being a~~

> ~~The reason~~ I enjoy horseback riding ~~is be~~

EXERCISE 8.3

Correct the mixed constructions in the following s

> designing
> The job that I want is ~~a person who designs~~ W

1. Because there are already an estimated 200,000 to
   for a living right now explains why many young pec
2. The fact that business is booming for independent W
   try that grows larger each year.
3. The reason many companies are going online is becau
   with people who use the Web.
4. The online domain of computer hackers has become routine
5. Some people think the industry standards expect that yc
   gramming languages to work with computers.
6. The information technology department is where a compan_ ,-cople to manage
   Web projects.
7. To figure out where in a corporation to look for a Web job, the personnel department
   is a resource.
8. Applicants for computer jobs located in San Francisco and New York are the primary
   centers for technology.
9. The most important qualification is applicants with Web experience.
10. By creating a personal Web page increases firsthand knowledge of the Internet.

9 ADJECTIVES AND ADVERBS

Adjectives and adverbs are powerful. Used appropriately, they can add precision
and force to your writing, as the following excerpt demonstrates.

> Seated cross-legged on a brocade pillow, wrapped in burgundy robes, was a short,
> rotund man with a shiny pate. He looked very old and very tired. Chhongba bowed
> reverently, spoke briefly to him in the Sherpa tongue, and indicated for us to come
> forward. JON KRAKAUER, *Into Thin Air*

Adjectives modify nouns or pronouns and indicate which one, what kind, or how
many. **Adverbs** modify verbs, adjectives, other adverbs, clauses, or entire sentences
and indicate how, when, where, how often, or to what extent (see also 1d and 1e).

The two most common errors involving adjectives and adverbs occur when
writers use (1) an adjective instead of an adverb (or vice versa) and (2) the wrong
form of an adjective or adverb in a comparison. Use the following guidelines to
identify and correct these and other common errors in your writing.

djectives, to modify verbs, adjectives, or other adverbs.

rsation you may often use adjectives in place of adverbs, you
ful in your writing to use adverbs to modify verbs, adjectives, or
rbs.

▶ Those pants are ~~awful~~ *awfully* expensive.

▶ The headlights shone ~~bright~~ *brightly*.

9b Use adjectives, not adverbs, after linking verbs.

Linking verbs, often forms of *be* and other verbs such as *feel, look, make,* and *seem,* express a state of being. A linking verb takes a **subject complement,** a word group that completes or renames the subject of the sentence. Verbs such as *feel* and *look* can also be action verbs. When they function as action verbs in a sentence, they may be modified by an adverb.

If you are not sure whether a word should be an adjective or adverb, determine how it is used in the sentence. If the word modifies a noun, it should be an adjective.

ADJECTIVE   Our *waiter* looked *slow.*

Slow modifies the word *waiter,* a noun. In this sentence, *looked* is a linking verb.

ADVERB   Our waiter *looked slowly* for some menus.

In this sentence, *looked* is expressing an action and is not a linking verb; *slowly* modifies *looked.*

9c Use *good* and *bad* as adjectives; use *well* and *badly* as adverbs.

▶ Einstein was not a *good student.*

The adjective *good* modifies the noun *student.*

▶ Einstein did not *perform well* in school.

The adverb *well* modifies the verb *perform.*

▶ He did ~~bad~~ *badly* in the leading role.

The adverb *badly* modifies the verb *did.*

When you are describing someone's health, *well* can also function as an adjective.

▶ The disease was in remission, but the *patients* were not yet *well.*

9d Be careful not to use adjectives such as *real* and *sure* to modify adverbs or other adjectives.

▶ The produce was crisp and ~~real~~ *really* fresh.

The adverb *really* modifies the adjective *fresh.*

9e Avoid double negatives.

A sentence with two negative words or phrases contains a **double negative**, which conveys a positive meaning. Do not use two negatives in a sentence unless you want to express a positive meaning (for example, *not uncommon* means "common").

▶ The company is not doing ~~nothing~~ *anything* to promote its incentive plan.

▶ No one under eighteen ~~can't~~ *can* vote in the presidential election.

POSITIVE MEANING INTENDED

Athletic sportswear is not uncommon as casual attire.

9f Use the comparative form of adjectives and adverbs to compare two things; use the superlative form to compare three or more things.

Adjectives and adverbs can be used to compare two or more persons, objects, actions, or ideas. The **comparative** form of an adjective or adverb compares two items. The **superlative** form compares three or more items. Use the list below to check the comparative and superlative forms of most regular adjectives and adverbs in your sentences.

	Comparatives	*Superlatives*
One-syllable adjectives and adverbs	Add *-er: colder, faster*	Add *-est: coldest, fastest*
Two-syllable adjectives	Add *-er: greasier**	Add *-est: greasiest**
Adjectives with three or more syllables or adverbs ending in *-ly*	Add *more* in front of the word: *more beautiful, more quickly*	Add *most* in front of the word: *most beautiful, most quickly*

*To form the comparative and superlative forms of adjectives ending in *-y,* change the *y* to *i* and add *-er* or *-est.*

Irregular adjectives and adverbs form their comparative and superlative forms in unpredictable ways, as the following list illustrates.

	Comparative	*Superlative*
Adjectives		
good	better	best
bad	worse	worst
little	less	least
Adverbs		
well	better	best
badly	worse	worst
Words That Function as Adjectives and Adverbs		
many	more	most
some	more	most
much	more	most

Do not use comparative or superlative forms with absolute concepts, such as *unique* and *perfect*. Something cannot be more or less unique, for example; it is either unique or not unique.

▶ This is ~~the most~~ ᵃ unique solution to the pollution problem.

9g Check your comparisons to be sure they are complete when using comparative and superlative forms.

An incomplete comparison can leave your reader confused about what is being compared.

INCOMPLETE	The Internet works more efficiently.
REVISED	For sending messages, the Internet works more efficiently than the postal service.
INCOMPLETE	The catcher sustained the most crippling knee injury.
REVISED	The catcher sustained the most crippling knee injury of his career.

9h Do not use *more* or *most* with the *-er* or *-est* form of an adjective or adverb.

▶ The hypothesis must be ~~more~~ clearer.

For more exercises on adjectives and adverbs, refer to the Parts of Speech and Adjectives and Adverbs sections of Exercise Central at www.bedfordstmartins .com/successfulwriting.

EXERCISE 9.1

Correct any errors involving adjectives and adverbs in the following sentences.

▶ Events on television seem important because television has more influence. *than any other medium.*

1. Television can have a more immediate impact because it is mainly visual.
2. Televised images from Vietnam made some Americans feel terribly about the war.
3. Military groups are now real careful about allowing reporters to film armed conflicts for television.
4. Politicians who look badly on television tend to perform badly in polls.
5. In 1960, John F. Kennedy was viewed more positively after a televised debate.
6. More Americans get their news from television and the Internet today.
7. Newspapers may describe important news stories clearer than television.
8. While television is better than newspapers at reporting stories with a strong visual element, it is worst at analyzing them.
9. News stories that are not visual may be treated very superficial on television.
10. People shouldn't never assume that what they read on the Internet or see on television is necessarily true.

EXERCISE 9.2

Correct any errors involving adjectives and adverbs in the following paragraph. Some sentences may be correct as written.

► Originating in China, *feng shui* is a ~~traditionally~~ art of balancing elements to achieve harmony.

Feng shui is taken very serious in many Asian societies. Some Hong Kong business executives, for example, will not feel comfortably working in an office until it has been approved by a *feng shui* master. Other people are more interested in *feng shui* for its elegance. A room designed with this idea in mind looks tranquilly. The name *feng shui* means "wind and water," and balancing elements is the more important aspect of the art. Some people believe that this balance brings good luck. Others will admit only that surroundings can have a psychological effect. It is easier to feel comfortable in a room designed according to *feng shui* principles. The placement of doors, windows, and furnishings contributes to the peaceful effect. Whether *feng shui* is magic or simple great interior design, something about it seems to work.

For more exercises on adjectives and adverbs, refer to the Parts of Speech and Adjectives and Adverbs sections of Exercise Central at www.bedfordstmartins .com/successfulwriting.

10 MISPLACED AND DANGLING MODIFIERS

A **modifier** is a word or group of words that describes, changes, qualifies, or limits the meaning of another word or group of words in a sentence.

► The contestant *smiled delightedly.*

The adverb *delightedly* modifies the verb *smiled.*

► *Pretending to be surprised,* he greeted the guests.

The adjective phrase *Pretending to be surprised* modifies the pronoun *he.*

Modifiers that are carefully placed in sentences give your readers a clear picture of the details you want to convey. However, when a sentence contains a **misplaced modifier,** it is hard for the reader to tell which word or group of words the modifier is supposed to be describing.

10a Place modifiers close to the words they describe.

MISPLACED   The mayor *chided* the pedestrians for jaywalking *angrily.*

The adverb *angrily* should be closer to the verb it modifies, *chided.* Here, the adverb appears to be modifying *jaywalking,* so the sentence is confusing.

REVISED   The mayor *angrily chided* the pedestrians for jaywalking.

MISPLACED   The press *reacted* to the story leaked from the Pentagon *with horror.*

The adverb phrase *with horror* should explain how the press reacted, not how the story was leaked, so the modifier should be closer to the verb *reacted.*

REVISED   The press *reacted with horror* to the story leaked from the Pentagon.

10b Make sure each modifier clearly modifies only one word or phrase in a sentence.

When a modifier is placed near or next to the word or phrase it modifies, it may also be near another word it could conceivably modify. When a modifier's placement may cause such ambiguity, rewrite the sentence, placing the modifier so that it clearly refers to the word or phrase it is supposed to modify.

UNCLEAR   The film's attempt to portray war accurately depicts a survivor's anguish.

Does the film attempt to portray war accurately, or does it accurately depict a survivor's anguish? The following revisions eliminate the uncertainty.

REVISED   *In its* ~~The film's~~ attempt to portray war accurately *, the film* depicts a survivor's anguish.

REVISED   The *film* ~~film's attempt to portray war~~ accurately depicts a survivor's anguish*, in its attempt to portray war realistically.*

10c Revise a dangling modifier by rewriting the sentence.

A **dangling modifier** is a word or phrase that does not modify or refer to anything in a sentence. Instead, it seems to modify something that has been left out of the sentence. A dangling modifier can make the meaning of a sentence unclear, inaccurate, or even comical. Most dangling modifiers appear at the beginning or end of sentences.

> DANGLING   **After singing a thrilling aria, the crowd surged toward the stage.**

This sentence suggests that the crowd sang the aria.

> DANGLING   **Laying an average of ten eggs a day, the neighboring farmer is proud of his henhouse.**

This sentence suggests that the farmer lays eggs.

To revise a sentence with a dangling modifier, follow these steps.

1. Identify the word or words that the modifier is supposed to modify.
2. Revise the sentence to correct the confusion either by changing the modifier into a clause with its own subject and verb or by rewriting the sentence so the word being modified becomes the subject.

>   *Pavarotti sang*
> ▶ After ~~singing~~ a thrilling aria, the crowd surged toward the stage.

>   *his prize chickens give*   *reason to be*
> ▶ Laying an average of ten eggs a day, the neighboring farmer ~~is~~ proud of his henhouse.

EXERCISE 10.1

Correct any misplaced or dangling modifiers in the following sentences.

>   *scientists have built*
> ▶ Hoping to get a message from outer space, a huge telescope. ~~has been built,~~

1. Solar systems exist throughout the galaxy like our own.
2. So far, no proof on other planets of the existence of life forms has been found.
3. A tremendously powerful telescope searches distant stars for signs of life in the Caribbean.
4. Astronomers monitor signals coming from other parts of the solar system carefully.
5. Wondering whether humans are alone in the universe, the telescope may provide answers.
6. Most of the signals have been caused by cell phone and satellite interference received so far.
7. While trying to intercept signals from other planets, a signal has also been sent from earth.
8. The message is on its way to other parts of our galaxy, containing information about earth.
9. The message will take twenty thousand years to reach its destination or more.
10. A signal sent to earth similarly would take a long time to reach us.

For more exercises on misplaced and dangling modifiers, refer to the Misplaced and Dangling Modifiers section of Exercise Central at www .bedfordstmartins.com /successfulwriting.

For more exercises on misplaced and dangling modifiers, refer to the Misplaced and Dangling Modifiers section of Exercise Central at www .bedfordstmartins.com /successfulwriting.

EXERCISE 10.2

Correct any misplaced or dangling modifiers in the following paragraph. Some sentences may be correct as written.

▶ The measurement is now based on atomic vibrations ~~of one second~~. *of one second,*

    Making sure standard weights and measures are the same all over the world is an important task. To trade internationally, a kilogram in Mexico must weigh the same as a kilogram in Japan. In the past, countries set standards for weighing and measuring individually. One English king declared a yard to be the distance from his nose to his thumb egotistically. Weight was once measured in barleycorns, so unethical merchants soaked barleycorns to make them heavier in water. Today, the metric system is the worldwide standard, and the weight of the U.S. pound is based even on the standard kilogram. In France, a cylinder is the world standard kilogram made of platinum. Securely, this official kilogram is kept in an airtight container. Nevertheless, losing a few billionths of a gram of weight each year, world standards might eventually be affected. Hoping to find a permanent solution, scientists want to base the kilogram measurement on an unchanging natural phenomenon.

USING PUNCTUATION CORRECTLY

11 END PUNCTUATION

The end of a sentence can be marked with a period (.), a question mark (?), or an exclamation point (!).

11a Use a period to mark the end of a sentence that makes a statement, gives an instruction, or includes an indirect question; use periods with most abbreviations.

An **indirect question** is a statement that reports what was asked or is being asked: *He asked where the classroom was.*

Writers seldom omit the period at the end of a sentence that makes a statement or gives directions.

STATEMENT   Amnesty International investigates human rights violations.

INSTRUCTION   Use as little water as possible during the drought.

Writers sometimes mistake an indirect question for a direct one, however.

▶ Most visitors want to know where the dinosaur bones were found?.

This sentence states what question was asked; it does not ask the question directly.

Many abbreviations use periods (*Mas., Co., St.,*). If you are not sure whether an abbreviation should include periods, check a dictionary.

When an abbreviation that uses periods ends a sentence, an additional period is not needed.

▶ My brother works for Apple Computer, Inc./

Note, however, that the Modern Language Association (MLA) recommends omitting periods in abbreviations that consist of capital letters (*IBM, USIA, BC*) but including periods in abbreviations that consist of lowercase letters (*a.m.*).

11b Use a question mark to end a sentence that asks a direct question.

DIRECT QUESTION   Why was the flight delayed?

When a question is also a quotation, the question mark is placed within the quotation marks (see also 15d).

▶ "What did she want?"? Marcia asked.

11c Use an exclamation point to end a sentence that expresses a strong emotion or a forceful command.

▶ Altering experimental results to make them conform to a hypothesis is never ethical!

Use exclamation points sparingly; they lose their impact when used too frequently.

▶ Government officials immediately suspected terrorism!.

For more exercises on the use of end punctuation marks, refer to the End Punctuation section of Exercise Central at www.bedfordstmartins .com/successfulwriting.

EXERCISE 11.1

Correct any errors in the use of end punctuation marks in the following sentences. Some sentences may be correct as written.

▶ Is it possible that hemophilia in the Russian czar's family contributed to the Russian Revolution./?

1. When the daughters of Queen Victoria of England, who carried the gene for hemophilia, married royalty in Germany and Russia, those royal families inherited hemophilia as well.
2. The Russian czar's only son and heir to the throne suffered from hemophilia.
3. You might ask if internal bleeding can occur when a hemophiliac receives a bruise?.
4. Czar Nicholas and his wife Alexandra often saw their little boy in terrible pain!.
5. A phony monk named Rasputin eased the child's pain, but was he a gifted healer or just a con man/?

12 COMMAS

A **comma** (,) is used to separate parts of a sentence from one another. Commas, when used correctly, make your sentences clear and help readers understand your meaning.

12a Use a comma before a coordinating word (*and, but, for, nor, or, so, yet*) that joins two independent clauses.

An **independent clause** contains a subject and verb and can stand alone as a sentence.

▶ The ball flew past the goalie, but the score did not count.

▶ Her dog was enormous, so many people found it threatening.

12b Use a comma to separate three or more items in a series.

A **series** is a list of three or more items—words, phrases, or clauses.

▶ Dancing, singing, and acting are just a few of her talents.

▶ Sunflowers grew on the hillsides, along the roads, and in the middle of every pasture.

Some writers omit the comma before the coordinating conjunction (such as *and, or*) in a brief series when using a casual or journalistic style. Occasionally this omission can create confusion, so it is better to include the final comma.

CONFUSING   She insured her valuable heirlooms, watches and jewelry.

Do her heirlooms consist entirely of watches and jewelry, or did she insure three kinds of items?

CLEAR   She insured her valuable heirlooms, watches, and jewelry.

A comma is not used after the last item in a series.

▶ Aphids, slugs, and beetles,/ can severely damage a crop.

(See also 13c on when to use semicolons to separate items in a series.)

12c Use a comma to separate two or more adjectives that modify the same noun when they are not joined by a coordinating word.

▶ Rescue workers found the frightened, hungry child.

To be sure a comma is needed, try reversing the two adjectives. If the phrase still sounds correct when the adjectives are reversed, a comma is needed. If the phrase sounds wrong, a comma is not needed.

▶ The airy, open atrium makes visitors feel at home.

The phrase *open, airy atrium* sounds right, so a comma is needed.

▶ Local businesses donated the bright red uniforms.

The phrase *red, bright uniforms* sounds wrong because *bright* modifies *red uniforms* in the original sentence. A comma is not needed.

12d Use a comma to separate introductory words, phrases, and clauses from the rest of a sentence.

INTRODUCTORY WORD   Above, the sky was a mass of clouds.

Without the comma, this sentence would be confusing.

INTRODUCTORY PHRASE   At the start of the project, the researchers were optimistic.

INTRODUCTORY CLAUSE   When alcohol was outlawed, many solid citizens broke the law.

Exception: A comma is not needed after a single word or short phrase or clause when there is no possibility of confusion.

▶ Then a rainbow appeared.

12e Use a comma to set off a nonrestrictive word group from the rest of the sentence.

A **nonrestrictive word group** describes or modifies a word or phrase in a sentence, but it does not change the meaning of the word or phrase. To decide whether a comma is needed, read the sentence without the word group. If the basic meaning is unchanged, a comma is needed.

▶ Most people either love or hate fruitcake, *which is a traditional holiday dessert.*

The meaning of *fruitcake* is not changed by the relative clause *which is a traditional holiday dessert,* so the word group is **nonrestrictive** and a comma is needed.

▶ The child *wearing a tutu* delights in ballet lessons.

The phrase *wearing a tutu* identifies which child delights in ballet lessons, so the word group is **restrictive**, necessary to explain what the word it modifies means, and a comma is not needed.

12f Use a comma to set off parenthetical expressions.

A **parenthetical expression** provides extra information. It can also be a transitional word or phrase (*however, for example, at the beginning*) that is not essential to the meaning of the sentence.

▶ *Furthermore,* his essay had not been proofread.
▶ Islamic countries were, *in fact,* responsible for preserving much classical scientific knowledge.

12g Use commas with dates, addresses, titles, and numbers.

▶ She graduated on June 12, 1994.

When you give only a month and year, a comma is not needed.

▶ She graduated in June 1994.

Place a comma after the date when it appears before the end of the sentence.

▶ Boswell met Johnson on May 16, 1763, in London.

When you give an address within a sentence, do not place a comma between the state and the ZIP code.

▶ Send the package to PO Box 100, McPherson, Kansas 67460.

Separate a name from a title with a comma.

▶ The featured speaker was Kate Silverstein, Ph.D.

Use commas in numbers that have more than four digits.

▶ Estimates of the number of protesters ranged from 250,000 to 700,000.

In a number with four digits, the comma is optional: *1500* or *1,500.*

12h Use a comma to separate a direct quotation from the words that explain it.

A **direct quotation** gives a person's *exact* words, either spoken or written, set off by quotation marks.

▶ She asked, "What's the score?"

Place the comma before the closing quotation mark.

▶ "Wait and see, "ˏwas his infuriating response.

(See also 15b and 15e.)

12i Use commas to set off the name of someone directly addressed, to set off an echo question, and with a "not" phrase.

DIRECT ADDRESS	"James, answer the question concisely." "Bail has not been granted, your honor."
ECHO QUESTION	More development will require a more expensive infrastructure, won't it?
"NOT" PHRASE	Labor Day, not the autumnal equinox, marks the end of summer for most Americans.

12j Omit unnecessary commas.

As you edit and proofread your papers, watch out for the following common errors in comma usage.

OMIT A COMMA BETWEEN A SUBJECT AND VERB.

subject verb

▶ The poet Wilfred Owenˏ was killed a week before World War I ended.

A **complement** is a word or group of words that describes or renames a subject or object.

OMIT A COMMA BETWEEN A VERB AND COMPLEMENT.

verb   complement

▶ The school referendum is considered / very likely to pass.

OMIT A COMMA BETWEEN AN ADJECTIVE AND THE WORD IT MODIFIES.

adjective   noun modified

▶ A growing family needs a large / house.

OMIT A COMMA BETWEEN TWO VERBS IN A COMPOUND PREDICATE.

compound predicate

▶ We sat / and waited for our punishment.

OMIT A COMMA BETWEEN TWO NOUNS OR PRONOUNS IN A COMPOUND SUBJECT.

compound subject

▶ Harold Johnson / and Margaret Simpson led the expedition.

OMIT A COMMA BEFORE A COORDINATING WORD JOINING TWO DEPENDENT CLAUSES.

dependent clause   dependent clause

▶ The band began to play before we arrived / but after the rain stopped.

OMIT A COMMA AFTER THE WORD *THAN* IN A COMPARISON.

▶ The Homestead Act made the cost of land to pioneers less than / the price the government had paid.

OMIT A COMMA AFTER *LIKE* OR *SUCH AS*.

▶ Direct marketing techniques such as / mass mailings and telephone solicitations can be effective.

OMIT COMMAS APPEARING NEXT TO A QUESTION MARK, EXCLAMATION POINT, OR DASH, OR BEFORE AN OPENING PARENTHESIS.

▶ "Where have you been? / " she would always ask.

▶ "Stop! / " the guard shouted.

▶ Keep spending to a minimum / — our resources are limited — and throw nothing away.

▶ Fast food / (which is usually high in fat) / is growing in popularity all over the world.

OMIT COMMAS AROUND WORDS THAT RENAME, AND RESTRICT, ANOTHER WORD BEFORE THEM.

If the words are **restrictive**—necessary to explain what the word they modify means—do not enclose them with commas.

▶ The man͵ who brought his car in for transmission work͵ is a lawyer.

For more exercises on the use of commas, refer to the Commas section of Exercise Central at www.bedfordstmartins .com/successfulwriting.

EXERCISE 12.1

Correct any errors in the use of commas in the following sentences. Some sentences may be correct as written.

▶ After slavery was abolished in New York in 1827͵ several black settlements were established in what is now New York City.

1. Seneca Village a crowded shantytown on the Upper West Side was the home of many poorer black New Yorkers.
2. The city of New York͵ bought the land where the Seneca villagers lived.
3. The land became part of Central Park͵and everyone͵ who lived there͵had to leave in the 1850s.
4. Household items from Seneca Village still turn up in Central Park today͵and a museum exhibit was recently devoted to life in the long-gone settlement.
5. In present-day Brooklyn, there was once a middle-class black settlement, called Weeksville.
6. James Weeks, an early resident͵owned much of the land.
7. Another, early, landholder, Sylvanus Smith, was a trustee of the African Free Schools of Brooklyn.
8. His daughter, Susan Smith McKinney-Steward, was born in Weeksville, and was the valedictorian of New York Medical College in 1870.
9. McKinney-Steward became the first, female, African American physician in New York, and the third in the United States.
10. Weeksville was a success story, for some of the houses survived into the twentieth century and have been preserved as historical monuments.

For more exercises on the use of commas, refer to the Commas section of Exercise Central at www.bedfordstmartins .com/successfulwriting.

EXERCISE 12.2

Correct any errors in the use of commas in the following paragraph. Some sentences may be correct as written.

▶ In June͵ 1998, fifty years after Korczak Ziolkowski began sculpting the Crazy Horse monument, the face of Crazy Horse was unveiled.

A monument to the Lakota Sioux warrior, Crazy Horse, is under construction in the Black Hills of South Dakota. Korczak Ziolkowski a sculptor, who also worked on Mount Rushmore, began the project in 1948. Ziolkowski was born on September 6, 1908,—thirty-one years to the day after Crazy Horse died. A Sioux chief asked Ziolkowski, if he would create a monument to honor Crazy Horse, and other Indian heroes. Ziolkowski designed a sculpture of Crazy Horse on horseback that, when it is completed, will be the largest statue in the world. The sculpture is being shaped from Thunderhead Mountain a six-hundred-foot granite rock. Tons of rock have been blasted, from the mountain. The sculptor died in 1982 but his widow, children, and grandchildren have carried on the work. There has been no government funding so, they have paid for the work entirely with donations and admission fees. By the middle of the twenty-first century the statue should be finished, and will depict the great Sioux hero pointing at the hills he loved.

13   SEMICOLONS

A **semicolon** (;) indicates a stronger pause than a comma but not as strong a pause as a period.

An independent clause contains a subject and a verb and can stand alone as a sentence.

13a Use a semicolon to join two closely related independent clauses.

Use a semicolon to join two closely related independent clauses not connected by a coordinating word (*and, but, for, nor, or, so,* or *yet*).

▶ In January and February, sunny days are rare and very short in northern countries; winter depression is common in the north.

For advice on other ways to join two independent clauses, see Section 4 of the Handbook.

A conjunctive adverb is a word (such as *also, however,* or *still*) that links two independent clauses.

13b Use a semicolon to join two independent clauses linked by a conjunctive adverb or transitional expression.

▶ The stunt pilot had to eject from the cockpit,; nevertheless, he was not injured.

▶ Mass transit is good for the environment; for example, as many people can fit in a bus as in fifteen cars.

13c Use semicolons to separate items in a series if commas are used within the items.

Semicolons help prevent confusion in a sentence that contains a series of items with one or more commas within the items.

▶ Fairy tales inspire children by depicting magical events, which appeal to their imaginations; clever boys and girls, who encourage young readers' problem-solving skills; evil creatures, who provide thrills; and good, heroic adults, who make the childhood world seem safer.

Also use a semicolon to separate a series of independent clauses that contain commas.

▶ He is stubborn, selfish, and conservative; she is stubborn, combative, and liberal; and no one is surprised that they do not get along.

(See also 12b on when to use commas to separate items in a series.)

13d Do not use a semicolon to introduce a list or to separate a phrase or dependent clause from the rest of the sentence.

▶ A growing number of companies employ prison inmates for certain jobs;: selling magazines, conducting surveys, reserving airplane tickets, and taking telephone orders.

(For more on introducing lists, see 14a.)

▶ On the other hand;, taking risks can bring impressive results.

▶ I'll always wonder; if things could have been different.

For more exercises on the use of semicolons, refer to the Semicolons section of Exercise Central at www.bedfordstmartins .com/successfulwriting.

EXERCISE 13.1

Correct any errors in the use of semicolons in the following sentences. Some sentences may be correct as written.

▶ Many people are in a hurry today;, yet they always seem to feel they are falling further behind.

1. One activity Americans do frequently is driving; to school, to work, to the store, or to leisure activities.
2. When too many people are driving in a hurry; tempers can flare.
3. For years, people have driven while angry, however, now the phenomenon is known as "road rage."
4. Angry drivers can make mistakes, such as forgetting basic safety precautions, they may take unnecessary risks, such as passing recklessly, they often drive too fast, and occasionally they even try to injure other drivers or damage other vehicles.
5. Drivers who are angry at other drivers commit dangerous offenses; following, racing, or even ramming other vehicles.
6. There have been incidents; when one driver has attacked another.
7. As Americans are beginning to realize; road rage endangers all drivers.
8. Drivers under the influence of road rage cause increasing numbers of accidents, and they must be stopped.
9. Public education campaigns are spreading, if people are aware of their reactions, they may control themselves better.
10. Every driver should realize that getting angry is never a solution; and may even make problems worse.

For more exercises on the use of semicolons, refer to the Semicolons section of Exercise Central at www.bedfordstmartins .com/successfulwriting.

EXERCISE 13.2

Correct any errors in the use of semicolons in the following paragraph. Some sentences may be correct as written.

▶ The word *placebo* is Latin for "I will please,"; placebos have long been used in medical experiments.

    In medicine, a placebo is a substance; often a sugar pill, that has no medicinal use. Placebos alone cannot cure any medical problem, nevertheless, many patients improve when taking them. Because patients who receive placebos do not know that the pills are useless, they think they are getting help for their condition; and they get better. This strange but true fact, recognized by doctors; pharmacists; and other professionals; is called the "placebo effect." Chemically, a placebo does nothing, theoretically, the patient should not respond, but somehow, this trick works on many people. The placebo effect is often seen in patients; but it is not widely understood. Since the Middle Ages, people have considered the mind and the body as separate; the placebo effect indicates that this separation may not really exist. The mind can play tricks on the body, for example, the brain produces phantom-limb pain in amputees. Doctors wonder; if the mind can also help to heal the body. If the answer is "yes," then the advances in medical knowledge could be enormous.

14 COLONS

You can use a **colon** (:) to introduce a list, an explanation, an example, or a further thought within a sentence. The information following the colon should clarify or offer specifics about the information that comes before it.

14a Use a colon to introduce a list or a series.

When you use a **colon** to introduce a list, make sure the list is preceded by a complete sentence.

▶ The archeologists uncovered several items: pieces of pottery, seeds, animal bones, and household tools.

                                                  common childhood illnesses

▶ All students must be immunized against: measles, mumps, and rubella.

14b Use a colon to introduce an explanation, an example, or a summary.

▶ In many ways, Hollywood is very predictable: Action movies arrive in the summer, dramas in the fall.

▶ One tree is particularly famous for its spectacular autumn colors: the sugar maple.

▶ Disaster relief efforts began all over the country: Volunteers raised forty million dollars.

Note: If the group of words following a colon is a complete sentence, the first word can begin with either a capital or a lowercase letter. Whichever option you choose, be consistent throughout your paper.

14c Use a colon to introduce a word or phrase that renames another noun.

▶ A hushed group of tourists stared at the most famous statue in Florence: Michelangelo's *David.*

14d Use a colon to introduce a lengthy or heavily punctuated quotation.

A quotation that is more than one or two lines long or that contains two or more commas can be introduced by a colon.

▶ Without pausing for breath, his campaign manager intoned the introduction: "Ladies and gentlemen, today it is my very great privilege to introduce to you the person on whose behalf you have all worked so tirelessly and with such impressive results, the man who is the reason we are all here today—the next president of the United States."

▶ The instructions were confusing: "After adjusting toggles A, B, and C, connect bracket A to post A, bracket B to post B, and bracket C to post C, securing with clamps A, B, and C, as illustrated in figure 1."

14e Use a colon to separate hours and minutes, in salutations for business letters, between titles and subtitles, and in ratios.

HOURS AND MINUTES	9:15 a.m.
SALUTATIONS	Dear Professor Sung:
TITLES AND SUBTITLES	*American Sphinx: The Character of Thomas Jefferson*
RATIOS	7:1

14f Use a colon only at the end of an independent clause.

A colon should always follow an independent clause, which could stand on its own as a complete sentence. Do not use a colon between a verb and its object, between a preposition and its object, or before a list introduced by such words as *for example, including, is,* and *such as.*

An independent clause contains a subject and a verb and can stand alone as a sentence.

▶ A medieval map is hard to read: The top of the map points to the east, not the north.

    A medieval map is hard to read is an independent clause.

▶ Even a small garden can produce: beans, squash, tomatoes, and corn.

▶ My cat had hidden a ball of twine under: the sofa.

▶ Bird-watchers are thrilled to spy birds of prey such as: peregrine falcons, red-tailed hawks, and owls.

For more exercises on the use of colons, refer to the Colons section of Exercise Central at www.bedfordstmartins .com/successfulwriting.

EXERCISE 14.1

Correct any errors in the use of colons in the following sentences. Some sentences may be correct as written.

▶ **Young, impeccably dressed couples participated in the latest craze: swing dancing.**

1. The shuttle launch is scheduled for precisely 10.00 a.m.
2. The proposed zoning change was defeated by a margin of 2/1.
3. On early rap records, listeners heard percussion from unusual sources such as: turntables, microphones, and synthesizers.
4. To find out whether a film is historically accurate, consult *Past Imperfect: History According to the Movies.*
5. He believes that the most American of all sports is: baseball.
6. As the entourage rushed past, the star's press agent snapped her orders: "No questions, no photos, no comment, no kidding!"
7. Travel advisories are in effect for the following areas, the northern Rocky Mountains and the upper Great Plains.
8. The neon lights gleamed: above stores and in diner windows.
9. We were not hungry, we had just eaten lunch an hour earlier.
10. Some music historians claim that the American songwriting tradition reached its peak in: the 1930s.

15   QUOTATION MARKS

A direct quotation gives a person's *exact* words, either spoken or written, set off by quotation marks.

Quotation marks (" ") are used to indicate **direct quotations** or to mark words used as words in your sentences. Quotation marks are always used in pairs. The opening quotation mark (") appears at the beginning of a word or quoted passage, and the closing mark (") appears at the end.

15a Place quotation marks around direct statements from other speakers or writers.

Be careful to include the *exact* words of the speaker or writer within the quotation marks.

▶ Lincoln recalled that the United States was "dedicated to the proposition that all men are created equal."

Because *dedicated to the proposition that all men are created equal* repeats Lincoln's exact words, quotation marks are required.

▶ Lincoln recalled that the United States was "dedicated to the ~~idea~~ *proposition* that all men are created equal."

Words in quotation marks must be quoted *exactly* as they appear in the original source.

In dialogue, place quotation marks around each speaker's words. Every time a different person speaks, begin a new paragraph.

> He said, "Sit down."
> "No, thank you," I replied.

With longer passages, indent prose quotations of more than four lines and verse quotations of more than three lines if you are following MLA style; do not use quotation marks. Indent the quotation ten spaces or one inch from the left margin. When you quote a poem, follow the line breaks exactly.

```
In "A Letter to Her Husband, Absent upon Public Employment," Ann
Bradstreet poignantly longs for him to return:
          My chilled limbs now numbed lie forlorn;
          Return, return, sweet Sol, from Capricorn;
          In this dead time, alas, what can I more
          Than view those fruits which through thy heat I bore?
          Which sweet contentment yield me for a space,
          True living pictures of their father's face. (11-16)
```

Note: If you are following APA style, indent quotations of forty or more words five spaces from the left margin. For more on the MLA and APA styles of documentation, see Chapter 20, (pages 716–56).

15b Place a comma or period that follows a direct quotation *within* the quotation marks.

▶ "Play it, Sam," Rick tells the piano player in *Casablanca.*

▶ Willie Sutton robbed banks because "that's where the money is."

15c Place colons and semicolons *outside* of quotation marks.

▶ The marching band played "Seventy-Six Trombones;"; the drum major's favorite song.

▶ A new national anthem should replace "The Star-Spangled Banner;"; no one can sing that song.

15d Place question marks and exclamation points according to the meaning of the sentence.

If the quotation is a question or exclamation, place the question mark or exclamation point *within* the closing quotation mark. If the punctuation mark comes at the end of a sentence, no other end punctuation is needed.

▶ "How does the bridge stand up?"? the child wondered.

▶ Poe's insane narrator confesses, "It is the beating of his hideous heart!"!

If the entire sentence, of which the quotation is part, is a question or exclamation, the question mark or exclamation point goes *outside* the closing quotation marks at the end of the sentence.

▶ Was Scarlett O'Hara serious when she said, "Tomorrow is another day?"?

15e Use a comma to separate a short quotation from an introductory or identifying phrase such as *he replied* or *she said*.

▶ "Video games improve eye-hand coordination," he replied.

▶ "The homeless population,", she reported, "grew steadily throughout the 1980s."

15f Use single quotation marks (' ') to indicate a quotation or a title within a quotation.

▶ The mysterious caller repeatedly insists, "Play 'Misty' for me."

15g Place quotation marks around the titles of short works.

SECTION OF A BOOK	Chapter 1, "Ozzie and Harriet in Spanish Harlem"
POEM	"Ode on a Grecian Urn"
SHORT STORY	"The Yellow Wallpaper"
ESSAY OR ARTICLE	"Their Malcolm, My Problem"

SONG	"I'll Be Around"
EPISODE OF A TELEVISION PROGRAM	"Larry's Last Goodbye"

15h Do not use quotation marks to call unnecessary attention to words or phrases.

▶ The manager who was originally in charge of the project "jumped ship" before the deadline.

Quotation marks can be used to mark words used as words (as an alternative to italics).

▶ The word "receive" is often misspelled.

EXERCISE 15.1

Correct any errors in the use of quotation marks in the following sentences. Some sentences may be correct as written.

▶ The hotel has an excellent restaurant specializing in "fresh" fish.

1. Her essay was entitled, ""To Be or Not to Be": Shakespeare and Existentialism."
2. Why did the professor assign "To an Athlete Dying Young?"
3. A movie line many teenagers imitated was "Do you feel lucky, punk"?
4. After September 11, 2001, President Bush said he was going to "fight terror".
5. "I have a dream," Martin Luther King Jr. told the civil rights marchers.
6. Come live with me and be my love, pleads the speaker in Marlowe's poem.
7. The grand jury was not "completely" convinced of the need for a trial.
8. It turned out that the pianist could play only Chopsticks.
9. O'Brien originally published the chapter called "Speaking of Courage" as a short story.
10. Our waitress announced, "The special is prime rib;" unfortunately, we are vegetarians.

For more exercises on the use of quotation marks, refer to the Quotation Marks section of Exercise Central at www.bedfordstmartins .com/successfulwriting.

16 ELLIPSIS MARKS

An ellipsis mark (. . .) is written as three equally spaced periods. It is used within a direct quotation to indicate where you have left out part of the original quotation. You use an **ellipsis mark** to shorten a quotation so that it includes just the parts you want or need to quote.

ORIGINAL QUOTATION	"The prison, a high percentage of whose inmates are serving life sentences, looked surprisingly ordinary."
SHORTENED	"The prison . . . looked surprisingly ordinary."

Notice that the two commas were also omitted when the quotation was shortened.

However, when you shorten a quotation, be careful not to change the meaning of the original passage. Do not omit any parts that will alter or misrepresent the writer's intended meaning.

ORIGINAL   "Magicians create illusions, but sometimes audience members want to believe that magic is real."

MEANING ALTERED   "Magicians . . . want to believe that magic is real."

When you omit the last part of a quoted sentence, add a sentence period, for a total of four periods (a period plus the ellipsis mark).

ORIGINAL QUOTATION   "In the sphere of psychology, details are also the thing. God preserve us from commonplaces. Best of all is to avoid depicting the hero's state of mind; you ought to try to make it clear from the hero's actions. It is not necessary to portray many characters. The center of gravity should be in two persons: him and her."

ANTON CHEKHOV, Letter to Alexander P. Chekhov

SHORTENED   "God preserve us from commonplaces. Best of all is to avoid depicting the hero's state of mind. . . . It is not necessary to portray many characters. The center of gravity should be in two persons: him and her."

An ellipsis mark is not needed to indicate that the quoted passage continues after the sentence ends.

▶ He is modest about his contributions to the abolitionist cause: "I could do but little; but what I could, I did with a joyful heart ⌢." (Douglass 54).

Do not use an ellipsis mark at the beginning of a quotation, even though there is material in the original that comes before it.

ORIGINAL QUOTATION   "As was the case after the recent cleaning of the Sistine Chapel, the makeover of the starry ceiling in Grand Central Station has revealed surprisingly brilliant color."

SHORTENED   "[T]he makeover of the starry ceiling in Grand Central Station has revealed surprisingly brilliant color."

Note: The first word of a quoted sentence should be capitalized. If you change from a lowercase to a capital letter, enclose the letter in brackets (see 18d).

If you are following MLA style, enclose ellipsis marks that you add to a quotation in brackets, as in the following shortened version of the Chekhov quotation given above.

SHORTENED   "In the sphere of psychology, details are also the thing. [. . .] Best of all is to avoid depicting the hero's state of mind; you ought to try to make it clear from the hero's actions" (Chekhov 1446).

(For more on MLA style for ellipsis marks, see Chapter 20, p. 711.)

EXERCISE 16.1

Shorten each of the following quotations by omitting the underlined portion and adding an ellipsis mark where appropriate.

For more exercises on the use of ellipsis marks, refer to the Ellipsis Marks section of Exercise Central at www.bedfordstmartins .com/successfulwriting.

▶ "Some people who call themselves vegetarians still eat less cuddly creatures such as chicken and fish."

1. "The structure of DNA, as Watson and Crick discovered, is a double helix."
2. "Although African Americans had won Academy Awards before, Halle Berry was the first African American woman to win the Academy Award for Best Actress.
3. Hamlet muses, "To be or not to be, that is the question."
4. "Many Americans do not realize that people of all classes receive financial help from the government."
5. "Cole Porter cultivated a suave, sophisticated urban persona even though he came from a small town in Indiana."
6. "From an anthropological perspective, Zora Neale Hurston's collections of folklore proved to be valuable."
7. "We take modern conveniences for granted today, but two hundred years ago households even had to make their own soap."
8. "Folic acid, doctors now believe, can help to prevent certain birth defects."
9. "Although saltwater aquariums are beautiful, they are difficult and expensive to maintain."
10. "She wrote rather doubtful grammar sometimes, and in her verses took all sorts of liberties with the metre" (Thackeray 136–37). (MLA style)

17 APOSTROPHES

An **apostrophe** (') has three functions: to show ownership or possession, to indicate omitted letters in contractions, and to form some plurals.

17a Use an apostrophe to indicate possession or ownership.

Add *-'s* to make a singular noun possessive, including nouns that end with *s* or the sound of *s* and **indefinite pronouns** (*anyone, nobody*).

An **indefinite pronoun** does not refer to a specific person, place, or object. It refers to people, places, or things in general (*anywhere, everyone, everything*).

▶ The *fox's* prey led it across the field.
▶ Whether she can win the nomination is *anybody's* guess.

Note that the possessive forms of personal pronouns do not take apostrophes: *mine, yours, his, hers, ours, theirs, its.*

▶ Each bee has it's function in the hive.

The possessive form of *who* is *whose* (not *who's*).

▶ Marie Curie, *whose* work in chemistry made history, discovered radium.

Add an apostrophe to a plural noun to make it possessive, or add -'s if the plural noun does not end in *s*.

▶ Both *farms'* crops were lost in the flood.
▶ Our *children's* children will reap the benefits of our efforts to preserve the environment today.

To show individual possession by two or more people or groups, add an apostrophe or -'s to each noun.

▶ Sam is equipment manager for both the *boys'* and *girls'* basketball teams.
 Sam works for two different teams.

To show joint possession by two people or groups, add an apostrophe or -'s to the last noun.

▶ The *coaches and players'* dream came true at the end of the season.

Add -'s to the last word of a compound noun to show possession.

▶ My *father-in-law's* boat needs a new engine.
▶ We were ushered into the *chairman of the department's* office.

17b Use an apostrophe to indicate the omitted letter or letters in a contraction.

▶ *I've* [I have] seen the answers.
▶ Jason *didn't* [did not] arrive last night.

17c Use an apostrophe to form the plural of a number, letter, symbol, abbreviation, or word treated as a word.

▶ There are three *5*'s on the license plate.
▶ She spells her name with two *C*'s.
▶ The *?*'s stand for unknown quantities.
▶ Using two *etc.*'s is unnecessary.
▶ Replace all *can*'s in the contract with *cannot*'s.

In the sentences above, note that numbers, letters, and words used as themselves are in italics. The -s ending should not be italicized, however. (For more on italics and underlining, see 23d.)

When referring to the years in a decade, no apostrophe is used.

▶ The fashions of the 1970s returned in the 1990s.

Apostrophes are used to signal the omission of the numerals that indicate the century.

the class of '03   music of the '90s

17d Avoid using apostrophes to form plurals and to form possessives for personal pronouns.

▶ The trapper⁀'s came to town to trade.

▶ She paid for my lunch as well as her⁀'s.

For more exercises on the use of apostrophes, refer to the Apostrophes section of Exercise Central at www.bedfordstmartins .com/successfulwriting.

EXERCISE 17.1

Correct the errors in the use of apostrophes in the following sentences. Some sentences may be correct as written.

▶ The 1960's was a decade of upheaval.

1. The Vietnam War became the focus of many young peoples' disagreements with their parents.
2. Young Americans felt that their parents' generation was more inhibited than theirs.
3. In the 1960s, "dropping out" was often an activists' choice.
4. Members of the World War II generation were often horrified by their sons and daughters' behavior.
5. When people recall that decade, they tend to remember it's excesses.

18 PARENTHESES AND BRACKETS

PARENTHESES

Parentheses—( )—are used to separate nonessential information from the rest of a sentence or paragraph.

18a Use parentheses to add words, phrases, or sentences that expand on, clarify, or explain the material that precedes or follows.

▶ The EPA (Environmental Protection Agency) is responsible for developing water pollution standards.

▶ The application fee for the four-day workshop (a total of $100, including the registration fee) is due Friday.

Be sure to use parentheses sparingly; they can clutter your writing.

18b Use parentheses to insert dates or abbreviations.

▶ Elizabeth Cady Stanton (1815–1902) helped to organize the first American women's rights convention.

▶ Guidelines for documenting research papers in the humanities are published by the Modern Language Association (MLA).

18c Check the placement of other punctuation used with parentheses.

Parenthetical information that appears at the end of a sentence should be inserted before the period that ends the sentence.

▶ Irish dance has become popular in the United States (probably because of the success of *Riverdance*).

When parenthetical information appears after a word that would be followed by a comma, the comma is always placed after the closing parenthesis.

▶ He called when his plane landed (or so he said), but no one answered.

When a complete sentence appears within parentheses, punctuate the sentence as you would normally.

▶ Timber companies propose various uses for national forests. (Public land can be leased for commercial purposes.)

Exception: If the material within the parentheses is a question, it should end with a question mark.

▶ A few innocent-looking plants (have you heard of the Venus's-flytrap?) capture and eat insects and animals.

BRACKETS

Brackets ([ ]) are used within quotations and within parentheses.

18d Use brackets to add information or indicate changes you have made to a quotation.

▶ Whitman's preface argued, "Here [the United States] is not merely a nation but a teeming nation of nations."

The explanation tells where *here* is.

▶ "Along came a spider and sat down beside [Miss Muffett]," who apparently suffered from a phobia.

The bracketed name replaces *her* in the original.

Use brackets to enclose the word *sic* when signaling an error in original quoted material.

▶ The incumbent's letter to the editor announced, "My opponent's [sic] claims regarding my record are simply not true."

The Latin word *sic* lets your readers know that the misspelled word or other error in the quoted material is the original author's error, not yours.

Note: If you are using MLA style, enclose ellipsis marks that you add to shorten a quotation in brackets (see Section 16 of the Handbook).

18e Use brackets to enclose parenthetical material in a group of words already enclosed in parentheses.

▶ The demonstrators (including members of the National Rifle Association [NRA]) crowded around the candidate.

EXERCISE 18.1

Correct the errors in the use of parentheses or brackets in the following sentences. Some sentences may be correct as written.

▶ Typhoid Mary would probably not have infected so many victims if she had stopped working (she was a cook,).

1. Nathan Hale regretted that he had "but one life to give for (his) country."
2. The Committee for Scientific Investigation of Claims of the Paranormal (CSICOP) tests claims of supernatural abilities.
3. Malcolm X [1925–1965] was an American political figure assassinated in the 1960s.
4. The invention of anesthesia made possible many advances in medicine (including lengthy surgery.)
5. Children believe what they see on television, (at least most of it) and therefore parents should monitor their children's viewing.

For more exercises on the use of parentheses and brackets, refer to the Parentheses and Brackets section of Exercise Central at www.bedfordstmartins .com/successfulwriting.

19 DASHES

Use a **dash** (—) to separate parts of a sentence. A dash suggests a stronger separation than a comma, colon, or semicolon does. To type a dash, hit the hyphen key twice (--), with no spaces before, between, or after the hyphens. Some word-processing programs automatically convert the two hyphens to a dash (—).

19a Use a dash or dashes to emphasize a sudden shift or break in thought or mood.

▶ Computers have given the world instant communication—and electronic junk mail.

19b Use a dash or dashes to introduce an explanation, an example, or the items in a series.

▶ The success of the D-Day invasion was almost miraculous—capturing the beaches of Normandy must have looked impossible in 1944.

When the added thought appears in the middle of the sentence, use two dashes to set it off.

▶ The music-hating monster in *Beowulf*—the poet withholds his name at the beginning—attacks the hall.

19c Use dashes sparingly.

Dashes are emphatic. Do not overuse them, or they will lose their effectiveness. Also be careful not to use a dash as a substitute for a **conjunction** or transition.

A **conjunction** is a word or words used to connect clauses, phrases, or individual words.

▶ Einstein's job in Switzerland was dull, ~~—~~ *but* it offered him plenty of time to think; ~~—~~ *while working there* he came up with the theory of relativity.

For more exercises on the use of dashes, refer to the Dashes section of Exercise Central at www.bedfordstmartins .com/successfulwriting.

EXERCISE 19.1

Add a dash or pair of dashes where they might be effective, and correct any errors in the use of dashes in the following sentences.

▶ Food—who eats what and why?—is now a subject studied by academics.

1. One issue particularly concerns scholars of food; why are certain foods acceptable in some cultures but not in others?
2. Some foods were once popular, but today—hardly anyone has heard of them.
3. In the 1990s, people in Great Britain were alerted to a new danger, mad cow disease.
4. In the 1960s, frozen foods—icy blocks of corn, peas, and string beans—were popular —and convenient—alternatives to fresh produce.
5. Today fresh fruits and vegetables are valued once again, unless a busy cook has no time for peeling and chopping.

20 CAPITALIZATION

Capitalize the first word of a sentence, **proper nouns**, and the pronoun *I*.

A **proper noun** names a particular person, place, thing, or group.

20a Capitalize the first word in a sentence and in a direct quotation.

▶ revision is important.

R (with caret before "revision")

Capitalize the first word in a direct quotation unless it is incorporated into your own sentence or it continues an earlier quotation.

▶ The union representative said, "that meeting did not take place."

(T above "that")

▶ Sam Verdon complained that "No one takes college athletes seriously."

(n above "No")

▶ "I prefer not to interpret my paintings," replied the famous watercolorist, "Because they should speak for themselves."

(b above "Because")

20b Capitalize proper nouns, including the names of specific people, places, things, and groups.

PEOPLE AND ANIMALS	Franklin Roosevelt, his dog Fala
CITIES, STATES, NATIONS	St. Paul, Minnesota, the United States
WELL-ESTABLISHED GEOGRAPHIC REGIONS	the Gulf Coast, the U.S. Southwest
GOVERNMENT AND OTHER PUBLIC OFFICES, DEPART-MENTS, AND BUILDINGS	the Pentagon, the Supreme Court, the Puck Building
SOCIAL, POLITICAL, BUSINESS, SPORT-ING, AND CULTURAL ORGANIZATIONS	League of Women Voters, National Basketball Association
MONTHS, DAYS OF THE WEEK, AND HOLIDAYS	February, Thursday, Labor Day

CHAPTER OR SECTION TITLES IN BOOKS	"Why America Has Changed"
NATIONALITIES AND LANGUAGES	Ethiopian, Dutch
RELIGIONS, RELIGIOUS FIGURES, AND SACRED BOOKS	Judaism, the Pope, the Koran
TRADE NAMES	Coca-Cola, Brillo
HISTORIC EVENTS	the Treaty of Versailles, Reconstruction
SPECIFIC COURSE TITLES	Organic Chemistry 101

20c Do not capitalize common nouns.

FAMILY MEMBERS	my uncle, his father
GENERAL AREAS OF THE COUNTRY	southwestern United States
SUBJECTS	I study chemistry.
CENTURIES	seventeenth-century England
GEOGRAPHICAL AREAS	the lake in the park

20d Capitalize the titles of literary and other works, such as books, articles, poems, plays, songs, films, and paintings.

Capitalize the first and last words of the title, the first word following a colon, and all other words except **articles, coordinating conjunctions,** and **prepositions.**

Articles are the words *a, an,* and *the.*

Coordinating conjunctions (*and, but, for, nor, or, so, yet*) connect sentence elements that are of equal importance.

Prepositions (such as *before, on,* and *to*) are used before a noun or pronoun to indicate time, place, space, direction, position, or some other relationship.

BOOK	*Confusion Is Next: The Sonic Youth Story*
ARTICLE	"Making History at Madison Park"
POEM	"My Last Duchess"
PLAY	*A Raisin in the Sun*
SONG	"Yellow Rose of Texas"
FILM	*Gone with the Wind*
PAINTING	*The Starry Night*

20e Capitalize a personal title only when it directly precedes a person's name.

▶ Vice President Maria Washington briefed the stockholders.

▶ Maria Washington was hired from a rival company to be the new vice president.

It is acceptable to capitalize the titles of certain high government officials regardless of whether they precede a name: *the President of the United States.*

EXERCISE 20.1

Correct the capitalization errors in the following paragraph.

>   *U*   *N*
> ▶ The united nations meets at its headquarters in New York City.
>   ^   ^

     During world war II, the governments of twenty-six countries pledged their willingness to continue fighting on behalf of the Allies. United States president Franklin Roosevelt came up with a name for the group: the united nations. The "Declaration By United Nations" promised the support of those twenty-six governments for the war effort. The Nations signed this document on New Year's day, 1942. By 1945, the number of countries involved in the united nations had grown to fifty-one. From April through June of that year, fifty Representatives attended the united nations Conference on International Organization in San Francisco. There, the Nations debated the contents of a charter. Although the War was nearing an end, the governments foresaw a need to continue international cooperation. The charter was ratified on October 24, 1945, by China, France, The Soviet Union, The United Kingdom, The United States, and a majority of the other Nations. Every year since then, October 24 has been known as united nations day.

For more exercises on capitalization, refer to the Capitalization section of Exercise Central at www.bedfordstmartins .com/successfulwriting.

21 ABBREVIATIONS

Abbreviations are shortened forms of words and phrases. It is acceptable to use abbreviations for some personal titles, names of organizations, time references, and Latin expressions. Most abbreviations use periods, but those composed of all capital letters often do not.

21a Abbreviate titles before and after a person's name.

Ms. Amy Tan	Arthur Rodriguez, M.D.
St. Mary	Bill Cosby, Ph.D.
Dr. C. Everett Koop	Martin Luther King Jr.

21b Abbreviate names of familiar organizations, corporations, and countries.

Use common abbreviations such as *PBS, CIA,* and *HIV* when you are certain that your readers will recognize them.

ABC	FBI	NATO
UNICEF	USA	VCR

21c Abbreviate time references that precede or follow a number.

▶ The meeting will begin at 10:15 a.m. and end at 12 p.m.

▶ The statues were carved in about 300 BCE.

The letters BCE stand for "before the common era." An alternative is BC ("before Christ").

▶ Alfred became king in AD 871.

The letters AD stand for the Latin term *anno Domini* and precede the date. The alternative CE ("common era") follows the date.

21d Use common abbreviations for Latin terms in parentheses, footnotes, or references.

It is acceptable to use abbreviations for Latin terms in parenthetical comments as well as in source notes or citations. Avoid using these abbreviations outside of parentheses in the text of your essay; use the English equivalent instead.

e.g.	for example
et al.	and others
etc.	and so forth
i.e.	that is
vs. *or* v.	versus

▶ Edison invented the light bulb, the motion picture camera, sound recording devices, etc.

[handwritten annotations: such items as ... and]

21e Do not abbreviate certain words and phrases when they are used in sentences.

Some abbreviations that are acceptable in scientific or technical writing should be spelled out in most other kinds of writing.

UNITS OF MEASUREMENT	ten inches [*not* ten in.]
GEOGRAPHICAL OR PLACE NAMES	I live in New York City [*not* N.Y.C.]. (*Exceptions: Washington, D.C.; U.S. when it is used as an adjective, as in U.S. Senate*)
PARTS OF WRITTEN WORKS	chapter 6 [*not* ch. 6]
DAYS, MONTHS, AND HOLIDAYS	Thursday [*not* Thurs.]

NAMES OF SUBJECT AREAS	biology [*not* bio]
PERSONAL TITLES USED WITHOUT A PROPER NAME	doctor [*not* Dr.]

EXERCISE 21.1

Correct the misused abbreviations in the following sentences.

> *political science*
> ► Students of ~~poli sci~~ know that public opinion often moves in cycles.

1. According to Washington Irving's story, Rip van Winkle fell asleep in the Catskill Mts. for twenty years.
2. The average American woman is five ft. four in. tall.
3. Since it is only ninety pp. long, the text is really a novella, not a novel.
4. The Great Depression began with the stock-market crash on Black Mon.
5. The Coen brothers have a reputation for creating unorthodox films: e.g., *Fargo* and *O Brother, Where Art Thou?*

For more exercises on abbreviations, refer to the Abbreviations section of Exercise Central at www.bedfordstmartins .com/successfulwriting.

22 NUMBERS

As a general rule, use numbers according to the rules of your field of study. Be sure to represent numbers as numerals or as words consistently.

22a Spell out numbers that begin sentences.

> *Two hundred ten*
> ► ~~210~~ students attended the lecture.

22b Spell out numbers that can be written in one or two words.

twenty-six checks	two hundred women
sixty students	one thousand pretzels

Use numerals for numbers that cannot be spelled out in one or two words.

> *375*
> ► There are ~~three hundred seventy-five~~ students enrolled this fall.

Use numerals in a sentence with more than one number where one number needs to be written in numerals.

> *28*
> ► Of the 420 students in my school, only ~~twenty-eight~~ have a driver's license.

When two numbers appear in succession, spell out one and give numerals for the other.

►   Each counselor is in charge of nine ~~three~~-year-olds.
                                            ³
                                            ^

22c Use numerals according to convention.

DATES	August 10, 1993; the 1960s
DECIMALS, PERCENTAGES, FRACTIONS	56.7, 50% *or* 50 percent, 1¾ cups
EXACT TIMES	9:27 a.m.
PAGES, CHAPTERS, VOLUMES	page 27, chapter 12, volume 4
ADDRESSES	122 Peach Street
EXACT AMOUNTS OF MONEY	$5.60, $1.3 million
SCORES AND STATISTICS	23–6 victory, a factor of 12

For more exercises on the use of numbers in sentences, refer to the Numbers section of Exercise Central at www .bedfordstmartins.com /successfulwriting.

EXERCISE 22.1

Correct the errors in the use of numbers in the following sentences. Some sentences may be correct as written.

                                                         77
►   The quotation you're looking for is on page ~~seventy-seven~~.
                                                         ^

1. 77% of those responding to the poll favored increased taxes on cigarettes.
2. The estimated cost was too low by eighty-seven dollars and fourteen cents.
3. Each window is composed of 100s of small pieces of colored glass.
4. All traffic stopped as a 90-car train went slowly past.
5. February twenty-two is George Washington's birthday, but Presidents' Day is always celebrated on a Monday.

23 ITALICS AND UNDERLINING

Italic or *slanted type* is used for emphasizing particular words or phrases. It is also used to set off titles of longer works, names of vehicles, non-English words, and words deserving special emphasis.

When writing by hand or using a typewriter, use <u>underlining</u> to indicate italics. Most word-processing programs provide italic type, but your instructor may prefer that you use underlining instead. For example, your instructor may require you to use underlining in a works-cited list. (For more on MLA guidelines, see

Chapter 20, p. 716.) In this chapter, most of the examples modeling the use of italics or underlining are shown in italic type.

23a Italicize or underline titles of works published separately.

BOOKS	*Great Expectations*
PLAYS	*Rent*
LONG POEMS	*The Iliad*
MAGAZINES AND JOURNALS	*Entertainment Weekly;* the *New York Review of Books*
NEWSPAPERS	the *Columbus Dispatch*
MOVIES AND VIDEOTAPES	*A Beautiful Mind*
LONG MUSICAL WORKS, RECORDINGS	*Exile on Main Street*
TELEVISION AND RADIO SERIES	*The Practice*
VISUAL WORKS OF ART (PAINTINGS, SCULPTURES)	*Birth of Venus*

The titles of shorter works, such as the titles of articles, short stories, and songs, should be enclosed in quotation marks (see 15g).

23b Italicize or underline the names of ships, trains, aircraft, and spacecraft.

Titanic	*Spirit of St. Louis*
Orient Express	space shuttle *Challenger*

23c Italicize or underline non-English words not in everyday use.

Words from other languages should be italicized unless they have become a part of the English language, such as "chic" or "taco." If you are unsure, check an English dictionary. If the word is not listed, it should be italicized.

▶ Our instructor lectured on the technique of *Verstehen.*

▶ Tacos are now as much a part of American cuisine as pizza.

23d Italicize or underline numbers, letters, words, or phrases called out for special emphasis.

Use italics for numbers, letters, or words used as terms.

▶ Every bottle has *33* on the label.

▶ Hester Prynne is forced to wear a scarlet *A*.

▶ Today, *ain't* is listed in most dictionaries.

Italicize a word or phrase that is being defined or emphasized.

▶ *Alliteration* — the same sounds repeated at the beginning of each word in a group — can be an effective literary device.

Use italics for emphasis sparingly. When you italicize too many words in a sentence or paragraph, the emphasis is lost.

▶ The U.S. National Park system is *extremely important* because it protects some of
     (no italics)
the most *beautiful* and *unusual* parts of this country.
     (no italics)   *(no italics)*

For more exercises on the use of italics in sentences, refer to the Italics and Underlining section of Exercise Central at www.bedfordstmartins .com/successfulwriting.

EXERCISE 23.1

Correct the errors in the use of italics in the following sentences. Some sentences may be correct as written.

▶ <u>Oedipus</u>, written by Sophocles in the fifth century BC, is possibly the most famous play of the classical period.

1. The exchange student greeted everyone with a hearty *"Bonjour!"*
2. His professor insisted that TV Guide was not an acceptable research source.
3. Cartoons like The Simpsons have become surprisingly popular with adult audiences.
4. The first European settlers at Plymouth arrived on the Mayflower.
5. His book is discussed in depth in the article *Africa: The Hidden History.*

24 HYPHENS

A **hyphen** (-) is used to join compound words, to connect parts of words, and to split words at the end of typewritten lines of text.

24a Use a hyphen to join words that function as a unit.

Some compound nouns and verbs are spelled as one word (*download*), some are spelled as two words (*washing machine*), and some are spelled using hyphens (*foul-up*). Check a dictionary when you are unsure; if you do not find the compound listed in your dictionary, spell it as two words.

Use a hyphen to join words that together modify a noun.

▶ An *icy-fingered* hand tapped on her shoulder.

However, when the first word of the compound ends in *-ly* or when the compound adjective follows the noun it modifies, no hyphen is used.

▶ The guard found a *clumsily hidden* duplicate key.

▶ Her voice was *well trained*.

24b Use a hyphen with some prefixes (*all-, ex-, great-, self-*) and suffixes (*-elect*).

▶ Most Americans' parents, grandparents, or *great-grandparents* came from another country.

▶ The *governor-elect* made a stirring victory speech.

Use a hyphen for clarity to prevent confusion with certain combinations of prefixes and base words.

▶ She wants the taxpayers to approve the funding for her ~~recreation~~ of the demolished town hall.

    re-creation

    Recreation has a different meaning from *re-creation*.

24c Use a hyphen when spelling out fractions and the numbers *twenty-one* to *ninety-nine,* in word-number combinations, and to indicate inclusive numbers.

    two-thirds finished   *twenty-two* sources

▶ The *675-yard* path winds through a landscaped garden.

▶ Pages *99-102* cover the military campaigns.

24d Use a hyphen between syllables to split a word at the end of a typewritten or handwritten line.

Although most word-processing programs automatically break the line before a long word and move the word to the next line, in typewritten or handwritten text you should use a hyphen to divide any words that fall at the end of a line. Divide words between syllables; never break a one-syllable word. Divide a compound word between its parts. Words can also be divided between a prefix and root or between a root and suffix. Check your dictionary if you are uncertain about where to break a word.

```
     Viking invaders failed to conquer Ireland
   because the country was governed by a num-
   ber of petty kings rather than by a central
```

```
authority that could be effectively over-
thrown; however, by the tenth century this
situation began to change.
```

For more exercises on hyphen use, refer to the Hyphens section of Exercise Central at www .bedfordstmartins.com /successfulwriting.

EXERCISE 24.1

Correct the errors in the use of hyphens in the following sentences. If you are not sure about a word, check your dictionary. Some sentences may be correct as written.

▶ Does any ~~teen-ager~~ really need liposuction?
    teenager

1. Adolescents today who are unhappy with their looks can turn to the increasingly-popular option of plastic surgery.
2. For many selfconscious teens and young adults, surgery seems to be the perfect solution.
3. Until recently, very few sixteen year olds considered making permanent surgical changes.
4. But as more adults pay for nose-jobs and tummy tucks, more teens are expressing interest.
5. Are images of people with apparently perfect bodies and faces unduly influencing less-than-perfect young Americans?

25 SPELLING

Misspelled words are among the most common errors for many student writers. Be sure to pay attention to spelling as you edit and proofread your papers and keep a dictionary close at hand. Misspellings can make your paper appear carelessly written. Use the tips in the accompanying box and the basic spelling rules that follow to help improve your spelling.

25a Remember to put *i* before *e* except after *c* or when pronounced as an *a* as in *neighbor* and *weigh*.

 i before *e:* achi*e*ve, thi*e*f

 except after *c*: conce*i*ve, rece*i*ve

 or when pronounced as an *a*: fr*ei*ght, th*ei*r

Memorize the exceptions, such as *either, foreign, height, leisure, neither, seize,* and *weird.*

25b Add *-s* or *-es* to form the plural of most nouns.

Singular common nouns ending in *-s, -ch, -sh,* or *-x* form the plural by adding *-es.* Nouns ending in *-o* usually form the plural by adding *-s* when the *-o* follows a vowel or *-es* when the *-o* follows a consonant.

> **TIPS FOR IMPROVING YOUR SPELLING**
>
> - **Purchase a collegiate dictionary and take the time to look up the correct spellings of unfamiliar words.**
> - **Use your word processor's spell-checker function.** Be sure to take advantage of the spell-checker as you edit and proofread your drafts. However, keep in mind that this function will not catch all spelling errors; for example, it cannot detect the incorrect use of *it's* versus *its* or of homonyms such as *there* versus *their* and *weather* versus *whether.* (See 25d for a list of homonyms.)
> - **Proofread your drafts for spelling errors.** To avoid being distracted by the flow of ideas in your essays, proofread them backwards, from the last word to the first, looking only for misspellings. For words that sound alike but have different spellings (*to/too/two, their/there*), stop to check their use in the sentence and determine whether you have used the correct word.
> - **Keep a list of words you commonly misspell.** Whenever you catch spelling errors in a draft or see misspellings marked by your instructor in papers returned to you, add the words to your list. Use your dictionary to locate the correct spelling and pronunciation of each word in the list. Review your list of words periodically and practice pronouncing and writing the words until you master their correct spellings and usage.
> - **Develop a spelling awareness.** As you read and write, pay attention to words and how they are spelled. When you encounter a new word, pronounce it slowly and carefully while taking note of its spelling. Try to create a mental image of each word, especially words with silent letters or unusual spellings.

| Add *-s:* | professor, professor*s* | zoo, zoo*s* |
| Add *-es:* | sandwich, sandwich*es* | hero, hero*es* |

To form the plural of common nouns ending in *-y,* change the *y* to *i* and add *-es* when the *y* is preceded by a consonant. Add only *-s* when the *y* is preceded by a vowel.

| story | stor*ies* | day | day*s* |
| baby | bab*ies* | key | key*s* |

Compound nouns form the plural by adding *-s* or *-es* to the most important word or, when all the words are equally important, to the last word of the compound.

mother-in-law	mother*s*-in-law
passerby	passer*s*by
stand-in	stand-in*s*

Proper nouns form the plural by adding *-s* or *-es* without changing the noun's ending.

Thursday	Thursday*s*
Mr. and Mrs. Jones	the Jones*es*

▶ The Gunderson*'s* met us for dinner last night.

25c Drop, keep, change, or double the final letter when adding endings to some words.

Drop the silent *e* when adding an ending that begins with a vowel (*a, e, i, o, u*). Keep the silent *e* when adding an ending that begins with a consonant.

hope	hop*ing*	care	care*ful*
force	forc*ing*	encourage	encourage*ment*
advise	advis*able*	love	love*ly*

For words that end in *y,* change the final *y* to *i* before adding an ending when the *y* follows a consonant. Keep the final *y* when the *y* follows a vowel, when the ending is *-ing,* or when *y* ends a proper name.

study	stud*ies*	buy	buy*er*
marry	marr*ied*	marry	marry*ing*
		Fahey	Fahey*s*

Exception: Drop the final *y* whenever you add *-ize.*

memory	memor*ize*
category	categor*ize*

When adding an ending to one-syllable words, double the final consonant if the ending starts with a vowel and the final consonant follows a single vowel. Do *not* double the consonant when two vowels or a vowel and another consonant precede it.

hop	hop*ped*	pair	pair*ed*
trek	trek*ked*	rent	rent*ed*

When adding an ending to words with two or more syllables, double the final consonant if a single vowel precedes it and the stress falls on the last syllable.

| transmit | transmit*ted* |
| refer | refer*ral* |

Do *not* double the final consonant when two vowels or a vowel and another consonant precede it.

| react | react*ed* |
| redeem | redeem*ing* |

Do *not* double the final consonant if the ending starts with a consonant.

| commit | commit*ment* |
| regret | regret*fully* |

25d Watch out for homonyms, groups of words that sound the same but are spelled differently.

The following list includes some commonly confused groups of words.

Homonyms	*Examples of Usage*
accept (to take or receive)	Most stores *accept* credit cards.
except (other than)	Everyone has arrived *except* Harry.
affect (to influence)	The new law will *affect* us.
effect (the result, outcome)	The *effect* of the storm was frightening.
already (by now)	Miriam is *already* in class.
all ready (fully prepared)	Geoffrey is *all ready*.
allusion (a reference to)	The poem contained an *allusion* to Greek mythology.
illusion (a fantasy)	Margaret is under the *illusion* that she is famous.
cite (to refer to)	Be sure to *cite* your sources.
sight (vision, or a tourist attraction)	Her *sight* is failing.
site (a place)	We visited the *site* of the accident.
complement (to complete, a counterpart)	The side dishes *complement* the main course.
compliment (praise)	Allison received numerous *compliments*.

(Continued on next page)

(Continued)

Homonyms	Examples of Usage
elicit (to bring out)	The film *elicits* an emotional response.
illicit (illegal)	The sale of *illicit* drugs is prohibited on campus.
its (possessive of *it*)	The show has found *its* audience.
it's (contraction of *it is*)	*It's* too late to go back.
lead (verb: to guide or direct)	Professor Hong will *lead* the discussion group.
led (past tense of verb *lead*)	Professor Hong *led* the discussion group.
lead (noun: a heavy metal)	*Lead* poisoning is dangerous.
loose (not securely attached)	The button was *loose*.
lose (to fail to keep)	I often *lose* my keys.
principal (most important, or a head of a school)	The citizens' *principal* concern is educational costs.
principle (a basic rule or truth)	This *principle* should govern all of your actions.
their (possessive of *they*)	The students brought *their* books to class.
there (in that place, opposite of *here*)	*There* is the bus.
they're (contraction of *they are*)	*They're* early.
to (toward)	Please move *to* the front of the class.
too (also, or excessively)	Harry is coming *too*.
two (following *one*)	The *two* speeches were similar.
who's (contraction of *who is*)	*Who's* taking a cab?
whose (possessive of *who*)	*Whose* book is this?
your (possessive of *you*)	*Your* experiment is well designed.
you're (contraction of *you are*)	*You're* passing the course.

25e Watch out for commonly misspelled words.

Commonly Misspelled Words

absence	accidentally	achievement	amateur	apologize
accept	accommodate	acquaintance	analysis	apparent
accessible	accuracy	acquire	analyze	appearance

Commonly Misspelled Words (continued)

argument	eighth	laboratory	privilege	thorough
ascend	eligible	leisure	probably	through
athlete	embarrass	length	proceed	tragedy
attendance	emphasize	library	professor	truly
beginning	environment	license	pronunciation	unanimous
believe	especially	lightning	psychology	usually
benefited	exaggerate	loneliness	quantity	vacuum
boundary	excellence	maintenance	quiet	vengeance
Britain	exercise	maneuver	receive	villain
bureaucracy	existence	marriage	recognize	weird
business	experience	mathematics	recommend	writing
calendar	explanation	miniature	reference	
cemetery	familiar	mischievous	referred	
changeable	fascinate	necessary	relieve	
characteristic	February	niece	repetition	
column	foreign	ninety	restaurant	
committee	forty	noticeable	rhythm	
conceive	fulfill *or* fulfil	occasionally	ridiculous	
conscience	government	occurrence	roommate	
conscious	grammar	omission	sacrifice	
convenience	guarantee	originally	schedule	
criticism	harass	parallel	secretary	
criticize	height	particularly	seize	
curiosity	humorous	permissible	separate	
deceive	hypocrisy	physical	sergeant	
decision	imagination	picnicking	several	
definitely	immediately	pleasant	similar	
descendant	incredible	possible	sincerely	
disappearance	inevitable	practically	sophomore	
disappoint	intelligence	precede	succeed	
disastrous	interest	preference	successful	
discipline	irresistible	prejudice	summary	
efficiency	judgment	preparation	surprise	
efficient	knowledge	prevalent	tendency	

25f Be alert for words that are formed from the same root (they may have different spellings) and for words with silent letters.

heir   heredity

aisle

pneumonia

For more exercises on catching spelling errors, refer to the Spelling section of Exercise Central at www.bedfordstmartins .com/successfulwriting.

EXERCISE 25.1

Correct the spelling errors in the following paragraph. If you are not sure about a word, check the list of commonly misspelled words on pages 938–39 or your dictionary. Some sentences may be correct as written.

       centuries
▶ After two ~~centurys~~ of isolation, Japan modernized very quickly.
          ^

  In 1542, the first European visiters arrived in Japan. Traders and missionarys from the West brought firarms, tobacco, and Christianity to the island nation, which was suffring from internal strife. Japanese rulers welcomed Christianity at first, seing it as a way to reunify the country. However, after large numbers of Japanese converted, some official intolerence toward Christianity appeared. Finally, the rebellion of a Catholic Japanese community ensured that the government would act to prevent Western missionaries and merchants from joining forces with Japanese dissidents. In 1640, a policy of isolation took affect. No foreiners were aloud to enter Japan, and no Japanese were permitted to travel abroad. This policy was finaly relaxed in 1853, and a new era began in 1868, with the arrival of a new imperial government. The new leaders were youthful and visionary, and they wanted to bring their country up to date. Although some Japanese who had enjoied privileges in the old society lost them during modernization, most people where delighted with the country's new direction.

26 NOUNS AND ARTICLES

The two primary types of nouns in English are proper nouns and common nouns. A **proper noun** names a specific, unique person, place, thing, calendar item, or idea and is always capitalized.

Sylvia Plath   Lake Erie   Toyota   Tuesday   Marxism

A **common noun** refers to a person, place, thing, or idea in general and is not capitalized.

writer   lake   car   day   ideology

Common nouns are classified as either count nouns or noncount nouns. A **count noun** names items that can be counted.

artists   books   towns

Count nouns have both singular and plural forms.

Singular Form	*Plural Form*
one artist	three artists
every book	most books
each town	all towns

A **noncount noun** names items that cannot be easily counted.

rain   traffic   mail

Most noncount nouns do not have a plural form.

Incorrect	*Correct*
advices	advice
informations	information
vocabularies	vocabulary

This chapter will help you use these categories—proper noun versus common noun, count noun versus noncount noun—to avoid errors in your writing, especially in your use of articles (*a, an,* and *the*).

26a Keep the following guidelines in mind for recognizing and using noncount nouns.

Nouns in the following categories are likely to be noncount nouns.

ABSTRACTIONS	advice, courage, grief, information, knowledge, love, satisfaction, wealth
FIELDS OF STUDY OR RESEARCH	chemistry, law, medicine, pollution, sociology, weather
SPORTS AND GAMES	chess, football, soccer, tennis
LIQUIDS	milk, water
THINGS THAT CANNOT BE EASILY COUNTED	rice, sand, snow

▶ He offered some good advices.

Do not use numbers or plural quantity words before noncount nouns.

▶ ~~Many~~ ^R^ rain ^s^ hit the windowpane.

Do not use the article *a* or *an* with noncount nouns.

▶ The horses were covered with ~~a~~ mud.

Noncount nouns are used with singular verbs.

▶ The milk ~~were~~ ^was^ sour.

Some nouns can be noncount or count, depending on whether they refer to something considered as a whole.

NONCOUNT	*Bread* is a staple in almost every cuisine. [*Bread* considered as a kind of food]
COUNT	Some *breads* are made without yeast. [Particular types of bread, such as rye or whole wheat]

26b Use an article or a demonstrative pronoun (*this, that, these, those*) with a count noun.

▶ Her client sent her ^a^ fax.

> *this*
> ▶ I found fax on my chair.
>   ^

26c Use *a* or *an* before a singular count noun that does not refer to a specific person, place, object, or concept.

▶ *A* computer is *a* useful tool.

▶ This country needs *an* electric car.

When using the articles *a* and *an,* remember that *a* is used before words beginning with a consonant sound and *an* is used before words beginning with a vowel sound.

a baby	an eagle
a city	an hour
a fish	an island
a hope	an orange
a unicycle	an outrage

26d Use *the* before a noun that refers to something specific.

▶ Mohammad pointed out *the* planets in *the* evening sky.

▶ *The* lamp on my desk is an antique.

Be sure not to omit the article.

> *the*
> ▶ He was awake before alarm rang.
>   ^

26e Use *a, an,* or *the* with most singular count nouns considered as general examples; no article is necessary for plural count nouns considered as general examples.

▶ *A* bird feeder is an entertaining addition to any yard.

▶ *The* cat is among the most agile creatures on earth.

▶ *Plants* add a cheery note to any room.

26f Use *the* with plural proper nouns (*the United States, the Joneses, the Koreans*) and certain types of singular proper nouns.

Some singular proper nouns use *the.*

PROPER NOUNS THAT CONSIST OF THE, A COMMON NOUN, AND OF	*the* Arch of Triumph, *the* state of Vermont, *the* University of Florida
NAMES OF BUILDINGS	*the* Eiffel Tower, *the* White House
COUNTRIES NAMED WITH A PHRASE	*the* Dominican Republic, *the* United Kingdom
NAMES OF HIGHWAYS	*the* Kensington Expressway
NAMES OF HOTELS AND MUSEUMS	*the* Guggenheim Museum, *the* Hilton Hotel
PARTS OF THE GLOBE	*the* Equator, *the* Northwest, *the* South Pole
HISTORICAL PERIODS AND EVENTS	*the* Industrial Revolution, *the* Renaissance
NAMES OF SEAS, OCEANS, GULFS, RIVERS, AND DESERTS	*the* Atlantic Ocean, *the* Gulf of Mexico, *the* Missouri River, *the* Red Sea, *the* Sahara
GROUPS OF ISLANDS	*the* Hawaiian Islands
MOUNTAIN RANGES	*the* Alps

26g Do not use an article with most other singular proper nouns.

▶ The houses are beautiful on ~~the~~ Maple Street.

For more exercises on articles, refer to the Nouns and Articles section of Exercise Central at www.bedfordstmartins .com/successfulwriting.

EXERCISE 26.1

For each of the following sentences, choose the correct article. Note that X = no article.

▶ For many Americans, (a/the) civil rights movement began when (X/the) Rosa Parks refused to give up her seat on a bus to a white man.

1. Rosa Parks, (an/the) African American woman living in Montgomery, Alabama, was riding (a/the) bus with sections reserved for white passengers.
2. (X/The) back of the bus, where African Americans were supposed to sit, was crowded.
3. Parks sat in (X/the) front of the bus, which took tremendous courage.
4. (A/The) bus driver forced her to get off (a/the) bus, but (X/the) incident set off the Montgomery bus boycott.
5. (X/The) people all over the United States heard (a/the) story of Rosa Parks, and the civil rights movement had its first hero.

27 VERBS

A **verb** shows an action, an occurrence, or a state of being. ESL writers need to pay special attention to their use of verb tenses, helping or modal verbs (also called auxiliary verbs), and verbs followed by an infinitive or a gerund.

27a Use the appropriate verb tense to express time accurately.

Verb tenses express time. They indicate when an action occurs, occurred, or will occur. The following sections will help you understand and form the simple, perfect, and progressive tenses.

The Simple Tenses

The simple tenses are used to show clear and simple time relationships. The following chart summarizes how each of the simple tenses is formed and used.

THE SIMPLE TENSES

Tense	How It Is Formed	Examples
Simple present Expresses an action or condition occurring at the time of speaking or writing, a statement of fact, or a habitual action	First- and second-person singular and plural, third-person plural: **base form** Third-person singular: base form + -s or -es	I *cook* for five people. They *cook* many unusual dishes. He *cooks* for a family of five.
Simple past Indicates that an action occurred in the past and was completed in the past	Regular verbs: base form + -d or -ed Irregular verbs: Forms vary; check the list on pages 840–42 or a dictionary.	We *played* field hockey yesterday. He *became* agitated when the doctor approached.
Simple future Indicates that an action will take place in the future	*will* or form of *be* + *going to* + base form	His doctor *will try* a new approach. Ron *is going to find* a way out.

The **base form** is the form of a verb as it appears in the dictionary.

THE PERFECT TENSES

Tense	How It Is Formed	Examples
Present perfect Indicates that a past action took place at an unspecified time or is continuing to the present	*has* or *have* + past participle	The landlord *has offered* to repair the damage. I *have worked* in this office for two years.
Past perfect Indicates that an action was completed in the past before some other past action	*had* + past participle	Rafika *had offered* to babysit, but she got sick.
Future perfect Indicates that an action will take place before some specified time in the future	*will* + *have* + past participle	By Monday, the team *will have offered* him a new contract.

The past participle of regular verbs is formed by adding -d, -ed, or -en to the verb's base form. It can be used as an adjective.

The present participle is the -ing form of a verb; it shows an action that is in progress or ongoing. It can be used as an adjective.

The Perfect Tenses

The perfect tenses are also used to show time relationships. A verb in one of the perfect tenses indicates an action that was or will be completed by or before some specified time. The perfect tenses are constructed by using a form of *have* along with the verb's **past participle.**

The chart at the top of this page summarizes how each of the perfect tenses is formed and used.

The Progressive Tenses

The simple progressive tenses describe actions in progress, indicating that an action did, does, or will continue. They are formed by using a form of *be* along with the **present participle.**

The perfect progressive tenses are used to describe actions that continue to the present or until another action takes place. They are often used to emphasize the length of time involved.

The chart on the next page summarizes how the progressive and perfect progressive tenses are formed and used.

EXERCISE 27.1

Choose the correct verb tense in the sentences on page 948.

THE PROGRESSIVE AND PERFECT PROGRESSIVE TENSES

Tense	How It Is Formed	Examples
Present progressive Indicates that an action began in the past, is happening now, and will end sometime in the future	form of *be* + present participle	Consultants *are changing* the workforce.
Past progressive Indicates that an action was in progress at a specified time in the past	*was* or *were* + present participle	He *was changing* a light bulb when the ladder collapsed. They *were driving* to the beach when their car stalled.
Future progressive Indicates that an action will begin and continue in the future. The time is often specified.	*will be* + present participle, or present tense of *be* + *going to be* + present participle	New parents *will be changing* diapers for at least two years. Exams *are going to be changing* under the new principal.
Present perfect progressive Emphasizes the ongoing nature of an action that began in the past and continues into the present	*has* or *have been* + present participle	Her secretary *has been running* errands all morning. They *have been planning* this party for several weeks.
Past perfect progressive Emphasizes the duration of an action that began and continued in the past and was completed before some other past action	*had been* + present participle	He *had been running* two miles a day until he broke his toe.
Future perfect progressive Emphasizes the duration of an action that will continue in the future for a specified amount of time before another future action	*will have been* + present participle	When she takes over, her family *will have been running* the company for four generations.

For more exercises on verb tense, refer to the Verbs section of Exercise Central at www .bedfordstmartins.com /successfulwriting.

▶ Ever since the invention of computers, people (predicted/have been predicting) that books would disappear.

1. Most people (enjoy/enjoyed) reading off a computer screen but not for long periods of time.

2. When computer books become easier to read, some people predict that paper books (will disappear/have disappeared).

3. Until recently, most book lovers (had purchased/purchase) all their books in local bookstores.

4. Now, however, publishers (are offering/will be offering) online editions of their books.

5. Books and computers both serve a purpose, and the demand for both probably (increase/will be increasing) for years to come.

27b Use helping verbs to form tenses and express your meaning precisely.

Helping verbs are used before main verbs to form certain tenses. Some helping verbs—*have, do,* and *be*—change form to indicate tense (see 27a). The helping verb *do* indicates tense in questions, inverted phrases, and negative sentences. *Do you know her? Little did I realize what would happen. She does not like him.* It is also used for emphasis: *The sentence does need a comma.* The forms of these helping verbs are as follows.

> have, has, had
> be, am, is, are, was, were, being, been
> do, does, did

Other helping verbs, called **modals,** do not change form. Modal verbs include *can, could, may, might, must, shall, should, will,* and *would.* Modals are used to express ability, necessity, permission, intention, and so forth. The accompanying chart summarizes the common uses of modals.

HOW TO USE MODALS

Meaning	Present or Future Time	Past Time
Ability	*can* Most five-year-olds *can* tie their own shoes.	*could* + *have* + past participle Jim *could have registered* early if he wanted to.
Necessity	*must* or *have to* International travelers *must* carry passports.	*had to* The governor *had to* work with other officials.

(Continued on next page)

HOW TO USE MODALS *(Continued)*

Meaning	Present or Future Time	Past Time
Necessity (continued)	*must* or *have to* Students *have to* read critically.	*had to*
Permission	*may, can* Anyone with a ticket *may* see the film. You *can* come in now.	*might* + *have* + past participle *could* + *have* + past participle You *might have waited* inside, out of the rain. We *could have gone* to the movies.
Intention	*will* He *will* encourage real estate development.	*would* + *have* + past participle I *would have hiked* last weekend, but it rained.
Advisability	*should, had better* Everyone *should* get an education. She *had better* buy a ticket.	*should* + *have* + past participle The trainee *should have read* the manual.
Possibility	*may, might* An accountant *may* work long hours during tax season.	*may* or *might* + *have* + past participle *could* + *have* + past participle The burglar *might have entered* through the window. They *could have lost* their keys.
Speculation	*would* He *would* like her.	*would* + *have* + past participle No one *would have recognized* him without his moustache.

For more exercises on modals, refer to the Verbs section of Exercise Central at www .bedfordstmartins.com /successfulwriting.

EXERCISE 27.2

In each sentence, fill in the blank with a modal from the list. In most cases, more than one modal will work in the sentence. Use each modal only once.

can	may	should	would
could have	might	will	would have

▶ Busy professionals who are looking for a husband or wife _can_ try video dating.

1. Other people feel that they _____ meet their potential mate in person.
2. The Internet _____ be another way to find romance.
3. In the past, few _____ imagined such uses for technology.
4. Now people fear that technology _____ soon replace many human activities, including matchmaking.
5. Human matchmakers _____ become obsolete if video dating grows more popular.

27c Use gerunds or infinitives following verbs according to convention.

Often, you will need to use an **infinitive** or a **gerund** as the object of a verb in a sentence, as in the following examples.

An **infinitive** is a verb form made up of *to* plus the base form (*to run, to see*).

A **gerund** is an *-ing* form of a verb that functions as a noun (*complaining, jogging*).

▶ Mustafa needs *to find* his lecture notes.

▶ Lara avoids *studying* in her dormitory.

When you use an infinitive or a gerund as an object, you need to remember that some verbs are followed by infinitives, some verbs are followed by gerunds, and some can be followed by either form without a change in meaning. The following guidelines will help you determine which form to use.

Verbs Followed by Infinitives

Some verbs, including the verbs listed here, are usually followed by an infinitive in English.

agree	claim	manage	promise
ask	decide	need	refuse
beg	expect	offer	venture
bother	fail	plan	want
choose	hope	pretend	wish

In general, use these verbs with an infinitive, not a gerund.

       to finish
▶ Margaret managed ~~finishing~~ the project.
         ^

Some verbs are followed by a noun or a pronoun and then by an infinitive. These verbs include *allow, cause, convince, hire, instruct, order, remind, tell,* and *warn.*

▶ The bank *reminded your office to send* proof of employment.

When using a negative word (such as *no* or *not*) in a sentence containing a verb followed by an infinitive, place the word carefully; its position in the sentence often affects meaning.

▶ Bella did *not* claim to know.

    She never mentioned it.

▶ Bella claimed *not* to know.

    She said she did not know.

The causative verbs *have, let,* and *make* are followed by a noun or a pronoun and the base form of the verb (without the word *to*).

▶ The noise made her *lose* her concentration.
▶ The hotel lets visitors *bring* pets.
▶ Have your assistant *type* those letters.

Verbs Followed by Gerunds

The following verbs are often followed by a gerund.

admit	dislike	postpone
appreciate	enjoy	practice
avoid	finish	recall
consider	imagine	resist
delay	keep	risk
deny	mention	suggest
discuss	miss	tolerate

Use these verbs with a gerund, not an infinitive.

▶ The zoning committee considered ~~to approve~~ the proposal. *[approving]*

In a sentence containing a gerund, place a negative word (such as *no* or *not*) between the verb and the *-ing* form.

▶ Some vacationers consider *not* returning to work.

Verbs Followed by Infinitives or Gerunds

Some verbs (such as *begin, continue, like,* and *prefer*) can be followed by an infinitive or a gerund with little or no change in meaning.

INFINITIVE	Anita likes to jog.
GERUND	Anita likes jogging.

Other verbs (such as *forget, remember, stop,* and *try*) can be followed by either an infinitive or a gerund, but the meaning of the sentence changes.

INFINITIVE	Dien remembered to answer the letter.

He remembered that he had an obligation to do something.

GERUND	Dien remembered answering the letter.

He remembered (the action of) doing something.

For more exercises on gerunds and infinitives, refer to the Verbs section of Exercise Central at www.bedfordstmartins .com/successfulwriting.

EXERCISE 27.3

Correct the errors in the use of gerunds and infinitives in the following sentences. Some sentences may be correct as written.

        to discover

▶ Archeologists hope ~~discovering~~ when the first Americans arrived.

1. Many archeologists have considered to change the date they estimate that humans arrived in the Americas.
2. Until recently, scientists didn't expect finding evidence of human inhabitants older than 11,000 years, the age of stone tools found in Clovis, New Mexico, in the 1930s.
3. Recently, however, after discovering older evidence in Monte Verde, Chile, and other sites, some scientists have suggested to change this date.
4. Archeologists began to reexamine their assumptions after it was established that Monte Verde was older than the Clovis site.
5. One site in Virginia may be over 15,000 years old, and archeologists who keep to dig deeper may find even older evidence.

28 THE PREPOSITIONS *IN, ON,* AND *AT*

These three common prepositions are used before nouns or pronouns to indicate time or location.

Time

Use *in* with
  Months: *in* April
  Years: *in* 2003
  Seasons: *in* the winter
  Certain parts of the day: *in* the morning, *in* the afternoon

Use *on* with
  Days of the week: *on* Tuesday
  Dates: *on* June 20, 2004

Use *at* with
> Specific times: *at* 8 p.m., *at* noon
> Other parts of the day: *at* night, *at* dawn, *at* dusk

Location

Use *in* with
> Geographic places: *in* San Francisco, *in* rural areas
> Enclosed areas: *in* the stadium

Use *on* with
> A surface: *on* a shelf
> Forms of public transportation: *on* the bus
> Street names: *on* Main Street
> Floors of buildings: *on* the fourth floor
> Some areas of the country: *on* the Gulf Coast

Use *at* with
> Specific addresses (number and street):   *at* 130 Washington Street
> Named locations: *at* Juanita's house
> General locations: *at* the college
> Locations with specific functions: *at* the library

For more on prepositions, see 1g.

EXERCISE 28.1

In the following sentences, fill in the blank with either *in, on,* or *at.*

▶ Every year __*in*__ the spring, filmmakers gather in Hollywood for the Academy Awards ceremony.

1. The Academy Awards ceremony was first televised _____ 1953.
2. The participants gathered in the RKO Pantages Theater _____ Hollywood, California.
3. In 2002, the ceremony moved from its previous location _____ the Dorothy Chandler Pavilion _____ Los Angeles to its new location _____ the Kodak Theatre _____ Hollywood.
4. The participants have to arrive _____ the middle of the afternoon because the show is timed for the evening _____ the East Coast.
5. The ceremony appears on television around the world, and many members of the audience watch it very late _____ night or early _____ the morning.

For more exercises on the prepositions in, on, *or* at, *refer to the Prepositions* In, On, and At *section of Exercise Central at www.bedfordstmartins.com/successfulwriting.*

29 ADJECTIVES

When using **adjectives**, ESL writers need to pay special attention to how adjectives are arranged when they modify the same noun and how adjectives are combined with prepositions. (For more on adjectives, see 1d and Section 9 of the Handbook.)

An **adjective** modifies a noun or pronoun.

29a Follow the conventional order when two or more adjectives modify the same noun.

Possessives come before numbers.

▶ *Anita's three* papers were accepted.

Ordinal numbers (*first, second*) come before cardinal numbers (*one, two*).

▶ James's *first three* requests were denied.

Descriptive adjectives should appear in the following order.

1. Article or possessive noun: *an, Dr. Green's, these*
2. Opinion: *favorite, hideous, lovely*
3. Size: *big, enormous, tiny*
4. Shape: *circular, rectangular, round*
5. Age: *elderly, teenaged, three-year-old*
6. Color: *black, blue, maroon*
7. National origin: *English, Nigerian, Vietnamese*
8. Religion: *Christian, Jewish, Muslim*
9. Matter or substance: *crystal, onyx, tweed*
10. Noun used as an adjective: *book* (as in *book jacket*), *picture* (as in *picture frame*), *record* (as in *record producer*)

     ▶ *beautiful large white* horse

     ▶ *Juan's old* coat

     ▶ *a valuable new red British* car

     ▶ *small oval* table

29b Combine adjectives with specific prepositions to express your meaning precisely.

Prepositions (such as *before, on,* and *to*) are used before a noun or pronoun to indicate time, place, space, direction, position, or some other relationship.

Keep a list of adjective-**preposition** combinations that you hear in conversation or notice in your reading. Consult an ESL dictionary when you are not sure whether a particular combination expresses the meaning you intend. Here are some common adjective-preposition combinations.

afraid of	grateful to (person)
ashamed of	interested in
full of	proud of
grateful for (thing)	responsible for (thing or action)

responsible to (person)   suspicious of

satisfied with   tired of

sorry for

For more exercises on avoiding misplaced adjectives, refer to the Adjectives section of Exercise Central at www.bedfordstmartins .com/successfulwriting.

EXERCISE 29.1

Correct the errors in the order of adjectives and in adjective-preposition combinations in the following sentences.

>   *insane Roman emperor*
> ▶ The ~~emperor Roman insane~~ Caligula succeeded his uncle, the emperor Tiberius.
>   ^

1. Caligula made favorite his horse a Roman senator.
2. He was also responsible to declaring war on the sea god Neptune.
3. Brief Caligula's violent reign made many Roman citizens afraid for their emperor.
4. The emperor's notorious temper led to the deaths of unfortunate those Romans who angered him.
5. Upstanding many citizens were relieved when assassins left Caligula dead.

---

30 COMMON SENTENCE PROBLEMS

As you edit and proofread your writing, watch out for the following problems involving word order, relative pronouns, and negatives.

30a Place sentence elements in the correct order.

Place words and phrases that indicate time or place at the beginning or at the end of a clause. Do not place them between the verb and its direct object (D.O.).

                  verb   D.O.

INCORRECT   We did this afternoon our homework.

                  verb   D.O.

CORRECT   We did our homework this afternoon.

Place the indirect object (I.O.) after the verb and before the direct object (D.O.).

           verb   I.O.   D.O.

▶ Ramon bought his sister a videotape.

           verb   I.O.   D.O.

▶ Ramon bought her a videotape.

Exception: When a prepositional phrase takes the place of an indirect object, the phrase should follow the direct object.

$$\overset{\text{verb}}{\underbrace{}} \quad \overset{\text{D.O.}}{\underbrace{}} \quad \overset{\text{prep. phrase}}{\underbrace{}}$$

► Ramon bought a videotape for his sister.

Some verbs (such as *describe, explain, illustrate, mention, open,* and *say*) cannot be followed by an indirect object.

INCORRECT	Lu described us the figurine.
CORRECT	Lu described the figurine to us.

For more exercises on common sentence problems, refer to the Common Sentence Problems section of Exercise Central at www.bedfordstmartins .com/successfulwriting.

EXERCISE 30.1

Correct the errors involving the placement of sentence elements in the following sentences. Some sentences may be correct as written.

to the visitors

► A park ranger explained ~~the visitors~~ the habits of the cave's bats.
                                                            ^

1. Every evening at sunset, thousands of bats hunt from the entrance of Carlsbad Caverns in New Mexico mosquitoes.
2. Bat experts tell people that bats are actually helpful to humans.
3. One bat can eat in a single night a huge number of insect pests.
4. At the cave entrance at dusk, the bats provide to curious onlookers a spectacular show.
5. They give the crowds who come to see them when they fly out of the cave a thrilling experience.

30b Do not omit a relative pronoun when it is the subject of a relative clause or the object of a verb or preposition within a relative clause.

A relative pronoun is a noun substitute that relates groups of words to nouns or other pronouns: *the patient who injured her leg.*

A dependent clause contains a subject and a verb but does not express a complete thought.

A **relative clause** is a **dependent clause** that begins with a **relative pronoun** (such as *that, which, who, whom,* or *whose*) and modifies a noun or pronoun. Sometimes a relative clause begins with a preposition followed by a relative pronoun (the reason *for which* I am writing).

INCORRECT	The firefighter rescued the child was given a hero's welcome.
REVISED	The firefighter *who* rescued the child was given a hero's welcome.
INCORRECT	Juanita found the book for she had been searching all morning.
REVISED	Juanita found the book for *which* she had been searching all morning.

Exception: The relative pronoun and the verb *be* are often omitted in relative clauses when the clause is restrictive (essential to the meaning of the word or phrase it modifies); they should usually be included in a nonrestrictive clause (not essential to the meaning of the word or phrase it modifies). For more on restrictive and nonrestrictive word groups, see 12e.

RESTRICTIVE   Michael grabbed the newspapers [that were] on the table.

That were is optional because the clause is restrictive; it tells which newspapers are meant.

NONRESTRICTIVE   Michael tripped over the stack of day-old newspapers, which were ready to be recycled.

The clause supplies additional but nonessential information about the newspapers. It is nonrestrictive, so *which were* should be included.

Use the relative pronoun *whose* to show possession with a relative clause.

INCORRECT   The committee sat at a table that its surface was scratched.

REVISED   The committee sat at a table whose surface was scratched.

Use relative pronouns, not personal pronouns, to introduce relative clauses.

INCORRECT   Computer terminals, they are scarce at certain times of the day, are an obsession for many students.

REVISED   Computer terminals, *which* are scarce at certain times of the day, are an obsession for many students.

EXERCISE 30.2

Correct the errors in the use of relative pronouns in the following sentences. Some sentences may be correct as written.

                 that
▶ The United States is a nation ˄ was founded by settlers from other lands.

1. Immigration in the United States is a controversial subject that its implications have been debated for a century.
2. Early laws, they were sometimes discriminatory, restricted immigrants from certain countries.
3. Both legal and undocumented immigrants, who continue to come to the United States in record numbers, often seek employment.
4. Some Americans want to limit immigration fear that new arrivals will compete for scarce jobs.
5. New immigrants, their dreams and wishes resemble those of many previous generations of Americans, continue to arrive.

For more exercises on common sentence problems, refer to the Common Sentence Problems section of Exercise Central at www.bedfordstmartins.com/successfulwriting.

30c Make a sentence negative by adding *not* or a negative adverb such as *never* or *seldom*.

Place *not* after the first helping verb.

▶ The speech will *not* begin on time.

In questions, the helping verb should be followed by *not* or the contraction for *not* (*-n't*). Place the helping verb and *not* before the subject and the main verb.

▶ *Didn't* I read that story in the newspaper yesterday?

Place negative adverbs before the main verb. In a sentence with a helping verb, place the negative adverb after the first helping verb.

▶ Arthur *seldom forgets* an assignment.

▶ Marguerite *may never play* the violin again.

If a negative adverb is used at the beginning of a clause, the helping verb *do* is needed.

▶ *Rarely* does one see a bald eagle.

EXERCISE 30.3

Correct the errors in the use of negatives in the following sentences. Some sentences may be correct as written.

                                      not

▶ Most reports of UFO sightings and aliens ~~not~~ are believed.

1. Reputable scientists have confirmed never a UFO sighting.
2. A simple explanation for a sighting is difficult seldom to find.
3. People who believe aliens have contacted them offer convincing proof almost never.
4. Isn't it possible that many people simply want to convince themselves that humans are not alone?
5. Aliens may exist, but they probably not have arrived on earth yet.

For more exercises on common ESL problems, refer to the ESL Trouble Spots section of Exercise Central at www .bedfordstmartins.com /successfulwriting.

SUMMARY EXERCISE FOR CHAPTERS 26–30

Review Sections 26–30, then correct the errors in standard English usage in the following paragraph.

        the   *one*

▶ In United States, educational ~~one~~ idea is very controversial.

     Bilingual education, that its value is questioned by some educators, is widespread in United States. In bilingual education theory, students that are not speaking English learn most subjects in their native language. On the same time, they receive the English instruction from a teacher who also speaks their language so that eventually they will be able to join native speakers in a regular class. Reality of bilingual education is often different. At California, some parents of students in bilingual education classes protested their children were not learning English. They go to court to abolish bilingual education classes. It is true that some students who were taught mainly in their native language has difficulty ever learning English well enough to function in an English-language environment. Educators not agree about the reason for this apparent problem with bilingual education. Some felt students should learn most subjects in English immediately, even if they not are comfortable at first. They argue that this method should give to students the advantage of learning English quickly. Other professionals blame previous students' education in their native countries. They argue that without bilingual education, the many students had dropped out. In addition, they claim that forcing student to learn English has been making them to forget their native language. People on both sides of the issue have contributed to this argument some useful informations, but the controversy continues.

ANSWERS TO EVEN-NUMBERED EXERCISES

Section 1

EXERCISE 1.1 *page 835*

Answers

2. They invaded England from northern Europe. [proper, proper]

4. The Normans, who came from France, later conquered England. [proper, proper, proper]

EXERCISE 1.2 *page 838*

Answers

2. Events that surprise us are especially hard to remember accurately. [relative, personal]

4. The students were later asked to fill out questionnaires in which untrue details of these incidents were suggested. [relative, demonstrative]

EXERCISE 1.3 *page 840*

Answers

2. A few months later, over four thousand miners had arrived. [helping, action-intransitive]

4. Most "forty-niners" soon grew disillusioned. [linking]

EXERCISE 1.4 *page 842*

Answers

2. Correct

4. Ali grew increasingly well known for his quick moves in the ring and his quick wit everywhere else.

6. He refused to be drafted that year for religious reasons and was banned from boxing and stripped of his title.

8. He got the title back in 1974 by defeating George Foreman.

10. Correct

EXERCISE 1.5 *page 845*

Answers

2. While its writers were developing the Constitution, they studied important documents from other societies. [past progressive, simple past]

4. The Constitution is adaptable and has been amended—for example, to ensure that female and nonwhite citizens have the right to vote. [simple present, present perfect, simple present]

EXERCISE 1.6 *page 846*

Answers

2. In the seventeenth century, the practice of smoking opium spread from Java to China. [indicative, active]

4. Morphine was used as an effective painkiller during the Civil War. [indicative, passive]

EXERCISE 1.7 *page 847*

Answers

2. These clusters have led some people to believe that the cancers have environmental causes. [limiting, limiting, article, descriptive]

4. The Love Canal site was one of the first clusters to alert the American public. [proper, article, limiting, article, proper]

EXERCISE 1.8 *page 848*

Answers

2. No adverbs

4. Ikebana arrangements are typically triangular.

EXERCISE 1.9 *page 850*

Answers

2. Since Snow wrote his speech, relations between the two groups have changed. [subordinating conjunction]

4. Today, some academics in the humanities have adopted not only scientific terms but also scientific theories in their work. [correlative conjunction]

EXERCISE 1.10 *page 852*

Answers

2. Prior to that time, he had been interested in Western thought, but he became fascinated with Indian art.

4. Ray's first film, *Pather Panchali,* won a prize at the Cannes Film Festival <u>in</u> 1955.

EXERCISE 1.11   *page 852*

Answers

2. Our coach is a good guy, but <u>hey</u>, the team has to win, too.

4. <u>Oh</u>, and a few good runners wouldn't hurt either.

Section 2

EXERCISE 2.1   *page 854*

Answers

2. (Would) [this <u>kind</u> of human and wildlife cooperation] (<u>work</u> in other areas)?

4. [This <u>custom</u>] (both <u>ensures</u> the workability of the Amboseli Reserve's unusual system and <u>indicates</u> the difficulty of trying the same system elsewhere). Compound predicate.

EXERCISE 2.2   *page 855*

Answers

2. The travelers made the <u>head of the wealthy Donner family</u> [direct object] <u>their official leader</u> [object complement].

4. Unfortunately, heavy snows trapped the few remaining <u>wagons</u> [direct object] in the Sierra Nevada mountains in October.

EXERCISE 2.3   *page 858*

Answers

2. *living in the United States:* participial phrase; *in the United States:* prepositional phrase; *to maintain ties with their homeland:* infinitive phrase; *with their homeland:* prepositional phrase

4. *In some cases:* prepositional phrase; *with a proposed match:* prepositional phrase

EXERCISE 2.4   *page 860*

Answers

2. If a <u>child has difficulty concentrating on ordinary tasks such as homework</u>, he or she may have ADD.

4. Some people wonder <u>whether ADD might be a phenomenon connected to modern life</u>.

EXERCISE 2.5   *page 862*

Answers

2. Compound-complex

4. Complex

Section 3

EXERCISE 3.1   *page 867*

Possible Revisions

2. In these days of computerized mailing lists, your name and address are certainly not private.

4. To put it another way, four trees per person per year contribute to this tide of printed waste.

6. Email advertisers can target specific audiences, such as small-business owners or college students.

8. Companies are choosing from among more than 20,000 mailing lists. For just pennies per name, firms can target recipients with mass mailings, either paper or electronic, and make a profit from a relatively low response.

10. Your name can be "sold" over and over until it's almost impossible to track it to the business that first listed it.

Section 4

EXERCISE 4.1   *page 872*

Possible Revisions

2. Shopping through Internet bookstores is convenient, but some people miss the atmosphere of a traditional bookstore.

4. In the 1960s many Americans treated Vietnam veterans disrespectfully, a situation that has changed dramatically since that time.

6. With large bodies and tiny wings, bumblebees have long been a puzzle. How do they fly?

8. The Supreme Court often makes controversial decisions because the justices must decide how to interpret the Constitution.

10. Restoring a painting is, indeed, delicate work, and too much enthusiasm can be dangerous.

Section 5

EXERCISE 5.1   *page 877*

Answers

2. A student in most non-English-speaking industrialized nations expects to spend six or more years studying English.

4. Working for laws that require all Americans to speak English is a fairly common U.S. political tactic.

6. Some linguists joke that a person who speaks two languages is called "bilingual," while a person who speaks one language is called "American."

8. Correct

10. Everyone who studies a foreign language is likely to benefit.

Section 6

EXERCISE 6.1   *page 880*

Answers

2. Cuba, an island that lies ninety miles off the Florida coast, provided them with an excuse to do so.

4. In addition, many people in the United States had wanted to take over Spain's territories for a long time.

6. Cuba was allowed to take control of its own affairs right away.

8. Correct

10. Many Puerto Ricans are worried that statehood would destroy the native culture of their island, and none of them wants that to happen.

Section 7

EXERCISE 7.1   *page 883*

Possible Revisions

2. Because of the importance of the information, it often must be transmitted secretly.

4. "Invisible ink," which cannot be seen until the paper is heated, was once a popular way to communicate secretly.

6. During World War II, U.S. government code specialists hired Navajo Indians because Navajo is a difficult and little-studied language.

8. Because these cryptograms are so simple, they are no longer used to transmit messages.

10. Alan Turing, a British civil servant and mathematical genius, finally solved the enigma code.

EXERCISE 7.2   *page 885*

Answers

2. A team of researchers might disagree on their conclusions about the disappearance of the dinosaur.

4. In one way, animals resemble plants: Some are "weeds" because they have the ability to thrive under many conditions.

6. When a "weed" and a delicate native species compete for their survival, the native species usually loses.

8. People should be more concerned about the extinction of plants and animals than they seem to be.

10. The earth has experienced several mass extinctions in its history, but another would take its toll on the quality of human life.

EXERCISE 7.3   *page 889*

Answers

2. Correct

4. Following the success of Mammoth Cave, many Kentucky cavers hoped to make a fortune from their spelunking.

6. In January of 1925, a falling rock trapped Collins, who was spelunking in a narrow passage in Sand Cave.

8. For several days, the most famous man in Kentucky was he. [*Or:* For several days, he was the most famous man in Kentucky.]

10. Their failing to save Collins was a terrible tragedy for his family and the rescuers.

Section 8

EXERCISE 8.1   *page 893*

Possible Revisions

2. We wondered whether our professor knew of the new theory and whether she agreed with it.

4. Most parents think they have a major influence on their children's behavior.

6. Children strongly desire peer acceptance, and they want to be different from adults.

8. Most adults recall that, in childhood, their friends' opinions were extremely important to them.

10. Anxious parents would be greatly relieved if this hypothesis were proven.

EXERCISE 8.3   *page 895*

Possible Revisions

2. Business is booming for independent Web development shops, an industry that grows larger each year.

4. Once the domain of computer hackers, the online world has become a routine destination for many nontechnical people.

6. The information technology department is often the part of a company where Web projects are managed.

8. Applicants for computer jobs should know that San Francisco and New York are the primary centers for technology.

10. By creating a personal Web page, you increase your firsthand knowledge of the Internet.

Section 9

EXERCISE 9.1   *page 898*

Answers

2. Televised images from Vietnam made some Americans feel terrible about the war.

4. Politicians who look bad on television tend to perform badly in polls.

6. More Americans get their news from television and the Internet today than from any other source.

8. While television is better than newspapers at reporting stories with a strong visual element, it is worse at analyzing them.

10. People should never assume that what they read on the Internet or see on television is necessarily true.

Section 10

EXERCISE 10.1   *page 901*

Possible Revisions

2. So far, no proof of the existence of life forms on other planets has been found.

4. Astronomers carefully monitor signals coming from other parts of the solar system.

6. Most of the signals received so far have been caused by cell phone and satellite interference.

8. The message, containing information about earth, is on its way to other parts of our galaxy.

10. A signal sent to earth would take a similarly long time to reach us.

Section 11

EXERCISE 11.1   *page 904*

Answers

2. Correct

4. Czar Nicholas and his wife Alexandra often saw their little boy in terrible pain.

Section 12

EXERCISE 12.1   *page 909*

Answers

2. The city of New York bought the land where the Seneca villagers lived.

4. Household items from Seneca Village still turn up in Central Park today, and a museum exhibit was recently devoted to life in the long-gone settlement.

6. James Weeks, an early resident, owned much of the land.

8. His daughter, Susan Smith McKinney-Steward, was born in Weeksville and was the valedictorian of New York Medical College in 1870.

10. Correct

Section 13

EXERCISE 13.1   *page 911*

Answers

2. When too many people are driving in a hurry, tempers can flare.

4. Angry drivers can make mistakes, such as forgetting basic safety precautions; they may take unnecessary risks, such as passing recklessly; they often drive too fast; and occasionally they even try to injure other drivers or damage other vehicles.

6. There have been incidents when one driver has attacked another.

8. Correct

10. Every driver should realize that getting angry is never a solution and may even make problems worse.

Section 14

EXERCISE 14.1   *page 914*

Answers

2. The proposed zoning change was defeated by a margin of 2:1.

4. Correct

6. Correct

8. The neon lights gleamed above stores and in diner windows.

10. Some music historians claim that the American songwriting tradition reached its peak in the 1930s.

Section 15

EXERCISE 15.1   *page 917*

Answers

2. Why did the professor assign "To an Athlete Dying Young"?

4. After September 11, 2001, President Bush said he was going to "fight terror."

6. "Come live with me and be my love," pleads the speaker in Marlowe's poem.

8. It turned out that the pianist could only play "Chopsticks."

10. Our waitress announced, "The special is prime rib"; unfortunately, we are vegetarians.

Section 16

EXERCISE 16.1   *page 919*

Answers

2. "Halle Berry was the first African American woman to win the Academy Award for Best Actress."

4. "[P]eople of all classes receive financial help from the government."

6. "Zora Neale Hurston's collections of folklore proved to be very valuable."

8. "Folic acid . . . can help prevent certain birth defects."

10. "She wrote rather doubtful grammar sometimes, and in her verses took [. . .] liberties with the metre" (Thackeray 136–37).

Section 17

EXERCISE 17.1   *page 921*

Answers

2. Correct

4. Members of the World War II generation were often horrified by their sons' and daughters' behavior.

Section 18

EXERCISE 18.1   *page 923*

Answers

2. Correct

4. The invention of anesthesia made possible many advances in medicine (including lengthy surgery).

Section 19

EXERCISE 19.1   *page 924*

Answers

2. Some foods were once popular, but today hardly anyone has heard of them.

4. In the 1960s, frozen foods—icy blocks of corn, peas, and string beans—were popular and convenient alternatives to fresh produce.

Section 21

EXERCISE 21.1   *page 929*

Answers

2. The average American woman is five feet four inches tall.

4. The Great Depression began with the stock-market crash on Black Monday.

Section 22

EXERCISE 22.1   *page 930*

Answers

2. The estimated cost was too low by $87.14.

4. All traffic stopped as a ninety-car train went slowly past.

Section 23

EXERCISE 23.1   *page 932*

Answers

2. His professor insisted that *TV Guide* was not an acceptable research source.

4. The first European settlers at Plymouth arrived on the *Mayflower*.

Section 24

EXERCISE 24.1   *page 934*

Answers

2. For many self-conscious teens and young adults, surgery seems to be the perfect solution.

4. But as more adults pay for nose jobs and tummy tucks, more teens are expressing interest.

Section 26

EXERCISE 26.1   *page 944*

Answers

2. The

4. The; the; the

Section 27

EXERCISE 27.1   *page 946*

Answers

2. will disappear

4. are offering

EXERCISE 27.2   *page 949*

Answers

2. may *or* might

4. will, may, *or* might

EXERCISE 27.3   *page 952*

Answers

2. Until recently, scientists didn't expect to find evidence of human inhabitants older than 11,000 years, the age of stone tools found in Clovis, New Mexico, in the 1930s.

4. Correct

Section 28

EXERCISE 28.1 *page 953*

Answers

2. in
4. in; on

Section 29

EXERCISE 29.1 *page 955*

Answers

2. He was also responsible for declaring war on the sea god Neptune.
4. The emperor's notorious temper led to the deaths of those unfortunate Romans who angered him.

Section 30

EXERCISE 30.1 *page 956*

Answers

2. Correct
4. At the cave entrance at dusk, the bats provide a spectacular show to curious onlookers. [*Or:* At the cave entrance at dusk, the bats provide curious onlookers with a spectacular show.]

EXERCISE 30.2 *page 957*

Answers

2. Early laws, which were sometimes discriminatory, restricted immigrants from certain countries.
4. Some Americans who want to limit immigration fear that new arrivals will compete for scarce jobs.

EXERCISE 30.3 *page 958*

Answers

2. A simple explanation for a sighting is seldom difficult to find.
4. Correct

Acknowledgments

Nell Bernstein. "Goin' Gansta, Choosin' Cholita: Claiming Identity." From *West* (1994). Copyright © 1994 by Nell Bernstein. Reprinted with the permission of the author.

Elizabeth Bishop. "Filling Station." From "The Complete Poems: 1927-1979" by Elizabeth Bishop. Copyright © 1979, 1983 by Alice Helen Methfesel. Reprinted by permission of Farrar, Straus & Giroux, LLC.

David Blankenhorn. "Life without Father" from *Fatherless America: Confronting Our Most Urgent Social Problems.* Copyright © 1995 by the Institute for American Values. Reprinted with the permission of Basic Books, a member of Perseus Books, LLC.

David Bodanis. "A Brush with Reality: Surprises in the Tube." From *The Secret House* by David Bodanis. Copyright © 1986 by David Bodanis. Reprinted with the permission of The Carol Mann Agency.

Gwendolyn Brooks. "The Bean Eaters" from *Blacks.* Copyright © 1991 by Gwendolyn Brooks. Reprinted by consent of Brooks Permissions.

Armond D. Budish. "Fender Benders: Legal Do's and Don'ts" from *Family Circle,* July 19, 1994. Copyright © 1994 by Armond D. Budish. Reprinted with the permission of the author.

Janice Castro. Dan Cook and Cristina Garcia, "Spanglish" from *Time* (July 11, 1988). Copyright © 1988 by Time, Inc. Reprinted by permission.

Mike Crissy. "Linguist Deciphers Users of Word 'Dude.'" From *Associated Press,* December 8, 2004. Copyright © Associated Press. Reprinted with permission. All rights reserved. Distributed by Valeo IP.

Mary Crow Dog (Mary Brave Bird). "The Sweat Bath Ritual" from *Lakota Woman.* Copyright © 1990 by Mary Crow Dog and Richard Erdoes. Reprinted with the permission of Grove/Atlantic, Inc.

Joseph A. DeVito. "Territoriality." From *Human Communications,* Seventh Edition, by Joseph A. DeVito. Published by Allyn & Bacon, Boston, MA. Copyright © 1997 by Pearson Education. Reprinted by permission of the publisher.

Susan Douglas. "Remote Control: How to Raise a Media Skeptic" from the *Utne Reader,* January/February 1997. Copyright © 1997 by Susan Douglas. Reprinted with the permission of the author.

Barbara Ehrenreich. Excerpt from "Selling in Minnesota" from *Nickel and Dimed: On (Not) Getting By in America.* Copyright © 2001 by Barbara Ehrenreich. Reprinted with the permission of Henry Holt and Company, LLC.

Ian Frazier. "Dearly Disconnected" Published in *Mother Jones Wire,* January/February 2000. Copyright © 2000, Foundation for National Progress. Reprinted with the permission of the publisher.

Robert Frost. "Two Look at Two" from *The Poetry of Robert Frost*, edited by Edward Connery Lathem. Copyright 1951 by Robert Frost. Copyright 1923, © 1969 by Henry Holt and Company, LLC. Reprinted with the permission of Henry Holt and Company, LLC.

Daniel Goleman. "For Man and Beast, Language of Love Shares Many Traits" from the *New York Times,* February 14, 1995. Copyright © 1995 by The New York Times Company. Reprinted with permission.

Daniel Goleman. "His Marriage and Hers: Childhood Roots" from *Emotional Intelligence.* Copyright © 1995 by Daniel Goleman. Used by permission of Bantam Books, a division of Random House, Inc.

Martin Gottfried. "Rambos of the Road." From *Newsweek,* September 8, 1996. Copyright © 1986 by Martin Gottfried. Reprinted with permission of the author. Martin Gottfried's biography, *Arthur Miller: His Life and Work,* was published in the United States, Canada, England, France, and Italy in 2005.

Bruce Gottlieb. "How Much is that Kidney in the Window?" from *The New Republic,* May 22, 2000. Copyright © 2000 by The New Republic, LLC. Reprinted with the permission of The New Republic.

Jennifer Jacobson. "Bad Conduct by the Numbers" from the *Chronicle of Higher Education* 50, no. 37 (May 20, 2004): A37. Copyright © 2004 by The Chronicle of Higher Education. Reprinted with permission.

Rachel Jones. "Not White, Just Right" from *Newsweek,* February 10, 1997. Copyright © 1997 by Newsweek, Inc. All rights reserved. Reprinted with permission.

Thomas Kinnear, Kenneth Bernhardt, and Kathleen Krentler. "Who's Eating What, and Why, in the United States and Europe" from Thomas Kinnear and Kenneth Bernhardt, *Principles of Marketing, Fourth Edition.* Copyright © 1995 by Kenneth Bernhardt. Reprinted with the permission of the author.

Ted Koerth. "Economic Affirmative Action." From the *Cavalier Daily,* April 9, 1996. Copyright © 1996 by Ted Koerth. Reprinted with the permission of the *Cavalier Daily.* Ted Koerth's column appears on the Opinion Page of the *Cavalier Daily.*

Donna Lopiano. "Purse Snatching" from *Ms.* October/November 1999. Copyright © 1999. Reprinted with the permission of *Ms.* magazine and the author.

Jeremy MacClancy. "Eating Chili Peppers" from *Consuming Culture: Why You Eat What You Eat.* Copyright © 1992 by Jeremy MacClancy. Reprinted with the permission of A. M. Heath & Company, Ltd.

Yleana Martinez. "Cracking Cascarones" from *Hispanic,* March 1996: 49–50. Copyright © 1996 by *Hispanic* magazine. Reprinted with the permission of the publisher.

Gilbert Meilaender. "'Strip-Mining' the Dead: When Human Organs Are for Sale" from *National Review,* October 11, 1999. Copyright © 1999 by National Review, Inc. Reprinted with permission.

John Merline. "Why Consumers Have Been Choosing SUVs" from *Consumers' Research* 86, no. 4, April 2003. Reprinted with permission.

Norma Molen. "Another Mother's Child: A Letter to a Murdered Son," *Catalyst,* Summer 1993. Reprinted in the *Utne Reader,* March 19, 1994. Reprinted with the permission of the author.

Kerry Pechter. "Pet Therapy for Heart and Soul" from *Prevention* (1985). Copyright © Kerry Pechter. Reprinted with the permission of the author.

Alberto Alvaro Ríos. "The Secret Lion" from *The Iguana Killer: Twelve Stories of the Heart.* Copyright © 1984 by Alberto Alvaro Ríos. Reprinted with the permission the author.

Clay Risen. "Sunday!" from the *New Republic,* April 12/19, 2004. Copyright © 2004 by The New Republic, LLC. Reprinted with the permission of The New Republic.

Melissa Russell-Ausley and Tom Harris. "How the Oscars Work" from www.HowStuffWorks.com /oscars.htm. Copyright © 1998–2005 by HowStuffWorks, Inc. Reprinted with permission.

William Safire. "Abolish the Penny" from the *New York Times,* June 2, 2004. Copyright © 2004 by The New York Times Company. Reprinted with permission.

Scott Russell Sanders. "The Men We Carry in Our Minds" from *The Paradise of Bombs* Athens: The University of Georgia Press, 1984. Originally in *Milkweed Chronicle.* Copyright © 1984 by Scott Russell Sanders. Reprinted with the permission of the Virginia Kidd Agency, Inc.

Peter Scott. "Selling Civility" Originally published in the *Wall Street Journal,* June 29, 2001. Copyright © 2001 By Peter Scott Reprinted with the permission of the author.

Andrew Simms. "Would You Buy a Car That Looked Like This?" from *New Statesman* 133, no. 4176, November 29, 2004. Copyright © New Statesman. Reprinted with permission. All rights reserved.

Roger Simon and Angie Cannon. "An Amazing Journey" from *U.S. News and World Report,* August 6, 2001. Copyright © 2001 by U.S. News & World Report, LP. Reprinted with permission.

Brent Staples. "Black Men and Public Space" from *Harpers,* 1987. Originally published in different form: "Just Walk On By: A Black Man Ponders His Power to Alter Pubic Space," from *Ms.* magazine (September 1986). Copyright © 1986 by Brent Staples. Reprinted with the permission of the author.

Lynn Steier. "When Volunteerism Isn't Noble" from the *New York Times,* April 22, 1997. Copyright © 1997 by The New York Times Company. Reprinted with permission.

Laurence Steinberg. "Part-Time Employment Undermines Students' Commitment to School" from *Beyond the Classroom: Why School Reform Has Failed and What Parents Need to Do.* Copyright © 1996 by Laurence Steinberg. Reprinted with the permission of Simon & Schuster Adult Publishing Group.

Gary M. Stern. "Hitting the 'Granite Wall'" from *Hispanic,* December 2004. Copyright © 2004 by Gary M. Stern. Reprinted with the permission of the author.

Amy Tan. "Inferior Decorating" from *The Opposite of Fate* (New York: Putnam, 2003). Originally published (as "Tête-à-Tête.") in *Elle Décor* (1992). Copyright © 1992 by Amy Tan. Reprinted with the permission of the author and Sandra Dijkstra Literary Agency.

Kathleen Vail. "Words That Wound" from *American School Board Journal,* September 1999. Copyright © 1999 by the National School Boards Association. All rights reserved. Reprinted with permission from the American School Board Journal. All rights reserved.

Alton Fitzgerald White. "Right Place, Wrong Face" from the *Nation* (October 11, 1999). Originally titled "Ragtime, My Time." Reprinted with permission. For subscription information, call 1-800-333-8536. Portions of each week's *Nation* magazine can be accessed at http://www.thenation.com.

Paula M. White. "Bringing Out Your Child's Gifts" from *Essence,* September 1997. Copyright © 1997. Reprinted with the permission of the author.

George F. Will. "A Dash of Comma Sense" from the *Washington Post,* May 21, 2004. Copyright © 2004 by The Washington Post Writers Group. Reprinted with permission.

Abigail Zuger. "Defining a Doctor, with a Tear, a Shrug, and a Schedule" from the *New York Times,* November 2, 2004. Copyright © 2004 by The New York Times Company. Reprinted with permission.

Pictures

xlvi: David Weintraub/Photo Researchers; **liii:** (left) Kevin Horan/Stock Boston, (right) Billy E. Barnes/PhotoEdit; **lv:** Bill Aron/PhotoEdit; **lix:** (bottom left) Michelle Bridwell, (bottom right) David Young-Wolff/ (both) PhotoEdit; **lxi:** By permission. From Merriam-Webster OnLine © 2005 by Merriam-Webster, Incorporated (www.Merriam-Webster.com); **2:** (all) David Young-Wolff/PhotoEdit; **20:** David Wells/The Image Works; **39:** Robert Beck/Sports Illustrated; **58:** Elaine Sulle/Image Bank/Getty Images; **86:** © Tee and Charles Addams Foundation; **106:** (top left) Jeff Greenberg, (top right) Bob Daemmrich Photography, (bottom) Ellen Senisi/ (all) The Image Bank; **146:** DOD Defense Visual Information Center, Riverside, CA/Photo by LCPL Keith Underwood; **172:** (bottom) Bob Schochet. Originally published in *The Wall Street Journal;* **198:** Tony Freeman/PhotoEdit; **238:** © Gaetano/CORBIS; **282:** Lisa M. Robinson/Photonica/Getty Images; **324:** (all) Courtesy of Sauder Woodworking Co., Archbold, Ohio; **370:** (top) A. Ramey/Woodfin Camp and Associates, (bottom) Vanessa Vick/Photo Researchers; **462:** John Giustina/Getty Images; **504:** © Nigel Cooke/Daytona Beach News/CORBIS-Sygma; **554:** Courtesy of the Jeep brand; **588:** By permission of The Population Institute; **638:** © Peter Marlow/Magnum Photos; **662:** Chuck Nacke/Woodfin Camp and Associates; **668, 669:** Images used with permission of Seattle Pacific University; **694:** Bill Horsman/Stock Boston; **727:** © 2005 Newsweek, Inc. All rights reserved. Reprinted by permission; **758:** John & Yva Momatiuk/The Image Works; **796:** (top) AP Wide World Photos, (bottom) © Sidney Harris; **820:** Tom Carter/PhotoEdit.

Index

REVISION SYMBOLS

The numbers and letters refer to chapters and sections in the Handbook. Page numbers are provided for references to sections outside of the Handbook.

abbr	Faulty abbreviation **21**		p	Punctuation **11–19**
ad	Misuse of adjective or adverb **1d, 1e, 9, 29**		⌃⸴	Comma **12**
agr	Faulty agreement **5, 7e, 7f, 7g**		no ⌃	No comma **12j**
appr	Inappropriate language *p. 187, 188*		;	Semicolon **13**
art	Article **26**		:	Colon **14**
awk	Awkward **7, 8, 10**		⌄	Apostrophe **17**
cap	Capital letter **20**		" "	Quotation mark **15**
case	Error in pronoun case **7h–7m**		. ? !	End punctuation **11**
cliché	Cliché *p. 190*		—	Dash **19**
coh	Coherence *p. 128*		( )	Parentheses **18a, 18b, 18c**
cs	Comma splice **4**		[ ]	Brackets **18d, 18e**
coord	Coordination *p. 179,* **1f**		. . .	Ellipsis mark **16**
dm	Dangling modifier **10c**		ref	Reference, pronoun **7a–7d**
ESL	ESL problem **26–30**		run-on	Run-on sentence **4**
exact	Inexact word *p. 189*		sexist	Sexist language **7e**
frag	Fragment **3**		shift	Shift **8a–g**
fs	Fused sentence **4**		sl	Slang *p. 187, 188*
hyph	Error in use of hyphen **24**		sp	Spelling **25**
irreg	Error in irregular verb **1c**		sub	Subordination *p. 180,* **1**
ital	Italics **23**		t	Error in verb tense **1c, 6e, 6f, 27a**
lc	Lowercase letter **20**		trans	Transition *p. 128*
mix	Mixed construction **8h, 8i, 8j**		v	Voice **6d**
mm	Misplaced modifier **10a, 10b**		var	Sentence variety *p. 177*
num	Number **22**		vb	Verb error **6, 27**
para, ¶	New paragraph *p. 118*		wrdy	Wordiness *p. 175*
pass	Ineffective passive *p. 185,* **6d**		//	Faulty parallelism *p. 184*
			⌒	Close up
			⌃	Insert
			X	Obvious error

HANDBOOK CONTENTS

FIGURES, FLOWCHARTS, AND BOXES